THE PRESIDENT STREET BOYS:

GROWING UP
MAFIA

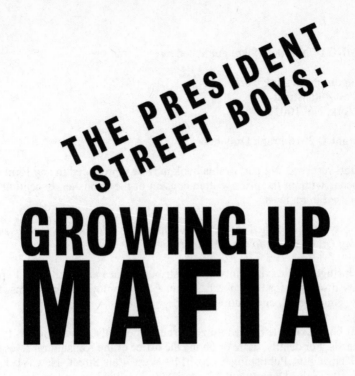

THE PRESIDENT STREET BOYS:

GROWING UP MAFIA

FRANK DIMATTEO

KENSINGTON PUBLISHING CORP.

www.kensingtonbooks.com

KENSINGTON BOOKS are published by

Kensington Publishing Corp.
119 West 40th Street
New York, NY 10018

Previously self-published by the author under the title *Lion in the Basement: Growing Up in the Gallo Crime Family.*

All Kensington titles, imprints, and distributed lines are available at special quantity discounts for bulk purchases for sales promotions, premiums, fund-raising, educational, or institutional use.

Special book excerpts or customized printings can also be created to fit specific needs. For details, write or phone the office of the Kensington sales manager: Kensington Publishing Corp., 119 West 40th Street, New York, NY 10018, attn: Sales Department; phone 1-800-221-2647.

KENSINGTON and the K logo are Reg. U.S. Pat. & TM Off.

ISBN-13: 978-1-4967-0547-1
ISBN-10: 1-4967-0547-5

First Trade Paperback Printing: August 2016

10 9 8 7 6 5 4 3 2 1

Printed in the United States of America

First Electronic Edition: August 2016

ISBN-13: 978-1-4967-0548-8
ISBN-10: 1-4967-0548-3

CONTENTS

"I'm gonna go get the papers, get the papers."
—Jimmy Two Times

"Are yous alone, or are yous by yourself?"
—FBI Mafia wiretap

"You can get further with a kind word and a gun than you can with just a kind word."
—Al Capone

"So I read something about the 'gay mafia' in Hollywood. What the hell is that—the kiss of death includes dinner and dancing?"
—Source unknown

"Y'know, that Japanese mafia, that Yakuza, those guys are smart. When they take someone for a ride, they get forty-five miles to the gallon."
—Vincent "Vinny Carwash" Vivino

"Six feet of earth makes everybody equal."
—Old Mafia proverb

INTRODUCTION
A DIFFERENT BREED OF GANGSTER

IT WAS BROOKLYN during the 1960s and my father was Richard "Ricky" Dimatteo, bodyguard for crime boss Larry Gallo. In one of the ballsiest moves in gangland history, the Gallo brothers, led by Crazy Joey Gallo, became what you might call independents. They didn't answer to any of the "five families" that ran New York back then. They didn't answer to *anybody*.

Larry and his brothers, Crazy Joe and Albert "Kid Blast" Gallo, were defiant gangsters who ran their own crew, had their own group of urban outlaws. By defiant, I mean they defied the Mob's Commission. That's a dangerous practice, but they didn't give a fuck. The Gallos were a different breed of gangster. They had their own style, their own way of operating, and they challenged the status quo of *La Cosa Nostra*—and that quo wasn't used to being defied. The old-school Dons didn't like the way the brothers were doing business.

Though they were originally part of the Profaci (later Colombo) Mafia family, the Gallo brothers went to war against the Profacis in 1961, and the streets of Brooklyn were littered with dead bodies.

Crazy Joe and his crew seemed to have a second set of balls. It didn't take long before the brothers, and their small but danger-

1

ous crew, were waging an all-out war with an established mob that had more men, more money, and more turf.

That was the beginning of the end.

Joe Gallo and his brothers and his crew ran their operation out of a storefront at the end of President Street near the Brooklyn waterfront (now called Red Hook; when I was a kid, it was known as South Brooklyn until the Brooklyn-Queens Expressway was built and cut it off from the rest of the world). The Gallo crew was among the most feared and ruthless gangs in the history of the American Mafia.

And that was the world I was born into.

This book tells an insider's story of the President Street crew. Unlike a lot of other Mafia books, this one's written by someone who knows what the fuck he's talking about. I was there.

It will explore the cause of, and the bloody battles of, the Gallo-Profaci War, fought for the most part on the streets of Brooklyn. The results were extensive, shaping the other New York crime families to this very day.

Here are detailed firsthand accounts of legendary Mafia meetings, harrowing crimes, violent confrontations, and inside dope on a mob murder or two that have remained a mystery until now.

The President Street Boys: Growing Up Mafia is a who's who of the American Mafia during the second half of the twentieth century: bosses, *capos*, street soldiers, as well as shady businessmen and even some celebrities. The sleazy world of pornography—long before the Internet—was also a huge moneymaker for the mob. I was a part of that world, too (though I never had to take my clothes off or anything).

I was reared on the knee of the Mafia, you might say. It's the only life I ever knew. It took me years before I realized that I didn't have a choice. For me, being in "the Life" was the only life I knew.

I knew the rules of the street better than I knew my ABCs. I knew that it was a harsh world and you had to be tough to survive. I also knew, at the time anyway, that those affiliated with the Gallos respected honor, while their asshole Mafia enemies did not.

I knew all the mobbed-up wiseguys and they all knew me, from the time I was born. Thanks in large part to movies like *The Godfather* and *Goodfellas*, and later, the TV show *The Sopranos,* the mob guys have been glorified, like they were America's modern-day equivalent to England's Arthurian legends, Robin Hood and his band of merry men. (And believe me, Robin Hood and his pals were bigger crooks than we ever were.)

The Mafia has been portrayed as evil, ruthless killers, heartless criminals loyal to no one and nothing except the almighty dollar. Nothing but a bunch of tax-evading, dope-smoking, coke-sniffing, money-laundering, weenie-wagging, wife-cheating, womanizing, lip-biting, lying, despicable, self-centered, self-serving, horns-waggling, double-dealing, power-hungry, money-grubbing thieves.

To me, a young kid from Brooklyn, where everyone in the neighborhood was mobbed up in one way or another, these "criminals" were also my family members, my neighbors, and my friends.

I'm not denying that some of the stuff in those movies is sure-as-hell true. But like the mob lawyer says in that great old gangster movie *The Asphalt Jungle*, "Crime is merely a left-handed form of human endeavor."

Me, I'm actually right-handed. But you get the idea.

THIS IS NOT A HISTORY LESSON

There are times when I've used published sources—books, newspapers, etc.—to better tell a story, to keep things in chronological order, and to give a little outside perspective.

But that doesn't mean this is a history lesson. This book is comprised in essence of memories that have history running through them on account of I happened to be where the action was.

This is not a tell-all—some things a guy has to protect. I'll promise this, though: This book contains *everything* that I've seen.

I knew and worked with some of the all-time most notorious and feared gangsters in mobdom, and I became an unwitting witness to some of gangland history's most infamous moments.

And for that, I have to thank my father.

As is true of a lot of guys, my dad was my idol. His name was Richard (Riccardo on his birth certificate), but everybody in the neighborhood called him Ricky. I wanted to be just like him when I grew up.

Who wouldn't?

He was good-looking, well-dressed, well-respected, made lots of money, drove fancy cars, and seemed to have the world by the balls. I didn't know back then in my youth that I was only seeing one part of the picture—the part my father wanted me to see.

You believe in Santa Claus because your folks tell you the fat fuck is real. In the same way, parents create a mythology around themselves and the rest of the world that ultimately becomes reality for a kid.

As adults, we again create false realities, put on the rose-tinted glasses, use denial. People who refuse to face facts have nothing to worry about. They are also notoriously lousy at balancing risk and reward.

I was that guy, looking at the world around me as if it were normal, and we all lived together in a glass-half-full world. To me, Ricky and the guys who hung out on President Street were gods in a world of devils.

I believed in the legendary version of the Mafia, the one that kept the people safe and happy (for a price) in a world in which government, law enforcement, and other gangs were all corrupt and needed to be defied.

It was okay if sometimes life in my neighborhood seemed to mimic an old Western movie, or a shoot-'em-up gangster picture taking place during Prohibition. It was okay because *we were the good guys*.

COLORFUL NICKNAMES

One thing Hollywood got right about the Mafia is the colorful nicknames. I remember the President Street Boys mostly by their nicknames: Little Angelo, Cockeyed Butchie, Ralphie Goodness, Stanley the Hat, Mooney, Smokey, Punchy, and Roy Roy.

And in charge were the Gallo brothers: Larry, Albert (aka Kid Blast), and Joey. When I was a little boy, the Gallos would pinch my cheeks so hard that there'd be tears in my eyes. I tried with all of my might to hide my pain from them, but they kept bearing down until they made me cry a little bit. They thought it was funny, and it was their way of showing affection. Eventually, I learned to tough it out, without my eyes watering. When you are around guys like that, you learn early on the value of being tough. So I got over the hard pinches of the cheek.

Pain, I was to learn, was a regular part of the business.

Dad's start in the Life came in 1958, just after he was discharged from the army. Ricky was a high school graduate from a poor Italian family, and he bounced around for a while, worked maintenance for American Airlines, discovered that he liked to box. It was something that many poverty-stricken kids turned to.

At that time, one of the best boxing venues in New York was the Sunnyside Gardens. It wasn't a big place (they tore it down in the late 1970s and put up a Wendy's in its place), but it was famous because during the late '40s and early '50s, it was from there that the old DuMont Television Network broadcast boxing matches on their weekly show. It was the sort of place where guys on their way up fought guys on their way down, with the newcomers being showcased on TV for bigger shows at Madison Square Garden.

Ricky fought in the preliminaries as a middleweight—but he was not a pugilist with top-ten level skills—and he was smart enough to cut his boxing career short while he still had his marbles.

After that he hooked up with Anthony "Little Augie Pisano" Carfano and Anthony "Tony Bender" Strollo, who were *caporegimes* in the Genovese Crime Family. Carfano and Strollo ran nightclubs in the city (that means Manhattan), and they were looking for a bouncer.

Little Augie was the key factor there. He was a man with a history and a lot of enemies. He was a mob killer, killed for Vito Genovese—and, unfortunately for Augie, sometimes he also shot people for Lucky Luciano and Frank Costello.

Six times Augie had been arrested for murder, but each time they'd had to cut him loose. Augie was in charge of collecting the Genoveses' cut from New York's garment district. Because of his garment district status, Augie also controlled labor unions there, and may have used his muscle to rig a few city elections.

He was a Genovese lieutenant, although he and the boss weren't chummy-chummy. Augie's allegiance was in question. In 1959, Vito had called for a meeting of his lieutenants because he was worried about family solidarity. Everybody showed up except Augie. He was discussed in his absence. Little Augie was about fifty, but he still enjoyed women as much as ever. He'd had a couple of wives. One was a cop's sister. A dapper dresser, he was known for his white felt fedora with black silk band, his finely tailored suits, and his shiny shoes.

Tony Bender was the guy who saw Ricky in one of his Sunnyside Garden fights, saw that he was tough as nails, and offered him a job interview. Quizzed and tested, Ricky demonstrated that he was good at handling himself and others, so he was hired.

He worked at two clubs in Manhattan: The V̶ The Gold Key. One night he got into a figh̶ who'd been spending too much time talking̶ no-no back then. Ricky floored him twice anᴜ̶ the club—and only later learned that the guy was En̶ who, in 1958, was just then starting his career as a pro ̶ Griffith went on to win belts as both a welter- and middleweighᴛ̶, but he is perhaps most frequently remembered as the boxer who killed a man in the ring on national TV. The fight, against the Cuban fighter Benny "Kid" Paret, was held at Madison Square Garden on March 24, 1962. At the weigh-in, Paret touched Griffith's buttocks and called him gay, which angered Griffith—and also turned out to be true. Griffith took out his anger in the ring and gave Paret a brutal, and fatal, beating. But on the night he encountered Ricky Dimatteo in a New York nightclub, he came out second best.

It was while working as a bouncer for the Genovese guys that Ricky got to know the Gallo brothers, especially Larry and Joey, who were at that time members of the Profaci Family of Brooklyn. They were friends of Carfano and Strollo and came into his clubs all the time. Ricky and Larry hit it off big, and became best buddies.

On September 25, 1959, Augie was shot in the back of his head while sitting at the wheel of his Cadillac. Augie's last date was with a married beauty queen named Janice Drake. She was married to comedian Alan Drake. The Drakes were swingers. One was just as apt to step out as the other. There was no jealous-husband angle.

For syndicate guys, a kiss from Janice Drake was like the kiss of death. She made a habit of getting next to hoods just before they were shuffled off the mortal coil. Janice was Albert Anastasia's dinner date the night before his date with destiny in the Park Sheraton barbershop. (More about that later.) She was also the

...te of garment district powerbroker Nat Nelson on the night he was ventilated.

Augie and Janice went out to dinner that night. After dinner they drove around in Augie's Cadillac. They were ambushed as they drove down a dark street in the borough of Queens, not far from the airport that was, at the time, known as LaGuardia Field. The car had continued on after the shooting and crashed into the curb. The hit became famous because a New York *Daily News* photographer was on the scene immediately. Photos showed Drake, slumped to one side but eyes open, staring at the windshield, with a bullet hole in the center of her forehead. Augie had fallen over to his right, so that his head now rested in Janice's lap.

The hit looked like the start of a war, so Larry Gallo needed a bodyguard. Larry came to the Peppermint Lounge in New York and asked Ricky to come over to Brooklyn with him. Ricky did, and from then on my dad was a fixture on President Street. He got a job in a bar, where he met my mom.

As a boy, I would go to the bar to make a few dollars. I'd clean up the place. Plus, I brought my shoe-shine box. When the guys came in, they laughed at me. They could see I was setting them up. They liked a kid who knew how to make money, and they'd give huge tips, ten dollars or more depending. The bigger the gangster, the bigger the tip. I made a good chunk of change. I could bring in $150 on a good Saturday afternoon. Not bad for a kid in the 1960s.

That was my world, as a kid, safe on a Saturday afternoon. At night there were bullets flying around. The hit on Augie had, as expected, precipitated a war between the Gallo and Profaci contingents.

The Gallos had tried to overpower then-boss Joe Profaci and seize control of the family. They had a laundry list of reasons why Profaci had to go, including the fact that he was greedy, imposing unnecessary financial "tribute" fees from all family members.

The coup didn't work, so the Gallos splintered off from Profaci and a civil war broke out. That meant the boys had to hide out, "hit the mattresses" on President Street, where they had their clubs and hangouts. They hid in safe places to be secure from attack and be able to plot their own offensives. The phrase "hitting the mattresses" was later made famous in *The Godfather* movies, where they slept on mattresses on the floor while hiding out. And that part was true. Guys did literally "hit the mattresses," because there weren't enough beds at the safe houses on President Street for all the crew that was hiding out.

JOEY'S PET LION

Roy Roy had a club there, and that's where a lot of the hiding was done. And so did Armando, a dwarf gangster who worked for Joey Gallo. Along with hosting a safe house, Armando's job was to walk Joey's pet lion. The lion was used as a demonstration tool only, to put the hurry-up in those too slow in paying their debts. The lion lent inspiration to a wide variety of enemies and other various victims. The lion never had to attack.

Everyone taken down those basement stairs got the idea: See the lion, the lion is hungry, pay the vig. The lion was exceptionally motivational, and debts were paid promptly.

Some of the crew hid out at Gargiulo's Flower Shop and Lefty Big Ears's joint. They had the street locked down. President Street was a sanctuary from the bullets of war. It was fairly secure geographically, sealed in at the east by the big trench dug to accommodate the Brooklyn-Queens Expressway, and on the west by the water. The street came to a T on both ends. Further protection was offered from the south by the entrance to and the mouth of the Brooklyn Battery Tunnel.

At the time of the war, Ricky was so new with the Gallo crew that he wasn't widely recognized by the Profaci side. He could move around fairly easily and remained unharmed. For this reason, he was chosen to be one of the shooters on the Carmine "The Snake" Persico hit.

Persico is a big name in the history of *La Cosa Nostra*, a future godfather of the Profaci Family. He was a Red Hook boy, a member of the Garfield Boys who once killed a rival with his bare hands during a rumble. His first claim to fame was being in on the barbershop killing of Albert "The Mad Hatter" Anastasia, and he was on the list of those who needed to be taken out to defeat the Profaci gang. Persico had been his own entity and an ally of the Gallos for a time, but Profaci offered Persico lucrative rackets in exchange for allegiance. Persico accepted. To demonstrate his allegiance, Persico executed a failed murder attempt on Larry Gallo, and thus ended up on the Gallo hit list. In retaliation for the botched execution, a group of gunmen, including my father, ambushed Persico in the dingy Gowanus section of Brooklyn, where a polluted canal slices through a charred brick cluster of warehouses and factories. A panel truck pulled alongside Persico's car one night and he was shot in the face, head, and shoulder. Persico lived, and my dad's job as bodyguard was more important than ever, which was easy for him because he and Larry Gallo had a strong and loyal friendship.

So there you have a taste. My father's life in the mob. My own life in the mob. Two generations. Four decades. An inside story like never before, a first-person eyewitness account of what it's like to grow up in the underworld. Revealed in brutal and inglorious detail, the men behind the headlines, in their raw day-to-day business affairs, the seduction, the inner workings. Details based on eyewitness reports and deathbed confessions about some of the Mafia's most notorious murders. It's quite a ride.

This book is fifty-eight years in the making. The result is the most personal and accurate testament to "the Life" that you'll ever read. Some myths will be dispelled, others enforced, but the record will be set straight regarding many of the infamous events of mob history.

I would like to thank my family: Richard Dimatteo, Amelia Dimatteo, Emily Dimatteo, Kristina Dimatteo, Frank Dimatteo, Matthew Dimatteo, Chris Chairamonte, Valory Dimatteo, Louis and Josephine Floridia, Tony Crispe, my three grand-kids—Salvatore, Frank III, and Luciano—and Carrol Torres. On the pro side, thanks to Michael Benson (author of *The Devil at Genesee Junction*) and to Gary Goldstein at Kensington Books for their expert support.

This book is dedicated to Richard "Silver Fox" Dimatteo. We all have parents, some good, some bad, some indifferent. I had Ricky and Dee. I was born into a crazy world of blood, guns, scores, and violence.

I had no say in the matter. But I learned from what I saw, things most kids don't ever see, plus I got to live a life most people are denied. I am not glorifying the life that Ricky led. It was his life to live the way he wanted to.

The family I lived with was comprised of the people I loved, and I have no regrets. I stand proud to have Ricky and Dee as parents. That statement has gone through a process over the years. There were a number of things I had to clarify in my mind before I could declare pride in my parents. I had to come to grips with the fact that the Life was a bad life, that those in it miss out on so much, and that it was my life, too—and that I, too, had missed out on a lot.

Ricky has passed on, may he rest in peace, and so has Bobby Darrow, Punchy, Uncle Joe Shep, and Roy Roy. Now I am left alone with only memories of the life we led, a life I share here in this book with you.

CHAPTER 1
WE CALLED IT
SOUTH BROOKLYN

TO UNDERSTAND WHY the people in these stories act the way we do, you've got to understand where we came from: South Brooklyn—with a focal point on a protruberance of land jutting into New York Harbor called Red Hook.

Red Hook was a part of the Town of Brooklyn right from the beginning, in the 1600s when the place was called "Breuckelen" on the East River, and Kings Highway (still a major thoroughfare wandering through the modern Brooklyn grid circumventing long-forgotten obstacles) was trafficked by the Dutch. Three hundred years later it was a big city, consolidated in 1898 as a borough of New York City. When they built the Brooklyn Bridge, Brooklyn grew fast, wrapping around the Narrows, through Coney Island, all the way past Sheepshead Bay to Canarsie, which were villages that were swallowed up.

It's not hard to figure out how Red Hook—originally Roode Hoek—got its name. It sticks out into the Upper Bay in a hook shape, curling across Buttermilk Channel toward the only-yards-away western shore of Governor's Island. And there's a redness to the soil, too—not that there's much visible soil left. In the nineteenth century, shipping companies built ports, called Basins. There was the Atlantic, the Erie, and the Brooklyn Basins.

By the 1900s, there were a lot of piers, where hard men could make a living loading up and unloading the oceangoing cargo ships. When the Depression came, there wasn't as much work, and times got tough for a lot of people.

People who lived in Red Hook didn't call it that. They called it "The Point," explaining that *hoek* in Dutch meant "point," or "corner"—not "hook." Whatever. In the 1920s and '30s, if you lived on the Point, you were probably poor.

The men who worked on the piers were immigrants, sons of immigrants, Italians and Germans and Irish, and they were all called longshoremen. They lived on the Point and worked on the Point.

Today if you go there, you see the Red Hook Housing Projects, but back in the 1930s that was the site of a shantytown for homeless guys who lived clustered in a community of shacks, and people called it a "Hooverville," named after the U.S. president held responsible for everyone being broke.

Today, real estate in many sections of the five boroughs is going sky-high, so the real estate brokers have assigned trendy names to subdivisions of the old neighborhood. Today there is not just Red Hook, but also Cobble Hill, Carroll Gardens, the Columbia Street Waterfront, and on and on. Back then we just called it South Brooklyn.

I was born at 113 First Place between Court Street and Smith Street in 1956. I lived there until I was five. When I looked out my bedroom window, I saw Scotto's Funeral Parlor and it was always busy, same old black hearse every time, pallbearers moving slowly and stiffly, widows behind veils with buckling knees.

When I was five we moved a couple of blocks up and over, to Sackett Street between Smith and Hoyt Streets. Now when I looked out my window I saw Saint Agnes Church, and sure enough, there always seemed to be a coffin going in and out. Even at that young age I could tell an omen when I saw one.

South Brooklyn was a mixed neighborhood, not blended, the ethnicities each having carved out their own chunk. The blacks had the Gowanus Projects. The Puerto Ricans stuck close to Smith Street. The Irish were sprinkled around. The Italians had just about everything from Court Street west.

There was very little trouble between peoples. For generations Brooklynites had the Dodgers in common. If you were an Italian and you were talking to a guy who was something else, you could always say, "Hey, how about that Pee Wee Reese?" or "How about that Carl Furillo?" And you were on the same team. Roy Campanella was everybody's hero. When the Dodgers left, the borough lost some of that, and every once in a while there was racial or ethnic bullshit.

Most of the Italian men in the neighborhood worked on the piers. The other advantage the Italians had early on was that we owned all of the stores. My favorite store when I was a kid was Helen's Candy Store, at the corner of Sackett and Smith Streets. Helen and her sister ran the place. The trick was to get Helen to smile, a very difficult thing to do. You had to do handstands. She had everything you wanted. That was where I went for my penny candy and baseball cards. Boy, I miss them.

Italians also owned the many pork stores, fresh vegetable markets, hero shops, bakeries, pastry shops, restaurants, and bars. On Court Street there was Romeo's Deli, owned by a brother and sister and their spouses. They ran it themselves, always served you with a smile and a warm word, and they treated you like family. Best prosciutto and mozzarella heroes in the history of the world. When the Romeos got old and closed, it was a great loss to the neighborhood.

Esposito Pork Store was owned by a friend of our family, Frank Esposito, the father. I bowled with him and hung out with him at the local club—one of the nicest men you'd ever want to meet. He had the best pork sausage and Italian imports in Brooklyn. Going to Esposito's was like attending a museum for great imported food. On display with class and pride were all the Italian *formaggi*: asiago, gorgonzola, Grana Padano, pecorino romano. Hanging from the ceiling was prosciutto, capicola, salami, soppressata, and pepperoni. When you walked in, the smell sent you back to Italy, whether you'd ever been there or not, which for some of the older gentlemen could be an emotional experience. It was a smell to make you weep for joy. The sons are there now keeping it alive.

The other big pork store was Aiellos. All of my friends worked there when they were young. If you needed a job that was the first place you checked, because they always needed someone. It was a huge store and had everything you could possibly need from Italy.

And the bakeries, each one better than the next. There was Caputo Bakery on Court Street, had the best Sicilian bread; Cammareri Bakery at the corner of Henry and Sackett Streets, made famous by the movie *Moonstruck*, had maybe the best bread in all of Brooklyn (they closed the Henry Street bakery but reopened in Bensonhurst); Mazzola Bakery has the best lard bread on earth, what can I say, they've been there for sixty years; Court Pastry on Court and Degraw Streets, where I had my first cannoli and cheesecake, and the best lemon ice. Some bakeries moved and then came back: Montelone Pastry on Court Street changed hands a few times, but they kept the same ingredients because the cookies are to die for—and they serve espresso while you wait.

Rainbow Vegetable Market was a small family-owned market at Court and Sackett, run by a father and his sons. They knew everyone by name. If you needed broccoli rabe, they had it. Escarole, they had it. The fruit melted in your mouth, and they would deliver to your house a two-dollar bag of anything. It's gone now, but not forgotten.

At Joe's Superette they had the best prosciutto balls and rice balls you ever ate. Joe got sick and passed away. Another store lost.

Union Street Market, at the corner of Union and Smith, was a grocery store that was there forever. If you were Italian and lived on the Smith Street side, that was where you went to shop or hang out.

I'll never forget the smell of Damico's Coffee at Court and Degraw. Frank and Alex were friends of the family. I grew up with their sons. You could smell the Italian coffee brewing in the morning from blocks away. It was a sad day when, with the neighborhood changing, the Damicos received a letter from the city. Stop the roasting, people are complaining about the smell. What a kick in the ass. They had to stop because the newbies, full of Wonder Bread and processed cheese food, didn't like it. I would have said, "Fuck you."

Sal's Pizza at Court and Degraw, fantastic. Johnny is a friend for a lifetime. Johnny today runs the place, trying to keep it the same as it always was, but it's a battle. The pizza is still good. If you want it the old-fashioned way or the new way, makes no difference, you still get to sit with Johnny, have a drink, and reminisce about the neighborhood. You can find me in there once a week talking John's ear off, complaining about something.

The tablecloth restaurants: Helen's, Gloria's, Angelo's, Queen. All on Court Street, all within six blocks of each other. All of them gave you good homemade Italian food made by the owners until they couldn't cook no more. I watched them all get old and go.

After dinner, you could go to Ebel's Ice Cream Parlor or Mr. and Mrs. Bauer's Ice Cream Parlor, old-school places that opened around 1900 and lasted for more than seventy-five years until everyone became too cool to go there anymore.

As a kid I remember being sent for ice cream with a dollar in my pocket, and I'd come back with a big white cardboard container, like the kind they put takeout Chinese food in now.

* * *

It felt like there was a bar on every corner. Some of the ones I remember the best are:

Butch's Inn on Court Street and Third Place. I saved Roy Roy's life there once. (More about *that* in chapter 21.) That bar has been gone for years, but if those walls could talk I wouldn't be here writing.

There was The Step Inn, for sixty years. My mother worked there in the 1960s. I hung out there after Ju Ju bought it. What a place. Martin Scorsese would pay a million bucks for the rights. All the wiseguys hung out at Ju Ju's. It was like a ride on the Coney Island Cyclone every night. Lauren Bacall drank there. I sat there with Punchy on many nights, but it's gone now.

And there was The Court Terrace at Court and Atlantic, run by the Gallo family. I was put there in the 1970s to help out. Got my first score from there. Again, if the walls could talk, my wife would walk.

At El Bolario, a Spanish bar on Court Street, I got my first pinch. I know it had a pool table, because I hit the owner in the head with a pool stick. It's gone now, too.

There was Guzzies Bar & Grill at Smith and Union. It's now called Red Roses. I'm not going to say anything about the place. My father always told me, "If you have nothin' nice to say, don't say nothin'." Back when it was Guzzies, in the 1970s, I hung out with Roy Roy and did a lot of drinking there. This was before drinking and driving was bad.

Our neighborhood movie house was the Rex. It opened in the 1920s, during the era of silent movies, and was later called the Cobble Hill, at Court and Butler. I used to pay fifty cents to see two movies there, a cartoon and a film of an old 1920s bike race. The bikes had numbers on them. If your ticket had the winning number, you got free popcorn. Ju Ju owned the place for a short time, and on weekends he had all the doo-wop groups there,

Bobby Lester and the Moonglows. They sang "The Ten Commandments of Love." The Drifters were there, The Five Satins, The Capris sang "There's a Moon Out Tonight." Ju Ju had everyone you could think of. That theater is still going strong in 2016 as a movie house.

On Columbia Street was another movie house called the Happy Hour Theater. It closed in the 1970s. Its backyard was next to Roy Roy's club, so we used to go in at night and take whatever looked good. We made off with about a hundred movie posters, but we eventually threw them out. Later we found out they were worth a lot of money. Who the fuck knew?

Also on Columbia Street, down on the Red Hook side where everything was a little bit more run-down, it was old school. We had "House of Calzone" at the time. They only had deep-fried calzones—the only kind they made in Brooklyn. It makes a great difference in taste. Anyway, the house is still there and we still go there for calzones even though the new workers are assholes. I don't deal with them. I have my children go there for me now.

Ferdinando's Focacceria. If you like panelle, tripe, or vastedda, it's the place to go. Open since 1904. Every hood in Brooklyn has stopped in there for a meal. I try to eat there once a month. One thing that makes it special: They had Manhattan Special on tap. That's coffee soda, made with real coffee on Manhattan Avenue in Greenpoint, Brooklyn.

Defontes Sandwich Shop, in Red Hook since 1922, was a small, beat-up place, but you couldn't beat the shrimp in red sauce or the roast beef sandwich with homemade gravy. It's still open and we still eat there.

Anthony's Bar on Van Brunt Street opened in the 1940s. When you turned eighteen (the legal drinking age back then), this was the place to go. It was only a couple of blocks from the projects, but you could go in there at four in the morning and not worry about trouble.

Cafiero's Restaurant, on President between Columbia and Hicks, was an old-school restaurant with corrugated-tin ceilings and walls, a tile floor, wicker chairs, wood tables with plain tablecloths, and a small menu of homemade Italian food like your mother made. If you were Italian, there was a small back room where the boys could hold meetings—a real hood haven. Cafiero got old, closed the place, and that was the last of the old-school restaurants.

For clothes you went to Marietta Men's Wear at Court and Carroll, open since the 1940s, run by Matty and Joe. Matty just passed away. As I write this, I just went to say good-bye to him, a great man. I still buy my Ginny T-shirts there.

One of the first stores I was ever in by myself was Frank's Clothing Store on Union Street, a family-run place where all of the longshoremen and their families went for pants, underwear, T-shirts, and socks, for cheap. My grandmother sent me there when I was just about old enough to walk. I went in there with her a few times, as well, at least once for pantaloons when she was about ninety-two.

On Court Street was Pop's Poolroom, one of the oldest pool rooms around. It was on the second floor, so if there was a fight it was a bitch to get out. All of the good players shot there. It might've been a little bit too old. The pool tables themselves were worse for wear, and it was already dingy by the time I started hanging out there. There was one table that was legendary, the table that Al Capone shot a game on. When the place closed, a friend of mine bought the Al Capone table.

The other pool hall on Court (this one at Butler), was Ju Ju's. He took over for Patty and renamed the place as Ju Ju's Pool Room. It stayed like that for years, then Ju Ju eventually sold the place to Sally Balsamo, who is gone now.

*   *   *

All of these great places up and down the well-kept and tree-lined streets of South Brooklyn, it was a great place to grow up. Every block you walked down, there was someone you knew, guys who hung out, guys with parents who spoke broken English. As kids we were out from morning till late at night, playing "Buck, Buck, How Many Horns Are Up?" and freeze tag, hit the stick, skullzy, stoop ball, box ball, and ringolevio (which was like team hide-and-seek). We flipped baseball cards. If you had a bike, the cards went into the spokes to make noise. We made scooters out of milk crates and roller skates. We wore Red Ball Keds ("Run faster, jump higher, stop on a dime") and PF Flyers, dungarees and Ginny T-shirts.

And, yeah, there were hoods everywhere, so ingrained into the fabric of the community that you didn't even think about it. That was just the way things were. We had a wiseguy on every corner, one in every store. Sometimes it was a representative of the Gallo brothers, or Old Man Profaci's crew. The Gambino guys had a club. Fuck, they all had clubs.

Point is, someone was always looking out for you. When your mom or your grandma wanted you, they just stuck their head out the window and called you, and you could hear them from blocks away. If you didn't hear, someone would relay the message: "Hey, Frankie Boy, they're calling you."

Per capita there were more infamous hoodlums from Red Hook and South Brooklyn than anywhere else in the country. In South Brooklyn, if you weren't a family member, you knew someone who was a family member. Everyone had an uncle or a cousin (or a father) who was a wiseguy.

Even if you didn't have a blood relative who was in the Life, the hoods knew you from the block and if you did something wrong, they would give you a kick in the ass. Curse in front of a woman, kick in the ass. Didn't help someone carry groceries, kick in the ass. I got kicked in the ass all the time, at least once a week. Sometimes I'd go home and tell my parents that I got kicked in the ass, and they'd kick me in the ass again. Those were the days.

No one was kidnapped or molested. No one got sick. And the kids from other neighborhoods were scared to mess with us. Man. Blink me the fuck back right now.

By the time you were old enough to hit the street you were known. All of the wiseguys knew you, all the families, every bartender. And you knew all the broads, good and bad.

Even though it was a small neighborhood, a lot of people came from the outside because commerce was good, and we had entertainment value. It was like a tourist trade, I guess, folks coming in to eat and drink in South Brooklyn, and it was all by word of mouth. Tourists came all the way from Canarsie and Clinton Hill to have a tablecloth meal on Court Street, and maybe go out for a couple of drinks after. Sure, it was the same cast of characters year after year, but there was variety to spice things up. You were meeting new people all the time.

There was good and bad. A lot of girls came to the bars because they knew there were wiseguys there, and they liked the action. Then there were guys who thought they were tough and would show up just to fuck with us.

For me it was all a learning experience for the Big Show. I had the inside track when it came to being successful with the guys on account of I was Ricky's kid.

CHAPTER 2
THE GALLO BROTHERS

DURING THE LATE 1920S there was a bloody power struggle raging through New York City's underworld. It was during that struggle between two Old World mob titans that the three Gallo brothers were born, boom, boom, boom, so maybe they were born to make war, born to use war to achieve mob supremacy. Larry was the oldest, born on November 23, 1927, followed by Joey on April 7, 1929, and Albert on June 6, 1930.

Joe "The Boss" Masseria had been in a war with Sal Maranzano. Both men wanted to be *capo di tutti capo*. Sal was a visionary of sorts. He saw a world in which the Families worked together rather than warring amongst themselves, thus increasing *La Cosa Nostra* power tenfold. Masseria couldn't have cared less about Maranzano's Big Picture. Masseria had a Big Picture of his own, one in which New York City was all his, and he shared it with no one.

The war went on for two years, lots of guys getting whacked on both sides. Bugsy Siegel, Meyer Lansky, and Lucky Luciano all had a clandestine meeting with Sal in the Bronx Zoo. There, while feeding peanuts to the elephants, they came up with a way to end the war: whack Joe the Boss. It was Luciano who asked Joe to join him for dinner at Scarpato's in Coney Island on April 15, 1931.

The men ate, and ate, and they drank Italian red wine. The feast lasted for three hours. Luciano patted himself on his belly, belched, and left the table to go to the can and take a piss. As soon as Masseria was alone at the table, four gunmen—Bugsy Siegel, Vito Genovese, Albert Anastasia, and Joe Adonis—burst into the restaurant and aerated Joe the Boss. Joe tried to hide but couldn't avoid the path of six bullets, at least one of which was fatal. Fourteen more slugs tore up the restaurant wall behind Masseria. Luciano came out of the restroom and left the restaurant before the police arrived. For the four gunmen, it wasn't a silky-smooth getaway. When the getaway driver stalled the car, Bugsy slugged him. But everyone escaped anyway. The Masseria hit, and its violent aftermath, proved to be a pivotal moment in mob history. It helped to put into place the mob leadership that would remain for most of the remainder of the century. I know this because my uncle Joe Schipani was a driver for Lucky and told me so.

The Gallos grew up on the mean streets of Red Hook, where nothing in the nation (maybe even the world) was as mob-dominated as the lucrative Red Hook waterfront. Joey Gallo was small in stature, both short and slight, but he had balls of steel. He was blond and blue-eyed despite his Mediterranean heritage.

Joey loved the movies, was fascinated by gangsters of the silver screen, especially Richard Widmark as vile Tommy Udo in *Kiss of Death* (1947). That character was evil through and through and laughed like a hyena. Joey did a dead-on impression of Widmark, his face curled into a snarl as he laughed, a laugh that sounded fiendishly psychopathic. He imitated that movie in other ways, too. Udo is portrayed as a hip cat who digs jazz, so Joey professed to be a jazz aficionado, as well. He dressed as Udo had dressed, wearing black suit, black shirt, white tie. Now, Widmark's portrayal of Udo *was* exceptional. He was nominated for an Oscar. But there were those among us kids who thought

Joey's Udo thing was a little weird, but we were smart enough to keep our mouths shut about it. After a while, once you got to know him, you said, "Ah, it's just Joey."

Joey left a lasting impression on me when I was little. His eyes gleamed when he smiled. He looked at you and made you feel special. He would pinch my cheek so fucking hard that it still hurts today. Joe first got arrested at age fifteen, and he had the balls to go into his Udo act during his court hearing. He was so effective that the judge sent him to King County Hospital for observation. The doctors checked him out and tagged him schizophrenic. Crazy Joey. Like a fox. His schizophrenia didn't stop him from outsmarting all of the doctors and waltzing right out of that hospital as soon as he was able.

Joey went to prison when I was seven and got out when I was sixteen. It would be ten years before I'd see him again, and he didn't forget me.

Hell, we didn't need a doctor to tell us that Joey was crazy. We'd seen the proof. He would go after guys twice his size. He'd work them over with his fists. If he had one handy, he'd beat them with a bat. If he didn't like the matchup he'd pull a gun— the great equalizer. Joey ran the streets of Red Hook with a small crew and was feared by everyone.

Brother Larry was also a small guy—but tough. He had heart and a temper, but unlike Joey, who got into everyone's face, Larry could control his volatility, and this was considered a sign of maturity, of leadership. Larry had charisma, another thing that made him seem like he was naturally in charge. He had a reputation for being rational. Guys would go to him seeking advice and Larry would dish out the wisdom.

Point is, Joey might have been the brother whom everyone was most afraid of, but Larry called the shots. He had a brain for concocting new ways to make money on the street. He understood the politics of the street. He knew that the best way to get in the good graces of the old-school bosses was to demonstrate that you were a good, smart *earner*. He used his brains over his fists. He didn't need his fists, he had Joey's at his disposal. Joey was the muscle, the guided torpedo that you sent to break someone's legs if they needed breaking. Because he was smart and he was a good earner, Larry worked his way into the mob by the 1950s. With Joey at his side, Larry figured he had the kind of juice he needed to be the boss of his own family. If fate hadn't taken a hand, he probably would have gone on to run the Profaci family.

Albert was the youngest of the Gallo brothers, and like his brothers, he was small but knew how to hold his own with larger tough guys. He was a good-looking guy, and he had a good head on his shoulders like Larry. He had something else in common with his brothers: a mean streak that always lurked in the background, ready to flare up. Being the baby, Albert was used to having his older brothers looking out for him. He learned to depend on them, which turned out to do him no good in the long run. His nickname was "Kid Blast," and he would have been better off if he'd become a scholar, a college professor or something like that. He didn't have the tools to follow his brothers into the Life. He ended up leaning on the Gallo name too much, and he never won the love or respect of the crew.

Umberto Gallo, whom everyone called Papa, was the Gallo brothers' dad. He arrived in the United States in 1920, from Torre Del Greco in Naples, Italy. As had many hoodlums who came over from the Old Country at that time, Papa capitalized on Prohibition and salted away a fortune in illegal booze money. When Prohibition ended, he used his nest egg to back a major loan-sharking operation.

The Gallos' mother was Mary, the clan's backbone. She kept the Gallo men in line, no easy task. Papa and Mary opened a diner called Jackie's Charcolette at Church and McDonald Avenues in the Kensington section of Brooklyn. The whole Gallo family worked there at one time or another, and the Gallo brothers held meetings there. On days when the joint was really bustling with hungry patrons, Blast and his sisters were the first to pitch in and help out in the kitchen, mainly by doing the cooking.

Toward the end of Papa Gallo's time on earth, I was one of the guys who picked up and dropped him off on Henry Street, where he loved to play cards. They had big, big card games twice a week. I just had to make sure I was on time, and I had his cigars, or I'd hear a lion's roar coming out of that little old man's mouth.

There was a Profaci mobster at the time, a captain under Joseph Magliocco and a made man with his own crew, named Johnny "Bath Beach" Oddo. He was accustomed to stopping in Red Hook and became familiar with the Gallo brothers and their exploits—so he took them under his wing.

There was concern among the higher-ups that Joey was really crazy, such a loose gun that he couldn't be trusted to do as he was told. They were always asking, "Joey on drugs?" Larry and Albert always said no. But the suspicions continued, and the idea was put forth that they should lock Joey in a room for a couple of days to see if he was on the junk. So they held Joey captive. They learned that he didn't have withdrawal symptoms, but he really was fucking crazy. It was the 1950s, but Joey acted like it was the 1930s.

Like all hoods, the Gallo brothers had to start at the bottom and work their way up. Their first assignments were small street crimes. But they were ruthless and efficient, so they were quickly promoted to a more important role as Profaci muscle. They roughed up victims under the regime of Frankie "Shots" Abbatemarco, who ran the family's million-dollar-a-year numbers racket.

You had to have balls of steel to keep from being eaten alive by the streets during those wild early days. Luckily, the Gallo brothers had them. Whomever Profaci wanted hurt, the Gallo brothers hurt. Legs were busted. Heads were busted. Whatever. The boss says you should shape up.

Profaci came to trust the Gallo brothers to be as violent as necessary without fucking up, and he assigned them one of the biggest hits of all time, a hit on Albert Anastasia, a boss, the underworld's high lord executioner. It was one of the biggest hits in mob history, setting a record that stands to this day. The hit team would consist of Joey and Larry, a young street hood from Red Hook named Carmine Persico, and Larry's number-one gunman, Joe "Jelly" Gioelli.

Anastasia was ordered to reap just what he sowed. For years Anastasia ran "Murder, Inc." He was a psychopath, in the clinical sense, a fancy word for reptilian, without feelings. And he was one tough fuck, a dangerous combo. Albert had ten killings under his belt by the time he was twenty-five. He started killing in the 1920s. During the 1950s, Anastasia worked his way up the ladder in the Mangano Crime Family, really old school. That was one of the original families that ran Brooklyn. Albert was a snake, and he killed Vincent and Philip Mangano, then took over their family. Then he got on the commission's shit list when he shot Arnold Shuster after Shuster ratted on the legendary bank robber Willie Sutton. Then word got around that Anastasia was selling buttons, taking cash to make a guy a made man. It was only a matter of time.

It was one of the most famous hits of all time, taking place on October 25, 1957, in the barbershop of the Park Sheraton Hotel, where Anastasia was getting a shave and a haircut. Here's something you might not know: Anastasia's driver, Anthony "Coppy" Coppola, says he was outside at the time of the shooting, "taking a little sun." Anastasia's bodyguard, James Squillante, wasn't the take-a-bullet type, and he ran when the shooters entered the barbershop. Ironically, Squillante was Anastasia's top gun, and had only a month earlier killed Frank Scalise. Coppola and Squillante, it turned out, had been given a heads-up by Vito Genovese and Carlo Gambino that Anastasia's shave was to be his last, and they knew to take a hike when the time came. The info was framed in a way they could easily understand: "Walk or die." Coppola and Squillante walked.

When Joey got back to President Street he was lit. The adrenaline from the hit had him sky-high, and he kept saying that he and his fellow shooters from then on needed to be referred to as "The Barbershop Quartet."

That was the Gallo brothers' big move. Not long after that, Joey, Larry, and Carmine Persico became made men. Joe Profaci didn't like it, but there was nothing he could do. The Gallos and Persico were clearly budding stars. He couldn't stop them, but he just had to hope that somewhere down the line he could contain them.

Over the next few months, the American Mafia began to get real publicity for the first time. J. Edgar Hoover, head of the FBI forever and ever, said there was no such thing as the Mafia. He said this sometimes just after being treated to a fine day at a thoroughbred racetrack where everything was free and he was fed the names of the winning horses before the races. People knew the mob existed, but they didn't know the details, at least not until the U.S. Senate, with Bobby Kennedy and others asking tough questions, called a bunch of hoods to testify, put them under oath, and then grilled them with everyone watching on television. There was much pleading of the fifth. The hearings started in early 1957 and continued until the next year. It was called the McClellan Committee, and its job was to investigate "corruption, criminal infiltration, and illegal activities in the nation's labor unions," which of course included the longshoremen. In 1958, Joey and Larry were subpoenaed and had to go down to D.C. to testify.

Joey found himself eye to eye with Bobby Kennedy. Bobby stared him down.

Joey looked down and said, "Nice rug to play a craps game on." Bobby Kennedy and the rest of the senators and lawyers then got to see Joey go into full Udo mode, cackling like a hyena, doing his Richard Widmark impression. That was the moment that Crazy Joey became legendary. They'd make a movie about him. It was a bad movie, but it was about Joey. Bob Dylan wrote a song about him. The Udo impression for Bobby Kennedy was what started all of that.

Once under oath and on the stand, Joey and Larry answered every question the same way, "I respectfully decline to answer on the grounds that the answer may tend to incriminate me."

When the boys got back to President Street, they were even fuller of themselves than ever.

"Bobby Kennedy is a fag!" they said.

Joey said, "Fucking Kennedy needed to be warned, he's fucking with Joey Gallo. It felt good telling the little prick to go fuck himself."

At that point, as the 1950s came to a close, the Gallo brothers had a crew of more than fifty guys. These guys were loyal. They would have gone to Washington and put a bullet through Bobby Kennedy's head if the Gallo brothers had wanted them to.

CHAPTER 3
MONDO ILLIANO

ONE OF THE GUYS who made South Brooklyn special when I was growing up was Armando "Mondo" Illiano. He was first cousin to Frank "Punchy" Illiano, and ran "Mondo's club" on President Street, a block from the piers, where the Gallo crew hung out. Punchy and Mondo were very close, and Punchy used to hold most of his meetings at his cousin's place.

My dad took me to Mondo's when I was six or seven to meet Punchy, and I met them at the same time. The thing that made Mondo different was that he was a dwarf, and I remember how weird I felt as a little kid because I was already taller than him. Mondo was also the kind of guy that made you like him. Little guy, big heart. Hell, he was just about the most popular guy in the whole neighborhood.

I also met Mondo's mom, who was known to all as "Mama Palma." She was a small woman who always dressed in black, and spoke broken English. She treated you like she was your grandma. All she wanted to do was feed you.

As I grew older and started to hang out on President Street more, I got to know Armando better. After a while, you didn't care that he was a dwarf. He was just one of the guys. He was loyal to Joey Gallo, and knew no fear. You had to love the Latin meaning of his name, which was "army man." And that was what he was: a soldier in Joey Gallo's army.

CLEO THE LION

At that time (around 1961), Joey Gallo knew a guy in the city named Tony, who had a shop with exotic animals. I think he knew Joey through the bookmaking operation. Something like that.

One day Tony called Joey and told him he had a monkey, a real monkey, like out of a zoo. Joey liked the idea of having a monkey around and told Tony to bring the animal down to President Street. But the monkey was not popular and only lasted a couple of weeks. Joey had to call Tony and tell him to come and take back the monkey. It was throwing shit all over the place.

Still, there persisted the notion that Mondo's club needed an exotic animal, to spice things up a bit, and to intensify the club's aura in a way that could be frightening to potential enemies.

So Tony says, "Mondo, I got a lion cub named Cleo." So the lion moved into Mondo's basement. It was little at first, with big, big paws.

Joey and Larry Gallo liked to tell a story about bringing Cleo home. Joey was driving, Larry sitting shotgun, and Cleo was in the middle. They were coming off the Brooklyn Bridge and pulling onto Flatbush Avenue and a cop car pulled up alongside. Man, did that cop do a double take. They couldn't stop laughing. (That's something you've got to keep in mind. As bad as these guys were, they loved to laugh. They saw the comedy in life and enjoyed every minute. Of course, if you pissed them off, everything could change in a flash.)

So Cleo took up residence in the basement of Mondo's club, where he grew and grew and grew. That basement wasn't finished and done up nice. It was just a cellar, but it had already had quite a history when it was converted into a lion's den. It was Mama Rosa's place years before, and they used to have all-night card games down there when my mom was a kid. After that, it became her daughter Dolly's place, but when they found out she was a thief they chased her, and Mondo and his mom took over, with Tarzan doing the cooking. (Tarzan had a joint on Ninth Street and Third Avenue called The Blue Beetle, named after his partner, who was a jockey.) It was often used as storage space for whatever swag the boys had picked up recently. And if it was wartime, guys would hide out down there.

That lion in the basement became like the night Reggie Jackson hit three home runs in one World Series game. Over the years, the number of guys who claim to have been there to see it in person has grown exponentially. If everyone who claimed to have seen Cleo was an actual eyewitness, then President Street would have been more crowded than the circus. In reality, the only guys who got to see the lion were crewmembers and the poor jerks who owed them money.

You can imagine what it was like. There would be some guy who owed the Gallo brothers money, whether it was from sports betting or a loan or whatever. He'd be invited over to Mondo's club to have a "discussion." The guy would already be scared, his heart pounding. Then they'd invite him into the basement. At the top of the stairs he would know something was up, from the smell. Then maybe he heard a roar. Already the guy was shitting his pants. By the time he actually saw the lion, he was planning to sell his house to pay back his debt. They never had to actually feed anyone to the lion. Just showing them Cleo was always enough!

Mondo was in charge of the maturing Cleo, and it wasn't long before Mondo's physical advantage had evaporated. Mondo couldn't handle her anymore and Cleo had to go.

From the very first time I came onto the block, Mondo treated me like family. He came over, asked me if I needed anything, asked, "How's Ricky?" And Mondo was like that every time I saw him, right up until the time he died.

* * *

Sonny Girard, who loved Mondo, remembers him as a guy who was barely four feet tall, yet a guy who made a big impression on those who knew him, even those who only briefly crossed his path. He was an integral part of a mob at war, a warrior/soldier, and yet one of the funniest guys around.

Sure, he kept a lion in his basement, that's legendary, but Girard remembered him best as a guy on the street walking a big German shepherd with illegal numbers receipts under his collar.

Being funny was Mondo's calling in life. He was funny when he was proprietor (along with his mom) of the club you were in, the Longshoreman's Club, and he hung out to entertain you. But he was even *funnier* when he was a guest at someone else's joint and could be in full party mode.

On some weekend night Sonny and the others would all be at the Coco Poodle, a bar on Coney Island Avenue and Cortelyou Road, where the Kensington section meets Ditmas Park in Brooklyn.

There were a lot of bars around there, and this one became a crew hangout. On these well-lubricated evenings, it became customary to take Mondo into an open but dimly lit back room area, where they would tie a red tablecloth around his neck like a cape, sit him on the back of a chair that was tipped over on the floor, then have two guys slide Mondo around the dance floor as the band blasted out the theme from the *Batman* TV show.

The sliding throne would skid to a halt at the center of the dance floor and Mondo would stand up and gyrate wildly to the music, then he was on the floor, his movements seemingly out of control, until you saw the method in his madness, as he bumped up and against and danced under the skirts of the female dancers. Once you've seen that, you get to laugh every time you think about it for the rest of your life.

Girard offers a Mondo story that couldn't be told if we didn't all live in a world in which men pretty much universally carried guns for self-protection, and Mondo wasn't a self-deprecating guy. He got the joke, he was four feet tall, it was funny. Girard wasn't there, he heard this story, but he believes it to be true. A few of the guys, including Armando, were coming back from New Jersey when they had a minor car accident, a fender-bender, with a female driver. As they pulled over to exchange licenses and registrations, Armando was slipped out of the car, laid on the ground, and then covered by one of the guys' suit jackets. During the document exchange, the woman was led around to the other side of the car, where Mondo was lying on the road, as still as death. The woman almost fainted when she saw him. She not only thought he'd been killed in the accident but that he was a normal-sized man who had been cut in half.

Joey Gallo and Mondo would go out. If anyone asked who the little guy was, Joey would introduce Mondo as his bodyguard.

One of the best photos of all time was taken the night after Joe Magnasco was killed. A bunch of the crew were picked up and run in, and there's a photo of the lineup, with Mondo's head coming no higher than the other guys' midsections.

Cops asked Mondo if he saw the killer.

"I saw his belt buckle," Mondo said. "Show me a lineup of belts and I might be able to recognize it."

Mondo was usually funny, but he could be gruff and grouchy sometimes with the guys in the crew, the guys he loved most of all.

Sonny Girard says he still sometimes finds himself daydreaming and remembering Armando Illiano, the littlest tough guy.

CHAPTER 4
THE ORIGINAL CREW

THE GALLO FAMILY was colorful, comprised of all types of characters. That in itself made it unique. The factions back in those days weren't exactly known for their diversity. For one thing, in other crews, everyone was Italian. It was very rare for a family to have a non-Italian in its employ. But the Gallos didn't care. The original crew had a few Arabs, a Greek, and a Pole. It was the United-fucking-Nations of the underworld. The other families frowned on their diversity, saying that you couldn't trust non-Italians. You couldn't trust anyone, they said, who hadn't been born into the Life. The question of mixed ethnicities in the crew was a thorn in Joey Gallo's side for a long time. The more people complained, the more Joey despised all of the old traditional rules.

Regardless of where their folks had been born, there was a colorful cast of characters that decorated President Street in the 1960s and '70s. One popular hoodlum of the day was Joe "Jelly" Gioelli. He was a childhood friend of the Gallos, grew up in South Brooklyn, short and stocky with wavy black hair and eyes as cold as ice. He became the main muscle for the crew early on. Even though most people don't know, he was one of the shooters in the famous Albert Anastasia hit, and he was also responsible for the disposal of Frankie "Shots" Abbatemarco.

35

Frankie was a guy who didn't broadcast the details of his child-hood, so little is known. He did a couple of years in prison during the Roaring Twenties on narcotics charges. He got his big push in mob politics when he ran numbers during the Depression for Joe Profaci. Money was tight at the time, and Frankie Shots was a brilliant earner. According to one source (and who knows which books he was looking at), the numbers were bringing in $7,000 a day at the peak. Like everyone else in the Profaci/Colombo family, Jelly was getting pissed off at Joe Profaci's ever-increasing tribute demands. You had guys who were scraping by in the old hood paying huge tribute to a guy who had estates in New Jersey and Florida. Frankie Shots was among those who refused to pay the tribute in protest, and when the debt got as high as $50,000, the contract went out. Frankie Shots breathed his last on November 4, 1959. The hit was given to Joey, who refused it, so it went to Carmine Persico. The hit was at Cardiello's on Fourth Avenue and Carroll Street, where Frankie Shots was ambushed by Per-sico and Jelly in topcoats and fedoras. Shots rang out. The front window of the saloon exploded into shards. Frankie Shots was hit at least once and tumbled back into the bar. The gunman got away, and Frankie Shots died on the barroom floor, his face in the sawdust. So the Gallos had taken out Frankie Shots on Joe Profaci's behalf in theory because Profaci had offered them a larger percentage of the numbers rackets, but Profaci reneged on the deal, thus contributing to the growing divide between the two factions.

Jelly was loyal to the end and had to be eliminated (gruesome details to come) on August 17, 1961, which was, of course, a big blow to the Gallo brothers.

During the war, a few good men were taken out much too soon. One, Joey "Mags" Magnasco, was a South Brooklyn prod-uct, a real concrete kind of fella. He was a solid player for the Gallos, with hands of steel and a "no holds barred" type of attitude. Joey Mags developed a deep hatred for Profaci early on, even before the war. He joined the Gallos just as the war was announced and became one of the war's first casualties, eliminated on a chilly night in October 1961, shot to death outside the Union Street Diner. (I was there, but I'll get to that.)

One of the non-Italians on the Gallo crew was Ali "Ali Baba" Hassen Waffa, an interesting guy—and one of the few crewmembers who'd once held down a real (that is, legitimate) job. He'd been a cook on a cruise line, but he spent most of his time in South Brooklyn. He eventually ran a string of gambling dens in all of New York's Arab neighborhoods, and a Shylock operation, as well. When the war came he became one of Joey's top hit men. He was terminated on June 15, 1963, while aboard a boat that had just docked in Hoboken, New Jersey.

Another close friend of the Gallos was Louie "Cadillac" Mariani. It is suspected (strongly suspected, in some circles) that Mariani was the shooter in the botched hit on Nicky "Jiggs" Forlano of the Profacis in October 1961. Louie was eliminated two years later in retaliation. On April 17, 1964, John Battista and Fat Tony Regina were sentenced for Mariani's murder. Then Joseph "Bats" Cardiello got killed in 1963, one of the brothers from the bar of that name, a Gallo loyalist, and a good guy from the neighborhood.

THE SYRIANS

The crew had two other non-Italians, Louie "The Syrian" Hubella and Sammy "The Syrian" Zahralbam. Louie was a standup guy and a charter member of the Gallo crew. He was tough as nails, a World War II vet, who ran a sports book and loaned money to Brooklyn's Arabs. There was a dense cluster of Arabs along Atlantic Avenue, the major thoroughfare that separated downtown Brooklyn from South Brooklyn. It was on Atlantic Avenue, out of a club he owned called The Court Terrace Lounge, that Louie conducted his business. Louie was known as an efficient gun-man, one of Joey Gallo's favorites. He could crack his knuckles and guys would shit their pants, so he was instrumental in convincing bar owners to go along with Joey's protection racket. Louie was *consigliere* to the Gallo brothers—and he would end up being a pallbearer at Joey's funeral.

Sammy the Syrian was another story. Sammy and Louie might have shared the same nickname (they were brothers-in-law), but they were opposites. Sammy was a stocky, nasty fella. He helped run the gambling dens and spoke like Edward G. Robinson. He was a real ass, and apparently not too bright, because he often got nasty to the wrong people. Down the road there was a falling-out.

ROY ROY AND PUNCHY

Now, some of these guys were gone when I was still a little kid, and some hung around to make a great impression on me. There was one member of the original crew who stood out for me for a very long time. He was Rosario "Roy Roy" Musico, born on President Street in 1942—and from day one he led a wild life. His mom was small but sassy, a petite firecracker, with a voice that carried the husk of every cigarette she'd ever smoked. She had a club from which she sometimes simultaneously served longshoremen and took numbers. Roy Roy grew up in the club, and got rough and tough when he was very young from all of the exposure. He was still just a kid when he became an asset to the Gallos—and he stayed an asset for a long time, as loyal as they come. Roy Roy's job was to groom all of the young guys on their way up, teach them the ropes. He was this wild combination of ruthless gangster and party animal. He could down a bottle of Scotch in the course of a night, and smoke a couple of joints on top of it to take the edge off. But he was rebellious. He didn't like to be told what to do. The rule with the crew was no mustaches and no beards, but Roy Roy wouldn't shave until Larry or Blast would yell at him.

The other original crewmember who had a big influence on me was Frank "Punchy" Illiano, Mondo's first cousin. He was tough as nails, fought in the Golden Gloves when he was a kid, and had hung out on President Street since day one. Later, he took the gloves off and used those hands to put a hurt on the Gallos' enemies. A lot of guys named Punchy are called that because they act like they've been on the receiving end too much, but this Punchy got the name for dishing them out, often in crisp and destructive combinations. He ran all of the street fairs in South Brooklyn and finally became a made man in the 1970s. Punchy was close to my father, and they stayed close their whole lives.

CHITOZ

Gennaro "Chitoz" Basciano was a real South Brooklyn tough guy, born and raised in the heart of Red Hook. He was a stone-cold killer, but you would never know it by speaking to him. He was right-hand man to Joey and Larry for many years. He was another guy who could've earned a living in the ring, a guy who could knock you cold with one shot. He was quiet but deadly—and loyal. He did a lot of work in the early days. He stuck by Larry and Joey until the end, and was a great friend to me.

COCKEYED BUTCH

Not all of the original crew got along with the Gallo boys all the time. One guy who was always in trouble was Joseph "Cockeyed Butch" Musemeci, who wore glasses as thick as coke bottles and drank like a fish. He went to bed with a netting on his head so he wouldn't muss his hair. He was a meticulous dresser but not a good-looking man. He looked like Mr. Magoo, and he was married to the niece of Joe Colombo. My parents were close for many years with him and his wife. It's just a symptom of the fucked-up way things were that Butch and my dad couldn't stay on the same side forever.

The thing with Butch was that he was a degenerate gambler

and was always getting yelled at by Larry. He took care of all of the gambling outside the neighborhood for the family. Larry set up an office for him at the Manhattan Beach Hotel, which was on the same sandbar as Coney Island and Brighton Beach, just a little bit farther east, just south of Sheepshead Bay. He had an easy job. He sat in there at the end of the bar and he took bets for horses and other sports. The problem was, being a degenerate, he couldn't even come close to controlling himself in that atmosphere, like an alcoholic who tends bar. My dad used to sit with him some days, and he saw Butch, for every bet he took, place a bet of his own going the other way. Larry kept yelling at him to stop. One time Larry got so mad that he punched Butch in the mouth and knocked out two of his front teeth. But Butch couldn't be trained. He kept doing it his own way. He lost a ton of money for Larry.

MOONEY

Here's a guy that nobody liked from day one: John "Mooney" Cutrone. I don't really know much about him, just that he was made by Profaci in the early 1950s, long before Larry or Joey got their buttons.

I didn't like him. Nobody liked him. My father wanted to kill him. I mean, it was an obsession with Ricky. It was all I heard him talk about for what seemed like years, how much he wanted to kill that fucking Mooney.

My dad would get into it in detail. He had different ways in which he wanted to kill fucking Mooney, and he would describe them to you vividly and with sadistic glee. A lot of the methods involved squeezing. Mooney, in the meantime, continued to breathe and annoy everyone. He was made, and therefore whack-proof.

Mooney was a small man with a sour puss and a nasty disposition. For some reason Larry liked him. That, and how the guy got made in the first place, are two unsolved mysteries. An old-time Profaci guy might know, but there aren't many of them left.

The instant that Mooney's magic shield began to lower, the contract went out on him, and seven guys raised their hands to volunteer for the job—a couple of them who had never even fired a gun before.

Ricky began complaining about Mooney when I was a little kid, and I was twenty fucking years old before it stopped.

NICKY BIANCO

Nicky was a guy I only knew for a short time, but he was important because he was instrumental in the "Gallo Peace Deal." He was a newcomer, born and raised in Rhode Island, and showed up in Brooklyn in the 1960s with reputed connections to the Patriarca crime family.

A tough guy with a few killings under his belt, he was involved with the Colombo family for a while, and then went back to Patriarca when they offered him a button. He was friends with the Gallo brothers right up until the point that the shit hit the fan, and then he moved on.

You'd think that we'd call him a fair-weather friend for that, but it turned out he was doing what he thought was best for the underworld in general. He went to the Patriarcas, after a period of time when he sided with the Gallos because he felt their gripe against Profaci, in particular Joseph Magliocco, was legit. Then the war started and it got out of hand, the carnage became too great, and Nicky felt he had to do something.

He went to Raymond Patriarca and asked if there wasn't something they could do to put an end to the madness. Full-fledged war on the streets of Brooklyn was bad for business. Patriarca agreed and assigned Nicky to broker a deal, which Nicky did.

So, maybe in the long run his leaving the Gallos for the Patriarcas was good for the Gallos. But my father didn't think so. Ricky always said that Nicky Bianco was a gypsy, that he had no roots, that he blew from one place to another, carried by the wind, rather than be fastened to a turf like all of the men Ricky admired. Ricky wasn't shy about his disdain, either.

In 1982, Nicky, back on his home turf, reportedly participated in the killing of Anthony Mirabella, an associate of the Patriarcas whose allegiance was fickle, in a restaurant in Providence, Rhode Island.

Nicky ended up being indicted on charges related to the Mirabella murder, but there was no trial as the judge quickly dismissed all charges for lack of evidence. The law didn't get to Nicky until 1991, when he was charged and convicted on RICO bullshit and sentenced to eleven years. He died behind bars on November 14, 1994.

Ricky never did warm up to him.

PETE "THE GREEK" DIAPOULIS

Pete the Greek is like Fred Merkle or Bill Buckner, respectable ballplayers who will be notorious forever because of the one time they fucked up big. Pete was muscle, a bodyguard. He was tall, heavyset, nobody you'd want to fuck with, always had a cigarette dangling from his mouth.

And you never would have heard his name if he hadn't been a bodyguard for Joey Gallo on the morning when the Colombo crew made the biggest mistake of their lives. We'll touch upon this a lot more later in the book, of course, but Pete the Greek fucked up big, so bad that some suspected it was "accidentally on purpose," and he had to spend the rest of his life dealing with what he'd done—or hadn't done.

The Greek could carry his weight, but he had no personality. He met Joey when they were young and got his start with the crew by tending bar at the Coco Poodle. Larry had Pete working the gambling operations in Brooklyn's Greek neighborhoods. Today, organized crime is more cross-cultural than it was back in the day. The Gallos were progressives when it came to pushing their operations into non-Italian neighborhoods.

Nobody liked Pete. There was nothing to like. He was all muscle, dull to the extreme when he wasn't hurting someone. When Joey got out of jail, he asked for Pete to be his bodyguard, a job that Pete did well every day—except for the last.

CARMINE PERSICO

Carmine "The Snake" Persico was a violent psychopath, born and raised in South Brooklyn. He started out in the Garfield Boys (so named because they hung out during the late 1940s and early '50s at Fifth Avenue and Garfield Place in Park Slope) and worked his way up to the Frankie "Shots" Abbatemarco crew. He was a friend of Joey and Larry Gallo from back when they were kids. Persico and the Gallo boys had a number of things in common, among them loan-sharking, bookmaking, burglaries, and hijacking. It turned out that Persico's real talent was for killing. Once he started to brutally kill, with eyes as cold as ice, he worked his way up quickly. He was in on the Anastasia hit, and on the Frankie Shots hit, as well.

I've known him since I was a kid, and I know for a fact he was well liked among his crew. He did everything his boss asked him to do, but deep down inside, Persico's only loyalty was to Persico. He was a psychopath, and they're selfish to a creepy level. He even double-crossed and set up his childhood friend Larry Gallo. That was how he got the name "The Snake."

ET AL.

There were many other guys who were with the Gallo brothers in the beginning, guys who stuck with them throughout the Gallo-Profaci War. They were shooting guys—and they were getting shot at. And most of the time they weren't getting paid very much to do it. It was all about brotherhood and allegiance.

There was SALVATORE "TOUGH SALLY" BALSAMO. He came from the neighborhood, had hands like baseball mitts. He was a money-making machine, big into swag. He stole stuff rather than money, mainly cigarettes. A double threat, he was good with his hands *and* ready to shoot. He ran Cobble Hill Car Service for many years, had a brother named Joey who was with us for a short time.

JOSEPH "SMOKEY" D'ANTUANO was another guy from Red Hook, grew up with the Gallos, and would do anything for Larry. He was a chubby bald guy, always pleasant to be around. His thing was money: He liked to make it and make it fast. He ran a sports book, took numbers, owned a car service. He was around until 1973, when he left with Mooney.

One compadre, JOHNNY "TARZAN" LUSTERINO, owned a bar at Third Avenue and Ninth Street called The Blue Beetle. The boys went to Tarzan's place often, and when war broke out it was Lusterino who came to President Street and cooked for the boys. He was there to do more than cook, though, and always let it be known that he and his gun were available for assignment. He was killed in 1973.

ANTHONY "ABBY" ABBATEMARCO was Frankie Shots's son. After Profaci whacked his old man, he knew his days were numbered in that organization and he hid out with the Gallos. Abby stayed on President Street until the late 1960s, when he got a better deal from the Colombos and went back.

Others left, too: Leonard "Lenny Dell" Dello, Joseph "Little Lollipop" Carna, Larry "Big Lollipop" Carna, Vincent "Chico" Regina, Salvatore "Sally Boy" Mangiamelli, and a few more. They went where the money was. The craziest thing about it was that these guys had all put their lives on the line to back up the Gallo brothers, only to skip to the other side the second the war was over. It only goes to show the power of money.

CHAPTER 5

RICKY & DEE

THE DI MATTEO FAMILY, with a space between the *i* and the *M* back then, came from Naples, Italy. One set of my paternal great-grandparents sailed to America in the 1890s, entering New York Harbor and sailing past Red Hook and the then-brand-new Statue of Liberty on their way to Ellis Island. My grandparents were Gabriel Di Matteo, born June 5, 1899, and Carmina Cassella, born November 29, 1908, both in Brooklyn. Shortly after meeting, Gabriel and Carmina took a boat to Bara Lotina, Italy, and were married. They returned to America in the 1930s, and had their first boy, John, in 1932.

Then, on March 4, 1937, Riccardo Antonio Dimatteo was born at Methodist-Episcopal Hospital in Park Slope, Brooklyn. When my dad was a little boy, they lived at Carroll Street and Third Avenue in the Gowanus section, then moved to Williamsburg. He grew up in an absolutely normal, poor Italian household. To make ends meet, Gabriel worked in construction and Carmina was a seamstress.

RICKY THE BOUNCER

My father's life in organized crime didn't begin until 1958, not long after he got out of the army. He was a high school graduate, which was a real accomplishment if you came from a poor Italian family, a sign you were smart.

Dad boxed, worked as a bouncer, and joined the Gallos. One of the first jobs my dad took as a member of the Gallo crew was at the Hilltop Bar on Prospect Avenue and Prospect Park West in Brooklyn. Larry and his crew had been put in there to run the place. There were Nicky Bianco, Bobby Darrow, and others.

My dad stayed with Abby, son of Frankie Shots (much more about them later), and Jimmy "Bats" Cardiello, who owned Cardiello's Tavern on Sackett Street.

But it was at the Hilltop Bar on Prospect Park West and Prospect Avenue where all of the action started. The Hilltop was a typical old bar with a four-by-four window in front looking out onto the street. There was a well-worn and beer-soaked bar, a small kitchen in the back, a few booths, and pictures of Frank Sinatra and Dean Martin on the walls. There was a cigarette machine, a jukebox, and an old wooden phone booth with numbers carved into its inner walls. During the 1970s, they filmed scenes for *Dog Day Afternoon* in the Hilltop Bar.

Now, my mother's name was Amelia Dominica Fiore, but Larry, Blast, and Ricky called her Dolly—don't know why, "Hello Dolly" was a hit song, maybe that was it—and Dolly eventually got shortened to Dee, and that was her name from then on.

She says Ricky was first to call her that. She's not sure why, but she suspects he didn't like the nickname she had at the time, which was Chubby. She'd been chubby as a baby, her mother called her "Chubby," and the nickname stuck. She, of course, didn't like the name, but that only served to make the name stick harder. The more she said, "That's not my name," the more it became her name.

Ricky put an end to that.

When they met she said, "Hi, I'm Chubby."

He said, "No, you're not," and she never was again.

MOM MEETS RICKY

Here's how it happened, according to my mom: I was about four, and she was hanging out with her girlfriends and they went to a neighborhood bar around the corner from one of her girlfriends' house, the Sackett Street Bar. A couple of fellows came in and they were talking to them. She was saying that she was looking for a job because she was living at home with her mother and father and wanted to help out with the bills.

One of the boys was named Rick, and he said, "What do you do?"

Mom said, "Work in a bank."

He said, "I don't have a bank, but I have a bar."

She told him she'd never been a barmaid and he promised to show her how to do it, and took her and her girlfriends to his bar, the Hilltop Bar. It really was on top of a hill.

"You want a drink?" Ricky asked her.

She said she did, but she didn't know what she wanted. "Surprise me," she said, so he mixed her an Orange Blossom: gin and orange juice. They got to talking.

She said, "You have a packed bar. If I have to count all that money and each drink is different I could never do it." He said he would help her, so she said okay.

He kept his word and he did help her, every day for a couple of weeks. Eventually Cupid's arrows struck them. But there were complications: Rick was married with a kid, a little girl. And that wasn't all of it.

As my mom puts it, "He had girlfriends. A *lot* of girlfriends."

She doesn't know much about Ricky's first marriage, just that between the bar and the girls he went out with, he never went home.

I MEET RICKY

If it wasn't for the Hilltop Bar, I wouldn't be around to tell this story. I'd like to think things happen because they were meant to happen.

I was about five years old when I met Ricky at the bar. He was well-dressed, stood about five-eight, well-built with a great smile, and he gave me a bow and arrow as a gift. He spoke softly to me, as if he'd known me for years. I felt his warmth and trust immediately.

I didn't know he was a hood. What did I know? I was five. Ricky was already in the Life when my mom met him. It's just the way it was.

THE FIORES

My mother's family, the Fiore family, came from Naples. It was my grandparents who came to the United States when they were very young. They came separately, and met here. Salvatore Fiore was born on December 15, 1897, and came to America in 1904. My grandmother, Amalia Decarrone, was born on October 2, 1902, and came to the United States in 1906. My grandfather lived for a while in the town of Croton-on-Hudson, up in Westchester County, then moved to South Brooklyn where, when he was old enough, he worked as a longshoreman. He worked on the piers all of his life, in Brooklyn and Manhattan. My grandmother always lived in Red Hook, where she worked odd jobs as a girl— at her brother's place and a few others. Salvatore and Amalia, now known as Mary, were married in 1919. My mother was born on September 7, 1934. She had one sister and five brothers, many of whom came to a tragic end. Two died as children. A brother burned to death at age three, and a brother named Salvatore died at childbirth. Martin died in World War II while on a mission. Mike died of a heart attack while still in his thirties, and Frank just passed away a couple of years ago from diabetes. My aunt is fighting diabetes now in a hospital in California. My mom is still doing okay.

"Too okay!" she says. "Maybe it's because I was the only one out of all of us to be born in a hospital—and I was fat!"

TOUGH TIMES

Mom was born at the time of the Great Depression. Things were rationed back then, you had to get your food with stamps issued by the government, so she learned early not to take things for granted.

Meat was a once-in-a-while thing, and she remembers going with my grandmother down to the chicken place to pick out a chicken. They ate one big meal a day—and that was it. People walked around Red Hook picking dandelions to make soup and salad. They lived together in an apartment on Baltic Street so small that they considered the alcove a room. There was only one real bedroom.

Mom doesn't remember a time when she didn't know there was a mob. My grandfather (called "Pa") would tell her stories. He was an eyewitness to a killing way back when in the neighborhood, when a guy named Silk Stockings was killed. I looked him up and he was a real guy, Johnny "Silk Stockings" Guistra. He ran with Frankie Yale and was muscle for the Mineo crime family. Pa would see him on the Brooklyn piers and in the neighborhood bars. Pa knew Johnny had a piece of Scotto's Funeral Home on First Place. Silk Stockings got whacked on May 10, 1931, on the Lower East Side in the city. He was suspected of knowing about the Masseria killing. Pa was having a beer when he saw Johnny during the last seconds of his life. Then he saw Johnny again, dead on the street. Pa ran home and never went back to that bar again. Pa said that Silk Stockings was as mean as they come, and when he walked on Court Street you could *feel* it.

DOCILE . . . TO A POINT

When my mother's brother Martin was killed in World War II, they moved from Baltic Street to First Place, just a few blocks to the south, but it was there that she *personally* became aware of the mob. It was a small world. Joey Gallo once dated my mother's girlfriend who lived next door to her on First Place. That was in the early 1950s, when they were all still teenagers.

My mom says that considering Joey was a homicidal maniac, a full-fledged psychopath, he could be very sweet—happy, friendly, hanging out, having dinner. At that time they all hung out at a place called Monte's.

"All of them was docile," she says. "Of course, if you twisted them the wrong way, you would see what happened."

The girlfriend who dated Joey lived in the same building as Frank "Punchy" Illiano and his parents. She was friends with Andy "Mush" Russo and Carmine Persico. When she first became acquainted with those guys, they were running numbers out of Punchy's father's house. So, you might say my mom was a "wise gal" from the start.

When my mom quit school, she went to work with my grandmother at my uncle Natole's place. She went to P.S. 142 right there on Henry Street and then to the High School of Home Making. She was South Brooklyn, born and raised.

I ENTER THE SCENE

Here's how I come into the story: My mother got married in 1954 to a pro boxer named Alphonzo "Funzi" Milone, from Coney Island, Brooklyn. When she was a young woman, my mom used to take the train to Coney Island all the time. In the summer, it was not only fun, there with the beach and the amusement parks, but those were the days before air-conditioning, and it was ten degrees cooler at Coney Island than home in Red Hook. Back then, there used to be a place for dancing underneath the boardwalk, with a jukebox. My mom loves to dance. One time she was dancing with a guy and Funzi cut in. He asked her a few times for a date. She finally went out with him, and he told her he was a boxer.

He told her he was a semi-pro because he had to work a real job in addition to fighting, but one look at his record (see the appendix) shows he was a full-fledged pro (although not necessarily well paid), and that he fought on the undercard of major shows.

Funzi fought as Al Milone and had a 16-15 record, taking on all comers. He started out fighting at the Fort Hamilton Arena, at Ninety-ninth Street and Fort Hamilton Parkway, in a spot that is now underneath an entrance ramp to the Verrazano-Narrows Bridge. He fought in Philadelphia, at the Fifth Regiment Armory in Paterson, New Jersey. He fought at the St. Nicholas Arena in the city, and at the Sunnyside Gardens in Queens. By the peak of his career he fought twice in Madison Square Garden.

Things might have proceeded more quickly between my mom and Funzi if it hadn't been for the policies of my grandfather, which were strict. Mom was only seventeen so she had to be sneaky. She was expected to be home by eight thirty, nine o'clock. If she was too late, my grandfather would lock the door, so she'd have to pound and my grandmother would come down and let her in.

"It was rough," she says.

On the other hand, if she wanted to go shopping she much preferred going with my grandfather, who couldn't say no and bought her whatever she wanted.

When she was nineteen, Funzi asked her to marry him. My uncle and his wife took Mom and Funzi to get married, and they moved to Bay Fiftieth Street to live with Funzi's parents and his sister Lucy.

Trouble started in the marriage when Mom learned that Funzi didn't like to work. He liked to run and train for fights, but bringing home a paycheck wasn't his thing. My mom walked on him and went home to my grandparents, where my grandfather still wouldn't let her go out, now because she was a married woman.

The separation lasted a year and Funzi said he wanted to make up. He was turning over a new leaf. She said okay. They got together, they fought, got together, fought. They couldn't make it. She left again, and then discovered she was pregnant.

She says, "I asked my father what to do. He said, 'Have the *bambino*.' At the time they didn't believe in anything else."

There was one last attempt to reconcile with Funzi, but by this time he was fooling around so that was that. They stayed friends, he got this, she got that, and they stayed nice. My mother never bad-mouthed Funzi to me.

I came along on May 30, 1956, and Mom was a single mother at twenty-two. Divorced and with a baby, she went nowhere. Fortunately, my grandfather was good with kids, including me, and my grandmother would get up in the morning and feed me.

DOLLY'S BAR TRICK

As I got a little bit older, no longer a baby, Mom met Ricky, went to work as a barmaid, and worked in a series of bars, some nicer than others. One was in Sunset Park, Third Avenue, under the BQE, where sometimes she was the only person in the joint who didn't speak Spanish. Another was on Eleventh Avenue, which she thinks was called Anthony's at the time. In there, the customers were easier to understand. She also spent a stint working as a hat-check girl in a fancier joint over on Avenue U.

While tending bar, she had a trick up her sleeve. When she gave back the change for a drink, she would push back the coins until they went under the bar's back padding and got stuck. At the end of the night she might have as much as fifty dollars in coins to dig out and put in her black plaster cat bank. Ricky was cleaning up the bar one day and he found the cat, full of coins, so he cut a hole in the bottom, emptied the bank, and put the bank back where he'd found it. She kept putting change in. Every once in a while, Ricky would empty it again. One day Ricky and Larry Gallo were sitting at the end of the bar, laughing. Ricky told my mom that Larry needed some change. My mom said she had some change in the cat bank and went to get it. When she lifted the bank and felt it was empty, she was furious. She threw the cat at

Ricky and Larry, just missing them, so hard that it struck the phone booth and broke the glass.

Ricky and Larry were laughing so hard that they almost fell off their bar stools.

"Do you really think that you're smarter than me?" Ricky asked.

My mother said, "Not in a million years, honey."

"That's right," Ricky said, and he gave her four hundred dollars, about the amount that he'd taken out of the bank. They laughed all night. The next day she went down the block and bought another black cat bank to replace the one she broke. The glass in the phone booth remained cracked for some time.

It was one of the good times sandwiched in between all of the bad times.

SCARIEST MOMENTS

The scariest moment my mom can remember about being with my dad came once when they were in a car and he flipped out. Ricky and Dee were sitting in the back, and a guy up front pissed Ricky off. She won't mention the asshole's name because he has a brother who's still alive.

Ricky pulled a gun and was going to shoot the guy. When the car stopped, she jumped out of the car and ran. Though there was no shooting that night, she always quickly points out that, evidently, not long after that incident, the guy did die—and it wasn't from natural causes.

That was the scariest moment when she was in his presence. Most of the fear came when he wasn't around, when he would all of a sudden have to go on the lam and she wouldn't know what was going on until the boys came around to brief her on the situation.

Actually, going on the lam became routine after a while. One time Ricky packed up some lunch bags and took me with him on the lam, so he'd have some company.

Sometimes Ricky would flee just far enough to stay out of the way until things cooled down. Sometimes, when it was more serious, he'd go all the way to California and stay there until he got a phone call to come back. Dee remembers she was working for the Chin's sister in a place called the Magic Lantern on Cropsey Avenue when Ricky took off for California. The Chin, that's Vincent Gigante to you, Genovese boss for almost a quarter of a century. She came home from work one night and all of Ricky's clothes were gone. She figured that was it. Then one night she was working and Ricky just walked into the bar. He was back.

Dee says she only met the Chin twice, but on one occasion she mentioned to him that there was only one kind of champagne she liked, and from then on, every Easter, the Chin would send her a case of Tattinger champagne.

DIAMOND RATS

When I was little I saw the bar mostly on weekends when I made money either by cleaning up or by bringing my shoe-shine box. I kept my eyes and ears open, because there was always all kinds of shit going on.

Swag. Cigarettes. Anything you could steal. Stuff that fell off the truck. The stuff came into the bar, and then it left. Ricky, I remember, once made a diamond score. He hid them in an envelope in a wall in the cellar. When he found a buyer, he went to get them and they were gone. He said, "No way," and got a flashlight and looked in the wall. Rats had opened up the envelope and had scattered the diamonds in between the beams. He had to break the cement wall and squeeze in. He put on a hat and gloves and fired shots at the rats to make them run. He found about ten of the forty diamonds he'd hidden there. Man, was he pissed.

It was while working at the bar that Ricky met the whole Gallo crew: Cockeyed Butch, Roy Roy, Smokey, Punchy, Bobby Darrow, Tarzan, The Syrians, The Greek, The Beard, Jelly, Mooney, Ali

Baba, and Chitoz. One bad-ass crew. They had card games in the back, a pot of espresso on, and there was always something to eat.

There was never a moment when the bar was open and no one from the crew was there. Guys were there waiting for the joint to open, always two or three guys there, everyone always in a suit and tie.

Just like Pearl Harbor changed America, the start of the first Profaci War changed South Brooklyn. Guys who were used to sitting on bar stools found themselves hitting the mattresses. Guys who used to wander Brooklyn establishments like a bee going from flower to flower now kept their heads low on President Street.

On President Street there were a number of safe houses available. Roy Roy and his mother, Fran, had a club. Mondo and his mom had the Longshoreman's Club. Gargiulo Flower Shop was a hideout. Some restaurants took guys in, as well: Lefty Big Ears's, Mama Rose's, then her daughter Dolly's (no relation to my mom). The boys would always eat at Lefty's. They had the block locked down.

Ricky, being fairly new to the crew, was able to move around with the enemy for a while. That is when Larry began calling Ricky by his code name: Mr. Goldberg.

CHAPTER 6
THE FIRST GALLO-PROFACI WAR

JOE PROFACI was an old-time greaseball, and Joey Gallo was getting sick of him. Profaci's organization had been around for close to thirty years, having been started in 1931 after the assassination of Salvatore Maranzano. The Profaci family started out totally old school—nothing but Sicilians allowed. Profaci had been a Maranzano gunman, but nonetheless, when he assumed power, he proved adept at making peace with the other New York mob leaders, Neapolitans many of them, like future bosses Vito Genovese, Frank Costello, Lucky Luciano, and Albert Anastasia. Profaci became a ranking member of the national committee. He blended legitimate businesses with his rackets, went to church, and lived a quiet life.

There was a glass ceiling in the Profaci organization, and the Gallos kept banging their heads against it. They did not get promoted and were limited to only doing individual jobs, after which they were allowed to keep only a tiny percentage of the take. When in 1959 Larry and Joey negotiated for a larger share of their street earnings, Profaci reacted by rote. He'd been there, done that, and he gave them a line of bullshit before taking the money back in tribute.

Joey and Larry went to the other members of the Profaci family to air out their gripe and to hopefully pick up support. They went to Frankie Shots and Johnny Bath Beach. They talked to Profaci captains like Nicholas "Jiggs" Forlano, Charles LoCicero, and Harry Fontana.

While all of this was going on, Profaci ordered the Gallo crew to kill Frankie Shots. If it had been anyone else, the Gallos would have had no problem, but they didn't want to be the ones to take out Frankie Shots, so they passed off the job to Carmine Persico and Joe Jelly.

The Gallos didn't want Frankie Shots hit at all. Frankie had been giving Larry and Joey some insider advice as to how to bring Profaci down. But Persico and Jelly took out Frankie Shots at Cardiello's, and afterward Profaci asked Larry and Joey to turn over Frankie's son Abby, but instead Abby hid out on President Street.

And that was the end of any allegiance between Profaci and the Gallos. Larry and Joey had the backing of many Profaci *capos* who wanted Profaci to share more of the wealth, and they announced that they were fed up.

In February 1961, Larry, Joey, and Tony Bender had a meeting at the Hilltop Bar. Tony was the one who pulled the short straw and went to the commission with the Gallo brothers' beef.

Left to their own devices, Tony, Joey, and Larry devised a plan to kidnap Joe and Frank Profaci, Joe Colombo, John Scimone, Joseph Magliocco, and Sally Musacchio.

On February 27, 1961, Joey sent out a crew to make the pickups. He sent Jelly, Chitoz, Big Lollipop, Little Lollipop, Punchy, Louie the Syrian, and Vincent "Chico" Regina. It went pretty smoothly. They kidnapped everyone on the list except for Joe Profaci, who caught wind of the plot and took off to Florida.

One of the hostages was future boss Joseph Magliocco, who pissed his pants while in captivity, a humiliation that left him with a lifelong hatred for the Gallos.

After a few weeks of his captains being held hostage, Profaci made a peace agreement just to get them back. What Profaci didn't know was that Joey and Larry were at odds over what to do with the hostages, so much so that they came to blows. Joey didn't trust Profaci and wanted to kill the captives one by one, starting with Magliocco. Larry talked him out of it. Joey had been right not to be trustful. Joe Profaci had no intention of keeping his word.

That was a moment that was often discussed in my house. Ricky always said that he loved Larry like a brother, and that Joey was a maniac, but in this case Joey had been right.

Larry, as it turned out, wasn't hardwired to be a war boss. He had some sense of fairness that ended up being exposed as naïveté. They say that all's fair in love and war, a fact that Larry didn't properly consider.

He thought that as long as he did the right thing, all of the other bosses would side with him. As it turned out, money wins over morality every time—not just in organized crime, but in life in general. Larry's decision to be fair backfired on him big-time.

In August 1961, Profaci did exactly what Joey said he would do. Profaci ordered the killings of Larry, Joey, and the rest of the Gallo crew, Punchy, Mooney, and Chitoz. Larry ordered them all to lie low on the block.

Joey put together a crew of guys who could shoot. Guys who wouldn't be recognized immediately, like Ricky and Tony, were sent out as scouts. If they spotted anyone on the list, they would get word back to President Street and a team of shooters would be sent out.

The one thing everyone remembers about this part of the war was that the Gallo brothers had the gang that couldn't shoot straight—and it was true. Joey's torpedoes were on the erratic side, and many more of Profaci's crew were shot at than shot.

As is true of all wars, there were agents, double agents, and triple agents. There were turncoats and snakes. Larry and Joey were led to believe that Persico and John Scimone were on their side, not aware that they were spies. The Gallo bothers met with them often and discussed tactics and strategy, unaware that the information was going directly to Joe Profaci. Larry had been naïve when it came to trusting Persico, but both Larry and Joey were naïve when they trusted everyone in their seemingly loyal crew.

On August 17, 1961, Sally D'Ambrosio and John Scimone invited Joe Jelly to come fishing with them off Sally's boat. Jelly liked to fish and had been on the boat before, so he had no reason to think anything was wrong. So that morning Jelly left his girlfriend's house for a relaxing day out on the ocean.

While on the boat, Sally shot Jelly, chopped off and wrapped up his ring finger, chopped the rest of his body into little pieces, put the pieces in a fifty-gallon drum, and dropped the drum into the sea.

Cut to August 20, three days later, when no one knew where Jelly was, but there was starting to be concern. That day Larry received an invitation to the Sahara Lounge, a bar in East Flatbush, for a meeting with Scimone and Persico.

No one was around, and the only person to take Larry to the meeting was Kid Blast. Larry had made a rule that none of the Gallo brothers should go anywhere together, so Larry went to the Sahara alone.

Bad move.

In later years, when Ricky told and retold this story to me, I always had the same questions: "Where were the guys from the crew? Why did Larry have to go alone?"

"He was the Boss," Ricky said.

"Where was Dell? Where was Chico?"

"Larry was like that. He had no fear. He was trusting. He got the call, and he went. Well . . . guess what happened?"

Larry was outnumbered three to one in the Sahara. While Larry was talking to Scimone and Persico, Sally put a rope around Larry's neck and tried to kill him. Luckily for Larry, a beat cop checking on the bar walked in just then and broke it up. Sally ran out and, during his hasty exit, shot one of the cops and got away.

Larry survived, but he had a mark around his neck for the rest of his life. It was after that that Larry gave Persico his nickname, "The Snake," which stuck with him for the rest of his days.

The same day as the meeting in the Sahara, a member of the Gallo crew named Alfonso took Joey's car to pick up guns at the Caribbean Lounge in Bed-Stuy, and was shot at. The shooters thought it was Joey—so the Profaci boys had essentially tried to kill Larry and Joey on the same day.

The next morning a car drove by Jackie's Charcolette and threw out the package containing Jelly's finger, along with his clothing, which had been stuffed with fish. That sent a message to the Gallos: "*Jelly sleeps with the fish.*"

The next casualties were a pair of Joey's low-key guys, Marco Morelli and Tony DiCarlo. They got whacked by Carmine Persico and Jiggs Forlano, which proved they would hit anybody associated with the Gallos, not just the major players.

Joey's fragile mental state was taxed by the pressure of the war, and he grew to become like a ticking time bomb. He sat low for about a month and considered the matter, bothered by the fact that he no longer could be sure whose side some people were on, so he decided to just kill everyone. He wanted to go into their houses, into their clubs, and kill them all. This was no longer just about Profaci; it was about being betrayed by old friends, which had Joey mad, in every sense of the word. He was overwhelmed with bloodlust. The whole point became to kill.

THE KILLING OF JOEY MAGS

In October, Punchy, Chitoz, and Joey Magnasco were driving up Union Street looking for Harry Fontana, a Profaci *capo*. They were looking for him because he was supposed to be on the Gallos' side but he didn't seem to be doing as much as he could. In fact, it seemed like he was actually avoiding the Gallo crew, as if he might have something to hide. They finally found him in front of the Union Diner at the corner of Union and Fourth Avenue. Joey Mags jumped out of the car and started arguing with Harry Fontana.

In the heat of the argument, Harry's bodyguard shot Joey Mags, killing him on the spot. I know this because I was there, just five years old, with my mother, visiting my mother's girlfriends Chickie and Lillian in their apartment, and we were standing just twenty feet away when Joey Mags was shot.

My mom, being an adult, remembers it clearly. She became aware that there was some running around, some commotion nearby, a scuffle, and then she remembers car horns blaring, and gunshots. She grabbed me and started heading away from the action. She saw a couple of guys running away, just a glimpse out of the corner of her eye, so she couldn't say for sure who they were. Not that she would have said anyway.

"I'm smart enough not to look," she says. "None of my business."

But I remember seeing Joey Mags yelling and then falling to the ground. I knew that these were friends of my father's, but I didn't realize until later that I had actually seen Joey Mags just die there on the street. Even when I did figure it out, which didn't take long, I was young and it didn't bother me very much.

Later, while doing research for this book, I found a photo that had been taken by a newspaper photographer of Joey—still on the sidewalk, looking for all the world like he was taking a nap, a police chalk mark around him, and a priest, Father Benny Calleja, administering the last rites. That's how I know the date, October 4, 1961.

A few days later, there was a raid by Chief Inspector Raymond

Martin on President Street at Mondo's club, and many members of the Gallo crew were arrested and held on twenty-five thousand dollars' bail. They were charged as material witnesses in a gang war. President Street was empty.

Behind bars were Larry, Joey, and Albert Gallo, along with Mondo, of course; Abby; Anthony Gargiulo; Mooney; Alfonso Sarrantino; Lenny Dell; Sally Mangiamelli; Punchy; Vincent Regina; and the Carna brothers.

During the subsequent court appearance, Joey went into full Tommy Udo mode, with Mondo at his side. He told everyone in the courthouse that the police were harassing him.

In the meantime, lawyer Joe Iovine (the Gallo brothers' uncle Cupie) fought the charges, finally had them dropped, and everyone got to go home, except Joey, who was scheduled to leave for prison. In December 1961, Carmine Persico and Sally D'Ambrosio dressed up like women, jumped in a car, and went looking for Joey Gallo, whom they hoped to kill before he went away. Luckily, they couldn't find him.

On December 21, 1961, Joey Gallo was sentenced to fourteen years in prison on extortion charges. The weird thing was that Joey could have fought it, but he wouldn't let his lawyers work it out. It was like Joey wanted to go away. Larry told him it would be easier for them to kill him in prison, but Joey didn't care. He really was fucking crazy.

I was only five years old when Joey left, but I didn't forget him. Hell, on his way up the river, he stopped, his blue eyes gleaming, to give my cheek one last pinch. It was hard to forget, because it hurt for a week. Truth was, back then, I didn't really know who Joey was. I thought everybody was an uncle. My dad didn't take Joey's departure too hard. He was new and his connection was more with Larry. He appreciated sanity. Larry was level-headed, whereas Joey would have been happy killing everyone in the world until he was all alone, listening to his own Udo laugh.

In prison, Joey became a social activist, of all things. Like all prisons, his was divided along racial lines, but Joey went against the grain. He worked on building an alliance between the African American and Italian prisoners, while working against the white supremacist groups, including the Ku Klux Klan, that were active back then.

Larry became the leader of what was becoming known in New York City as the "Sixth Family." There were five established crime families, and the Gallos were the sixth.

At this time, maybe ten or so of the fifty Gallo crewmembers were shooters. The Gallo crew had collective balls of steel, fearing no one, bowing to no one—not even Carlo Gambino, who was not just the head of his own family, but the godfather of godfathers, the head of New York's five crime families.

The whole idea of being a rebel crew was unheard of—on account of it was considered suicidal. As the war continued, there were guys on President Street who hadn't left the block in a long time. Others left only tentatively, to get supplies or to go on a scouting mission. In February 1962, a couple of guys were on their way back to President Street, when they heard some kids screaming from a house on the block. There was a fire, and kids were trapped inside the building. Two days later, the *New York Times* reported the details: Seven Gallo gang members had saved six children from a top-floor apartment at 73 President Street, when a burning mattress filled the apartment with smoke. The newspaper gave the address of the "Gallo headquarters" as 51 President Street—not good for security—and said the men had just finished eating at a nearby restaurant when they saw the smoke. The apartment was occupied by Mrs. Sista Biaz, and her six children, who ranged in age from ten months to six years. The mom had been out shopping, and the kids had started the fire by playing with matches.

The crew ran into the house and then up the stairs to the top floor, where the fire was. They busted down the door. Lenny and Roy Roy smothered the fire with their jackets and Punchy, Larry, and Blast grabbed the kids and got them out of there. Even though Evelyn, age five, burned her hair, all of the other kids were carried out unharmed. The paper listed the heroes as: Larry Gallo, 31, who suffered from smoke inhalation but refused treatment; Albert J. Gallo, 32; Frank Illiano, 34; Anthony Abbatemarco, 39; Alfonso Serantonio, 22; Leonard Delio, 37; and John Commarato, 37.

Mrs. Biaz gushed, "They saved the lives of my children!"

Fire Chief Alexander Steier said, "They had the fire out and the kids out—a very good job."

NYPD Chief Inspector Raymond Martin offered only tempered praise, wishing the experience would turn the Gallo boys into "decent citizens."

The news guys wanted to take photos of the brave hoods, but Larry didn't want to be photographed. Anyway, the guys were heroes for a day.

In March 1962, Joe Profaci's son Salvatore had a couple of bullets whiz past his head, but he was unharmed.

On April 8, 1962, we lost Tony Bender, a sixty-two-year-old onetime high-ranking *capo* of the Genovese family, who grew up on the city's Lower East Side. Vito Genovese ordered the hit on Tony Bender. Vito had been pinched for drugs and believed it was Tony who had set him up. Plus, Tony was gaining power as an underboss and Vito didn't like that. Tony was also friendly with the Gallos and Vito didn't like that, either. But the final straw was the fact that Tony had gotten involved with Albert Anastasia and was selling buttons for cash.

Tony's death was a big deal at my house. Sadness and anger filled the air. He was the guy who'd seen my dad fight at the Sunnyside Gardens and had first offered him a job, the whole reason Ricky was in the crew in the first place.

Vito thought there were some *capos* in his organization who were too close to the "renegade" Gallo brothers. The Gallos, tougher than they were smart, were painting themselves into a strategic corner.

Gambino tried to talk Profaci, now a very sick man, into negotiating peace with the Gallos.

He said, "No way. There will be blood."

On June 6, Profaci died of cancer, and Joe Magliocco, Profaci's brother-in-law, took over for him. Nepotism was the order of the day in that family, as even Joe Profaci held sway with organized crime in other areas of the country through family and marriage.

The *New York Times* called Magliocco a "benign-looking man," born in Sicily, and a speaker of broken English.

Whenever he was questioned by police, Magliocco would pretend to be weak and mentally slow. The Suffolk County Police once hauled him in on a murder case. Magliocco grabbed his heart, took some pills, and acted confused.

His lifestyle could not have been in sharper contrast to the boys on President Street. Magliocco was sixty-five years old, lived in a mansion behind a stockade fence in East Islip, Long Island. One building in his compound housed steam baths. He had a stable and rode horses. He grew an acre of tomatoes. He had a thirty-five-foot yacht, on which he entertained his rich and old friends.

Larry Gallo, on the other hand, might be found at Mondo's club, sleeping on a mattress and not standing in front of windows. Instead of needing money to feed the horses and pay the servants, the Gallo crew was young and wild. They needed money for booze and broads, and they lived in tenements in low-rent apartments, on a dead-end street that was practically under siege by Profaci gunmen.

The Gallos were young, not rich, and when confronted by law enforcement or their enemies, they never ever acted weak or confused.

Joey Gallo talked to cops the same way he talked to everyone else. One time a detective told him that Frank Costello "owned New Orleans," meaning that he was in charge of the rackets in the Big Easy. Joey Gallo thought that was a joke. "Who gave him the city?" Joey asked. "Eisenhower? Anyone strong enough could take those rackets away from Frank Costello."

It didn't take the Gallos long to figure out that Magliocco was an even bigger prick than Profaci. He was one of the guys whom the Gallos had kidnapped, the one who'd pissed his pants while a captive, a humiliation he now sought to avenge.

For the rest of 1962, the Gallo crew hid out on President Street, and sometimes a team of shooters would go out with orders to find Profaci men and shoot them on sight.

In March 1963, Joey sent a team to kill Carmine Persico, the Snake. They put a bomb under Persico's Caddy, unaware that the car had a steel plate under the driver's seat. The bomb went off, but the plate saved Persico's life. He walked away, bleeding and dazed with a concussion, hearing loss, and cuts and bruises as Punchy, Ricky, and Chitoz just watched in shock.

On May 10, the Gallo crew's pattern of failed assassination attempts continued as Magliocco captain Johnny "Bath Beach" Oddo was shot at while sitting in his car. The bullet missed Johnny but took out the car's engine.

On May 19, Ricky was one of the assassins for the next attempted hit on the Snake. It was Ricky, Punchy, Chitoz, and Pete the Greek. They rode in a panel truck, pulled up alongside Persico's car, and opened fire.

With Persico in the car was Sal D'Ambrosio, who was wounded

but walked away. Persico was shot up pretty good. He took shots to the shoulder and the face, and was even said to have spit out a bullet after the shooting. At first, some people thought he'd caught the fucking bullet with his teeth, but a better theory is that the bullet coursed its way through a lot of Carmine's body before finally coming to a rest in his mouth.

Bottom line was, Persico was still breathing, and he'd seen his shooters. So Ricky left us and went to live in California for three months, after which Larry called him back.

That's when things got deadly. On June 6, 1963, D-day, a local businessman who'd been good to the Gallos, a guy named Emile Colantuano, was found shot to death. Six days later, Punchy was shot at.

Chitoz found out that Vincent DiTucci was the shooter. Chitoz went out and shot DiTucci to death, either to avenge the attempt on Punchy or maybe because that was the only Profaci guy Chitoz could find that night.

On June 15, 1963, the *New York Times* ran an article informing the world that thirty-three-year-old Gennaro Basciano (that is, Chitoz) of President Street, an occasional longshoreman, was a witness and person of interest in the shooting death of Profaci gang member, thirty-four-year-old Vincent DiTucci, who'd been found sitting in his car in the Ozone Park section of Queens with five bullets in his head. Officially, the victim had been unemployed since he'd gotten out of prison four years earlier on a burglary conviction. The paper reported that Chitoz was arrested while standing in front of the Gallo crew headquarters at 51 President Street, that he was being held without bail, and that he'd been ID'd by witnesses from an array of photos. It said that hostilities between the Profacis and the Gallos went back to the early 1950s, and that the Gallos were known to own several companies dealing in coin-operated machines. Larry and his sixty-two-year-old dad, Albert Gallo, were in trouble for trying to illegally obtain

a government-insured bank loan, and there were deportation proceedings under way for the Gallo brothers' father. The paper did
some arithmetic and reported that Big Albert and his sons had, all
together, been arrested more than a hundred times.

It got to the point that there was more than one shooting on the
same night, sometimes hit-hit and sometimes hit-counter-hit.
Joseph Cardiello was killed the same night that the Profacis
killed Cadillac Louis Mariani. On July 24, Ali Baba bought it in
Hoboken, New Jersey.

On December 28, 1963, Magliocco died. Massive heart attack.
For the second time in two years, natural causes had taken out the
leader of the Profacis. This time the man assuming power was
Joseph Colombo, and it was no longer known as the Profaci family. Now it was the Colombo family.

Joe Colombo had a mob pedigree. His dad, Anthony, was an
early member of the Profacis, and was killed along with his mistress in his car in 1938, dead by strangulation. Joe Colombo had
a whole biography that didn't include him being a hood, which
helped when he was negotiating with the legit world. He went to
New Utrecht High for a couple of years, dropped out to join the
Coast Guard, and was discharged for a psychological difficulty.
He was a longtime longshoreman, a meat salesman, and finally a
real estate agent. He was disabled during his last few years.

Now Colombo, with an outside assist from the Patriarca family
of Rhode Island, sent Nicky Bianco to negotiate a peace settlement
with Larry and Blast. The war was over. The Gallo brothers would
be allowed to keep their crew together on President Street. There
followed eight years of relative peace.

By the fall of 1964, eighteen members of the Gallo gang were
under arrest and charged with twenty counts, including conspiracy to murder a rival gang, and violations of weapons laws.

The trial, before Justice Dominic S. Rinaldi in the Supreme Court, didn't last long. A deal was cut. Seventeen of the crew-members, including Larry and Blast, pleaded guilty to a misde-meanor, which carried only a light sentence, and the eighteenth, Mrs. Gloria Patane, the Gallos' aunt, had the charges against her dismissed.

The deal came about in face of the possibility that the district attorney's wiretap evidence might be tossed out as improper. The charge to which the seventeen pleaded guilty was "conspiring to commit an assault."

The indictment said that the Gallos' vendetta against the Pro-faci contingent had resulted in at least a dozen murders, dating back to 1960.

The court questioned each defendant before accepting his guilty plea. For example:

"Are you Larry Gallo?"

"Yes, sir."

"Were you familiar with the hideaways on Ocean Avenue, and Foster Avenue between 1960 and 1963?"

"Yes, sir."

"Did you and these other people plan and scheme to assault those who were interfering with whatever business you people were in?"

"Yes, sir."

"Are you guilty?"

"Yes, sir."

Seventeen times the judge went through the rigmarole. Mrs. Patane was deemed to have been punished enough and her charges were dismissed. Her husband, Santo "Uncle Sam" Patane, was among the other seventeen, and Mrs. Patane wept quietly in the courtroom even as she was let off the hook.

The Gallos had been vocal about what they considered "harass-ment" from law enforcement, to which an official talking to the

Times replied, "It's the first time an entire mob has been picked up and pleaded guilty."

Now, during all of this time, with the exception of being within spitting distance of the killing of Joey Mags, my life was pretty normal. According to my mom, I was a good kid. Well-behaved, didn't give her any problems. Seriously. Hard to believe now.

Even as I got a little bit older, it wasn't that I was bad. I was just careless sometimes. My mom remembers Ricky telling her, "I don't mind the stuff that Frankie is doing. He's just got to learn to watch his ass, because I'm not always going to be around."

I might make it sound like it was perfect. Sometimes, if I didn't do what I was told, Ricky would make me stand in the corner and sing "Old MacDonald." Ha, child abuse! I started kicking the wall when I sang, so Ricky told me I could stop. Otherwise I'd've put a hole in the wall.

Another time, as a punishment or just to yank me around, Ricky gave me a paper bag and sent me to the gas station to get him some compressed air.

The biggest trouble I got into as a kid came when I was climbing up one of the fire alarm poles they used to have on the street, before cell phones, placed there so you could send for the fire department even if you were stuck outside. I hit the triggering mechanism with my foot—by mistake, honest!—and set off the alarm.

CHAPTER 7
THE COCO POODLE

IN LATE 1964, the Gallo crew headed to the Coco Poodle, a bar on Coney Island Avenue in Brooklyn, owned by a guy we called George the Jew. Coney Island Avenue goes all the way from the parade grounds at the south edge of Prospect Park, to Coney Island on the Atlantic Ocean, as straight as an arrow, lined up so that when you're heading toward the park, you get a perfect view of the Empire State Building poking up from the horizon at the end of the road.

The bar was old, with a four-by-four front window looking out onto the street. The bar itself took up more than half of the Coco Poodle's square footage. There were a couple of booths and a jukebox that couldn't be beat, filled with great 45s by Jimmy Roselli, Frank Sinatra, Dean Martin, Sammy Davis, Jerry Vale. That jukebox was always playing.

The bar had a nice feel, what they call in the restaurant biz *ambience*. It attracted passionate broads from as far as New Jersey who liked to hang out with wiseguys. These women didn't play games. They weren't ashamed to tell you exactly why they were there. It was a relaxed atmosphere, because you knew you were going to go home with one of them at the end of the night. Right across the street was George's Diner, open all night, so we always had a good meal, even if it was five o'clock in the morning.

JIMMY ROSELLI

It was Larry Gallo's idea. He was the first to hear of Jimmy Roselli, who, at that time, was a kid in Hoboken, New Jersey, but who was supposed to be a rising star with real talent.

So Larry grabbed my dad and Punchy, and they went to a club to see Jimmy. They found that it was all true. The guy had it. What a voice. My mom says the meeting was at Hester and Mulberry, but I think it was actually in Hoboken. They met Roselli. The meeting went well, and Larry helped Roselli get some gigs in New York.

Since jukeboxes were a big part of business back then, Larry bought up a bunch of Jimmy Roselli records, and other Italian records, as well, to put in the jukeboxes.

From then on, the Gallo crew had carte blanche at all of Roselli's shows—front seats until the day he retired, backstage afterward for drinks, dinners with Roselli and his wife. When Roselli sang at the San Gennaro Feast, we were there. After a while Jimmy Lefty and Pete Carvella managed Roselli. Jimmy Lefty was a crewmember with the Gallos for years, and Carvella was Lefty's legit sidekick. At one of the clubs one night, Roselli had his seven-year-old daughter on stage singing, and she was good!

Sometimes we would travel to see him: Connecticut and New Jersey. One time Roselli sent a limo for Mom and Dad to see him in Atlantic City.

My mom says, "It wasn't even like a celebrity thing. It was more personal friends. He got all la-dee-da, but he still kept in touch."

Roselli accomplished a lot in show business, and there were plenty of folks, especially those who spoke Italian, who preferred Jimmy Roselli even to Frank Sinatra—they were both from Hoboken, so the rivalry was natural. Folks from the Old

Country preferred Roselli because he could sing in Italian, with a perfect Neapolitan accent.

My mom says that it was the tone of Jimmy Roselli's voice that made him so popular. Even people who didn't speak Italian would love the songs he sang in that language, because they could feel the emotion, and they could relate.

His big hit was "*Mala Femmena* (Bad Woman)." Roselli was most popular in and around New York City, but he had national and international fame, as well. He appeared three times on *The Ed Sullivan Show*, and he sang the theme song to the Gina Lollobrigida movie *Buona Sera, Mrs. Campbell*.

Over the years, Jimmy Roselli did some really nice things for me, standup things. He was a nice guy—no matter what some people say. His song "Little Pal" is still the mob's anthem, and it still brings tears to their eyes.

My father spent a lot of time at the Poodle. He'd pick up Larry and they'd go there and have meetings with the rest of the crew—Little Angelo, Cockeyed Butchie, Ralphie Goodness, Stanley "The Hat" Mooney, Punchy, Tony Bernardo, and Roy Roy. Trust me, that's a lot of characters.

They'd score and bring all kinds of swag into the Poodle—diamonds, gold, watches, TVs, men's suits, and guns. They would've stolen dogs and cats if they'd thought they could be sold. They brought so much shit to the bar that I thought it was a fucking store. There was variety, but the operation that took up most of the time involved cigarettes.

CIGARETTE RUNS AND THE VAN OF A DIFFERENT COLOR

It was during the Poodle era that Larry Gallo, Ricky, and Roy Roy would make bootleg cigarette runs to Carolina. At first Larry went with Roy Roy, then Ricky went with Roy Roy.

They used Larry's Chrysler, because they could remove the

backseat and pack that area with cartons of cigarettes, buy them cheap and bring them north to sell them in the clubs.

They were supplying a lot of clubs, and back then everyone smoked. There were so many orders at one point that Larry's Chrysler wouldn't do the trick, so they rented a van and packed that. Business was great; for a while they were making two runs a week.

After a while, cops wised up to the operation. Roy Roy and Ricky were loaded up and heading home, driving the van down a dark road late at night, when they noticed they were being followed by a detective's car.

Ricky went into evasive mode, made a few unexpected turns, and lost the tail. But now they knew the cops knew, and that complicated the operation. Only minutes after losing the police car, Ricky pulled over at a rest stop, grabbed a can of paint that was in the van, and hurriedly painted the van a different color. They were carrying a second set of license plates, so they changed plates and drove the van of a different color back to Brooklyn. They dropped off the cigarettes and returned to President Street, where they found a pair of federal investigators having a discussion with Blast.

Blast said to Ricky and Roy Roy, "Tell the dicks how you got away."

This was against everything Ricky and Roy Roy stood for. They kept their mouths shut. But Blast was persistent.

"Do it! Tell the Law," Blast said.

Roy Roy couldn't stand it and finally said, "Blast, what the fuck are you talking about?"

"The Law said to stop going on the runs and they won't arrest anyone," Blast replied. "But you got to tell them how you got away."

So Ricky and Roy told the cops about their evasive maneuvers, the can of paint, and the spare license plates. Everyone got a big laugh out of it, and that was the end of the cigarette runs.

THE BLACKOUT

A couple months before the 1965 blackout, the one that turned off the lights in the whole northeast part of the country, I met Sonny Girard. I was, what? Nine. And he was a real character who had come in to the Poodle with tons of men's clothes—suits, overcoats, ties, sports jackets, hats, all good stuff—and he was getting the boys to buy.

The night of the blackout, we were in the Poodle. Ricky was there with some of his friends and they were drinking. Dad was always drinking. Dewar's and water was his drink of choice. They had a transistor radio on listening to the blackout news, drinking to candlelight, and scheming about the number of places they would be able to rob before the lights came back on.

Now, I don't know what exactly happened that night. All I know is that the next day the bar's basement contained a lot of new stuff—tools, car rims, gold serving trays, women's clothes, and a three-foot model of the Frankenstein monster, which they gave to me. They had it standing at the bottom of the stairs at the bar. Man, I thought everything was great.

During the summer of 1966, a long, hot summer, the New York City Youth Board employed Larry and Blast to help ease race relations in Brooklyn. There had been disturbances in some of the more rapidly changing neighborhoods of Brooklyn.

A later court ruling, heavily critical of the hiring, complained that the city had given the Gallo brothers "official authority" when it came to quelling unrest. The hiring, the court said, was "inimical to proper law enforcement and damaging to the prestige of duly constituted authority."

The brothers' role in all of this quelling was ill-defined. They were supposed to work to "cool" white youths in the troubled neighborhoods, and hopefully cut down on the number of rumbles. To help the cause, the Youth Board had given the Gallos, in letter form, intelligence that would help them identify and stop potential trouble. The Gallos really did do the job they said they would, making efforts to keep the peace in Flatbush during July and in East New York in August.

All of this was controversial enough, so that once again the Gallo brothers were in the newspapers. Some folks thought it was a mockery of justice to give official juice to known gangsters, while others, citing the actual work that Larry and Blast did, said they should get a fucking medal. Some feared that the Gallos had been promised a deal or some form of immunity in exchange for their efforts to smooth out racial animosity, noting that the brothers were under investigation by a grand jury for racketeering. The brothers had done recent stints in jail for refusing to testify, and when the grand jury came to a decision, it was thumbs-up, insufficient evidence to warrant any indictments.

Conspiracy theorists snorted knowingly.

ROOTING FOR FAT LOUIE TO DIE

Then there were times when I knew things were not great. At the end of 1966, my dad had to go away for a couple of weeks. Mom told me he was on a trip with the boys, but then I saw the guys come over to our house and give Mom money. I heard them say to her that Ricky "would be on the lam." He was going to have to hide out for a little while longer until "the problem" was fixed.

"The problem" turned out to be a top-notch nineteen-year-old asshole named "Fat Louie," who'd fucked with my dad and gotten hurt real bad. There was some tension on account of Fat Louie was in the hospital, ICU, and they were waiting to see whether or not he would die. Fat Louie was a moron, they said, and had taken three bullets, none of which took out a vital organ.

So, he was lingering and they were still trying to figure out what they were going to do. For the time being, Ricky needed to be in an unknown location. They were pulling for Fat Louie to die. Survivors sing.

As it turned out, Fat Louie did recover from his gunshot wounds, but he had learned wisdom during his convalescence and he kept his mouth shut regarding the circumstances of his perforation.

So Dad was back and it was great to see him. Fat Louie died exactly a year later at age twenty. Roy Roy said it couldn't have happened to a nicer guy, that the prick had lived 364 days too long. Fat Louie would've died years earlier, Roy Roy said, except for his uncle was a big shot with the Gambino family.

BLAST HOLDS THE PAN

One night my mom got a call that Ricky had been shot, but was okay—and again he had to go on the lam. Ricky and Roy, I heard, had gone to "do a piece of work" (that is, kill somebody), and Ricky got shot in the knee.

So they called a doctor who had an office right on President Street. They took him there, and the doctor gave him something for the pain. The doctor stuck a leather belt between my dad's teeth and told him to bite down. He then took a hammer and chisel and knocked the bullet out of Ricky's knee bone. Ricky was one tough fuck.

It's amazing what loyal friends will do for one another in a time of crisis. While Ricky was on the table having the bullet removed from his knee, he had to take a piss, so he rolled over and pissed in a pan that Blast held for him. When Ricky was finished, Blast took the pan out and threw it away.

When it was all over, that was all they could talk about. Forget about the fact that Ricky had been shot in the knee—Blast had to catch Ricky's piss! Now, that was news. All of that pain and these guys were laughing like it was the funniest thing in the world.

I should have known then, even though I was only a kid, that these guys were not normal. When they got shot, they stopped the bleeding and went on the lam until everything cooled down.

RICKY AND MOONEY HAVE A BEEF

When Ricky came back to the Poodle, he got into an argument with Mooney. It wasn't hard to do. Mooney was a made man with no respect for anyone and a bad attitude.

On this night, Ricky was in no mood for Mooney's shit. Button or no button, Ricky went to go get his gun, because he was going to fucking kill Mooney. Ricky was not two steps out of the bar when Larry Gallo got a phone call: *Ricky and Mooney have a beef, Ricky's talking crazy.*

By the time Ricky got back to the bar, now armed and ready, Larry was standing out front waiting for him. It was three o'clock in the morning.

"What are you doing, Ricky?"

"Nothing."

"I know that Mooney is an asshole, but he's a made man and he's with me, so you can forget about what you want to do."

Ricky smiled and went into the bar to have a drink with Larry. Mooney was long gone. It was over. For now.

THE USED CAR DEALER WITH THE BIG MOUTH

One night my mom was waiting for Ricky at the Coco Poodle, sitting with the owner, George the Jew. A guy came in whom they recognized as the owner of a local used car dealership just up the street.

Seconds later Ricky and Larry came in, Larry announcing that he wanted a drink before he went home. They sat down at the bar—and the used car dealer said the wrong thing to Larry.

Ricky told George to lock the door. He told my mother to go behind the bar and "pretend to serve drinks." I think Ricky would've handled it, except Larry told him not to butt in, and Larry was the boss.

Larry then turned and started to beat the guy.

"You think (*smack*) you're tough (*smack*) with your (*smack*) fucking (*smack*) mouth (*smack*). This is what you get (*smack,*

smack), and if you call the cops that's fine, I'll come to your home and kill you! (*smack, smack, smack*)"

Larry had hands like stone, Roberto Duran hands, and he beat the guy until he broke every fucking bone in his body. Then they threw him in the street.

1968, A CRAZY YEAR

Man, 1968 was a crazy year. It was crazy everywhere, but especially in South Brooklyn. Ricky went to do a piece of work, and put his gun inside his pants at the small of his back. The gun went off, and Ricky shot himself in the ass. Bobby Bornhold took him to the hospital. Bobby was a young hood on his way up at the time, and Ricky was his mentor. He was a nice guy, tall, young, blond. Once they got to the emergency room and checked in, they realized they had a problem. Hospitals are required to report gunshot wounds.

The cops were on the way, so, instead of sticking around and explaining the mishap to the authorities, they ran out of the hospital. I remember my dad and Bobby coming back home. Ricky was still bleeding, so they put him on the couch, gave him a belt to bite down on, poured some Scotch on the bullet hole, and used a pair of pliers to pull the bullet out. They packed the hole with gauze. Ricky drank the rest of the Scotch and fell asleep.

Bobby Bornhold wasn't around long. One night Ricky came to the club and told some of the guys that Bobby was out on a stickup that had gone bad and he ended up shooting and killing a cop. He was caught, convicted, and got a life bid, and that was the last we saw of him.

THE OLD SAHARA

Every now and again Ricky would hang out at a place called the Old Sahara, on Utica Avenue in East Flatbush, the same place where Larry had almost gotten killed. This was back in late 1968. Today, the place is called The Lion's Den. Back then, the place was owned by Johnny One-Eye, a gay tough guy. One night while in there, Ricky got into an argument with an off-duty cop. My mother was sitting with Ricky at the bar, and the cop started coming on like a smart-aleck.

Ricky didn't want to make trouble with my mom there. She said, "Let's just leave," so they got up and left the bar—but the cop followed them out. He started to fuck with Ricky some more, and then pulled a gun. At that point, Ricky had had enough of this guy's shit. He jumped on him, took his gun away, and beat him up so badly that they had to reconstruct the cop's face. Later they joked that Ricky did him a favor because the guy was better-looking after the beating.

Because the guy was a cop, the police *had* to investigate, although they probably didn't want to. They hauled in my mom and questioned her. She said she'd been in the ladies' room the whole time and didn't see a thing of what had happened outside. Eventually it all went away.

RICKY KILLS A GUY

The worst trouble Ricky got into that year was in a bar in Bensonhurst, on Thirteenth Avenue. The story goes that there was a guy in the bar drinking who started to act like a real tough guy. He got real nasty and started calling out guys to fight. He caught Ricky in the right mood, and started an argument, which soon rolled out onto the street. Ricky won the fight—and the guy died. Ricky was arrested and went to trial. But in the meantime Ricky and Roy Roy had both stopped shaving, and had full beards. Roy Roy sat in the front row of the courtroom's gallery section, right behind Ricky at the defense table—and that fucked up the witness. He couldn't tell them apart! He failed to identify Ricky, and they threw the murder case out.

Many years later, I got an e-mail from the son of the guy who'd gotten killed. He said a cop told his mother that it was my father who'd killed his father. The guy said it wasn't nice that I was then promoting my father, who was a killer.

I told him, "If you weren't there, you'll never know the real story. Maybe you were told that your father was a regular guy, but that's not what I know." I told him that I was sorry for his loss, but that if it had been my dad who died in the fight, I wouldn't be e-mailing him. The losing side always complains. It was the "other guy's" fault. The winner goes to jail and the loser goes to the hospital or maybe the cemetery, and it doesn't make a fucking difference who's right or wrong. That's how it works.

It is my personal opinion that if two people are willing to do bodily harm to each other and one loses, the other really shouldn't be punished for it.

POODLE IN HEAT

After a while, because of the occasional commotion, the Coco Poodle got hot. A regular visitor was Detective Lambert, head of the NYPD's so-called Pizza Squad, formed to keep an eye on the "Gallo crime family." Every once in a while, the squad would hit President Street, or the Coco Poodle, and round up the crew—just to bust their balls. Lambert would grab Punchy, Roy Roy, or Sonny Hats, maybe Blast, Nicky Bianco, Louie, Chitoz, charge them with vagrancy, and bring them into the Lawrence Street Police Station.

The guys, while they were waiting to see a judge, would always bring along a deck of cards and play pinochle to pass the time. Then they'd go before the judge, and the judge would throw it out and yell at Detective Lambert: "Don't bring them in again!" Next week they'd do it all over again.

But the bottom line was that the Coco Poodle finally got too hot to stay at, so we were off again.

CHAPTER 8
FREEPORT, LONG ISLAND

THE YEAR 1968 had some serious ups and downs. On the one hand, I went suburban. Ricky and his friend Dickey scored the catering concession at the Freeport Yacht Club, out near the south shore of Long Island, just east of Oceanside.

On the other hand, my mother was arrested for bearer-bond fraud in Brooklyn. Her attorney, the Gallo lawyer, was a fellow named Bob Weiswasser. She had no priors and probably should've gotten a slap on the wrist. But the prosecutor wanted to make a deal: probation in exchange for info. They wanted to know where she was getting the bearer bonds, but she kept her mouth shut. She was convicted, and at her sentencing hearing Weiswasser again tried to get her probation, but the judge said that she was a part of—his words—"organized crime," and he gave her three sentences of three years apiece to run concurrently. She ended up serving eighteen months. Ricky was convinced it was the lawyer's fault.

I can remember Ricky saying, "Weiswasser was no fucking good, and he's going to pay for it one day."

I went to live at my grandparents' house for a few weeks. Ricky would come visit me to see if I needed anything.

Sometimes he'd pick me up and we'd go to visit my mother in

prison. It wasn't what I expected. I guess I thought it would look like Sing Sing or The Tombs, but instead it was more like a camp.

It was in Alderson, West Virginia. A few famous women had spent time there, like Billie Holiday, and some Cuban woman who shot at a diplomat. Most of the women were there for drugs.

Today, my mom says, "I can't say it was rough. I had my job at the bakery, I worked for an hour and a half, changed my clothes, went to the cafeteria and had breakfast, and I had the rest of the day to myself. You could go outside and take some sun. Sometimes they had entertainment there—and we used to make our own hooch. At lockup time a female guard would come around and check you into your room. I know I couldn't leave, but I didn't live like an animal."

I was twelve years old, and I guess I thought it was a little weird to have a mom in prison, but I didn't say much about it and no one else did, either. When Ricky commented at all, he said, "It is what it is."

Then Ricky picked me up for good, and I moved with him out to Freeport. It was a great setup for me. We stayed at the yacht club, which was a cool place, and Dickey had three daughters who couldn't keep their hands off of me. We were young. They were so nice to me. So I was occupied, and only vaguely aware that Ricky was always going back and forth with Larry to take care of business in Brooklyn.

I wanted for nothing. Every night there was all you could eat. There was a pool table, arcade games, an Olympic-sized swimming pool, tennis courts—everything we wanted.

Larry Gallo's son Steven was like a big brother to me. He was five years older and lived in the next town over, Merrick. He would always come by to see if I needed anything. Sometimes he'd just pick me up and we'd ride around—and riding around with Steven was exciting because he liked to drive fast.

THE FREEPORT STOCKS

Sometimes we'd go to the stock-car racetrack right there in my town, Saturday night in the seven-thousand-seat Freeport Stadium in Freeport, Long Island. The quarter-mile track was built around the outside of a sports field where they played baseball and football.

Even back in the late '60s, the Freeport track had an "old feel." They'd been featuring car races there since 1934, a starting ground for drivers that became famous, including some of the guys who drove the first NASCAR races, like Bruno "The Flying Mailman" Brackey.

There was a lot of side-betting going on in the stands, of course, but Freeport stayed in operation by not awarding prize money to the drivers. If Steve won the race, he got a medal or a trophy and a kiss from a pretty girl—but no cash. It was all for fun.

Steven Gallo had a canary-yellow Corvette, souped up, 1968 or '69, and I'd go with him when he went to the Freeport Stocks to race it. Those were great times. Steven and I, as we say in South Brooklyn, "stood friends" for many years.

THE WHORE WIVES OF YACHT CLUB ASSHOLES

There were a lot of rich folks around the yacht club. But it wasn't classy money. The guys were all blue-collar slobs with a scheme who'd rigged the system and skimmed themselves a fortune.

It was at the yacht club that I learned to hate people.

There was a lot of wheeling and dealing going on, and there were times when my dad and his friends were right in the middle of it. I could feel the change in atmosphere when the crew showed up. Everyone knew that the mob was there. The men all looked like they were shitting their pants, and their whorish wives all looked like they were coming in their panties.

To this day I have never seen a congregation of nymphomaniacs like the wives of the Freeport Yacht Club. They were desperate housewives long before that was a thing. And their husbands had pretensions of legitimacy, well connected with law enforcement, politics, and the Brooklyn judicial system.

Those esteemed male citizens would cluck their tongues at the Italians who frequented the place, "those hoodlums." And it was a riot, because their wives couldn't wait to give those same hoodlums blow jobs in every dark corner of the club.

Then those men, oblivious to their wives' behavior, would start ragging on the very heavy hitters who'd gotten them where they were, all of the corrupt judges, and councilmen, and police chiefs.

Even as a kid I couldn't stand any of them. All I could think was: *What a bunch of assholes.*

ANGLO-SAXON PRICKS

I know, you're way ahead of me. Here's a place with a lot of rich assholes, sharing space with guys from President Street. If you thought that might lead to trouble, well, you were right.

One night the members were having a party at the club. There were three guys standing near the stairs. One of them, an asshole of an excruciating nature, got ballsy with my father.

"All you greaseballs think you're in the mob," the guy said to Ricky.

"Excuse me, sir. I'd appreciate it if you'd cool it with your mouth," Ricky said, as polite as he could be.

"What the fuck you think you're going to do about my mouth?" the guy said. He must've felt untouchable to say that shit. This was a false assumption. Turned out he was very touchable.

The next thing I saw, the guy's teeth were on the floor next to the hot food trays, and two other guys were sprawled out on the floor, too, taking an impromptu snooze. It was all over in a flash.

Dickey rushed Ricky out of the place through the kitchen. It took the casualties a half hour to get up off the floor (with assistance) and get out. About two hours later, the cops showed up and talked to Ricky. Some words were exchanged, and when they left they took my father with them. He said he had no choice on account of the assholes used an ethnic epithet. They took him to the station house.

We were worried about Ricky. He had positioned himself as a guy unlikely to get any favors from the district attorney, Dennis Dillon. In fact, the last time Ricky had seen the DA, just a few weeks earlier, he'd said, "Hey, your wife gives a great blow job."

It wasn't a very smart thing to say, so we thought Ricky might be detained indefinitely for the scuffle at the club. But, happily, he was only at the station house for a couple of hours. The guys from the club decided that they didn't want to press charges, so the police let Ricky go.

A week later, the three guys who'd been standing near the staircase sent a message through a mediator to Ricky. They begged my father to let it go. They apologized, claiming they were drunk. They were wrong, wrong, wrong.

Bullshit, Ricky thought. Those guys had learned who Ricky was—that was what that was all about. They now knew what they didn't know before: that my father was not a greaseball who thought he was in the mob, but rather Larry Gallo's personal bodyguard, and all that that implied. If you said the wrong thing to Ricky, which they had, you would soon learn that you had fucked with the wrong guy and you might go missing. That was why those Anglo-Saxon pricks came back asking for their asses.

I sometimes think back on those assholes who bad-mouthed Italians. Now I can see that they were jealous, on account of we had two sets of balls and they had none.

RICKY'S GREAT PARTY

Parties at the yacht club were always exciting, sometimes in a good way, and sometimes bad. The *worst* Freeport party took place when a guy named Sonny Franzese, a *capo* in the Colombo family and a good friend of Ricky's from Brooklyn, threw a party at the yacht club for his girlfriend, who was Johnny Lion's sister. The party came. Sonny didn't show up. Turns out he was pissed off at his girlfriend for something and was out with another broad. She got extremely upset and threw a fit. The club had to call some of Sonny's guys to come and get her out.

Then there was the best party . . .

One Labor Day, Ricky was throwing a barbecue party for all of the club members and their families. There were ten barbecue pits set up to accommodate an anticipated three hundred guests.

At first, things went great. As the people came in, Ricky would start up the barbecue pits, so he always had just as many pits as he needed going. The food was being cooked and served as if by a well-oiled machine.

Then suddenly there was a rush of people who all showed up at once, so Ricky had to get the rest of the pits going quickly. Patience wasn't his strongest attribute. He grabbed a can of lighter fluid and began to squirt it on the coals.

When the flames didn't flare up quickly enough for him, he went back and squirted some more. Well, this time all the fluid went up at once, blew fluid back onto Ricky, and in a big, bright *poof*, he was on fire.

The guys reacted quickly but not intelligently to the instant emergency. As Ricky was starting to look like the Human Torch, the guys started throwing their Scotch at him.

Other guys threw water. Towels. One guy threw a chair. Thanks. By the time the fire was out, my dad had lost half an ear, was burned on half of his face, and the entire left side of his body was blistered.

Off to the hospital he went. The party raged on. It was unanimous: That Ricky Dimatteo sure knew how to throw a great party!

About a week later, my dad was out of the hospital and every-thing got back to normal. The catering business was thriving, and Ricky was making a lot of money. The place was even booked a year ahead—and then the bottom fell out.

The club members got together and voted Ricky and Dickey out, on the grounds that the place was being run by organized crime. But that wasn't the real reason. Once they saw that the place was making money, the cocksuckers wanted to put their own people in there. That's why I never liked white-collar goodie-goodies. They are the "Legal Mafia," and they go both ways—just like their wives.

One of the things the club prided itself on was this huge aquar-ium that ran the length of the bar. On his way out, Ricky, as pissed as he could be, took a bottle of liquor and poured it all in the tank. The fish died happy.

NADINE AND DONNA

I met my first girlfriend in Freeport. Nadine. Summertime. Junior high. I met her at the pool. We were young and it didn't last long. I never forgot her. She was a sweet one. After that, there was Donna, when I was fifteen, sixteen. Met her at the bowling alley. That was a little bit more serious. Man, was she beautiful. She looked like Cher.

THE QUIET RIDE

It was just about the time we started to lose the yacht club. Dad told me to take a ride with him to pick up Larry and drive him home. Ricky said that Larry wasn't feeling well. So we did. It was a quiet ride. Dad and Larry were talking about old times, talking about some business. They talked about bringing Jimmy Roselli to New York, about Joey getting out of prison soon, and about how he was worried about his little brother. It ended with a few laughs and a hug. Then Larry grabbed my cheek, but not as hard as usual, and he gave me a hug as he said good-bye. And that was the last time I ever saw Larry Gallo. Soon after that, he checked in to Nassau Hospital in Mineola, Long Island, and on May 17, 1968, he died in his sleep of cancer.

Larry's death was important enough to warrant a big obituary in the *New York Times*, where it listed Larry's business interests as "illegal profits from gambling, the policy racket"—that means numbers—"and loan-sharking, as well as the underworld control of vending machines, pinball machines, and the jukebox business."

The paper mentioned the Gallo-Profaci War and reported that about a dozen hoods were killed, the majority of them Gallo soldiers. The war, it said, ended in 1965 because Joe Colombo took over the Profacis and arranged a settlement. The obituary concluded with a retelling of the story of how Larry's life was saved when a beat cop wandered into the bar while he was being strangled. Larry, it said, was survived by his wife, Gloria, and his brothers, Joey and Albert, Joey residing at that time in Greenhaven State Prison. Larry, the paper reported, lived in Merrick, Long Island, and his body was laid out at Prospero's Funeral Home on Eighty-sixth Street in the shadow of the elevated train in Bensonhurst. The requiem high mass was held at St. Rose of Lima's Roman Catholic Church at Parkville Avenue and Ocean Parkway in Brooklyn, after which Larry was buried in St. Charles Cemetery in Farmingdale, Long Island.

My father and Larry were so close that part of Ricky died that day, as well. I remember my father being changed, like a light had gone out. He said things like, "We're fucked now."

Ricky's big fear was that, now that Larry was gone and Joey was still in prison, the Gallo crew was vulnerable and other opportunistic families would move in on us, cause some problems.

MOM COMES HOME

We were still living in Freeport when my mom was released from prison. Ricky went to pick her up. They made a stop in South Brooklyn to see my grandmother, and then came out to Freeport.

It was great having her home. We weren't going to be staying on Long Island for much longer. I had no ties there. I'd already been kicked out of school; after ten suspensions I was expelled, and I was only in seventh grade.

I didn't go to school much. I hated it. One day, instead of going to school I walked with a friend all the way back to the neighborhood in Brooklyn. Twenty fucking miles! The school told my mom I was missing, but she had a good idea where to look. Roy Roy eventually found me and took me back home.

That summer my mom and dad were staying a lot with Abby, Jimmy Bats, and their wives. On weekends we would go to the Seven Lakes upstate and have a blast. We were living in a hotel on a lake one summer and one hot day my parents and I went out on the lake in a rowboat.

Ricky decided he wanted to have some fun and jumped off the boat and started to swim back to shore. My mom was screaming. She didn't swim and was struggling with the oars to get the boat to move.

Ricky saw that she was having a hard time so he swam back, but when he got back to the boat my mom hit him with the oar and wouldn't let him back in the boat. So he had to swim back to shore again, but this time he started to cramp up and almost didn't make it.

By the time he made it ashore he was exhausted. He just stretched out on the ground and panted.

Jimmy and Abby came up to him and said, "Don't worry, Ricky. We had your back."

Ricky said, "Fuck you!"

HERO IN HIS UNDERWEAR

Back at the hotel we had dinner and saw a show, the adults had a few drinks, and then I went to bed. That night as we were sleeping, Mom heard loud sounds next door in Jimmy's room.

Dad had a gun under his pillow, so he grabbed it and moved toward the door. He ran for a few steps and then dropped to the floor and rolled the rest of the way to the door. He determined that the sounds were coming from the next room over, so he went out into the hall, with his gun and in his underwear. There was a cleaning woman in the hallway. She screamed and ran. It sounded like somebody was getting beat up in Jimmy Bats' room.

Ricky knocked on Jimmy's door and charged in, a hero in his BVDs. What he saw was Jimmy sleeping, and making those sounds.

Jimmy's wife said, "Ricky, what's going on?"

"I heard noises, thought Jimmy needed help."

"Oh he always makes those sounds when he sleeps," she said.

Jimmy smacked his lips a couple of times, rolled over, and became quiet. My dad came back to our room. He told my mom what happened, adding, "I told you, Dee, they are fucking weird. Jimmy was fighting in his sleep."

CHAPTER 9
BACK TO BROOKLYN

AND SO, ONE ERA OVER, another beginning, the Dimatteos returned to Brooklyn. It was the end of 1969, and I remember being on Sackett Street with my grandfather and grandmother, Sal and Mary Fiore, two of the nicest people you'll ever meet in your life.

All these years later I remember them like it was yesterday. They took me places, sometimes touristy places that people visiting from out of town see all the time but where locals usually don't go. I went with my grandparents to see the Empire State Building and the Statue of Liberty.

We rode *The Circle Line*, which is a boat ride that goes all the way around the island of Manhattan. Other times they just took me to Coney Island, where there was both a beach and an amusement park. It was there that you could ride the Cyclone, one of the world's oldest roller coasters.

Today's modern roller coasters are scary because of how fast and high they go, with loop-dee-loops and parts of the ride where you're upside down. The Cyclone was terrifying because it was so old and rickety, you felt like the thing was going to fall apart at any second. (Today, in 2015, the Cyclone is still there, still rickety, scarier than ever, and has yet to collapse.)

On less ambitious days, my grandparents took me to the Carroll Street playground, where I would play ball while they watched.

It occurs to me today that the Fiores were using me as an excuse to visit these places and do these things themselves. They were born in Italy, had lived in the United States for fifty years, and this was the first opportunity they'd had to see the sights.

My grandfather was a longshoreman who worked the Brooklyn and Manhattan piers—and he was as straight as an arrow. He didn't have a crooked bone in his body. I once saw him refuse to pick a penny up off the floor. "It's not mine," he would say.

Sometimes I overheard my grandfather talking to my mother in a warning tone. "You better keep an eye on that Ricky," he would say. "I think he's, you know, one of *those* guys."

"Pa, what are you talking about?" my mother would reply. "He's a prize fighter and he owns a bar."

My grandfather would shake his head. "You can't-a bullshit-a me. I know more than you think-a."

Then my grandmother would get in the act. "Why you no shutta up, Sal?"

And Grandpa would yell back, *"Sta' zitta atto!"* ("Keep your mouth shut!") And that was the end of the conversation.

My grandmother thought I could do no wrong. When my hands were cold, she would put them under her arms. She would tell me her belly was a pillow, and I could rest my head on it. If I said I was hungry, there would be food in front of me in two minutes.

There were a couple of times, not very many, when my grandfather would yell at me for something or other, me acting up, and my grandmother would go at him like a tiger.

I was lucky. I had my maternal grandparents for thirty-seven years. Now it's been more than twenty years with a tear in my eye.

Those years, at the end of the 1960s in Brooklyn, were some

of the best of my life. I made a lot of friends whom I've stayed close to through the years.

STAYING OUT LATE

It was around 1970 that the Gallos began working on a deal with Al Goldstein, the editor and publisher of *Screw* magazine. People who grew up in New York probably remember that rag. It looked like a newspaper, but it only had the news from the world of sex, what was new in blow jobs and stories like that.

Inside there were ads for every illegal sex operation in the whole fucking city, and hard-core porn photographs, the kind you could only get in the shops of Times Square at that time, only *Screw* was sold at newsstands throughout the city.

To be better situated to the new operation, we moved to an apartment on Foster Avenue that was about four, five miles southeast of the old neighborhood, so despite the move I continued to hang out on Court Street with my cousin Blake and some new friends like Marty, Tommy, Brian, Steven, and of course "Goomba Louie."

That was my jock period. I was always playing some kind of ball, baseball in the summer, football in the winter. There was stickball, softball, handball, box ball, punch ball, Wiffle Ball—I played them all, with one exception: basketball. They tried to get me to play that, but I said no. Fuck that game. I just didn't like it.

That was life. After playing ball all day, we went back to the block to hang out. It was stupid to go to Foster Avenue to eat and then come back to hang out, so I often ate at one of my friends' houses. Most of us didn't go to school, so we stayed out late.

MEETING JU JU

We would sit at the corner of Douglass and Court Streets, drink some beers, and bullshit about anything. Most of the time we hung out at Ju Ju's, which was between Butler and Douglass on Court. Before Ju Ju bought the place, when we first started hanging out there, it was called Patty's Pool Room.

Every guy from north of Union Street shot pool there. There were great players like Willie Pepitone, we called him Willie Pep, who once shot against Minnesota Fats. Pep was a long-shoreman who lived on Douglass Street, and he was at the pool hall every night teaching us how to shoot and taking our money. We had the run of the place, and we did a lot of drinking there.

Ju Ju's father was an old-time wiseguy from New York, the Gambino family. The man known as "Mr. Leone" told Ju Ju to take over Patty's Pool Room so he'd have a place to come to when he was in Brooklyn.

I met Ju Ju around that time. It happened when Marty's seven-year-old nephew came running to Douglass Street from the direction of the pool hall. He was crying.

I asked what happened, and the nephew said some guy in the pool hall had kicked him in the ass.

"What did you do?"

"I didn't do nothin'!" the kid cried.

So I walked the kid back to the pool room and asked him who did it. It was Ju Ju.

"Hey, mister, you should refrain from striking the kid," I said, or words to that effect.

"Who are you?" Ju Ju asked.

I said, "I'm Frankie, Ricky's son from President Street."

He knew my dad, and so he was nice. He smiled and said, "Okay." Ju Ju could have kicked my ass from one corner to another if he'd wanted to. Instead he called my father, told him that he'd just met me and liked the way I conducted myself.

MY FIRST JOBS

After that Ju Ju put me to work. I was still a kid, but I was already six feet tall and everyone thought I was older, assumed I could drive. So I've been driving since I was thirteen, fourteen years old.

Ju Ju and I would go almost to Coney Island, to the Esplanade

Inn at the ass end of Cropsey Avenue, all the way down on the corner of Bay Fiftieth Street. He needed to go there and pick up the "Shylock" money, and I would drive. That was the beginning of a thirty-year friendship.

Meanwhile, the Gallo crew, which at that time was comprised of about sixty guys, was still under the rule of the Colombo family. But the Gallo crew was a feared entity because—and you can't sugarcoat it—they were both tough and cruel.

They had to be that way. It was a matter of survival. They were outmanned and outgunned by their enemies. They had to compensate by being the baddest motherfuckers in Brooklyn. Otherwise, they would never have survived the 1960s.

They were bad, and they had their hand in almost every racket known to man: gambling, loan-sharking, construction, bars, restaurants, cigarettes, and music. I say "almost" because there were no drugs.

The Gallos had control of all the bookies and sports gambling in Bed-Stuy. No one could have a jukebox or a pinball machine or a cigarette machine in their bar without paying the Gallos, and that included wiseguys.

JOEY GOES TO SEE VALACHI

Here's a Joey story from way back that'll give you an idea. Joey, all twitchy and crackling with crazy, went to see Joe Valachi, who later became famous when he turned A-1 rat and became the first guy to admit in public that the Mafia actually existed. Up until then, a lot of law enforcement, including J. Edgar Hoover's FBI, told the public that organized crime was a figment of the press' imagination. Valachi sang, and his tune made the feds look like a bunch of idiots, which they probably were.

Anyway, that was later. Joey went to see Valachi and told him he had to put one of his jukeboxes in his place.

Later, when Valachi blabbed, the subject of Joey Gallo came

up. Valachi said, "Joey was one crazy fuck. I was going to pay anyway, because I had to. Joey didn't need to be that crazy."

ITALIAN WOODSTOCK

During the summer of 1970, we got a call instructing us to get down to Columbus Circle, at the southwest edge of Central Park in the city, for a rally of the Italian-American Civil Rights League. I went with my father, Roy Roy, Bobby Darrow, and Steven Cirillo.

Ever since Valachi spilled the beans and the feds *had* to attack organized crime, the FBI had been watching Colombo's every move, and he was sick of it. The League was formed to support Colombo's primary cause, and that was that the feds were persecuting Italian Americans, conducting their investigations based on myth and prejudice rather than on actual evidence.

The scene at Columbus Circle was wild. It was like Italian Woodstock. It had been proclaimed "Italian-American Unity Day," and it said in the papers that there were 150,000 people there.

Many prominent entertainers performed. There were five congressmen there, all of whom gave speeches that were way too long. Everyone in the Gallo crew was very uncomfortable going, as it seemed like a public support of Colombo, which rubbed the fellas the wrong way.

We got out of that fucking madhouse as soon as we could. It meant we had to commingle with the enemy, you see. We all knew that Joey was getting out soon and he didn't like Joseph Colombo at all.

ONE EYE ON THE REARVIEW

By the end of 1970, I started going with my father and some friends to the San Su San Nightclub out in Mineola, on Long Island, a joint owned by Sonny Franzese.

Other times we went to Sonny's Pan Am Hotel in Queens. There was a place to be, with great entertainment at night, and guys from all of the families went there. You could see Jimmy Roselli, Joe Barone, Lily Ann Carol.

One night at the San Su San, I was drinking Scotch and water. I must've had ten or more drinks. I know I put a hurting on a bottle, and I was feeling no pain. On the way home, Ricky tossed me the car keys and told me to drive.

I still didn't have a license or a permit or nothing. While other dads were telling their sons to drive carefully, two hands on the wheel, to expect the unexpected, my dad told me to drive with one eye on the rearview mirror to make sure we weren't being followed. It's funny, I still do that to this day.

I started driving Ricky wherever he needed to go. I'd drive him to Queens to the Golden Chariot to see Pasquale "Paddy Mac" Macchiarole, a *capo* in the Genovese family. Ricky used to bring him tripe. Mac loved the way my uncle Joey Click Click made tripe. Sometimes I'd drive my dad up to President Street to see Blast.

I started picking up my godfather, Bobby Darrow. He was a character, a small guy with big balls, a lovable lunatic. He drank and smoked pot like every day was his last, was a soft-spoken man who could turn in an instant like an animal. I don't think he wanted to be a gangster, it was more like he didn't have a choice—a natural gangster. He lived in the Sutton Apartments next to Washington Cemetery on Ocean Parkway. I would go in his apartment, and he would be all dressed up like he was going out at night, except it was morning and he'd be just sitting there sipping a cup of coffee.

We would have coffee together, and then he would open the window and throw the rest of the coffee out the window, into the cemetery below. He'd say, "The dead need their coffee in the morning, too." To this day, I still don't know how crazy he was.

My mom and dad may have moved back to Brooklyn after the yacht club deal went bad, but they kept a summer house in Freeport. I was the one who had to drive Bobby Darrow out there. I don't think Bobby drove.

We would go out there during the summer and sometimes on weekends during other seasons, whenever we could. It was good to get out of the city, get some fresh air.

In the summer, my dad would have parties there and everyone from the crew came: Blast, Louie the Syrian, Punchy, Roy Roy, Steven Cirillo, and Al Goldstein from *Screw* magazine. They would stay for a few days and my mother would cook for everyone. We had a pool in the backyard and we ate outside in the back most of the time. The neighbors used to get nervous. They'd see Cadillacs coming and going all of the time, with guys whose pictures they'd seen in the newspapers getting in and out. We'd laugh because we'd see them looking at us, and then running back into their houses.

I can't blame them. We didn't see our neighbors for the whole summer. Between the Italian music and the guys who did a lot of yelling even when they were just talking, I would have run away, too.

BOMBS BURSTING IN AIR

On the Fourth of July, 1971, we had a party in Freeport. In keeping with the occasion, a few of the guys brought fireworks over. There was some discussion: set them off one at a time and make them last throughout the night, orrrrrrr set them off all at once and see what happened?

They went for the big boom and, man, did they get it. They blew out the windows in our house. Those same neighbors who had run inside when they saw wiseguys getting out of luxury automobiles, now called the cops.

When the cop car pulled up, Blast hid in the basement. Cops saw the broken windows, so we couldn't very well say nothing happened.

"Some kids ran by, threw the fireworks, and then ran away," Ricky said. "God's honest truth, Officer." Cops asked to see ID. You should've seen their faces when they saw some of the names of the guys they were dealing with.

"How long you fellas staying in town?" one cop asked.

"We're going to be here all weekend," one of our guests said happily.

From that night on, there was an unmarked cop car on the corner, and it stayed there for the rest of the summer.

THE CRAZY KAT

One night we were all drinking homemade wine that Bobby Darrow had brought over, and we all got lit. At that time we had a boat, a twenty-one-footer called *The Crazy Kat*, docked nearby. Everyone went to sleep from the wine except Bobby, who went to look at the boat.

It was about five o'clock in the morning when we heard a knock on the door. Ricky answered, and it was a cop.

"Richard Dimatteo?"

"That's right."

"You know that guy in the car?"

Sitting in the backseat of the cop car parked out front was Bobby, looking at him like the cat that just ate the canary.

Ricky had to wait until he stopped laughing before he could talk.

"Yeah, I know him. What did he do?"

"Harbor Patrol caught him operating a boat while drinking. He didn't have any papers for it. We told him we needed to arrest him, but he said it was your boat and you'd vouch for him."

"I'll vouch for him," Ricky said.

The cop gave Bobby a ticket and told him to stay away from the water. As soon as the cop left, Bobby was pissed. It turned out he'd taken his brand-new gun on board with him and he'd had to throw it overboard when he saw the Harbor Patrol shining their spotlight on him.

Ricky said, "Bobby, what the fuck were you doing out there on the water?"

Bobby said, "I was fishing for dinner."

"But, Bobby, you didn't bring no fishing pole."

"I was shooting the fish!"

That was my godfather, a nut.

JOEY'S HOME

We had many parties at the Freeport summer house, and it was good to see the crew having so much fun, to hear all of the laughter and see all of those smiles. It would all be over soon.

The change occurred the instant Joey Gallo got out of prison. I'll never forget the day when Joey came home to President Street. I was hanging out on the block with my good friend Anthony "Goombabiel" Russo, and a big black Cadillac pulled up to the curb.

Joey Gallo got out and looked at me.

"You're Ricky's kid," he said.

"Yeah," I replied.

He said, "You know, if anything ever happens to Ricky, you'll always have a home on the block."

"Thanks, Joey." What else could I say?

He pinched both of my cheeks and started to walk away. Then he stopped and turned.

"Do me a favor, kid. Go wash the car." So me and Goombabiel washed Joey's car.

I saw Joey a few times more. He wasn't staying much on the block. Not long after Joey came home, Ricky told me to get off the block for a while. The cops were all over the fucking place. Joey was starting in, fucking with Joe Colombo, not just fucking around.

Joey said that from then on no one in the crew was to go to Colombo for anything. The crew was not to take any money to Joe, no scores, nothing. We were not to do our drinking in any Colombo bars, and we were not to partner up with any of Colombo's crew in any of our operations.

This was a nightmare. Ever since the peace treaty, the Gallo and Colombo crews had worked together on a lot of shit. We'd been doing business with them and everything was cool. Now the bullets were going to start flying again. Like a bad breeze coming off the Gowanus Canal, you could smell it.

When Larry was alive, he'd run the crew pretty much like he was the boss of a family, but he still had to okay sit-downs and moves through Colombo or there would have been a problem.

After Larry died, Blast slacked off and was listening to Joe Colombo. Now Joey was home and he laid down one simple rule: "Fuck Joe Colombo."

CHAPTER 10
THE MOD SQUAD

THERE WAS A NEW GENERATION of hoods on President Street, sons of and nephews of, who were all coming of age more or less at the same time. Blast was the youngest of the three brothers; he was in charge of the young studs, and he called them the Mod Squad.

The late 1960s and early '70s were a time of great changes, and fashion in the world of wiseguys changed, as well. Hair and sideburns got longer. Bell-bottoms were in. Some of the guys were so good at looking like a hippie that they stopped looking like hoods.

Blast did his best, but it was hard keeping a line on these guys. They didn't follow the old rules. They were drinking, out smoking pot, out being flashy. It wasn't just the hair and clothes that were changing. The schemes were different, too.

Blast was like an uncle and a mentor to me. He could have asked me to do anything and I would not have refused. He yelled at me when I had growing pains and he complimented me when I did well. Because I was still so young, he never had me do anything that put me in harm's way.

Part of it was that I was young, but there was another factor. I was Ricky's son, and if I got hurt or in trouble, there would be a problem with Ricky, and Blast didn't want to fuck with Ricky.

My father had been so close to Larry for so long that he'd become like a fourth Gallo brother, and if there was a problem, there were guys in the crew who would come to Ricky before they came to Blast. I ran the streets for many years on the strength of being with the Gallo crew, but the fact that I was Ricky's son carried its own immeasurable weight.

Here they are, the Mod Squad:

STEVIE G.

Steven Gallo, son of Larry Gallo, was so close to us that my mom and dad called him "son." My kids called him Uncle Steve. We were so close, and yet he broke my father's heart. We no longer see eye to eye. I don't want to write anything bad about him in this book for two reasons: I was asked not to, plus he has no way of defending himself. Let me leave it at this: It just goes to show that you can't trust anyone, no matter how close you feel like you are with them. Even after all of the good and bad times, the birth of my children, New Year's parties, barbecues, funerals, and weddings, it turns out I was putting my ass on the line with these guys all for nothing, just to have my family thrown to the wolves, especially my mother.

MY GODFATHER: BOBBY DARROW

Robert "Bobby Darrow" Bongiovi was born on May 28, 1937. He was my godfather, and a cousin to Rocco Miraglia, a *capo* with Joe Colombo. He was a born psychopath from the streets of East Flatbush, Brooklyn, but when he walked into a room you knew it. He was one of a kind. He'd grown up as one of the 1950s street gang, the Farragut Road Boys. By the time he turned twenty-one, he had already killed two guys. By the time he became a member of the Gallo crew, he was a full-fledged madman. He loved his Scotch and he loved his pot, and he lived every day like it might be his last.

His only function was to kill. He would just sit around waiting for the call. He had a great smile, he loved women, and women loved him. He always had a beautiful woman on his arm. I drove him around for two years.

Carmine "The Doc" Lombardozzi, a made man in the Gambino family, had to leave his wife to marry one of Bobby's exes. They had a daughter together. The ex was the daughter of a made man, Stabato Muro from the Profaci family.

Carmine started going out with her and he really fucked up, got himself into a bad situation. The edict came down: Marry her or die. The girl wasn't so happy, but Carmine took care of her for the rest of her life.

Driving Bobby Darrow around for two years, you see a lot of shit.

STEVEN CIRILLO

Steven C. was a great guy. If you saw him on the street, you'd think he was just the guy next door. He was born in Red Hook, born tough, a guy with no fear, and he was one of the family's shooters.

I was with him on President Street day and night for two years, sometimes with his wife, Jo Ann; we'd go into the city and have dinner. He was a good guy, but deadly. The night before he was killed, my wife and I, and my mom and dad, went to dinner at La Margarita, which was one of the top clubs in the city. We had a great night, but the next day was a nightmare.

PRESTON GERITANO

Preston Geritano was another one who, in the long run, got a raw deal from the Gallo family. He was a weird guy, a strange guy, born in Red Hook, also a Gallo shooter. He didn't say much, but he had eyes that gleamed so much you felt like you'd be able to see him in the dark. You could look at him and tell right away that this was a guy you didn't want to fuck with.

Preston had two brothers in the crew. They were one tough family, but they always showed great respect to me and my father. (We were close to him until he was released to the Genovese family. We didn't see much of him after that. He was eventually killed by his brother-in-law on April 22, 2004.)

BOBBY BORRIELLO

Bobby Borriello was a real home-grown tough guy—and big; he stood six-six. He was always smiling, called everybody "Muggs," and hit like a mule. I spent many nights with him and his wife before he went to jail.

In jail he met John Gotti, and when he got out of jail he was released to the Gambinos. He was a shooter and had his hands in everything. Him going to the Gambinos was a big loss for the Gallos.

He was a moneymaker who was respected and feared. Hard to replace. If you needed anything, you would ask Bobby.

When he came over to our house he'd say, "Dolly, got a minute?"

My mom would go over to him and say, "Bobby, what's up?"

He would say, "I like your apron," and he'd reach over and stick "fagazy" (that is, highly questionable) credit cards in her apron pocket. "Go and use them now," he'd say with a laugh.

He didn't have to do that. That was just the kind of guy he was. If he was doing well, his friends were going to be doing well, too. We stayed close to Bobby until the day he was killed, April 13, 1991, at age forty-seven. His death was a big loss to the family, and if you knew Bobby you'd know why.

STEVEN BORRIELLO

Bobby's brother was another guy who got a bum deal from the Gallos. He's still living. Another home-grown guy, a tough one from Clinton Street in Red Hook. You wish there were a hundred guys like Steve B. We had a ton of fun in the old days. He was like a big brother to me.

We haven't spoken in a while. His mind was poisoned by Stevie G. I respect him and I will leave it at that. His father, Patty, was a good man and is truly missed.

TONY THE BEARD

Tony "The Beard" Bernardo was small in frame—five-four, 140 pounds—with gleaming blue eyes, and balls bigger than bowling balls. He was on many hit lists. He was on the hit that took out the lawyer, Bob Weiswasser. He was a guy who played them close to his vest, and you couldn't tell whether he liked you or not. Thank God he liked me! He was partners with his pal Angelo P. for years, then he ran away in the 1980s with a ton of Gallo Shylock money. I heard he died of natural causes.

JOE THE RICAN

Joe "The Rican" Castro was from the streets of Brooklyn, not too smart, but there when you needed him. He could kill with no remorse. He took me on my first two scores. He used to come to the house to pick up Ricky a few times a week. That was during a time when guys always rode two in a car, one driver and one guy sitting shotgun.

Joe was a big guy, taller than six-foot, and mean as they come. His big mistake came when he killed his girlfriend's doctor because he thought she was cheating with him, and now he's doing life in prison.

GOOMBABIEL

Anthony Russo, I called him Goombabiel, was my good friend. In my mind he was always smiling. I think it was because of all the pot he smoked. He was born in South Brooklyn, and I spent many evenings with him from 1970 when I was thirteen, until

1986, when I was thirty! Roy Roy told him to watch over me, like a guardian angel. That, to tell the truth, wasn't that great of an idea. Now you had me and Goombabiel—who was going to watch over us?

After a few weeks we were out doing scores, drinking every night, and getting into arguments. We were partners taking bets with football tickets. He used to go on the *Screw* magazine paper route with me—more about that later. We opened a club on Sixth Avenue and Twentieth Street in Brooklyn, a neighborhood now called South Slope.

Whatever we could do wrong we did, and we laughed about it as we did it. He was a loyal guy who would do anything for you. At one point he started to sleep at my house so he could get up five days a week at five in the morning and give my wife, Emily, a ride to work on Long Island.

Many years later, when we went our separate ways, I called him for a favor and he said yes. Thank goodness, as it turned out, I ended up not needing the favor, but there he was, willing to go. One of my true friends.

RALPHIE GOODNESS

Ralphie Goodness was once married to Blast's sister-in-law, and he was with the Gallos dating back to the 1960s. He was a fixture at the Coco Poodle, a professional gambler, and a thief. I was told that if it looked like there was going to be a fight, he had your back—for what it was worth, because if real trouble started he wasn't good with his hands. But he was there, and sometimes that was enough.

Ralphie was a pretty boy and always concerned about his looks. Every hair was always in place, and he was always dressed to a T. As I write this, I learned that Ralphie had kept in touch with my friend Sonny Girard, who told me Ralphie passed away at home in Florida while cooking a sauce.

ANTHONY "BULL EYE" PRANO

Anthony was always with Steven Gallo, like his other half. We called them Martini & Rossi because they went everywhere together. Bull Eye was a small guy with thick-lensed glasses. He must've been blind as a bat without them. I still don't know what Bull Eye's function was.

FRANK "PROSCIUTTO" FARELLA

My dear friend, born in Red Hook, he was with me and Goombabiel on President Street through it all. Frank was what you call a real "street guy," a throwback to the old gangster days. He was a tough fuck, but he lost his way. We lost him to the *babonya*. Heroin. He died too young.

VINNIE CAPISCE

Here's a guy who was liked by a great number of people, including my father. Vinnie is still alive and living in "The Hook." If you needed something, all you had to do was ask Vinnie. He was a real standup guy and very close to Roy Roy.

COCO

Coco was a young Puerto Rican kid from the neighborhood. I don't think he was even ten years old, but he looked as old as us, and he acted like it, too. He was there with us all through "the war." He cooked for us and ran for anything we needed. He left us after the war, and joined the police force. Now retired.

"RED"

We called him "Red." He's still living. He was Punchy's right-hand man for years, a fixture in Red Hook, and a standup guy. I haven't seen much of him for a while. He had to be a good guy to have stayed with Punchy for so long.

JOHN THE ARAB

John the Arab was another native-born Red Hook guy. We were neighbors when we were kids, both lived on Douglass Street. He was close to Roy Roy. I spent a lot of nights drinking with him in Roy's club. John had his hands in everything. If you needed him, he was there with no fear.

He was another guy who drank the Stevie G. Kool-Aid. But I got to speak with him and got him to see the light. I was friends with him until the end. He died too young. His liver went bad.

RICHIE

Still alive and well. I've known him now for, what? Forty years. He was loyal to Punchy and was there for him until the day Punchy died. If you saw Punchy, you saw Richie. Many, many men would love to have a friend like Richie.

There were many guys who came to President Street to do business. Many would come and go, but in the end there weren't many guys left in the Gallo crew.

These days, if you're not going to make any money, you're gone. There is no loyalty.

I see Wonder Bread and American cheese writers who throw around the words *omerta* and *la cosa nostra* like they know what the fuck they are talking about. Not one of those WASP bastards lived the Life, or has ever gotten burnt. It's easy to have shit come out of your mouth.

CHAPTER 11

JOEY'S HOME

WHEN JOEY GALLO got out of prison, there was a powwow with all the regulars at the club on President Street. Joey's time in prison had done nothing to pump up his sanity. Here was a guy who when in prison sided with the Black Muslims over the neo-Nazis, which might've been a good business move—lots of black people in Brooklyn with money to spend, neo-Nazis are harder to find—but it was a war that was clearly color-coded, and going black couldn't have been a relaxing way to do his time.

Now home, he was every bit as crazy as ever, and the tone around the block changed with him there. Right away he started ranting that Joe Colombo was fucking his crew out of a ton of money and that Blast was sucking up to Joe too much. Joey pointed out that come Christmastime Joe Colombo gave shitty ties as presents, while Blast gave him big envelopes of cash or a set of golf clubs.

"No more," Joey said.

Joey set up a meeting with Joe Colombo. Instead of coming himself, Colombo sent Nicky Bianco and Rocco Miraglia with a $1,000 gift. Joey threw it back at them and told them to give Colombo a message: "*I want the $100,000 that's owed to me. Tell him that is nonnegotiable.*" As best as anyone could tell, that hundred grand represented the business—loan-sharking, kickbacks from restaurants, garbage—Colombo had gotten on account of Joey was away.

When Nicky and Rocco left, Joey said to Blast and Louie the Syrian, "Colombo didn't have the fucking balls to come see me himself. The last time Nicky Bianco sat on a deal we got fucked." He was talking about the 1962 peace deal with Profaci that Profaci reneged on.

Nicky came back a week later with a message from Colombo: "It's not going to happen."

Joey replied, "In that case, you can tell Joe to go fuck himself."

This time, after Nicky left, Joey said, "We're no longer going to answer to Joe Colombo. If we have to go to war, let's go!"

So Joey started calling in the crew. For the rest of that year, Joey was gearing up for war with Colombo, stocking away guns, getting some cash together to hold them over when it came time to "hit the mattresses."

During the gearing-up phase, Joey was also learning which of the crew would be loyal and which would hightail it out of there when they sensed trouble coming. Sure enough, as soon as Joey started using the word "*war*," some of the guys became scared. Sally Balsamo's brother Joe was gone. Anthony Peanuts took off. And I didn't see Ralphie Goodness anymore.

THE SHOOTING OF COLOMBO

We were told not to go to the 1971 Italian-American Civil Rights League rally at Columbus Circle in the city, because that would have been construed as showing support for Joe Colombo. The year before, the rally had been a major success, a real Italian Woodstock, and the crew had gone but didn't like it and left early. The League scored a major victory in November 1970 when they held a benefit at Madison Square Garden and Sinatra showed up to sing. Colombo scheduled the second annual Italian-American

Unity Day in Columbus Circle in hopes of repeating the first one's success.

Colombo must've known that this year's event, to be held on June 28, 1971, was on shakier ground than the first one, for the simple reason that Joey Gallo once again walked the streets.

Colombo's activities had been interrupted as of late by African American interference. Colombo had heard that Joey had gotten tight with some of the brothers from Bed-Stuy while in prison, and he naturally blamed Joey for these incidents.

Now this Gallo crew doctrine—"don't go to the rally"—became very important, because Joe Colombo got shot at that rally. He was on his way to the podium to give his speech, when a Harlem street hustler named Jerome Johnson approached wearing League press credentials and disguised as a photojournalist. Johnson pulled an automatic and fired three shots into Colombo's head. Colombo's kid and another guy wrestled Johnson to the ground, at which point another man stepped forward and shot Johnson to death. The second shooter escaped. His identity remains unknown. There was a half-hearted attempt to continue the show, but everyone split after the shooting. Colombo didn't die, not right away anyway.

As Joey Gallo liked to say, "Colombo got *vegetabled*."

Colombo lingered in a coma for years and didn't die until 1978.

Of course, the Colombos blamed the Gallo crew.

But no one had to tell us. We knew that Joey wasn't behind it, although there might've been an effort to make it look like the Gallos were responsible. Sure, Joey hated Colombo's guts and wanted him dead, and he'd go into a fucking rage whenever Colombo's name came up, and it was only a matter of time before Joey made something happen regarding the health of Joe Colombo, but still, the hit at the rally didn't come from us.

There were three major reasons the boys on President Street

knew right away that the hit on Colombo came from elsewhere: (1) Sending a black guy to kill Colombo would have been stupid and the Gallo brothers weren't stupid, (2) my father would have known about the hit in advance if it had come from the Gallos, and he would have told me, and (3) we wouldn't have just been walking around the street like assholes if it had been us. There would have been some consideration to blowback, and as it was guys like Punchy, Roy Roy, and Louie found themselves vulnerable, open targets. And that's also stupid. If the Gallo crew had been in on the hit, we might not have been told precisely what was going to happen, but we would have been informed that something was going to go down so we'd have known to lie low.

None of those reasons had anything to do with public opinion, though. Everybody thought we did it. The papers printed that we did it. We were innocent, and yet the heat was on us. (We found out later that the hit was set up by Colombo captains just to get rid of their boss, so they set it up to look like Joey Gallo did it.) Carlo Gambino wanted Colombo out of the way, and he gave his blessing for the hit.

Now, if you could speak to Greg Scarpa or Carmine Persico, you would hear the real story, how it went down, because that's where the hit on Colombo came from.

Cops pulled Joey and Blast in and questioned them about Colombo's shooting. The brothers said, "Seriously, not us." Police had to let them go after a short time. Then Punchy and Chitoz got pulled in. Same deal. Then it was Tony Bernardo. and Ricky. The Law did that for a couple of weeks, then they gave up because no one knew anything.

WHOM TO TRUST?

The shooting of Joseph Colombo signaled a big change in my life. I stayed on the block a lot after that. I knew a lot of shit was going on because there were a lot of guys coming and going. We sorted out who was with us and who was full of shit. We accumulated supplies.

The most important supply was guns. That was the big question: Where were the guns going to come from? To fight a war on the streets of Brooklyn, you needed a lot of guns, because when the Law was on your trail you were always throwing them away.

In Joey's mind, keeping track of loyalties was even more important than maintaining an adequate arsenal. He had lists: guys who were loyal no matter what, guys who were loyal but lacked balls (and so they could be persuaded), guys who were neutral, guys who were double agents trying to play both sides against the middle, and guys who were completely full of shit.

Whom to trust? Guys can flip real easy. Wannabes are the first ones to open their mouths. Wannabes will start trouble and then, when it comes, they'll run and leave you standing there with your balls in your hands.

Sitting there in Roy Roy's club, I remember listening to the endless conversation, who was really siding with whom and who was full of shit. I learned a lot, but it didn't register at first. I was sixteen, although I looked twenty, and I didn't have an open mind. I only looked at things in one way, the old Three Musketeers line: "All for one and one for all." I would have done anything those guys asked me to do. Thank God, Roy Roy kept me out of everything. He would point to his eye, then smile. He said that the young guys were off-limits and that we would be safe. Then he told me to go over to Court Street and hang out with my friends. If he needed me to come back to President Street, he would call me.

So I moved around a lot. Scores were far apart, and we had to eat and drink. I was still working on the newspaper routes for an income. The good thing was that a Scotch and water was two dollars and a slice of pizza was only 25 cents, so there was plenty of money for that.

When I was on President Street with Roy Roy, I would sit and watch everything, try to learn stuff. One thing I learned was that there were guys in the crew whom I didn't like. In fact, I thought they were real assholes. First and foremost on that list was Sammy the Syrian. What a jerk-off. He was the guy who sounded like Edward G. Robinson, that real "gingerilla," tough-guy shit. He spoke to me like I was an asshole. He had no respect for anyone. I told Ricky and Roy Roy that I didn't like Sammy's attitude. They said, "Don't mind him. He's an asshole." They didn't like him, either.

Some of these guys were off on account of delusions of grandeur. Take Pete the Greek. Another asshole. He thought he was Al Capone. Ricky thought Pete was weak sauce. "His next fight will be his first," Ricky would say. The only reason the boys on President Street tolerated him was that he was Joey's driver. Joey, for some unknown reason, liked him.

On the other side of the coin, there were guys hanging out whom I liked a lot. Louie the Syrian was a great man, a gentleman, soft-spoken and smart. He was *consiglia*. That means he was the guy who had the boss's ear, and he was authorized to represent the boss at meetings. If you needed help, you went to him—and I did many times.

And of course, I loved Mondo. He was always friendly and he made sure you were fed. I used to watch in amazement as he had a way with the ladies, too. He wouldn't go out with another little person. He always seemed to have a six-foot blonde on his arm. Well, maybe they just looked six-foot because they were standing next to Mondo. He used to put his face right in their box when he danced with them. We used to laugh our asses off. And he'd do this with his mother right there in the kitchen watching him!

UNION STREET SHOOTING

When I got called back to the block, I was sleeping at an apartment we had at 16 President Street, staying with Goomba and

Frankie Prosciutto. If we weren't in the club with Roy, we'd be in that apartment for days at a time.

After a few weeks of lying low, a change of scenery started to sound really nice, and I'd get itchy to get off the block. One night, when my wanderlust was particularly acute, I went into Blast's club and asked if maybe I could go out someplace and get something to eat.

Blast said, "Okay."

Louie the Syrian said, "No."

Bobby B. said, "It's safe if the kid goes."

Louie was outvoted, and me and Goomba took my new 1966 Cadillac convertible, which I'd recently purchased from Mooney, and I drove. We went to the end of President Street, took a right on Van Brunt Street, then another right on Union. We had gone less than a quarter mile, halfway around the fucking block, when a car pulled up next to us, squeezed off five or six shots, and took off.

Holy shit. I lost control of the car, hopped the curb, and plowed into a johnny pump (a "fire hydrant" in the rest of the world). Me and Goomba got out of the car and ran around the block to President Street, yelling at the top of our lungs.

Everyone had heard the shots, the crew, the Law, all the neighbors. The cops reacted quickly and a car with the Organized Crime Squad was hot off in pursuit of the shooters.

We went running into Blast's club. Blast was already on the move.

"You boys hold down the fort," he said, and he was out the door, disappearing into the night.

About five minutes later, a car came careening down President Street and smashed through the police barricade at the beginning of the block. A couple of electric-orange traffic cones and a big blue wooden horse went flying. From inside they fired a couple of shots at the club. The boys left inside the club spilled outside and scattered. Some of them ran for their own cars to chase down the shooters. Some stood around with their hands on their hips for a couple of minutes and then went back into the club to finish their fucking espressos.

After a while the boys who'd hopped into their cars came back to the block. The car from the Organized Crime Squad returned. The bad guys got away—and everyone was pissed off. It was at this point that everyone realized the drive-by shooters had tossed out a hand grenade, and the damn thing was sitting there on the fucking sidewalk unexploded, so then there was more fuss as a bomb unit took it away without incident.

Eventually we made friends with the police. There were a couple of guys who practically lived on the block for months, so we got to know them. Every once in a while, someone would run out and give them some food and coffee. We tried to make their job pleasant.

After Goomba and I were shot at, Detective Charles Bartell told us that the cops figured it was a planned move—that the enemy was out there waiting for someone to leave the block so they could try to kill them. They knew the shooting nearby would draw the cop car off the block and thus allow a drive-by attack on the club.

When the excitement was over, me and Goomba went back into the club and had a few more Scotches.

Ricky was never on the block. He was always out on the streets looking for someone to shoot. He used to call in to the club, and he'd talk to Blast or Louie or me and identify himself only as "Mr. Goldberg." My mom didn't see him for weeks at a time. The Gallo crew had safe houses all over Brooklyn and in the city, and sometimes Mr. Goldberg would indicate his location in code and I would venture out and take him money or a gun or whatever it was he needed.

The first thing I did was to make sure no one was following me. The rule was that I was too young to be touched, but the rules didn't seem to matter anymore, as the attack on Goomba and me indicated. So I kept my eyes on the rearview mirror just as Ricky had taught me. Better safe than sorry. If they killed me even though I was too young, what was I going to do, complain? I always carried a gun. When I was in the car driving, I'd stick it under the dashboard.

Before I made my delivery, I'd go into a nearby bar, have a few drinks, leave with a girl, and anyone who might be watching me would think I was just out partying. Then I'd take the girl with me for the delivery. The location was usually a bar or a restaurant in the city, which was fine with me. It was just a place to have another drink. And there was a lot of drinking, sometimes a bottle of Dewar's a night.

Then, once Ricky had the gun, he'd find a hidden spot to watch, like a deer hunter up in a tree, and he'd wait for Apples MacIntosh and Joe Yacovelli. Ricky had a hunter's patience. He could wait for days. But they never happened by while he was ready for them. They were either lucky, or they had someone telling them they had an armed stalker.

CHAPTER 12
THE COURT TERRACE

ONE DAY I GOT A CALL to go to a bar called The Court Terrace Lounge at Court Street and Atlantic Avenue. It was one of Joey Gallo's bars, run by this guy called Rocky Trimatano. They needed someone to "help watch the place," so they picked me. Big mistake.

The first day I opened the bar and was waiting for the barmaid to come in, when three guys I recognized came to the door. I let them in. One of them wanted a drink. So, being the nice guy that I am, I went behind the bar, fixed him a drink, and gave it to him.

When he finished the drink, he slid his empty glass toward me and said, "You owe me a drink."

"Why?" I asked.

"You walked past the cash register with a hat on. It's an old superstition; you walk past the cash register with your hat on, you owe the bar a drink."

I said, "Fuck you. I'm not giving you a fucking thing—and if you're going to keep busting my balls, I'm going to throw you out."

My memories are sketchy about what happened next. I threw a left hook, and one of the guys hit the jukebox hard as I was trying to push him out of the bar. Then the door flew open and Rocky, the guy who ran the place, came bursting in to see what was going on.

"Let him go," Rocky said to me.

I let the guy go. I explained the situation and Rocky told me the guy hadn't made up the story—it was a true tradition. But I still felt I was right. The guy was an asshole for pulling that on me. I'd like to say that that was the worst thing that happened to me at The Court Terrace, but the truth was, that was only the beginning—the start of an eight-month hell-ride.

By the way, the guy I threw into the jukebox was named Phillie Jukebox. It was a little bit funny, and afterward he and I made friends.

ANOTHER SUIT RUINED

Within my first couple of weeks at the bar, I had some of my guys there with me—Goomba, Marty, Blake, and Steve. We ran the place with no trouble, until one night when four 350-pound college football players came in. They got drunk and started to fuck with me.

I swear, I was using all of my interpersonal skills to keep things from getting out of control, and it was getting me nowhere. Then Marty smashed a beer mug into one football player's face, and all hell broke loose.

There were six of us, but the heaviest among us had to weigh 150 pounds soaking wet. It was a battle—and it went on forever. I was on the floor most of the time with my legs wrapped around this monster, and I was punching the shit out of him. My cousin Blake was on him, too, and sometimes we were hitting each other.

When it was all over and the cops came, they had to take two of the football players out on stretchers, and the other two crawled out on their hands and knees. The cops told them they should be ashamed of themselves and asked us if we wanted to press charges. We said no, and they all left. I had some broken knuckles. The guys had a couple of things broken and there were a few black eyes—but you should have seen the other guys. They were fucked up.

THE DRUNKEN NORWEGIAN SAILOR

We had a lot of good nights at The Court Terrace. The music was great, and there were always a lot of broads. One night we got real drunk and got into an argument with a drunken Norwegian sailor. He'd wandered in from Montero's Bar, which was farther up Atlantic Avenue. Trouble started when we decided it was time for him to leave and he didn't want to go.

I wound up getting in a fight with him that spilled out onto the street. I hit him so many times that I broke my hand—so I started to kick the shit out of him. I kicked him so hard and often that I busted my new alligator shoes, and that pissed me off even more. The soles were hanging off and I had to limp back into the bar. That really sucked! I'd paid two hundred dollars for them at Layton's in the city.

When I got back in the bar, I noticed that my white gold diamond ring was missing. We locked the bar down.

"No one leaves until I find that ring!" I said.

Some people wanted to leave. I said no. We thought that maybe one of them had found it, so I pulled out my gun for emphasis, adding, "Nobody is leaving."

Some people were looking harder than others. There was one girl who was really tenacious. She was a heavy girl, couldn't have weighed a pound less than 300, and she was down on her hands and knees with the sawdust and the cigarette butts.

"I found it!" she screamed. It was in a crack in the floor. She was so happy she was crying. I thanked her and went over to give her a hug, but I couldn't get my arms around her. Turned out, she wasn't happy because I got my ring back, but because she finally got to go home, which she did—and none of us ever saw her again.

The rest of the night went okay, but the next day I got a call to come down to President Street.

Louie the Syrian said, "Frankie, I heard about the thing that happened at the bar last night. I didn't like the thing about the gun."

He told me he didn't want me to get in trouble, drinking and having a gun. Pulling a gun in the bar was bad for business for one thing, and bad for another because if the cops came I was fucked.

"I'm sorry, Louie," I said.

"Okay," he said.

We kissed and I went on my way.

THE FIGHT AT EL BOLEROS

A week later I was in The Court Terrace drinking with two guys, both named Raymond, when another guy came running into the bar all excited.

"Marty's in a fight at the El Boleros," the guy said, spitting out the words between gasps for breath. He was talking about my good friend Marty, and the El Boleros was another bar down the block on Court Street.

So me and the two Raymonds ran out and headed down the block. When we got to the El Boleros, we found that everyone was fighting. It looked like one of those brawls in a TV Western: One guy throws a punch and in a flash everyone is hitting each other over the head with breakaway prop chairs. I tried to find Marty so I could tell the good guys from the bad guys.

"Marty, who we fighting?" I said, but he didn't have to answer. I figured it out on my own after I hit a couple of guys and a ton of guys hit me back. I hit the owner with a bar stool, which was *not* a breakaway TV prop, and I busted his head open.

I looked off to one side just in time to see a guy shove a knife into Marty's stomach. Seconds later, one of the Raymonds was stabbed. I needed a weapon fast, so I grabbed a pool stick, and I was hitting everyone I could reach with it, in the meantime backing up toward the door so I could get the fuck out of there before someone stuck a blade in my liver.

Just as I got to the door, something hit me in the arm, and my whole arm went dead, just hanging there useless at my side. I had to take Marty and both of the Rays to the hospital—the second Ray had also been cut—so we all ended up in the hospital.

We were still in the process of getting patched up when the cocksucking owner of the bar, his head bandaged, came up to us in the company of a beat cop named Officer Gannon.

The cop looked at me and said, "Oh no."

We were all arrested for assault. Two of us (including me) had to stay in the hospital while the two others who didn't need a hospital bed got to spend two days in jail.

While I was in the hospital, Blast, Louie, Punchy, Roy Roy, Bobby B., and Joe the Rican went to El Boleros. They'd heard I was in a battle, and they wanted to find out what the fuck was up. That made me feel good, that those guys would put their lives on the line and leave the block for me. It made me feel like I was really a member of the crew. They probably went for Ricky's sake, but it still made me feel good.

Lawyers talked the charges down to "pay restitution." I never paid. When the bar owner found out I was Ricky's son, he said he didn't want my money. A few weeks later, we found out that the owner was arrested. He was a big drug dealer, had had a beef with a guy in the bar weeks before the fight with Marty. The owner had killed the guy and buried him in the bar's basement. It was all over the papers. Someone ratted him out.

This was happy news for me and Goomba. I took a certain pride in having busted the head of the guy who'd buried a murder victim in his basement.

"That's right, I fucked him up," I would say, and we'd both crack up.

Goomba would say, "Fuck you. You just got lucky."

"Fuck, no," I'd say. "He's lucky I didn't put *him* in the basement."

JOE THE RICAN'S GOOD SCORE

Weeks went by, and everybody healed up. It was midwinter, and Kings County was encased in a polar air mass. There were a lot of indoor activities going on. We were playing pool in Ju Ju's when Joe the Rican came in. You met him earlier: big, dumb, dangerous, and mean, but a Gallo guy.

I'm shooting pool, chalking up my stick, when Joe the Rican came in, came up to me, and pulled me aside.

"What?"

"I need to talk to you, Frankie."

"I didn't do nothing."

"I know. You're a good boy. Listen, I heard about a good score," he said.

"What's it about?"

"Shipment of coke coming off a ship at the piers. Divers are gonna unload the shit."

I figured out right away that the only way Joe the Rican was telling me this shit at all was because he wanted me in on the score somehow.

"What do you need?" I asked.

"I need three guys to watch the water, spotters, see when the divers are doing what they do, so when they get the thing ashore, we can take it away from them."

"Where do we stand?"

"On the Promenade. You see the divers and you beep me. I go down to the dock and youse come down and give me a hand."

"Okay," I said, and I got Marty and Goomba to be the other two guys. I got guns and a car.

It was the coldest night of the winter. And we stood there on

the Promenade from ten at night until five the next morning looking for fucking divers down there bobbing around in the inky
water.

We had to shut the car off so no one would notice us, froze our
asses off and almost got frostbite. When it got light out, we took off.

As soon as we got back to the club, Joe the Rican called and
said, "Where the fuck were you?"

"The sun was coming up. We left," I said.

"They just made the drop-off," he said.

"They must've made us and waited till we left."

We later learned from some guys we knew from Third Avenue
that the divers did make us, and they knew who we were. We
were lucky that they didn't just come up and kill us. I was told
some things I hadn't known before: that the Gallo crew had been
ordered by the Colombo crew to stay the fuck off the piers, and
that this was a Colombo pier and a Colombo score.

Well, all I got out of Joe the Rican's "good score" was a head
cold and almost being killed. Win some, lose some.

Joe the Rican didn't give up on me. He had another idea not
long after the first. It was hard to imagine a light bulb going on
over his head, so maybe somebody was spoon-feeding him inspiration. The second attempt was the charm, though, and I was in
on my first score that worked.

MY FIRST SCORE THAT WORKED

Joe needed some guys to pull a diamond heist in the city. I
called Marty and Steven C. and we went with him. The Rican
and Marty went in first, bum-rushed the Jewish guy in there, hit
him in the head with a pistol. Me and Steven came in a few seconds later and cleaned out what we could find in diamonds. Joe
and Marty tied up the guy and we took off. After Joe fenced the
diamonds, we got about five thousand dollars each.

Joe's staff didn't receive a large percentage of the take. Being that we were young guys and hadn't paid our dues yet, I guess that was okay.

I was busy spending my money in the pool room when a guy came running up and said they were talking about the diamond heist on TV. I ran over to the set to watch. They were talking to the Jewish guy, and he seemed very pleased with himself, explaining that the thieves did not get the really good diamonds, which were hidden in a secret drawer. But I didn't feel too bad because the guy had a big bandage on his head—that took the edge off of his smugness.

Everyone in the pool room started to crack up, laughing at the guy's fucked-up head. At least we had some money. I went to the city to get some new clothes, bought new alligator shoes, some knit sweaters, and several pairs of black pants like the pair that got ruined in the fight with the football players.

CHAPTER 13
SCREW MAGAZINE AND THE
WORLD OF PORN

THE GALLO CREW had a deal with Al Goldstein, the owner of *Screw* magazine: exclusive distribution rights in the five boroughs. Between 1955 and 1975, porn had gone from stag parties and mail order to mainstream newsstands, growing into a billion-a-year industry. In the view of hoodlums, porn was a good earner, so naturally the Mafia found a way to sink its teeth into smut.

The mob and the porn industry make very strange but profitable bedfellows. The President Street gang first formed a partnership with the pornography industry in 1971. One problem the porn press had always had was finding a way to distribute the stuff. The mails were federally owned and had restrictions. States had varying laws regarding what was and wasn't obscene, and the "straight" newspaper and magazine distributors in the country were hesitant to distribute stuff that might cause trouble with the Law.

They said shit like, "We are afraid of being brought up on obscenity charges by associating with such graphic material."

So the boys saw the opening and quickly filled it, formed their own distribution companies, and distributed the stuff that no one else wanted to deal with, like *Screw* magazine, a variety of more sharply focused hard-core newsprint magazines, one per fetish it seemed, and big-print dirty paperback novels cranked out at a pace of eight a week by a team of writers typing as fast as they could into primitive, refrigerator-sized word processors.

The business grew so rapidly that by the mid-1980s the distribution of almost every major pornographic newspaper and magazine in the United States was controlled by one of two mob-ruled entities: Star Distributors or Astro News Distributors. The latter of those two, that was us.

Star was the largest national porn distributor at the time. They were located at 150 Lafayette Street in Manhattan. The other, Astro, was located at 118 Eighth Street in Brooklyn. It had the Gowanus on one side and the Fourth Street Basin on the other, so you could always smell the waterway no matter which way the wind was blowing.

Both were mob. Star was run by Robert DiBernardo, who was known in circles as DB. He made his bones with the DeCavalcante crew from New Jersey (the family that *The Sopranos* was based on), and later became *caporegime* in the Gambino family. Officially, DB was vice president of Star Distributors. On paper, he was listed as a suit-and-tie corporate officer, but on the street where it mattered he was the Man, the absolute last word regarding Star and its business decisions.

Astro News was another story. It was the major New York City distributor of pornographic newspapers, and was operated by my father, Ricky Dimatteo, who ran the company for the Gallos.

Here's a quick summary of how that came to be: Astro's biggest client at the time was Milky Way Productions, Inc., which published *Screw*, a weekly tabloid-sized porn paper with a circulation of about 100,000. Between Astro and Star, we were distributing close to 300,000 papers every week.

How did *Screw* come to be distributed by a mob-run company? According to Al Goldstein, the publisher/editor, he didn't have a choice in the matter.

"We have no options as to who we deal with," he said. "No legitimate distributor will touch us. I'd deal with Hitler if I had to. I'll deal with anyone I can do business with."

Before he went mob, Goldstein tried to get his newspaper distributed by some legitimate but inexperienced people who turned out to be incompetent. He was desperate for a New York–based distributor that knew what they were doing. He wound up turning to a friend of his who was the brother-in-law of Pete the Greek, who was a business partner of Bobby Darrow, my godfather, and both were members of the Gallo gang. After getting the okay from the Gallos, the Greek, Darrow, and Roy Roy started distributing *Screw* for Goldstein.

It was Roy Roy's job to make sure the newsstands in the five boroughs all knew that it would be a big mistake if they refused to take *Screw*. He went to the big newsstands first, like Nathan's at Forty-fourth and Broadway, and Block at Forty-second and Eighth Avenue, and he told them flat-out that if they didn't take the paper, when they came to work in the morning, their stands wouldn't be there.

They all said, sure, they would take the paper. And it turned out to be a smart move, as those two large newsstands were each selling upwards of ten thousand copies of *Screw* every week. Sometimes we had to make two or three deliveries per week to those places to keep them in supply.

The initial problem didn't come from the newsstands, but rather from the crew of amateurs who'd been distributing *Screw* before we took over. It turned out they were not only clueless when it came to business, but they also had no idea who they were dealing with. They went to Goldstein and adamantly protested their firing. They said some things. It had to stop. So the Greek and Darrow rounded up some guys from President Street—including Ricky and me—and we destroyed their trucks with baseball bats.

The independent distributor was never heard from again. Gallo *consigliere* Louie the Syrian handed off the distribution business to Ricky to run. The business was so profitable that they had to set up a separate company just for porn distribution.

Goldstein was thrilled. *Screw* was getting out there and it was selling. Still, having the mob as your business partner had its ups and downs.

The upside was that if anyone tried to wrestle any type of control away from Goldstein or fuck with him in any way, he had the Gallos to protect him. There was a time when some guys approached Goldstein about leaving the Gallos and going with them instead, but Goldstein told Ricky about it and it was taken care of immediately.

The downside of the partnership was that Goldstein and his Milky Way company had little control over his product's printing, distribution, and bookkeeping. Astro News and, by extension, the mob, handled it all from start to finish, including the sharing and distribution of profits.

THE PROCESS

The process was as follows: When a paper was ready for publication, it was taken from Milky Way's offices at 116 West 114th Street in the city to the printer on Kings Highway in Brooklyn. The printed papers were loaded on Astro News trucks and delivered bundle by bundle to the newsstands and stores. The resulting earnings were split 60/40, with us getting the larger share, and Goldstein having to pay all overhead—employee salaries, legal fees, etc.—out of his.

The Gallo crew didn't necessarily support or approve of Goldstein's paper; they were mostly ambivalent. They usually only complained that Goldstein went too far when he criticized the Catholic Church.

Goldstein was an opinionated guy, and along with pictures of women giving blow jobs and the like, every issue of *Screw* came

laden with a piece of Goldstein's mind. On the subject of the
Church, Goldstein and the Gallos did not see eye to eye.

To inform Goldstein of the distributor's dissatisfaction with
his editorial content, Blast had a meeting with him in the back of
a black Cadillac. Goldstein listened for a while as Blast explained
that it would be in his best interests to tone down the anti-Church
rhetoric, to which Goldstein surprisingly told Blast to go fuck
himself. To further express his fury, Goldstein not only didn't
turn his anti-Church comments down a notch, he turned them up
to full volume.

There was nothing Goldstein liked less than being told what to
do. He told Blast that his guys were in charge of the distribution,
he was in charge of the content, and the subject wasn't open for
discussion.

Blast gave in. Goldstein was a good earner, and besides, he
was nuts. It wasn't just that he was stubborn, but he had all sorts
of beliefs and self-myths working. He was convinced that he was
more than just a producer of newsprint porn, he was a crusader,
an anti-censorship pioneer in the spirit of the controversial comedian Lenny Bruce.

Blast thought Goldstein's claims of having a higher purpose
were so much bullshit. Deep down inside, Goldstein was just a
degenerate, so he was in the right business.

Despite the fact that Goldstein was sometimes difficult to deal
with, and clearly he and his distributors were different types of
people, everyone got along for the most part. When the money is
flowing freely, things can be like that.

Life was very old school on President Street, and the boys
were conservative in their worldview. They were walking, talking contradictions. At night they were out committing crimes, but
during the day they supported zealous law-and-order politicians
like Ronald Reagan and Richard Nixon. They looked upon Goldstein as a flake, a hippy-dippy flower child whose newspapers

filled with naked women with hard-ons in their mouths meant nothing to them.

When Goldstein was being an asshole, it almost always involved his ego. He thought that it was *important* that he was showing the world hard dicks and pussies. His distributors didn't understand any of that. They looked at him and all they saw were dollar signs.

Goldstein was a cash cow, and as long as he remained so, he could be as flaky as he liked. Money is the great deodorant that can cover up the foulest stench. Business was always going to come first.

As far as Goldstein was concerned, the only thing that kept him even the slightest bit humble was the fact that the Mafia owned him and his business. He talked a good game and walked around with a chip on his shoulder like he wasn't afraid of anybody, like nobody was going to tell him what to do. Deep down, he knew that if push came to shove, these men who were his partners would have a bullet put into his head if he ever tried to do something foolish.

Goldstein had an actual partner, the guy who'd put up money to get *Screw* started, and his name was Jim Buckley. He was not in favor of doing business with the mob, and he was petrified of them.

Funny thing was, Goldstein's distributors liked Goldstein's sense of bravado more than the cowering cowardice of Buckley. They liked Goldstein because he could defuse tensions with his sarcasm and off-color remarks.

That was Goldstein's greatest skill, in fact. He could look the toughest tough guy right in the eye and make his point, but do it in a humorous enough of a way to keep from infuriating anybody.

Goldstein also knew his place. He knew that his situation was a good one. He liked having a distributor that no one was going to mess with.

CESSPOOLS

I got along with Al Goldstein for the most part. Blast set it up so that Goldstein only had to deal with Ricky. All New York distribution issues were run by and through my father. There were no papers, no lawyers. There was a handshake between Blast and Goldstein and it was a done deal.

I was working closely with my dad at that point and so I got to see some of the sleazy world of pornography. I remember going into S&M clubs, sex clubs, and fetish joints for numerous meetings. Sometimes I was shocked by the things I saw in these cesspools.

One time I was in a Manhattan sex club called The Nutcracker Suite that catered to every immoral depravity one could think of: twisted orgies, sex slaves, men locked in cages and on dog leashes.

One night while I was sitting at a bar waiting for someone I was supposed to meet, I glanced over, and there, a few feet away, was a grown man in nothing but a diaper and a bonnet, sitting in a playpen like a baby.

To make it even more comical, the guy weighed about three hundred pounds. I started to laugh uncontrollably, and when he saw me laughing, he became highly insulted.

He looked at me with a straight face, like I'd just caught him doing something mundane like mailing a letter, and he said, "Why are you laughing at me?"

I didn't feel like I needed to state the obvious, but I did anyway: "Because you're dressed up like a fucking baby and you're a grown man."

He pouted and crawled away.

There was another place called the Hellfire. Guys would be standing at the bar, and they'd jerk off right there on the floor at your feet. I saw women putting cigarettes out on guys, and you could see the marks where they'd done it before. And guys would get charged off on that.

It was surreal, like a nightmare but you couldn't wake up,

like being trapped inside an episode of that HBO series Real Sex, troubling, with strange people doing strange things out in the open for everyone to see.

I've seen it all, believe me. My whole life I have been around career criminals, even contract killers, but none of them were as bizarre as the freaks I encountered in those fetish joints.

THE WELL-OILED MACHINE

The mob was making tons of money off of *Screw*, and every week they fed Al Goldstein an envelope of cash. Everybody was getting their fair share and the paper was getting out there to the public without a hitch.

As time went on, my family became friendly with Goldstein and we spent a lot of social time together, including barbecues at our home.

Goldstein was also close with Robert "DB" DiBernardo, whom he'd known from even before the *Screw* magazine days. Al had written for other sex magazines that DB circulated. They got along very well.

Circulation peaked in the 1970s with an issue that bragged on its cover, "Exclusive Photos! Jackie Kennedy Naked!" That issue (Number 206) sold more than 300,000 copies.

Everyone was playing by the rules. People were satisfied. Nobody was getting hurt. But all of that was about to change.

DB'S DEMISE

DB was a well-respected *capo* and a good earner for the Gambino family. In addition to his pornography distribution operation, he was also involved in labor unions and other legitimate businesses. He was intelligent and articulate, and many guys thought he would make a great boss one day. DB's one flaw, and it turned out to be a fatal flaw, was that he was a loner. He came and went on his own, no posse, no entourage. He paid his tribute, but he had his own mind. He expressed his own opinion, which could be dangerous, especially in a family that was in major upheaval after Big Paul Castellano was gunned down outside Sparks Steakhouse nine days before Christmas in 1985. DB became a victim of his own success. Guys in the ranks grew jealous of DB's position; some owed him a lot of money. Those closest to the new boss, John Gotti—namely Sammy "The Bull" Gravano and Angelo Ruggiero—began to conspire against DB. They had Gotti's ear, and they filled it with negative stuff about DB. Gotti became convinced that DB had been bad-mouthing him, saying he was an ineffective leader. Gotti came to see DB as a threat to his power. DB had no love for Gotti, but he stuck with him. In June 1986, DB was called to a meeting in the basement of Gravano's drywall company in Bensonhurst.

DB came to my home to speak to Ricky about being called in.

"Don't go or bring someone with you," Ricky advised.

"Why?"

"If you've heard grumbling, that's enough," Ricky said.

DB smiled and said, "Don't worry. I make all their money for them."

He had his coffee with us and left.

DB visiting our home wasn't unheard of. Only a few weeks earlier he'd knocked on the door and asked Ricky how they blew up the car that Frank Decicco was in. Ricky said it was a remote control.

So DB went to his meeting at Gravano's drywall company alone, and there he was shot in the back of the head without ceremony by Gravano's main shooter, Joe Paruta.

Here's proof of just how fragile everyone's position in the Mafia is. DB was a guy who seemed to have everything going for him. He had the respect of just about everyone around him, and he was one of the highest earners—two traits that should offer you some longevity in the Life.

Alphonse, Mooney, Blast, Butch, Chico, Little Mondo, and Larry in a police lineup, August 1961.
A detective asked Little Mondo, "Did you see the shooter?" Mondo replied, "Only his belt."
(author photo)

Emily, the future Mrs. Dimatteo, and yours truly hanging out on the corner of Douglass and Court Streets in Brooklyn, 1973. This was a candid shot, hence our surprised expressions. Wiseguys don't like getting their pictures taken unless they know it's being done. *(author photo)*

Steven Cirillo, Bobby Darrow, my mom (on the chaise lounge), Tony, Joann,
and future *Screw* magazine publisher Al Goldstein, relaxing on a summer's day, circa 1973.
(author photo)

Roy Roy, Bobby Darrow (my godfather), and me visiting Bobby in prison, 1974. *(author photo)*

That's me on the right side (second from the back), wearing the striped jacket.
I still have that jacket, but Emily won't let me wear it anymore.
(author photo)

My father, Ricky Dimatteo, at home, holding court over an antipasto, with Anthony Rotondo,
a capo in the DeCavalcante family. The DeCavalcantes were, in part, the inspiration for the TV show
The Sopranos. You'll note who's doing the talking and who's doing the listening.
(author photo)

My father, Ricky, and me clowning around at the Dis & Dat Lounge in Mill Basin, Brooklyn.
Ricky owned a piece of it. There was a shootout there, and a barmaid was killed.
(author photo)

That's my godfather, Bobby
"Bobby Darrow" Bongivoni (far left),
and the Farragut Street boys.
These were some tough mugs.
How tough?
They drank Rheingold beer.
(author photo)

My blond alibi, Emily,
at Albert "Blast" Gallo's wedding.
I'm not sure what she's holding
in her left hand.
Probably dessert.

Albert "Blast" Gallo's wedding. The smart-ass emcee asked,
"Do we have any Italians here tonight at this reception?
Raise your guns!" Virtually everyone in the room did.
(author photo)

Me, my lovely wife, Emily, Mom, and Dad. We are on our way to hear Jimmy Roselli sing at the San Su San nightclub on Long Island. When Roselli sang "When Your Old Wedding Room Was New," you'd see some of the toughest, meanest, deadliest mobsters crying into their Cutty Sark. *(author photo)*

At Albert "Blast" Gallo's wedding. I don't remember who the gal is on the right, but she's one of the reasons I miss the 1970s. *(author photo)*

DB's murder was the beginning of the end for *Screw* magazine and the distribution business. We continued with the business, but over time *Screw*'s circulation was dropping. Goldstein had legal troubles. Legitimate papers and magazines began running escort ads, and the rapidly growing Internet was becoming the new home of porn. The world didn't need a raunchy underground sex newspaper anymore.

THE FAMILY BUSINESS

The arrangement between Astro and Goldstein was one that benefited both parties for many years. Goldstein could be a pain in the ass at times. He would grumble and groan about the distribution of profits, but in the end it was his gravy train, and he didn't really want to do or say anything that would jeopardize that.

We were all making a boatload of money. As strange as it may sound, distributing *Screw* and other porn papers and magazines became the family business.

I started working for Astro as a helper to the drivers on the trucks when I was only thirteen years old. On Mondays, Tuesdays, and Wednesdays, I was on the trucks. I stayed in the office on Fridays and dropped off the payments to Goldstein. I was the boss's son, after all, so I (sometimes) got the easier assignments, and I wasn't complaining. It all ended in 2003 when *Screw* finally went out of business.

CHAPTER 14
JOEY'S KILLING

JOEY GALLO came to President Street once or twice a week. He was in the city most of the time with his new wife and friends. Pete or Bobby would pick him up if he had to go on a "meet." Most of the time he was just walking alone without a bodyguard.

Joey had no fear and was always saying things like, "They ain't going to kill nobody."

As winter turned to spring in 1972, Blast tried to talk Joey into being more careful. He didn't like him living in the city, going out to clubs at night, and visiting Mulberry Street in Little Italy.

"You're acting like you are invincible and it ain't safe," Blast would say, but Joey didn't listen.

"I got Darrow and the Greek with me, don't worry. I know what I'm doing," Joey would say, and Blast would just throw up his hands.

Joey had a reputation for being shrewd and clever, but not on April 7, 1972. It was Joey's forty-third birthday. We all saw him that day and wished him a happy birthday, in our own way.

That night Joey was having a dinner party with his wife, step-daughter, sister Carmela, Pete the Greek and his girl, and Bobby Darrow. Joey was meeting some new friends at the Copacabana in the city. Pete and Darrow were Joey's only bodyguards for the night. Blast told Joey there were going to be other wiseguys at the club and he should bring more protection, but Joey insisted he had enough.

"Only Pete and Darrow, that's the way I want it," Joey said.

At the Copa, people were sending drinks over to Joey's table, but it was getting late. Pete had introduced Darrow to a girl earlier in the night, and Darrow was at her table rapping with her. Bobby wasn't going to pass on a piece of ass.

It got to be time to call it.

Pete came over to Bobby and said, "I'm taking Joey home."

Bobby said, "Okay, let's go."

When they got back to Joey's table, Joey told Bobby he didn't need to come along.

"Go take the broad and get laid," Joey said.

Bobby looked at Pete.

"Go," Pete said. "I'll take Joey home."

On the way home, Joey wanted what was commonly referred to at the time as "chink food"—that is, Chinese. They drove through Chinatown, but the restaurant they liked was closed.

(I have to admit, I've never quite believed that part of the story. We went for chinks at five in the morning all the time.)

Joey said, "Go to Mulberry Street."

Pete said, "No."

Joey said, "Yes."

Pete was driving along Mulberry, and as they passed Hester Street, they saw a new place that had just opened, owned by Matty "The Horse" Ianniello, a *capo* with the Genovese family. So they went in. They stopped to speak to Matty first and he gave them a table in the back. The party consisted of Joey and his bride (they'd only been married for three weeks), her ten-year-old daughter, Joey's sister Carmela, Pete the Greek, and Pete's date.

They were eating and talking there for a while, unaware that a low-key hood by the name of Joe Luparelli had been sitting at the clam bar with a friend when they came in. Joe knew that there was an open hit out on Joey, so he dropped his spoon, picked it up, and then hurried out of the restaurant. He went two blocks down Mulberry to his club and called Joey "Yak" Yacovelli, who was at that time the acting boss of the Colombos ever since Joe Colombo got vegetabled at Columbus Circle. Yak told Luparelli to get a few guys and kill Joey. So Luparelli got Sonny "Pinto" DiBiase (a former Genovese guy, now with the Colombos), Philip Gambino (a Colombo man despite his last name), and "two clowns" who might've been brothers. They went back to Ian-niello's restaurant on Mulberry and Hester. They brought two cars, one of which was to serve as the crash car, to intercept any car that might be trying to interfere with their getaway.

Now, everyone knows what happened next. These guys went into the restaurant, killed Joey, and shot Pete in the ass. They split and hid out in Nyack, which was across the George Washington Bridge and about fifteen minutes north. That part everyone agrees on. Everything else comes in *versions*.

One version has it that, right after the shooting, apparently with a bullet still in his buttock, Pete went up to Matty the Horse and said, "If you set up Joey, you're a dead man." But that didn't make any sense. Matty was a made man and wasn't going to set anyone up in his own place with him in it and bullets flying all over the place.

Joey was simply at the wrong place at the wrong time. Or maybe it wasn't so simple, because everything was wrong from the very beginning. Pete, if he had been a good bodyguard, wouldn't have allowed Joey to get in that position. He should've said something like, "Joey, it's late and you have your wife and your little girl with you." Or maybe, "It's late and you know all the assholes are out at this time in the morning." If Joey had re-spected Pete, he would've listened.

Another thing, Joey and Pete were sitting with their backs to the door. If Pete were a real bodyguard, he would have *never* turned his back to the door. He would have jumped on Joey when the shooting started. Instead he yelled at Matty, which gave Joey a chance to go outside unprotected, and the bullet that killed Joey hit him when he was outside.

Joey's decision-making wasn't at its best that night, either. Joey liked Pete, but Pete was not a real bodyguard.

CHAOS

After Joey got killed, all hell broke loose on President Street. All the guys came down to the block to see what happened and what to do. Mooney was the only made guy in the crew and was trying to be the big shot. I was in Roy Roy's club and Roy was in a bad mood. I never saw him like that before, so I kept quiet. My father didn't get there until late the next night. Same with Blast. All the talk was "Why shoot Joey?" And, "What are we going to do about it?"

At first no one knew who did it. The Greek was in the hospital with his ass in a sling, and my godfather, Bobby Darrow, was nowhere to be found. It was chaos.

Louie the Syrian was trying to calm everyone down. It was decided that the first thing that needed to be done was to make arrangements for Joey's funeral. And we had to deal with Mama and Pop Gallo—not to mention sister Carmela, who was there when Joey got killed and was a wreck.

The wake was at Guido's Funeral Home on Clinton Street. There were over three hundred mourners, including some celebrity wiseguys, not counting the ridiculous shitload of plainclothes cops.

As we left Guidos to go to the church, the hearse drove past President Street so Joey could go by the block one last time.

Mary Gallo, Joey's mom, lost it at the funeral and began to scream. "The streets are going to run with blood!" she said.

Hearing that, I was convinced she was right. Mama Gallo's knees buckled as she was leaving the church, and there was a photo in the papers of her being held up by a couple of the guys as she was coming down the church stairs.

As it turned out, the resulting carnage was not as extensive as perhaps Mary Gallo had hoped it would be.

SORTING IT OUT

After everything calmed down, as much as was possible, Bobby Darrow got to the club, and Louie asked him the important question: "What the fuck happened? Why wasn't you there with Joey?"

Bobby told him the story: They were partying at the Copa, Pete introduced Bobby to a girl, they got lovey-dovey. When it got late, Pete said he would take Joey home and told Bobby it was okay for him to leave with the broad. Bobby said he went to Joey to see if that was okay, Joey said it was, they kissed, and Bobby left.

Bobby realized what this line of questioning meant. Guys were muttering under their breath that they thought Bobby had left because he knew what was up, and that he might have had something to do with setting Joey up.

Bobby didn't like having suspicion cast upon him, not one fucking bit. Finally he'd had it: "You think I set up Joey? That what you think? If anyone thinks that, kill me now!"

Then he left in a huff—perhaps smarter than giving a roomful of highly emotional hoods a chance to think about the proposition. In the long run, my godfather got a pass. He might have been a pot-smoking, pill-taking maniac, but he'd killed five men for the Gallo family, and he would have taken a bullet to protect Joey. One thing about this crew: They were loyal.

I'll never forget it. Bobby went to my father's house and sat down with Ricky. They sat at the small bar my father had overlooking the bay. I made drinks.

We drank.

My father put his hand on Bobby's hand and said, "Bobby, you know I love you. I want to know what happened."

"Ricky, Pete and Joey told me to leave."

"Okay. Okay, I'll speak to Blast."

"You know what I think, Ricky? I think Pete set up Joey. You know what I'm going to do. I'm going to fucking kill Pete and everyone else involved in the hit," Bobby said.

"You are going to do fucking nothing. You are going to stay low and on the block."

Three and a half weeks after Joey's murder, the *New York Times* ran a story at the top of their front page about the killing and its aftermath, with a headline bigger than the other top story of the day, the death of longtime FBI director J. Edgar Hoover. The story reported that Luparelli turned himself in to the FBI and admitted that he and four other men were the ones who'd hit Joey. The article named Yacovelli as the guy who authorities believed ordered the hit.

Later, there was all kinds of bullshit. There was an Irishman who wrote a book saying he was the guy who killed Joey Gallo— and Jimmy Hoffa, as long as he was at it. Everybody knew it was bullshit.

THE SECRET MEETING

What happened next? Well, not much, at first. Cooler heads prevailed, and blood did not run in the streets. Blast maybe didn't have the power to go the distance.

After a few weeks following Joey's death, the question at the club stopped being so much "What the fuck happened?" and it became more like, "Who the fuck is in charge now?"

Mooney was the only made man, and he wanted to be boss. Blast had the Gallo name but lacked leadership qualities. His brothers had always been in charge. The crew hated Mooney, but they suspected Blast might not be able to handle the job.

There was a secret meeting at a club at Woodhull and Hicks Streets. In attendance were Ricky, Bobby B., Steve B., Steven C., Preston, Smokey, Sammy the Syrian, Louie, Chitoz, Sally B., Roy Roy, Punchy, and a few more guys—low-key guys.

Also there to offer his opinion was my uncle Joe Shep, a Genovese *capo* and well-respected man who started with Lucky Luciano and Frank Costello. Uncle Joe said we should stick with Blast.

Others had other ideas. Someone suggested that Ricky should be boss. Ricky said it was simple: It was Blast's family name, so it was Blast's family.

"I could never go against Blast," Ricky said. He didn't always like Blast's ways, but he'd taken an oath with his brother Larry and would die by it.

That night the boss of the Genovese family, Frank "Funzi" Tieri, also came to find out what was going to happen. That's another one of those moments I'll never forget. I was hanging out in the front room with Goombabiel and Frankie Prosciutto when Tieri came in. There was music playing. The boys were in the back room.

I swear, the instant Tieri came through the door the music stopped. He had on a three-quarter-length black leather jacket and a pea cap. I remember my heart racing as I greeted him. He was a scary guy, soft-spoken but demanding.

I later learned that there were guys in the crew who really didn't want Blast to be in charge, regardless of his last name, and they felt so strongly that there was a split. Mooney took Sammy, Jerry, Tarzan, Smoky, and four more guys and broke away. They went back to the Colombos, and it was that split that started the second Gallo-Colombo War.

THE NEAPOLITAN NOODLE SHOOTING

In August 1972, word was out that Carmine "The Snake" Persico, Jerry "Lang" Langella, and Hugh "Apples" MacIntosh were going to be in a meeting at Neapolitan Noodle, a restaurant on East Seventy-ninth Street in the city.

I wasn't "in" on any of this, and it all comes from stuff I heard later, secondhand, and some of it doesn't jibe in my mind, but I'll get to that.

Just for the occasion, I was told, an outside hit man named Ted was imported from Las Vegas to kill them all, right there in the restaurant. The problem was, Ted didn't know what his targets looked like.

So Bobby Darrow was added to the op. His job was to point out for Ted where Persico and the others were sitting. After the point-out was made, however, the targets left the bar and switched to a table.

Result: Ted shot four innocent guys. Two died.

Okay, there are problems with the story. Ted, obviously, was not that great of a professional or this wouldn't have happened. A real pro wouldn't have fired until he had made a personal ID of his target, at least from a photograph. Also, Bobby Darrow had known some of those guys since they were kids. Bobby had even shot "Apples MacIntosh" in the balls a few years earlier so he knew him well. He would have noticed and alerted the hit man if table-switching was taking place. The hit was fucked up. How it was fucked up, I think anyway, is still open to interpretation. I later heard that the real spotter was a young guy who also knew the targets well by sight, but who pointed out the wrong table and then disappeared. Word is, he went straight. I think the whole idea was off to begin with. The thinking was that an outside shooter was necessary because all of the Gallo boys were recognizable and couldn't do the hit. It was a bad idea, but what the fuck do I know?

WRONG THING TO SAY TO A WACKO

On March 11, 1973, Bobby Darrow went in the Broadway Pub, in the Times Square area in the city, a much nicer part of town today than it was then. Then it was like the funkiest place on earth, a land outside the Law.

Bobby got into a "who has bigger balls" contest with the bartender, a guy named Sam Wuyak.

At some point Wuyak said the magic words, "I'm with Joey Yacovelli." Wuyak must've known that Yacovelli was the guy who set up Joey and that Bobby was in Joey's crew. Right?

Anyway, it was the wrong thing to say to a wacko. Bobby followed him into the men's room and shot him twice with deadly accuracy.

The cops, the DA, and the papers didn't see it Bobby's way at all. The papers only reported that the poor bartender got shot. They didn't include that he was a hood, or a wannabe hood, that he was a stupid guy, too stupid to realize there are things you don't say to a crazy man.

WHAT THE PRESS HAD TO SAY

On March 15, 1973, Nicholas Gage reported in the *New York Times* that thirty-six-year-old Robert Bongiovi, an "alleged gunman" who was with Joey Gallo on the night he was hit, had been charged with a murder police believed to be linked to the Gallo killing. The murder in question was that of Sam Wuyak, the night manager at the Broadway Pub on West Forty-fifth Street late the previous Saturday night.

Gage reported that Bongiovi and another man came into the pub on Saturday night, where Wuyak was overheard telling the men that he was a friend of Joseph Yacovelli, reputedly the acting boss of the Colombo family.

A confessed participant in Joey's killing, Joseph Luparelli, turned himself in to the FBI because he thought his accomplice was going to rat on him. He told police that Yacovelli had ordered the Joey hit. He told police that he'd been in Umberto's when Joey came in, and quickly ran to a nearby restaurant to inform four members of the Colombo family.

According to a female witness in the Broadway Pub (who was one of Matty the Horse's girlfriends), after mentioning Yacovelli, Wuyak was led by Bongiovi into a restroom at the back of the bar, where he was later discovered shot twice in the head. The *Times* didn't report the name of the second man, but mentioned police believed that he was a close friend of Bongiovi's.

My godfather was held without bail. Robert Tanenbaum, assistant district attorney, called it an "execution-style slaying" and said a grand jury would be convened to hear evidence in the case. Bobby's lawyer, Robert I. Weiswasser, said his client had been invited to testify before the grand jury but had declined.

The alert reporter noted that Umberto's, where Joey was killed, and the Broadway Pub were both owned by brothers of Matthew Ianniello, ID'd by the feds as a member of the Genovese family. At the scene of Joey's death, a Joey bodyguard named Peter Diapoulis was overheard saying to Ianniello, "I'm going to blow your head off. You set Joey up."

The article noted that the Colombo boys blamed the Gallo boys for starting the war, that it began when Gallo shot Joseph Colombo at Columbus Circle on June 30, 1971. The *Times* noted that Bongiovi was alleged to have played a key role in the war. The FBI dug out info that Bongiovi had more than an accomplice/rat to worry about. His was one of five names, the FBI learned, on whom the Colombos had issued murder contracts. Another name on that list, Gage reported, was forty-three-year-old Albert "Kid Blast" Gallo, who had taken charge following Joey's death.

Bongiovi, the article concluded, was hanging out at the Gallo group's headquarters at 76 President Street in Carroll Gardens (they published the address), when he was arrested for murder on March 14.

A VERY SHORT TRIAL

So my godfather was arrested on President Street, went to trial. His lawyer was Bob Weiswasser, the same guy who'd tried to get my mom's fraud charges dismissed but instead bought her eighteen months in jail.

Things went no better for Bobby. In the shortest trial in history, bing, bang, boom, Bobby was convicted and sentenced to life without chance of parole. He was convicted of murder one, premeditated murder.

How? We're still trying to figure it out. This was mid-Gallo-Colombo War and the mayor needed a scapegoat. How did the Law know it was premeditated when Bobby didn't even know himself? My dad said Weiswasser was a bad man.

I wondered, *Who the hell is going to give the dead their coffee now?*

CHAPTER 15

EMILY

I'LL NEVER FORGET THE DAY I met Emily—or the date: March 4, 1973. It was my father's birthday, and I was with my cousin Blake hanging out and eating pizza at Sal's Pizzeria at Court and Sackett Streets, like we did every day.

I saw a girl walking down Court Street and I said to Blake, "Look at that chick. She's got a nice ass."

"I know her," Blake said. "Hang on."

He went over to the chick with the nice ass and her sister, they talked for a little while, and then all three of them came into the pizzeria. Blake introduced me to my future girlfriend, wife, and the mother of my children.

Her name was Emily. At first her sister did most of the talking, but after a while Emily began to join in, as well.

"Do you have a boyfriend?" I asked her.

"Not really," she said.

"Would you like to go out some night for a few drinks?"

"I'm fifteen!"

"So what?"

She laughed at me.

"Give me your phone number?"

"I don't think so. I'll see you in the neighborhood."

The girls said they had to leave, so we said our good-byes.

After the girls were gone I turned to Blake: "So how do you know them?"

"I don't," he said with a laugh. "I just went over to them and said you wanted to meet them."

"You're an asshole!"

Blake laughed even harder and we went back to eating our pizza. When we finished we went back to the pool room.

Emily stayed on my mind. I did some detective work and found out where she lived. Instead of going over there myself and pounding on her door, I decided a more indirect approach was warranted.

It was about the middle of March when I went into Sal's Flower Shop and talked to a girl I knew named Geraldine who worked there. I sent her over to Emily's house with a dozen roses and she got Emily's phone number for me. About a month later Emily and I started dating.

One day she told me that she'd been reading the newspapers and saw that a guy affiliated with the Gallos had just been arrested for murder. I told her that was my godfather, Bobby Darrow, and I knew all about it.

I was a little worried that she wouldn't want to go out with me on account of the family business. There was no way I could hide the fact that my dad was a Gallo guy. It was a small neighborhood and everyone knew.

Now my godfather was a murderer. I had no idea how she was going to take that. She gave me a funny look but it didn't go any further. She didn't know very much about the Life, but the reality was starting to sink in.

My feet got into great shape. Emily and I would walk everywhere. That's what we did. We walked around and talked about stuff. She was still going to school, and she had to be home for dinner, but in between she'd hang out at the pool room, and we'd go for a walk up to Brooklyn Heights, where the streets were narrow and shaded by huge trees, the brownstones were some of the most expensive anywhere in the five boroughs, there was a promenade that overlooked the piers and the lower Manhattan skyline (the same promenade where I'd frozen my ass off looking for cocaine-smuggling divers), and Montague Street with lots of cool shops and restaurants, like Brooklyn's own version of Greenwich Village.

That phase of our relationship was interrupted near the end of 1973, when I had to stay on President Street more often and I didn't get to see her as much.

MOM TO THE RESCUE

My mother found out that I was dating a girl but couldn't see her as often as I wanted because I had to stay on the block.

"Give me her phone number?" my mom said.

"Mom, why?"

"Just give it to me," she said, snapping her fingers impatiently.

I did as I was told.

So my mom called Emily and told her she was coming to pick her up and bringing her to see me, and that she wasn't going to take no for an answer. So she went to Emily's house in the car, parked outside, and honked the horn.

Emily came running out.

My mom said, "Get in the car. Let's go."

Emily had never met my mom before. It must have been quite a shock. My mom loves to tell the story. They drove back to President Street. At the end of the block was the usual police barricade. According to my mom, Emily had a memorable look on her face, like she just wanted to die.

Before they could get on the block, they had to pass through a police barricade. Only after they gave the right answers could they get passed through. Finally, after what must've seemed to Emily like a frightening ordeal, she and my mom made it to Roy Roy's club. I remember standing there unable to blink for a minute as my mother and my girlfriend came walking through the door together. Emily looked like she was in a state of shock. Her hands were shaking. Emily looked at me with wide eyes.

I sat her down at a table and got her a glass of wine. After a few minutes she began to relax a little bit. Then, one by one, all of the guys came over to introduce themselves to her. Looking back on it, I can understand why she might have been a little overwhelmed.

It was like we were on a receiving line as the boys came over: Roy Roy, Bobby Borriello, Steven Cirello, Bull Eye, Punchy, Louie the Syrian. They were great guys, but not one of them looked anything like Valentino. It was normal to me, but she was young and hadn't grown up with gangsters.

They were rough characters, but they were very nice to Emily. Some of those guys had girlfriends who were hanging out at Blast's club on the other side of the street. The guys had to stay in Roy's club for security reasons. Pretty soon some of the girl-friends came over to introduce themselves to Emily, as well.

Emily visibly relaxed. She became quick friends with some of those girls from across the street, and after that she began to come to the club on weekends to hang out. She would get a kick out of Mondo. He was always extra-special nice to her, and Emily became very fond of him and his mother.

FIGHT WITH A COP

Emily was coming to the block often. One night while I was waiting for her, I went outside the club to get a little fresh air and have a cigarette. I knew the Organized Crime Squad was always on the block lurking. You couldn't fart without their noses up your ass.

I was standing on the corner when one of these dicks, a thick-necked Irishman with chins, came over to me and said, "Get off the corner."

"Pardon me?"

"Get off the corner," he repeated, using his "command voice" that some of them learned in grade school when they were bullies.

I wasn't in the mood.

"Are you kidding me? Fuck, no," I said. I sniffed a little bit, like something might smell bad.

Again. "Get off the corner, greaseball."

Now, I was a boxer at the Luna Boxing Club, right around the corner on Columbia Street. I was a guy with both length and skills. I gave the cop a once-over and plotted my strategy: a quick one-two to stun him, maybe rock him a little with one on the button, bend his nose, then work the body, fold him over, and an uppercut to finish him off. My blood father was a legendary boxer at Coney Island. I had chromosomes jam-packed with pugilistic skill, so why take shit from a fat Irish cop?

I threw a left jab, came up woefully short, and the cop beat the living shit out of me, beat me down the block and into Roy Roy's club. He beat me through the club, and we were almost to the back doors when Roy Roy and Punchy intervened, pulling the cop off me, pinning him down, and having someone run to get the other dick at the end of the block.

I was hurt pretty bad.

The next day Louie the Syrian told Ricky what had happened.

Ricky said, "Louie, I am coming to the block and there is going to be one dead Irishman."

Ricky was out of control, so Louie got in touch with Detective Charles Bartell of the Organized Crime Squad and said, "Charley, Ricky's in a rant."

When Ricky got to the block, he found Charley and four dicks with their hands up. The fat Irish cop was nowhere to be seen.

"He's gone, Ricky. We had him shipped out of here," they said.

So Ricky, Charley, and Louie sat down and talked for hours. I couldn't hear everything that was being said, but I could see the way Ricky's hands were working as he talked, so I had a pretty good idea what he was saying and it was pretty powerful shit.

"I am going to shoot the motherfucking Irishman in the head. All the dicks can go fuck themselves. If they don't like it, go do what you want to do."

The detectives were apologizing to him, and the more Ricky griped the harder they apologized. They drank coffee, and eventually the dicks left, at which point Ricky came over to poor, battered me and said, "Just remember, we have all the time in the world and he lives as long as we say so. One year or maybe two, but you'll always have the time. Who knows, maybe you'll forgive him."

He pinched my cheek and went on his way.

THE GARBAGE TRUCK

It took me a couple of weeks to recoup from my bumps and bruises. After I healed I picked up Emily to go for a ride in my green four-door 1964 Cadillac, in excellent condition for a nine-year-old car. The best thing about the car was its radio, which came with a button on the floor near the gas pedal so you could change stations with your foot.

We had a lot of fun with that radio, the reason being that Emily didn't know the floor button was there, and I had her convinced that the radio responded to voice command, so for a whole summer she talked to the radio to change stations and it always worked.

One night I was with Emily, it was about five in the morning and we were at Regine's nightclub in the city. Waiter told me I had a call. It was Tony B.

"Louie got arrested. You need to go to the precinct."

So I rushed Emily home, to Smith and Butler Streets, and as I was driving up Butler Street, a garbage truck was in the way. I honked my horn.

I stuck my head out the window. "I got an emergency. Can you move a little and let me by?"

Guy said, "Wait a minute."

I said, "Okay."

About five minutes passed, I again asked, not quite so nicely, if they could move just enough for me to pass.

"You can fuckin' wait!" the guy said.

I pulled out my .25 automatic—a girl gun really, but we all had them because they fit in our pockets—and I shot at him. He jumped in the garbage bin with all the garbage.

I was out of the car, right past the guy I'd just shot at, to the driver's side window. The .25 was still in my hand, puny but potentially deadly if you got in close.

"Move the fucking truck or I'll blow your fucking head off."

He moved the truck.

As I slid the Caddy past the truck, I saw the guy climbing out of the back of the truck, brushing garbage off of himself. At the end of the block, I looked up again at my rearview mirror and the guy was doing an angry dance in the street and giving me the finger.

For a second I thought I should really go back there and kill him. The fucking balls that guy had, giving the finger to an armed and angry man. But wisdom prevailed. I needed to get to the precinct. There really was an emergency. So I let it go.

I got to the Seventy-sixth Precinct, the "Seven-Six." I couldn't go in with my gun, so I hid it under the dash near the radio. I parked and went in.

"I'm looking for Tony B. and Louie."

"They're in the holding cells."

I walked up a flight of stairs and then down a hall. There was a door that said DETECTIVE UNITS, and it was partially open so I could see inside. In there was a chalkboard on the wall. On it were about a hundred photos of everybody connected with the Gallos—including me!

When I got to the holding cells, I asked Tony B. and Louie what they needed.

"Please get us some espresso," they said, "and get some for the dicks, as well."

It was still too early for stores to be open. I made a phone call to a guy I knew across the street who had a small store, and asked him if he could open up early and get the boys some coffee. The old man was nice and rushed to open. I went across the street to pick up the coffee, and on my way back I see the garbage men there making a complaint. As I walked by I looked them right in the face and smiled. They scratched their heads like, *That guy looks a lot like the guy who just shot at us.* But it didn't compute. I was walking into the Seventy-sixth Precinct like I owned the place with a carton full of coffee containers. I was relaxed and as happy as can be, in sharp contrast to the aggravated guy who'd shot at them only minutes before. Thank God those guys didn't get my license plate number or I would've been dead. As I went up the flight of stairs a second time with the coffee, I thought to myself, *What a perfect alibi.*

I started laughing, and I was still laughing when I handed out the coffee.

Louie said, "What's so goddamned funny?"

I couldn't tell them. They would have gone totally fucking nuts on me.

"The old man at the store said something funny to me, that's all." I changed the subject. "What else can I do for you guys?"

Tony said, "Go to Roy Roy and tell him we're here. He'll know what to do."

I had to wake Roy Roy up. I explained the situation.

"Okay," Roy said. "You go get some sleep. You look like shit and we are going to have to go and bail them out soon."

Later that day, we went to the courthouse and bailed out Tony and Louie. They went to the club and I went home. That night I was taking Emily to see Jimmy Roselli at the 802 Club on Sixty-fourth Street and Eighth Avenue in Bay Ridge, Brooklyn. My mom and dad were going to meet us at the club.

Before the show, Em and I went to the dressing room and sat with Roselli.

"Where's Ricky?" Roselli asked.

"They're on their way," I said.

The show had already started by the time my mom and dad came in. Jimmy stopped the song he was singing and said, "Hey, Ricky, you finally made it. You want me to start over?"

Ricky laughed, then sat and watched the show.

After it ended we all went back and had a few drinks. My mom and dad left, and then, after an interval, Emily and I left. That was in case Ricky was being followed, so that Emily and I would not be in harm's way.

CHAPTER 16
THE SHIT HITS THE FAN

IN 1973, while I was meeting and falling in love with my future wife and the mother of my children, the shit was hitting the fan on President Street. The war between the Gallos and the Colombos heated up when Mooney split from Blast and took a few of the crewmembers with him. Along with Mooney, Sammy the Syrian, Chitoz, Smokey, and Tarzan had gone over to the other side.

I remember how fucked up this all felt to me at the time. I knew bullets were going to fly. Guys I'd known all my life, guys I looked up to, guys I hung out with, were now expected to come back and try to kill us. The world was turning upside down. What a fucking kick in the ass.

At first Louie the Syrian thought I should stay on the block, but my dad and the guys spoke about it and said I could move around, keep doing what I was doing, that the old rules applied: The young guys wouldn't be involved in the war.

It wasn't like I could go anywhere I wanted to, though. There were places that were considered relatively secure, and I stuck to them as much as I could. My dad set stuff up. A guy who wandered into the wrong place with the wrong attitude could get hurt quick, and I was already smart enough to know the benefits of staying in places where I had friends around me.

The guys in the crew weren't the only ones concerned about my safety. The police were looking out for me, as well. When I went to leave the block, Detective Charles Bartell of the always-present Organized Crime Squad grabbed me and asked me where I was going.

"What are you leaving for?" he asked.

"I got my Astro paper run to do."

"Okay," he said and let go of my arm. "Keep your nose clean."

BOWLING FOR DOLLARS

After the routes, Dad dropped me off at Leader Lanes, a bowling alley on Coney Island Avenue. I was staying there. The owner was a friend of my father's, a guy named Cha Cha, an older fellow who'd been in the Life forever.

While I was there, I hung out at the bar. I wasn't a bowler. Guys would come in and play for money. They'd challenge me, and I'd have to shake them off.

One day Cha Cha saw this happen and the fucking light bulb went on over his head.

"Frankie, I am going to teach you how to bowl," he said.

I said, "No."

A couple of weeks later, he once again declared his intention to teach me how to be a kegler. This time I caved. Turned out, I was a natural, bowled a one-fucking-eighty in my first game ever.

"Beginner's luck," Cha Cha said.

But I bowled another 180, and another and another.

"You don't have to teach me to bowl. I taught myself," I said.

"You're a *ringer*!"

"Am not!"

"I can still get you to bowl a lot better," he said.

"Let's go!" I replied.

Thus began a two-week bowling intensive. All I did was bowl,

and when it was over I was ready to bowl for money. Cha Cha
and I bowled as a team. We won a lot of money, and would have
won more except sometimes we got too drunk.

I had a great time during the bowling-with-Cha Cha era. It made
those tough weeks in 1973 go by fast. I stayed at Leader Lanes until
Cha Cha had a heart attack and was no longer able to be there. I'd
lost my "rabbi"—that is, my protector—so I moved on.

One day I was doing the paper route along Court Street, dropping
off the new issue of *Screw*. When I came back to the truck, I saw
Detective Charles Bartell leaning on my jacket, which was lying
across the seat. We were on a first-name basis by this time.

"Hey, Charley."

"Hello, Frankie. How's everything going?"

"Uhhh, fine."

"When you're done with the papers, you going right back to
the block?"

"Yeah."

I knew what was up. He was leaning on my jacket and he
could feel the gun in my pocket. I thought I was fucked, but he
gave me a pass. He wasn't there to get me in trouble; he wanted
to get me back on the block because he'd heard things were about
to get out of control.

So I went to the block. When I got there, Charley was standing
there with Roy Roy and Louie the Syrian. Roy called me an asshole and gave me a little smack on the back of the head. I was an
idiot to leave my gun in my jacket pocket when I wasn't wearing
my jacket.

"What are you going to do if there is trouble?" Roy said. "You
gonna say, 'Time-out, while I get my gun'? If you're going to
have a gun, then it's got to be on you."

Louie didn't agree. He didn't think I should be carrying at all.

Charley the dick was funny. He said, "I don't know what you
guys are talking about at all," and walked away with a smile.

That night Roy Roy and I got drunk. He started out ripping me a new asshole about the gun. But the drunker we got, the funnier it got, until every time Roy Roy mentioned the gun we'd laugh until there were tears in our eyes. Eventually we got to the point where we didn't even know what we were talking or laughing about.

What wasn't so funny was that I was told it was time for me to hit the mattresses. There was chicken wire on all the windows. We ate at Lefty Big Ears's club at night, where the food was great, like a restaurant. I was in Roy Roy's club every night, and it was during this time that he and I grew close. He was a peculiar guy, but he taught me a lot of things I was going to need to know.

Roy continued to keep me away from a lot of the things that were going on. He would send Goombabiel or Prosciutto or one of the other young guys to run an errand—to pick up some swag or numbers. Because I was Ricky's son, I was handled with kid gloves.

Me and Goombabiel stayed together day and night. Coco, he was a good kid, would bring our clothes to the cleaners. Some mornings we'd wake up and Coco would make breakfast for us— that was me, Stevie G., and Goombabiel. We never went hungry.

We were sleeping in an apartment on the block. We had the whole building, all the young guys were in there, and I got to tell you, there were so many broads going in and out of that place, you couldn't tell if it was the Mod Squad's hideout or a whorehouse!

I wasn't partaking in any of that. I was thinking about Emily, whom I wasn't seeing as much of as I wanted because of the tight security. I missed her a lot, but I wasn't worried about her. All the guys in the neighborhood knew that she was my girlfriend and she would be okay.

There was an incident, however. Roy Roy's brother Jake was at the pool room one day being an ass. Emily and some of her girlfriends were in there and Jake got a little mouthy with her.

"Go fuck yourself," Emily said.

Then Jake got real nasty.

"I'm telling Ricky," she said.

Jake realized he'd made a mistake and ran to the block to tell Roy Roy what had happened. Should he talk to Ricky before Emily had a chance to? What should he do?

Roy told him he had two choices, first, to go back to the pool room and apologize to Emily.

"What's the second choice?"

"Get a shovel and dig a hole, because you're going to be in it."

So Jake went back and apologized, and Emily forgave him, and we all stayed friends for many years after that.

THE PIZZA RUN

One day Cosmo the Barber came to the block to cut our hair. He was from the Gamesman Barbershop on Court Street. Barbers do more house calls than you might think: shut-ins, the elderly, guys on lockdown. He came to the block once a week and brought with him a pretty manicurist who was going out with a local light-heavyweight who was born Eddie Gregory but by this time fought as Eddie Mustafa Muhammad. He had a WBA belt for a while, and she was hot.

One night after Cosmo cut everyone's hair, Blast sent me and Goombabiel to a pizzeria on Court Street to pick up ten pies for the boys. It was raining like a motherfucker. We didn't want to go. We were all dressed up in Roy Roy's club, freshly groomed and looking good. I remember I was wearing my alligator shoes with a custom silk sharkskin suit. Trouble was, we had to go out in the fucking monsoon. We got the money from Blast, jumped in my car, and drove up Union to Smith Street.

As I was making the left onto Smith, Goombabiel said, "We got a tail."

I kept an eye on them. We got as far as Warren Street, when three detective cars, one coming head-on at us, and two behind, stopped us with guns drawn, and screamed for us to put our hands on the wheel. We did.

The Law came over to the car and pulled us out into the monsoon.

"Where you fellas headed?"

"To get pizza!"

"Bullshit."

"Call the pizzeria. We're going to pick up!"

They laughed and proceeded to take apart my whole fucking car, piece by piece. They didn't say what they were looking for, but we knew it was guns. They thought we were on our way to give them to one of the crewmembers.

When they didn't find anything, they said, "Put your car back together and get the fuck back on the block."

I looked at Goombabiel and said, "What the fuck are we going to do now?"

There were a hundred pieces of the car in the street and on the sidewalk. First we put the seats back in, then we went to work on the smaller parts. We were drenched. I was so wet that my alligator shoes were squeaking.

We didn't go straight back to the block like the dicks told us to. Fuck them. We went and picked up the pies, then went back to the block, where everyone laughed at us because we looked like fucking drowned rats. We didn't think it was funny at all.

We were griping about being harassed and this and that until Roy Roy put a stop to it.

"Stop the shit," he said. "It's part of being here"—although he couldn't say it with a straight face. He couldn't stop laughing at us. The rest of the night went good. A few broads showed up that night, and thank God we had dry clothes to change into.

Late in 1973, a hit team was sent out to kill Johnny "Tarzan" Lusterino. Steven C. and Tony B. knew they had to hit him because he was a stone-cold killer and they were afraid of him.

They hit him fast. He had been close to Joey, but Joey was dead and Tarzan was back with the Colombos.

Then, on July 2, 1974, a hit squad was sent to kill Sammy the Syrian and Chitoz. Preston, Steven C., and Ricky were sent to the Henryville Social Club on Thirty-ninth Street and Fort Hamilton Parkway in the Borough Park section of Brooklyn. The guys sat there for hours waiting for their targets to come out. Just as Sammy and Chitoz stepped out of the club, traffic backed up, so at the key moment there were cars in the way. A couple of shots were fired, but they were only slightly wounded. It just seemed like we didn't have any luck.

LOSING STEVEN C.

During this time I'd gotten very close to Steve Cirillo and his wife, Jo Ann. He was with my dad a lot, and we would go to dinner together at La Maganetta, a place in New York. Then, on the block, we would sit around and talk about things that had nothing to do with the mob. I would talk about Emily and he would talk about Jo Ann and his son, Stevie, how much he loved them.

I'll never forget the night of August 4, 1974, for the rest of my life. I was hanging around doing nothing like usual, having a few drinks with Goombabiel, when Roy Roy got a call that Steve Cirillo had just gotten killed. He'd been running a gambling night ("Las Vegas Nite") in the basement of the B'nai Israel of Sheepshead Bay on Ocean Avenue, an event sponsored by the orthodox synagogue's Men's Club, and someone shot and killed him with a high-powered rifle. Man, I felt like someone had just ripped my heart out. I got scared, then so fucking mad, I could have ripped the heart out of the chest of the guy who did it—and eaten it! What a waste of a human life! I don't have the words to fully describe my feelings about this.

Police told reporters that there were somewhere between forty and seventy-five persons in the basement at the time of the shooting. Many thought someone had set off firecrackers until Jo Ann began to scream that her husband had been shot. When police arrived, Jo Ann said she'd been at another table and hadn't seen who did the shooting. Detectives found a rifle and a handgun hidden in a children's playground next to the temple. The police theorized that the shots had been fired from outside through an open basement window. Steve was an easy target because he was standing in front of that window under bright lights.

SWITCHING CARS

It was getting pretty bad out on the street after Steve Cirillo got killed. I had to get out of the neighborhood. I had the Caddy convertible, and the bad guys knew it was mine, so I needed another car.

I called Goomba Louie and told him to meet me at Bay Parkway, in the Korvette's parking lot. It was dark, and when I got there I saw Louie's car, but no Louie. So I waited a while until I got tired of waiting.

I took out my gun and went over to inspect the car. I looked in the side window and saw Louie and his girlfriend, Josephine, on the floor, hiding. They saw me and started screaming. They scared the shit out of me, and afterward we laughed so hard we cried.

Louie then gave me the car and some cash and I went on my way. Louie took the Caddy. Later he told me he drove all the way home with his head hanging out the window so the bad guys would be able to see that he wasn't me.

The *very next night*, Louie and his girlfriend were in the Caddy, and they stopped at a light at Court and Degraw Streets, when three unmarked cop cars surrounded them with guns drawn. Louie and Josephine shit themselves.

"Where's Frankie Dimatteo?" the dicks asked. "Better question yet, where's Ricky Dimatteo?"

Louie shrugged.

"Why you driving Frankie's car?"

"Mine's in the shop."

"What shop?"

"I don't know. Frank took it there."

"If he brought it there, then where is he?"

"He was home last I spoke to him."

"You're a bad liar, Louie. Tell Ricky there was a hit on him and he should come in to the precinct."

"Okay, I'll relay the message," Louie said, and the cops let him go.

While that was going on, Emily and I were at the Playboy Club in New Jersey.

STANDING ON THE CORNER WITH LOUIE THE SYRIAN

A week later I got back to the block. I stayed at the club and didn't go anywhere. Three weeks went by, till September 2, 1974. It was a clear night, and I was standing at the corner of President and Columbia Street talking to Louie the Syrian, the other Louie. He was talking to Angelo Perfuma, and Angelo handed him a piece of paper, something to read. Louie looked like he was playing trombone for a second.

Louie sent me back into the club. "Ask Roy Roy to give you my glasses," he said.

"Sure, Louie," I said, and turned to go in search of Roy.

As I walked away, I heard a shot. I spun around in time to see Louie hit the ground. I hit the ground, too, coming down hard on my elbows. Louie was still and there was blood coming from his head. I'd never been so scared before. I popped up to my feet and ran like a fucking deer into the club. The guys poured out of the club and onto the street to see what happened. By the time they came back inside, I didn't have to say anything to them.

They just asked if I was okay, and I said yes. Then I drank a bottle of Scotch with bandages on my elbows and said shit like, "What the fuck is going on here?"; "Are we just going to sit here and let ourselves be picked off one by one?"; and, "Fuck this." I sat there all night, until the bottle was empty.

Roy Roy got sick of listening to me. "Calm the fuck down, Frankie. Everything is under control." I think he drank more than me. I remember he had a dead look in his eyes.

The cops came to question me.

"What happened? What did you see?"

"I saw my body hitting the fucking floor."

That was the end of that. We locked down for a while. Louie the Syrian lived but was in Long Island College Hospital. Then we were told there was going to be a sit-down.

PUNCHY GETS SHOT

But the sit-down didn't come quick enough. On September 11, 1974, I was standing at President and Columbia Streets talking with Punchy, who was forty-six years old at the time, and I swear, as God is my witness, that they shot Punchy as we were getting a hot dog from Louie the Hot Dog Guy, who had a cart there on the corner.

If Punchy hadn't bent over a little to say something to Tony B., he would have been shot in the head. Instead he took it in the neck and shoulder. I was about twenty feet away, and again I hit the deck hard. I ran back into the club, just as I had after Louie the Syrian was shot. Only this time I was lost in the commotion, so much so that everybody forgot about me. After all of the press and the Law left, I was just sitting there.

It was a madhouse, like something out of a movie. Just then my mom called me.

"Is everything okay?"

"Why, Mom?" I said, trying to sound normal.

"I had a funny feeling that you were in trouble."

"No. But Punchy just got shot."

She hung up. Talk about a mother's intuition.

Roy Roy sent me to the hospital to keep an eye on Punchy while he was there. The theory was that if I went, it wouldn't look like Punchy had a bodyguard. I was sent with a pistol, which I hid under one of the chairs in Punchy's room.

Police learned that the bullet that hit Punchy in the right shoulder was fired by a rifle from a roof two hundred feet away.

Sometime after that, I was at the hospital when the Law got wind of a plot. "Someone's supposed to come to the hospital to kill Punchy," they said, and there were police in and out of his room all night, looking out the window.

They kicked me out, and I had to leave the pistol behind. I came back the next day and snuck it out.

About a month later, Louie the Syrian got out of the hospital. Punchy was released a few months after that.

NEW WORLD ORDER

When the sit-down finally did take place, my uncle Joe Schipani, a Genovese *capo*, mediated a truce between the Gallos and the Colombos. The talks were leaning toward a dismantling of the Gallo crew, whose members would go over to the Genovese family.

At the meeting Blast had been forced to give a list of everyone in his crew, and me and Goombabiel were on the list. The perk of the deal would be that Blast, Punchy, and Ricky would become made men.

The new world order worked out for a while. It felt like everything was back to normal. No more ducking every time a fucking car backfired, or some asshole threw a cherry bomb. I was hanging out in the neighborhood with my girlfriend at my side. Louie the Syrian and Punchy were back on the block, but neither of them were ever the same.

Ricky had to do a short stint in jail on a gun charge. He was on his way to Long Island to kill Mooney when he was pulled over. We still don't know how the cops knew who he was. He was in a rented car. Maybe Mooney had guardian angels everywhere.

It was just about the time when Ricky got out of jail, April 1975, that Emily and I got engaged, and we had a party to celebrate at the Victorian House, a party hall run by our heavy-drinking friend Victor Palermo, a great guy with one arm.

On the night of the party, I was worried about whether or not my dad would make it. He'd had to go on the lam a couple of days earlier because he'd pulled a truck heist, furs at JFK Airport, with Paddy Mac Macchiarole.

On the night of the party, his whereabouts were unknown. It got a little bit late at the party and we'd given up on my father, when Ricky came walking in—with Jimmy Roselli!

Jimmy chatted a little bit, congratulated me, kissed Emily, posed for a few photos, and then he and Ricky were gone into the night. I never knew what was going to happen from minute to minute.

Later I learned the details of why Ricky had to go on the lam. They'd had the truck of furs and made their getaway, but were followed. They dumped the truck and took off. Police confiscated the truck, impounded it, and started to build a case against Paddy Mac.

All was not lost, however. My father still had the key to the truck. With the invisibility of a stealthy secret agent, and the calm of a stone-cold hunter, Ricky walked one moonless night into the police impounded-vehicle area, and drove the truck full of furs right out the front gate.

The case against Paddy was dropped for lack of evidence!

CHAPTER 17
HITTING THE STREETS

AFTER EVERYTHING CALMED DOWN on President Street, we again moved around the neighborhood freely. It felt great. The stress of keeping my head low all the time eased, and pretty soon I was back to hanging out on Court Street without worrying about having my hair parted by a drive-by bullet.

We were starting to feel the power we'd gained by surviving the war. Peacetime brought a shift, and the young guys from the Gallo crew had moved up in the pecking order.

One night I went to Goomba Louie's house on Douglass Street. Some of his family from Texas were visiting, and my Emily and Josephine had appointed themselves South Brooklyn's goodwill ambassadors. They wanted to take Louie's relatives on a walking tour through the neighborhood, to see the sights.

The tour was marred when a car full of loudmouths pulled up alongside them and the male passengers tried to talk to the women.

The come-on came to a screeching halt when a guy in the backseat yelled, "Holy shit! Let's get the fuck out of here—that's Frankie Milone's girl!" The car pulled away so fast that the guy's head snapped back. (That was my name back then. Ricky adopted me, and I officially changed my name to Frank Dimatteo when I turned eighteen. My parents paid for the lawyer and the paperwork, a gift for my eighteenth birthday.)

As the girls told the story, they made it seem as if they didn't like the things those guys said, and just to make sure we got mad, she told us that these guys had her feeling "like a prisoner."

"So, get in a car and go look for them," I said. "Who gives a fuck?"

That frustrated them. It took more than shouting out of a car at women to start trouble just then. Shooting, yes; shouting, no. We were tired of trouble. Besides, once the guy saw who Emily was they'd done the right thing. No harm, no foul, as they say.

Just about then, a guy I knew came to Louie's house and knocked on the door, said he needed to talk to me for a second. Louie and I went outside with him. There was a car out front with four guys in it. He explained that they were the guys who had talked to Emily, but they didn't know at first who she was, but when they figured it out they shut it down. They were very sorry, and they wanted to make sure I wasn't mad at them.

"Thank you for coming to me. I'm not mad," I said. "I thought it was funny."

"We were thinking about running home and begging our parents for help," the guy said. "We didn't know whether to cry or shit."

"Forget about it. We'll see you later at Ju Ju's for a drink."

After they left, Louie said it looked like we were getting real "reps." His relatives couldn't have been more impressed. Louie and I were "big shots from Brooklyn." Louie had been telling them who I was, *bragging* about our exploits, and it was good for the myth that a couple of guys wanted to kiss our fucking rings while the relatives were visiting.

THE HOT HOTWIRE

We had power, all right. Guys would come to us with a score if they had a problem. We went to the local bars and most guys bought us drinks. We knew some guys who ran a pot distribution operation. They asked us for protection, and they gave us five hundred dollars. If there was ever trouble with a vendor, we had to say it was "our pot." Guys would back off because they didn't want to fuck with us.

That was passive income, though. We went out and aggressively earned, as well. We sold swag, hijacked some stuff. One day Goombabiel's brother acquired the key to a stereo warehouse, which we planned to use to clean out the place.

THIS TRUCK IS ON FIRE

On the chosen night, as it turned out, we had a key for the warehouse but not for the truck. Marty had hotwired a truck that was inside the warehouse and loaded up with stereos and other electronic equipment.

During the getaway, I followed the truck in a van. We got as far as Fourth Avenue, and *poof,* the truck caught on fire. Flames, smoke, no power. In order to get the engine started, I pushed the burning truck with my van, but that didn't work. Then we heard police sirens, so everyone piled into my van and we got away, but we had to abandon the truck full of stereos.

"What happened, Marty? Why is that truck on fire?"

"I must've fucked up when I crossed wires to start the engine."

All that work and we got shit. Nothing. What could we do? We went to the pool room, had a couple of drinks, and laughed about it.

THE BLUE ANGEL

We started going to some of the better clubs in the city, like the Blue Angel, in midtown Manhattan. I used to meet Bull Eye and Stevie G. there. Those guys were together so much we called them Martini & Rossi. Stevie G. was a character, a small guy with thick glasses and a comb-over.

I used to meet Bull Eye at the Gamesman Shop on Court Street once a week. I was there for a manicure and he'd get his hair fixed. He spoke like a street guy but would always ask how Ricky was and if I was being a good boy and staying out of trouble. I'd say, "Why, you the only one who can have fun?"

The broads were beautiful at the Blue Angel, and they all wanted to talk to me. I was feeling like some big shot, a broad under either arm, being scorchingly charming.

They say that once a broad starts making you feel handsome, the meter is usually running. All I know was that these gals were stacked and they cracked up at everything I said.

When Stevie told me they were probably high-priced hookers, it didn't dampen my mood as much as you'd think. They were hot, and I was a young man.

PUNCHY'S CLUB

After the Blue Angel we'd go over to Punchy's club on Second Avenue and Sixty-seventh Street. One night Punchy's was packed and some guys we knew from Red Hook came in, guys who were trouble wherever they went, and there was no reason to think this night was going to be different. It was like trying to have a good time with a time bomb ticking in the room.

Sure enough, about midnight it blew. One of the Red Hook guys got into an argument. We stepped in right away and tried to nip it in the bud. For a while it looked like peace might prevail, then the guy from Red Hook went downstairs to take a leak. As he was coming back up the stairs, the guy he'd argued with was coming down the stairs. So the Red Hook asshole stabbed this guy in the belly and took off.

It was time to leave. On the sidewalk out in front of Punchy's, a dikey broad came over to my cousin Blake and hit him. So Blake knocked her out. Cold.

"What the fuck is all that about?" I asked my cousin.

"There's a lesbian bar next door," Blake said.

"I know that. You stopped in for a drink?"

"No! A lesbian came into Punchy's, about an hour ago. Maybe not that long. She told me she was a switch-hitter."

"So?"

"I bought her a drink."

"And then she got mad and hit you."

"No, I guess she went back to the lesbo joint and told her girlfriend that she liked me. That was the girlfriend who attacked me."

As we were having this conversation, there was an unconscious lesbian on the sidewalk and an ambulance was pulling up for the stab victim inside on the stairs. Now we had a couple of reasons to get the fuck out of there.

But wait, there's more. Blake's lesbian friend ran up, saw her girlfriend unconscious, decided she was in love with Blake, and fell in under his arm. Now she was with us.

I'd love to say that it was just another night at Punchy's, but it wasn't. The Law was all over the joint because of the stabbing, and they shut the place down.

THE DRIFT INN

It was back to Brooklyn for us after that. Our new hangout was The Drift Inn. A gangster named Louie Pizza owned the joint. We hung out there with his son, who was a roly-poly guy, always smiling.

Louie was a friend of my dad's, and he invited me into his little crew. It was a small, dark bar, with excellent oldies on the jukebox. A lot of broads and knock-around guys hung out there. There was always a lot of dancing.

The bar was at the southern end of Coney Island Avenue, not far from the beach, so it was common to make a "Nathan's run," load up on hot dogs, and then return for more drinking. When it wasn't dogs, we stuffed our faces with fried shrimp, chow mein, or buns and fries.

Like a lot of young men, I had anger issues. I was pissed off at the world. For the most part I kept it in, but a few drinks and I'd be ranting and raving, looking for a reason to sock someone.

At The Drift Inn I'd walk in and say to the barmaid, "Give the bar a drink." She would smile. She knew my strategy. Buy a round early, for five or six guys, and before long they'd all buy you one back, by which time the bar would be crowded with people trying to buy you a drink.

Not only would the club fill up but my anger would grow, and it seemed like I was always getting into a fight before the night was through. If nobody started something with me, I imagined they did and fought them anyway.

Bottom line was, I was becoming a dysfunctional alcoholic, and alcohol was frying my brain, leading me into increasingly self-destructive behaviors. Luckily, drinks were cheap.

I'M A LUCKY FUCK

One night a group of my "nice" friends—that is, guys with girlfriends who were supposed to be behaving themselves—came and joined me at The Drift Inn. We were all chatting up the broads and dancing, having a great time.

I was out in front smoking a cigarette and talking with someone when I saw something up the street that sent a chill up and down my spine. No, it wasn't a hood pulling a gun. It was Emily and the girlfriends of my friends in a car. They saw me and pulled over to park.

I butted out my cigarette and ran into the bar to warn my friends. I got to some of them, but not all by the time the girls entered the bar with a sense of purpose in their stride.

They walked right up to me. I greeted them with my biggest smile.

"Hey! What's up? Can I buy you girls a drink?" I said.

"Why did you run inside?" Emily said. "You saw us and ran inside!"

"Me? No way!" I said.

"I know why!" one of the girls said and broke off into the club. She found her boyfriend, my friend Andy, with a girl on his lap, kissing. Man, was she pissed. Andy caught hell.

"I'm never going out with you again, Frankie!" Andy later said.

"What the fuck did I do? You guys came to me," I said.

Everything was always my fault.

Emily just smiled and said, "You lucky fuck!"

YOU SAID A MOUTHFUL

One night I walked into The Drift Inn and the place was kind of quiet. The vibe was off.

I asked, "What's up?"

They told me that one of Louie Pizza's guys, a guy named Joey, had left the bar the night before to see a broad who was a wiseguy's girlfriend. He got caught and they cut off his prick and balls, stuffed them into his mouth, and then beat him to death and tied him to a tree in a Staten Island cemetery.

"That's fucked up," I said.

And we drank the night away.

A FAKE STEVE

One night, just before we stopped going to The Drift Inn, I was standing at the bar and the place was packed. The unbelievably hot barmaid came over to me and said there was some guy farther down the bar who was claiming to be Stevie Gallo.

She pointed him out and I recognized him as a guy I knew slightly—lived on Court Street, named Steve Honda. I went over to him and clasped my hand on his shoulder.

"Steve Gallo, what a surprise running into you here," I said. I gave his shoulder a menacing squeeze.

He shit.

"I didn't know you were here," he said, sweating bullets.

"Just finish your drink and go," I said.

He didn't even bother to finish his drink. He ran out the door.

I said to the barmaid, "Let it go. He was just a moron."

"Who was he?"

"I didn't know him," I lied. If I'd told her who he was, Stevie G. would have been obligated to give the guy "a smack."

"I knew he wasn't Steven because I'm fucking Steven," she said with a laugh.

STEVE B. GETS SHOT

We didn't stop going to The Drift Inn because of anything we did. Louie Pizza, as it turned out, was dealing dope out of the joint and over time it got hot. Nobody wants to drink while under surveillance so we moved on.

Not long after that we heard Louie had been killed. It was only a matter of time. It was Louie Pizza who'd gone with Bobby Darrow to kill a wiseguy named Apples MacIntosh, a friend of Carmine the Snake's. Bobby, if you'll recall, shot Apples in the balls. Apples never got a hard-on again and was waiting for the right time to get revenge on Louie. Apparently this was it. Besides, Louie was dealing in junk, big-time.

Right around this time we were moving to the other side of Brooklyn. My father bought a place in Gerritsen Beach right on the water. How he found it I'll never know. It was in no-man's-land, smack in the middle of an Irish neighborhood. It took an hour to get from the house to the streets I still considered home.

Blast was staying with us, so I had to give up my Gerritsen Beach bedroom for him. I didn't care that much. I was out all night most of the time during this period, so when I eventually got home it was light outside and I just passed out on the couch.

One night in February 1976 I got a call to go to President Street. When I got there my dad told me that Steve Borriello had been shot. This was like hearing bad news about a big brother.

"How bad is it?"

"Bad," Ricky said. "He got shot in the face. They don't think he's going to make it."

Blast was trying to figure out motive. We'd thought hostilities were over. So Blast went to Chin to make a beef. They found out Mooney and Chitoz were behind it. They'd been called in but didn't show. Being defiant, they were open for a hit.

We knew it was them. They'd used the same MO as the shooters of Punchy, Louie, and Steven C. Thank God, Steven B. survived, but he was never the same and had to have years of surgery.

I wasn't told at the time who was sent to kill Chitoz. The boss had everyone on a don't-need-to-know basis. Only the guys in on the hit knew who was in on the hit. The word I got later was that it was Bobby B. and Preston.

Whoever it was, they caught Chitoz on June 16, 1976, in Frank's Diner on Nevins Street. When I found out, I wasn't happy. I liked Chitoz and thought he was a good guy. I'd known him since I was a kid. I knew his sons. My mother was friends with his wife. My father always referred to Chitoz as a "real man"—no higher praise from Ricky.

Why did this have to happen? I'd known that Chitoz was one of the guys who was unhappy with Blast being boss—but I also knew that Chitoz and the Gallo crew had done a lot of things together. They couldn't let him walk away. It hurt, but not as much as Steven C., Louie, Punchy, or Steven B. getting shot. I should have opened my eyes to what it was all about right then. But I was a stupid kid, and I didn't see.

After Chitoz was killed, Mooney was called in again, and was told the Chitoz hit would end it, but he had to go. Too much bad blood—but now it was over. (As it turned out, not quite.)

NO ONE STEERING THE BOAT

For the Fourth of July, 1976, my dad threw a big pool party out at the house. Everyone from the crew was there. There must've been a hundred people in and out. Dad had a thirty-two-foot boat and everyone wanted to go out for a ride.

We were taking guys back and forth. I remember on one trip a boat came up alongside us to tell us that no one was steering the boat, but when they got closer they saw it was Mondo at the wheel.

We laughed our asses off.

It was around that time that Bob Dylan put out an album called *Desire*, and on it was an eleven-minute song called "Joey" about Joey Gallo. Sometimes when you're too close to something, you don't realize how famous it is. We knew the Gallo crew made it into the papers now and then, but Bob Dylan singing about President Street made us feel special, and I liked the song, too. Two years earlier Peter Boyle had played Joey in a movie called *Crazy Joe*, but it was so corny and bogus that we weren't that impressed by it. Dylan seemed more legit.

SHOOT THE MOONEY

On October 5, 1976, in Big Danny's Luncheonette on East Second Street and Avenue M in Midwood, Tony B. and Ricky caught fifty-six-year-old Mooney sipping coffee at the lunch counter. They were wearing ski masks.

Ricky was the only one who spoke: "Everybody hit the deck," he said.

Everyone did as told, including the owner, Donald "Big Danny" Murer—except Mooney, who got off his stool and ran toward the back of the diner. He made it as far as the door to the kitchen, where he was machine-gunned in the back of the head.

He was dead. *Now* it was over.

According to the *Daily News* the next day, witnesses gave police the plate number of the getaway car.

Sure, I felt power on Court Street and could frighten morons and idiots by being Ricky's kid, but there was a downside to the new world order, as well. We were now part of the Genovese family, and the Gallo crew was technically broken up. Going to the city with the Chin's family was like being adopted. Blast and Punchy got made. Ricky was passed up. Ricky had done a ton of work and had earned it. He always felt there was a Judas in the discussion.

CHAPTER 18
THE TILTING DRESSER

Blast got married and had his wedding party in Queens, at Paddy Mac's restaurant. Dad was in jail again, so I took my mom and Emily.

I said to Emily, "I'm going to call you my Blond Alibi."

"How come?" she asked.

"Because you always look like a million dollars and are always there for me."

When we got to the wedding, Blast—the groom!—grabbed me and said, "Stay with me." So, instead of dancing with my beautiful wife, for the rest of the night I walked around with him. If he went out for a cigarette, I was there. If he needed anything, I went for it. Thinking back on it, I never even got a thank-you. That's fucked up.

MY SECRET ROOM

In 1977, me and Goomba Louie found a storefront on Twentieth Street and Sixth Avenue, in south Park Slope. It was just up the block from Toddo Marino's Dixie Tavern.

We put a ton of arcade games in our club, and built a small bar. I had a secret room in the back. The only access was from behind the bar. You had to move a liquor shelf to get to the door. That was where we held meetings, nightly card games, and hid our swag. It was hooked up nice. I had a bed back there.

We were making $3,000, $4,000 a week. I was there for almost three years before I gave the place to Louie, who had Matty Square coming in as a partner. This may cause you to wonder: Why walk away from something so lucrative? It all started with some neighborhood wannabes.

WANNABE ASSHOLES

One night there was trouble in the club. The above-mentioned assholes were yapping that they were with Aniello Dellacroce. That wasn't just any name to throw out there. That was a heavy claim.

When Big Paulie Castellano was named boss of the family after Carlo Gambino's death in 1976, many members of the family, including John Gotti, were irritated because they felt that this was nepotism at work, since Paulie was Don Carlo's brother-in-law. They felt that the new godfather should have been Aniello Dellacroce, who had served as Don Carlo's underboss since 1965. Dellacroce stayed on as underboss and oversaw the family's blue-collar crimes, while Castellano oversaw the white-collar side of the operation.

So these guys in my club are claiming to be Dellacroce boys and I said, "I don't give a fuck who you are, I'm throwing you out of here on your ass." And I did.

An hour later my cousin heard a knock on the door. He answered the door, and some guy hit him. We all ran out to help. The guys I'd thrown out were back, and they had brought help.

We all went around the block to a schoolyard to fight. As soon as the first punch was thrown, the cops were there. I had a gun, which I heaved as far as I could. When we came out of the schoolyard we were held while police went in, found the gun, and we were all arrested. After two days in jail, we all got out because no one took responsibility for the gun. They couldn't hold six guys for one gun.

A few weeks later, Louie and Matty had a beef with the same assholes. Matty called us down to help out. When we pulled up, Matty was fighting one of them—and the guy was biting Matty's thumb! Everyone was trying to get him to stop, and there must've been thirty, forty guys out there.

So we pulled a sawed-off shotgun out of the trunk of our car, and let go a blast. That guy's teeth released Matty's thumb instantly. Everyone scattered, and again the cops were on the scene in a snap of your fingers.

This time we got away, into the car and out of there. We thought the Law knew it was us, and so we hid out on Long Island for a week. Turned out they didn't know shit.

And that still wasn't the end of it. Those assholes made a beef about us at Toddo Marino's, and I got called to that bar for a meeting with my father and Aniello Dellacroce! One of the assholes was there, too, looking like a smug-faced snitch.

"What happened?" Aniello asked.

I told him.

"Is it true you said you didn't give a fuck if they were with me or not?"

"I did, but I didn't mean it that way," I said, and thank God he laughed.

"You should never say things like that, Frankie, because when you are right, it can make you wrong."

Then Aniello turned to the asshole and made a small gesture. One of his bodyguards smacked the asshole hard in the face. That took the smirk off.

"Never use my name," Anniello said, "and get the fuck out of the neighborhood."

It was over. And so was the club, now too hot to keep open.

The story, however, doesn't quite end there. I ran into those

guys from the beef two years later in Fort Lauderdale, Florida, at
the 4 O'Clock Club. I was in there with Louie and Goombabiel.
The second we walked in, I spotted them.

"We're fucked," I said. "Let me handle it."

They saw me and walked over. I put my "fuck you" face on. I
didn't need to, though. Those guys wanted to shake hands, be
friends, and buy us a drink.

I'm a guy with a suspicious nature and I didn't buy it at first.

"If you are going to do it, do it now," I said.

"No, no, no, we're talking to a few girls over there, come join us."

And it was peaceful. We had a drink with them, and maybe
even smiled a bit. Everybody tried to make light of the past, but I
never got to the point where I trusted them, and I was very happy
when we got out of there with nobody hitting nobody.

What were the odds? Small fucking world.

WHACKING WEISWASSER

If you remember back to my mom getting arrested for fraud and
the negotiations that led to her going away for a year and a half,
my dad blamed the lawyer, the one who did legal work for the
whole Gallo crew, a guy named Bob Weiswasser. In fact, my dad
said he was "no fucking good." Later Weiswasser defended Bobby
Darrow on his murder charge, and sold Bobby down the road.

But it wasn't until the summer of 1979 that his luck ran out.

The word was that it was debt that finally fucked Weiswasser.
He was in to a lot of guys for a lot of money. He had no grip on
his gambling urge and let it get out of hand. The theory went that
Weiswasser had gone rat and was paying debts with soft money
when he fucked up cases involving Gallo people.

On July 22, 1979, Weiswasser was found shot twice in the
back of the head, in his car in Manhattan. That night I went to
Roy Roy's club. Ricky, Punchy, Tony B., and Roy were smiling
and having a toast.

"To that cocksucker!" they said cheerfully. Two of the four took him out, but everyone was equally pleased.

EMILY AND I GET HITCHED

At the end of 1979, I got married to Emily at Sacred Hearts Church on Summit Street, just on the other side of the Brooklyn-Queens Expressway from the President Street block.

It was a Dee Dimatteo production, starting with the bridal shower at Michael's Restaurant in the back room there. There were seventy-five to a hundred people there, music, gifts galore. It was supposed to last four hours, and it went seven. She remembers going with Emily to Mr. Kleinfeld's to pick out a wedding gown. She tried on a bunch of them and then she put one on and everyone came running into the room. That was the one.

It was, as Billy Idol would say, a white wedding. We could not have looked more pure. The bride was in white, I was in white, the twelve members of the wedding party, all dressed in white.

The reception was at The Riviera on Stillwell Avenue in Coney Island, more than three hundred guests, including someone from each of the New York crime families. The place was owned by a guy named Zach, and it had just been redone with a big glass dome. They had the bride and groom and the wedding party sitting at a dais, and the priest was giving a speech. He said that we all looked holy, like we were at the Last Supper. I looked at Louie and we started to laugh. Pretty soon everyone was laughing at the notion that we were holy, and the poor priest didn't know what was so funny.

TEXAS RESTAURANT

After the wedding, Emily and I left for Texas to meet up with Louie and Josephine. We opened an Italian restaurant down there in Clear Lake, and returned to Brooklyn, leaving Louie in charge down there.

At the end of 1981, Louie called me and said that the restaurant wasn't earning.

I said, "Come back home."

Louie had just had a daughter, Danielle, and Emily and I had just had our first, Kristina. Responsibilities were growing, and we weren't going to be patient with businesses that underperformed.

"We can open a restaurant here!" I said hopefully, and I went up and down Court Street scouting locations. I found a storefront at Court and Amity. I got started building the restaurant even before Louie returned north.

We opened in March 1982 as Brooklyn House of Pasta and Seafood. We all worked there. Louie could cook, and he taught me how to make every item on the menu. Emily and Jo worked the front.

We had a ton of people come in and they liked the food. Lou Rawls, the great singer, used to come in. We got show biz celebs and mob celebs. Anthony "Shorty" Mascuzzio loved us. He was a good fellow from the Gambino family, and he loved our seafood.

Operating the restaurant was a trip, but we still weren't making any money, so it was short-lived. Louie and I had little mouths to feed.

TONS OF HAITIAN POT

In 1980, Ricky, Mosh, and I went down to Florida, to meet with a good friend. While down there I called my uncle Bobby. We set up a marijuana deal with some Cubans.

We put up $75,000 for a plane and the pot to come in from Haiti. What we didn't know was that we were setting up the deal with an undercover DEA special agent.

We had meetings with this guy first at the Fontainebleau Hotel, and then at a private joint called the Cricket Club, both in Miami Beach. At night we were partying at all of the hot spots, and during the day we rode on Uncle Bobby's cigarette boat with a ton of broads, drinking and eating like pimps.

We got the deal done. A week later, the pilot landed the plane in Florida, unloaded the pot into trucks, and *bam!* Everyone got pinched. I was the lucky one. I just got a subpoena.

Ricky, Bobby, Mosh, and the pilot were all arrested. Bobby and I ended up walking, but Ricky and Mosh, after all the appeals, got three years. They went to jail in 1984, Allenwood Federal Prison Camp, and they got out in July 1987.

THE FLYING LEG

Upon our return, I went with Jimmy Springers and Roy Roy to visit Bobby Darrow at the state prison in Dannemora, New York, up by the Canadian border. Jimmy was an old wheel guy for the Gallos. He was dying of diabetes. They kept cutting off his limbs, but he wouldn't quit smoking. We visited Bobby for a few hours and talked about his case. The Dannemora prison was a hellhole, looked like a fort, had to be the worst prison in the state. That anyone could serve time there is a miracle.

That night, after we left the prison, we went out to eat and had a few drinks. The hotel was a broken-down piece of shit, the only place to stay in the whole town. It was snowing heavily, and to get to our room we had to go to the back of the building, then up a flight of wooden stairs.

Roy went first. Then Springers, with his wooden leg. Then me. Springers was halfway up when his fake foot got caught in the stairs and his leg came off, flew into the air, and hit me before sliding down the rest of the steps.

Roy and I never laughed so hard in our lives.

"Frankie, what the fuck are you doing? Go get Jimmy's leg for him!" Roy said through his tears.

"Okay, Roy."

So I got Jimmy's leg, he put it on, and we made it to our

room without further incident. Roy busted Jimmy's balls all night long. Never once did Jimmy act like he thought it was funny. All he did was curse his fucking wooden leg, and that just made Roy and me laugh even harder.

LOSING PRESIDENT STREET

Not long after I got back from Florida, in the late 1970s, we lost President Street. For years the Law wanted the Gallo crew off the block, but they couldn't find a way.

But it finally got to the point where the Law was no longer going to be denied. I don't know how many lawyers and corrupt politicians put their heads together to come up with the scheme, but legal or not, it worked.

They decided to turn the whole block into a stinking shithole until no one could live there anymore.

The Borough of Brooklyn decided to put new sewers on President Street between Columbia and Van Brunt Streets. It was like a fucking invasion. They came in with big equipment and tore up the street.

The crew reacted loudly but ineffectively. Some of the cursing from the boys was in Italian and some in English, but the air was blue. The sewer repair guys didn't give a fuck.

Almost immediately a source inside City Hall leaked to members of the crew that the decision had come from on high and this was the start of a plan to get the Gallo boys off the block.

Roy Roy laughed at the source. Bullshit conspiracy theory! But not for long. It all came true.

The press caught on. A newswoman from Channel 7, Rose Ann Scamardella, who was from the neighborhood, came to the block to interview the house owners. Roy told her to "get off the fucking block" or he would "give her a kick in the ass." She left fast.

A few weeks later, the pumps that were stopping the water from seeping into the big hole in the middle of the street stopped working. The hole filled up with water and undermined the foundations of all of the houses on the block.

The city promptly condemned all of the houses, and that was the end of President Street. Mission accomplished. A whole block of one-hundred-year-old homes were torn down because four of them were owned by the Gallo crew. The rest were all owned by innocent people who'd had those buildings in their families for generations.

The Law didn't care. They got what they wanted. I'll never forget seeing Mondo sitting at the window of Toddo's club. His mom had passed away, he was alone, and now his home was gone. Thank God for Toddo. His club was outside the disaster area.

You could see it in Mondo's face, it was over—and it broke my heart.

(Jumping ahead for a bit, the last things that Mondo ever said to me were, "How's Ricky?"; "How's Dolly?"; and "Are you being a good boy? You need anything?" I was in my late thirties at the time. I can't forget it, because this came from a guy who had lost everything he had, a sick man, and still he had time to ask me if I needed anything. He was a big man in my eyes.)

LEMMON 714

In 1983 I got in touch with one of my street partners and said, "I need to make some money."

I was living off of the $300 to $500 a week I was making from a drug deal I'd had working since 1980. I had the connection with the stuff and vouched for credit for my new partner.

It was a sweet deal. I didn't have to do anything. He did everything, and I counted my money. My father had made a connection with a Canadian guy for quaaludes, the real thing: Lemmon 714.

The op was crazy big; fifty thousand fucking pills a month crossing the border. I'd meet my guy in the parking lot of the

Skyway Hotel, on Conduit near JFK Airport in Queens, or the
Jade East Motel in Jamaica, Queens. I took the bails out of his
car trunk, put them in mine, and went home. We paid fifty cents
a 'lude and sold them for two bucks apiece.

We were making a ton of money. If you wanted 'ludes, you
came to us. And they did, from all directions: Long Island, New
Jersey, Connecticut. Things were rolling along nicely.

Then we got greedy and decided to expand the operation,
which involved putting our hands on other shit. When someone
asked for it, we said we could get it, and we did.

And the money continued to roll in. Every time I came home
with money, I gave some to Emily, who was like the bank in a
game of Monopoly. At night as I was trying to go to sleep, I'd
look at our dresser and see it was starting to tilt. Emily had been
stuffing cash under the dresser until no more could fit.

CHAPTER 19

DIS & DAT LOUNGE

RICKY AND MY UNCLE JOE SHEP took over a bar on Mill Avenue in the Mill Basin section of Brooklyn. Some of the most expensive houses in all of New York are in Mill Basin, on the waterfront, but for the most part it's a middle-class neighborhood.

They bought the bar from Nicky Tango. My father used to drink there many years before and was an old friend of Nicky's. Back then, the road was still unpaved dirt. A lot of the old school guys would go there. It was off the beaten path, on the east side of Flatbush Avenue and in an alcove south of Avenue U, so it was a good place to hide away.

When the place went up for sale, Ricky grabbed it. We cleaned it up and opened the kitchen. It was doing well. I worked there three nights a week. My father and Goomba would do the rest of the nights.

My cousin Debby was the coat check girl. She dated Steven Gallo, so he was there often. We had four barmaids, one of them a friend of Sal "Brother" Sorrentino's. He knew her from Red Hook. The girl, who was Latina, was dating a big-time Latino drug dealer, so she was connected coming and going.

One Friday night I was sick, so I called in to see if one of the guys could cover for me. My father told me that he had planned on being there anyway, and that I should stay home in bed.

That night two guys came into the bar looking for the Latina barmaid. When she saw them come in, she went straight to Ricky and said, "Those guys are bad news."

BAD NEWS

Ricky went over to them and asked them to leave, at which point they each pulled out a pistol and started shooting. They shot Ricky in the face, they shot the barmaid, and they shot another girl who was just there having a drink.

Ricky shot one of them as they ran. The other turned and shot Ricky a second time. Twice wounded now, Ricky chased them out the door and down the block. When he knew he couldn't catch them, he ditched his own gun somewhere along the street. One of the young guys who had been at the bar grabbed Ricky and drove him to the hospital. When he got to the hospital, still bleeding badly, he finally passed out.

I was lying there in my sickbed and the phone rang. It was the bar, telling me there'd been a shooting.

"Come over now!" the voice said.

By the time I got there, the cops were already there, and they had the place roped off. I went in and it looked like a war zone. The cops were talking to my cousin Debby and Jackie Randazzo.

EMS guys were tending to the barmaid. I saw a body on the floor with a cover over it. They told me it was a girl who'd just turned twenty-one and was out for a birthday drink. She knew no one in the bar, and now she was dead.

I went over to Jackie and asked what happened. She told me as best as she could remember. She said she was pretty sure Ricky was shot, and the guys who came in were shot, too. They all ran out and didn't come back.

My brain was filled with about twenty voices, all of them screaming. I didn't know what the fuck to do. Not long after that, I got a call from the hospital. I was the next-of-kin and I needed to get there right away.

When I got to the hospital, a priest was giving Ricky the last rites. They told me they didn't think he was going to make it, but there was an urgency in the way they wheeled him off to surgery, so I knew there was a chance.

Everything started to spin. I had to take a knee and get oxygen to my brain. I got it together and learned for the first time the details of Ricky's wounds. He'd been shot in the mouth, the bullet blasting out his teeth. He'd also taken a bullet in the arm that went through-and-through, entered his chest, and stopped at his heart.

He made it through surgery. The next day detectives came from the precinct and arrested him. When he recovered, he went to court and was released on bail. He got the case turned around.

"I was the victim!" he cried, and finally the Law agreed.

The arrest had just been their form of pressure because they wanted him to ID the guys who had shot him. Ricky said he didn't see them well enough to identify them, which might've actually been true.

Slowly but surely we figured out what had happened. The Latina barmaid had, without our knowledge, been blabbing to the Law about her drug-dealing boyfriend. When the boyfriend and his bosses found out, they put a hit out on her. They didn't know that Ricky owned the bar. If they had, then they would have taken care of things someplace else. The two shooters were both shot in return, by Ricky, and they were arrested when they went to the hospital.

After that, the barmaid went to court and testified against them. They went to jail for killing the girl and shooting the barmaid. The case against Ricky was thrown out completely. There was a sit-down and it was determined that when the shooters were released, they were going to have to pay for shooting Ricky and killing his innocent customer.

Years later, when the shooters did get out of jail, they were only free for a month before both were found dead. But that was later. In the present, the shooting and its aftermath hurt the Dis & Dat badly.

THE ONE-PUNCH KNOCKOUT

I did a lot of drinking at Beefsteak Charlie's in Sheepshead Bay, because my good friend Nicky hung out there. I'd go with him to drop off the night deposit. He took me because I had a gun, and he always treated me well.

I remember one night in that bar I was talking to a couple of girls whom I knew, when I noticed there were two guys behind me, one of whom was a real asshole.

He was making some gestures at the girls and making them nervous and uncomfortable. I spun around and caught the guy making faces at them.

"What the fuck are you doing?" I asked.

He was a little guy, but his friend was as big as a house.

"You want to fuck with us?" the big one asked.

I hit the little one first and knocked him out with one punch. His friend figured to be more of a challenge. I took one step toward him and he showed me his palms, saying "no fight."

That would have been that, until I heard somebody say that the little guy had hit his head on the bar's foot rail on his way down. "He isn't moving," I heard someone say. The next thing I knew, my friend Nicky had me by the arm. "Let's get the fuck out of here," he said. I held a bar rag over my face and Nicky began to lead me out toward the kitchen.

My escape didn't go smoothly. We ran into a couple of Sheepshead Bay locals, a little bit older than me, regulars at the bar. They obstructed my exit through the kitchen.

"We don't like what you did out there," one of them said.

I turned to confront him, and after a little scuffle Nicky pulled me away. So there was a delay, but I eventually made it out the back door and miraculously Frankie Horn's cousin, a friend of mine, was already sitting in a car with the motor running, so all we had to do was climb in, she hit the gas, and we were out of there.

We went to a local bar and hung out together. She made a phone call and learned the guy was still alive but in bad shape. When he regained consciousness, he told cops that someone hit him but he didn't know who.

Afterward there were tensions between my friends and me and the guys we'd encountered in the kitchen. Nicky did his best to smooth things over and got them to say it was over, but I could tell those guys didn't like me.

I returned to the bar, and the big guy, the friend of the guy I hit, came up to me.

"My friend has a big mouth and is always getting himself slugged." He still wanted no trouble from me.

It was near the end of the night, and he said he didn't have a car, so could I give him a ride home? I said sure. As I drove him home, I was waiting for something to happen. If he tried anything, I figured I'd shoot him in the face.

When I got him home, there, waiting outside, was his father. The big guy seemed friendly. He said he was looking forward to seeing me the next week at the bar. I was confused.

"Yeah. Sure. I guess," I said, still not sure if I was supposed to whack him or be his friend.

TURN OUT THE LIGHTS—THE PARTY'S OVER

A couple of weeks later, I heard that Beefsteak Charlie's was closing so I went there to get drunk and say good-bye to the place. I got plenty drunk, pulled a gun, and began to shoot out the wall lights. You know, what the fuck? They weren't going to be needed anymore. Turn out the lights, the party's over, *bang, bang, bang.*

Joining me was a real tough guy named Dukie, who sounded like that old disc jockey Wolfman Jack, like he'd gargled with fucking rocks. He pulled out his gun and shot out a few lights with me.

Then Dukie and me had a contest to see who could shoot out the most lights, a test of skill that was in full swing when a girl screamed that there were two tables back there, now completely in the dark. Then all of the girls started to scream. Everyone's ears were ringing. I thought the shooting of the lights had given the joint some atmosphere. Dukie and me hid behind the bar for a while, and we could hear Nicky trying to smooth out things with distraught patrons, and then we snuck out like two kids who were in trouble.

NICKY FRISKS ME

With Beefsteak Charlie's closing their doors, Nicky would be out of work. He was a good manager and had a huge following. Whatever bar he hung out at was bound to have steady customers. I recommended Nicky to Ricky, saying he would be perfect for our place. We could announce that we were under new management and make it seem like we ourselves weren't there anymore.

So Nicky managed our place and it began to make money again. I only went in there every once in a while. One time I visited Nicky with a few guys from my crew. The next day, Nicky called my father and complained. He was trying to change the ambience of the place, to make it seem like it wasn't the sort of place that was going to be shot up like the Old West, and having me and my crew in there wasn't getting with the program. Besides, my guys didn't pay. Ricky told me that from then on the guys in my crew would pay for their own drinks at the bar. I said okay. That gives you an idea of how much Ricky wanted to keep Nicky happy.

A while later, I went in there with my friend Mike the electrician. I didn't have to pay for my drinks, but when Mike went to pay his tab, Nicky waved him off. "Good luck," he said. Nicky pulled me aside and said he didn't mean that shit about my friends having to pay; he was just looking out for the joint, you know? I said, "No problem," and he grabbed me in a kind of hug, like maybe he was patting me down.

The next day Ricky summoned me.

"I don't want you going into the bar with a gun. Leave it in the car," he said.

"Okay."

That night I went to do a pickup with Mike the electrician and I told him about Nicky frisking me.

"Nicky's got something up his sleeve," Mike said.

A few weeks later, Mike and I had been together all day, drinking and making pickups. By nighttime I had a snootful and I said, "Let's go the bar."

Mike went in ahead of me and walked right up to Nicky, informing him that I was in an "advanced stage" of the evening, and that my mind was stormy with trouble. Nicky thanked him for the heads-up.

By the time I got to Nicky, he was already on the defensive.

"Come on, Frankie, don't bust my balls," he said.

I took my gun out of my pocket and shot twice. Luckily, I was so hammered that Nicky couldn't have been safer, because he was what I was aiming at. One bullet went into the mirror behind the bar, and another went between Nicky and Mike.

I was about to shoot again, when I glanced to one side and saw four old people sitting in a booth with horrified expressions on their faces, looking at me like I was some kind of monster.

And you know what? I realized, maybe for the first time in my life, that they were right. I was out of control. There was an ass-hole of a monster in the room—and he was me.

I placed the gun gently on the bar, put my hands in the air, and said, "Sorry."

I looked down the bar, and I could see Mike contorting himself with adrenaline. "Do you know what you just did?" Mike said. "Ricky is going to be pissed."

I laughed, but not at Ricky being pissed. That part actually scared me a little. It was Mike's contortions that were funny; he was bending and straightening at the waist with his arms down between his legs.

Nicky was all shook up. "Why shoot me? I didn't do nothing," he said, pouring shots, leaving the bottle on the bar.

As we drank I said, "You are a fucking rat and you stabbed me in the back. *I put you here*." Then I said, "It's over," and left.

Mike and I made it to his house, but he couldn't find his keys. He was too fat to crawl in through a window, so I did. In another life-time, I'd have made a great B&E man. For a tall guy I'm pretty stealthy. I found my way back to the door in the dark and let him in.

"You got to be quiet," he said loudly.

I stumbled into the bedroom, and fell onto the bed—right on top of Mike's wife, Cindy.

She said, "What did you two morons do now?"

Mike told her. I passed out and woke up with Cindy putting coffee under my nose.

"Your father is looking for you," she said. "For both of you assholes."

"Does he know I'm here?"

"No, Dimatteo! I told your wife that you and Mike called to say you were upstate."

Mike said, "We're fucked. What are we going to do?"

There was only one choice. "Hide!" I said.

The next day Sal "Brother" Sorrentino came over to Mike's and said with a laugh that he'd talked to Ricky and calmed him down, and that everything was okay. I asked him how and he just smiled.

The next night, Ricky, Mike, and I went to the bar to talk to Nicky. Dad told me to never, ever go to the Dis & Dat again if I'd been drinking. Nicky told Ricky he couldn't do it anymore, but that he'd hang in until another manager could be found to replace him.

FAT DOM

To fill the managerial opening, I got in touch with an old friend of Ricky's, Fat Dom. He earned his nickname and then some, and he always had a cigar clamped in his mouth. He had experience, having run the Intermission Lounge for years. I'd known Fat Dom since I was a kid. I used to drink at Dom's bar, and he'd always treated me good. He wasn't doing anything, so he agreed to come out and run the Dis & Dat for Ricky.

Not long after Dom took over, Ricky had to go to jail and serve time for some bullshit.

NO STITCHES

Flash back to a Fat Dom story: A few years before, I was driving down Coney Island Avenue and I passed out at the wheel. I hit a parked car, pushing it into the street, my car sliding perfectly into the parking spot it had vacated. I hit my head and face on the windshield going up and then on the steering wheel on the way back down. It's a bad way to wake up. I stumbled out of the car, and I could see there was a bar right across the street, the Island Lounge, which I recognized as a cop bar. So instead of going there, I walked farther up the block to George's Diner. The second I entered, people started to scream. My head, it turned out, looked like one gigantic blood ball.

I fled the screaming people and returned to my car, where a group of people had gathered. Someone grabbed my arm and began to tug me across the street. It was Fat Dom, and he took me into the Island Lounge.

He was talking to me, but I couldn't understand what he was saying. A concussion on top of a good all-day drunk leaves you feeling like you're underwater. My memories of all of this are surreal, like it was part-dream and all real.

The next thing I knew, I was in a cop car heading for the hospital. I started to sober up a bit. I had a few scratches on my head, but the big problem was my mouth, which, according to the emergency room doctor, needed an estimated forty stitches, under my lips, both top and bottom.

I asked the doctor if it would heal without stitches, and he said it would if they could ever stop the bleeding, but that could take a long time.

I said, "Let me go."

Sounds like I was being a tough guy, but no. Truth is, the thought of a needle and thread going through my body freaked me out.

Dom called Ricky to tell him I was in the hospital but okay, and that he should report the car stolen. I left the hospital and there was a car waiting for me. I made it home and passed out. When I woke up the next morning, I was in so much pain that I wanted to die. Emily got me some painkillers and I stayed in bed for a week. My mouth felt like it had nuts in it, and I continued to bleed for days.

The point of the story is that Fat Dom covered the whole thing up for us, and so I knew he was a guy we could trust. But now that Fat Dom was at the Dis & Dat, I thought he was different somehow, a guy who played them closer to the vest than before.

I got the feeling that he wanted the bar all to himself and that I was in the way.

VISITING BOBBY DARROW

When Ricky returned home, I went with him and Roy Roy to see Bobby Darrow at Auburn State Prison. He'd been away for more than ten years, but it felt like yesterday when he'd left.

It felt odd seeing him in there. We talked like he was coming home the next day instead of never. We sat and talked, but no one said too much because the Law was listening.

Bobby said he had a hard-on (that is, a beef) with Pete the Greek, as well as with his motherfucking lawyer, Bob Weiswasser. Ricky and Roy told him to stop bullshitting, that they'd taken care of Weiswasser and he was dead.

Bobby recalled the night Joey was killed, and said that Pete's story, that Bobby had met a girl and asked to leave, was bullshit. He said that the part of the story about being unable to find an open restaurant in Chinatown was bullshit.

"It just don't add up," Bobby said.

We talked about President Street. Roy said that money was getting harder to make. Bobby called Blast a "Judas." When we left, Bobby was still smiling, like he was coming home soon.

That night we went to eat at the "hick restaurant" in the hotel. After eating, we hung out at the bar, where we stuck out like white guys at a Black Panther meeting. Everyone in the place knew we were from Brooklyn, probably the second we entered, but certainly by the end of the night. Every broad in the joint was talking to us. We had everyone singing, "Bad, bad Leroy Brown . . ." We went to bed whacked.

The next morning we drove back to Brooklyn, and Ricky and Roy spent the whole ride debating whether or not Pete the Greek was a rat who'd set up Joey.

Ricky said, "If he did his job, body-guarding Joey, he wouldn't be dead."

They went over it again and again. Why was Pete shot in the ass? Why did Joey run outside? Joey got hit inside but was killed outside. Why was Pete yelling at Matty the Horse and not with Joey outside?

They agreed that Joey would still be alive if he'd had other people with him.

Ricky said, "I never liked that Greek, but we can't say he's bad until we prove it, or our asses are on the line."

When we got back to the block, Ricky and Roy went into Roy's club. They stayed there for hours talking, then moved to Mondo's club.

I asked my dad, "So, how did it go?"

He said, "You'll know if need be."

CHAPTER 20
THE PINCH

LOUIE AND I were running the Brooklyn House of Pasta, trying to build it up so we could get some time off. Louie was burned out from all the hours he spent in the kitchen. I was in front, where it was easier, but it was the drinking that was burning me out. I had two little kids and I needed more money.

In 1984, there was an undercover operation from Long Island that was on to us. A prick whom we knew, a guy named Mal who'd been a friend of my uncle Chubby, got pinched for drugs and made a deal with the Law to become a criminal informant, a CI. They'd give him a break and he'd give them us.

Mal got in touch with Ricky to buy 'ludes. Mal was wired for the exchange. Now they had us, so they started a sting operation. Mal kept coming back every week for more. Now, Mal said, he wanted a key of coke. That was a little bit more than two pounds. I got a call from Mal, contacted the seller, and set it up. When the deal went down, Mal was with an undercover cop, and there were cops on the roofs of the surrounding buildings. We were sitting at a table, waiting for the seller, and waiting. Emily sat down and we ate. Mal was telling stories. I went outside to call the seller but got no answer.

It was getting late, so I went back inside and said, "I don't think he's coming."

Mal said, "Okay, let's set it up for another night."

The next morning, the seller told me he showed up but saw the cops all around and so he took off.

"You're kidding," I said.

"Fuck no."

"Why don't you just drop off the package to me?"

"No, Frankie. You're hot."

I called Ricky and told him what had happened.

Ricky said, "Chubby heard Mal was not good. I didn't believe him. Are you sure what you said happened?"

"I didn't see no Law," I told him.

"Okay, I'll take care of it," Ricky said.

MEETING WITH MAL

I wanted to open a fast-food chicken store on Smith Street, so I rented a storefront for five hundred dollars a month. I grabbed a friend who operated Globe Monte's, a maker of restaurant supplies, and I made him put everything I needed into my store.

We opened in October of 1984, and everything was going fine until I once again heard from Mal. He wanted to know about a meeting that was scheduled, he said, to be held in my store.

I said, "Really? This is the first I've heard of it."

I called Ricky and learned the meeting was real.

"Our friend Phil is doing a deal with Mal. Make sure they get a nice table."

"Okay."

That week I got tons of calls from Mal with all kinds of non-vague questions like, "How good is the stuff?" and, "When do you expect it." I got a bad feeling. To get along in this Life, you need a sixth sense about hoods who might be prompting you to incriminate yourself. Mal had my sixth sense buzzing.

I clammed up. "I don't know the answers to your fucking questions, Mal. Ask the guy when you see him."

When the meeting at my chicken joint came, Mal was first to

arrive. With him was an undercover cop, and the two of them were waiting for our friend Phil. There was some small talk.

The undercover cop asked me, "Got any 'ludes?"

I said, "No, I'm busy in restaurants." That ended the small talk.

Phil came in and asked me which guy was Mal, so I introduced them. That was what you might call an A-number-one bad move. They all went into the back room, made the deal, and on the way out, everyone said good-bye to me.

"WE'RE IN TROUBLE"

On March 22, 1985, 8:00 a.m., I was at home sleeping. The phone rang and Emily answered. She woke me up.

"There's a detective on the phone who wants to speak to you."

"Okay." I woke up fast.

The first thing the guy said to me was, "I know you've got two kids, so I didn't want to come to the house. Let's talk at your restaurant."

I said, "I'll be right there." I hung up the phone and said to Emily, "We're in trouble." I called my lawyer, Jay Holick, and told him what I thought was going down and that he needed to meet me at the restaurant right away.

When I got there, I was met by two detectives who told me I was under arrest for drug sales. Holick told me to go with the detectives and that he would take care of it. At Central Booking I was booked and then held for about four hours. The detectives returned and told me I was leaving with them. They took me to Queens, to a jail there. They said they didn't want me. So, it was back in the car, and into Manhattan, to Chambers Street, where they told me they needed to pick up some papers. I was left in the car with no handcuffs and the motor running. By this time it was about 9:00 p.m., and it had been a long day.

When the detectives came back to the car, they asked, "Hungry?"

I said I was.

"Let's go back to your restaurant then and have dinner," they said. I called Louie and told him to expect us. So I had dinner with the detectives. We drank two bottles of wine.

Somewhere during the second bottle, they told me what had happened. They wanted to arrest me, but they couldn't get the paperwork right—Nassau County crime, Kings County bust, it confused them.

"Go home, go to bed. But be in court tomorrow morning at nine," they said, and I said okay.

The next morning, my lawyer called and talked to Emily.

"Emily, get ready to bail Frankie out," he said.

"I don't have to bail him out, Jay. He's right here asleep." She gave the phone to me.

"How the hell did you get out? Once you're booked, only a judge can release you."

"I'm fucking talking to you, ain't I?" I said.

I got to court at nine, with my wife, my lawyer, and the two detectives at my side. Everyone was very positive with me, keeping my spirits up. I should be able to make bail and go home, everyone assured me.

So that is why I practically shit myself when the judge whacked his gavel and said, "I don't have the case in front of me, so I have to set bail high. Bail is set for two million dollars. Next case!"

Fuck. We couldn't make bail, so I was off to jail. Phil and Ricky had also been arrested. Phil made his bail immediately, and Ricky was held for a few hours in the Atlantic Avenue tombs. I saw him there for about an hour and then he also made bail.

It took a month, going back and forth to hearings, with lots of delays because they still didn't have my fucking paperwork straight. When they did get their ducks in order, it wasn't good. I was charged with four A-1 felonies, all narcotics related, and all with potential punishments of twenty-five to life.

We had to put up twenty-five thousand dollars in cash and someone's home, and then finally I was out. Out but scared shit-less. The thought of going away for twenty-five years was terri-fying. I was twenty-eight years old with a wife and a three- and two-year old at home.

Then, a few months later, my lawyer, Jay Holick, died of stom-ach cancer, so I needed a new guy. Benny the Sidge, a Gambino *capo*, told me to go to his lawyer, who was highly recommended. He was Santo Sgarlato Jr. I met him and he wanted $100,000, but I said sure.

Where was I going to get the money? Who knew? I did know it was worth it, though. As Santo reminded me, "If you blow just one of these charges, you get twenty-five years in prison."

Later I said to Emily, "Where the fuck am I going to get a hun-dred thousand dollars?"

She said, "Something always comes along to make money."

A few nights later, I got a call from a junkie I knew. He said he had a shitload of diamonds. We met at the restaurant, and sure enough, he had about $75,000 worth of diamonds.

Confession time. I gave some serious thought to killing the junkie and just taking the diamonds. It's a good thing that he gave me a nice price, or I might've. I was that desperate.

I bought the diamonds for $2,500, and sold them for $50,000. I gave the cash to Santo, and he said I could pay the rest of his fee over time as I got the money. There was no telling how long that was going to take.

At that time, I was having trouble making money. Most of the money I could save came from my paper route. It wasn't that I was lazy. I had a twenty-four-hour tail, and I couldn't say boo without detectives crawling up my ass.

Everywhere I went, the Law went. After a while, even the money I was getting from the old drug deal was becoming hard to get ahold of. My partner had to find creative ways to pay me. He was smart. Every other night he would call Emily and ask if she needed anything for the kids. She would complain that she needed something, and so he would come to the house carrying a bag of baby food or diapers or toys or something, and always in the bag was an envelope of cash. The first time he brought the bag Emily threw it out.

I came home and asked her, "Where's the money?"

She said, "He didn't give me anything."

"No way."

I looked in the garbage and there was the envelope containing five hundred dollars.

"There will always be money in the bag," I said, and Emily just laughed.

After a while, when I came home at night I'd go over to the detectives and tell them that I was home for the night so they could go home.

"If you're fucking with us, it's the last thing you'll do," they would always say. They'd go home and come back in the morning, and I knew not to fuck with them. I couldn't win.

This went on for nineteen months. At the court hearings the judge was having trouble figuring out all of the paperwork. There were still Nassau/Brooklyn jurisdictional issues. Plus, a few times the paperwork referred to me as "Ricky," and the judge didn't like that.

It got to the point where we were preparing for pretrial hearings and the DA asked to have a meeting with me.

He said, "Look, no matter how this goes, you are going to jail for at least seventeen years. But all you've got to do is say your father is the boss and we will knock your charges down to an E felony and you'll be out in three years."

I said, "Go fuck yourself." And I walked out.

Santo told me that they had something they weren't telling him.

In October 1986, the trial was scheduled to begin Monday, but when we got there, the first thing the judge did was delay the start until Thursday. Santo didn't know why, so I sent him to find out. He tried, but got no answer.

So Thursday we were back in court, waiting for the case to start and I went into the men's room. While I was in there pissing, the DA came in and took the urinal next to mine.

"Good morning, Mr. Dimatteo."

"Hello."

"I feel like this is going to be a good day."

"We'll see," I said.

When my case was called, the DA started to speak, but Judge Renzi interrupted him immediately.

"Mr. Crowe," the judge said to the prosecutor, "I am going to ask you three questions. I want a yes or no answer, you understand me?"

"Yes, Your Honor."

"Number one: Is there any evidence that Frank Dimatteo made any money on this sale?"

"No, but . . ."

"Just yes or no!"

"No."

"Number two: Do you have any evidence that Frank Dimatteo ever possessed any narcotics in his own hand?"

"No, but . . ."

"Yes or no!"

"No."

"Number three: Do you have any evidence that Frank Dimatteo put this deal together?"

"No, but his father . . .

"Yes or no!"

"No."

The judge slammed his gavel, a little bit angrily I thought, and said, "We're taking a thirty-minute break."

When the judge came back, he told the DA that he had a hundred felony cases on his docket and never to bring him a case like that again. The judge then turned to me and said, "Mr. Dimatteo, go home."

I turned to Santo and said, "What just happened?"

He said, "I don't know, let's just go."

The judge threw all of the charges out, giving the district attorney's office thirty days in which to re-indict me, which didn't happen.

A week later, Louie and Josephine took Emily and me to Bermuda for a week. It felt great being free. When we got back home, Louie, Goombabiel, and I then took off to Florida for a few weeks.

When I got back, Ricky was leaving for prison due to the Florida pot case and the two 'lude deals. The coke case against him was thrown out. He was convicted on the remaining charges, sentenced to three years, and served one.

AMELIA'S

While he was away, I converted the Dis & Dat into a restaurant. I went there every day and did whatever needed to be done until we got it opened, and we renamed it Amelia's after my mother.

People with money came in to eat. We had a ton of wiseguys: Carmine Lamandozzi, the Clemenza brothers, Benny the Sidge's crew, and Joe Shep—all regulars. The place did better as a restaurant than it ever did as a bar.

When Ricky got out of jail, he wanted to change some things in the place. He didn't like stem glasses, so he called Bobby Brooksey from the Gemini Lounge and asked him if he had any glasses. Bobby said yes and sent over four cases of glasses that I still have to this day.

Ricky said, "Wiseguys don't like stem glasses."

I said, "I didn't hear anyone complaining."

"I'm old school, Frankie. I like things old-fashioned."

He didn't like the booze I was selling, either. Grey Goose vodka, what the hell was that? He didn't think it would sell. So we got the older brands to make him happy. We sold a case of Grey Goose for every bottle of Smirnoff's, but we kept the Smirnoff's on hand anyway just to keep Ricky happy.

A few months after he got home, he was able to speak to the guys. He invited a few of the guys and their girls to his house for a welcome back get-together. Ricky, Punchy, Blast, and Joe Shep were sitting around drinking, and it did really feel like the old days for a while.

One time Goomba and I were sitting in the living room. The boys were at the little bar area my dad had set up near the bay window, laughing and telling stories. It was snowing like a motherfucker outside. Punchy was drinking campia and soda, Blast had a glass of wine or two, and Ricky drank Dewar's and water. The old boys were putting them away, and then Blast dared Punchy to jump into the bay behind the house! They were joking about how cold the water in the bay was, and there were actually chunks of ice floating in it.

So Punchy jumped out the window, ran down the deck where the boats were, and jumped in the fucking water. By the time we got to him, he was trying to get back on the deck, but it was slippery and he was having a tough time. We grabbed him and pulled him up on the deck. By the time we got him back up, we were all soaked. We got Punchy back into the house, and Ricky got him some dry clothes to put on. We all sat back at the bar, and Punchy was so freezing that it took him a long time to get warm.

After a while Blast and Ricky said to Punchy, "Are you fucking crazy?"

Punchy said, "It was nothing. Wasn't even c-c-c-c-cold."

"You're fucking nuts," the others said, and they continued to drink and laugh into the night.

CHAPTER 21
ON THE WAY TO NEW YORK

BLAST MOVED TO LITTLE ITALY. He'd had an opportunity to get in on La Casa Bella, a restaurant at Mulberry and Hester Streets, and he took it. He said good-bye to President Street, leaving behind a sinking ship. But a handful of the faithful were still there to the end.

From then on, the meetings were held at La Casa Bella, and sometimes I went along with Ricky or whoever else was left. After a while, I didn't see much of the old guys anymore. You saw them if you were doing something with them, but otherwise no.

Officially, we were with Blast. But "official" didn't mean shit anymore. In reality, we were pretty much broken up. We all had to go out and make a living. Louie and I started hanging out at La Casa Bella.

It was a new deal for us. Up till then we never went into the city much. We hung around the neighborhood joints, and if we traveled it was to other parts of Brooklyn. In Manhattan I felt a different kind of sophistication.

At La Casa Bella, there was a guy and his mother who sang Italian music. They were great. Whenever they played, Louie and I would take the girls there. One time we were having dinner there and Blast came over and sat at our table.

Louie was Blast's favorite. Blast liked smart young guys, and he thought Louie was smart. Louie impressed him, talked about school—he was still going to Pace University, fooling around.

So Blast said, "What are you doing with Frankie?" What he meant was: *With a dummy like Frankie.*

Louie said, "Don't think Frankie isn't smart. I've been learning a lot from him—and not all bad things."

Blast said, "I like that you didn't miss a beat."

They laughed.

Blast said to me, "You got a good friend there. Where's your dad?"

"With Al Goldstein."

"I hope he's making money with that fat fucking Jew," Blast said, and laughed again.

For the rest of the night, Louie and I enjoyed the food and the music. A lot of the guys came in. We spent a lot of money, but it was okay because we were also making a lot of money.

I really liked Blast, even though he wasn't the type of guy to be friendly. But I knew that since I was a kid, so I wasn't in awe; that's Albert Gallo. It was more like he was an uncle.

The day after Louie and I had that conversation with Blast, Louie got a call from someone he knew in the NYPD, who said the joint was bugged and we were being recorded. Louie was warned: "Stay the fuck out of there."

Louie called me over to his house and told me what he'd heard. I went to Blast and told him what Louie had been told. Blast didn't say a word. He turned on his heel and walked away, smart enough not to question me about it.

After I gave Blast that news, I hung out for a few Dewar's. I saw Mike the Owl's son Nicky, who was there with his girl. He was a good guy from the neighborhood, a guy you could count on if you came up short and needed quick funds.

ONE NIGHT IN MANHATTAN . . .

A few weeks later, me and a friend of mine named Stevie left La Casa Bella and went to Rodney Dangerfield's comedy club at First and Sixty-fourth in the city for a meeting with a few guys and a pot dealer who was making twenty thousand dollars a week.

The dealer was just a guy who knew someone who knew us, and he needed our help. Armenians were trying to move in on his business, selling pot, uppers, coke, and smack on his turf.

So, to keep the peace and head off any potential beefs, we met with the four Armenians around the corner in a joint called the Hippopotamus and explained what was up.

The Armenians said they'd give us two thousand dollars a week to make the pot dealer back off. Well, we weren't going to get nearly that much from the pot dealer, so we went back to him at Dangerfield's and told him he had better back off or the Armenians would kill him. He gave us a look like, *Man, did I just get fucked*.

As Stevie and I were about to leave Dangerfield's, we ran into two girls we knew from Ju Ju's. They asked if I could give them a ride back to the Hook, and I said no problem.

I was driving down Second Avenue when I came upon a guy who was blocking the intersection, having a fucking conversation with someone. I got out of the car and asked him to please move.

He told me to go fuck myself.

I pulled my .25 automatic and shot at him three times. I missed, but he moved his car pretty damn quick. I got back in the car, and as I was putting the gun back in my pocket, it went off, nearly hitting Stevie and me.

The two girls in the back started to scream. They thought someone was shooting at us, and I told them to calm down, that it was just me trying to put the gun away, and they cried all the way back to Ju Ju's.

At Ju Ju's I went in with them, bought them a couple of drinks, and tried to get them to relax. They told me that I was a sick fuck and that they were never going to ride with me again.

But as the alcohol continued to flow, and they thought about all of that sexy danger they'd just experienced, they began to come on to me, turning one wild night in Manhattan into an even wilder night back in Brooklyn.

LIKE COWBOYS

Roy Roy was still staying in the neighborhood. He didn't like to go to New York. He said Blast was all bullshit, so he stayed local. In fact, he didn't leave his club very much.

One night I went into a bar named Butch's Inn on Court Street. I was meeting Roy there. He was at the corner of the bar with Hugh "Apples" MacIntosh, the castrated Colombo killer, a mean motherfucker, and I could tell the instant I entered the place that Apples was giving Roy a hard time.

Roy caught my eye and gave me a quick flash of a look that said, *Go away*. But as going away isn't my style, I silently walked over to the bar, stood next to Roy, and ordered a drink.

MacIntosh noticed me and leaned over toward me to be sure I heard what he said, which was, "What are you going to do when I blow his brains all over you?"

I said, "You better have two bullets."

MacIntosh turned to Roy and asked, "Who the fuck is that?"

Roy said, "Ricky's son."

Mac grinned and walked out. He had respect for Ricky so he just walked out.

Roy started to yell at me, but I interrupted him: "What the fuck did you expect me to do? I just saved your ass."

Roy looked at me with a shocked expression, then he snapped out of it and bought me a drink. That was the last we ever spoke of it. I overheard the barmaid saying, "They're just like cowboys. Another wild night at Butch's."

SICILIAN SAMMY

Celebrities were pretty common. Jerry Orbach, the actor from the TV show *Law & Order*, was a friend of Joey's and Blast's, so we saw him all the time. Punchy and Bobby Darrow ran in a circle in Manhattan and that way they got in touch with a lot of people.

Sammy Davis Jr. once called my house looking for Dad. Al Goldstein picked up. I was standing there listening in.

"This is Sammy. Where's Ricky?"

Goldstein handed me the phone.

"Who's this?" I said.

"Sammy Davis."

I said, "Get out!"

"Really. It is. Who's this?"

"Frankie, Ricky's son."

"I'll be there in five minutes."

Five minutes later, a limo pulled up out front. Sammy was in there with a blonde and his mother.

"We're going out. Let's go," Sammy said.

So we went into the city to a "swinger's club" called Plato's Retreat. Inside, Sammy ran around with a couple of girls and left me in the lounge with the blonde and his mom. He didn't give a fuck. The limo driver brought in some real champagne and we drank the shit out of it.

Sammy was in town for about a month, so for a few weeks I ran with him to every bar and club in Manhattan.

He would say to me, "You're looking at a black Jew who's hooked up with the Mafia."

"How does that work?" I asked.

"I'm really from Sicily, but Dino told me to tell everyone I was black."

I looked at him like he was fucking nuts, and then his eyes would start to twinkle, even the glass one, and he'd break out into a big smile and start to laugh so hard he had to slap his knee.

We got close for a time, but he died shortly thereafter on May 16, 1990.

The night after I saved Roy Roy, Punchy called me and said, "Meet me at Ju Ju's."

Ju Ju's Bar was actually the old Park Inn at Court and Carroll Streets. My mom worked there back in the old days. It was an old tavern with a small stage next to the bar—and when I say "small," I mean it could hold maybe one guy playing guitar.

I got there at five thirty. Punchy was sitting at the end of the bar with the legendary movie star Lauren Bacall and Tanya Roberts, who was best known for being one of Charlie's Angels on TV.

He introduced me and said, "We're going out tonight, and you're driving."

Punchy and Lauren got along well, and she was a regular on the block for a while. Once we went to the Red Velvet, a piano bar on Sixtieth Street and First Avenue in New York. They had a fat broad playing piano and singing who was out of this world. I pretty much had to babysit Tanya Roberts during this time. We bounced from club to club, and got back to Brooklyn at eight o'clock in the morning. I got home and Emily was already up ironing my underwear.

The next night, Louie and I took the girls to the Crazy Country Club in Bay Ridge. It really was nuts. They had a microphone in the ladies' room hooked up to speakers in the club. There was an air nozzle in the floor just inside the entrance so that air could be blown up the skirts of the women as they came in. I still felt like shit from the night before, but I was doing what I had to do.

There were other celebrities who came in, such as Joan Hackett, who was an old movie star, and Liza Minnelli, who was a young one at that time. They were friends of Punchy and Joey and liked to drink on Court Street.

Liza in particular enjoyed a cocktail, but she wouldn't sing, no matter how many sheets to the wind she was. She said that singers were like whores: When they started giving it away, they'd be out of business.

BYE-BYE, BLAST

A few weeks rolled by. We were still going back and forth to La Casa Bella. Blast liked us there. He was comfortable when Ricky was with him. Ricky was still officially with Blast, but that was about to come to an end.

One morning we got a call to come to the restaurant for a noon meeting. When we got there, Blast was at the bar. He took us upstairs, where a few guys from the crew were sitting around: Preston, Stevie G., Bull Eye, and Steven B.

Blast sat Ricky down and told him that Vincent "The Chin" Gigante had found out that we were selling drugs, was pissed off, and was calling us in. Blast told Chin that it had nothing to do with him, because Ricky wasn't with him anymore.

Ricky looked at him, smiled, and said that was fine with him. Ricky's loyalty to the Gallos was unwavering, but he'd pledged that allegiance to a Gallo brother who had now been dead a long time, and while leaving Blast might've been the end of an era, it wasn't breaking my father's heart.

Still, deep down inside, it hurt him when he was passed up for being made with Blast and Punchy. At least now he knew why. Bobby Darrow had called Blast a "Judas." Ricky was hurt because way back when, he'd had an offer to be made from Tony Bender, and he'd turned it down.

Ricky turned to the others, saying, "I hope you guys weren't here to scare me, because I'd hate to think that about any of you. I hope none of you are here to kill me."

The others said no, no, no, that Blast had just called them to come in and they didn't know what was going on. Everyone kissed and we left.

We got in the car, and as I was driving us back to Brooklyn, no one said a word. The only sound was Ricky muttering to himself and grinding his teeth. Finally Ricky said, "Blast did the right thing. If Chin thought we were with Blast, he would've had us killed."

The Chin was really, really anti-drugs. If you were with the Chin, you didn't sell drugs, and if you did, you didn't get caught.

Ricky told me that we weren't off the hook yet. If the Chin wanted us dead, it would be someone from Blast's crew who would get the job. So now I had to keep an eye out for friends (or *former* friends) as well as for enemies. I now had to look out for guys I'd grown up with.

When the wiseguys found out that Ricky wasn't with Blast anymore, they came to the restaurant in Mill Basin. They were like recruiters, like those you'd find in the army. Guys from the Bonanno crew showed up. The Lucchese crew came by, and they both tried to get Ricky to join up.

Ricky said, "Like I always said, if you need me for anything, just call me, but for now let me do what I'm doing."

In 1991 a new era began, when a third family made their pitch. Our guests were Rudy Farone and Louie T., *capos* in the New Jersey family of Sammy "The Plumber" DeCavalcante. They said Sammy was expanding his operation and setting up a few crews in Brooklyn.

Anthony Rotondo, a new DeCavalcante *capo*, was running one of the crews and Sammy wanted Ricky to help him. Ricky said yes—and he said yes because Anthony's father, Jimmy, was a dear friend who'd been killed a few years earlier.

So now we were part of the DeCavalcante crew.

Here we go again!

EPILOGUE
REFLECTIONS

I'D LIKE TO THINK I'm not just older but wiser now as I write this, that I can reflect back on the things that have happened to me and around me during my youth and young adulthood with some sort of perspective.

I've seen friends kill friends. I've seen guys grow up and kill their mentors. I've seen mentors kill the guys they were grooming. Why? Usually it was because they were paranoid. They got so scared from so much time in the Life that they could no longer tell the good guys from the bad guys. Or maybe that was the trouble: Maybe we were all bad guys.

I've seen guys so loyal they would die for each other and then break up over money or rank in the crew. In this world, you're good as long as you're needed. Looking back over everything I've seen and heard, I feel like my life in the Life took place in a mirror, built on backward rules and never quite real. It was an oxymoronic world based on loyalty and comprised of rats. You were expected to be loyal to bosses who were in turn ratting on you. I thought they were gods, but they all died.

Ricky lived much longer than he should have, after having been shot three different times and surviving two bad car crashes. The joke was that Ricky had nine lives—like a cat. We always said he was so bad that even the devil wouldn't take him. When he was actually dying, in 2010, we still suspected he might pull through. His mind was still there, but his body was failing him.

The last words that I ever spoke with him were over the phone. I didn't want to go to Florida to visit him, because I didn't want to see him actually dying. I didn't want to believe it. On the phone I could pretend it wasn't really true.

He said to me, "Hey, pal, don't worry. I'm going to be fine."

I told him I knew it.

"You come down here, and we'll have dinner and drinks," he said.

Then he died and left me all alone. It was a shock, because he'd never left me alone in the fifty years I'd been with him.

The following year, 2011, my mom and I visited my godfather, Bobby "Darrow" Bongiovi, at the Coxsackie Medical Center, where he was dying of throat cancer, just finishing up his life sentence for killing that guy in the men's room of the bar way back in 1973. He was a sick man, but when he saw me he still smiled.

He'd refused treatment for his cancer. He knew he was going to die. Why prolong the inevitable? He spoke to me with a raspy voice, "The only thing I have left is my hair, and I'm not losing it."

He had with him two mirrors, a comb, and a stack of letters—his entire lot of worldly possessions after seventy-four years of life.

He told me it was time for him to go and be with my dad. He apologized for not being at Ricky's funeral. I told him he had a good excuse. I knew he would've been there if he could.

We laughed and talked about the times when he was young and I was a kid and all of the good times we'd had. He asked me if I remembered him picking me up and driving around. I did. I asked him if he remembered throwing coffee out the window of his Avenue L apartment into the cemetery below. He did.

"I still think that's nuts," I said.

"Why, do you think we're normal?" he asked with a smile.

It was getting late, and I knew I wouldn't be seeing him again.

I said, "Besides being in prison, what do you regret?"

He said, "Frankie Boy, I have a few regrets. One, I should never have gotten caught for killing that prick in the bar. The Law railroaded me, and the guys left me out to rot. Two, I never got the chance to kill Pete the Greek, the bodyguard with Joey Gallo the night Joey got whacked. Pete was involved. I should have realized something was up when he told me to leave the Copa, that he had it covered. He couldn't protect himself, never mind Joey. Pete got a gun pinch, then I got picked up, and I never got a chance to kill the mutt. Three, if I had known that Albert was the piece of shit that he is, I wouldn't have wasted the bullet on that prick in the bar. He left me here like a dog. What a mutt!"

(Note to Albert: If you are reading this book, I am just reporting the words that came out of Bobby's mouth. I have no opinion on the matter. I'm just telling the story. Even after we left the Gallos, I always stood up for you when anyone would say any not-so-nice things. I believe that if you're with someone, it's got to be all the way, and you never did anything wrong to me—nothing serious, anyway.)

I said, "Bobby, you've been in here for thirty-seven years. You've had a lot of time to think about it. You don't regret doing any of this shit at all?"

He said, "Frankie Boy, I did so much more work. This is what I am. If I regret it, I'm going to hell as a punk. I'd rather go to hell recommended."

There was a little more talk, and I knew he was growing weaker, so I said to my mother, "Let's go."

I leaned over and kissed Bobby good-bye, and with a tear in my eye, I left.

Driving home, I said to my mom, "I just lost the two guys I

loved the most within a year." I got that scary feeling of being alone again. Two days later we got the call: Bobby had died in his sleep.

Mom and I went to see Punchy at his restaurant on Columbia Street. I didn't realize how long it had been since I'd last seen him. He was a tough, hard guy, but he'd grown old.

I felt a little bit nostalgic for the old days, but not entirely. Punchy had always been good to me, but he'd never really stopped seeing me as a kid, and I had to get away from him because he wasn't treating me like a grown man.

No matter what I did, I got no recognition. I know that in this Life you don't always get a pat on the back or a star in your book, but there are still ways to let people know that what they did in the Life is recognized, and I could have used more of that from Punchy. Now I saw how much time had changed him, and all I could think about was how old I now was. When I saw Punchy, I got a flashback to the day he'd gotten shot on President Street while standing with Tony Bernardo, getting a hot dog. I didn't mind when they had me staying with him in the hospital. I liked him and he was one of the big boys. I thought guarding him would be a feather in my cap. Now I looked at him after years of not seeing him, and it felt like my world was coming to an end—again. He looked old, sick, and frail. It was still him, but I felt like he wasn't there.

We talked for just a few minutes. He asked me how I was, wanted to know what I was up to. My mother came over to him and they sat and spoke for a bit. I don't know what they talked about. I walked away. I had that feeling again. I was being left alone.

Frank "Punchy" Illiano passed away in January of 2014, the last of the gods. I have no urge to justify what they did in their lives. The Lord will judge them, not me. I lived in a world of gangsters, some of them murderers, but that was what they *did for a living*. I knew them as husbands, fathers, brothers, uncles, and friends.

And today, I know, they are turning over in their graves over what has happened to "this thing of ours." I can hear Ricky saying to Punchy, "What a joke!"

If you've made it this far in the book, I guess I can tell you a secret. After Larry died and Joey was killed, Blast was the leader in name only. Ricky was really in charge. He called the shots. I had a lot of advantages because Ricky was my father, yet sometimes I wake up in the morning and I ask myself, "Has this been a dream or a nightmare?"

There's still a huge portion of my story that remains untold. For that, you'll have to wait for my second book: It's all about ten years with the DeCavalcante crime family, the craziest decade yet, with its *Partying* with a capital *P*, drug deals in Miami, porn video companies, and the "Soprano" tapes, then finally being put up to be made in 1999.

To the families of the guys written about in this book, let me say, these men were my gods, and it is a history I needed to tell as I saw it. These are my memories. I didn't tell everything that happened, but what I told was the truth.

To you readers from Brooklyn, I'd like to point out that if you ever crossed the Cropsey Avenue Bridge into Coney Island and you saw a guy on the bridge shadow-boxing, that was my birth father, Alphonzo "Funzi" Milone.

A BIG "FUCK YOU"

I'd like to finish my story with a big "Fuck You" to any of you out there planning to give me shit because you think I'm breaking the fucking code, by telling tales out of school. Here's what I have to say to that: Everybody in my book is now dead. Nobody is going to jail because of anything I've written. That's more than

I can say for the tales told by a lot of guys, the "Real Rats," guys who are hanging around movie sets and signing autographs. They talk about "our thing" and how "I know someone." Once again, *Fuck You*, because everyone knows someone. So I'm making a list. If you feel like busting my balls, here's a list of rats whose balls need busting, so go and bust theirs. But be careful because about half of them could give you the beating of your life. But what the fuck do I know?

MEMBERS WHO HAVE FLIPPED

Genoroso "Jimmy the General" Barbieri (soldier), Paul Cantarella (soldier), Richard "Shellackhead" Cantarella (*capo*/acting underboss), Dominick Cicale (soldier/acting *capo*), Frank Coppa (*capo*), Joseph "Joey Mook" D'Amico (soldier), Frank "Curly" Lino (*capo*), Michael "Sonny" Maggio (soldier), Joseph "Big Joey/The Ear" Massino (boss), Nicholas "P.J." Pisciotti (soldier/acting *capo*), James "Jimmy Tag/Big Lou" Tartaglione (*capo*), Salvatore "The Chief" Vitale (soldier/underboss), Dominic "Fat Dom" Borghese (soldier), Primo Cassarino (soldier), Joseph "Little Joe" D'Angelo (soldier), Michael "Mikey Scars" DiLeonardo (*capo*), Frank "Frankie Fapp" Fappiano (soldier), Salvatore "Sammy the Bull" Gravano (underboss), Robert Mormando (soldier), Nicholas "Nicky Skins" Stefanelli (soldier), "Big" Dino Calabro (*capo*), Joseph "Joe Camp" Campanella (soldier), Joseph "Joey Caves" Competiello (soldier), Michael "Mikey" Franzese (soldier/acting *capo*), Reynold "Ren" Maragni (*capo*), Salvatore "Big Sal" Miciotta (soldier/acting *capo*), John Pate (*capo*), Alan Quatrache (soldier), Anthony Russo (acting *capo*), Sebastiano "Sebby" Saracino (soldier), Carmine Sessa (*consiglieri*), Michael "Mikey" Souza (soldier), Frank "Frankie Blue Eyes" Sparaco (soldier), Anthony "Bingy" Arillotta (soldier), Vincent "Fish" Cafaro (soldier), Renaldi "Ray" Ruggiero (*capo*), Felix Tranghese (*capo*), Anthony "Tumac" Accetturo (*capo*), Anthony "Gas Pipe" Casso (underboss), Peter "Fat Pete" Chiodo (*capo*), Alphonse "Little Al" D'Arco (*capo*/acting boss), Joseph D'Arco (soldier), Joseph "Little Joe/Joe D" Defede (soldier/acting boss), Frank Gioia Sr. (soldier), Frank Gioia Jr. (soldier), Steve LaPella (soldier), Thomas "Tommy" Ricciardi (soldier), Vincent "Vinny Baldy" Salanardi (soldier), Frank "Goo Goo" Suppa (soldier), Anthony Rotundo (*capo*), Vinnie Ocean (boss), Chris Paciello, Frank Cullotta, Dino Basino, and Frank Calabrese Jr.

I could go on forever. People just want to break the wrong guy's balls.

APPENDIX: AL MILONE'S BOXING RECORD

Born: September 16, 1933
Middleweight, Brooklyn, New York
Won 16, Lost 15, Draw 1, No Contest 1

DATE	OPPONENT	LOCATION	RESULT
Aug. 12, 1954	Walter Monforte	Ft. Hamilton Arena	W (dec.)
April 16, 1956	Art Lusby	St. Nicholas Arena	W (dec.)
May 7, 1956	Jimmy Landron	St. Nicholas Arena	W (dec.)
May 24, 1956	Danny Jones	Sunnyside Garden	W (KO)
June 11, 1956	Jose Lopez	St. Nicholas Arena	W (dec.)
July 2, 1956	Art Lusby	St. Nicholas Arena	L (dec.)
July 30, 1956	Jimmy Landron	St. Nicholas Arena	W (dec.)
Sept. 3, 1956	Tony Sansone	St. Nicholas Arena	W (dec.)
Oct. 8, 1956	Bill Flamio	St. Nicholas Arena	L (dec.)
Nov. 8, 1956	Jimmy Archer	Sunnyside Garden	L (TKO)
Feb. 4, 1957	Fred McArthur	St. Nicholas Arena	W (TKO)
March 18, 1957	Stefan Redl	St. Nicholas Arena	L (TKO)
May 4, 1957	Stefan Redl	Paterson (NJ) Armory	L (TKO)
Aug. 26, 1957	Joe Lissy	St. Nicholas Arena	L (dec.)
Sept. 23, 1957	Tony DiBiase	St. Nicholas Arena	L (TKO)
Dec. 16, 1957	Eddie Prince	St. Nicholas Arena	L (dec.)

DATE	OPPONENT	LOCATION	RESULT
Feb. 27, 1958	Gene Hamilton	Sunnyside Garden	W (dec.)
Aug. 19, 1958	Harvey McCullough	Milford, CT	W (dec.)
Sept. 29, 1958	Tommy Holmes	St. Nicholas Arena	L (dec.)
April 20, 1959	Jimmy Landron	St. Nicholas Arena	L (dec.)
May 11, 1959	Angelo Allegue	St. Nicholas Arena	W (dec.)
May 25, 1959	Angelo Allegue	St. Nicholas Arena	W (KO)
June 26, 1959	Bobby Bartels	Madison Square Garden	L (TKO)
Sept. 28, 1959	Eddie Woods	Philadelphia Arena	No Contest*
Jan. 19, 1960	George Chimenti	Trenton, NJ	L (dec.)
Feb. 1, 1960	Bruce Gibson	Philadelphia Arena	L (dec.)
Feb. 29, 1960	Jimmy Landron	St. Nicholas Arena	W (dec.)
March 31, 1960	Isaac Jenkins	Sunnyside Garden	W (dec.)
April 21, 1960	Jay Anderson	Plaza Hotel (Paterson, NJ)	Draw
June 6, 1960	Obdulio Nunez	St. Nicholas Arena	L (TKO)
Dec. 5, 1960	Johnny Torres	St. Nicholas Arena	W (dec.)
Dec. 17, 1960	Johnny Torres	Madison Square Garden	W (dec.)
March 18, 1961	Tito Velez	St. Nicholas Arena	L (dec.)

*Referee stopped fight after fifth round because neither fighter could continue.

BIBLIOGRAPHY

Books and Periodicals

Anderson, David. "Gallo Trial, Barely Begun, Ends; 17 Plead Guilty, and 18th Is Freed." *New York Times*, September 23, 1964.

Davila, Albert, and Paul Meskil. "Gallo Gang Veteran Is Rubbed Out." *Daily News*, October 6, 1976.

Gage, Nicholas. "Alleged Gallo Aide Held in Mob Killing." *New York Times*, March 15, 1973.

——————. "Pornographic Periodicals Tied to Organized Crime." *New York Times*, October 13, 1975.

——————. "Story of Joe Gallo's Murder: 5 in Colombo Gang Implicated," *New York Times*, May 3, 1972.

——————. "Gallo Gang Member Is Shot in Brooklyn." *New York Times*, September 3, 1974.

——————. "Gallo Gang Saves 6 Children in Fire in Brooklyn Flat." *New York Times*, February 1, 1962.

——————. "Gallo Man Held in Gang Slaying: Photo Picked by Witnesses in Ozone Park Shooting." *New York Times*, June 15, 1963.

——————. "Gallo Reprisal Held Motive in Shooting." *New York Times*, July 3, 1974.

Kihss, Peter. "Gallo Aide Slain at a Dice Table; Reputed Mobster
    Shot While at Benefit in Synagogue, Weapons Discovered."
    New York Times, August 5, 1974.

——————. "Larry Gallo Dies in Sleep at 41; Fought in Brook-
    lyn Gang War." *New York Times*, May 19, 1968.

Perlmutter, Emanuel. "Roots of the Gallo-Profaci War: Youth vs.
    Age, Need vs. Plenty," *New York Times*, December 11,
    1963.

——————. "Use of the Gallos in Race Unrest Is Scored by
    Jury." *New York Times*, September 8, 1966.

Websites

"Frank 'Frankie Shots' Abbatemarco—The Precursor to the Pro-
    faci-Gallo War." Americanmafiahistory.com. Accessed
    April 11, 2015.

"Joey Gallo Biography." www.biography.com/people/joey-gallo-
    20701997?_escaped_fragment. Accessed April 22, 2015.

VERBATIM CONVERSATION, ME AND MY MOM, 2015

"I'M GONNA TELL YOU NOW, FRANKIE. I heard what happened in Cousin's with you and David, with the guns!"

"What are you talking about?"

"You must've been really drunk, Frankie! You forgot what happened in Cousin's with David with the guns?"

"No, no, David wasn't there."

"Who was there?"

"I was there with Emily. Guys from Third Avenue came in, and Chi Chi from Douglass Street came in. And these guys were taking turns busting my balls telling me the others were bothering them. So at the end of the night, I said to both of them, why don't you just go fucking do something? So I shot the gun, and I threw them all out of the bar."

"Who's the one ran out to the trunk of the car, got guns out?"

"That was on Seventh Avenue."

"With David."

"At the club."

"See, that's another thing."

The operations manager at the great radar pulse generator Excalibur did not even inform his supervisor the first time a strange blip appeared on his data processing display. He thought it was an artifact, a bogey created by an anomalous processing algorithm. When the signature repeated several times, though, he paid closer attention. The manager called in the chief Excalibur scientist, who analyzed the data and decided that the object was a long period comet. It was another two months before a graduate student proved that the signature belonged to a smooth body at least forty kilometers in its longest dimension.

By 2197 the world knew that the object hurtling through the solar system toward the inner planets was a second extraterrestrial spacecraft. The International Space Agency concentrated its resources to prepare a mission that would intercept the intruder just inside the orbit of Venus in late February of 2200. Again the eyes of humanity looked outward, toward the stars, and the deep philosophical questions raised by the first Rama were again debated by the populace on Earth. As the new visitor drew nearer and its physical characteristics were more carefully resolved by the host of sensors aimed in its direction, it was confirmed that this alien spacecraft, at least from the outside, was identical to its predecessor. Rama had returned. Mankind had a second appointment with destiny.

"A STRONGLY PLOTTED, COMPELLING
ADVENTURE STORY."
—*Science Fiction Chronicle*

"MUCH BETTER THAN *RENDEZVOUS WITH RAMA*."
—*San Diego Tribune*

"THE NOVEL IS PACKED WITH THE TECHNICAL BRILLIANCE THAT IS CLARKE'S FORTE, BUT IT IS ALSO A CAPTIVATING STRUGGLE AMONG VARIED HUMAN NATURES."
—*Chicago Tribune*

"CONTINUES THE ENTERTAINING, HARD-SF TRADITION CLARKE VIRTUALLY INVENTED."
—*The Detroit News*

"CLARKE AND LEE TOSS READERS MYSTERY AFTER MYSTERY, CLUE AFTER CLUE, BUILDING . . . TO AN ENDING THAT LEAVES US WANTING MORE."
—*Philadelphia Inquirer*

Bantam Books by Arthur C. Clarke
Ask your bookseller for the books you have missed

ASTOUNDING DAYS
RENDEZVOUS WITH RAMA
TALES FROM PLANET EARTH

With Gentry Lee
RAMA II

RAMA II
ARTHUR C. CLARKE
AND
GENTRY LEE

BANTAM BOOKS
NEW YORK · TORONTO · LONDON · SYDNEY · AUCKLAND

RAMA II

A Bantam Spectra Book
Bantam hardcover edition / December 1989
Bantam paperback edition / December 1990

ISBN 0-553-28658-7

Published simultaneously in the United States and Canada

Bantam Books are published by Bantam Books, a division of Bantam Doubleday Dell Publishing Group, Inc. Its trademark, consisting of the words "Bantam Books" and the portrayal of a rooster, is Registered in U.S. Patent and Trademark Office and in other countries. Marca Registrada. Bantam Books, 666 Fifth Avenue, New York, New York 10103.

PRINTED IN THE UNITED STATES OF AMERICA

OPM   0 9 8 7 6 5 4 3 2 1

RAMA REVISITED

I never imagined, until a few years ago, that I would ever collaborate with another writer on a work of fiction. *Non*-fiction was different: I've been involved in no less than fourteen multi-author projects (two with the editors of *Life*, and you don't get more multiplex than that). But fiction—no way! I was quite sure I would never let any outsider tamper with my unique brand of creativity. . . .

Well, a funny thing happened on the way to the word processor. Early in 1986 my agent, Scott Meredith, called me in his most persuasive "Don't-say-no-until-I've-finished" mode. There was, it seemed, this young genius of a movie producer who was determined to film something—*anything* —of mine. Though I'd never heard of Peter Guber, as it happened I had seen two of his movies (*Midnight Express*, *The Deep*), and been quite impressed by them. I was even more impressed when Scott told me that Peter's latest, *The Color Purple*, had been nominated for half a dozen Oscars.

However, I groaned inwardly when Scott went on to say that Peter had a friend with a brilliant idea he'd like me to develop into a screenplay. I groaned, because there are no new ideas in s.f., and if it really was brilliant I'd have thought of it already.

Then Scott explained who the friend was, and I did a double-take. The project suddenly looked very exciting indeed, for reasons that had nothing to do with Peter Guber, but a lot to do with Stanley Kubrick.

Flashback. Twenty years earlier, in *2001: A Space Odyssey*, Stanley and I had visited the moons of Jupiter, never dreaming that these completely unknown worlds would, in fact, be reconnoitered by robots long before the date of our movie. In March and July 1979, the two *Voyager* probes revealed that Io, Europa, Ganymede, and Callisto were stranger places than we'd dared to imagine. The stunning views of Jupiter's giant satellites made it possible—no, imperative—for me to write *2010: Odyssey Two*. This time around, the Jovian sequences could be based on reality, not imagination; and when Peter Hyams filmed the book in 1984, he was able to use actual images from the *Voyager* spacecraft as backgrounds for much of the action.

Spectacular though the results of the 1979 missions were, it was confidently hoped that they would be quite surpassed within a decade. The *Voyager* spacecraft spent only a few hours in the vicinity of Jupiter, hurtling past the giant planet and its moons on the way to Saturn. But in May 1986, NASA planned to launch *Galileo*, an even more ambitious space probe. This would make not a brief fly-by, but a *rendezvous; Galileo* would spend two years, starting in December 1988, on a detailed survey of Jupiter and its major moons. By 1990, if all went well, there would be such a flood of new information about these exotic worlds that a third Space Odyssey would be inevitable. *That* was what I was planning to write; I'd hitched my wagon to *Galileo*, and could hardly care less about some amateur science fiction author's ideas. How to turn him down politely? I was still pondering this when Scott continued:

"Peter Guber wants to fly out to Sri Lanka, just for thirty-six hours, to introduce this guy to you. His name is Gentry Lee, and let me explain who he is. He works at the Jet Propulsion Laboratory, and he's the chief engineer on Project Galileo. Have you heard of that?"

"Yes," I said faintly.

"And before that, he was director of mission planning for the *Viking* landers, that sent back those wonderful pictures from Mars. Because he felt the public didn't appreciate what was going on in space, he formed a company with your friend Carl Sagan to make *Cosmos*—he was manager of the whole TV series—"

"Enough!" I cried. "This man I have to meet. Tell Mr. Gabor to bring him here right away."

"The name," said Scott, "is *Guber*. Peter Guber."

Well, it was agreed that the two of them would fly out to Sri Lanka, and if I liked Gentry's idea (and, equally important, Gentry) I'd develop an outline—perhaps a dozen pages—which would give characters, locations, plot, and all the basic elements from which any competent script writer could generate a screenplay.

They arrived in Colombo on February 12, 1986—just two weeks after the *Challenger* disaster. 1986 was going to be *the* Big Year for Space, but now the entire NASA program was in total disarray. In particular, *Galileo* would be delayed for years. It would be 1995 before there could be any further news from the moons of Jupiter. I could forget about *Odyssey Three*—just as Gentry could forget about doing anything with *Galileo* except getting it back from the Cape and putting it in mothballs.

Happily, the Guber-Lee-Clarke Summit went well, and for the next few weeks I filled floppy disks with concepts, characters, backgrounds, plots—anything which seemed even remotely useful to the story we'd decided to call *Cradle*. Gentry liked my four-thousand-word outline and flew out to Sri Lanka again so that we could fill in the details. From then onward, we were able to collaborate by making frequent phone calls and flying yards of printout across the Pacific.

The writing took the best part of a year, though of course we were both involved in other projects as well. When I discovered that Gentry had a considerably better background in English *and French* literature than I did (by now I was immune to such surprises) I heroically resisted all attempts to impose my own style on him. This upset some longtime ACC readers, who when *Cradle* appeared under our joint names were put out by passages where I should have done a little more sanitizing. The earthier bits of dialogue, I explained, were the result of Gentry's years with the hairy-knuckled, hard-drinking engineers and mathematicians of JPL's Astrodynamics Division, where the Pasadena cops often have to be called in to settle bare-fisted fights over Bessel Functions and nonlinear partial differential equations.

Though I'd greatly enjoyed working with Gentry, when

we'd finished rocking *Cradle* I had no plans for further collaboration—because Halley's Comet was now dominating my life, as it had failed to dominate terrestrial skies. I realized that its next appearance, in 2061, would provide a splendid opportunity for a third Space Odyssey. (If the much-delayed *Galileo* does perform as hoped in 1995 and beams back megabytes of new information from the Jovian system, there may be a Final Odyssey. But I make no promises.)

By the summer of 1987, *2061: Odyssey Three* was doing very nicely in the bookstores, thank you, and I was once again beginning to feel those nagging guilt pains that assail an author when he's not Working On A Project. Suddenly, I realized that one was staring me right in the face.

Fifteen years earlier, the very last sentence of *Rendezvous With Rama* had read: "The Ramans do everything in threes." Now, those words were a last-minute afterthought when I was doing the final revision. I had not—cross my heart—any idea of a sequel in mind; it just seemed the correct, open-ended way of finishing the book. (In real life, of course, no story ever ends.)

Many readers—and reviewers—jumped to the conclusion that I had planned a trilogy from the beginning. Well, I hadn't—but now I realized it was a splendid idea. And Gentry was just the man for the job: He had all the background in celestial mechanics and space hardware to deal with the next appearance of the Ramans.

I quickly outlined a spectrum of possibilities, very much as I had done with *Cradle*, and in a remarkably short time Scott had sold a whole package to Bantam's Lou Aronica. *Rama II*, *The Garden of Rama*, and *Rama Revealed* would be written and delivered during the 1989–91 period.

So once again Gentry Lee is commuting across the Pacific for brainstorming sessions in the Sri Lankan hills, and the postman is complaining about the bulky printouts he has to balance on his bicycle. This time around, however, technology has speeded up our intercontinental operations. The fax machine now allows us to exchange ideas almost in real time; it's far more convenient than the Electronic Mail link Peter Hyams and I used when scripting *2010* (see *The Odyssey File*).

There is much to be said for this kind of long-distance collaboration; if they are too close together, co-authors may waste a lot of time on trivia. Even a solitary writer can think of endless excuses for not working; with two, the possibilities are at least squared.

However, there is no way of demonstrating that a writer is neglecting his job; even if his snores are deafening, his subconscious may be hard at work. And Gentry and I knew that our wildest excursions into literature, science, art, or history might yield useful story elements.

For example, during the writing of *Rama II* it became obvious that Gentry was in love with Eleanor of Aquitaine— don't worry, Stacey, she's been dead for 785 years—and I had to tactfully dissuade him from devoting pages to her amazing career. (If you wonder how E of A could have the remotest connection with interstellar adventures, you have pleasures in store.)

I certainly learned a lot of French and English history from Gentry that they never taught me at school. The occasion when Queen Eleanor berated her son, the intrepid warrior-king Richard the Lion Heart, *in front of his troops* for failing to produce an heir to the throne must have been one of the more piquant moments in British military history. Alas, there was no way we could work in this gallant but gay Corleone, who was often a godfather, never a father . . . very unlike Gentry, whose fifth son arrived toward the end of *Rama II*.

But you will meet Gentry's most cherished creation, the yet-to-be-born St. Michael of Siena. One day, I am sure, you'll encounter him again, in books that Gentry will publish under his own name, with the minimum of help or hindrance from me.

As I write these words, we're just coming up to the midway point of our four-volume partnership. And though we think we know what's going to happen next, I'm sure the Ramans have quite a few surprises in store for us. . . .

—Arthur C. Clarke

1
RAMA RETURNS

The great radar pulse generator Excalibur, powered by nuclear explosions, had been out of service for almost half a century. It had been designed and developed in a frantic effort during the months following the transit of Rama through the solar system. When it was first declared operational in 2132, Excalibur's announced purpose was to give Earth ample warning of any future alien visitors: one as gigantic as Rama could be detected at interstellar distances—years, it was hoped, before it could have any effect on human affairs.

That original commitment to build Excalibur had been made even before Rama had passed perihelion. As the first extraterrestrial visitor rounded the sun and headed out toward the stars, armies of scientists studied the data from the only mission that had been able to rendezvous with the intruder. Rama, they announced, was an intelligent robot with absolutely no interest in our solar system or its inhabitants. The official report offered no explanations for the many mysteries encountered by the investigators; however, the experts did convince themselves that they understood one basic principle of Raman engineering. Since most of the major systems and subsystems encountered inside Rama by the human explorers had two functional backups, it appeared that the aliens engineered everything in threes. Therefore, since the entire giant vehicle was assumed to be a machine, it was considered highly likely that two more Rama spacecraft would be following the first visitor.

But no new spaceships entered the solar neighborhood from the empty reaches of interstellar space. As the years passed the people on Earth confronted more pressing problems. Concern about the Ramans, or whoever it was that had created that drab cylinder fifty kilometers long, abated as the lone alien incursion passed into history. The visit of Rama continued to intrigue many scholars, but most members of the human species were forced to pay attention to other issues. By the early 2140s the world was in the grip of a severe economic crisis. There was no money left to maintain Excalibur. Its few scientific discoveries could not justify the enormous expense of assuring the safety of its operation. The great nuclear pulse generator was abandoned.

Forty-five years later it took thirty-three months to return Excalibur to operational status. The primary justification for the refurbishment of Excalibur was scientific. During the intervening years radar science had flourished and produced new methods of data interpretation that had greatly enhanced the value of the Excalibur observations. As the generator again took images of the distant heavens, almost nobody on Earth was expecting the arrival of another Rama spacecraft.

The operations manager at Excalibur Station did not even inform his supervisor the first time the strange blip appeared on his data processing display. He thought it was an artifact, a bogey created by an anomalous processing algorithm. When the signature repeated several times, however, he paid closer attention. The manager called in the chief Excalibur scientist, who analyzed the data and decided the new object was a long period comet. It was another two months before a graduate student proved that the signature belonged to a smooth body at least forty kilometers in its longest dimension.

By 2197 the world knew that the object hurtling through the solar system toward the inner planets was a second extraterrestrial spacecraft. The International Space Agency (ISA) concentrated its resources to prepare a mission that would intercept the intruder just inside the orbit of Venus in late February of 2200. Again the eyes of humanity looked outward, toward the stars, and the deep philosophical questions raised by the first Rama were again debated by the populace on Earth. As the new visitor drew nearer and its physical characteristics were more carefully resolved by the host of sensors aimed in its direction, it was confirmed that this alien spacecraft, at least from the outside, was identical to its predecessor. Rama had returned. Mankind had a second appointment with destiny.

2
TEST AND TRAINING

The bizarre metallic creature inched along the wall, crawling up toward the overhang. It resembled a skinny armadillo, its jointed snail body covered by a thin shell that curled over and around a compact grouping of electronic gadgetry astride the middle of its three sections. A helicopter hovered about two meters away from the wall. A long flexible arm with a pincer on the end extended from the nose of the helicopter and just missed closing its jaws around the odd creature.

"Dammit," muttered Janos Tabori, "this is almost impossible with the 'copter bouncing around. Even in perfect conditions it's hard to do precision work with these claws at full extension." He glanced over at the pilot. "And why can't this fantastic flying machine keep its altitude and attitude constant?"

"Move the helicopter closer to the wall," ordered Dr. David Brown.

Hiro Yamanaka looked at Brown without expression and entered a command into the control console. The screen in front of him flashed red and printed out the message, COMMAND UNACCEPTABLE. INSUFFICIENT TOLERANCES. Yamanaka said nothing. The helicopter continued to hover in the same spot.

"We have fifty centimeters, maybe seventy-five, between the blades and the wall," Brown thought out loud. "In another two or three minutes the biot will be safe under the overhang. Let's go to manual and grab it. Now. No mistakes this time, Tabori."

For an instant a dubious Hiro Yamanaka stared at the balding, bespectacled scientist sitting in the seat behind him. Then the pilot turned, entered another command into the console, and switched the large black lever to the left position. The monitor flashed, IN MANUAL MODE. NO AUTOMATIC PROTECTION. Yamanaka gingerly eased the helicopter closer to the wall.

Engineer Tabori was ready. He inserted his hands in the instrumented gloves and practiced opening and closing the jaws at the end of the flexible arm. Again the arm extended and the two mechanical mandibles deftly closed around the jointed snail and its shell. The feedback loops from the sensors on the claws told Tabori, through his gloves, that he had successfully captured his prey. "I've got it," he shouted exultantly. He began the slow process of bringing the quarry back into the helicopter.

A sudden draft of wind rolled the helicopter to the left and the arm with the biot banged against the wall. Tabori felt his grip loosening. "Straighten it up," he cried, continuing to retract the arm. While Yamanaka was struggling to null the rolling motion of the helicopter, he inadvertently tipped the nose down just slightly. The three crew members heard the sickening sound of the metal rotor blades crashing against the wall.

The Japanese pilot immediately pushed the emergency button and the craft returned to automatic control. In less than a second, a whining alarm sounded and the cockpit monitor flashed red. EXCESSIVE DAMAGE. HIGH PROBABILITY OF FAILURE. EJECT CREW. Yamanaka did not hesitate. Within moments he blasted out of the cockpit and had his parachute deployed. Tabori and Brown followed. As soon as the Hungarian engineer removed his hands from the special gloves, the claws at the end of the mechanical arm relaxed and the armadillo creature fell the hundred meters to the flat plain below, smashing into thousands of tiny pieces.

The pilotless helicopter descended erratically toward the plain. Even with its onboard automatic landing algorithm active and in complete control, the damaged flying machine bounced hard on its struts when it hit the ground and tipped over on its side. Not far from the helicopter's landing site, a portly man, wearing a brown military suit covered with ribbons, jumped down from an open elevator. He had just descended from the mission control cen-

ter and was clearly agitated as he walked briskly to a
waiting rover. He was followed by a scrambling lithe
blond woman in an ISA flight suit with camera equipment
hanging over both her shoulders. The military man was
General Valeriy Borzov, commander-in-chief of Project
Newton. "Anyone hurt?" he asked the occupant of the
rover, electrical engineer Richard Wakefield.

"Janos apparently banged his shoulder pretty hard during the ejection. But Nicole just radioed that he had no
broken bones or separations, only a lot of bruises."

General Borzov climbed into the front seat of the rover
beside Wakefield, who was sitting behind the vehicle control panel. The blond woman, video journalist Francesca
Sabatini, stopped recording the scene and started to open
the back door of the rover. Borzov abruptly waved her
away. "Go check on des Jardins and Tabori," he said,
pointing across the level plain. "Wilson's probably there
already."

Borzov and Wakefield headed in the opposite direction
in the rover. They traveled about four hundred meters
before they pulled alongside a slight man, about fifty, in a
new flight suit. David Brown was busy folding up his
parachute and replacing it in a stuff bag. General Borzov
stepped down from the rover and approached the American scientist.

"Are you all right, Dr. Brown?" the general asked,
obviously impatient to dispense with the preliminaries.

Brown nodded but did not reply. "In that case," General Borzov continued in a measured tone, "perhaps you
could tell me what you were thinking about when you
ordered Yamanaka to go to manual. It might be better if
we discussed it here, away from the rest of the crew."

"Did you even see the warning lights?" Borzov added
after a lengthy silence. "Did you consider, even for a
moment, that the safety of the other cosmonauts might be
jeopardized by the maneuver?"

Dr. David Brown eventually looked over at Borzov with
a sullen, baleful stare. When he finally spoke in his own
defense, his speech was clipped and strained, belying the
emotion he was suppressing. "It seemed reasonable to
move the helicopter just a little closer to the target. We

had some clearance left and it was the only way that we could have captured the biot. Our mission, after all, is to bring home—"

"You don't need to tell me what our mission is," Borzov interrupted with passion. "Remember, I helped write the policies myself. And I will remind you again that the number one priority, *at all times*, is the safety of the crew. Especially during these simulations. . . . I must tell you that I am absolutely flabbergasted by this crazy stunt of yours. The helicopter is damaged, Tabori is injured, you're lucky that nobody was killed."

David Brown was no longer paying attention to General Borzov. He had turned around to finish stuffing his parachute into its transparent package. From the set of his shoulders and the energy he was expending on this routine task, it was obvious that he was very angry.

Borzov returned to the rover. After waiting for several seconds he offered Dr. Brown a ride back to the base. The American shook his head without saying anything, hoisted his pack onto his back, and walked off in the direction of the helicopter and the elevator.

3
CREW CONFERENCE

Outside the meeting room in the training facility, Janos Tabori was sitting on an auditorium chair underneath an array of small but powerful portable lights. "The distance to the simulated biot was at the limit of the reach of the mechanical arm," he explained to the tiny camera that Francesca Sabatini was holding. "Twice I tried to grab it and failed. Dr. Brown then decided to put the helicopter on manual and take it a little closer to the wall. We caught some wind . . ."

The door from the conference room opened and a smiling, ruddy face appeared. "We're all here waiting for you," said General O'Toole pleasantly. "I think Borzov's becoming a little impatient."

Francesca switched off the lights and put her video camera back in the pocket of her flight suit. "All right, my Hungarian hero," she said with a laugh, "we'd better stop for now. You know how our leader dislikes waiting." She walked over and put her arms gently around the small man. She patted him on his bandaged shoulder. "But we're really glad you're all right."

A handsome black man in his early forties had been sitting just out of the camera frame during the interview, taking notes on a flat, rectangular keyboard about a foot square. He followed Francesca and Janos into the conference room. "I want to do a feature this week on the new design concepts in the teleoperation of the arm and the glove," Reggie Wilson whispered to Tabori as they sat down. "There are a bunch of my readers out there who find all this technical crap absolutely fascinating."

"I'm glad that the three of you could join us," Borzov's sarcastic voice boomed across the conference room. "I was

starting to think that perhaps a crew meeting was an
imposition on all of you, an activity that interrupted the
far more important tasks of reporting our misadventures or
writing erudite scientific and engineering papers." He
pointed at Reggie Wilson, whose ubiquitous flat keyboard
was on the table in front of him. "Wilson, believe it or
not, you're supposed to be a member of this crew first and
a journalist second. Just one time do you think you can
put that damn thing away and listen? I have a few things
to say and I want them to be off the record."

Wilson removed the keyboard and put it in his briefcase. Borzov stood up and walked around the room as he
talked. The table in the crew conference room was a long
oval about two meters across at its widest point. There
were twelve places around the table (guests and observers, when they attended, sat in the extra chairs over
against the walls), each one equipped with a computer
keyboard and monitor slightly inset into the surface and
covered, when not being used, by a polished grain top
that matched the quality simulated wood on the rest of the
table. As always, the other two military men on the expedition, European admiral Otto Heilmann (the hero of the
Council of Governments intercession in the Caracas crisis)
and American air force general Michael Ryan O'Toole,
flanked Borzov at one end of the oval. The other nine
Newton crew members did not always sit in the same
seats, a fact that particularly frustrated the compulsively
orderly Admiral Heilmann and, to a lesser extent, his
commanding officer Borzov.

Sometimes the four "nonprofessionals" in the crew would
cluster together around the other end of the table, leaving
the "space cadets," as the five cosmonaut graduates of the
Space Academy were known, to create a buffer zone in the
middle. After almost a year of constant media attention,
the public had relegated each member of the Newton
dozen to one of three subgroups—the nonpros, consisting
of the two scientists and two journalists; the military troika;
and the five cosmonauts who did most of the skilled work
during the mission.

On this particular day, however, the two nonmilitary
groups were thoroughly mixed. The famed Japanese inter-

disciplinary scientist Shigeru Takagishi, widely regarded as the foremost expert in the world on the first Raman expedition seventy years earlier (and also the author of the *Atlas of Rama* that was required reading for all of the crew), was sitting in the middle of the oval between Soviet pilot Irina Turgenyev and the brilliant but often zany British cosmonaut/electrical engineer Richard Wakefield. Opposite them were life science officer Nicole des Jardins, a statuesque copper brown woman with a fascinating French and African lineage, the quiet, almost mechanical Japanese pilot Yamanaka, and the stunning Signora Sabatini. The final three positions at the "south" end of the oval, facing the large maps and diagrams of Rama on the opposite wall, were occupied by American journalist Wilson, the inimitable and garrulous Tabori (a Soviet cosmonaut from Budapest), and Dr. David Brown. Brown looked very businesslike and serious; he had a set of papers spread out in front of him as the meeting began.

"It is inconceivable to me," Borzov was saying while he strode purposefully around the room, "that any of you could ever forget, even for a moment, that you have been selected to go on what could be the most important human mission of all time. But on the basis of this last set of simulations, I must admit that I am beginning to have my doubts about some of you.

"There are those who believe that this Rama craft will be a copy of its predecessor," Borzov continued, "and that it will be equally disinterested and uninvolved with whatever trifling creatures come to survey it. I admit it certainly appears to be at least the same size and same configuration, based on the radar data that we have been processing for the past three years. But even if it does turn out to be another dead ship built by aliens that vanished thousands of years ago, this mission is still the most important one of our lifetime. And I would think that it demands the very best effort from each of you."

The Soviet general paused to collect his thoughts. Janos Tabori started to ask a question but Borzov interrupted him and launched again into his monologue. "Our performance as a crew on this last set of training exercises has been absolutely abominable. Some of you have been

outstanding—you know who you are—but just as many of
you have acted as if you had no idea what this mission was
about. I am convinced that two or three of you do not
even read the relevant procedures or the protocol listings
before the exercises begin. I grant you that they are dull
and sometimes tedious, but all of you *agreed,* when you
accepted your appointments ten months ago, to learn the
procedures and to follow the protocols and project policies. Even those of you with no prior flight experience."

Borzov had stopped in front of one of the large maps on
the wall, this one an inset view of one corner of the city of
"New York" inside the first Raman spaceship. The area of
tall thin buildings resembling Manhattan skyscrapers, all
huddled together on an island in the middle of the Cylindrical Sea, had been partially mapped during the previous
human encounter. "In six weeks we will rendezvous with
an unknown space vehicle, perhaps one containing a city
like this, and all of mankind will depend on us to represent them. We have no way of knowing what we will find.
Whatever preparation we will have completed before then
may well be not enough. Our knowledge of our pre-
planned procedures must be perfect and automatic, so
that our brains are free to deal with any new conditions we
may encounter."

The commander sat down at the head of the table.
"Today's exercise was nearly a complete disaster. We could
easily have lost three valuable members of our team as
well as one of the most expensive helicopters ever built. I
want to remind you all, one more time, of the priorities of
this mission as agreed to by the International Space Agency
and the Council of Governments. The top priority is the
safety of the crew. Second priority is the analysis and/or
determination of any threat, if it exists, to the human
population of the planet Earth." Borzov was now looking
directly down the table at Brown, who returned the commander's challenging look with a stony stare of his own.
"Only after those two priorities are satisfied and the Raman
craft is adjudged harmless does the capturing of one or
more of the biots have any significance."

"I would like to remind General Borzov," David Brown
said almost immediately in his sonorous voice, "that some

of us do not believe the priorities should be blindly applied in a serial fashion. The importance of the biots to the scientific community cannot be overstated. As I have said repeatedly, both in cosmonaut meetings and on my many television news appearances, if this second Rama craft is just like the first—which means that it will ignore our existence completely—and we proceed so slowly that we fail even to capture a single biot before we must abandon the alien ship and return to Earth, then an absolutely unique opportunity for science will have been sacrificed to assuage the collective anxiety of the world's politicians."

Borzov started to reply but Brown stood up and gestured emphatically with his hands. "No, no, hear me out. You have essentially accused me of incompetence in my conduct of today's exercise and I have a right to respond." He held up some computer printout and waved it at Borzov. "Here are the initial conditions for today's simulation, as posted and defined by *your* engineers. Let me refresh your memory with a few of the more salient points, in case you've forgotten. Background condition number one: It is near the end of the mission and it has already been firmly established that Rama II is totally passive and represents no threat to the planet Earth. Background condition number two: During the expedition biots have only been seen sporadically, and never in groups."

Brown could tell from the body language of the rest of the crew that his presentation had had a successful beginning. He drew a breath and continued. "I assumed, after reading those background conditions, that this particular exercise might represent the last chance to capture a biot. During the test I kept thinking what it would mean if we could bring one or several of them back to the Earth—in all the history of humanity, the only absolutely certain contact with an extraterrestrial culture took place in 2130 when our cosmonauts boarded that first Rama spaceship.

"Yet the long-term scientific benefit from that encounter was less than it might have been. Granted, we have reams of remote sensing data from that first investigation, including the information from the detailed dissection of the spider biot done by Dr. Laura Ernst. But the cosmonauts brought home only one artifact, a tiny piece of some kind of biomechanical flower whose physical characteristics had already irreversibly changed before any of its mysteries could be understood. We have nothing else in the way of souvenirs from that first excursion. No ashtrays, no drinking glasses, not even a transistor from a piece of equipment that would teach us something about Raman engineering. Now we have a second chance."

Brown looked up at the circular ceiling above him. His voice was full of power. "If we could somehow find and return two or three different biots to the Earth, and if we could then analyze these creatures to unlock their secrets, then this mission would without doubt be the most significant historical event of all time. For in understanding in depth the engineering minds of the Ramans, we would, in a real sense, achieve a first contact."

Even Borzov was impressed. As he often did, David Brown had used his eloquence to turn a defeat into a partial victory. The Soviet general decided to alter his tactics. "Still," Borzov said in a subdued tone during the pause in Brown's rhetoric, "we must never forget that human lives are at stake on this mission and that we must do nothing to jeopardize their safety." He looked around the table at the rest of the crew. "I want to bring back biots and other samples from Rama as much as any of you," he continued, "but I must confess that this blithe assumption that the second craft will be exactly like the first disturbs me a great deal. What evidence do we have from the first encounter that the Ramans, or whoever they are, are benevolent? None at all. It could be dangerous to seize a biot too soon."

"But there's no way of ever being certain, Commander, one way or the other." Richard Wakefield spoke from the side of the table between Borzov and Brown. "Even if we verify that this spaceship is exactly like the first one almost seventy years ago, we still have no information about what will happen once we make a concerted effort to capture a biot. I mean, suppose for a moment that the two ships are just supersophisticated robots engineered millions of years ago by a now vanished race from the opposite side of the galaxy, as Dr. Brown has suggested in his articles. How can we predict what kinds of subroutines might be programmed into those biots to deal with hostile acts? What if the biots are integral parts, in some way that we have not been able to discern, of the fundamental operation of the ship? Then it would be natural, even though they are machines, that they would be programmed to defend themselves. And it is conceivable that what might look like an initial hostile act on our part could be the trigger that changes the way the entire ship functions. I remember reading about the robot lander that crashed into the ethane sea on Titan in 2012—it had stored entirely different sequences depending on what it—"

"Halt," Janos Tabori interrupted with a friendly smile. "The arcana of the early robotic exploration of the solar system is not on the agenda for today's postmortem." He looked down the table at Borzov. "Skipper, my shoulder is hurting, my stomach is empty, and the excitement of today's exercise has left me exhausted. All this talk is wonderful, but if there's no more specific business would it be out of line to suggest an early end to this meeting so that we will have adequate time, for once, to pack our bags?"

Admiral Heilmann leaned forward on the table. "Cosmonaut Tabori, General Borzov is in charge of the crew meetings. It is up to him to determine—"

The Soviet commander waved his arm at Heilmann. "Enough, Otto. I think that Janos is right. It has been a long day at the end of an extremely busy seventeen days of activity. This conversation will be better when we are all fresh."

Borzov stood up. "All right, we will break for now. The shuttles will leave for the airport right after dinner." The crew started preparing to leave. "During your short rest period," Borzov said as an afterthought, "I want all of you to think about where we are in the schedule. We have left only two more weeks of simulations here at the training center before the break for the end-of-the-year holiday. Immediately thereafter we begin the intensive prelaunch activities. This next set of exercises is our last chance to get it right. I expect each of you to return fully prepared for the remaining work—and recommitted to the importance of this mission."

4

THE GREAT CHAOS

The intrusion of the first Raman spacecraft into the inner solar system in early 2130 had a powerful impact on human history. Although there were no immediate changes in everyday life after the crew headed by Commander Norton returned from encountering Rama I, the clear and unambiguous proof that a vastly superior intelligence existed (or, as a minimum, *had* existed) somewhere else in the universe forced a rethinking of the place of homo sapiens in the overall scheme of the cosmos. It was now apparent that other chemicals, doubtless also fabricated in the great stellar cataclysms of the heavens, had risen to consciousness in some other place, at some other time. Who were these Ramans? Why had they built a giant sophisticated spacecraft and sent it on an excursion into our neighborhood? Both in public and private conversation, the Ramans were the number one topic of interest for many months.

For well over a year mankind waited more or less patiently for another sign of the Ramans' presence in the universe. Intense telescopic investigations were conducted at all wavelengths to see if any additional information associated with the retreating alien spaceship could be identified. Nothing was found. The heavens were quiet. The Ramans were departing as swiftly and inexplicably as they had arrived.

Once Excalibur was operational and its initial search of the heavens turned up nothing new, there was a noticeable change in the collective human attitude toward that first contact with Rama. Overnight the encounter became a historical event, something that *had* happened and was now completed. The tenor of newspaper and magazine

articles that had earlier begun with phrases like "when the
Ramans return . . ." changed to "if there is ever another
encounter with the creatures who built the huge spaceship
discovered in 2130 . . ." What had been a perceived threat,
a lien in a sense on future human behavior, was quickly
reduced to a historical curiosity. There was no longer an
urgency to deal with such fundamental issues as the return
of the Ramans or the destiny of the human race in a
universe peopled by intelligent creatures. Mankind relaxed, at least for a moment. Then it exploded in a parox-
ysm of narcissistic behavior that made all previous historical
periods of individual selfishness pale by comparison.

The surge of unabashed self-indulgence on a global scale
was easy to understand. Something fundamental in the
human psyche had changed as a result of the encounter
with Rama I. Prior to that contact, humanity stood alone
as the only known example of advanced intelligence in the
universe. The idea that humans could, as a group, control
their destiny far into the future had been a significant
linchpin in almost every working philosophy of life. That
the Ramans existed (or had existed—whatever the tense,
the philosophic logic came to the same conclusion) changed
everything. Mankind was not unique, maybe not even
special. It was just a question of time before the prevailing
homocentric notion of the universe was to be irrevocably
shattered by clearer awareness of the Others. Thus it was
easy to comprehend why the life patterns of most human
beings suddenly veered toward self-gratification, reminding literary scholars of a similar time almost exactly five
centuries earlier, when Robert Herrick had exhorted the
virgins to make the most of their fleeting time in a poem
that began, "Gather ye rosebuds while ye may / Old time
is still a-flying. . . ."

An unrestrained burst of conspicuous consumption and
global greed lasted for just under two years. Frantic acqui-
sition of everything the human mind could create was
superimposed on a weak economic infrastructure that had
been already poised for a downturn in early 2130, when
the first Raman spaceship flew through the inner solar
system. The looming recession was first postponed throughout 2130 and 2131 by the combined manipulative efforts of

governments and financial institutions, even though the
fundamental economic weaknesses were never addressed.
With the renewed burst of buying in early 2132, the world
jumped directly into another period of rapid growth. Production capacities were expanded, stock markets exploded,
and both consumer confidence and total employment hit
all-time highs. There was unprecedented prosperity and
the net result was a short-term but significant improve-
ment in the standard of living for almost all humans.

By the end of the year in 2133, it had become obvious
to some of the more experienced observers of human
history that the "Raman Boom" was leading mankind toward disaster. Dire warnings of impending economic doom
started being heard above the euphoric shouts of the
millions who had recently vaulted into the middle and
upper classes. Suggestions to balance budgets and limit
credit at all levels of the economy were ignored. Instead,
creative effort was expended to come up with one way
after another of putting more spending power in the hands
of a populace that had forgotten how to say wait, much
less no, to itself.

The global stock market began to sputter in January of
2134 and there were predictions of a coming crash. But to
most humans spread around the Earth and throughout the
scattered colonies in the solar system, the concept of such
a crash was beyond comprehension. After all, the world
economy had been expanding for over nine years, the last
two years at a rate unparalleled in the previous two centuries. World leaders insisted that they had finally found the
mechanisms that could truly inhibit the downturns of the
capitalistic cycles. And the people believed them—until
early May of 2134.

During the first three months of the year the global
stock markets went inexorably down, slowly at first, then
in significant drops. Many people, reflecting the superstitious attitude toward cometary visitors that had been prev-
alent for two thousand years, somehow associated the
stock market's difficulties with the return of Halley's Comet.
Its apparition starting in March turned out to be far brighter
than anyone expected. For weeks scientists all over the
world were competing with each other to explain why it

was so much more brilliant than originally predicted. After it swooped past perihelion in late March and began to appear in the evening sky in mid-April, its enormous tail dominated the heavens.

In contrast, terrestrial affairs were dominated by the emerging world economic crisis. On May 1, 2134, three of the largest international banks announced that they were insolvent because of bad loans. Within two days a panic had spread around the world. The more than one billion home terminals with access to the global financial markets were used to dump individual portfolios of stocks and bonds. The communications load on the Global Network System (GNS) was immense. The data transfer machines were stretched far beyond their capabilities and design specifications. Data gridlock delayed transactions for minutes, then hours, contributing additional momentum to the panic.

By the end of a week two things were apparent—that over half of the world's stock value had been obliterated and that many individuals, large and small investors alike, who had used their credit options to the maximum, were now virtually penniless. The supporting data bases that kept track of personal bank accounts and automatically transferred money to cover margin calls were flashing disaster messages in almost twenty percent of the houses in the world.

In truth, however, the situation was much much worse. Only a small percentage of the transactions were actually clearing through all the supporting computers because the data rates in all directions were far beyond anything that had ever been anticipated. In computer language, the entire global financial system went into the "cycle slip" mode. Billions and billions of information transfers at lower priorities were postponed by the network of computers while the higher priority tasks were being serviced first.

The net result of these data delays was that in most cases individual electronic bank accounts were not properly debited, for hours or even days, to account for the mounting stock market losses. Once the individual investors realized what was occurring, they rushed to spend whatever was still showing in their balances before the

computers completed all the transactions. By the time
governments and financial institutions understood fully
what was going on and acted to stop all this frenetic
activity, it was too late. The confused system had crashed
completely. To reconstruct what had happened required
carefully dumping and interleaving the backup checkpoint
files stored at a hundred or so remote centers around the
world.

For over three weeks the electronic financial management system that governed all money transactions was
inaccessible to everybody. Nobody knew how much money
he had—or how much anyone else had. Since cash had
long ago become obsolete, only eccentrics and collectors
had enough bank notes to buy even a week's groceries.
People began to barter for necessities. Pledges based on
friendship and personal acquaintance enabled many people to survive temporarily. But the pain had only begun.
Every time the international management organization that
oversaw the global financial system would announce that
they were going to try to come back on-line and would
plead with people to stay off their terminals except for
emergencies, their pleas would be ignored, processing
requests would flood the system, and the computers would
crash again.

It was only two more weeks before the scientists of the
world agreed on an explanation for the additional bright-
ness in the apparition of Halley's Comet. But it was over
four months before people could count again on reliable
data base information from the GNS. The cost to human
society of the enduring chaos was incalculable. By the
time normal electronic economic activity had been restored, the world was in a violent financial downspin that
would not bottom out until twelve years later. It would be
well over fifty years before the Gross World Product would
return to the heights reached before the Crash of 2134.

5

AFTER THE CRASH

There is unanimous agreement that The Great Chaos profoundly altered human civilization in every way. No segment of society was immune. The catalyst for the relatively rapid collapse of the existing institutional infrastructure was the market crash and subsequent breakdown of the global financial system; however, these events would not have been sufficient, by themselves, to project the world into a period of unprecedented depression. What followed the initial crash would have been only a comedy of errors if so many lives had not been lost as a result of the poor planning. Inept world political leaders first denied or ignored the existing economic problems, then overreacted with a suite of individual measures that were baffling and/or inconsistent, and finally threw up their arms in despair as the global crisis deepened and spread. Attempts to coordinate international solutions were doomed to failure by the increasing need of each of the sovereign nations to respond to its own constituency.

In hindsight, it was obvious that the internationalization of the world that had taken place during the twenty-first century had been flawed in at least one significant way. Although many activities—communications, trade, transportation (including space), currency regulation, peacekeeping, information exchange, and environmental protection, to name the most important—had indeed become international (even interplanetary, considering the space colonies), most of the agreements that established these international institutions contained codicils that allowed the individual nations to withdraw, upon relatively short notice, if the policies promulgated under the accords no longer served the interests of the country in question. In

short, each of the nations participating in the creation of
an international body had the right to abrogate its national
involvement, unilaterally, when it was no longer satisfied
with the actions of the group.

The years preceding the rendezvous with the first Raman
spaceship in early 2130 had been an extraordinarily stable
and prosperous time. After the world recovered from the
devastating cometary impact near Padua, Italy, in 2077,
there was an entire half century of moderate growth.
Except for a few relatively short, and not too severe,
economic recessions, living conditions improved in a wide
range of countries throughout the time period. Isolated
wars and civil disturbances did erupt from time to time,
primarily in the undeveloped nations, but the concerted
efforts of the global peacekeeping forces always contained
these problems before they became too serious. There
were no major crises that tested the stability of the new
international mechanisms.

Immediately following the encounter with Rama I, however, there were rapid changes in the basic governing
apparatus. First, emergency appropriations to handle
Excalibur and other large Rama-related projects drained
revenues from established programs. Then, starting in
2132, a loud clamor for tax cuts (to put more money into
the hands of the individuals) reduced even further the
allocations for needed services. By late 2133, most of the
newer international institutions had become understaffed
and inefficient. Thus the global market crash took place in
an environment where there was already growing doubt in
the minds of the populace about the efficacy of the entire
network of international organizations. As the financial
chaos continued, it was an easy step for the individual
nations to stop contributing funds to the very global organizations that might have been able, if they had been used
properly, to turn the tide of disaster.

The horrors of The Great Chaos have been chronicled
in thousands of history texts. In the first two years the
major problems were skyrocketing unemployment and bank-
ruptcies, both personal and corporate, but these financial
difficulties seemed unimportant as the ranks of the homeless and starving continued to swell. Tent and box commu-

nities appeared in the public parks of all the big cities by the winter of 2136–37 and the municipal governments responded by striving valiantly to find ways to provide services to them. These services were intended to limit the difficulties created by the supposedly temporary presence of these hordes of idle and underfed individuals. But when the economy did not recover, the squalid tent cities did not disappear. Instead they became permanent fixtures of urban life, growing cancers that were worlds unto themselves with an entire set of activities and interests fundamentally different from the host cities that were supporting them. As more time passed and the tent communities turned into hopeless, restless caldrons of despair, these new enclaves in the middle of the metropolitan areas threatened to boil over and destroy the very entities that were allowing them to exist. Despite the anxiety caused by this constant Damocles' sword of urban anarchy, the world squeaked through the brutally cold winter of 2137–38 with the basic fabric of modern civilization still more or less intact.

In early 2138 a remarkable series of events occurred in Italy. These events, focused around a single individual named Michael Balatresi, a young Franciscan novitiate who would later become known everywhere as St. Michael of Siena, occupied much of the attention of the world and temporarily forestalled the disintegration of the society. Michael was a brilliant combination of genius and spirituality and political skills, a charismatic polyglot speaker with an unerring sense of purpose and timing. He suddenly appeared on the world stage in Tuscany, coming seemingly out of nowhere, with a passionate religious message that appealed to the hearts and minds of many of the world's frightened and/or disenfranchised citizens. His following grew rapidly and spontaneously and paid no heed to international boundaries. He became a potential threat to almost all the identified leadership coteries of the world with his unwavering call for a collective response to the problems besetting the species. When he was martyred under appalling circumstances in June of 2138, mankind's last spark of optimism seemed to perish. The civilized world that had been held together for many months by a flicker of hope and a slim thread of tradition abruptly crumbled into pieces.

The four years from 2138 to 2142 were not good years to be alive. The litany of human woes was almost endless. Famine, disease, and lawlessness were everywhere. Small wars and revolutions were too numerous to count. There was an almost total breakdown in the standard institutions of modern civilization, creating a phantasmagoric life for everyone in the world except the privileged few in their protected retreats. It was a world gone wrong, the ultimate in entropy. Attempts to solve the problems by well-meaning groups of citizens could not work because the solutions they conceived could only be local in scope and the problems were global.

The Great Chaos also extended to the human colonies in space and brought a sudden end to a glorious chapter in the history of exploration. As the economic disaster spread on the home planet, the scattered colonies around the solar system, which could not exist without regular infusions of money, supplies, and personnel, quickly became the forgotten stepchildren of the people on Earth. As a result almost half of the residents of the colonies had left to return home by 2140, the living conditions in their adopted homes having deteriorated to the point where even the twin difficulties of readjustment to Earth's gravity and the terrible poverty throughout the world were preferred over continuing to stay (most likely to die) in the colonies. The emigration process accelerated in 2141 and 2142, years characterized by mechanical breakdowns in the artificial ecosystems at the colonies and the beginning of a disastrous shortage of spare parts for the entire fleet of robot vehicles used to sustain the new settlements.

By 2143 only a very few hard core colonists remained on the Moon and Mars. Communications between Earth and the colonies had become intermittent and erratic. Monies to maintain even the radio links with the outlying settlements were no longer available. The United Planets had ceased to exist two years previously. There was no all-human forum addressing the problems of the species; the Council of Governments (COG) would not be formed for five more years. The two remaining colonies struggled vainly to avoid death.

In the following year, 2144, the last significant manned space mission of the time period took place. The mission was a rescue sortie piloted by an amazing Mexican woman named Benita Garcia. Using a jerryrigged spacecraft thrown together from old parts, Ms. Garcia and her three-man crew somehow managed to reach the geosynchronous orbit of the lame cruiser *James Martin*, the final interplanetary transport vehicle in service, and save twenty-four members from the crew of a hundred women and children being repatriated from Mars. In every space historian's mind, the rescue of the passengers on the *James Martin* marked the end of an era. Within six more months the two remaining space stations were abandoned and no human lifted off the Earth, bound for orbit, until almost forty years later.

By 2145 the struggling world had managed to see the importance of some of the international organizations neglected and maligned at the beginning of The Great Chaos. The most talented members of mankind, after having eschewed personal political involvement during the benign early decades of the century, began to understand that it would only be through the collective skills of the brightest and most capable humans that any semblance of civilized life could ever be restored. At first the monumental cooperative efforts that resulted were only modestly successful; but they rekindled the fundamental optimism of the human spirit and started the renewal process. Slowly, ever so slowly, the elements of human civilization were put back into place.

It was still another two years before the general recovery finally showed up in economic statistics. By 2147 the Gross World Product had dwindled to 7 percent of its level six years earlier. Unemployment in the developed nations averaged 35 percent; in some of the undeveloped nations the combination of unemployed and underemployed amounted to 90 percent of the population. It is estimated that as many as one hundred million people starved to death during the awful summer of 2142 alone, when a great drought and concomitant famine girdled the world in the tropical regions. The combination of an astronomical death rate from many causes and a minuscule birthrate (for who wanted to bring a child into such a hopeless world?) caused the world's population to drop by almost a billion in the decade ending in 2150.

The experience of The Great Chaos left a permanent scar on an entire generation. As the years passed, and the children born after its conclusion reached adolescence, they were confronted by parents who were cautious to the point of phobia. Life as a teenager in the 2160s and even the 2170s was very strict. The memories of the terrible traumas of their youth during The Chaos haunted the adult generation and made them extremely rigid in their application of parental discipline. To them life was not a joyride at an amusement park. It was a deadly serious affair and only through a combination of solid values, self-control, and a steady commitment to a worthwhile goal was there a chance to achieve happiness.

The society that emerged in the 2170s was therefore dramatically different from the freewheeling laissez-faireism of fifty years earlier. Many very old, established institutions, among them the nation-state, the Roman Catholic church, and the English monarchy, had enjoyed a renaissance during the half century interim. These institutions had prospered because they had adapted quickly and taken leadership positions in the restructuring that followed The Chaos.

By the late 2170s, when a semblance of stability had returned to the planet, interest in space began to build again. A new generation of observation and communication satellites was launched by the reconstituted International Space Agency, one of the administrative arms of the COG. At first the space activity was cautious and the budgets were very small. Only the developed nations participated actively. When piloted flights recommenced and were successful, a modest schedule of missions was planned for the decade of the 2190s. A new Space Academy to train cosmonauts for those missions opened in 2188 and had its first graduates four years later.

On Earth growth was achingly slow but regular and predictable for most of the twenty years preceding the discovery of the second Raman spaceship in 2196. In a technological sense, mankind was at approximately the same overall level of development in 2196 as it had been, sixty-six years earlier, when the first extraterrestrial craft had appeared. Recent spaceflight experience was much less, to be certain, at the time of the second encounter; however, in certain critical technical areas like medicine and information management, the human society of the last decade of the twenty-second century was considerably more advanced than it had been in 2130. In one other component the civilizations encountered by the two Raman spacecraft were markedly different: Many of the human beings alive in 2196, especially those who were older and held the policy-making positions in the governing structure, had lived through some of the very painful years of The Great Chaos. They knew the meaning of the word "fear." And that powerful word shaped their deliberations as they debated the priorities that would guide a human mission to rendezvous with Rama II.

6
LA SIGNORA SABATINI

"So you were working on your doctorate in physics at SMU when your husband made his famous prediction about supernova 2191a?"

Elaine Brown was sitting in a large soft chair in her living room. She was dressed in a stark brown suit, sexless, with a high-collar blouse. She looked stiff and anxious, as if she were ready for the interview to be completed.

"I was in my second year and David was my dissertation adviser," she said carefully, her eyes glancing furtively at her husband. He was across the room, watching the proceedings from behind the cameras. "David worked very closely with his graduate students. Everybody knew that. It was one of the reasons why I chose SMU for my graduate work."

Francesca Sabatini looked beautiful. Her long blond hair was flowing freely over her shoulders. She was wearing an expensive white silk blouse, trimmed by a royal blue scarf neatly folded around her neck. Her lounging pants were the same color as the scarf. She was sitting in a second chair next to Elaine. Two coffee cups were on the small table between them.

"Dr. Brown was married at the time, wasn't he? I mean during the period when he was your adviser."

Elaine reddened perceptibly as Francesca finished her question. The Italian journalist continued to smile at her, a disarmingly ingenuous smile, as if the question she had just asked was as simple and straightforward as two plus two. Mrs. Brown hesitated, drew a breath, and then stammered slightly in giving her response. "In the beginning, yes, I believe that he still was," she answered. "But his divorce was final before I finished my degree." She stopped again and then her face brightened. "He gave me an engagement ring for a graduation present," she said awkwardly.

Francesca Sabatini studied her subject. *I could easily tear you apart on that reply,* she thought rapidly. *With just a couple more questions. But that would not serve my purpose.*

"Okay, cut," Francesca blurted out suddenly. "That's a wrap. Let's take a look and then you can put all the equipment back in the truck." The lead cameraman walked over to the side of robot camera number one, which had been programmed to stay in a close-up on Francesca, and entered three commands into the miniature keyboard on the side of the camera housing. Meanwhile, because Elaine had risen from her seat, robot camera number two was automatically backing away on its tripod legs and retracting its zoom lens. Another cameraman motioned to Elaine to stand still until he was able to disconnect the second camera.

Within seconds the director had programmed the automatic monitoring equipment to replay the last five minutes of the interview. The output of all three cameras was shown simultaneously, split screen, the composite picture of both Francesca and Elaine occupying the center of the monitor with the tapes from the two close-up cameras on either side. Francesca was a consummate professional. She could tell quickly that she had the material she needed for this portion of the show. Dr. David Brown's wife, Elaine, was young, intelligent, earnest, plain, and not comfortable with the attention being focused on her. And it was all clearly there in the camera memory.

While Francesca was wrapping up the details with her crew and arranging to have the annotated interview composite delivered to her hotel at the Dallas Transportation Complex before her flight in the morning, Elaine Brown came back into the living room with a standard robot server, two different kinds of cheese, a bottle of wine, and plenty of glasses for everyone. Francesca glimpsed a frown on David Brown's face as Elaine announced that there would now be "a small party" to celebrate the end of the interview. The crew and Elaine gathered around the robot and the wine. David excused himself and walked out of the living room into the long hall that connected the back of the house, where all the bedrooms were, with the living quarters in the front. Francesca followed him.

"Excuse me, David," she said. He turned around, his impatience clear. "Don't forget that we still have some unfinished business. I promised an answer to Schmidt and Hagenest upon my return to Europe. They are anxious to proceed with the project."

"I haven't forgotten," he replied. "I just want to make certain first that your friend Reggie is finished interviewing my children." He heaved a sigh. "There are times when I wish I was a total unknown in the world."

Francesca walked up close to him. "I don't believe that for a minute," she said, her eyes fixed on his. "You're just nervous today because you can't control what your wife and children are saying to Reggie and me. And nothing is more important to you than control."

Dr. Brown started to reply but was interrupted by a shriek of "*Mommeee*" reverberating down the hall from its origin in a distant bedroom. Within seconds a small boy, six or seven years old, swept past David and Francesca and raced pell-mell into the arms of his mother, who was now standing in the doorway connecting the hall and the living room. Some of Elaine's wine sloshed out of her glass from the force of the collision with her son; she unconsciously licked it off her hand as she sought to comfort the little boy.

"What is it, Justin?" she asked.

"That black man broke my dog," Justin whined between sobs. "He kicked it in the butt and now I can't make it work."

The little boy pointed back down the hall. Reggie Wilson and a teenage girl—tall, thin, very serious—were walking toward the rest of the group. "Dad," said the girl, her eyes imploring David for help, "Mr. Wilson was talking to me about my pin collection when that damned robot dog came in and bit him on the leg. After peeing on him first. Justin had programmed him to make mischief—"

"She's lying," the crying little boy interrupted her with a shout. "She doesn't like Wally. She's never liked Wally."

Elaine had one hand on the back of her nearly hysterical son and the other firmly around the stem of her wineglass. She would have been unsettled by the scene even if she hadn't noticed the disapproval she was receiving from her husband. She quaffed the wine and put the glass on a nearby bookshelf. "There, there, Justin," she said, looking embarrassed, "calm down and tell Mom what happened."

"That black man doesn't like me. And I don't like him. Wally knew it, so he bit him. Wally always protects me."

The girl, Angela, became more agitated. "I knew something like this would happen. When Mr. Wilson was talking to me, Justin kept coming into my room and interrupting us, showing Mr. Wilson his games, his pets, his trophies, and even his clothes. Eventually Mr. Wilson had to speak sharply to him. Next thing we know Wally is running wild and Mr. Wilson has to defend himself."

"She's a liar, Mom. A big liar. Tell her to stop—"

Dr. David Brown had had enough of this commotion. *"Elaine,"* he shouted angrily above the din, "get . . . *him* . . . out of here." He turned to his daughter as his wife pulled the weeping little boy through the door into the living room. "Angela," he said, his anger now raw and unconcealed, "I thought I told you not to fight with Justin today under any circumstances."

The girl recoiled from her father's attack. Tears welled up in her eyes. She started to say something but Reggie Wilson walked between her and her father. "Excuse me, Dr. Brown," he interceded, "Angela really didn't do anything. Her story is basically correct. She—"

"Look, Wilson," David Brown said sharply, "if you don't mind, I can handle my own family." He paused a moment to calm his anger. "I'm terribly sorry for all this confusion," he continued in a subdued tone, "but it will all be finished in another minute or so." The look he gave his daughter was cold and unkind. "Go back to your room, Angela. I'll talk to you later. Call your mother and tell her that I want her to pick you up before dinner."

Francesca Sabatini watched with great interest as the entire scene unfolded. She saw David Brown's frustration, Elaine's lack of self-confidence. *This is perfect,* Francesca thought, *even better than I might have hoped. He will be very easy.*

*   *   *

The sleek silver train cruised the North Texas countryside at two hundred and fifty kilometers per hour. Within
minutes the lights from the Dallas Transportation Complex appeared on the horizon. The DTC covered a mammoth area, almost twenty-five square kilometers. It was
part airport, part train station, part small city. Originally
constructed in 2185 both to handle the burgeoning long-
distance air traffic and to provide an easy nexus for trans-
ferring passengers to the high-speed train system, it had
grown, like other similar transportation centers around the
world, into an entire community. More than a thousand
people, most of whom worked at the DTC and found life
easier when there was no commute, lived in the apartments that formed a semicircle around the shopping center south of the main terminal. The terminal itself housed
four major hotels, seventeen restaurants, and over a hundred different shops, including a branch of the chic Donatelli
fashion chain.

"I was nineteen at the time," the young man was saying
to Francesca as the train approached the station, "and had
had a very sheltered upbringing. I learned more about
love and sex in that ten weeks, watching your series on
television, than I had learned in my whole life before. I
just wanted to thank you for that program."

Francesca accepted the compliments gracefully. She was
accustomed to being recognized when she was in public.
When the train stopped and she descended onto the platform, Francesca smiled again at the young man and his
date. Reggie Wilson offered to carry her camera equipment as they walked toward the people mover that would
take them to the hotel. "Does it ever bother you?" he
asked. She looked at him quizzically. "All the attention,
being a public figure?" he added in explanation.

"No," she answered, "of course not." She smiled to
herself. *Even after six months this man does not understand me. Maybe he's too engrossed with himself to figure
out that some women are as ambitious as men.*

"I knew that your two television series had been popular," Reggie was saying, "before I met you during the
personnel screening exercises. But I had no idea that it

would be impossible to go out to a restaurant or to be seen in a public place without running into one of your fans."

Reggie continued to chat as the people mover eased out of the train station and into the shopping center. Near the track at one end of the enclosed mall a large group of people were milling around outside a theater. The marquee proclaimed that the production inside was *In Any Weather*, by the American playwright Linzey Olsen.

"Did you ever see that play?" Reggie idly asked Francesca. "I saw the movie when it first came out," he continued without waiting for her to answer, "about five years ago. Helen Caudill and Jeremy Temple. Before she was really big. It was a strange story, about two people who had to share a hotel room during a snowstorm in Chicago. They're both married. They fall in love while talking about their failed expectations. As I said, it was a weird play."

Francesca was not listening. A boy who reminded her of her cousin Roberto had climbed into the car just in front of them at the first stop in the shopping center. His skin and hair were dark, his facial features handsomely chiseled. *How long has it been since I have seen Roberto?* she wondered. *Must be three years now. It was down in Positano with his wife, Maria.* Francesca sighed and remembered earlier days, from long ago. She could see herself laughing and running on the streets of Orvieto. She was nine or ten, still innocent and unspoiled. Roberto was fourteen. They were playing with a soccer ball in the piazza in front of Il Duomo. She had loved to tease her cousin. He was so gentle, so unaffected. Roberto was the only good thing from her childhood.

The people mover stopped outside the hotel. Reggie was looking at her with a fixed stare. Francesca realized that he had just asked her a question. "Well?" he said, as they descended from their car.

"I'm sorry, dear," she answered. "I was daydreaming again. What did you ask?"

"I didn't know I was that boring," Reggie said without humor. He turned dramatically to ensure that she was paying attention. "What choice did you make for dinner tonight? I had narrowed it down to Chinese or Cajun."

At that particular moment the thought of having dinner

with Reggie did not appeal to Francesca. "I'm very tired tonight," she said. "I think I'll just eat by myself in the room and do a little work afterward." She could have predicted the hurt look on his face. She reached up and kissed him lightly on the lips. "You can come by my room for a nightcap about ten."

Once inside her hotel suite, Francesca's first action was to activate her computer terminal and check for messages. She had four altogether. The printed menu told her the originator of each message, the time of its transmission, the duration of the message, and its urgency priority. The Urgency Priority Network (UPN) was a new innovation of International Communications, Inc., one of the three surviving communications companies that were finally flourishing again after massive consolidation during the middle years of the century. A UPN user entered his daily schedule early in the morning and identified what priority messages could interrupt which activities. Francesca had chosen to accept forwarding of only Priority One (Acute Emergency) messages to the terminal at David Brown's house; the taping of David and his family had to be accomplished in one day and she had wanted to minimize the chances of an interruption and delay. The rest of her messages had been retained at the hotel.

She had a single Priority Two message, three minutes long, from Carlo Bianchi. Francesca frowned, entered the proper codes into the terminal, and turned on the video monitor. A suave middle-aged Italian dressed in après-ski clothes, sitting on a couch with a burning fireplace behind him, came into view. "*Buon giorno, cara*," he greeted her. After allowing the video camera to pan around the living room at his new villa in Cortina d'Ampezzo, Signor Bianchi came right to the point. Why was she refusing to appear in the advertisements for his summer line of sportswear? His company had offered her an incredible amount of money and had even tailored the advertising campaign to pick up on the space theme. The spots would not be shown until after the Newton mission would be over, so there was no conflict with her ISA agreements. Carlo acknowledged that they had had some differences in the past, but according to him they were many years ago. He needed an answer in a week.

Screw you, Carlo, Francesca thought, surprised at the intensity of her reactions. There were few people in the world who could upset Francesca, but Carlo Bianchi was one of them. She entered the necessary commands to record a message to her agent, Darrell Bowman, in London. "Hi Darrell. It's Francesca in Dallas. Tell that weasel Bianchi I wouldn't do his ads even if he offered me ten million marks. And by the way, since I understand that his main competition these days is Donatelli, why don't you find their advertising director, Gabriela something or other, I met her once in Milano, and let her know that I would be happy to do something for them after Project Newton is over. April or May." She paused for a moment. "That's it. Back in Rome tomorrow night. My best to Heather."

Francesca's longest message was from her husband, Alberto, a tall, graying, distinguished executive almost sixty years old. Alberto ran the Italian division of Schmidt and Hagenest, the multimedia German conglomerate that owned, among other things, over one third of the free newspapers and magazines in Europe as well as the leading commercial television networks in both Germany and Italy. In his transmission Alberto was sitting in the den in their home, wearing a rich charcoal suit and sipping a brandy. His tone was warm, familiar, but more like a father than a husband. He told Francesca that her long interview with Admiral Otto Heilmann had been on the news throughout Europe that day, that he had enjoyed her comments and insights as always, but that he had thought Otto came across as an egomaniac. *Not surprising,* Francesca had mused when she heard her husband's comment, *since he absolutely is. But he is often useful to me.*

Alberto shared some good news about one of his children (Francesca had three stepchildren, all of whom were older than she) before telling her that he missed her and was looking forward to seeing her the next night. *Me too,* Francesca thought before responding to his message. *It is comfortable living with you. I have both freedom and security.*

*   *   *

Four hours later Francesca was standing outside on her balcony, smoking a cigarette in the cold Texas December air. She was wrapped tightly in the thick robe supplied to the rooms by the hotel. *At least it's not like California,* she thought to herself as she pulled a deep drag into her lungs. *At least in Texas some of the hotels do have smoking balconies. Those zealots on the American West Coast would make smoking a felony if they could.*

She walked over to the side of the railing so that she would have a better view of a supersonic airliner approaching the airport from the west. In her mind's eye she was inside the plane, as she would be the next day on her flight home to Rome. She imagined that this particular flight had come from Tokyo, the undisputed economic capital of the world before The Great Chaos. After being devastated by their lack of raw materials during the lean years in the middle of the century, the Japanese were now prosperous again as the world returned to a free market. Francesca watched the plane land and then looked up at the sky full of stars above her. She took another pull on her cigarette and then followed the exhaled smoke as it drifted slowly away from her into the air.

And so, Francesca, she reflected, *now comes what may be your greatest assignment. A chance to become immortal? At least I should be remembered a long time as one of the Newton crew.* Her mind turned to the Newton mission itself and briefly conjured up images of fantastic creatures who might have created the pair of gargantuan spaceships and sent them to visit the solar system. But her thoughts jumped back quickly to the real world, to the contracts that David Brown had signed just before she had left his home that afternoon.

That makes us partners, my esteemed Dr. Brown. And completes the first phase of my plan. And unless I miss my guess, that was a gleam of interest in your eyes today. Francesca had given David a perfunctory kiss when they had finished discussing and signing the contracts. They had been alone together in his study. For a moment she had thought he was going to return the kiss with a more meaningful one.

Francesca finished her cigarette, stubbed it out in the ashtray, and went back into her hotel room. As soon as she opened the door she could hear the sound of heavy breathing. The oversized bed was in disarray and a naked Reggie Wilson was lying across it on his back, his regular snores disturbing the silence of the suite. *You have great equipment, my friend,* she commented silently, *both for life and for lovemaking. But neither is an athletic contest. You would be more interesting if there was some subtlety, perhaps even a little finesse.*

7
PUBLIC RELATIONS

The solitary eagle soared high above the marshes in the early morning light. It banked on a gust of wind coming from the ocean and turned north along the coast. Far below the eagle, starting at the light brown and white sands beside the ocean and continuing through the collection of islands and rivers and bays that stretched for miles toward the western horizon, an intermittent complex of diverse buildings connected by paved roads broke up the grassland and swamp. Seventy-five years earlier, the Kennedy Spaceport had been one of a half dozen locations on the Earth where travelers could disembark from their high-speed trains and airplanes to catch a shuttle flight up to one of the LEO (Low Earth Orbit) space stations. But The Great Chaos had changed the spaceport into a ghostly reminder of a once flourishing culture. Its portals and fancy connecting passageways were abandoned for years to the grasses, water birds, alligators, and ubiquitous insects of Central Florida.

In the 2160s, after twenty years of complete atrophy, the reactivation of the spaceport had begun. It had been used first as an airport and then had evolved again into a general transportation center serving the Florida Atlantic coast. When launches to space recommenced in the mid-2170s, it was natural that the old Kennedy launch pads would be recommissioned. By December of 2199 more than half of the old spaceport had been refurbished to handle the steadily growing traffic between Earth and space.

From one of the windows of his temporary office Valeriy Borzov watched the magnificent eagle glide gracefully back to its nest high in one of the few tall trees within the center. He loved birds. He had been fascinated by them for years, beginning in his early boyhood in China. In his most vivid recurring dream General Borzov was always living on an amazing planet where the skies swarmed with flying creatures. He could still remember asking his father if there had been any flying biots inside the first Rama spacecraft and then being acutely disappointed with the reply.

General Borzov heard the sound of a large transport vehicle and looked out his west-facing window. Across the way, in front of the test facility, the propulsion module that would be used by both Newton vehicles was emerging from its test complex, carried on a huge platform moving on multiple tracks. The ·repaired module, sent back to the subsystem test area because of a problem with its ion controller, would be placed that afternoon inside a cargo shuttle and transferred to the spacecraft assembly facility at space station LEO-2, where it would be retrofitted prior to the final integrated vehicle tests just before Christmas. Both of the two Newton flight spacecraft were currently undergoing final checkout and test at LEO-2. All of the simulation exercises for the cosmonauts, however, were conducted over at LEO-3 with the backup equipment. The cosmonauts would only use the actual flight systems at LEO-2 during the last week before launch.

On the south side of the building, an electric bus pulled to a stop outside the office complex and discharged a small handful of people. One of the passengers was a blond woman wearing a long-sleeved yellow blouse with vertical black stripes and a pair of black silk pants. She walked with an effortless grace over to the building entrance. General Borzov admired her from a distance, reminding himself that Francesca had been a successful model before becoming a television journalist. He wondered what it was that she wanted and why she had insisted on seeing him privately before the medical briefing this morning.

A minute later he greeted her at the door to his office. "Good morning, Signora Sabatini," he said.

"Still so formal, General," she replied, laughing, "even when there's only the two of us? You and the two Japanese men are the only members of the team who refuse to call me Francesca." She noticed that he was staring strangely at her. She looked down at her clothing to see if something was wrong. "What's the matter?" she asked him after a momentary hesitation.

"It must be your blouse," General Borzov answered with a start. "For just a moment I had the distinct impression that you were a tiger poised to pounce on a hapless antelope or gazelle. Maybe it's old age. Or my mind has started playing tricks on me." He invited her to come into his office.

"I have had men tell me before that I resemble a cat. But never a tiger." Francesca sat down in the chair beside the general's desk. She meowed with a mischievous smile. "I'm just a harmless tabby housecat."

"I don't believe that for a moment," Borzov said with a chuckle. "Many adjectives can be used to describe you, Francesca, but harmless would never be one of them." He suddenly became very businesslike. "Now, what can I do for you? You said that you had something very important to discuss with me that absolutely could not wait."

Francesca pulled a large sheet of paper out of her soft briefcase and handed it to General Borzov. "This is the press schedule for the project," she said. "I reviewed it in detail only yesterday with both the public information office and the world television networks. Notice that of the in-depth personal interviews with the cosmonauts, only five have already been completed. Four more were originally scheduled for this month. But notice also that when you added that extra three-day simulation to this coming set of exercises, you wiped out the time that had been allotted to interview Wakefield and Turgenyev."

She paused for a moment to make sure he was following her. "We can still catch Takagishi next Saturday and will tape the O'Tooles on Christmas Eve in Boston. But both Richard and Irina say that they now have no time for their interviews. In addition, we still have an old problem: Neither you nor Nicole is scheduled at all—"

"You insisted on a meeting at seven-thirty this morning to discuss this *press* schedule," Borzov interrupted, his voice clearly conveying the relative importance that he assigned to such activities.

"Among other things," Francesca answered nonchalantly. She ignored the implied criticism in his comment. "Of the people on this mission," she continued, "the polls show that the public has the greatest interest in you, me, Nicole des Jardins, and David Brown. So far, I have been unable to pin you down on a date for your personal interview and Madame des Jardins says that she does not intend to have one at all. The networks are unhappy. My prelaunch coverage is going to be incomplete. I need some help from you."

Francesca looked directly at General Borzov. "I am asking you to cancel the additional simulation, to set a definite time for your personal interview, and to talk to Nicole on my behalf."

He frowned. The general was both angered and annoyed by Francesca's presumption. He was going to tell her that the scheduling of personal publicity interviews was not high on his priority list. But something held him back. Both his sixth sense and a lifetime of experience in dealing with people told him to hesitate, that there was more to this discussion than he had yet heard. He temporized by changing the subject.

"Incidentally, I must tell you that I am growing increasingly concerned about the lavish scope of this New Year's Eve party that your friends in the Italian government/business coalition are hosting. I know we agreed at the beginning of our training that we would participate, as a group, in that one social function. But I had no idea that it was going to be billed as the party of the century, as it was called last week by one of those American personality magazines. You know all those people; can't you do something to reduce the scope of the party?"

"The gala was another item on my agenda," Francesca replied, carefully avoiding the thrust of his comment. "I need your assistance there as well. Four of the Newton cosmonauts now say that they do not plan to attend and two or three more have suggested that they may have other commitments—even though we all agreed to the party back in March. Takagishi and Yamanaka want to celebrate the holiday with their families in Japan and Richard Wakefield tells me that he has made reservations to go scuba diving in the Cayman Islands. And then there's that Frenchwoman again, who simply says that she's not coming and refuses to offer any kind of explanation."

Borzov could not suppress a grin. "Why are you having such a hard time with Nicole des Jardins? I would think that since both of you are women, you would be able to speak to her more easily than the others."

"She is entirely unsympathetic with the role of the press in this mission. She has told me so several times. And she is very stubborn about her privacy." Francesca shrugged her shoulders. "But the public is absolutely fascinated with her. After all, not only is she a doctor and a linguist and a former Olympic champion, but also she is the daughter of a famous novelist and the mother of a fourteen-year-old daughter, despite never having been married—"

Valeriy Borzov was looking at his watch. "Just for my information," he interrupted, "how many more items are on your 'agenda,' as you call it? We are due in the auditorium in ten more minutes." He smiled back at Francesca. "And I feel compelled to remind you that Madame des Jardins went out of her way today to accommodate your request for press coverage of this briefing."

Francesca studied General Borzov for several seconds. *I think he's ready now,* she thought to herself. *And unless I misjudged him he will understand immediately.* She pulled a small cubic object out of her briefcase and handed it across the desk. "This is the only other item on my agenda," she said.

The Newton commander-in-chief seemed puzzled. He turned the cube over in his hands. "A free-lance journalist sold it to us," Francesca said in a very serious tone. "We were assured it was the only copy in existence."

She paused a moment while Borzov loaded the cube into the appropriate part of his desk computer. He blanched noticeably when the first video segment from the cube appeared on the monitor. He watched the wild rantings of his daughter, Natasha, for about fifteen seconds. "I wanted to keep this out of the hands of the tabloid press," Francesca added softly.

"How long is the tape?" General Borzov asked quietly.

"Almost half an hour," she replied. "I'm the only one who has seen the entire thing."

General Borzov heaved a sigh. This was the moment his wife, Petra, had dreaded ever since it was first made official that he would be the commanding officer of the Newton. The institute director at Sverdlovsk had promised that no reporters would have access to his daughter. Now here was a videotape with a thirty-minute interview with her. Petra would be mortified.

He stared out the window. In his mind he was assessing what would happen to the mission if his daughter's acute schizophrenia were paraded before the public. It would be embarrassing, he conceded, but the mission would not be damaged in any serious way. . . . General Borzov looked across at Francesca. He hated making deals. And he wasn't certain that Francesca herself had not commissioned the interview with Natasha. Nevertheless . . .

Borzov relaxed and forced a smile. "I guess I could thank you," he said, "but somehow it doesn't seem appropriate." He paused for a moment. "I assume I'm expected to show some gratitude."

So far, so good, Francesca thought. She knew better than to say anything just yet.

"All right," the general continued after the lengthy silence, "I will cancel the extra simulation. Others have already complained about it." He turned the data cube over in his hands. "And Petra and I will come to Rome early, as you once suggested, for the personal interview. I will remind all the cosmonauts tomorrow about the party on New Year's Eve and tell them that it is their duty to attend. But neither I nor anyone else can require Nicole des Jardins to talk to you about anything except her work." He stood up abruptly. "Now it's time for us to go to that biometry meeting."

Francesca reached up and kissed him on the cheek. "Thank you, Valeriy," she said.

8

BIOMETRY

The medical briefing had already begun when Francesca and General Borzov arrived. All the rest of the cosmonauts were present, as well as twenty-five or thirty additional engineers and scientists associated with the mission. Four newspaper reporters and a television crew completed the audience. At the front of the small auditorium stood Nicole des Jardins, wearing her gray flight outfit as always, and holding a laser pointer in her hand. To the side of her was a tall Japanese man in a blue dress suit. He was listening carefully to a question from the audience. Nicole interrupted him to acknowledge the new arrivals.

"*Sumimasen*, Hakamatsu-san," she said. "Let me introduce our commander, General Valeriy Borzov of the Soviet Union, as well as the journalist-cosmonaut Francesca Sabatini."

She turned toward the latecomers. "*Dobriy Utra*," Nicole said to the general, quickly nodding a greeting in Francesca's direction as well. "This is the esteemed Dr. Toshiro Hakamatsu," Nicole said. "He designed and developed the biometry system that we are going to use in flight, including the tiny probes that will be inserted into our bodies."

General Borzov extended his hand. "I am glad to meet you, Hakamatsu-san," he said. "Madame des Jardins has made us all very much aware of your outstanding work."

"Thank you," the man replied, bowing in the direction of Borzov after shaking his hand. "It is an honor for me to be part of this project."

Francesca and General Borzov took the two empty seats at the front of the auditorium and the meeting continued. Nicole aimed her pointer at a keyboard on the side of a small podium and a full-scale, multicolored male model of the human cardiovascular system, with veins marked in blue and arteries in red, appeared as a three-dimensional holographic image in the front of the room. Tiny white markers circulating inside the flowing blood vessels indicated the direction and rate of flow. "The Life Sciences Board of the ISA just last week gave final approval to the new Hakamatsu probes as our key health monitoring system for the mission," Nicole was saying. "They withheld their approval until the last minute so that they could properly assess the results of the stress testing, in which the new probes were asked to perform in a wide variety of off-nominal situations. Even under those conditions there was no sign that any rejection mechanisms were triggered in any of the test subjects.

"We are fortunate that we will be able to use this system, for it will make life much easier both for me, as your life science officer, and for you. During the mission you will not be subjected to the routine injection/scanning techniques that have been used on previous projects. These new probes are injected one time, maybe twice at the most during our one-hundred-day mission, and they do not need to be replaced."

"How did the long-term rejection problem get solved?" came a question from another doctor in the audience, interrupting Nicole's train of thought.

"I will discuss that in detail during our splinter session this afternoon," she replied. "For now, it should be sufficient for me to mention that since the key chemistry governing rejection focuses on four or five critical parameters, including acidity, the probes are coated with chemicals that adapt to the local chemistry at the implantation site. In other words, once the probe arrives at its destination, it noninvasively samples its ambient biochemical environment and then exudes a thin coating for itself that is designed to be consistent with the chemistry of the host and thereby avoid rejection.

"But I am getting ahead of myself," Nicole said, turning to face the large model showing blood circulation in the human being. "The family of probes will be inserted here, in the left arm, and the individual monitors will disperse according to their prescribed guidance programs to thirty-two distinct locales in the body. There they will embed themselves in the host tissue." The inside of the holographic model became animated as she spoke and the audience watched as thirty-two blinking lights started from the left arm and scattered throughout the body. Four went to the brain, three more to the heart, four to the primary glands of the endocrine system, and the remaining twenty-one monitors spread out to assorted locations and organs ranging from the eyes to the fingers and toes.

"Each of the individual probes contains both an array of microscopic sensors to sample important health parameters and a fancy data system that first stores and then transmits the recorded information upon receipt of an enabling command from the scanner. In practice, I would expect to scan each of you and dump all your health telemetry once a day, but the recorders can handle data covering up to four days if necessary." Nicole stopped and looked at the audience. "Are there any questions so far?" she asked.

"Yes," said Richard Wakefield in the front row. "I see how this system gathers trillions of bits of data. But that's the easy part. There's no way you or any other human being could look at all that information. How does the data get synthesized or analyzed so that you can tell if anything irregular is happening?"

"You'd make a great straight man, Richard," Nicole said with a smile. "That's my next subject." She held up a small, flat, thin object with a keyboard on it. "This is a standard programmable scanner that permits the monitored information to be sampled in many different ways. I can call for a full dump from any and/or all channels, or I can request transmission only of warning data . . ."

Nicole saw many confused looks in her audience. "I'd better back up and start this part of the explanation again," she said. "Each measurement made by each instrument has an *expected* range—one that will vary of course from individual to individual—and a much wider *tolerance* range used to identify a true emergency. If a particular measurement only exceeds the expected range, it is entered in the warning file and that specific channel is marked with an alarm identifier. One of my options using the scanner is to read out only these warning lists. If an individual cosmonaut is feeling fine, my normal procedure would be just to see if there are any entries in the warning buffer."

"But if you have a measurement outside the tolerance range," interjected Janos Tabori, who was the backup life science officer, "then watch out. The monitor turns on its emergency transmitter and uses all its internal power to send out a *beep, beep* noise that is frightening. I know. It happened to me during a short test with what turned out to be improper tolerance values. I thought I was dying." His comment caused general laughter. The image of little Janos walking around emitting a high-pitched beep was amusing.

"No system is foolproof," Nicole continued, "and this one is only as good as the set of values that are entered to trigger both the warnings and the emergencies. So you can see why calibration data is essential. We have examined each of your medical histories with extreme care and entered initial values in the monitors. But we must see actual results with the real probes inserted in your bodies. That's the reason for today's activity. We will insert your probe set today, monitor your performance during the four final simulation exercises that begin on Thursday, and then update the trigger values, if necessary, before we actually launch."

There was some involuntary squirming as the cosmonauts thought about the prospect of tiny medical laboratories indefinitely embedded in their critical organs. They were accustomed to the regular investigative probes that were placed in the body to obtain some specific information, like the amount of plaque blocking the arteries, but those probes were temporary. The thought of permanent electronic invasion was disquieting, to say the least. General Michael O'Toole asked two questions that were bothering most of the crew.

"Nicole," he inquired in his usual earnest manner, "can you tell us how you make sure that the probes actually go to the right places. Even more important, what happens if one malfunctions?"

"Of course, Michael," she answered pleasantly. "Re-

member these things will be inside me as well and I had
to ask the same questions." Nicole des Jardins was in her
middle thirties. Her skin was a shiny copper brown, her
eyes dark brown and almond-shaped, her hair a luxurious
jet black. There was an unshakable self-confidence radiating from her that was sometimes mistaken for arrogance.
"You won't leave the clinic today until we have verified
that all the probes are properly positioned," she was saying.
"Based on recent past experience, one or two of you may
have a monitor wander off course. It is an easy matter to
track it with the lab equipment and then send overwrite
commands as necessary to move it to the proper spot.

"As far as the malfunction issue is concerned, there are
several levels of fault protection. First, each specific monitor tests its own battery of sensors more than twenty times
a day. Any individual instrument failing a test is turned off
immediately by the executive software in its own monitor.
In addition, each of the probe packages undergoes a full
and rigorous self-test twice a day. Failure of self-test is one
of many fault conditions that causes the monitor to secrete
chemicals causing self-destruction, with eventual harmless
absorption by the body. Lest you become unduly concerned, we have rigorously verified all these fault paths
with test subjects during the past year."

Nicole wound up her presentation and stood quietly in
front of her colleagues. "Any more questions?" she asked.
After a few seconds' hesitation she continued, "Then I
need a volunteer to walk up here beside the robot nurse
and be inoculated. My personal probe set was injected
and verified last week. Who wants to be next?"

Francesca stood up. "All right, we'll start with *la bella
signora* Sabatini," Nicole said with uncharacteristic flare.
She gestured to the television personnel. "Focus those
cameras on the tracer simulation. It's quite a show when
these electronic bugs swarm through the bloodstream."

9
DIASTOLIC IRREGULARITY

Through the window Nicole could barely discern the Siberian snowfields in the oblique December light. They were more than fifty thousand feet below her. The supersonic plane was slowing now as it moved south toward Vladivostok and the island of Japan. Nicole yawned. After only three hours of sleep, it would be a fight all day to keep her body awake. It was almost ten in the morning in Japan but back home at Beauvois, in the Loire Valley not far from Tours, her daughter, Genevieve, still had four more hours of sleep until her alarm would awaken her at seven o'clock.

The video monitor in the back of the seat in front of Nicole automatically turned on and reminded her that in only fifteen minutes the plane would land at the Kansai Transportation Center. The lovely Japanese girl on the screen suggested that now would be an excellent time to make or confirm ground transportation and housing arrangements. Nicole activated the communication system in her seat and a thin rectangular tray with a keyboard and small display area slid in front of her. In less than a minute Nicole arranged both her train ride to Kyoto and her electric trolley passage from there to her hotel. She used her Universal Credit Card (UCC) to pay for all transactions, after first correctly identifying herself by indicating that her mother's maiden name was Anawi Tiasso. When she was finished a small printed schedule listing her train and trolley identifiers, along with the times of arrival and transit (she would reach her hotel at 11:14 A.M. Japanese time), popped out of one end of the tray.

As the plane prepared for its landing, Nicole thought about the reason for her sudden trip one third of the way around the world. Just twenty-four hours ago she had been planning to spend this day around her home, alternating some office work in the morning with some language practice for Genevieve in the afternoon. It was the beginning of the holiday break for the cosmonauts and, except for that stupid party in Rome at the end of the year, Nicole was supposedly free until she had to report to LEO-3 on January 8. But while she had been sitting in her office at home the previous morning, routinely checking the biometry from the final set of simulations, Nicole had come across a curious phenomenon. She had been studying Richard Wakefield's heart and blood pressure during a variable gravity test and had not understood a particularly rapid surge in his pulse rate. She had then decided to check Dr. Takagishi's detailed heart biometry for comparison, since he had been engaged in a strenuous physical activity with Richard at the time of the pulse surge.

What she had found when she had examined a full dump of Takagishi's heart information had been an even bigger surprise. The Japanese professor's diastolic expansion was decidedly irregular, maybe éven pathological. But no warnings had been issued by the probe and no data channels had been alarmed. What was going on? Had she detected a malfunction in the Hakamatsu system?

An hour's worth of detective work had resulted in the identification of more peculiarities. During the full set of simulations, there had been four separate intervals during which Takagishi's problem had occurred. The abnormal behavior was sporadic and intermittent. Sometimes the extra long diastole, reminiscent of a valve problem during the filling of the heart with blood, would not appear for as long as thirty-eight hours. However, the fact that it did recur four different times suggested that there was definitely an abnormality of some kind.

What had mystified Nicole was not the raw data itself—it was the failure of the system to trigger the proper alarms in the presence of the wildly irregular observations. As part of her analysis she had traced laboriously through the Takagishi medical history, paying special attention to the cardiology report. She had found no hint of any kind of abnormality, so had convinced herself that she was seeing a sensor error and not a true medical problem.

So if the system was working correctly, she had reasoned, *the onset of the long diastole should have immediately sent the heart monitor outside the expected range and triggered an alarm. But it didn't. Neither the first time nor any other time. Is it possible that we have a double failure here? If so, how did the unit continue to pass self-test?*

At first Nicole had thought about phoning one of her assistants in the life science office at ISA to discuss the anomaly she had found, but she decided instead, since it was a holiday for ISA, to telephone Dr. Hakamatsu in Japan. That phone call to him had completely bewildered her. He had told her flatly that the phenomenon she had observed must have been in the patient, that no combination of component failures in his probe could have produced such strange results. "But then why were there no entries in the warning file?" she had asked the Japanese electronics designer.

"Because no expected range values were exceeded," he answered confidently. "For some reason an extremely wide expected range must have been entered for this particular cosmonaut. Have you looked at his medical history?"

Later on in the conversation, when Nicole told Dr. Hakamatsu that the unexplained data had actually come from the probes inside one of his countrymen, namely cosmonaut-scientist Takagishi, the usually restrained engineer had actually shouted into the phone. "Wonderful," he had said, "then I'll be able to clear up this mystery in a hurry. I'll contact Takagishi-san over at Kyoto University and let you know what I find."

Three hours later Nicole's video monitor had revealed the somber face of Dr. Shigeru Takagishi. "Madame des Jardins," he had said very politely, "I understand that you have been talking with my colleague Hakamatsu-san about my biometry output during the simulations. Would you be kind enough to explain to me what you have found?"

Nicole had then presented all the information to her fellow cosmonaut, concealing nothing and expressing her personal belief that the source of the erroneous data had indeed been a probe malfunction.

A long silence followed Nicole's explanation. At length

the worried Japanese scientist had spoken again. "Haka-matsu-san just visited me here at the university and checked out the probe set inside me. He will report that he found no problems with his electronics." Takagishi had then paused, seemingly deep in thought. "Madame des Jardins," he had said a few seconds later, "I would like to ask you a favor. It is a matter of the utmost importance to me. Could you possibly come to see me in Japan in the very near future? I would like to talk with you personally and explain something that may be related to my irregular biometry data."

There had been an earnestness in Takagishi's face that Nicole could neither overlook nor misinterpret. He was clearly imploring her to help him. Without asking any more questions, she had agreed to visit him immediately. A few minutes later she had reserved a seat on the over-night supersonic flight from Paris to Osaka.

"It was never bombed during the great war with Amer-ica," Takagishi said, waving his arms at the city of Kyoto spread out below them, "and it suffered almost no damage when the hoodlums took over for seven months in 2141. I admit that I am prejudiced," he said, smiling, "but to me Kyoto is the most beautiful city in the world."

"Many of my countrymen feel that way about Paris," Nicole answered. She pulled her coat tightly around her. The air was cold and damp. It felt as if it might snow at any moment. She was wondering when her associate was going to start talking about their business. She had not flown five thousand miles for a tour of the city, although she did admit that this Kyomizu Temple set among the trees on a hillside overlooking the city was certainly a magnificent spot.

"Let's have some tea," Takagishi said. He led her to one of the several outside tearooms flanking the main part of the old Buddhist temple. *Now*, Nicole said to herself as she stifled a yawn, *he's going to tell me what this is all about*. Takagishi had met her at the hotel when she had arrived. He had suggested that she have some lunch and a short nap before he returned. After he had picked her up at three o'clock, they had come directly to this temple.

He poured the thick Japanese tea into the two cups and waited for Nicole to take a sip. The hot liquid warmed her mouth even though she didn't care for the bitter taste. "Madame," Takagishi began, "you are doubtless wondering why I have asked you to come all the way to Japan on such short notice. You see," he spoke slowly but with great intensity, "all my life I have dreamed that perhaps another Rama spacecraft would return while I was still alive. During my studies at the university and during my many years of research I was preparing myself for one single event, the return of the Ramans. On that March morning in 2197 when Alastair Moore called me to say that the latest images from Excalibur indicated that we had another extraterrestrial visitor, I nearly wept with joy. I knew immediately that the ISA would mount a mission to visit the spaceship. I resolved to be part of that mission."

The Japanese scientist took a drink from his tea and looked to his left, out across the manicured green trees and the slopes above the city. "When I was a boy," he continued, his careful English barely audible, "I would climb these hills on a clear night and stare into the sky, searching for the home of the special intelligence that had created that incomparable giant machine. Once I came with my father and we huddled together in the cold night air, looking at the stars, while he told me what it had been like in his village during the days of the first Rama encounter twelve years before I was born. I believed on that night"—he turned to look at Nicole and she could again see the passion in his eyes—"and I still believe today, that there was some reason for that visit, some purpose for the appearance of that awesome spaceship. I have studied all the data from that first encounter, hoping to find a clue that would explain why it came. Nothing has been conclusive. I have developed several theories on the subject, but I do not have enough evidence to support any of them."

Again Takagishi stopped talking to drink some of his tea. Nicole had been both surprised and impressed by the depth of feeling he had exhibited. She sat patiently and said nothing while she waited for him to continue. "I knew that I had a good chance to be selected as a cosmonaut," he said, "not only because of my publications, including the *Atlas*, but also because one of my closest associates, Hisanori Akita, was the Japanese representative on the selection board. When the number of scientists remaining in the competition had been reduced to eight and I was one of them, Akita-san suggested to me that it looked as if the two leading contenders were myself and David Brown. You'll recall that up until that time, no physical examinations of any kind had been conducted."

That's right, Nicole remembered. *The potential crew was first reduced to forty-eight and then we were all taken to Heidelberg for the physicals. The German doctors in charge insisted that each of the candidates must pass every single medical criterion. The academy graduates were the first group tested and five out of twenty failed. Including Alain Blamont.*

"When your countryman Blamont, who had already flown half a dozen major missions for the ISA, was disqualified from consideration because of that trivial heart murmur—and the Cosmonaut Selection Board subsequently upheld the doctors by denying his appeal—I completely panicked." The proud Japanese physicist was now staring directly into Nicole's eyes, entreating her to understand. "I was afraid that I was going to lose the most important opportunity of my career because of a minor physical problem that had never before affected any part of my life." He paused to choose his words carefully. "I know that what I did was wrong and dishonorable, but I convinced myself at the time it was all right, that my chance to decipher the greatest puzzle in man's history should not be blocked by a group of small-minded doctors defining acceptable health only in terms of numerical values."

Dr. Takagishi told the rest of his story without embellishment or obvious emotion. The passion he had fleetingly demonstrated during his discussion of the Ramans had vanished. His monotonic recital was crisp and clear. He explained how he had cajoled his family physician into falsifying his medical history and providing him with a new drug that would prevent the occurrence of his diastolic irregularity during the two days of his physical at Heidelberg. Although there had been some risk of deleterious side effects from the new drug, everything went according to plan. Takagishi passed the rigorous physical and was ultimately selected as one of the two mission scientists, along with Dr. David Brown. He had never thought again about the medical issue until about three months ago, when Nicole had first explained to the cosmonauts that she was planning to recommend the usage of the Hakamatsu probe system during the mission instead of the standard temporary probe scans once every week.

"You see," Takagishi explained, his brow now starting to furrow, "under the old mission technique I could have used that same drug once a week and neither you nor any other life science officer would ever have seen my irregularity. But a permanent monitoring system cannot be fooled—the drug is much too dangerous for constant use."

So you somehow worked out a deal with Hakamatsu, Nicole thought, jumping ahead of him in her own mind. *Either with or without his explicit knowledge. And you input expected value ranges that would not trigger in the presence of your abnormality. You hoped that nobody analyzing the tests would call for a full biometry dump.* Now she understood why he had summoned her urgently to Japan. *And you want me to keep your secret.*

"*Watakushi no doryo wa, wakarimas,*" Nicole said kindly, changing into Japanese to show her sympathy for her colleague's anguish. "I can tell how much distress this is causing you. You need not explain in detail how you tampered with the Hakamatsu probes." She paused and watched his face relax. "But if I understand you correctly, what you want is for me to become an accomplice to your deception. You recognize of course that I cannot even consider preserving your secret unless I am absolutely convinced that your minor physical problem, as you call it, represents no possible threat to the mission. Otherwise I would be forced—"

"Madame des Jardins," Takagishi interrupted her, "I have the utmost respect for your integrity. I would never, *never* ask you to keep my heart irregularity out of the record unless you agreed that it was really an insignificant problem." He looked at her in silence for several seconds. "When Hakamatsu first phoned me last evening," he continued quietly, "I thought originally that I would call a press conference and then resign from the project. But while I was thinking about what I would say in my resignation, I kept seeing this image of Professor Brown. He is a brilliant man, my American counterpart, but he is also, in my opinion, too certain of his own infallibility. The most likely replacement for me would be Professor Wolfgang Heinrich from Bonn. He has published many fine papers about Rama but he, like Brown, believes that these celestial visits represent random events, totally without connection in any way to us and our planet." The intensity and passion had returned to his eyes. "I cannot quit now. Unless I have no choice. Both Brown and Heinrich might miss the clue."

Behind Takagishi, on the path that led back to the main wooden building of the temple, three Buddhist monks walked briskly past. Despite the cold, they were dressed lightly in their usual charcoal gray smocks, their feet exposed to the cold in open sandals. The Japanese scientist was proposing to Nicole that they spend the rest of the day at the office of his personal physician, where they could study his complete and uncensored medical history dating back to his childhood. If she would be willing, he added, they would give her a data cube containing all the information to take back to France and study at her leisure.

Nicole, who had been listening intently to Takagishi for almost an hour, momentarily diverted her attention to the three monks now purposefully climbing the stairs in the distance. *Their eyes are so serene*, she thought. *Their lives so free of contradiction. Onemindedness can be a virtue. It makes all the answers easy.* For just a moment she was envious of the monks and their ordered existence. She wondered how well they would handle the dilemma that Dr. Takagishi was presenting her. *He is not one of the space cadets*, she was now thinking, *so his role is not absolutely critical to mission success. And in a sense he is right. The doctors on the project have been too strict. They never should have disqualified Alain. It would be a shame if . . .*

"*Daijobu*," she said before he had finished talking. "I will go with you to see your doctor and if I don't find anything that bothers me, I will take the entire file home with me to study during the holidays." Takagishi's face lit up. "But let me warn you again," she added, "if there is anything in your history that I find questionable, or if I have the slightest shred of evidence that you have withheld any information from me, then I will ask you to resign immediately."

"Thank you, thank you so much," Dr. Takagishi replied, standing and bowing to his female colleague. "Thank you so much," he repeated.

10

THE COSMONAUT
AND THE POPE

General O'Toole could not have slept more than two hours altogether. The combination of excitement and jet lag had kept his mind active all night long. He had studied the lovely bucolic mural on the wall opposite the bed in his hotel room and counted all the animals twice. Unfortunately, he had remained wide awake after he had finished both counts.

He took a deep breath, hoping that it would help him relax. *So why all this nervousness?* he thought. *He is just a man like all the rest on Earth. Well, not exactly.* O'Toole sat up straight in his chair and smiled. It was ten o'clock in the morning and he was sitting in a small anteroom inside the Vatican. He was about to have a private audience with the Vicar of Christ himself, Pope John-Paul V.

During his childhood, Michael O'Toole had often dreamed of someday becoming the first North American pope. "Pope Michael," he had called himself during the long Sunday afternoons when he had studied his catechism alone. As he had repeated the words of his lessons over and over and committed them to memory, he had imagined himself, maybe fifty years in the future, wearing the cassock and papal ring, celebrating mass for thousands in the great churches and stadia of the world. He would inspire the poor, the hopeless, the downtrodden. He would show them how God could lead them to a better life.

As a young man Michael O'Toole had loved all learning, but three subjects had especially intrigued him. He could not read enough about religion, history, and physics. Somehow his facile mind found it easy to jump between these different disciplines. It never bothered him that the epistemologies of religion and physics were one hundred and eighty degrees apart. Michael O'Toole had no difficulty recognizing which questions in life should be answered by physics and which ones by religion.

All three of his favorite scholastic subjects merged in the study of creation. It was, after all, the beginning of everything, including religion, history, and physics. How had it happened? Was God present, as the referee perhaps, for the kickoff of the universe eighteen billion years ago? Wasn't it He who had provided the impetus for the cataclysmic explosion known as the Big Bang that produced all matter out of energy? Hadn't He foreseen that those original pristine hydrogen atoms would coalesce into giant clouds of gas and then collapse under gravitation to become the stars in which would be manufactured the basic chemical building blocks of life?

And I have never lost my fascination for creation, O'Toole said to himself as he waited for his papal audience. *How did it all happen? What is the significance of the particular sequence of events?* He remembered his questions of the priests when he was a teenager. *I probably decided not to become a priest because it would have limited my free access to scientific truth. The church has never been as comfortable as I am with the apparent incompatibilities between God and Einstein.*

An American priest from the Vatican state department had been waiting at his hotel in Rome the previous evening when O'Toole had returned from his day as a tourist. The priest had introduced himself and apologized profusely for not having responded to the letter that General O'Toole had written from Boston in November. It would have "facilitated the process," the priest had remarked in passing, if the general had pointed out in his letter that he was *the* General O'Toole, the Newton cosmonaut. Nevertheless, the priest had continued, the papal schedule had been juggled and the Holy Father would be delighted to see O'Toole the next morning.

As the door to the papal office swung open, the American general instinctively stood up. The priest from the night before walked into the room, looking very nervous, and quickly shook O'Toole's hand. They both glanced toward the doorway, where the pope, wearing his normal white cassock, was concluding a conversation with a member of his staff. John-Paul V came forward into the anteroom, a pleasant smile on his face, and extended his hand toward O'Toole. The cosmonaut automatically dropped to one knee and kissed the papal ring.

"Holy Father," he murmured, astonished at the excited pounding of his heart, "thank you for seeing me. This is indeed a great honor for me."

"For me as well," the pope replied in lightly accented English. "I have been following the activities of you and your colleagues with great interest."

He gestured toward O'Toole and the American general followed the church leader into a grand office with high ceilings. A very large, dark wood desk stood on one side of the room under a life-size portrait of John-Paul IV, the man who had become pope during the darkest days of The Great Chaos and had provided both the world and the church with twenty years of energetic and inspirational leadership. The gifted Venezuelan, a poet and historical scholar in his own right, had demonstrated to the world between 2139 and 2158 how positive a force the organized church could be at a time when virtually every other institution was collapsing and was, therefore, unable to give any succor to the bewildered masses.

The pope sat down on a couch and motioned for O'Toole to sit next to him. The American priest left the room. In front of O'Toole and the pope were great windows that opened onto a balcony overlooking the Vatican gardens some twenty feet below. In the distance O'Toole could see the Vatican museum where he had spent the previous afternoon.

"You wrote in your letter," the Holy Father said, without referring to any notes, "that there were some theological issues that you would like to discuss with me. I assume these are in some way related to your mission."

O'Toole looked at the seventy-year-old Spaniard who was the spiritual leader of a billion Catholics. The pope's skin was olive, his features sharp, his thick black hair now mostly gray. His brown eyes were soft and clear. *He certainly doesn't waste any time*, O'Toole thought, recalling an article in *Catholic* magazine in which one of the leading cardinals in the Vatican administration had praised John-Paul V for his management efficiency.

"Yes, Holy Father," O'Toole said. "As you know, I am about to embark on a journey of the utmost significance for humankind. As a Catholic, I have some questions that I thought it might be helpful for me to discuss with you." He paused for a moment. "I certainly don't expect you to have all the answers. But maybe you can guide me a little with your accumulated wisdom."

The pope nodded and waited for O'Toole to continue. The cosmonaut took a deep breath. "The issue of redemption is one that's bothering me, even though I guess it's just a part of a bigger concern that I have in reconciling the Ramans with our faith."

The pope's brow furrowed and O'Toole could tell that he was not communicating very well. "I have no trouble whatsoever," the general added as an explanation, "with the concept of God creating the Ramans—that's easy to comprehend. But did the Ramans follow a similar pattern of spiritual evolution and therefore need to be redeemed, at some point in their history, like human beings on Earth? And if so, did God send Jesus, or perhaps his Raman equivalent, to save them from their sins? Do we humans thus represent an evolutionary paradigm that has been repeated over and over throughout the universe?"

The pope's smile broadened almost into a grin. "Goodness, General," he said with humor, "you have romped over a vast intellectual territory very quickly. You must know that I do not have fast answers to such profound questions. The church has had its scholars addressing the issues raised by Rama for almost seventy years and, as you would expect, our research has recently intensified because of the discovery of the second spacecraft."

"But what do you personally believe, Your Holiness?" O'Toole persisted. "Did the creatures who made these two incredible space vehicles commit some original sin and also need a savior sometime in their history? Is the story of Jesus unique for us here on Earth, or is it just one small chapter in a book of nearly infinite length that covers all sentient beings and a general requirement for redemption to achieve salvation?"

"I'm not certain," the Holy Father replied after several seconds. "Sometimes it is nearly impossible for me to fathom the existence of other intelligence in any form out there in the rest of the universe. Then, as soon as I acknowledge that it certainly wouldn't look like us, I struggle with images and pictures that sidetrack my thinking from the kinds of theological questions that you have raised this morning." He paused for a moment, reflecting. "But most of the time I imagine that the Ramans too had lessons to learn in the beginning, that God did not create them perfect either, and that at some time in their development He must have sent them Jesus—"

The pope interrupted himself and looked intently at General O'Toole. "Yes," he continued softly, "I said Jesus. You asked me what I believed personally. To me Jesus is both the true savior and the only son of God. It would be He who would be sent to the Ramans also, albeit in a different guise."

O'Toole's face had brightened at the end of the pontiff's remarks. "I agree with you, Holy Father," he said excitedly. "And therefore all intelligence is united, everywhere throughout the universe, by a similar spiritual experience. In a very, very real sense, assuming that the Ramans have also been saved, we are all brothers. After all, we are made from the same basic chemicals. That means that Heaven will not be limited just to humans but will encompass all beings everywhere who have understood His message."

"I can see where you might come to that conclusion," John-Paul replied. "But it is certainly not one that is universally accepted. Even within the church there are those who have an altogether different view of the Ramans."

"You mean the homocentric group that uses quotations from St. Michael of Siena for support?"

The pope nodded.

"For myself," General O'Toole said, "I find their narrow interpretation of St. Michael's sermon on the Ramans much too confining. In saying that the extraterrestrial spacecraft might have been a herald, like Elijah or even

Isaiah, foretelling the second coming of Christ, Michael was not restricting the Ramans to having only that particular role in our history and no other function or existence. He was simply explaining one possible view of the event from a human spiritual perspective."

Again the pontiff was smiling. "I can tell that you have spent considerable time and energy thinking about all this. My advance information about you was only partially correct. Your devotion to God, the church, and your family were all cited in your dossier. But there is little mention of your active intellectual interest in theology."

"I consider this mission to be by far the most important assignment of my life. I want to make certain that I properly serve both God and mankind. So I am trying to prepare myself in every possible way, including discovering whether or not the Ramans may have a spiritual component. It could affect my actions on the mission."

O'Toole paused a few seconds before continuing. "By the way, your holiness, have your researchers found any evidence of possible Raman spirituality, based on their analysis of the first rendezvous?"

John-Paul V shook his head. "Not really. However, one of my most devout archbishops, a man whose religious zeal sometimes overshadows his logic, insists that the structural order inside the first Raman craft—you know, the symmetries, geometric patterns, even the repetitive redundant designs based on the number three—is suggestive of a temple. He could be right. We just don't know. We don't see any evidence either way about the spiritual nature of the beings who created that first spaceship."

"Amazing!" said General O'Toole. "I had never thought of that before. Imagine if it really was created as some kind of a temple. That would stagger David Brown." The general laughed. "Dr. Brown insists," he said in explanation, "that we poor ignorant human beings would not have any chance of ever determining the purpose of such a spaceship, for the technology of its builders is so far advanced beyond our comprehension that it would be impossible for us ever to understand any of it. And, according to him, of course there could be no Raman religion. In his opinion they would have left all the superstitious mumbo

jumbo behind eons before they developed the capability
to construct such a fabulous interstellar spacecraft."

"Dr. Brown is an atheist, isn't he?" the pope asked.

O'Toole nodded. "An outspoken one. He believes that
all religious thinking impairs the proper functioning of the
brain. He regards anyone who doesn't agree with his point
of view as an absolute idiot."

"And the rest of the crew? Are they as strongly opinionated on the subject as Dr. Brown?"

"He is the most vocal atheist, although I suspect Wakefield, Tabori, and Turgenyev all share his basic attitudes.
Strangely enough, my intuitive sense tells me that Commander Borzov has a soft spot in his heart for religion.
That's true of most of the survivors of The Chaos. Anyway,
Valeriy seems to enjoy asking me questions about my
faith."

General O'Toole stopped for a moment as he mentally
completed his survey of the religious beliefs of the Newton crew. "The European women des Jardins and Sabatini
are nominally Catholic, although they would not be considered devout by any stretch of the imagination. Admiral
Heilmann is a Lutheran on Easter and Christmas. Takagishi
meditates and studies Zen. I don't know about the other
two."

The pontiff stood up and walked to the window. "Somewhere out there a strange and wonderful space vehicle,
created by beings from another star, is headed toward us.
We are sending a crew of a dozen to rendezvous with it."
He turned toward General O'Toole. "This spaceship may
be a messenger from God, but probably only you will be
able to recognize it as such."

O'Toole did not reply. The pope stared out the window
again and was quiet for almost a minute. "No, my son," he
finally said softly, as much to himself as to General O'Toole.
"I do not have the answers to your questions. Only God
has them. You must pray that He will provide the answers
when you need them." He faced the general. "I must tell
you that I am delighted to find you so concerned with
these issues. I am confident that God also has purposely
selected you for this mission."

General O'Toole could tell that the audience was coming to an end. "Holy Father," he said, "thank you again for seeing me and sharing this time. I feel deeply honored."

John-Paul V smiled and walked over to his guest. He embraced him in the European manner and escorted General O'Toole out of his office.

11

ST. MICHAEL OF SIENA

The exit from the subway station was opposite the entrance to the International Peace Park. As the escalator deposited General O'Toole on the upper level and he walked out into the afternoon light, he could see the domed shrine to his right, not more than two hundred meters away. To his left, at the other end of the park, the top of the ancient Roman Colosseum was visible behind a complex of administrative buildings.

The American general walked briskly into the park and turned right on the sidewalk leading to the shrine. He passed a lovely small fountain, part of a monument to the children of the world, and stopped to watch the animated, sculptured figures playing in the cold water. O'Toole was full of anticipation. *What an incredible day,* he was thinking. *First I have an audience with the pope. And now I finally visit the shrine of St. Michael. I definitely saved the best day for last.*

When Michael of Siena was canonized in 2188, fifty years after his death (and, perhaps more significantly, three years after John-Paul V had been elected as the new pope), there had been an immediate consensus that the perfect place to locate a major shrine in his honor would be in the International Peace Park. The great park stretched from the Piazza Venezia to the Colosseum, wandering around and among those few ruins from the old Roman fora that had somehow survived the nuclear holocaust. Choosing the exact spot for the shrine had been a delicate process. The Memorial to the Five Martyrs, honoring those courageous men and women who had dedicated themselves to the restoration of order in Rome during the months immediately following the disaster, had been the feature attraction of the park for years. There was considerable feeling that the new shrine to St. Michael of Siena must not be allowed to overshadow the dignified, open, marble pentagon that had occupied the southeast corner of the park since 2155.

After much debate it was decided that St. Michael's shrine should be located in the opposite, northwest corner of the park, its foundation symbolically centered on the actual epicenter of the blast, only ten yards from the place where Trajan's Column had stood until it was instantaneously vaporized by the intense heat at the core of the fireball. The first floor of the round shrine was entirely for meditation and worship. There were twelve alcoves or chapels attached to the central nave, six with sculpture and artwork following classical Roman Catholic motifs and the other six each honoring one of the world's major religions. This eclectic partition of the ground floor was purposely designed to provide comfort for the many non-Catholics who made pilgrimages to the shrine to pay their respects to the memory of the beloved St. Michael.

General O'Toole did not spend much time on the first level. He knelt and said a prayer in the chapel of St. Peter, and looked briefly at the famous wood sculpture of Buddha in the nook beside the entrance, but like most tourists he could not wait to see the incomparable frescoes on the second floor. O'Toole was overwhelmed by both the size and the beauty of the famous paintings the moment he stepped out of the elevator. Directly in front of him was a life-size portrait of a lovely girl of eighteen with long blond hair. She was bending down in an old church in Siena on Christmas Eve in 2115 and leaving behind a curly-haired baby, wrapped in a blanket and placed in a basket, on the cold church floor. This painting represented the night of St. Michael's birth and was the first in a sequence of twelve panels of frescoes that completely circled the shrine and told the story of the saint's life.

General O'Toole walked over to the small kiosk beside the elevator and rented a forty-five-minute audio tour cassette that was ten centimeters square and easily fit in his coat pocket. He picked up one of the tiny disposable receivers and clipped it into his ear. After choosing En-

glish as his language, he pushed the button marked
INTRODUCTION and listened as a lovely feminine British
voice explained what he was about to see.

"Each of the twelve frescoes is six meters high," the
woman was saying as the general was studying the features
of the baby Michael in the first panel. "The lighting in the
room is a combination of natural light from the outside,
coming through filtered skylights, and artificial illumination from the electronic arrays in the dome. Automatic
sensors determine the ambient conditions and mix the
natural with the artificial light so that the viewing of
the frescoes is always perfect.

"The twelve panels on this level correspond to the
twelve alcoves on the floor below. The arrangement of
the frescoes themselves, which follow the life of the saint
in a chronological order, flows in a clockwise direction. Thus
the final painting, commemorating Michael's canonization
ceremony at Rome in 2188, is right next to the painting of
his birth in the Siena cathedral seventy-two years earlier.

"The frescoes were designed and implemented by a
team of four artists, including the master Feng Yi from
China, who appeared suddenly in the spring of 2190 without any prior notification. Despite the fact that very little
was known outside China of his skill, the other three
artists, Rosa da Silva from Portugal, Fernando Lopez from
Mexico, and Hans Reichwein from Switzerland, immediately welcomed Feng Yi to their team on the strength of
the superb sketches that he had brought with him."

O'Toole glanced around the circular room as he listened
to the lyrical voice on the cassette. On this last day of
2199, there were more than two hundred people on the
second floor of St. Michael's shrine, including three tour
groups. The American cosmonaut progressed slowly around
the circle, stopping in front of each panel to study the
artwork and listen to the discussion on the cassette.

The major events of St. Michael's life were depicted in
detail in the frescoes. The second through fifth panels
featured his days as a Franciscan novitiate in Siena, his
fact-finding tour around the world during The Great Chaos,
the beginning of his religious activism when he returned
to Italy, and Michael's use of the church resources to feed

the hungry and house the homeless. The sixth painting showed the tireless saint inside the television studio donated by a wealthy American admirer. Here Michael, who spoke eight languages, repeatedly proclaimed his message of the fundamental unity of all humanity and the requirement for the wealthy to care for the less fortunate.

The seventh fresco was Feng Yi's portrait of the confrontation in Rome between Michael and the old and dying pope. It was a masterpiece of contrast. Using color and light brilliantly, the painting conveyed the image of an energetic, vibrant, and vital young man being wrongly censured by a world-weary prelate anxious to live out his final days in peace and quiet. In Michael's facial expression could be seen two distinctly different reactions to what he was being told: obedience to the papacy and disgust that the church was more concerned with style and order than substance.

"Michael was sent to a monastery in Tuscany by the pope," the audio guide continued, "and it was there that the final transformations in his character took place. The eighth panel depicts God's appearances to Michael during this period of solitude. According to the saint, God spoke to him twice, the first time in the middle of a thunderstorm and the second time when a magnificent rainbow filled the sky. It was during the long and violent storm that God shouted out, on the claps of thunder, the new "Laws of Life" which Michael later proclaimed at his Easter sunrise service at Bolsena. On His second visitation God informed the saint that his message would be spread to the ends of the rainbow and that He would give the faithful a sign during the Easter mass.

"That most famous miracle of Michael's life, one that was watched on television by over a billion people, is shown in the ninth panel. The painting presents Michael preaching Easter mass to the multitudes gathered around the shores of Lake Bolsena. A vigorous spring shower is drenching the crowd, most of whom are dressed in the familiar blue robes that had become associated with his following. But while the rain falls all around St. Michael, not a drop ever falls on the pulpit or on the sound equipment being used to amplify his voice. A perpetual radiant spotlight from the Sun bathes the young saint's face as he announces God's new laws to the world. It was this cross-over from being a purely religious leader—"

General O'Toole switched off the cassette as he walked toward the tenth and eleventh paintings. He was familiar with the rest of the story. After the mass at Bolsena, Michael was beset by a flock of troubles. His life abruptly changed. Within two weeks most of his cable television licenses were rescinded. Stories of corruption and immorality among his young devotees, whose numbers had grown into the hundreds of thousands in the Western world alone, were constantly in the press. There was an assassination attempt, which was foiled at the last minute by his staff. There were also baseless reports in the media that Michael had proclaimed himself the second Christ.

And so the leaders of the world became afraid of you. All of them. You were a threat to everyone with your Laws of Life. And they never understood what you meant by the final evolution. O'Toole stood in front of the tenth fresco. It was a scene he knew by heart. Almost every other educated person in the world would also recognize it instantly. The television replays of the last seconds before the terrorist bomb exploded were shown every year on June 28, the first day of the Feast of St. Peter and St. Paul and the anniversary of the day that Michael Balatresi and almost a million others had perished in Rome on a fateful early summer morning in 2138.

You had called them to come to Rome to join you. To show the world that everyone was united. And so they came. The tenth painting showed Michael in his blue robes, standing high on the steps of the Victor Emmanuel Monument next to the Piazza Venezia. He was in the middle of a sermon. Around him in all directions, spilling over into the Roman fora along the jam-packed Via dei Fori Imperiali leading to the Colosseum, was a sea of blue. And faces. Eager, excited faces, mostly young, looking up and around the monuments of the ancient city to catch a glimpse of the boy-man who dared to suggest that he had a way, God's way, out of the despair and hopelessness that had engulfed the world.

Michael Ryan O'Toole, a fifty-seven-year-old American

Catholic from Boston, fell on his knees and wept, like thousands before him, when he looked at the eleventh panel in the sequence. This painting depicted the same scene as the previous panel, but the time was more than an hour later, an hour *after* the seventy-five-kiloton nuclear bomb hidden in a sound truck near Trajan's Column had exploded and sent its hideous mushroom-shaped cloud into the skies above the city. Everything within two hundred meters of the epicenter had been instantly vaporized. There was no Michael, no Piazza Venezia, no huge Victor Emmanuel Monument. In the center of the fresco was nothing but a hole. And around the perimeter of that hole, where the vaporization had not been quite as complete, were scenes of agony and horror that would shatter the complacency of even the most self-protected individuals.

Dear God, General O'Toole said to himself through his tears, *Help me to comprehend the message in Saint Michael's life. Help me to understand how I can contribute, in whatever small way, to Your overall plan for us. Guide me as I prepare to be Your emissary to the Ramans.*

12

RAMANS AND ROMANS

"So, what do you think?" Nicole des Jardins stood up and turned around slowly in front of the camera beside the monitor. She was wearing a form-fitting white dress made from one of the new stretch fabrics. The hem of the dress was cut just below her knees and the long sleeves were marked by one black stripe that passed under her elbow as it ran from the shoulder to the wrist. The wide, jet-black belt matched both the color of the stripe and the color of her hair and high-heeled shoes. Her hair was pulled together by a comb at the back of her head and then left to tumble freely almost to her waist. Her only jewelry was a gold tennis bracelet containing three rows of small diamonds that she was wearing around her left wrist.

"You look beautiful, Mom," her daughter, Genevieve, answered her from the screen. "I've never seen you before both dressed up *and* with your hair down. What happened to your normal sweatsuit?" The fourteen-year-old grinned. "And when does the party start?"

"At nine-thirty," Nicole replied. "Very fashionably late. We probably won't have dinner until an hour after that. I'm going to eat something in the hotel room before I leave so that I won't starve."

"Mom, now don't forget your promise. Last week's *Aujourd'hui* said that my favorite singer, Julien LeClerc, would definitely be one of the guest entertainers. You have to tell him that your daughter thinks he's absolutely *divine!*"

Nicole smiled at her daughter. "I will, darling, for you. Although it will probably be misinterpreted. From what I have heard your Monsieur LeClerc thinks that every woman in the world is in love with him." She paused for a moment. "Where's your grandfather? I thought you said he would be joining you in a few minutes."

"Here I am," Nicole's father said as his weathered, friendly face appeared on the screen next to his granddaughter. "I was just finishing up a section of my new novel on Peter Abelard. I didn't expect you to call this early." Pierre des Jardins was now sixty-six years old. A successful historical novelist for many years, his life since the early death of his wife had been blessed by fortune and accomplishment. "You look stunning!" he exclaimed after seeing his daughter in her evening wear. "Did you buy that dress in Rome?"

"Actually, Dad," Nicole said, again turning around so that her father could see the entire outfit, "I bought this for Francoise's wedding three years ago. But of course I never had a chance to wear it. Do you think it's too simple?"

"Not at all," Pierre replied. "In fact, I think it's just perfect for this kind of extravaganza. If it's like the big fetes that I used to attend, every woman there will be wearing her fanciest and most expensive clothing and jewelry. You will stand out in your simple black and white. Particularly with your hair down like that. You look perfect."

"Thanks," Nicole said. "Even though I know you're prejudiced, I still like to hear your compliments." She looked at her father and daughter, her only two close companions for the last seven years. "I'm really surprisingly anxious. I don't think I'll be this nervous on the day we encounter Rama. I often feel out of my element at big parties like this and tonight I have a peculiar sense of foreboding that I can't explain. You remember, Dad, like I felt the day before our dog died when I was a child."

Her father's face became serious. "Maybe you'd better consider staying in the hotel. Too many of your premonitions have been accurate in the past. I remember your telling me that something was wrong with your mother two days before we received that message—"

"It's not that strong a feeling," Nicole interrupted. "And besides, what would I give as an excuse? Everyone's expecting me, especially the press, according to Francesca

Sabatini. She's still annoyed with me for refusing to have a personal interview with her."

"Then I guess you should go. But try to have some fun. Don't take things so seriously for this one night."

"And remember to say hello to Julien LeClerc for me," Genevieve added.

"I'll miss you both when midnight comes," Nicole said. "It will be the first time I've been away from you on New Year's Eve since 2194." Nicole paused for a moment, remembering their family celebrations together. "Take care, both of you. You know I love you very much."

"I love you, too, Mom," Genevieve shouted. Pierre waved good-bye.

Nicole switched off the videophone and checked her watch. It was eight o'clock. She still had an hour before she was supposed to meet her driver in the lobby. She walked over to the computer terminal to order something to eat. With a few commands she requested a bowl of minestrone and a small bottle of mineral water. The computer monitor told her to expect them both in between sixteen and nineteen minutes.

I really am high-strung tonight, Nicole thought as she leafed through the magazine *Italia* and waited for her food. The feature story in *Italia* was devoted to an interview with Francesca Sabatini. The article covered ten full pages and must have had twenty different photographs of *"la bella signora."* The interviewer discussed both of Francesca's highly successful documentary projects (the first on modern love and the second on drugs), stressing the point, in the middle of some questions about the drug series, that Francesca repeatedly smoked cigarettes during the conversation.

Nicole perused the article in a hurry, noting as she read that there were facets to Francesca she had never considered. *But what motivates her?* Nicole wondered to herself. *What is it that she wants?* Near the end of the magazine story, the interviewer had asked Francesca her opinion of the other two women in the Newton crew. "I feel that I'm actually the only woman on the mission," Francesca had answered. Nicole slowed down to read the rest of the paragraph. "The Russian pilot Turgenyev thinks and acts

like a man and the French-African princess Nicole des
Jardins has purposely suppressed her femininity, which is
sad because she could be such a lovely woman."

Nicole was only slightly angered by Francesca's glib
comments. More than anything, she was amused. She felt
a brief competitive surge but then chided herself for such
a childish reaction. *I'll ask Francesca about this article at
just the right time*, Nicole thought with a smile. *Who
knows? Maybe I'll even ask her if seducing married men
qualifies her as feminine.*

The forty-minute drive from the hotel to the party at
Hadrian's Villa, which was located on the outskirts of the
Roman suburbs not far from the resort town of Tivoli, was
passed in total silence. The other passenger in Nicole's car
was Hiro Yamanaka, the most taciturn of all the cosmonauts. In her television interview two months earlier with
Yamanaka, a frustrated Francesca Sabatini, after ten minutes of two- and three-word, monosyllabic responses to all
her questions, had asked Hiro if the rumor about his being
an android were true.

"What?" Hiro Yamanaka had asked.

"Are you an android?" Francesca had repeated with a
mischievous smile.

"No," the Japanese pilot had responded, his features
remaining absolutely expressionless while the camera
zoomed in on his face.

When the car turned off the main road between Rome
and Tivoli to drive the final mile to the Villa Adriana, the
traffic became congested. Progress was very slow, not only
because of the many cars carrying people to the gala, but
also because of the hundreds of curious onlookers and
paparazzi who were lining the small two-lane road.

Nicole took a deep breath as the automobile finally
pulled into a circular drive and stopped. Outside her
tinted window she could see a bevy of photographers and
reporters, poised to pounce on whoever climbed out of
the car. Her door opened automatically and she stepped
out slowly, pulling her black suede coat around her and
trying to be careful not to catch her heels.

"Who's that?" she heard a voice say.

"Franco, over here, quick—it's cosmonaut des Jardins."

There was a smattering of applause and the flash of many cameras. A kindly looking Italian gentleman came forward and took Nicole by the hand. People moiled around her, several microphones were stuck in her face, and it seemed as if she were being given a hundred simultaneous questions and requests in four or five different languages.

"Why have you refused all personal interviews?"

"Please open your coat so we can see your dress."

"Do the other cosmonauts respect you as a doctor?"

"Stop a moment. Please smile."

"What is your opinion of Francesca Sabatini?"

Nicole said nothing as the security men held back the crowd and led her to a covered electric cart. The four-passenger cart moved slowly up a long hill, leaving the crowd behind, as a pleasant Italian woman in her mid-twenties explained in English to Nicole and Hiro Yamanaka what they were seeing around them. Hadrian, who had ruled the Roman empire between A.D. 117 and 138, had built this immense villa, she told them, for his own enjoyment. The architectural masterpiece represented a blending of all the building styles Hadrian had seen on his many journeys to the distant provinces and was designed by the emperor himself on three hundred acres of plain at the foot of the Tiburtini Hills.

The initial cart ride past the ancient assortment of buildings was apparently an integral part of the evening's festivities. The lighted ruins themselves were only vaguely suggestive of their previous glory, for roofs were mostly missing, the decorative statuary had all been removed, and the rough stone walls were bare of adornment. But by the time the cart wound past the ruins of the Canopus, a monument built around a rectangular pool in the Egyptian style (it was the fifteenth or sixteenth building in the complex—Nicole had lost count), a general sense of the huge extent of the villa had definitely emerged.

This man died over two thousand years ago, Nicole thought to herself, remembering her history. *One of the smartest humans who ever lived. Soldier, administrator, linguist.* She smiled as she recalled the story of Antinous.

Lonely most of his life. Except for one brief, all-consuming passion that ended in tragedy.

The cart came to a stop at the end of a short walkway. The woman guide finished her monologue. "To honor the great Pax Romana, an extended time of world peace two millennia ago, the Italian government, helped by generous donations from the corporations listed underneath the statue over there on your right, decided in 2189 to construct a perfect replica of Hadrian's Maritime Theater. You may recall that we passed the ruins of the original at the beginning of the ride. The goal of the reconstruction project was to show what it would have been like to have visited a part of this villa during the emperor's lifetime. The building was finished in 2193 and has been used for state events ever since."

The guests were met by formally clad young Italian men, uniformly tall and handsome, who escorted them along the walkway, up to and through Philosopher's Hall, and finally into the Maritime Theater. There was a brief security check at the actual entrance and then the guests were free to roam as they pleased.

Nicole was enchanted by the building. It was basically round in shape, about forty meters in diameter. An annulus of water separated an inner island—on which was located a large house with five rooms and a big yard—from the wide portico with its fluted columns. There was no roof above the water or the inner part of the portico, the open skies giving the entire theater a wonderful feeling of freedom. Around the building the guests mixed and talked and drank; advanced robot waiters rolled around carrying large trays of champagne and wine and other alcoholic spirits. Across the two small bridges that connected the island with its house and yard to the portico and the rest of the building, Nicole could see a dozen people, all dressed in white, working to set up the dinner buffet.

A heavy blond woman and her pint-size, jocular husband, a bald man wearing an old-fashioned pair of spectacles, were rapidly approaching Nicole from about thirty feet away. Nicole prepared for the coming onslaught by taking a small sip of the champagne and cassis cocktail that had been handed to her by a strangely insistent robot a few minutes before.

"Oh, Madame des Jardins," the man said, waving at her and closing in with great speed. "We just have to talk to you. My wife is one of your biggest fans." He walked up beside Nicole and gestured to his wife. "Come on, Cecelia," he shouted, "I've got her."

Nicole took a deep breath and forced a wide smile. *It's going to be one of those evenings,* she said to herself.

Finally, Nicole was thinking, *maybe I'll have a few minutes of peace and quiet.* She was sitting by herself, her back purposely toward the door, at a small table in the corner of the room. The room was at the rear of the island house in the middle of the Maritime Theater. Nicole finished the last few bites of her food and washed them down with some wine.

Whew, she thought, trying without success to remember even half the people she had met in the last hour. She had been like a prized photograph, passed from person to person and praised by everyone. She had been embraced, kissed, hugged, pinched, flirted with (by both men and women), and even propositioned by a rich Swedish shipbuilder who had invited her to his "castle" outside the city of Göteborg. Nicole had hardly said a word to any of them. Her face ached from polite smiling and she was a trifle tipsy from the wine and champagne cocktails.

"Well, as I live and breathe," she heard a familiar voice behind her say, "I believe the lady in the white dress is none other than my fellow cosmonaut, the ice princess herself, Madame Nicole des Jardins." Nicole turned and saw Richard Wakefield staggering toward her. He bounced off a table, reached out to stabilize himself on a chair, and nearly fell in her lap.

"Sorry," he said, grinning and managing to seat himself beside her. "I'm afraid I've had too much gin and tonic." He took a big gulp from the glass that had miraculously remained unspilled in his right hand. "And now," he said with a wink, "if you don't mind, I'm going to take a nap before the dolphin show."

Nicole laughed as Richard's head hit the wooden table

with a splat and he feigned unconsciousness. After a moment she leaned over playfully and forced one of his eyelids open. "If you don't mind, comrade, could you not pass out until after you explain to me the bit about the dolphin show."

With great effort Richard sat up and began rolling his eyes. "You mean you don't know? You, who always know *all* the schedules and *all* the procedures? That's impossible."

Nicole finished her wine. "Seriously, Wakefield. What are you talking about?"

Richard opened one of the small windows and stuck his arm through it, pointing at the pool of water that encircled the house. "The great Dr. Luigi Bardolini is here with his intelligent dolphins. Francesca is going to introduce him in about fifteen minutes." He stared at Nicole with wild abandon. "Dr. Bardolini is going to prove, here and tonight," he shouted, "that his dolphins can pass our university entrance exams."

Nicole pulled back and looked carefully at her colleague. *He really is drunk,* she thought to herself. *Maybe he feels as out of place as I do.*

Richard was now gazing intently out the window. "This party is really some zoo, isn't it?" Nicole said after a long silence. "Where did they find—"

"That's it," Wakefield interrupted her suddenly, giving the table a triumphant pounding. "That's why this place has seemed familiar to me since the moment we walked in." He glanced at Nicole, who was eyeing him as if he had lost his mind. "It's a miniature Rama, don't you see?" He jumped up, unable to contain his happiness at his discovery. "The water surrounding this house is the Cylindrical Sea, the porticoes represent the Central Plain, and we, lovely lady, are sitting in the city of New York."

Nicole was beginning to comprehend but could not keep up with the racing thoughts of Richard Wakefield. "And what does similarity of design prove?" he thought out loud. "What does it mean that human architects two thousand years ago constructed a theater with some of the same guiding principles of design as those used in the Raman ship? Similarity of nature? Similarity of culture? Absolutely not."

He stopped, now aware that Nicole was staring fixedly at him. "Mathematics," he said emphatically. A quizzical expression told him that she still didn't understand completely. "Mathematics," he said again, surprisingly lucid all of a sudden. "That's the key. The Ramans almost certainly didn't look like us and clearly evolved on a world far different from the Earth. But they must have understood the same mathematics as the Romans."

His face brightened. "Hah," he shouted again, causing Nicole to jump. He was pleased with himself. "Ramans and Romans. That's what tonight is all about. And at some level of development in between is modern-day homo sapiens."

Nicole shook her head as Richard exulted in the joy of his wit. "You don't understand, lovely lady?" he said, extending his hand to help her up from her seat. "Then perhaps you and I should go to watch a dolphin show and I will speak to you of Ramans there and Romans here, of cabbages and kings, of dum-de-dum and sealing wax, and whether pigs have wings."

13

HAPPY NEW YEAR

After everyone had finished eating and all the plates had been cleared, Francesca Sabatini appeared in the center of the yard with a microphone and spent ten minutes thanking all the gala sponsors. Then she introduced Dr. Luigi Bardolini, suggesting that the techniques he had pioneered to communicate with the dolphins might prove extremely useful when humans try to talk to any extraterrestrials.

Richard Wakefield had disappeared just before Francesca had started speaking, ostensibly to find the rest room and obtain another drink. Nicole had caught sight of him briefly five minutes later, just after Francesca had finished with her introduction. He had been surrounded by a pair of buxom Italian actresses, both of whom were laughing heartily at his jokes. He had waved at Nicole and winked, pointing at the two women as if his actions were self-explanatory.

Good for you, Richard, Nicole had thought, smiling to herself. *At least one of us social misfits is having a good time.* She now watched Francesca walk gracefully across the bridge and start to move the crowd back from the water so that Bardolini and his dolphins would have plenty of room. Francesca was wearing a tight black dress, bare on one shoulder, with a starburst of gold sequins in the front. A gold scarf was tied around her waist. Her long blond hair was braided and pinned against her head.

You really belong here, Nicole thought, truthfully admiring Francesca's ease in large crowds. Dr. Bardolini began the first segment of his dolphin show and Nicole turned her attention to the circular pool of water. Luigi Bardolini was one of those controversial scientists whose work is brilliant but never quite as exceptional as he

himself wants others to believe. It was true that he had
developed a unique way of communicating with the dolphins and had isolated and identified the sounds of thirty
to forty action verbs in their portfolio of squeaks. But it
was not true, as he so often claimed, that two of his
dolphins could pass a university entrance exam. Unfortunately, the way the twenty-second century international
scientific community operated, if your most outrageous or
advanced theories could not be substantiated, or were
held up to ridicule, then your other discoveries, no matter
how solid, were often disparaged as well. This behavior
had induced an endemic conservatism in science that was
not altogether healthy.

Unlike most scientists, Bardolini was a brilliant show-
man. In the final segment of his show he had his two most
famous dolphins, Emilio and Emilia, take an intelligence
test in a real-time competition against two of the villa
guides, one male and one female, who had been selected
at random that evening. The construct of the competitive
test was enticingly simple. On two of the four large electronic screens (one pair of screens was in the water and
another pair was in the yard), a three-by-three matrix was
shown with a blank in the lower right-hand corner. The
other eight elements were filled with different pictures
and shapes. The dolphins and humans taking the test were
supposed to discern the changing patterns moving from
left to right and top to bottom in the matrix, and then
correctly pick out, from a set of eight candidates displayed
on the companion screen, the element that should be
placed in the blank lower right corner. The competitors
had one minute to make their choice on each problem.
The dolphins in the water, like the humans on the land
above them, had a control panel of eight buttons they
could push (the dolphins used their snouts) to indicate
their selection.

The first few problems were easy, both for the humans
and for the dolphins. In the first matrix, a single white ball
was in the upper left corner, two white balls in the second
column of the first row, and three white balls in the matrix
element corresponding to row one and column three.
Since the first element of the second row was a single ball

as well, half white and half black, and since the beginning
element of the third row was another single ball, now fully
black, it was easy to read the entire matrix quickly and
determine that what belonged in the blank lower right
corner were three black balls.

Later problems were not so easy. With each successive
puzzle, more complications were added. The humans made
their first error on the eighth matrix, the dolphins on the
ninth. Altogether Dr. Bardolini exhibited sixteen matrices, the last one so complicated that at least ten separate
changing patterns had to be recognized to properly identify what should be entered as the last element. The final
score was a tie, Humans 12, Dolphins 12. Both pairs took
a bow and the audience applauded.

Nicole had found the exercise fascinating. She wasn't
certain if she believed Dr. Bardolini's assertion that the
competition was fair and unrehearsed, but it didn't matter
to her. What she thought was interesting was the nature of
the competition itself, the idea that intelligence could be
defined in terms of an ability to identify patterns and
trends. *Is there a way that synthesis can be measured?* she
thought. *In children. Or even adults, for that matter.*

Nicole had participated in the test along with the human and dolphin contestants and had correctly answered
the first thirteen, missing the fourteenth because of a
careless assumption, and just finishing the fifteenth accurately before the buzzer sounded the end of the allocated
time. She had had no idea where to begin on the sixteenth. *And what about you Ramans?* she was wondering,
as Francesca returned to the microphone to introduce
Genevieve's heartthrob, Julien LeClerc. *Would you have
been able to answer all sixteen correctly in one tenth the
time? One hundredth?* She gulped, as she realized the full
range of possibilities. *Or maybe even one millionth?*

"I never lived, 'til I met you. . . . I never loved, 'til I
saw you. . . ." The soft melody of the old recorded song
swam in Nicole's memory and brought back an image from
fifteen years before, from another dance with another man
when she had still believed that love could conquer everything. Julien LeClerc misread her body signals and pulled

her closer to him. Nicole decided not to fight it. She was already very tired and, if the truth were known, it felt good being held tightly by a man for the first time in several years.

She had honored her agreement with Genevieve. When Monsieur LeClerc had finished his short set of songs, Nicole had approached the French singer and given him the message from her daughter. As she had anticipated, he had interpreted her approach to mean something entirely different. They had continued talking while Francesca had announced to the partygoers that there would be no more formal entertainment until after midnight and that all the guests were free to drink or snack or dance to the recorded music until then. Julien had offered his arm to Nicole and the two of them had walked back over to the portico, where they had been dancing ever since.

Julien was a handsome man, in his early thirties, but he was not really Nicole's type. First of all, he was too conceited for her. He talked about himself all the time and did not pay any attention when the conversation switched to other topics. Although he was a gifted singer, he had no other particularly outstanding characteristics. *But*, Nicole reasoned as their continued dancing brought stares from the other guests, *he's all right as a dancer and it beats standing around twiddling my thumbs.*

At a break in the music Francesca came over to talk to them. "Good for you, Nicole," she said, her open smile appearing genuine. "I'm glad to see that you're enjoying yourself." She extended a small tray with half a dozen dark chocolate balls lightly sprayed with white, possibly a sugar confection. "These are fantastic," Francesca said. "I made them especially for the Newton crew."

Nicole took one of the chocolates and popped it into her mouth. It was delicious. "Now I have a favor to ask," Francesca continued after several seconds. "Since I was never able to schedule a personal interview with you and our mail indicates that there are millions of people out there who would like to find out more about you, do you think that you could come over to our studio here and give me ten or fifteen minutes before midnight?"

Nicole stared intently at Francesca. A voice inside her

was sending out a warning, but her mind was somehow garbling the message.

"I agree," Julien LeClerc said while the two women looked at each other. "The press always talks about the 'mysterious lady cosmonaut' or refers to you as 'the ice princess.' Show them what you've shown me tonight, that you're a normal, healthy woman like everybody else."

Why not? Nicole finally decided, suppressing her interior voice. *At least by doing it here I don't have to involve Dad and Genevieve.*

They had started to walk toward the makeshift studio on the other side of the portico when Nicole saw Shigeru Takagishi across the room. He was leaning against a column and talking to a trio of Japanese businessmen dressed in formal attire. "Just a minute," Nicole said to her companions, "I'll be right back."

"*Tanoshii shin-nen,* Takagishi-san," Nicole greeted him. The Japanese scientist turned, startled at first, and smiled as he saw her approach. After he formally introduced Nicole to his associates, and they all bowed to acknowledge her presence and accomplishments, Takagishi started a polite conversation.

"*O genki desu ka?*" he asked.

"*Okagesama de,*" she replied. Nicole leaned across to her Japanese colleague and whispered in his ear. "I only have a minute. I wanted to tell you that I have carefully examined all your records and I am in complete agreement with your personal physician. There is no reason to say anything about your heart anomaly to the medical committee."

Dr. Takagishi looked as if he had just been told that his wife had given birth to a healthy son. He started to say something personal to Nicole but remembered he was in the midst of a group of his countrymen. "*Domo arrigato gozaimas,*" he said to the retreating Nicole, his warm eyes conveying the depth of his thanks.

Nicole felt great as she waltzed into the studio between Francesca and Julien LeClerc. She posed willingly for the still photographers while Signora Sabatini ensured that all the television equipment was in working order for the interview. She sipped some more champagne and cassis, making intermittent small talk with Julien. Finally she took a seat beside Francesca underneath the klieg lights. *How wonderful*, Nicole kept thinking about the earlier interaction with Takagishi, *to be able to help that brilliant little man*.

Francesca's first question was innocent enough. She asked Nicole if she was excited about the coming launch. "Of course," Nicole answered. She then gave a lively summary of the training exercises that the cosmonaut crew had been undergoing while waiting for the opportunity to rendezvous with Rama II. The entire interview was conducted in English. The questions flowed in an orderly pattern. Nicole was asked to describe her role in the mission, what she expected to discover ("I don't really know, but whatever we find will be extremely interesting"), and how she happened to go to the Space Academy in the first place. After about five minutes, Nicole was feeling at ease and very comfortable; it seemed to her that she and Francesca had fallen into a complementary rhythm.

Francesca then asked three personal questions, one about her father, a second about Nicole's mother and the Senoufo tribe in the Ivory Coast, and the third about her life with Genevieve. None of them were difficult. So Nicole was totally unprepared for Francesca's last question.

"It is obvious from your daughter's photographs that her skin is considerably lighter than yours," Francesca said in the same tone and manner that she had used for all the other questions. "Genevieve's skin color suggests that her father was probably white. Who was the father of your daughter?"

Nicole felt her heart rate surge as she listened to the question. Then time seemed to stand still. A surprising flood of powerful emotions engulfed Nicole and she was afraid she was going to cry. A brilliant hot image of two entwined bodies reflected in a large mirror burst into her mind and made her gasp. She momentarily looked down at her feet, trying to regain her composure.

You stupid woman, she said to herself as she struggled to calm the combination of anger and pain and remembered love that had crashed upon her like a tidal wave. *You should have known better*. Again the tears threatened

and she fought them. She looked up at the lights and
Francesca. The gold sequins on the front of the Italian
journalist's dress had grouped into a pattern, or so it
seemed to Nicole. She saw a head in the sequins, the head
of a large cat, its eyes gleaming and its mouth with sharp
teeth just beginning to open.

At last, after what seemed to be forever, Nicole felt that
she again had her emotions under control. She stared
angrily at Francesca. *"Non voglio parlare di quello,"* Nicole said quietly in Italian. *"Abbiamo terminato questa
intervista."* She stood up, noticed that she was trembling,
and sat down again. The cameras were still rolling. She
breathed deeply for several seconds. At length Nicole rose
from her chair and walked out of the temporary studio.

She wanted to flee, to run away from everything, to go
someplace where she could be alone with her private
feelings. But it was impossible. Julien grabbed her as she
exited from the interview. "What a bitch!" he said, waving
an accusing finger in Francesca's direction. There were
people all around Nicole. All of them were talking at the
same time. She was having trouble focusing her eyes and
ears in all the confusion.

In the distance Nicole heard some music that she vaguely
recognized but the song was more than half over before
she realized it was "Auld Lang Syne." Julien had his arm
around her back and was singing lustily. He was also
leading the group of twenty or so people clustered around
them in singing the final words. Nicole mouthed the last
bar mechanically and tried to maintain her equilibrium.
Suddenly a moist pair of lips was pressed against hers and
an active tongue was trying to pry open her mouth and
force its way inside. Julien was kissing her feverishly,
photographers were snapping pictures all around, there
was an incredible amount of noise. Nicole's head began to
spin and she felt as if she were going to faint. She struggled hard, finally succeeding in freeing herself from Julien's grasp.

Nicole staggered backward and bumped into an angry
Reggie Wilson. He pushed her aside in his haste to grab a
couple sharing a deep New Year's kiss in the flashing
lights. Nicole watched him disinterestedly, as if she were

in a movie theater, or even in one of her own dreams. Reggie pulled the pair apart and raised his right arm as if he were going to slug the other man. Francesca Sabatini restrained Reggie as a confused David Brown retreated from her embrace.

"Keep your hands off her, you bastard," Reggie shouted, still threatening the American scientist. "And don't think for one minute that I don't know what you're doing." Nicole could not believe what she was seeing. Nothing made any sense. Within seconds the room was full of security guards.

Nicole was one of many people ushered summarily away from the fracas while order was being restored. As she left the studio area she happened to pass Elaine Brown, sitting by herself in the portico with her back against a column. Nicole had met and enjoyed Elaine when she had gone to Dallas to talk to David Brown's family physician about his allergies. At the moment Elaine was obviously drunk and in no mood to talk to anybody. "You shit," Nicole heard her mutter, "I never should have showed you the results until after I had published them myself. Then everything would have been different."

Nicole left the gala as soon as she was able to arrange her transportation back to Rome. Francesca unbelievably tried to escort her out to the limousine as if nothing had happened. Nicole curtly rejected her fellow cosmonaut's offer and walked out alone.

It started to snow during the ride back to the hotel. Nicole concentrated on the falling snowflakes and was eventually able to clear her mind enough to assess the evening. Of one thing she was absolutely certain. There had been something unusual and very powerful in that chocolate ball she had eaten. Nicole had never before come so close to losing complete control of her emotions. *Maybe she gave one to Wilson too,* Nicole thought. *And that partially explains his eruption. But why?* she asked herself again. *What is she trying to accomplish?*

Back at the hotel she prepared quickly for bed. But just as she was ready to turn out the lights, Nicole thought she heard a light knock on the door. She stopped and listened, but there was no sound for several seconds. She had almost decided that her ears were playing tricks on her when she heard the knock again. Nicole pulled the hotel robe around her and approached the locked door very cautiously. "Who's there?" she said forcefully but not convincingly. "Identify yourself."

She heard a sound of scraping and a piece of folded paper was thrust under the door. Nicole, still wary and frightened, picked up the paper and opened it. On it was written, in the original Senoufo script of her mother's tribe, three simple words: *Ronata. Omeh. Here.* Ronata was Nicole's name in Senoufo.

A mixture of panic and excitement caused Nicole to open the door without first checking on the monitor to see who was outside. Standing ten feet away from the door, his amazing old eyes already locked on hers, was an ancient, wizened man with his face painted in green and white horizontal streaks. He was wearing a full-length, bright green tribal costume, similar to a robe, on which were gold swashes and a collection of line drawings of no apparent meaning.

"Omeh!" Nicole said, her heart threatening to jump out of her chest. "What are you doing here?" she added in Senoufo.

The old black man said nothing. He was holding out a stone and a small vial of some kind, both in his right hand. After several seconds he stepped deliberately forward into the room. Nicole backpedaled with each of his steps. His gaze never wavered from her. When they were in the center of her hotel room and only three or four feet apart, the old man looked up at the ceiling and began to chant. It was a ritual Senoufo song, a general blessing and spell invocation used by the tribal shaman for hundreds of years to ward off evil spirits.

When he had finished the chant the old man Omeh stared again at his great-granddaughter and began to speak very slowly. "Ronata," he said, "Omeh has sensed strong danger in this life. It is written in the tribal chronicles that the man of three centuries will chase the evil demons away from the woman with no companion. But Omeh cannot protect Ronata after Ronata leaves the kingdom of

Minowe. Here," he said, taking her hand and placing the stone and vial in it, "these stay with Ronata always."

Nicole looked down at the stone, a smooth, polished oval about eight inches long and four inches in each of the other two dimensions. The stone was mostly creamy white with a few strange brown lines wriggling across its surface. The small green vial that he had given her was no bigger than a traveling bottle of perfume.

"The water from the Lake of Wisdom can help Ronata," Omeh said. "Ronata will know the time to drink." He tilted his head back and earnestly repeated the earlier chant, this time with his eyes closed. Nicole stood beside him in puzzled silence, the stone and the vial in her right hand. When he was finished singing, Omeh shouted three words that Nicole did not understand. Then he abruptly turned around and walked quickly toward the open door. Startled, Nicole ran out into the hall just in time to see his green gown disappear into the elevator.

14

GOOD-BYE, HENRY

Nicole and Genevieve walked arm in arm up the hill through the light snow. "Did you see the look on that American's face when I told him who you were?" Genevieve said with a laugh. She was very proud of her mother.

Nicole shifted her skis and poles over to the other shoulder as they approached the hotel. *"Guten Abend,"* an old man who would have made a perfect Santa Claus mumbled as he ambled by. "I wish you wouldn't be so quick to tell people," Nicole said, not really chastizing her daughter. "Sometimes it's nice not to be recognized."

There was a small shed for the skis beside the entrance to the hotel. Nicole and Genevieve stopped and placed their equipment in a locker. They exchanged their ski boots for soft snow slippers and walked back out into the fading light. Mother and daughter stood together for a moment and looked back down the hill toward the village of Davos. "You know," said Nicole, "there was a time today, during our race down that back piste toward Klosters, when I found it impossible to believe that I will actually be way out there (she gestured at the sky) in less than two weeks, headed for a rendezvous with a mysterious alien spacecraft. Sometimes the human mind balks at the truth."

"Maybe it's only a dream," her daughter said lightly.

Nicole smiled. She loved Genevieve's sense of play. Whenever the day-to-day drudgery of the hard work and tedious preparation would begin to overwhelm Nicole, she could always count on her daughter's easy nature to bring her out of her seriousness. They were quite a trio, the three of them that lived at Beauvois. Each of them was sorely dependent on the other two. Nicole did not like to think how the hundred-day separation might affect their harmonious accord.

"Does it bother you that I will be gone so long?" Nicole asked Genevieve as they entered the hotel lobby. A dozen people were sitting around a roaring fire in the middle of the room. An inconspicuous but efficient Swiss waiter was serving hot drinks to the après-ski crew. There would be no robots in a Morosani hotel, not even for room service.

"I don't think of it that way," her cheerful daughter responded. "After all, I'll be able to talk with you almost every night on the videophone. The delay time will even make it fun. And challenging." They walked past the old-fashioned registration desk. "Besides," Genevieve added, "I'll be the center of attention at school for the whole mission. My class project is already set; I'm going to draw a psychological portrait of the Ramans based on my conversations with you."

Nicole smiled again and shook her head. Genevieve's optimism was always infectious. It was a shame—

"Oh, Madame des Jardins." The voice interrupted her thought. The hotel manager was beckoning to her from the desk. Nicole turned around. "There's a message for you," the manager continued. "I was told to deliver it to you personally."

He handed her a small plain envelope. Nicole opened it and saw just the tiniest portion of a crest on the note card. Her heart raced into overdrive as she closed the envelope again. "What is it, Mother?" Genevieve inquired. "It must be special to be hand delivered. Nobody does things like that these days."

Nicole tried to hide her feelings from her daughter. "It's a secret memo about my work," she lied. "The delivery-man made a terrible mistake. He should never have given it even to Herr Graf. He should have put it in my hands only."

"More confidential medical data about the crew?" Genevieve asked. She and her mother had often discussed the delicate role of the life science officer on a major space mission.

Nicole nodded. "Darling," she said to her daughter, "why don't you run upstairs and tell your grandfather that

I'll be along in a few minutes. We'll still plan dinner for seven-thirty. I'll read this message now and see if any urgent response is required."

Nicole kissed Genevieve and waited until her daughter was on the elevator before walking back outside into the light snow. It was dark now. She stood under the streetlight and opened the envelope with her cold hands. She had difficulty controlling her trembling fingers. *You fool,* she thought, *you careless fool. After all this time. What if the girl had seen. . . .*

The crest was the same as it had been on that afternoon, fifteen and a half years ago, when Darren Higgins had handed her the dinner invitation outside the Olympic press area. Nicole was surprised by the strength of her emotions. She steeled herself and finally looked at the rest of the note below the crest.

"Sorry for the last-minute notice. Must see you tomorrow. Noon exactly. Warming hut #8 on the Weissfluhjoch. Come alone. Henry."

The next morning Nicole was one of the first in line for the cable car that carried skiers to the top of the Weissfluhjoch. She climbed into the polished glass car with about twenty others and leaned against the window while the door automatically shut. *I have seen him only once in these fifteen years,* she thought to herself, *and yet . . .*

As the cable car ascended, Nicole pulled her snow glasses down over her eyes. It was a dazzling morning, not unlike the January morning seven years earlier when her father had called for her from the villa. They had had a rare snowfall at Beauvois the night before and, after much pleading, she had let Genevieve stay home from school to play in the snow. Nicole was working at the hospital in Tours at the time and was waiting to hear about her application to the Space Academy.

She had been showing her seven-year-old daughter how to make a snow angel when Pierre had called a second time from the house. "Nicole, Genevieve, there's something special in our mail," he had said. "It must have come during the night." Nicole and Genevieve had run to the villa in their snowsuits while Pierre posted the full text of the message on the wall videoscreen.

"Most extraordinary," Pierre had said. "It seems we've all been invited to the English coronation, including the private reception afterward. This is extremely unusual."

"Oh, Grandpapa," Genevieve said excitedly, "I want to go. Can we go? Do I get to meet a real king and queen?"

"There is no queen, darling," her grandfather replied, "unless you mean the queen mother. This king has not yet married."

Nicole read the invitation several times without saying anything. After Genevieve had calmed down and left the room, her father had put his arms around Nicole.

"I want to go," she had said quietly.

"Are you certain?" he had asked, pulling away and regarding her with an inquisitive stare.

"Yes," she had answered firmly.

Henry had never seen her until that evening, Nicole was thinking as she checked first her watch and then her equipment in preparation for her ski run down from the summit. *Father had been wonderful. He had let me disappear at Beauvois and almost nobody knew I had a baby until Genevieve was almost a year old. Henry never even suspected. Not until that night at Buckingham Palace.*

Nicole could still see herself waiting in the reception line. The king had been late. Genevieve had been fidgety. At last Henry had been standing opposite her. "The honorable Pierre des Jardins of Beauvois, France, with his daughter, Nicole, and granddaughter, Genevieve." Nicole had bowed very properly and Genevieve had curtsied.

"So this is Genevieve," the king had said. He had bent down for only a moment and put a hand under the child's chin. When the girl had lifted up her face he had seen something that he recognized. He had turned to look at Nicole, a trace of questioning in his glance. Nicole had revealed nothing with her smile. The crier was calling out the names of the next guests in the line. The king had moved on.

So you sent Darren to the hotel, Nicole thought as she schussed a short slope, aimed for a small jump, and was airborne for a second or two. *And he hemmed and hawed and finally asked me if I would come have tea.* Nicole dug her edges into the snow and came to an abrupt stop. "Tell Henry I can't," she remembered saying to Darren in London seven years earlier.

She looked again at her watch. It was only eleven o'clock, too early to ski to the hut. She eased over to one of the lifts and took another ride to the summit.

It was two minutes past noon when Nicole arrived at the small chalet on the edge of the woods. She took off her skis, stuck them in the snow, and walked toward the front door. She ignored the conspicuous signs all around her that said EINTRITT VERBOTEN. From out of nowhere came two burly men, one of whom actually jumped between Nicole and the door to the hut. "It's all right," she heard a familiar voice say, "we're expecting her." The two guards vanished as quickly as they had appeared and Nicole saw Darren, smiling as always, occupying the doorway to the chalet.

"Hi there, Nicole," he said in his normal friendly fashion. Darren had aged. There were a few flecks of gray around his temples and some salt with the pepper in his short beard. "How are you?" he asked.

"I'm fine, Darren," she answered, aware that despite all her lectures to herself, she was already starting to feel nervous. She reminded herself that she was now a professional, as accomplished in her own way as this king she was about to see. Nicole then strode forcefully into the chalet.

It was warm inside. Henry was standing with his back to a small fireplace. Darren closed the door behind her and left the two of them alone. Nicole self-consciously removed her scarf and opened her parka. She took off her snow glasses. They stared at each other for twenty, maybe thirty seconds, neither saying a word, neither wanting to interrupt the powerful flow of emotions that was carrying each of them back to two magnificent days fifteen years before.

"Hello, Nicole," the king said finally. His voice was soft and tender.

"Hello, Henry," she replied. He started to walk around

the couch, to come close to her, perhaps to touch her, but there was something in her body language that stopped him. He leaned on the side of the couch.

"Won't you sit down?" he invited.

Nicole shook her head. "I'd prefer to stand, if it's all right with you." She waited a few more seconds. Their eyes again locked in a deep communication. She felt herself being drawn to him despite her strong internal warnings. "Henry," she blurted out suddenly, "why did you summon me here? It must be important. It's not normal for the king of England to spend his days sitting in a chalet on the side of a Swiss ski mountain."

Henry walked toward the corner of the room. "I brought you a present," he said as he bent down with his back to Nicole, "in honor of your thirty-sixth birthday."

Nicole laughed. Some of the tension was easing. "That's tomorrow," she said. "You're a day early. But why—"

He extended a data cube toward her. "This is the most valuable gift I could find for you," he said seriously, "and it has taken many marks from the royal treasury to compile it."

She looked at him quizzically.

"I have been worried for some time about this mission of yours," Henry said, "and in the beginning I could not understand why. But about four months ago, one night when I was playing with Prince Charles and Princess Eleanor, I realized what was bothering me. My intuitive sense tells me that this crew of yours will have problems. I know it sounds crazy, particularly coming from me, but I'm not worried about the Ramans. That megalomaniac Brown is probably right, the Ramans couldn't care less about us Earthlings. But you're about to spend a hundred days in confined quarters with eleven other . . ."

He could tell that Nicole was not following him. "Here," he said, "take this cube. I had my intelligence agents put together full and complete dossiers on every member of the Newton dozen, including you." Nicole's brow furrowed. "The information, most of which is not available in the official ISA files, confirmed my personal view that the Newton team contains quite a few unstable elements. I didn't know what to do with—"

"This is none of your business," Nicole interrupted angrily. She was affronted by Henry's involvement in her professional life. "Why are you meddling—"

"Hey, hey, calm down, will you," the king replied. "I assure you my motives were all good. Look," he added, "you probably won't even need all this information, but I thought that maybe it could be useful. Take it. Throw it away if you like. You're the life science officer. You can treat it however you want."

Henry could tell that he had botched the meeting. He walked away and sat down in a chair facing the fire. His back was toward Nicole.

"Take care of yourself, Nicole," he mumbled.

She thought for a long moment, put the data cube inside her parka, and walked over behind the king. "Thank you, Henry," she said. Nicole let her hand fall on his shoulder. He didn't turn around. He reached up with his hand and very slowly wrapped his fingers around hers. They remained in that position for almost a minute.

"There was some data that eluded even my investigators," he said in a low voice. "One fact in particular in which I was extremely interested."

Nicole could hear her heart amid the crackle of the logs in the fireplace. A voice inside her shouted *Tell him, tell him.* But another voice, full of wisdom, counseled silence.

She slowly withdrew her fingers from his. He turned around to look at her. She smiled. Nicole walked over to the door. She put her scarf back on her head and zipped her parka before going outside. "Good-bye, Henry," she said.

15

ENCOUNTER

The combined Newton spacecraft had maneuvered so that Rama filled the expanded viewport in the control center. The alien spaceship was immense. Its surface was a dull, drab gray, and its long body was a geometrically perfect cylinder. Nicole stood beside Valeriy Borzov in silence. For each of them, this first sight of the entire Rama vehicle in the sunlight was a moment to savor.

"Have you detected any differences?" Nicole said at length. "Not yet," Commander Borzov replied. "It looks as if the two of them came off the same assembly line." They were quiet again.

"Wouldn't you love to see that assembly line?" Nicole asked.

Valeriy Borzov nodded. A small flying craft, like a bat or a hummingbird, zoomed past the viewport in the near field and headed off in the direction of Rama. "The exterior drones will confirm the similarities. Each of them has a stored set of images from Rama I. Any variations will be logged and reported within three hours."

"And if there are no unexplained variations?"

"Then we proceed as planned," General Borzov answered with a smile. "We dock, open up Rama, and release the interior drones." He glanced at his watch. "All of which should take place about twenty-two hours from now, provided the life science officer asserts that the crew is ready."

"The crew is in fine shape," Nicole reported. "I've just finished looking at a synopsis of the cruise health data again. It's been surprisingly regular. Except for hormonal abnormalities in all three women, which were not totally unexpected, we have seen no significant anomalies in forty days."

"So physically we're all ready to go," the commander said thoughtfully, "but what about our psychological readiness? Are you troubled about this recent spate of arguments? Or can we chalk it up to tension and excitement?"

Nicole was silent for a moment. "I agree these four days since the docking have been a little rough. Of course, we knew about the Wilson-Brown problem even before launch. We partially solved it by having Reggie on your ship during most of the cruise, but now that we've joined the two spacecraft and the team is all together again, those two seem to be at each other at every opportunity. Particularly if Francesca is around."

"I tried to talk to Wilson twice while the two ships were separated," Borzov said in a frustrated tone. "He wouldn't discuss it. But it's clear that he is very angry about something."

General Borzov walked over to the control panel and started fiddling with the keyboards. Sequencing information appeared on one of the monitors. "It must involve Sabatini," he continued. "Wilson didn't do much work during cruise, but his log indicates that he spent an inordinate amount of time on the videophone with her. And he was always in a foul mood. He even offended O'Toole." General Borzov turned and looked intently at Nicole. "As my life science officer, I want to know if you have any official recommendations about the crew, especially with respect to psychological interactions among the team members."

Nicole had not expected this. When General Borzov had scheduled this final "crew health assessment" with her, she had not thought that the meeting would extend to the mental health of the Newton dozen as well. "You're asking for a professional psychological evaluation also?" she asked.

"Certainly," General Borzov replied. "I want an A5401 from you that attests to both the physical and psychological readiness of every one of the crew members. The procedure clearly states that the commanding officer, before each sortie, should request crew certification from the life science officer."

"But during the simulations you asked only for physical health data."

Borzov smiled. "I can wait, Madame des Jardins," he said, "if you'd like time to prepare your report."

"No, no," Nicole said after some reflection. "I can give my opinions now and then officially document them later tonight." She hesitated several more seconds before continuing. "I wouldn't put Wilson and Brown together as crew members on any subteam, at least not in the first sortie. And I'd even have some qualms, although this opinion is certainly not as strong, about combining Francesca in a group with either of the two men. I would place no other limitations of any kind on this crew."

"Good. Good." The commander grinned broadly. "I appreciate your report, and not just because it confirms my own opinions. As you can understand, these matters can sometimes be fairly delicate." General Borzov abruptly changed the subject. "Now I have another question of an altogether different nature to ask you."

"What's that?"

"Francesca came to me this morning and suggested that we have a party tomorrow night. She contends that the crew is tense and in need of some kind of release before the first sortie inside Rama. Do you agree with her?"

Nicole reflected for a moment. "It's not a bad idea," she replied. "The strain has been definitely showing. . . . But what kind of party did you have in mind?"

"A dinner all together, here in the control room, some wine and vodka, maybe even a little entertainment." Borzov smiled and put his arm on Nicole's shoulder. "I'm asking your professional opinion, you understand, as my life science officer."

"Of course," Nicole said with a laugh. "General," she added, "if you think it's time for the crew to have a party, then I'd be delighted to lend a hand. . . ."

Nicole finished her report and transferred the file by data line over to Borzov's computer in the military ship. She had been very careful in her language to identify the problem as a "personality conflict" rather than any kind of behavioral pathology. To Nicole, the problem between Wilson and Brown was straightforward: jealousy, pure and simple, the ancient green-eyed monster itself.

She was certain that it was wise to prevent Wilson and Brown from working closely together during sorties inside Rama. Nicole chastised herself for not having raised the issue with Borzov on her own. She realized that her mission portfolio included mental health as well, but somehow she had difficulty thinking of herself as the crew psychiatrist. *I avoid it because it's not an objective process,* she thought. *We have no sensors yet to measure good or bad mental health.*

Nicole walked down the hall of the living area. She was careful to keep one foot on the floor at all times; she was so accustomed to the weightless environment that it was almost second nature. Nicole was glad that the Newton design engineers had worked so hard to minimize the differences between being in space and on the Earth. It made the job of being a cosmonaut much simpler by allowing the crew to concentrate on the more important elements of their work.

Nicole's room was at the end of the corridor. Although each of the cosmonauts had private quarters (the result of heated arguments between the crew and the system engineers, the latter having insisted that sleeping in pairs was a more efficient use of the space), the rooms were very small and confining. There were eight bedrooms on this larger vehicle, called the scientific ship by the crew members. The military ship had four more small bedrooms. Both spacecraft also had exercise rooms and "lobbies," common rooms where there was more comfortable furniture as well as some entertainment options not available in the bedrooms.

As Nicole passed Janos Tabori's room on her way to the exercise area, she heard his unmistakable laugh. His door was open as usual. "Did you really expect me," Janos was saying, "to trade bishops and leave your knights in command of the center of the board? Come on, Shig, I may not be a master, but I do learn from my mistakes. I fell for that one in an earlier game."

Tabori and Takagishi were involved in their usual post-prandial chess match. Almost every "night" (the crew had stayed on a twenty-four-hour day that coincided with Greenwich Mean Time) the two men played for an hour or so before sleeping. Takagishi was a ranked chess master but he was also softhearted and wanted to encourage Tabori. So in virtually every game, after establishing a solid position, Takagishi would allow his edge to be eroded.

Nicole stuck her head in the door. "Come in, beautiful," Janos said with a grin. "Watch me destroy our Asiatic friend in this pseudo-cerebral endeavor." Nicole had started to explain that she was going to the exercise room when a strange creature, about the size of a big mouse, scurried through her legs and into Tabori's room. She jumped back involuntarily as the toy, or whatever it was, headed for the two men.

> "The ousel cock, so black of hue
> With orange-tawny bill,
> The throstle, with his note so true,
> The wren with little quill . . ."

The robot was singing as it skipped toward Janos. Nicole dropped down on her knees and examined the curious newcomer. It had the lower body of a human and the head of a donkey. It continued to sing. Tabori and Takagishi stopped their game and both laughed at the bewildered expression on Nicole's face.

"Go on," said Janos, "tell him that you love him. That's what the fairy queen Titania would do."

Nicole shrugged her shoulders. The little robot was temporarily quiet. As Janos urged again, Nicole mumbled "I love you" to the twenty-centimeter Athenian with a mule's head.

The miniature Bottom turned to Nicole. "Methinks, mistress, you should have little reason for that. And yet, to say the truth, reason and love keep little company together nowadays."

Nicole was amazed. She reached out to pick up the tiny figure but stopped herself when she heard another voice.

"Lord, what fools these mortals be. Now where is that player I changed into an ass. Bottom, where art thou?"

A second small robot, this one dressed as an elf, leapt into the room. When he saw Nicole, he jumped up from the floor and hovered at eye level for several seconds, his tiny back wings beating at a frantic pace. "I be Puck, fair lass," he said. "I've not seen thee before." The robot dropped to the ground and was silent. Nicole was now dumbfounded.

"What in the world—" she started to say.

"*Shh . . .*" Janos said, motioning for her to be quiet. He pointed at Puck. Bottom was sleeping in the corner near the edge of Janos' bed. Puck had now found Bottom and was spraying him with a fine light dust from a small pouch. As the three human beings watched, Bottom's head began to change. Nicole could tell that the small plastic and metal pieces making up the asshead were simply rearranging themselves, but even she was impressed by the scope of the metamorphosis. Puck scampered off just as Bottom awakened with his new human head and started talking.

"I have had a most rare vision," Bottom said. "I have had a dream, past the wit of man to say what dream it was. Man is but an ass if he go about to expound this dream."

"Bravo. Bravo," Janos shouted as the creature fell silent.

"*Omedeto,*" Takagishi added.

Nicole sat down in the single unoccupied chair and looked at her companions. "And to think," she said, shaking her head, "that I actually told the commander you two were psychologically sound." She paused two or three seconds. "Would one of you please tell me what is going on here?"

"It's Wakefield," Janos said. "The man is absolutely brilliant and, unlike some geniuses, also very clever. In addition he's a Shakespeare fanatic. He has a whole family of these little guys, although I think Puck is the only one that flies and Bottom's the only one that changes shape."

"Puck doesn't fly," Richard Wakefield said, coming into the room. "He is barely capable of hovering, and only for a short period." Wakefield seemed embarrassed. "I didn't know you were going to be here," he said to Nicole.

"Sometimes I entertain these two in the middle of their chess game."

"One night," Janos added as Nicole remained speechless, "I had just conceded defeat to Shig when we heard what we thought was a fracas in the hall. Moments later, Tybalt and Mercutio entered the room, swearing and slashing their swords at each other."

"This is a hobby of yours?" Nicole asked after several seconds, indicating the robots with a wave of her hand.

"My lady," Janos interrupted before Wakefield could answer, "never, *never* mistake a passion for a hobby. Our esteemed Japanese scientist does not play chess as a hobby. And this young man from The Bard's hometown of Stratford-on-Avon does not create these robots as a hobby."

Nicole glanced at Richard. She was trying to imagine the amount of energy and work that was necessary for the creation of sophisticated robots like the ones she had just seen. Not to mention talent and, of course, passion. "Very impressive," she said to Wakefield.

His smile acknowledged her compliment. Nicole excused herself and started to leave the room. Puck zoomed around her and stood in the doorway.

> "If we shadows have offended,
> Think but this, and all is mended,
> That you have but slumbered here,
> While these visions did appear."

Nicole was laughing as she stepped over the sprite and waved good night to her friends.

Nicole stayed in the exercise room longer than she expected. Ordinarily thirty minutes of hard bicycling or running in place was enough to release her tensions and relax her body for sleep. On this evening, however, with the goal of their mission now so close at hand, it was necessary for her to work out for a longer time to calm her hyperactive system. Part of her difficulty was her residual concern about the report she had filed recommending that Wilson and Brown be separated on all important mission activities.

Was I too hasty? she asked herself. *Did I let General Borzov sway my opinion?* Nicole was very proud of her professional reputation and often constructively second-guessed her major decisions. Toward the end of her exercise she convinced herself again that she had filed the proper report. Her tired body told her that it was ready to sleep.

When she returned to the living area in the spacecraft, it was dark everywhere except in the hallway. As she started to turn left into the corridor that led to her room, she happened to glance beyond the lobby, in the direction of the small room where she kept all the medical supplies. *That's strange,* she thought, straining her eyes in the dim light. *It looks as if I left the supply room door open.*

Nicole walked across the lobby. The supply door was indeed ajar. She had already activated the automatic lock and had started to close the door when she heard a noise inside the dark room. Nicole reached in and turned on the light. She surprised Francesca Sabatini, who was sitting in the corner at a computer terminal. There was information displayed on the monitor in front of her and Francesca was holding a thin bottle in one of her hands.

"Oh, hello, Nicole," Francesca said nonchalantly, as if it were normal for her to be sitting in the dark at the computer in the medical supply room.

Nicole walked slowly over to the computer. "What's going on?" she said casually, her eyes scanning the information on the screen. From the coded headings, Nicole could tell that Francesca had requested the inventory subroutine to list the birth control devices available onboard the spacecraft.

"What is this?" Nicole now asked, pointing at the monitor. There was a trace of irritation in her voice. All the cosmonauts knew that the medical supply room was off limits to everyone but the life science officer.

When Francesca still did not reply, Nicole became angry. "How did you get in here?" she demanded. The two women were only a few centimeters apart in the small alcove next to the desk. Nicole suddenly reached over and grabbed the bottle out of Francesca's hand. While Nicole was reading the label, Francesca pushed her way through the narrow space and headed for the door. Nicole discovered that the liquid in her hand was for inducing abortions and quickly followed Francesca into the lobby.

"Are you going to explain this?" Nicole asked.

"Just give me the bottle, please," Francesca said finally.

"I can't do that," answered Nicole, shaking her head. "This is a very strong medicine with serious side effects. What did you think you were going to do? Steal it and have it pass unnoticed? As soon as I completed an inventory comparison I would have known that it was gone."

The two women stared at each other for several seconds. "Look, Nicole," Francesca said at length, managing a smile, "this is really a very simple matter. I have discovered recently, much to my chagrin, that I am in the very early stages of pregnancy. I wish to abort the embryo. It's a private matter and I did not want to involve you or any of the rest of the crew."

"You can't be pregnant," Nicole replied quickly. "I would have seen it in your biometry data."

"I'm only four or five days. But I'm certain. I can already feel the changes in my body. And it's the right time of the month."

"You know the proper procedures for medical problems," Nicole said after some hesitation. "This might have been very simple, to use your phrase, if you had first come to me. Most likely I would have respected your request for confidentiality. But now you've given me a dilemma—"

"Will you stop with the bureaucratic lecture," Francesca interrupted sharply. "I'm really not interested in the goddamn rules. A man has made me pregnant and I intend to remove the fetus. Now, are you going to give me the bottle, or must I find another way?"

Nicole was outraged. "You are amazing," she responded to Francesca. "Do you really expect me to hand you this bottle and walk away? Without asking any questions? You may be that cavalier about your life and health, but I certainly am not. I have to examine you first, check your medical history, determine the age of the embryo—only then would I even *consider* prescribing this medicine for you. Besides, I would feel compelled as well to point out to you that there are moral and psychological ramifications—"

Francesca laughed out loud. "Spare me your ramifications, Nicole. I don't need your upper class Beauvois morality passing judgment on my life. Congratulations to you for raising a child as a single parent. My situation is much different. The father of this baby purposely stopped taking his pills, thinking my being pregnant would rekindle my love for him. He was wrong. This baby is unwanted. Now, should I be more graphic—"

"That's enough," Nicole interrupted, pursing her lips in disgust. "The details of your personal life are really none of my business. I must decide what is best for you and for the mission." She paused. "In any event, I must insist on a proper examination, including the normal pelvic internal image set. If you refuse, then I won't authorize the abortion. And of course I'd be forced to make a complete report—"

Francesca laughed. "You don't need to threaten me. I am not *that* stupid. If it will make you feel better to stick your fancy equipment between my legs, then be my guest. But let's do it. I want this baby out of me before the sortie."

Nicole and Francesca hardly exchanged a dozen words during the next hour. They went together to the small infirmary, where Nicole used her sensitive instruments to verify the existence and size of the embryo. She also tested Francesca for her acceptability to receive the abortion liquid. The fetus had been growing inside Francesca for five days. *Who might you be?* Nicole thought as she looked on the monitor at the microscopic image of the tiny sac embedded in the walls of the uterus. Even in the microscope on the probe there was no way to tell that the collection of cells was a living thing. *But you are already alive. And much of your future is already programmed by your genes.*

Nicole had the printer list for Francesca what she could expect physically once she had ingested the medicine. The fetus would be swept away, rejected by her body, within twenty-four hours. There could possibly be some slight cramping with the normal menstruation that would follow immediately.

Francesca drank the liquid without hesitation. As her patient was dressing, Nicole thought back to the time when she had first suspected her own pregnancy. *Never once did I consider . . . And not just because her father was a prince. No. It was a question of responsibility. And love.*

"I can tell what you're thinking," Francesca said when she was ready to leave. She was standing by the infirmary door. "But don't waste your time. You have enough problems of your own."

Nicole did not reply. "So tomorrow the little bastard will be gone," Francesca said coldly, her eyes tired and angry. "It's a damn good thing. The world doesn't need another half-black baby." Francesca didn't wait for Nicole's response.

16

RAMA RAMA
BURNING BRIGHT

The touchdown near the entry port to Rama was smooth and without incident. Following the precedent of Commander Norton seventy years earlier, General Borzov instructed Yamanaka and Turgenyev to guide the Newton to a contact point just outside the hundred-meter circular disc centered on the spin axis of the giant cylinder. A set of low, pillbox-shaped structures temporarily held the spacecraft from Earth in place against the slight centrifugal force created by the spinning Rama. Within ten minutes strong attachments anchored the Newton firmly to its target.

The large disc was, as anticipated, the outer seal of the Raman air lock. Wakefield and Tábori departed from the Newton in their EVA gear and started searching for an embedded wheel. The wheel, which was the manual control for the air lock, was in exactly the predicted place. It turned as expected and exposed an opening in the outer shell of Rama. Since nothing about Rama II had yet varied from its predecessor in any way, the two cosmonauts continued with the entry procedure.

Four hours later, after considerable shuttling back and forth in the half kilometer of corridors and tunnels that connected the great hollow interior of the alien spaceship to the external air lock, the two men had finished opening the three redundant cylindrical doors. They had also deployed the transportation system that would ferry people and equipment from the Newton to the inside of Rama. This ferry had been designed by the engineers on Earth to

slide along the parallel grooves the Ramans had cut into
the walls of the outer tunnels unknown ages ago.

After a short break for lunch, Yamanaka joined Wakefield and Tabori and the three of them constructed the
planned Alpha communications relay station at the inside
end of the tunnel. The patterns of the arrayed antennas
had been carefully engineered so that, if the second Raman
vehicle was identical to the first, two-way communication
would be possible between cosmonauts located anywhere
on the stairways or in the northern half of the Central
Plain. The master communication plan called for the es-
tablishment of another major relay station, to be called
Beta, near the Cylindrical Sea; the pair of stations would
provide strong links everywhere in the Northern Hemicylinder and would even extend to the island of New
York.

Brown and Takagishi took their positions in the control
center once the operation of the Alpha relay station was
verified. The countdown to interior drone deployment
proceeded. Takagishi was obviously both nervous and excited as he finished his preflight tests with his drone.
Brown seemed relaxed, even casual, as he completed his
final preparations. Francesca Sabatini was sitting in front
of the multiple monitors, ready to select the best images
for real-time transmission to the Earth.

General Borzov himself announced the major events in
the sequence. He paused for a dramatic breath before
issuing the command to activate the two drones. The
drones then flew away into the dark emptiness of Rama.
Seconds later the main screen in the control center, whose
picture came directly from the drone being commanded
by David Brown, was flooded with light as the first flare
ignited. When the light became more manageable, the
outline of the first wide-angle shot could be seen. It had
always been planned that this initial picture would be a
composite of the Northern Hemisphere, covering all the
territory from the bowl-shaped end where they had entered down to the Cylindrical Sea at the midpoint of the
artificial world. The sharp image that was eventually frozen on the screen was overwhelming. It was one thing to

read about Rama and to conduct simulations inside its replica; it was quite another to be anchored to the gigantic spaceship near the orbit of Venus, and to be taking a first look inside. . . .

That the vista was familiar barely lessened the wonder of the image. In the end of the crater-shaped bowl, starting from the tunnels, a complex of terraces and ramps fanned out until they reached the main body of the spinning cylinder. Trisecting this bowl were three wide ladders, resembling broad railroad tracks, each of which later expanded into enormous stairways with more than thirty thousand steps each. The ladder/stairway combinations resembled three equally spaced ribs of an umbrella and provided a way to ascend (or descend) from the flat bottom of the crater to the vast Central Plain wrapped around the wall of the spinning cylinder.

The northern half of the Central Plain spread out to fill most of the picture on the screen. The huge expanse was broken into rectangular fields that had irregular dimensions except immediately around the "cities." The three cities in the wide-angle image, clusters of tall slim objects, resembling man-made buildings, that were connected by what looked like highways running along the edges of the fields, were immediately recognized by the crew as the Paris, Rome, and London named by the first Raman explorers. Equally striking in the image were the long straight grooves or valleys of the Central Plain. These three linear trenches, ten kilometers long and a hundred meters wide, were equally spaced around the curve of Rama. During the first Raman encounter these valleys had been the sources of the light that had filled the "worldlet" shortly after the melting of the Cylindrical Sea.

The strange sea, a body of water running completely around the huge cylinder, was at the far edge of the image. It was still frozen, as expected, and in its center was the mysterious island of towering skyscrapers that had been called New York since its original discovery. The skyscrapers stretched off the end of the picture, the looming towers beckoning to be visited.

The entire crew stared silently at the image for almost a

minute. Then Dr. David Brown started hooting. "All right,
Rama," he said in a proud voice. "You see, all you disbe-
lievers," he shouted loud enough for everyone to hear, "it
is *exactly* like the first one." Francesca's video camera
turned to record Brown's exultation. Most of the rest of
the crew were still speechless, transfixed by the details on
the monitor.

Meanwhile, Takagishi's drone was transmitting narrow-
angle photos of the area just under the tunnel. These
images were featured on the smaller screens around the
control center. The pictures would be used to reverify the
designs of the communication and transportation infrastructure to be established inside Rama. This was the real
"job" of this phase of the mission—comparing the thousands of pictures that would be taken by these drones to
the existing camera mosaics from Rama I. Although most
of the comparisons could be done digitally (and therefore
automatically), there would always be differences that would
require human explanation. Even if the two spaceships
were identical, the differing light levels at the times
the images were taken would create some artificial miscompares.

Two hours later the last of the drones returned to the
relay station and an initial summary of the photographic
survey was complete. There were no major structural
differences between Rama II and the earlier space vehicle
down to a scale of a hundred meters. The only significant
region of miscompares at that resolution was the Cylindrical Sea itself, and ice reflectivity was a notoriously difficult
phenomenon to handle with a straightforward digital comparison algorithm. It had been a long and exciting day.
Borzov announced that crew assignments for the first sortie would be posted in an hour and that a "special dinner"
would be served in the control center two hours later.

"You cannot do this," an angry David Brown shouted,
bursting into the commander's office without knocking,
and brandishing a hard-copy printout of the first sortie
assignments.

"What are you talking about?" General Borzov responded.
He was annoyed by Dr. Brown's rude entrance.

"There must be some kind of mistake," Brown continued in a loud voice. "You can't really expect me to stay here on the Newton during the first sortie." When there was no response from General Borzov, the American scientist changed tactics. "I want you to know that I don't accept this. And the ISA management won't like it either."

Borzov stood up behind his desk. "Close the door, Dr. Brown," he said calmly. David Brown slammed the sliding door. "Now *you* listen to me for a minute," the general continued. "I don't give a damn who you know. I am the commanding officer of this mission. If you continue to act like a prima donna, I'll see to it that you *never* set foot inside Rama."

Brown lowered his voice. "But I demand an explanation," he said with undisguised hostility. "I am the senior scientist on this mission. I am also the leading spokesman for the Newton project among the media. How can you possibly justify leaving me onboard the Newton while nine other cosmonauts go inside Rama?"

"I don't have to justify my actions," Borzov replied, for the moment enjoying his power over the arrogant American. He leaned forward. "But for the record, and because I anticipated this childish outburst of yours, I will tell you why you're not going on the first sortie. There are two major purposes for our first visit: to establish the communications/transportation infrastructure and to complete a detailed survey of the interior, ensuring that this spaceship is exactly like the first one—"

"That's already been confirmed by the drones," Brown interrupted.

"Not according to Dr. Takagishi," Borzov rebutted. "He says that—"

"Shit, General, Takagishi won't be satisfied until every square centimeter of Rama has been shown to be exactly the same as the first ship. You saw the results of the drone survey. Do you have any doubt in your mind—"

David Brown stopped himself in midsentence. General Borzov was drumming on his desk with his fingers and regarding Dr. Brown with a cold stare. "Are you going to let me finish now?" Borzov said at length. He waited a few more seconds. "Whatever you may think," the commander continued, "Dr. Takagishi is considered to be the world expert on the interior of Rama. You cannot argue even for a minute that your knowledge of the details approaches his. I need all five of the space cadets for the infrastructure work. The two journalists must go inside, not only because there are two separate tasks, but also because world attention is focused on us at this time. Finally, I believe it is important for my subsequent management of this mission that I myself go inside at least once, and I choose to do it *now*. Since the procedures clearly state that at least three members of the crew must remain outside Rama during the early sorties, it is not difficult to figure out—"

"You don't fool me for a minute," David Brown now interrupted nastily. "I know what this is all about. You've concocted an apparently logical excuse to hide the real reason for my exclusion from the first sortie team. You're jealous, Borzov. You can't stand the fact that I am regarded by most people as the real leader of this mission."

The commander stared at the scientist for over fifteen seconds without saying anything. "You know, Brown," he said finally, "I feel sorry for you. You are remarkably talented, but your talent is exceeded by your own opinion of it. If you weren't such a—" This time it was Borzov's turn to stop himself in midsentence. He looked away. "Incidentally, since I know that you will go back to your room and immediately whine to the ISA, I should probably tell you that the life science officer's fitness report explicitly recommends against your sharing any mission duties with Wilson—because of the personal animosity that both of you have demonstrated."

Brown's eyes narrowed. "Are you telling me that Nicole des Jardins actually filed an official memorandum citing Wilson and me by name?"

Borzov nodded.

"The bitch," Brown muttered.

"It's always someone else who is at fault, isn't it, Dr. Brown?" General Borzov said, smiling at his adversary.

David Brown turned around and stalked out of the office.

For the banquet, General Borzov ordered a few precious bottles of wine to be opened. The commanding officer was in an excellent mood. Francesca's suggestion had been a good one. There was a definite feeling of camaraderie among the cosmonauts as they brought the small tables together in the control center and anchored them to the floor.

Dr. David Brown did not come to the banquet. He remained in his room while the other eleven crew members feasted on game hens and wild rice. Francesca awkwardly reported that Brown was "feeling under the weather," but when Janos Tabori playfully volunteered to go check the American scientist's health, Francesca hurriedly added that Dr. Brown wanted to be left alone. Janos and Richard Wakefield, both of whom had several glasses of wine, bantered with Francesca at one end of the table while Reggie Wilson and General O'Toole engaged in an animated discussion about the coming baseball season at the opposite end. Nicole sat between General Borzov and Admiral Heilmann and listened to their reminiscences of peacekeeping activities in the early post-Chaos days. Cosmonauts Turgenyev and Yamanaka were their usual taciturn selves, contributing to the conversation only when asked a direct question.

When the meal was over, Francesca excused herself. She and Dr. Takagishi disappeared for several minutes. When they returned Francesca asked the cosmonauts to turn their chairs to face the large screen. Then, with the lights out, she and Takagishi projected a full exterior view of Rama on the monitor. Except that this was not the dull gray cylinder everyone had seen before. No, this Rama had been cleverly colored, using image processing subroutines, and was now a black cylinder with yellow-gold stripes. The end of the cylinder looked almost like a face. There was a momentary quiet in the room before Francesca began to recite.

> "Tyger, tyger, burning bright,
> In the forests of the night,

What immortal hand or eye,
Could frame thy fearful symmetry?"

Nicole des Jardins felt a cold chill run up her spine as she listened to Francesca begin the next verse.

"In what distant deeps or skies,
Burnt the fire of thine eyes? . . ."

That is the real question after all, Nicole was thinking. *Who made this gargantuan spacecraft? That's much more important for our ultimate destiny than why.*

"What the hammer? What the chain?
In what furnace was thy brain?
What the anvil? What dread grasp
Dare its deadly terrors clasp? . . ."

Across the table General O'Toole was also mesmerized by Francesca's recitation. His mind was again struggling with the same fundamental questions that had been bothering him since he originally applied for the mission. *Dear God,* he was wondering, *how do these Ramans fit into your universe? Did You create them first, before us? Are they our cousins in some sense? Why have You sent them here at this time?*

"When the stars threw down their spears
And water'd heaven with their tears,
Did He smile His work to see,
Did He who made the Lamb make thee?"

When Francesca finished the short poem there was a brief silence and then spontaneous applause. She graciously mentioned that Dr. Takagishi had provided all the image processing intelligence and the likable Japanese cosmonaut took an embarrassed bow. Then Janos Tabori stood at his chair. "I think I speak for all of us, Shig and Francesca, in congratulating you on that original and thought-provoking performance," he said with a grin. "It almost, but not quite, made me feel serious about what we are doing tomorrow."

"Speaking of which," General Borzov said, rising at the head of the table with his recently opened bottle of Ukrainian vodka, from which he had already taken two strong belts, "it is now time for an ancient Russian tradition—the toasts. I brought along only two bottles of this national treasure and I propose to share them both with you, my comrades and colleagues, on this very special evening."

He placed both bottles in General O'Toole's hands and the American adroitly used the liquid dispenser to channel the vodka into small covered cups that were passed around the table. "As Irina Turgenyev knows," the commander continued, "there is always a small worm in the bottom of a bottle of Ukrainian vodka. Legend has it that he who eats the worm will be endowed with special powers for twenty-four hours. Admiral Heilmann has marked two of the cup bottoms with an infrared cross. The two people who drink from the marked cups will each be allowed to eat one of the vodka-saturated worms."

"Yuch," said Janos a moment later, as he passed the infrared scanner to Nicole. He had first verified that he had no cross on the bottom of his cup. "This is one contest I am glad to lose."

Nicole's cup did have a marking on the bottom. She was one of the two lucky cosmonauts who would be able to eat a Ukrainian worm for dessert. She found herself wondering, *Must I do this?* and then answering her own question affirmatively as she saw the earnest look on her commanding officer's face. *Oh well,* she thought, *it probably won't kill me. Any parasites have probably been rendered harmless by the alcohol.*

General Borzov himself had the second cup with a cross on the bottom. The general smiled, placed one of the two tiny worms in his own cup (and the other in Nicole's), and raised his vodka toward the ceiling of the spacecraft.

"Let us all drink to a successful mission," he said. "For each of us, these next few days and weeks will be the greatest adventure of our lives. In a real sense, we dozen

are human ambassadors to an alien culture. Let us
each resolve to do our best to properly represent our
species."

He took the cover off his cup, being careful not to jiggle
it, and then drank it all in one gulp. He swallowed the
worm whole. Nicole also swallowed the worm quickly,
commenting to herself that the only thing she had ever
eaten that tasted worse than the worm was that awful
tuber during her Poro ceremony in the Ivory Coast.

After several more short toasts the lights in the room
began to dim. "And now," General Borzov announced
with a grand gesture, "direct from Stratford, the Newton
proudly presents Richard Wakefield and his talented robots." The room became dark except for a square meter to
the left of the table that was spotlit from above. In the
middle of the light was a cutaway of an old castle. A
female robot, twenty centimeters high and dressed in a
robe, was walking around in one of the rooms. She was
reading a letter at the beginning of the scene. After a few
steps, however, she dropped her hands to her sides and
began to speak.

"Glamis thou art, and Cawdor; and shalt be
What thou art promised. Yet do I fear thy nature:
It is too full o' th' milk of human kindness
To catch the nearest way. Thou wouldst be
    great . . ."

"I know that woman," Janos said with a grin to Nicole.
"I have met her somewhere before."

"*Shh,*" replied Nicole. She was fascinated by the precision in the movements of Lady Macbeth. *That Wakefield
really is a genius,* she was thinking. *How is he able to
design such extraordinary detail into those little things?*
Nicole was astonished by the range of expressions on the
robot's face.

As she concentrated, the tiny stage began to swim in
Nicole's mind. She momentarily forgot she was watching
robots in a miniature performance. A messenger came in
and told Lady Macbeth both that her husband was draw-

ing near and that King Duncan would be spending the night in their castle. Nicole watched Lady Macbeth's face explode with ambitious anticipation as soon as the messenger had departed.

> ". . . Come you Spirits
> That tend on mortal thoughts. Unsex me here
> And fill me, from the crown to the toe, top-full
> Of direst cruelty! Make thick my blood . . ."

My God, Nicole thought, blinking her eyes to make certain they were not playing tricks on her, *she's changing!* Indeed she was. As the words "Unsex me here" came from the robot, her (or its) shape began to change. The impression of the breasts against the metal gown, the roundness of the hips, even the softness of the face all disappeared. An androgynous robot played on as Lady Macbeth.

Nicole was spellbound and floating in a fantasy induced both by her wild imagination and the sudden intake of alcohol. The new face on the robot was vaguely reminiscent of someone she knew. She heard a disturbance to her right and turned to see Reggie Wilson talking avidly with Francesca. Nicole glanced back and forth quickly from Francesca to Lady Macbeth. *That's it,* she said to herself. *This new Lady Macbeth resembles Francesca.*

A burst of fear, a premonition of tragedy, suddenly overwhelmed Nicole and plunged her into terror. *Something terrible is going to happen,* her mind was saying. She took several deep breaths and tried to calm herself but the eerie feeling would not go away. On the little stage King Duncan had just been greeted by his gracious hostess for the evening. To her left Nicole saw Francesca offer General Borzov the last sips of the wine. Nicole could not quell her panic.

"Nicole, what's the matter?" Janos asked. He could tell she was distressed.

"Nothing," she said. She gathered all her strength and rose to her feet. "Something I ate must have disagreed with me. I think I'll go to my room."

"But you'll miss the movie after dinner," Janos said humorously. Nicole forced a pained smile. He helped her stand up. Nicole heard Lady Macbeth berating her husband for his lack of courage and one more wave of premonitory fear surged through her. She waited until the adrenaline burst had subsided and then excused herself quietly from the group. She walked slowly back to her room.

17

DEATH OF A SOLDIER

In her dream Nicole was ten years old again and playing in the woods behind her home in the Paris suburb of Chilly-Mazarin. She had a sudden feeling that her mother was dying. The little girl panicked. She ran toward the house to tell her father. A small snarling cat blocked her path. Nicole stopped. She heard a scream. She left the path and went through the trees. The branches scraped her skin. The cat followed her. Nicole heard another scream. When she awakened a frightened Janos Tabori was standing over her. "It's General Borzov," Janos said. "He's in excruciating pain."

Nicole jumped swiftly out of bed, threw her robe around her, grabbed her portable medical kit, and followed Janos into the corridor. "It looks like an appendicitis," he mentioned as they hurried into the lobby. "But I'm not certain."

Irina Turgenyev was kneeling beside the commander and holding his hand. The general himself was stretched out on a couch. His face was white and there was sweat on his brow. "Ah, Dr. des Jardins has arrived." He managed a smile. Borzov then tried to sit up, winced from the pain, and let himself lie back down. "Nicole," he said quietly, "I am in agony. I've never felt anything like this in my life, not even when I was wounded in the army."

"How long ago did it start?" she asked. Nicole had pulled out her scanner and biometry monitor to check all his vital statistics. Meanwhile Francesca and her video camera had moved over right behind Nicole's shoulder to film the doctor performing the diagnosis. Nicole impatiently motioned for her to back away.

"Maybe two or three minutes ago," General Borzov said with effort. "I was sitting here in a chair watching the movie, laughing heartily as I recall, when there was an intense, sharp pain, here on my lower right side. It felt as if something were burning me from the inside."

Nicole programmed the scanner to search through the last three minutes of detailed data recorded by the Hakamatsu probes inside Borzov. She located the onset of the pain, easily identifiable in terms of both heart rate and endocrine secretions. She next requested a full dump over the time period of interest from all channels. "Janos," she then said to her colleague, "go over to the supply room and bring me the portable diagnostician." She handed Tabori the code card for the door.

"You have a slight fever, suggesting your body is fighting some infection," Nicole told General Borzov. "All the internal data confirms that you are feeling severe pain." Cosmonaut Tabori returned with a small electronic array shaped like a box. Nicole extracted a small data cube from the scanner and inserted it into the diagnostician. In about thirty seconds the little monitor blinked and the words 94% LIKELY APPENDICITIS appeared. Nicole pressed a key and the screen displayed the other possible diagnoses, including hernia, internal muscle tear, and drug reaction. None were, according to the diagnostician, more than 2 percent probable.

I have two choices at this juncture, Nicole was thinking rapidly as General Borzov winced again from the pain. *I can send all the data down to Earth for a complete diagnostic, per the procedure* . . . She glanced at her watch and quickly computed twice the round-trip light time plus the minimum duration of a physician's conference after the electronic diagnosis was complete. *By which time it might be too late.*

"What does it say, Doctor?" the general was asking. His eyes were entreating her to end the pain as quickly as possible.

"Most likely diagnosis is appendicitis," Nicole answered.

"Dammit," General Borzov responded. He looked around at all the others. Everyone was there except Wilson and Takagishi, both of whom had skipped the movie. "But I won't make the project wait. We'll go ahead with the first and second sorties while I'm recuperating." Another sharp pain jolted him and his face contorted.

"Whoa," said Nicole. "It's not certain yet. We need a little more data first." She repeated the earlier data dump, now using the extra two minutes of information that had been recorded since she arrived in the lobby. This time the diagnosis read 92% LIKELY APPENDICITIS. Nicole was about to routinely check the alternative diagnoses when she felt the commander's strong hand on her arm.

"If we do this quickly, before too much poison builds up in my system, then this is a straightforward operation for the robot surgeon, isn't it?"

Nicole nodded.

"And if we spend the time to obtain a diagnostic concurrence from the Earth—*ouch*—then my body may be in deeper trauma?"

He is reading my mind, Nicole thought at first. Then she realized that the general was only displaying his thorough knowledge of the Newton procedures.

"Is the patient trying to give the doctor a suggestion?" Nicole asked, smiling despite Borzov's obvious pain.

"I wouldn't be that presumptuous," the commander answered with just a trace of a twinkle in his eye.

Nicole glanced back at the monitor. It was still blinking 92% LIKELY APPENDICITIS. "Do you have anything to add?" she said to Janos Tabori.

"Only that I have seen an appendicitis before," the little Hungarian answered, "once, when I was a student, in Budapest. The symptoms were exactly like this."

"All right," Nicole said. "Go prepare RoSur for the operation. Admiral Heilmann, will you and cosmonaut Yamanaka help General Borzov to the infirmary please?" She turned around to Francesca. "I recognize that this is big news. I will allow you in the operating room on three conditions. You will scrub like all the surgical staff. You will stand quietly over against the wall with your camera. And you will absolutely obey any order that I give you."

"Good enough." Francesca nodded. "Thank you."

Irina Turgenyev and General O'Toole were still waiting in the lobby after Borzov left with Heilmann and Yamanaka.

"I'm certain that I speak for both of us," the American said in his usual sincere manner. "Can we help in any way?"

"Janos will assist me while RoSur performs the operation. But I could use one more pair of hands, as an emergency backup."

"I would like to do that," O'Toole said. "I have some hospital experience from my charity work."

"Fine," replied Nicole. "Now come with me to clean up."

RoSur, the portable robot surgeon that had been brought along on the Newton mission for just this kind of situation, was not in the same class, in terms of medical sophistication, as the fully autonomous operating rooms at the advanced hospitals on Earth. But RoSur was a technological marvel in its own right. It could be packed in a small suitcase and weighed only four kilograms. Its power requirements were low. And there were more than a hundred configurations in which it could be used.

Janos Tabori unpacked RoSur. The electronic surgeon didn't look like much in its stowed configuration. All of its spindly joints and appendages were neatly arranged for easy storage. After Janos rechecked his *RoSur User's Guide*, he picked up the central control box of the robot surgeon and affixed it, as suggested, to the side of the infirmary bed where General Borzov was already lying. His pain had only subsided a little. The impatient commander was urging everyone to hurry.

Janos entered the code word identifying the operation. RoSur automatically deployed all its limbs, including its extraordinary scalpel/hand with four fingers, in the configuration needed to remove an appendix. Nicole then entered the room, her hands in gloves and her body covered with the white gown of the surgeon.

"Have you finished the software check?" she said.

Janos nodded.

"I'll complete all the preoperation tests while you scrub," she said to him. She motioned for Francesca and General O'Toole, both of whom were standing right outside the door, to enter the small room. "Any better?" she said to Borzov.

"Not much," he grumbled.

"That was a light sedative I administered. RoSur will give you the full anesthetic as the first step in the operation." Nicole had done all her memory refreshing in her room while she was dressing. She knew this operation inside out; it had been one of the surgical procedures they had performed during the test simulations. She entered Borzov's personal data file into RoSur, hooked up the electronic lines that would bring patient monitor information to RoSur during the appendectomy, and verified that all the software had passed self-test. As her last check, Nicole carefully tuned the pair of tiny stereo cameras that worked in concert with the surgical hand.

Janos came back into the room. Nicole pressed a button on the robot surgeon's control box and two hard copies of the operations sequence were quickly printed. Nicole took one and handed the other to Janos. "Is everyone ready?" she asked, her eyes on General Borzov. The commanding officer of the Newton moved his head up and down. Nicole activated RoSur.

One of the robot surgeon's four hands gunned an anesthetic into the patient and in one minute Borzov was unconscious. As Francesca's camera recorded every move of this historic operation (she was whispering occasional comments into her ultrasensitive microphone), the scalpel hand of RoSur, aided by its twin eyes, made the incisions necessary to isolate the suspect organ. No human surgeon had ever been so swift or deft. Armed with a battery of sensors checking hundreds of parameters every microsecond, RoSur had folded back all the requisite tissue and laid the appendix bare within two minutes. Programmed into the automatic sequence was a thirty-second inspection time before the robot surgeon would continue with the removal of the organ.

Nicole bent over the patient to check the exposed appendix. It was neither swollen nor inflamed. "Look at this, quick, Janos," she said, her eye on the digital clock counting down the inspection period. "It looks perfectly healthy." Janos leaned over from the opposite side of the operating table. *My God,* Nicole thought, *we're going to remove . . .* The digital clock read 00:08. "Stop it," she shouted. "Stop the operation." Nicole and Janos both reached for the robot surgeon control box at the same time.

At that instant the entire Newton spacecraft lurched sideways. Nicole was thrown backward, against the wall. Janos fell forward, smacking his head against the operating table. His outstretched fingers landed on the control box and then slowly released as he slumped to the floor. General O'Toole and Francesca were both thrown against the far wall. A *beep, beep* from one of the inserted Hakamatsu probes indicated that someone in the room was in serious trouble physically. Nicole checked briefly to see that O'Toole and Sabatini were all right and then struggled against the continuing torque to regain her position next to the operating table. With great effort she pulled herself across the room on the floor, using the anchored legs of the table. When she was beside the table she steadied herself, still holding on to the legs, and stood up.

Blood spattered Nicole as her head crossed the plane of the operating table. She stared with disbelief at Borzov's body. The entire incision was full of blood and RoSur's scalpel/hand was buried inside, apparently still cutting away. It was Borzov's probe set that was going *beep, beep*, despite the fact that Nicole had inserted, by command, significantly wider emergency values just before the operation.

A wave of fear and nausea swept through Nicole as she realized that the robot had not aborted its surgical activities. Holding on tight against the powerful force trying to push her against the wall again, she somehow managed to reach over to the control box and switch off the power. The scalpel withdrew from the pool of blood and restowed itself against a stanchion. Nicole then tried to stop the massive hemorrhaging.

Thirty seconds later the unexplained force vanished as suddenly as it had appeared. General O'Toole clambered to his feet and came over beside the now desperate Nicole. The scalpel had done too much damage. The commander was bleeding to death before her eyes. "Oh, no. Oh, God," O'Toole said as he surveyed the wreckage of his friend's body. The insistent *beep, beep* continued.

Now the life system alarms around the table sounded as well. Francesca recovered in time to record the final ten seconds of Valeriy Borzov's life.

It was a very long night for the entire Newton crew. In the two hours immediately after the operation, Rama went through a sequence of three more maneuvers, each, like the first one, lasting one or two minutes. The Earth eventually confirmed that the combined maneuvers had changed the attitude, spin rate, and trajectory of the alien space-ship. Nobody could ascertain the exact purpose of the set of maneuvers; they were just "orientation changes," according to the Earth scientists, that had altered the incli-nation and line of apsides of the Rama orbit. However, the energy of the trajectory had not been changed significantly—Rama was still on a hyperbolic escape path with respect to the Sun.

Everyone onboard the Newton and on Earth was stunned by the sudden death of General Borzov. He was eulogized by the press of all nations and his many accomplishments were lauded by his peers and associates. His death was reported as an accident, attributed to the untimely motion of the Rama spacecraft that had taken place during the middle of a routine appendectomy. But within eight hours after his death, knowledgeable people everywhere were asking tough questions. Why had the Rama spacecraft moved at exactly that time? Why had RoSur's fault protec-tion system failed to stop the operation? Why were the human medical officers presiding over the procedure not able to switch off the power before it was too late?

Nicole des Jardins was asking herself the same ques-tions. She had already completed the documents required when a death occurs in space and had sealed Borzov's body in the vacuum coffin at the back of the military ship's huge supply depot. She had quickly prepared and filed her report on the incident; O'Toole, Sabatini, and Tabori had all done the same. There was only one significant omission in the reports. Janos failed to mention that he had reached for the control box during the Raman maneu-ver. At the time Nicole did not think his omission was important.

The required teleconferences with ISA officials were extremely painful. Nicole was the person who bore the brunt of all the inane and repetitive questioning. She had to reach deep inside herself for extra reserves to keep from losing her temper several times. Nicole had expected that Francesca might hint at incompetence on the part of the Newton medical staff in her teleconference, but the Italian journalist was evenhanded and fair in her reportage.

After a short interview with Francesca, in which Nicole discussed how horrified she had been at the moment she had first seen Borzov's incision filled with blood, the life science officer retired to her room, ostensibly to rest and/or sleep. But Nicole did not allow herself the luxury of resting. Over and over she reviewed the critical seconds of the operation. Could she have done anything to change the outcome? What could possibly explain RoSur's failure to stop itself automatically?

In Nicole's mind there was little or no probability that RoSur's fault protection algorithms had a design flaw; they wouldn't have passed all the rigorous prelaunch testing if they contained errors. So somewhere there must have been a human error, either negligence (had she and Janos, in their haste, forgotten to initialize some key fault protection parameter?) or an accident during those chaotic seconds following the unexpected torque. Her fruitless searching for an explanation and her almost total fatigue made her extremely depressed when she finally fell asleep. To her, one part of the equation was very clear. A man had died and she had been responsible.

18

POSTMORTEM

As expected, the day after General Borzov's death was full of turmoil. The ISA investigation into the incident expanded and most of the cosmonauts were subjected to another long cross-examination. Nicole was interrogated about her sobriety at the time of the operation. Some of the questions were ugly and Nicole, who was trying to husband her energy for her own investigation of the events surrounding the tragedy, lost her patience twice with the interrogators.

"Look," she exclaimed at one point, "I have now explained four times that I had two glasses of wine and one glass of vodka three hours before the operation. I have admitted that I would not have drunk any alcohol prior to surgery, *if* I had known that I was going to operate. I have even acknowledged, in retrospect, that perhaps one of the two life science officers should have remained completely sober. But that's all hindsight. I repeat what I said earlier. Neither my judgment nor my physical abilities was in any way impaired by alcohol at the time of the operation."

Back in her room, Nicole focused her attention on the issue of why the robot surgeon proceeded with the operation when its own internal fault protection should have aborted all activities. Based on the *RoSur User's Guide*, it was evident that at least two separate sensor systems should have sent error messages to the central processor in the robot surgeon. The accelerometer package should have informed the processor that the environmental conditions were outside acceptable limits because of the untoward lateral force. And the stereo cameras should have transmitted a message indicating that the observed images were at variance with the predicted images. But for some reason neither sensor set was successful in interrupting the ongoing operation. What had happened?

It took Nicole almost five hours to rule out the possibility of a major error, either software or hardware, in the RoSur system itself. She verified that the loaded software and data base had been correct by doing a code comparison with the benchmark standard version of the software tested extensively during prelaunch. She also isolated the stereo imaging and accelerometer telemetry from the few seconds right after the spacecraft lurched. These data were properly transmitted to the central processor and should have resulted in an aborted sequence. But they didn't. Why not? The only possible explanation was that the software had been changed by manual command between the time of loading and the performance of the appendectomy.

Nicole was now out of her league. Her software and system engineering knowledge had been stretched to the limit in satisfying herself that there had been no error in the loaded software. To determine whether and when commands might have changed the code or parameters after they were installed in RoSur required someone who could read machine language and carefully interrogate the billions of bits of data that had been stored during the entire procedure. Nicole's investigation was stalled until she could find someone to help her. *Maybe I should give this up?* a voice inside her said. *How could you,* another voice replied, *until you know for certain the cause of General Borzov's death?* At the root of Nicole's desire to know the answer was a desperate yearning to prove for certain that his death had not been her fault.

She turned away from her terminal and collapsed on her bed. As she was lying there, she remembered her surprise during the thirty-second inspection period when Borzov's appendix had been in plain view. *He definitely wasn't having an appendicitis,* she thought. Without having any particular motive, Nicole returned to her terminal and accessed the second set of data that she had had evaluated by the electronic diagnostician, just prior to her decision to operate. She glanced only briefly at the 92% LIKELY APPENDICITIS on the first screen, moving instead to the backup diagnoses. This time DRUG REACTION was listed as the second most likely cause, with a 4 percent probability. Nicole now called for the data to be displayed in another way. She asked a statistical routine to compute the likely cause of the symptoms, *given* the fact that it could not be an appendicitis.

The results flashed up on the monitor in seconds. Nicole was astonished. According to the data, if the biometry information input from Borzov's probe set was analyzed under the assumption that the cause for the abnormalities could *not* be an appendicitis, then there was a 62 percent chance that it was due to a drug reaction. Before Nicole was able to complete any more analysis, there was a knock on her door.

"Come in," she said, continuing to work at her terminal. Nicole turned and saw Irina Turgenyev standing in the doorway. The Soviet pilot said nothing for a moment. "They asked me to come for you," Irina said haltingly. She was very shy around everyone except her countrymen Tabori and Borzov. "We're having a meeting of the crew down in the lobby."

Nicole saved her temporary data files and joined Irina in the corridor. "What sort of meeting is it?" she asked.

"An organizational meeting," Irina answered. She said nothing more.

There was a heated exchange in process between Reggie Wilson and David Brown when the two women reached the lobby. "Am I to understand, then," Dr. Brown was saying sarcastically, "that you believe the Rama spacecraft *purposely* decided to maneuver at precisely that moment? Would you like to explain to all of us *how* this asteroid of dumb metal happened to know that General Borzov was having an appendectomy at that very minute? And while you're at it, will you explain why this supposedly malevolent spaceship has allowed us to attach ourselves and has done nothing to dissuade us from continuing our mission?"

Reggie Wilson glanced around the room for support. "You're logic-chopping again, Brown," he said, his frustration obvious. "What you say always sounds logical on the surface. But I'm not the only member of this crew that found the coincidence unnerving. Look, here's Irina

Turgenyev. She's the one who suggested the connection to me in the first place."

Dr. Brown acknowledged the arrival of the two women. There was an authority in the way he was asking the questions that suggested he was in control of the gathering. "Is that right, Irina?" David Brown asked. "Do you feel, like Wilson, that Rama was trying to send us some specific message by performing its maneuver during the general's operation?"

Irina and Hiro Yamanaka were the two cosmonauts who spoke the least during crew meetings. With all eyes turned toward her, Irina mumbled "No" very meekly.

"But when we were discussing it last night—" Wilson insisted to the Soviet pilot.

"That's enough on that subject," David Brown interrupted imperiously. "I think we have a consensus, shared by our mission control officers on Earth, that the Raman maneuver was coincidence and not conspiracy." He looked at the fuming Reggie Wilson. "Now we have other more important issues to discuss. I would like to ask Admiral Heilmann to tell us what he has learned about the leadership problem."

Otto Heilmann stood up on cue and read from his notes. "According to the Newton procedures, in the event of the death or the incapacity of the commanding officer, the crew is expected to complete all sequences then under way in accordance with previous directions. However, once those in-process activities are finished, the cosmonauts are supposed to wait for the Earth to name a new commanding officer."

David Brown jumped back into the conversation. "Admiral Heilmann and I started discussing our situation about an hour ago and we quickly realized that we had valid reasons for being concerned. The ISA is wrapped up in their investigation of General Borzov's death. They have not even begun to think about his replacement. Once they do start, it may take them weeks to decide. Remember, this is the same bureaucracy that was never able to select a deputy for Borzov, so they eventually decided that he didn't need one." He paused several seconds to allow the rest of the crew members to consider what he was saying.

"Otto suggested that maybe we should not wait for the Earth to decide," Dr. Brown continued. "It was his idea that we should develop our own management structure, one that is acceptable to all of us here, and then send it to the ISA as a recommendation. Admiral Heilmann thinks they will accept it because it will avoid what could be a protracted debate."

"Admiral Heilmann and Dr. Brown came to see me with this idea," Janos Tabori now chimed in, "and emphasized how important it is for us to get started with our mission inside Rama. They even laid out a strawman organization that made sense to me. Since none of us has the broad experience of General Borzov, they suggested that maybe we should now have two leaders, possibly Admiral Heilmann and Dr. Brown themselves. Otto would cover the military and spacecraft engineering issues; Dr. Brown would lead the Rama exploration effort."

"And what happens when they disagree or their areas of responsibility overlap?" asked Richard Wakefield.

"In that case," Admiral Heilmann responded, "we would submit the item in question to a vote of all the cosmonauts."

"Isn't this cute?" said Reggie Wilson. He was still angry. He had been taking notes on his keyboard but now he stood up to address the rest of the cosmonauts. "Brown and Heilmann just happened to be worrying about this critical problem and they just happened to have developed a new leadership structure in which all the power and responsibility are divided between them. Am I the only one here who smells something fishy?"

"Now come on, Reggie," Francesca Sabatini said forcefully. She dropped her video camera to her side. "There is sound logic in the strawman proposal. Dr. Brown is our senior scientist. Admiral Heilmann has been a close colleague of Valeriy Borzov's for many years. None of us has a solid overall command of all aspects of the mission. To split the duties would be—"

It was difficult for Reggie Wilson to argue with Francesca. Nevertheless, he did interrupt her before she was finished. "I disagree with this plan," he said in a subdued tone. "I think we should have a single leader. And based on what I have observed during my time with this crew, there's only one cosmonaut that we could all easily follow. That's General O'Toole." He waved in the direction of his fellow American. "If this is a democracy, I nominate him as our new commanding officer."

There was a general uproar as soon as Reggie sat down. David Brown tried to restore order. "Please, please," he shouted, "let's work one issue at a time. Do we want to decide our own leadership and then hand it to the ISA as a fait accompli? Once we handle that question, then we can settle who those leaders should be."

"I had not thought about any of this before the meeting," Richard Wakefield said. "But I agree with the idea of cutting the Earth out of the loop. They have not lived with us on this mission. More important, they are not on-board a spaceship affixed to an alien creation somewhere just inside the orbit of Venus. We are the ones who will suffer if a bad decision is made; we should decide our own organization."

It was clear that everyone, with the possible exception of Wilson, preferred the idea of defining the leadership structure and then presenting it to the ISA. "All right," Otto Heilmann said a few minutes later, "we must now choose our leaders. One strawman proposal has been advanced, suggesting a leadership split between myself and Dr. Brown. Reggie Wilson has nominated General Michael O'Toole as the new commanding officer. Are there any other suggestions or discussion?"

The room was silent for about ten seconds. "Excuse me," General O'Toole then said, "but I would like to make a few observations." Everyone listened to the American general. Wilson was correct. Despite O'Toole's known preoccupation with religion (which he didn't force anyone else to share), he had the respect of the entire cosmonaut crew. "I think we must be careful at this point not to lose the team spirit that we have worked so hard to develop during the past year. A contested election at this point could be divisive. Besides, it's not all that important or necessary. Regardless of who becomes our nominal leader, or leaders, each of us is trained to perform a specific set of functions. We will do them under any circumstances."

Heads were nodding in agreement around the lobby.

"For myself," General O'Toole continued, "I must admit that I know little or nothing about the inside-Rama aspects of this mission. I have never trained to do anything except manage the two Newton spacecraft, assess any potential military threat, and act as a communications nexus onboard. I'm not qualified to be the commanding officer." Reggie Wilson started to interrupt but O'Toole continued without a pause. "I'd like to recommend that we adopt the plan offered by Heilmann and Brown and move on with our primary task—namely the exploration of this alien leviathan that has come to us from the stars."

At the conclusion of the meeting the two new leaders informed the rest of the cosmonauts that a rough draft of the first sortie scenario would be ready for review the following morning. Nicole headed for her room. On the way she stopped and knocked on the door of Janos Tabori. At first there was no response. When she knocked a second time, she heard Janos yell, "Who is it?"

"It's me—Nicole," she answered.

"Come in," he said.

He was lying on his back on the small bed with an uncharacteristic frown on his face.

"What's the matter?" Nicole asked.

"Oh, nothing," Janos answered. "I just have a headache."

"Did you take something?" Nicole inquired.

"No. It's not that serious." He still didn't smile. "What can I do for you?" he asked in an almost unfriendly tone.

Nicole was puzzled. She approached her subject cautiously. "Well, I was rereading your report on Valeriy's death—"

"Why were you doing that?" Janos interrupted brusquely.

"To see if there was anything we might have done differently," Nicole responded. It was obvious to her that Janos did not want to discuss the subject. After waiting a few seconds, Nicole spoke again. "I'm sorry, Janos. I'm imposing on you. I'll come back another time."

"No. No," he said. "Let's get this over with now."

That's a curious way of putting it, Nicole was thinking as she formulated her question. "Janos," she said, "nowhere in your report did you mention reaching for RoSur's control box right before the maneuver. And I could have sworn I saw your fingers on the keyboard panel as I was being swept over against the wall."

Nicole stopped. There was no expression of any kind on Cosmonaut Tabori's face. It was almost as if he were thinking of something else. "I don't remember," he said at length, without emotion. "You may be right. Perhaps my hitting my head erased part of my memory."

Stop now, Nicole said to herself as she studied her colleague. *There's nothing more you can learn here.*

19

RITE OF PASSAGE

Genevieve suddenly broke into tears. "Oh, Mother," she said. "I love you so much and this is absolutely awful."

The teenager hurriedly moved out of the camera frame and was replaced by Nicole's father. Pierre looked off to his right for a few seconds, to make certain that his granddaughter was out of earshot, and then turned toward the monitor. "These last twenty-four hours have been especially hard on her. You know how she idolizes you. Some of the foreign press have been saying that you bungled the surgery. There was even a suggestion this evening from an American television reporter that you were drunk during the operation."

He paused. The strain was showing on her father's face as well. "Both Genevieve and I know that neither of these allegations is true. We love you completely and send all our support."

The screen went dark. Nicole had initiated the videophone call and had, at first, been cheered by talking to her family. After her second transmission, however, when her father and daughter had reappeared on the screen twenty minutes later, it had been obvious that the events onboard the Newton had unsettled life at Beauvois as well. Genevieve had been particularly distraught. She had cried intermittently while talking about General Borzov (she had met him several times and the avuncular Russian had always been especially nice to her) and had barely managed to compose herself before breaking into tears again right before the end of the call.

So I have embarrassed you as well, Nicole thought as she sat down on her bed. She rubbed her eyes. She was extremely tired. Slowly, without being aware of how depressed she had become, she undressed for bed. Her mind was plagued with pictures of her daughter at school in Luynes. Nicole winced as she imagined one of Genevieve's friends asking her about the operation and Borzov's death. *My darling daughter,* she thought, *you must know how much I love you. If only I could spare you from this pain.* Nicole wanted to reach out and comfort Genevieve, to hold her close, to share one of those mother-daughter caresses that chase away the demons. But it could not be. Genevieve was a hundred million kilometers away.

Nicole lay in bed on her back. She closed her eyes but did not sleep. She was aware of a deep and profound loneliness, a sense of isolation more acute than any she had felt before in her life. She knew that she was longing for some sympathy, for some human being who would tell her that her feelings of inadequacy were overblown and not consistent with reality. But there was nobody. Her father and daughter were back on Earth. Of the two Newton crew members she knew best, one was dead and the other was behaving suspiciously.

I have failed, Nicole was thinking as she was lying on her bed. *On my most important assignment I have failed.* She recalled another feeling of failure, when she was only sixteen. At that time Nicole had competed for the role of Joan of Arc in a huge national contest associated with the 750th anniversary of the death of the Maid. If she had won, Nicole would have portrayed Joan in a series of pageants over the next two years. She had thrown herself totally into the contest, reading every book she could find about Joan and watching scores of video presentations. Nicole had scored at the top in virtually every test category except "suitability." She should have won, but she didn't. Her father had consoled her by telling Nicole that France was not ready for its heroines to have dark skin.

But that was not exactly a failure, the Newton life science officer told herself. *And anyway I had my father to comfort me.* An image of her mother's funeral came to Nicole's mind. She had been ten years old at the time. Her mother had gone to the Ivory Coast by herself to visit their African relatives. Anawi had been in Nidougou when a virulent epidemic of Hogan fever had swept through the village. Nicole's mother had died quickly.

Five days later Anawi had been cremated as a Senoufo queen. Nicole had wept while Omeh chanted her mother's soul through the nether world and into the Land of Preparation, where beings rested while waiting to be selected for another life on Earth. As the flames had mounted the pyre and her mother's regal dress had begun to burn, Nicole had felt an overpowering sense of loss. And loneliness. *But that time also my father was there beside me,* she recalled. *He held my hand as we watched Mother disappear. Together it was easier to bear. I was much more lonely during the Poro. And more frightened.*

She could still remember the mixture of terror and helplessness that had filled her seven-year-old body at the Paris airport on that spring morning. Her father had caressed her very tenderly. "Darling, darling Nicole," he had said. "I will miss you very much. Come back safely to me."

"But why must I go, Papa?" she had replied. "And why are you not coming with us?"

He had bent down beside her. "You are going to become part of your mother's people. All Senoufo children go through the Poro at the age of seven."

Nicole had started crying. "But Papa, I don't want to go. I'm French, not African. I don't like all those strange people and the heat and the bugs . . ."

Her father had placed his hands firmly on her cheeks. "You must go, Nicole. Your mother and I have agreed." Anawi and Pierre had indeed discussed it many times. Nicole had lived in France all her life. All she knew of her African heritage was what her mother had taught her and what she had learned from two month-long visits to the Ivory Coast with her family.

It had not been easy for Pierre to agree to send his beloved daughter off to the Poro. He knew that it was a primitive ceremony. He also knew that it was the cornerstone of the Senoufo traditional religion and that he had promised Omeh, at the time of his marriage to Anawi, that all their children would return to Nidougou for at least the first cycle of the Poro.

The hardest part for Pierre was staying behind. But Anawi was right. He was an outsider. He would not be able to participate in the Poro. He would not understand it. His presence would distract the little girl. There was an ache in his heart as Pierre kissed his wife and daughter and put them onto the plane to Abidjan.

Anawi was also apprehensive about the rite of passage ceremony for her only child, her little girl of barely seven years. She had prepared Nicole as well as she could. The child was a gifted linguist and had picked up the rudiments of the Senoufo language very easily. But there was no doubt that she was at a severe disadvantage with respect to the rest of the children. All of the others had lived their whole lives in and around the native villages. They were familiar with the area. To alleviate the orientation problem a little, Anawi and Nicole arrived in Nidougou a week ahead of time.

The fundamental idea of the Poro was that life was a succession of phases or cycles and that each transition should be carefully marked. Each cycle lasted seven years. There were three Poros in every normal Senoufo life, three metamorphoses that were necessary before the child could be transformed into an adult in the tribe. Despite the fact that many of the tribal customs faded away with the arrival of modern telecommunications devices in the Ivory Coast villages in the twenty-first century, the Poro remained an integral part of Senoufo society. In the twenty-second century, tribal practices enjoyed a renaissance of sorts, especially after The Great Chaos proved to most of the African leaders that it was dangerous to depend too much on the outside world.

Anawi kept a good acting smile upon her face during the afternoon that the tribal priests came to take Nicole away for the Poro. She didn't want her fear or anxiety to be transferred to her daughter. Nevertheless, Nicole could tell that her mother was troubled. "Your hands are cold and sweaty, Mama," she whispered in French as she hugged Anawi before departing. "Don't worry. I'll be all right." Nicole, in fact—the only brown face among the dozen dark black girls climbing into the carts—seemed almost cheery and expectant, as if she were going to an amusement park or a zoo.

There were four carts altogether, two carrying the little girls and two that were covered and unexplained. Nicole's friend from four years earlier, Lutuwa, who was actually one of Nicole's cousins, explained to the rest of the girls that the other wagons contained the priests and the "instruments of torture." There was a long silence before one of the little girls had the courage to ask Lutuwa what she was talking about.

"I dreamed it all two nights ago," Lutuwa said matter-of-factly. "They are going to burn our nipples and stick sharp objects in all our holes. And as long as we don't cry, we won't feel any pain." The other five girls in Nicole's cart, including Lutuwa, hardly said a word for the next hour.

By sunset they had traveled a long way east, past the abandoned microwave station, into the special area known only to the tribal religious leaders. The half dozen priests threw up temporary shelters and started building a fire. When it was dark, food and drink were served to the initiates, who sat cross-legged in a wide circle around the fire. After dinner the costumed dancing began. Omeh narrated the four dances, each of which featured one of the indigenous animals. Music for the dances came from tambourines and crude xylophones, the rhythm being maintained by the monotonic beat of the tom-tom. Occasionally an especially meaningful point in the story would be punctuated by a blast on the oliphant, the ivory hunting horn.

Just before bedtime Omeh, still wearing the great mask and headdress identifying him as the chieftain, handed each of the girls a large kit made of antelope hide and told them to study its contents very carefully. There was a flask of water, some dried fruit and nuts, two chunks of native bread, a cutting implement, some rope, two different kinds of unguents, and a tuber from an unknown plant.

"Tomorrow morning each child will be removed from this camp," Omeh said, "and placed in a specific location not too far away. The child will have only the gifts in the antelope hide. The child is expected to survive on her own and return to the same spot by the time the sun is full in the sky on the following day.

"The hide contains everything that is needed except for wisdom, courage, and curiosity. The tuber is something very special. Eating the fleshy root will terrify the child, but may also give abnormal powers of strength and vision."

20

BLESSED SLUMBER

The little girl had been alone for almost two hours before she really understood what was happening to her. Omeh and one of the younger priests had placed Nicole right near a small, brackish pond, surrounded on all sides by the high grasses of the savanna. They had reminded her that they would return in the middle of the next day. Then they were gone.

At first Nicole had reacted as if the entire experience were a great game. She had taken out her kit made of antelope hide and carefully inventoried the contents. She had mentally divided the food into three parts, planning what she would eat for dinner, breakfast, and midmorning snack. There was not excessive food, but little Nicole judged that it would be enough. On the other hand, when she had visually measured the flask to determine the adequacy of her water supply, she had concluded that it was marginal. It would be good if she could find a spring or some pure running water that could be used in an emergency.

Nicole's next activity had been to create a mental map of her location, paying special attention to any landmarks that would help her identify the brackish pond from a distance. She was an extremely organized little girl and, back at Chilly-Mazarin, often played by herself in a wooded vacant lot very close to her house. In her room at home Nicole had maps of the wood that she had carefully drawn by hand, her secret hiding places marked with stars and circles.

It was when she came upon four striped antelope, grazing calmly under the steady afternoon sun, that Nicole first understood how utterly isolated she was. Her first

instinct was to look for her mother, to show Anawi the
beautiful animals she had found. *But mother is not here*,
the little girl thought, her eyes scanning the horizon. *I am
all alone.* The last word echoed through her mind and she
felt an inchoate despair. She fought against the despair
and looked off into the distance to see if she could find any
indication of civilization. There were birds all around and
some more grazing animals on the horizon at the limit of
her vision, but no sign of any human beings. *I am all
alone*, Nicole said to herself again, a slight shiver of fear
running through her body.

She remembered that she wanted to find another source
of water and walked off in the direction of a large grove of
trees. The little girl had no idea about distances in the
open savanna. Although she did carefully stop every thirty
minutes or so to ensure that she could still find her way
back to the pond, it amazed her that the distant grove did
not appear to be coming any closer. She walked on and
on. As the afternoon waned, she became tired and thirsty.
She stopped to drink some of her water. The tsetse flies
surrounded her, buzzing around her face as she tried to
drink. Nicole took out the two unguents, smelled them
both, and applied the worse smelling of the two to her
face and arms. Her choice was apparently correct; the flies
also found the unguent noisome and kept their distance.

She reached the trees about an hour before dark. She
was delighted to find that she had fortuitously stumbled
upon a small oasis in the middle of the great stretch of
savanna. There was a strong spring in the grove where the
water rushed out of the ground and formed a circular pool
about ten meters in diameter. The excess water in turn
trickled out of one edge of the pool and became a creek
that ran from the oasis back into the savanna. Nicole was
exhausted and sweaty from her long walk. The water in
the pool was inviting. Without thinking she pulled off her
clothes, except for her underpants, and jumped in for a
swim.

The water invigorated and soothed her tired little body.
With her head underwater and her eyes closed, she swam
and swam and fantasized that she was in the community
pool in her suburb near Paris. In her imagination she had

gone to the piscine, as she generally did once a week, and was playing water sports with her friends. The memory comforted her. After a long time Nicole rolled over on her back and took a few strokes. She opened her eyes and looked at the trees above her. The rays from the late afternoon sun were making magic as they cut through the branches and the leaves.

Seven-year-old Nicole stopped swimming and treaded water for several seconds, looking around the edge of the pool for her clothes. She didn't see them. Puzzled, she scanned the perimeter of the pool more carefully. Still she saw nothing. In her mind she reconstructed all the scenes of her arrival in the grove and conclusively remembered exactly where she had placed both her clothes and the kit made from antelope hide. She climbed out of the water and examined the spot more closely. *This is definitely the place*, she thought. *And my clothes and the kit are gone.*

There was no way to quell the panic. It overpowered her in an instant. Her eyes flooded with tears, a wail broke from her throat. She closed her eyes and wept, hoping that this was all a bad dream and that she would wake up in the next few seconds and see her mother and father. But when she opened her eyes again, the same scene was still there. A half-naked little girl was alone in the wilds of Africa with no food, no water, and no hope of rescue before the middle of the next day. And it was almost dark.

With great effort Nicole managed at last to control both her fright and her tears. She decided to look for her clothes. Where they had been before, she found fresh prints of some kind. Nicole had no way of knowing what kind of animal might have made the tracks, so she assumed that it was one of the gentle antelope that she had seen that afternoon in the savanna. *That would make sense*, the little girl thought logically. *This is probably the best water hole in the area. They stopped here and were curious about my things. My splashing must have scared them away.*

As the light faded she followed the tracks along a tiny pathway through the trees. After a short trek she found the antelope hide, or rather what was left of it, discarded

on the side of the path. The kit was torn completely open.
All the food was gone, the water flask was mostly drained,
and everything else had fallen out except the unguents
and the tuber. Nicole finished the water that was left in
the flask and put it with the tuber in her right hand. She
discarded the messy unguents. She was about to continue
following the path when she heard a sound, halfway between a yelp and a cry. The sound was very close. The
path opened into the savanna about fifty meters ahead.
Nicole strained her eyes and thought she saw motion, but
she couldn't make out anything specific. Then she heard
the yelp again, louder this time. She dropped down on
her stomach and crawled slowly along the path.

There was a small rise fifteen meters before the end of
the grove. From that vantage point little Nicole saw the
source of the yelp. Two lion cubs were playing with her
green dress. Their watchful mother was on the opposite
side, staring out into the savanna twilight. Nicole froze in
terror as she comprehended that she was not visiting a
zoo, that she was out in the wild and a real African lioness
was only twenty meters away. Trembling with fear, she
inched back along the path, very slowly, very quietly, lest
she call attention to her presence.

Back near the pool she resisted the urge to jump up and
run pell-mell into the savanna. *Then the lioness will see
me for certain,* she thought. But where to spend the
night? *I'll find a ditch among the trees,* she reasoned,
away from the path. And lie still. Then maybe I'll be safe.
Still clutching the flask and the tuber, Nicole walked softly
over to the spring. She took a drink and filled her flask.
Next she crawled into the grove and found a ditch. Then,
convinced that she was as safe as she could possibly be
under the circumstances, the exhausted little girl fell asleep.

She woke up suddenly with a sensation that bugs were
crawling all over her. She reached down and rubbed her
bare stomach. It was covered with ants. Nicole screamed,
and then she realized what she had done. In a flash she
heard the lioness crashing through the brush, searching
for the creature that had made the noise. The little girl
shuddered and scraped the ants off with a stick. Then she
saw the lioness staring at her, the feral eyes piercing the

dark. Nicole was near collapse. In her fright she somehow remembered what Omeh had said about the tuber. She put the dirt-covered root into her mouth and chewed vigorously. It tasted awful. She forced herself to swallow.

A moment later Nicole was rushing through the trees with the lioness chasing her. Branches and leaves cut her face and chest. She slipped once and fell. When she reached the pool she did not stop. Nicole ran across the water, her feet barely touching the top. She flapped her arms. They had changed to wings, white wings. She was no longer touching the water. She was a great white heron soaring up, up into the night sky. She turned and looked at the puzzled lioness far below her. Laughing to herself, Nicole intensified her wing motion and rose above all the trees. The great savanna unfolded below her. She could see for over a hundred kilometers.

She flew across to the brackish pond, turned west, and spotted a campfire. She zoomed toward it, her bird shrieks piercing the calm of the night. Omeh awakened with a start, saw the solitary bird spread out against the sky, and made a loud bird cry of his own. "Ronata?" his voice seemed to ask. But Nicole did not answer. She wanted to fly higher, even above the clouds.

On the other side of the clouds the Moon and stars were clear and bright. They beckoned to her. She thought she heard music in the distance, a tinkling like crystal bells, as she soared higher and higher. She tried to flap her wings. They would barely move. They had changed into control surfaces, which now extended to increase the lift in the ultrathin air. Her aft rockets began to fire. Nicole was now a silver shuttle, thin and sleek, leaving the Earth behind.

The music was louder out in orbit. There it was a magnificent symphony, enhancing the beauty of the majestic Earth below her. She heard her name being called. From where? Who could be calling way out here? The sound came from beyond the Moon. She changed her heading, pointed toward the void of deep space, and fired her rockets again. She swept past the Moon, heading away from the Sun. Her speed was still increasing exponentially. Behind her the Sun was growing smaller and smaller. It became a tiny light and then disappeared altogether.

There was blackness all around. She held her breath and came to the surface of the water.

The lioness was prowling back and forth on the edge of the pool. Nicole could vividly see all the muscles in her powerful shoulders and read the expression on her face. *Please leave me alone,* Nicole said. *I won't hurt you or your babies.*

"I recognize your smell," the lioness answered. "My cubs were playing with that smell."

I too am a cub, Nicole continued, *and I want to return to my mother. But I am afraid.*

"Come out of the water," the lioness replied. "Let me see you. I do not believe that you are what you say."

Summoning all her courage, her eyes riveted on the lioness, the little girl walked slowly out of the water. The lioness didn't move. When the water was only waist deep, Nicole shaped her arms into a cradle and began to sing. It was a simple, peaceful melody, the one she remembered from the beginning of her life, when her mother or father would kiss her good night, put her down in the crib, and then turn out the light. The little animals in the mobile would go around and around while a woman's soft voice sang the Brahms lullaby.

"Lay thee down, now, and rest. . . . May thy slumber be blessed."

The lioness rocked back on her haunches and threatened to pounce. The girl, still softly singing, continued walking toward the animal. When Nicole was completely out of the water and only about five meters away, the lioness jumped aside and leapt back into the grove. Nicole kept walking, the soothing song giving her both comfort and strength. In a few minutes she was back out at the edge of the savanna. By sunrise she had reached the pond, where she lay down among the grasses and fell fast asleep. Omeh and the Senoufo priests found her lying there, half naked and still asleep, when the sun was high in the sky.

She could remember it all as if it were yesterday. *Almost thirty years ago now,* she recalled as she lay still awake in her small bed on the Newton, *and the lessons I learned have never stopped being valuable.* Nicole thought about the little seven-year-old girl who had been stranded in a completely alien world and had managed to survive. *So why am I feeling sorry for myself now?* she thought. *That was a much tougher situation.*

Immersing herself in her childhood experience had given her unexpected strength. Nicole was no longer depressed. Her mind was working overtime again, trying to formulate a plan that would give her the crucial answers to what had happened during the operation on Borzov. She had pushed her loneliness aside.

Nicole realized that she would have to stay onboard the Newton during the first sortie if she wanted to do a thorough analysis of all aspects of the Borzov incident. She resolved to bring up the issue with Brown or Heilmann in the morning.

At length the exhausted woman fell asleep. As she was drifting into the twilight world that separates waking and sleeping, Nicole was humming a tune to herself. It was the Brahms lullaby.

21
PANDORA'S CUBE

Nicole could see David Brown sitting behind the desk.
Francesca was leaning over him, pointing at something on
a large chart that was spread out in front of the two of
them. Nicole knocked on the door of the commander's
office.

"Hello, Nicole," Francesca said, as she opened the door.
"What can we do for you?"

"I came to see Dr. Brown," Nicole replied. "About my
assignment."

"Come on in," Francesca said.

Nicole shuffled in slowly and sat in one of the two chairs
opposite the desk. Francesca sat in the other. Nicole
looked at the walls of the office. They had definitely
changed. General Borzov's photographs of his wife and
children, along with his favorite painting, a picture of a
solitary bird with outstretched wings soaring above the
Neva River in Leningrad, had been replaced by huge
sequencing charts. The charts, each one headed by a
different name (First Sortie, Second Sortie, etc.), covered
the side bulletin boards from one end of the wall to the
other.

General Borzov's office had been warm and personal.
This room was definitely sterile and intimidating. Dr.
Brown had hung laminated replicas of two of his most
prestigious international scientific awards on the wall behind his desk. He had also raised the height of his chair so
that he looked down on anyone else in the room who
might be sitting.

"I have come to see you about a personal matter,"
Nicole said. She waited several seconds, expecting David
Brown to ask Francesca to leave the room. He said noth-

ing. Finally Nicole glanced in Francesca's direction to make her concern obvious.

"She has been helping me with my administrative duties," Dr. Brown explained. "I find that her feminine insight often detects signals that I have missed altogether."

Nicole sat silently for another fifteen seconds. She had been prepared to talk to David Brown. She had not expected that it would be necessary also for her to explain everything to Francesca. *Maybe I should just leave*, Nicole thought fleetingly, somewhat surprised to find that she was irritated about Francesca's being there.

"I have read the assignments for the first sortie," Nicole said eventually in a formal tone, "and I would like to make a request. My duties, as outlined in the sequence, are minimal. Irina Turgenyev, it seems to me, is also underworked for the three-day sortie. I recommend that you give my nonmedical tasks to Irina and I will stay onboard the Newton with Admiral Heilmann and General O'Toole. I will follow the progress of the mission carefully and can be available immediately if there is any significant medical problem. Otherwise Janos can handle the life science responsibilities."

Again there was silence in the room. Dr. Brown stared at Nicole and then at Francesca. "Why do you want to stay onboard the Newton?" Francesca responded at length. "I would have thought that you couldn't wait to see the inside of Rama."

"As I said, it's mostly personal," Nicole answered vaguely. "I'm still extremely tired from the Borzov ordeal and I have a lot of paperwork to finish. The first sortie should be straightforward. I would like to be fully rested and prepared for the second."

"It's a highly irregular request," David Brown said, "but under the circumstances, I think we can do it." He glanced again at Francesca. "But we'd like to ask a favor of you. If you're not going into Rama, then perhaps you'd be willing to spell O'Toole as communications officer from time to time? Then Admiral Heilmann could go inside—"

"Certainly," Nicole answered before Brown had finished.

"Good. Then I guess we're all agreed. We'll change the manifests for the first sortie. You will remain onboard the

Newton." After Dr. Brown was through talking, Nicole still made no move to leave her chair. "Was there something else?" he asked impatiently.

"According to our procedures, the life science officer prepares certification memoranda on the cosmonauts prior to each sortie. Should I give a copy to Admiral—"

"Give all those memos to me," Dr. Brown interrupted her. "Admiral Heilmann is not concerned with personnel matters." The American scientist looked directly at Nicole. "But you don't need to prepare new reports for the first sortie. I've read all the documents you wrote for General Borzov. They are quite adequate."

Nicole did not let herself be cowed by the man's penetrating gaze. *So you know what I wrote about you and Wilson*, she thought, *and you think I should feel guilty or embarrassed. Well, I don't. My opinions have not changed just because you are now nominally in charge.*

That night Nicole continued with her investigation. Her detailed analysis of the biometry data from General Borzov showed that he had had extraordinary levels of two strange chemicals in his system just before his death. Nicole could not figure out where they had come from. Had he been taking medication without her knowledge? Could these chemicals, which were known to trigger pain (they were used, according to her medical encyclopedia, to test pain sensitivity in neurologically distressed patients), somehow have been manufactured internally in some kind of allergic reaction?

And what about Janos? Why couldn't he remember reaching for the control box? Why had he been reticent and withdrawn since Borzov's death? Just after midnight she stared at the ceiling of her small bedroom. *Today the crew enters Rama and I will be here alone. I should wait until then to continue my analysis.* But she couldn't wait. She was unable to push aside all the questions that were flooding her mind. *Could there be a connection between Janos and the drugs in Borzov? Is it possible that his death was not completely accidental?*

Nicole took her personal briefcase out of the tiny closet. She opened it hastily and the contents spilled into the air.

She grabbed a group of family photographs that were floating above her bed. Then she gathered up most of the rest of the items and returned them to her briefcase. Nicole retained in her hand the data cube that King Henry had given her in Davos.

She hesitated before inserting the cube. At last she took a deep breath and placed it into the reader. Eighteen menu items were immediately displayed on the monitor. She could choose any of the twelve individual dossiers on the cosmonauts or six different compilations of crew statistics. Nicole called for the dossier on Janos Tabori. There were three submenus for his biography: Personal Data, Chronological Summary, and Psychological Assessment. She could tell from the listed file sizes that the Chronological Summary contained most of the details. Nicole accessed Personal Data first to gain familiarity with the format of the dossiers.

The brief chart did not tell her much that she didn't already know. Janos was forty-one and single. When he was not on duty for the ISA, he lived alone in an apartment in Budapest, only four blocks away from where his twice-divorced mother lived by herself. He had received an honors engineering degree from the University of Hungary in 2183. In addition to mundane items like height, weight, and number of siblings, the chart listed two other numbers: IE (for Intelligence Evaluation) and SC (for Socialization Coefficient). Tabori's numbers were +3.37 for IE and 64 for SC.

Nicole returned to the main menu and called up the Glossary to refresh her memory about the definitions of IE and SC. The IE numbers supposedly represented a composite measure of overall intelligence, based on a comparison with a similar worldwide student population. All students took a set of standardized tests at specified times between the ages of twelve and twenty. The index was actually an exponent in a decimal measuring system. An IE number of zero was average. An IE index of +1.00 meant the individual was above 90 percent of the population; +2.00 was above 99 percent of the population; +3.00 above 99.9 percent, etc. Negative IE indices indicated below-average intelligence. Janos' score of +3.37 placed him in the middle of the upper one tenth of one percent of the population in intelligence.

The SC numbers had a more straightforward explanation. They too were based on a battery of standardized tests administered to all students between the ages of twelve and twenty, but the interpretation here was easier to understand. The highest SC score was 100. A person scoring close to 100 was liked and respected by virtually everybody, would fit into almost any group, was almost never quarrelsome or moody, and was very dependable. A footnote to the explanation of the SC scores acknowledged that written tests could not accurately measure personality traits in all cases, so the numbers should be used with discretion.

Nicole reminded herself to do a comparison sometime of all the cosmonaut IE and SC scores. Then she accessed the Chronological Summary file for Janos Tabori. The next sixty minutes was an eye-opening experience for Nicole. As the life science officer, she had of course studied the official ISA personnel files for the entire crew. But if the information about Janos Tabori on the cube given to her by King Henry was correct (and she had no way of knowing one way or the other), then the ISA files were woefully incomplete.

Nicole had known previously that Janos had twice been selected as the outstanding engineering student at the University of Hungary; she had not known that he had been president for two years of the Gay Students Association of Budapest. She was aware that he had entered the Space Academy in 2192 and had graduated in only three years (because of his previous experience with major Soviet engineering projects); she had never been told that he had applied to the Academy twice previously and had been rejected both times. Despite sensational entrance scores, he had twice failed his personal interview—both times the interview committee had been headed by General Valeriy Borzov. Janos had been active in various gay organizations until 2190. Subsequently he had resigned from them all and never rejoined or participated in any organized gay activities. None of this information had been in his ISA file.

Nicole was stunned by what she had learned. It wasn't that Janos had been (or was) gay that disturbed her; she was free of prejudices where sexual orientation was concerned. What bothered her most was the likelihood that his official file had been deliberately censored to remove all references both to his homosexuality and to his earlier interactions with General Borzov.

The last entries in the Tabori Chronological Summary were also surprising for Nicole. According to the dossier, Janos had purportedly signed a contract with Schmidt and Hagenest, the German publishing conglomerate, in the last week of December, just before launch. His task was to perform unspecified "consulting" for a wide variety of post-Newton media endeavors in support of what was referred to as the Brown-Sabatini project. Cosmonaut Tabori was paid an initial fee of three hundred thousand marks for signing. Three days later his mother, who had been waiting almost a year for one of the new artificial brain implants that reversed the damage from Alzheimer's disease, entered the Bavarian Hospital in Munich for neurological surgery.

Her eyes weary and burning, Nicole finished reading the extensive dossier on Dr. David Brown. During the hours that she had been studying his Chronological Summary, she had created a special subfile for herself of those items in the summary that were of particular interest to her. Before trying again to sleep, Nicole scrolled through this special subfile one more time.

Summer 2161: Brown, eleven, enrolled in Camp Longhorn by father over strenuous objections of mother. Typical outdoor summer camp in hill country of Texas for upper class boys, featuring athletics of all kinds, riflery, crafts, and hiking. Boys lived ten to a barracks. Brown was extremely unpopular immediately. On fifth day bunkmates seized him coming out of shower and painted his genitals black. Brown refused to move from bed until mother had traveled almost two hundred miles to pick him up and take him home. Father apparently ignored son altogether after this incident.

September 2166: After being valedictorian from private high school, Brown enrolled as freshman in physics at Princeton. Remained in New Jersey only eight weeks. Completed undergraduate work at SMU while living at home.

June 2173: Awarded Ph.D. in physics and astronomy by Harvard. Dissertation advisor Wilson Brownwell called Brown "an ambitious, diligent student."

June 2175: Brown completed postdoctorate research on the evolution of stars with Brian Murchison at Cambridge.

April 2180: Married Jeannette Hudson of Pasadena, California. Ms. Hudson had been graduate student in astronomy at Stanford. Only child, daughter Angela, born in December 2184.

November 2181: Was refused tenure in astronomy department at Stanford because two members of evaluation committee believed Brown had falsified scientific data in several of his many scholarly publications. Issue was never resolved.

January 2184: Appointed to first ISA Advisory Committee. Prepared comprehensive plans for series of major new astronomical telescopes on far side of the moon.

May 2187: Brown named chairman of Department of Physics and Astronomy at SMU in Dallas, Texas.

February 2188: Fistfight with Wendell Thomas, Princeton professor, in atrium outside AAAS meeting in Chicago. Thomas insisted that Brown had stolen and published ideas they had discussed together.

April 2190: Electrified scientific world by not only publishing breakthrough models of supernova process, but also predicting nearby supernova to occur in mid-March 2191. Research done in collaboration with SMU doctoral student, Elaine Bernstein of New York. Strong suggestion from graduate associates of Ms. Bernstein that she was actually one with the new insights. Brown catapulted to fame as a result of his bold and correct prediction.

June 2190: Brown divorced wife, from whom he had been separated for eighteen months. Separation had started three months after Elaine Bernstein had begun graduate work.

December 2190: Married Ms. Bernstein in Dallas.

March 2191: Supernova 2191a filled night sky with light, as predicted by Brown et al.

June 2191: Brown signed two-year science reporting contract with CBS. Jumped to UBC in 2194 and then, at recommendation of agent, to INN in 2197.

December 2193: Brown awarded top ISA medal for Distinguished Scientific Achievement.

November 2199: Signed exclusive multimillion mark, multiyear contract with Schmidt and Hagenest to "exploit" all possible commercial applications of Newton mission, including books, videos, and educational material. Teamed with Francesca Sabatini as other principal, cosmonauts Heilmann and Tabori as consultants. Signing bonus of two million marks deposited in secret account in Italy.

Her alarm awakened her after she had been asleep for only two hours. Nicole dragged herself out of bed and freshened up in the retractable washbasin. She moved slowly into the corridor and turned toward the lobby. The other four space cadets were gathered around David Brown in the control center, excitedly reviewing the details of the initial sortie.

"All right," Richard Wakefield was saying, "first priorities are the lightweight individual chairlifts by the right and left stairways and one heavy load elevator from the hub to the Central Plain. Then we set up a temporary control center at the edge of the plain and assemble and test the three rovers. Crude campsite tonight, base camp at the Beta site near the edge of the Cylindrical Sea tomorrow. We will leave the assembly and deployment of the two helicopters for tomorrow, the icemobiles and motorboats for Day Three."

"That's an excellent summary," Dr. Brown replied. "Francesca will go with the four of you while you're setting up the infrastructure this morning. When the lightweight lifts are installed and operational, Admiral Heilmann and I will join you along with Dr. Takagishi and Mr. Wilson. We'll all sleep inside Rama tonight."

"How many long-duration flares do you have?" Janos Tabori asked Irina Turgenyev.

"Twelve," she answered. "That should be plenty for today."

"And tonight, when we go to sleep in there, it will be the darkest night that any of us have ever seen," Dr. Takagishi said. "There will be no moon and no stars, no reflection off the ground, nothing but blackness all around."

"What will the temperature be?" Wakefield asked.

"We don't know for certain," the Japanese scientist answered. "The initial drones carried only cameras. But the temperature in the region around the end of the tunnel was the same as in Rama I. If that's any indication, then it should be about ten degrees below freezing at the campsites." Takagishi paused for a moment. "And getting warmer," he continued. "We're now inside the orbit of Venus. We expect the lights to come on in another eight or nine days, and the Cylindrical Sea to melt from the bottom soon thereafter."

"Hey," kidded Brown. "It sounds as if you're becoming converted. You no longer qualify *all* your statements, just some of them." Takagishi replied, "With each datum that indicates this spaceship is like its predecessor seventy years ago, the probability that they are identical increases. Thus far, if we ignore the exact timing of the correction maneuver, everything about the two vehicles has been the same."

Nicole approached the group. "Well look who's here," Janos said with his usual grin. "Our fifth and final space cadet." He noticed her swollen eyes. "And our new commander was right. You do look as if you might benefit from some rest."

"I, for one," Richard Wakefield interjected, "am disappointed that my rover assembly assistant will now be Yamanaka instead of Madame des Jardins. At least our life science officer talks. I may have to recite Shakespeare to myself to stay awake." He elbowed Yamanaka in the ribs. The Japanese pilot almost smiled.

"I wanted to wish you all good luck," Nicole said. "As I'm sure Dr. Brown has told you, I felt I was still too tired to be very helpful. I should be fresh and ready by the second sortie."

"Well," Francesca Sabatini remarked impatiently after her camera had panned around the room and captured one final close-up of each face. "Are we finally ready?"

"Let's go," said Wakefield. They headed toward the airlock at the front of the Newton spacecraft.

22

DAWN

Richard Wakefield worked quickly in the near darkness. He was halfway down the Alpha stairway, where the gravity due to the centrifugal force created by the spin of Rama had grown to more than one fourth of a gee. The light from his headgear illuminated the near field. He was almost finished with another pylon.

He checked his air supply. It was already below the midpoint. By now they should have been deeper into Rama, closer to where they could breathe the ambient air. But they had underestimated how long it would take them to install the lightweight chairlifts. The concept was extremely simple and they had practiced it several times in the simulations. The upper part of the job, when they had been in the vicinity of the ladders and virtually weightless, had been relatively straightforward. But at this level the installation of each pylon was a different process because of the increasing and changing gravity.

Exactly a thousand steps above Wakefield, Janos Tabori finished wrapping anchor lines around the metal banisters that lined the stairway. After almost four hours of tedious, repetitive work, he was becoming fatigued. He remembered the argument the engineering director had advanced when he and Richard had recommended a specialized machine for the installation of the lifts. "It's not cost-effective to create a robot for nonrecurring uses," the man had said. "Robots are only good for recurring tasks."

Janos glanced below him but could not see as far as the next pylon, two hundred and fifty steps down the stairway. "Is it time for lunch yet?" he said to Wakefield on his commpak.

"Could be," was the response. "But we're way behind.

We didn't send Yamanaka and Turgenyev over to Gamma stairway until ten-thirty. At the rate we're going, we'll be lucky to finish these lightweight lifts and the crude camp-site today. We'll have to postpone the heavy load elevator and the rovers until tomorrow."

"Hiro and I are already eating," they both heard Turgenyev say from the other side of the bowl. "We were hungry. We finished the chair rack and the upper motor in half an hour. We're down to pylon number twelve."

"Good work," Wakefield said. "But I'll warn you that you're in the easy part, around the ladders and the top of the stairway. Working weightless is a snap. Wait until the gravity is measurably different at each location."

"According to the laser range finder, Cosmonaut Wake-field is exactly eight-point-one-three kilometers away from me," everyone heard Dr. Takagishi interject.

"That doesn't tell me anything, Professor, unless I know where the hell you are."

"I'm standing on the ledge just outside our relay station, near the bottom of the Alpha stairway."

"Come on, Shig, won't you Orientals ever go along with the rest of the world? The Newton is parked on the *top* of Rama and you are at the *top* of the stairway. If we can't agree on up and down, how can we ever hope to communicate our innermost feelings? Much less play chess together."

"Thank you, Janos. I am at the *top* of the Alpha stair-way. By the way, what are you doing? Your range is increasing rapidly."

"I'm sliding down the banister to meet Richard for lunch. I don't like eating fish and chips by myself."

"I'm also coming down for lunch," Francesca said. "I just finished filming an excellent demonstration of the Coriolis force using Hiro and Irina. It will be great for elementary physics classes. I should be there in five minutes."

"Say, signora"—it was Wakefield again—"do you think we could talk you into some honest-to-goodness work? We stop what we're doing to accommodate your filming—maybe we can make a trade with you."

"I'm willing," answered Francesca. "I'll help after lunch.

But what I would like now is some light. Could you use one of your flares and let me capture you and Janos having a picnic on the Stairway of the Gods?"

Wakefield programmed a flare for a delayed ignition and climbed eighty steps to the nearest ledge. Cosmonaut Tabori arrived at the same spot half a minute before the light flooded them. From two kilometers above, Francesca panned across the three stairways and then zoomed in on the two figures sitting cross-legged on the ledge. From that perspective, Janos and Richard looked like two eagles nesting in a high mountain aerie.

By late afternoon the Alpha chairlift was finished and ready for testing. "We'll let you be the first customer," Richard Wakefield said to Francesca, "since you were good enough to help." They were standing in full gravity at the foot of the incredible stairway. Thirty thousand steps stretched into the darkness of the artificial heavens above them. Beside them on the Central Plain the ultralight motor and the self-contained portable power station for the chairlift were already in operation. The cosmonauts had transported the electrical and mechanical subsystems in unassembled pieces on their backs and assembly had required less than an hour.

"The little chairs are not permanently connected to the cables," Wakefield explained to Francesca. "At each end there is a mechanism that attaches or detaches the chairs. That way it's not necessary to have an almost infinite number of seats."

Francesca hesitantly sat down in the plastic structure that had been pulled away from a group of similar baskets hanging from a side cable. "You're certain this is safe?" she said, staring at the darkness above her.

"Of course," Richard said with a laugh. "It's exactly like the simulation. And I'll be in the next chair behind you, only one minute or four hundred meters below. Altogether the ride takes forty minutes from bottom to top. Average speed is twenty-four kilometers per hour."

"And I don't do anything," Francesca remembered, "except sit tight, hold on, and activate my breathing system about twenty minutes from the summit."

"Don't forget to fasten your seat belt," Wakefield reminded her with a smile. "If the cable were to slow down or stop near the top, where you are weightless, your momentum could cause you to sail out into the Raman void." He grinned. "But since the entire chairlift runs beside the stairway, in the event of any emergency, you could always climb out of your basket and walk back up to the hub along the stairs."

Richard nodded and Janos Tabori switched on the motor. Francesca was lifted off the ground and soon disappeared above them. "I'll go right over to Gamma after I'm certain you're on your way," Richard said to Janos. "The second system should be easier. With all of us working together, we should be finished by nineteen hundred at the latest."

"I'll have the campsite ready by the time you reach the summit," Janos remarked. "Do you think we're still going to stay down here tonight?"

"That doesn't make much sense," David Brown said from above. He or Takagishi had monitored all cosmonaut communications throughout the day. "The rovers aren't ready yet. We had hoped to do some exploring tomorrow."

"If we each bring down a few subsystems," Wakefield replied, "Janos and I could assemble one rover tonight before we go to sleep. The second rover will probably be operational before noon tomorrow if we don't encounter any difficulties."

"That's a possible scenario," Dr. Brown responded. "Let's see how much progress we have made and how tired everyone is three hours from now."

Richard climbed into his tiny chair and waited for the automatic loading algorithm in the processor to attach his seat to the cable. "By the way," he said to his companion as he started his ascent, "thanks a lot for your good humor today. I might not have made it without the jokes."

Janos smiled and waved at his friend. Looking upward from his moving chair, Richard Wakefield could barely make out the light from Francesca's headgear. *She's more than a hundred floors above me,* he thought. *But only two and a half percent of the distance from here to the hub. This place is immense.*

He reached in his pocket and pulled out the portable meteorological station that Takagishi had asked him to carry. The professor wanted a careful profile of all the atmospheric parameters in the north polar bowl of Rama. Of particular importance for his circulation models was the density and temperature of the air versus the distance below the airlock.

Wakefield watched the pressure readings, which started at 1.05 bars, fall below Earth levels, and continue their steady monotonic decline. The temperature held fixed at a cold minus eight degrees Celsius. He leaned back and closed his eyes. It was a strange feeling, riding a basket upward, ever upward in the dark. Richard turned down the volume of one channel on his commpak; the only ongoing conversation was between Yamanaka and Turgenyev and neither of them ever had very much to say. He increased the volume on Beethoven's Sixth Symphony, which was playing in the background on another channel.

As he listened to the music, Richard was surprised at how his internal visions of brooks and flowers and green fields on Earth evoked a powerful feeling of homesickness. It was almost impossible for him to fathom the miraculous concatenation of events that had carried him from his boyhood home in Stratford to Cambridge to the Space Academy in Colorado and finally to here, to Rama, where he was riding a chairlift in the dark along the Stairway to the Gods.

No, Prospero, he said to himself, *no magician could ever have conceived of such a place*. He remembered seeing *The Tempest* for the first time as a boy and being frightened by the portrayal of a world whose mysteries might be beyond our comprehension. *There is no magic*, he had said at the time. *There are only natural concepts that we cannot yet explain*. Richard smiled. *Prospero was not a mage; he was only a frustrated scientist*.

A moment later Richard Wakefield was stupefied by the most amazing sight he had ever seen. As his chair was sailing soundlessly upward, parallel to the stairway, dawn burst upon Rama. Three kilometers below him, cut into the Central Plain, the long straight valleys that ran from the edge of the bowl to the Cylindrical Sea suddenly exploded with light. The six linear suns of Rama, three in each hemicylinder, were carefully designed to produce a balanced illumination throughout the alien world. Wakefield's first feelings were of vertigo and nausea. He was suspended in air by a thin cable, thousands of meters above the ground. He closed his eyes and tried to maintain his bearings. *You will not fall,* he said to himself.

"*Aieee,*" he heard Hiro Yamanaka yell.

From the ensuing conversation he could tell that Hiro, startled by the burst of light, had lost his footing near the middle of the Gamma stairway. He had apparently fallen twenty or thirty meters before he had adroitly (and luckily) managed to grab part of the banister.

"Are you all right?" David Brown asked.

"I think so," Yamanaka answered breathlessly.

With the short crisis over, everyone started talking at once. "This is fantastic!" Dr. Takagishi was shouting. "The light levels are phenomenal. And this is all happening *before* the thawing of the sea. It's different. It's altogether different."

"Have another module ready for me as soon as I reach the top," Francesca said. "I'm almost out of film."

"Such beauty. Such indescribable beauty," General O'Toole added. He and Nicole des Jardins were watching the monitor onboard the Newton. The real-time picture from Francesca's camera was being transmitted to them through the relay station at the hub.

Richard Wakefield said nothing. He simply stared, entranced by the world below him. He could barely discern Janos Tabori, the chairlift apparatus, and the half-completed campsite down at the bottom of the stairway. Nevertheless, the distance to them gave him some measure of this alien world. As he looked out across the hundreds of square kilometers of the Central Plain, he saw fascinating shapes in every direction. There were two features, however, that overwhelmed his imagination and vision: the Cylindrical Sea and the massive, pointed structures in the southern bowl opposite him, fifty kilometers away.

As his eyes grew more accustomed to the light, the gigantic central spire in the southern bowl seemed to grow larger and larger. It had been called Big Horn by the first explorers. *Can it really be eight kilometers tall?* Wakefield asked himself. The six smaller spires, surrounding the Big Horn in a hexagonal pattern and connected both to it and the walls of Rama by enormous flying buttresses, were each larger than anything made by man on Earth. Yet they were dwarfed by this neighboring prominence originating from the very center of the bowl and growing straight along the spin axis of the cylinder.

In the foreground, halfway between Wakefield's position near the north pole and that mammoth construction in the south, a band of bluish white ringed the cylindrical world. The frozen sea seemed illogical and out of place. It could never melt, the mind wanted to say, or all the water would fall toward the central axis. But the Cylindrical Sea was held in its banks by the centrifugal force of Rama. None knew better than the Newton crew that on its shore a human being would have the same weight as he would standing beside a terrestrial ocean.

The island city in the middle of the Cylindrical Sea was Rama's New York. To Richard its skyscrapers had not been too imposing in the views that had been offered by the light from the flares. But under the light of the Raman suns, it was clear that this city held center stage. The eyes were drawn to New York from any point inside Rama—the dense oval island of buildings was the only break in the orderly annulus that formed the Cylindrical Sea.

"Just look at New York!" Dr. Takagishi was gushing excitedly into his commpak. "There must be almost a thousand buildings over two hundred meters tall." He paused only a second. "That's where *they* live. I know it. New York must be our target."

After the initial outbursts there was a protracted silence while each of the cosmonauts privately integrated the sunlit world of Rama into his own consciousness. Richard could now clearly see Francesca, four hundred meters above him, as his chair crossed the transition between the stairways and the ladders and closed in on the hub.

"Admiral Heilmann and I have just had a quick conversation," David Brown said, breaking the silence, "with some advice from Dr. Takagishi. There seems to be no obvious reason to change our plans for this sortie, at least not the early part. Unless something else unexpected occurs, we will go forward with Wakefield's suggestion. We will finish the two chairlifts, carry the rover down for assembly later this evening, and all sleep in the campsite at the foot of the stairway as planned."

"Don't forget me," Janos hollered into his commpak. "I'm the only one who doesn't have much of a view."

Richard Wakefield unfastened his seat belt and stepped out onto the ledge. He looked down to where the stairway disappeared from view. "Roger, Cosmonaut Tabori. We have arrived back at Station Alpha. Whenever you give the signal, we will hoist you up to join us."

23

NIGHTFALL

. . . Considering the regular abuse that he received from his neurotic father and the emotional scars that must remain from his youthful marriage to British actress Sarah Tydings, Cosmonaut Wakefield is remarkably well adjusted. He underwent two years of professional therapy after his celebrated divorce, concluding a year before he entered the Space Academy in 2192. His scholastic record at the academy is still unequaled to this day; his professors in electrical engineering and computer sciences all insist that by the time of his graduation, Wakefield knew more than any member of the faculty. . . .

". . . Except for a wariness where intimacy is concerned (particularly with women—he has apparently had no sustained emotional involvements since the breakup of his marriage), Wakefield exhibits none of the antisocial behavior usually found in abused children. Although his SC was low as a youth, he has grown less arrogant as he has matured and is now less likely to force his brilliance upon others. His honesty and character are unassailable. Knowledge, not power or money, seems to be his goal. . . ."

Nicole finished reading the Psychological Assessment for Richard Wakefield and rubbed her eyes. It was very late. She had been studying the dossiers ever since the crew inside Rama had settled down to sleep. They would be awakening for their second day in that strange world in less than two hours. Her six-hour shift as communications officer would start in another thirty minutes. *So out of this entire bunch*, Nicole was thinking, *there are only three that are beyond question. Those four with their illegal media contract have already compromised themselves. Yamanaka and Turgenyev are unknowns. Wilson is mar-*

*ginally stable and has his own agenda anyway. That leaves
O'Toole, Takagishi, and Wakefield.*

Nicole washed her face and hands and sat down again at
the terminal. She exited from the Wakefield dossier and
returned to the main menu of the data cube. She scanned
the comparative statistics available and keyed a pair of
displays to appear side by side on the screen. On the
left-hand side was the ordered set of IE scores for each
member of the crew; opposite, for comparison, Nicole had
displayed the SC indices for the Newton dozen.

IE		SC	
Wakefield	+5.58	O'Toole	86
Sabatini	+4.22	Borzov	84
Brown	+4.17	Takagishi	82
Takagishi	+4.02	Wilson	78
Tabori	+3.37	des Jardins	71
Borzov	+3.28	Heilmann	68
des Jardins	+3.04	Tabori	64
O'Toole	+2.92	Yamanaka	62
Turgenyev	+2.87	Turgenyev	60
Yamanaka	+2.66	Wakefield	58
Wilson	+2.48	Sabatini	56
Heilmann	+2.24	Brown	49

Although Nicole had very quickly glanced through most
of the information in the dossiers earlier, she had not read
all the charts on all the crew members. Some of the
indices she now saw for the first time. She was particularly
surprised by the very high intelligence rating for Francesca Sabatini. *What a waste,* Nicole thought immediately.
All that potential being used for such ordinary pursuits.

The overall intelligence level of the crew was quite
impressive. Every cosmonaut was in the top one percent
of the population. Nicole was "one in a thousand" and she
was only in the middle of the dozen. Wakefield's intelligence rating was truly exceptional and placed him in the
supergenius category; Nicole had never before personally
known someone with such high scores on the standardized
tests.

Although her training in psychiatry had taught her to

distrust attempts to quantify personality traits, Nicole was intrigued by the SC indices as well. She herself would have intuitively placed O'Toole, Borzov, and Takagishi at the top of the list. All three men seemed confident, balanced, and sensitive to others. But she was astonished by Wilson's high socialization coefficient. *He must have been an altogether different person before he became involved with Francesca.* Nicole wondered for a brief moment why her own SC index was no higher than a seventy-one; then she remembered that as a young woman she had been more withdrawn and self-centered.

So what about Wakefield? she asked herself, realizing that he was the only viable candidate to help her understand what had happened inside the RoSur software during Borzov's operation. Could she trust him? And could she enlist Richard's help without revealing some of her farfetched suspicions? Again the thought of abandoning her investigation altogether seemed very appealing. *Nicole,* she said to herself, *if this conspiracy idea of yours turns out to be a waste of time . . .*

But Nicole was convinced that there were enough unanswered questions to warrant continuing her investigation. She resolved to talk to Wakefield. After determining that she could add her own files to the king's data cube, she created a new file, a nineteenth file, simply called NICOLE. She called in her word processing subroutine and wrote a brief memorandum:

> 3-3-00—Have determined for certain that RoSur malfunction during Borzov procedure due to external manual command after initial load and verification. Enlisting Wakefield for support.

Nicole pulled a blank data cube from the supply drawer adjacent to her computer. She copied onto it both her memorandum and all the information stored on the cube that she had been given by King Henry. When she dressed for her work shift in her flight suit, she put the duplicate cube in her pocket.

General O'Toole was dozing in the CCC (Command and

Control Complex) of the military spacecraft when Nicole arrived to give him a break. Although the visual displays in this smaller vehicle were not quite as breathtaking as those in the scientific ship, the layout of the military "C-Cubed" as a communications center was far superior, especially from a human engineering point of view. All the controls could easily be handled by a single cosmonaut.

O'Toole apologized for not being awake. He pointed to the three monitors that showed three different views of the same scene—the rest of the crew fast asleep inside the crude campsite at the foot of Alpha stairway. "This last five hours has not been what you would call exciting," he said.

Nicole smiled. "General, you don't need to apologize to me. I know you've been on duty for almost twenty-four hours."

General O'Toole stood up. "After you left," he summarized, checking his electronic log on one of the six monitors in front of him, "they finished dinner and then they started the assembly of the first rover. The automatic navigation program failed its self-test, but Wakefield found the problem—a software bug in one of the subroutines that was changed in the last delivery—and fixed it. Tabori took the rover for a test drive before the crew prepared for sleep. At the end of the day Francesca did a stirring short piece for transmission to the Earth." He paused for a moment. "Would you like to see it?"

Nicole nodded. O'Toole activated the far right television monitor and Francesca appeared in a close-up outside the enclosed campsite. The frame showed a portion of the bottom of the stairway and the equipment for the chairlift as well. "It is time to sleep in Rama," she intoned. She looked up and around her. "The lights in this amazing world came on unexpectedly about nine hours ago, showing us in more detail the elaborate handiwork of our intelligent cousins from across the stars." A montage of still photographs and short videos, some taken by the drones and some taken by Francesca herself on that day, punctuated her tour of the artificial "worldlet" that the crew was "about to explore." At the end of the brief segment the camera was again fixed on Francesca.

"Nobody knows why this second spacecraft in less than

a century has invaded our little domain at the edge of the galaxy. Perhaps this magnificent creation has no explanation that would be even remotely comprehensible to us human beings. But perhaps somewhere in this vast and precise world of metal we will find some keys that will unlock the mysteries enshrouding the creatures who constructed this vehicle." She smiled and her nostrils flared dramatically. "And if we do, then perhaps we will have moved one step closer to an understanding of ourselves . . . and maybe our gods as well."

Nicole could tell that General O'Toole was moved by Francesca's oratory. Despite her personal antipathy for the woman, Nicole begrudgingly acknowledged again that Francesca was talented. "She captures my feelings about this venture so well," O'Toole said enthusiastically. "I just wish I could be that articulate."

Nicole sat down at the console and entered the handover code. She followed the listed procedure on the monitor and checked out all the equipment. "All right, General," she said as she turned around in her chair, "I believe I can handle it from here."

O'Toole lingered behind her. It was obvious that he wanted to talk. "I had a long discussion with Signora Sabatini three nights ago," he said. "About religion. She told me that she had become an agnostic before finally coming back to the church. She told me that thinking about Rama had made her a Catholic again."

There was a long silence. For some reason, the fifteenth century church in the old village of Sainte Etienne de Chigny, eight hundred meters down the road from Beauvois, came into Nicole's mind. She remembered standing inside the church with her father on a beautiful spring day and being fascinated by the light scattering through the stained glass windows.

"Did God make the colors?" Nicole had asked her father.

"Some say so," he had answered laconically.

"And what do you think, Daddy?" she had then asked.

"I must admit," General O'Toole was saying as Nicole forced herself to return to the present, "that this entire voyage has been spiritually uplifting for me. I feel closer to God now than I have ever felt before. There's something about contemplating the vastness of the universe that humbles you and makes you—" He stopped himself. "I'm sorry," he said, "I have imposed—"

"No," Nicole answered. "No, you haven't. I find your religious certitude very refreshing."

"Nevertheless, I hope I haven't offended you in any way. Religion is a very private matter." He smiled. "But sometimes it's hard not to share your feelings, particularly since both you and Signora Sabatini are Catholics as well."

As O'Toole left the control complex, Nicole wished him a sound sleep during his nap. When he had gone, she removed the duplicate data cube from her pocket and placed it in the CCC cube reader. *At least this way,* she said to herself, *I have backed up my information sources.* Into her mind came a picture of Francesca Sabatini listening intently while General O'Toole waxed philosophical about the religious significance of Rama. *You're an amazing woman,* Nicole thought. *You do whatever it takes. Even immorality and hypocrisy are acceptable.*

Dr. Shigeru Takagishi stared in rapt silence at the towers and spheres of New York four kilometers away. From time to time he would walk over to the telescope that he had temporarily set up on the cliff overlooking the Cylindrical Sea and study a particular feature in that alien landscape.

"You know," he said at length to Cosmonauts Wakefield and Sabatini, "I don't believe the reports the first crew gave on New York are entirely accurate. Or else this is a different spaceship." Neither Richard nor Francesca responded. Wakefield was engrossed in the last stages of assembly of the icemobile and Francesca, as usual, was busy video recording Wakefield's efforts.

"It looks as if there are certainly three identical parts to the city," Dr. Takagishi continued, primarily to himself, "and three subdivisions within each of those parts. But all nine sections are not *absolutely* the same. There appear to be subtle differences."

"There," said Richard Wakefield, standing up with a satisfied smile. "That ought to do it. A full day ahead of schedule. I'll just quickly test all the important engineering functions."

Francesca glanced at her watch. "We're almost half an hour behind the revised timeline. Are we still going to take a fast look at New York before dinner?"

Wakefield shrugged his shoulders and looked at Takagishi. Francesca walked over to the Japanese scientist. "What do you say, Shigeru? Shall we take a quick run across the ice and give the people on Earth a close-up view of the Rama version of New York?"

"By all means," Takagishi answered. "I can't wait—"

"Only if you will be back at camp by nineteen thirty at the latest," David Brown interrupted. He was in the helicopter with Admiral Heilmann and Reggie Wilson. "We need to do some serious planning tonight. We may want to revise the deployments for tomorrow."

"Roger," said Wakefield. "If we forget about the pulley system for now and have no problem carrying the icemobile down the stairs, we should be able to cross the sea in ten minutes each way. That would get us back to camp in plenty of time."

"We've overflown many of the features of the Northern Hemicylinder this afternoon," Brown said. "No biots anywhere. The cities look like duplicates of each other. There were no surprises anywhere in the Central Plain. I personally think that maybe we should attack the mysterious south tomorrow."

"New York," Takagishi shouted. "A detailed reconnaissance of New York should be our goal for tomorrow." Brown didn't answer. Takagishi walked out to the edge of the cliff and stared down at the ice fifty meters below. To his left the unimposing narrow stairway cut in the cliff descended in short steps. "How heavy is the icemobile?" Takagishi asked.

"Not very," Wakefield answered. "But it's bulky. Are you certain you don't want to wait for me to install the pulleys? We can always go across tomorrow."

"I can help carry it," Francesca interjected. "If we don't at least see New York, we will not be able to make educated inputs at the planning meeting tonight."

"All right," Richard replied, shaking his head in amusement at Francesca. "Anything for journalism. I'll go first, so that most of the lifting is on my back. Francesca, get in the middle. Dr. Takagishi at the top. Watch out for the runners. They are sharp on the edges."

The climb down to the surface of the Cylindrical Sea was uneventful. "Goodness," Francesca Sabatini said as they prepared to cross the ice, "that was easy. Why is a pulley system needed at all?"

"Because sometimes we may be carrying something else or, perish the thought, we may need to defend ourselves during ascent or descent."

Wakefield and Takagishi sat in the front of the icemobile. Francesca was in the back with her video camera. Takagishi became more and more animated as they drew closer to New York. "Just look at that place," he said when the icemobile was about five hundred meters from the opposite shore. "Can there be any doubt that this is the capital of Rama?"

As the trio approached the shore, the breathtaking sight of the strange city silenced all conversation. Everything about New York's complicated structure spoke of order and purposeful creation by intelligent beings; yet the first set of cosmonauts, seventy years earlier, had found it as empty of life as the rest of Rama. Was this vast complex, broken into nine sections, indeed an enormously complicated machine, as the first visitors had suggested, or was the long thin island (ten kilometers by three) actually a city whose denizens had long ago disappeared?

They parked the icemobile on the edge of the frozen sea and walked along a path until they found a stairway leading to the ramparts of the wall surrounding the city. The excited Takagishi loped along about twenty meters in front of Wakefield and Sabatini. As they ascended, more and more of the details of the city became apparent.

Richard was immediately intrigued by the geometrical shapes of the buildings. In addition to the normal tall, thin skyscrapers, there were scattered spheres, rectangular solids, even an occasional polyhedron. And they were definitely arranged in some kind of a pattern. *Yes*, he thought to himself as his eyes scanned the fascinating complex of structures, *over there is a dodecahedron, there a pentahedron* . . .

His mathematical ruminations were interrupted when all the lights were suddenly extinguished and the entire interior of Rama was plunged into darkness.

24
SOUNDS IN
THE DARKNESS

At first Takagishi could see absolutely nothing. It was as if he had suddenly been struck blind. He blinked twice and stood motionless in the total darkness. The momentary silence on the commlinks erupted into hopeless noise as all the cosmonauts began to talk at the same time. Calmly, fighting against his growing fear, Takagishi tried to remember the scene that had been in front of his eyes at the moment the lights were extinguished.

He had been standing on the wall overlooking New York, about a meter from the dangerous edge. In the final second he had been looking off to the left and had just glimpsed a staircase descending into the city about two hundred meters away. Then the scene had vanished. . . .

"Takagishi," he heard Wakefield calling, "are you all right?"

He turned around to acknowledge the question and noticed that his knees had become weak. In the complete darkness he had lost his orientation. How many degrees had he turned? Had he been facing the city directly? Again he recalled the last image. The elevated wall was twenty or thirty meters above the floor of the city. A fall would be fatal.

"I'm here," he said tentatively. "But I'm too close to the edge." He dropped down on all fours. The metal was cold against his hands.

"We're coming," Francesca said. "I'm trying to find the light on my video camera."

Takagishi turned down the volume on his commpak and listened for the sound of his companions. A few seconds later he saw a light in the distance. He could barely make out the forms of his two associates.

"Where are you, Shigeru?" Francesca asked. The light from her camera illuminated only the area immediately around her.

"Up here. Up here." He waved before he realized that they could not see him.

"I want complete quiet," David Brown shouted over the communications system, "until everyone is accounted for." The conversations ceased after a few seconds. "Now," he continued, "Francesca, what's going on down there?"

"We're climbing the stairway up the wall, on the New York side, David, about a hundred meters from where we parked the icemobile. Dr. Takagishi was ahead of us, already at the top. We have the light from my camera. We're going to meet him."

"Janos," Dr. Brown said next, "where are you in rover number two?"

"About three kilometers from camp. The headlights are working fine. We could return in ten minutes or so."

"Go back there and man the navigation console. We'll stay airborne until you verify that the homing system is operational from your side. . . . Francesca, be careful, but come back to camp as fast as you can. And give us a report every two minutes or so."

"Roger, David," she said. Francesca switched off her commpak and called for Takagishi again. Despite the fact that he was only thirty meters away, it took Francesca and Richard over a minute to find him in the dark.

Takagishi was relieved to touch his colleagues. They sat down beside him on the wall and listened to the renewed chatter on the commpak. O'Toole and des Jardins verified that there had been no other observed changes inside Rama at the time the lights had gone out. The half dozen portable scientific stations that had already been deployed in the alien spaceship had exhibited no meaningful perturbations. Temperatures, wind velocities and directions, seismic readings, and near field spectroscopic measurements were all unchanged.

"So the lights went out," Wakefield said. "I admit that it was scary, but it was no big deal. Probably—"

"*Shh*," said Takagishi abruptly. He reached down and turned off both his and Wakefield's commpak. "Do you hear that noise?"

To Wakefield the sudden silence was nearly as unnerving as the total darkness had been a few minutes before. "No," he said in a whisper, after listening for several seconds, "but my ears are not very—"

"*Shh*." Now it was Francesca's turn. "Are you talking about that distant, high-pitched scraping sound?" she whispered.

"Yes," said Takagishi, quietly but excitedly. "Like something is brushing against a metallic surface. It suggests movement."

Wakefield listened again. Maybe he could hear something. Maybe he was imagining it. "Come on," he said to the others out loud, "let's go back to the icemobile."

"Wait," said Takagishi as Richard stood up. "It seemed to stop just as you spoke." He leaned over to Francesca. "Turn off the light," he said softly. "Let's sit here in the darkness and see if we can hear it again."

Wakefield sat back down beside his companions. With the camera light off it was absolutely black around them. The only sound was their breathing. They waited a full minute. They heard nothing. Just as Wakefield was about to insist that they leave, he heard a sound from the direction of New York. It was like hard brushes dragging across metal, but there was also an embedded high-frequency noise, as if a tiny voice were singing very fast, that punctuated the nearly constant scraping. The sound was definitely louder. And eerie. Wakefield felt his spine tingle.

"Do you have a tape recorder?" Takagishi whispered to Francesca. The scraping stopped at the sound of Takagishi's voice. The trio waited another fifteen seconds.

"Hey there, hey there," they heard David Brown's loud voice on the emergency interrupt channel. "Is everybody all right? You're way overdue for a report."

"Yes, David," Francesca replied. "We're still here. We heard an unusual sound coming from New York."

"Now's not the time for dilly-dallying. We have a major crisis on our hands. All our new plans have assumed that Rama would be constantly lit. We need to regroup."

"All right," Wakefield responded. "We're leaving the wall now. If all goes well we should be back to the campsite in less than an hour."

Dr. Shigeru Takagishi was reluctant to leave New York with the mystery of the strange sound unresolved. But he understood completely that now was not the appropriate time for a scientific foray into the city. As the icemobile raced across the frozen Cylindrical Sea, the Japanese scientist smiled to himself. He was happy. He knew that he had heard a new sound, something decidedly different from any of the sounds catalogued by the first Rama team. This was a good beginning.

Cosmonauts Tabori and Wakefield were the last two to ride up the chairlift beside the Alpha stairway. "Takagishi was really quite irritated with Dr. Brown, wasn't he?" Richard was saying to Janos as he helped the little Hungarian disembark from the chair. They glided along the ramp toward the ferry.

"I've never seen him so angry," Janos replied. "Shig is a consummate professional and he has great pride in his knowledge of Rama. For Brown to discount the noise you guys heard in such an offhand manner suggests an absence of respect for Takagishi. I don't blame Shig for being irritated."

They climbed onboard the ferry and activated the transportation module. The vast darkness of Rama retreated behind them as they eased through the lighted corridor toward the Newton.

"It was a very strange sound," Richard said. "It really gave me the chills. I have no idea if it was a new sound, or if maybe Norton and his team heard the same thing seventy years ago. But I do know that I had a bad case of the willies while I was standing there on the wall."

"Francesca was even pissed off at Brown at first. She wanted to do a feature interview with Shig for her nightly report. Brown talked her out of it, but I'm not certain he completely convinced her that strange noises are not news. Luckily she had enough of a story with just the lights going out."

The two men descended from the ferry and approached

the air lock. "Whew," said Janos. "I'm bushed. It has been a couple of long and hectic days."

"Yeah," Richard agreed. "We thought we would be spending the next two nights at the campsite. Instead we're back up here. I wonder what surprises are in store for us tomorrow."

Janos smiled at his friend. "You know what's funny about all this?" he said. He did not wait for Wakefield to answer. "Brown really believes he's in charge of this mission. Did you see how he reacted when Takagishi suggested that we could explore New York in the dark? Brown probably thinks it was *his* decision for us to return to the Newton and abort the first sortie."

Richard looked at Janos with a quizzical smile. "It wasn't, of course," Janos continued. "Rama made the decision for us to leave. And Rama will decide what we do next."

25

A FRIEND IN NEED

In his dream he was lying on a futon in a seventeenth century ryokan. The room was very large, nine tatami mats in all. To his left, in the yard on the other side of the open screen, was a perfect miniaturized garden with tiny trees and a manicured stream. He was waiting for a young woman.

"Takagishi-san, are you awake?"

He stirred and reached out for the communicator. "Hello," he said, his voice betraying his grogginess. "Who is it?"

"Nicole des Jardins," the voice said. "I'm sorry to call you so early, but I need to see you. It's urgent."

"Give me three minutes," Takagishi said.

There was a knock on his door exactly three minutes later. Nicole greeted him and entered the room. She was carrying a data cube. "Do you mind?" she said, pointing to the computer console. Takagishi shook his head.

"Yesterday there were half a dozen separate incidents," Nicole said gravely, pointing at some blips on the monitor, "including the two largest aberrations I have ever seen in your heart data." She looked at him. "Are you certain that you and your doctor provided me with complete historical records?"

Takagishi nodded.

"Then I have reason for concern," she continued. "The irregularities yesterday suggest that your chronic diastolic abnormality has worsened. Perhaps the valve has sprung a new leak. Perhaps the long periods of weightlessness—"

"Or perhaps," Takagishi interrupted with a soft smile, "I became overly excited and my extra adrenaline aggravated the problem."

Nicole stared at the Japanese scientist. "That's possible, Dr. Takagishi. One of the major incidents occurred just after the lights went out. I guess it was when you were listening to your strange sound."

"And the other, by chance, could it have been during my argument with Dr. Brown in the campsite? If so, that would support my hypothesis."

Cosmonaut des Jardins touched several keys on the console and her software entered a new subroutine. She studied the data displayed on two sides of a split screen. "Yes," she said, "it looks right. The second incident took place twenty minutes before we started leaving Rama. That would have been toward the end of the meeting." She moved away from the monitor. "But I can't dismiss the bizarre behavior of your heart just because you were excited."

They stared at each other for several long seconds. "What are you trying to tell me, Doctor?" Takagishi said softly. "Are you going to confine me to my quarters on the Newton? Now, at the most significant moment in my professional career?"

"I'm considering it," Nicole answered directly. "Your health is more important to me than your career. I've already lost one member of the crew. I'm not certain that I could forgive myself if I lost another."

She saw the entreaty in her colleague's face. "I know how critical these sorties into Rama are to you. I'm trying to find some kind of rationalization that will allow me to overlook yesterday's data." Nicole sat down at the far end of the bed and looked away. "But as a doctor, not a Newton cosmonaut, it's very, very tough."

She heard Takagishi approach and felt his hand gently on her shoulder. "I know how difficult it has been for you these last few days," he said. "But it was not your fault. All of us are aware that General Borzov's death was unavoidable."

Nicole recognized the respect and friendship in Takagishi's gaze. She thanked him with her eyes. "I very much appreciate what you did for me before launch," he continued. "If you feel compelled to limit my activities now, I will not object."

"Dammit," said Nicole, standing up quickly, "it's not that simple. I've been studying your overnight data for almost an hour. Look at this. Your chart for the last ten hours is perfectly normal. There's not a trace of any anomaly. And you had had no incidents for weeks. Until yesterday. What is it with you, Shig? Do you have a bad heart? Or just a weird one?"

Takagishi smiled. "My wife told me once that I had a strange heart. But I think she was referring to something altogether different."

Nicole activated her scanner and displayed the data on the monitor in real-time. "There we are again"—she shook her head—"the signature of a perfectly healthy heart. No cardiologist in the world would argue with my conclusion." She moved toward the door.

"So what's the verdict, Doc?" Takagishi asked.

"I haven't decided," she answered. "You could help. Have another one of your incidents in the next few hours and make it easy for me." She waved good-bye. "See you at breakfast."

Richard Wakefield was coming out of his room as Nicole headed down the hall after leaving Takagishi. She made a spontaneous decision to talk to him about the RoSur software.

"Good morning, princess," he said as he approached. "What are you doing awake at this hour? Something exciting, I hope."

"As a matter of fact," Nicole replied in the same playful tone, "I was coming to talk to you." He stopped to listen. "Do you have a minute?"

"For you, Madame Doctor," he answered with an exaggerated smile, "I have *two* minutes. But no more. Mind you, I'm hungry. And if I am not fed quickly when I'm hungry, I turn into an awful ogre." Nicole laughed. "What's on your mind?" he added lightly.

"Could we go into your room?" she asked.

"I knew it. I knew it," he said, spinning around and sliding quickly toward his door. "It's finally happened, just like in my dreams. An intelligent, beautiful woman is going to declare her undying affection—"

Nicole could not suppress a chortle. "Wakefield," she interrupted, still grinning, "you are hopeless. Are you never serious? I have some business to discuss with you."

"Oh, darn," Richard said dramatically. "Business. In that case I'm going to limit you to the two minutes I allocated you earlier. Business also makes me hungry . . . and grumpy."

Richard Wakefield opened the door to his room and waited for Nicole to enter. He offered her the chair in front of his computer monitor and sat down behind her on the bed. She turned around to face him. On the shelf above his bed were a dozen tiny figurines similar to the ones she had seen before in Tabori's room and at the Borzov banquet.

"Allow me to introduce you to some of my menagerie," Richard said, noticing her curiosity. "You've met Lord and Lady Macbeth, Puck, and Bottom. This matched pair is Tybalt and Mercutio from *Romeo and Juliet*. Next to them are Iago and Othello, followed by Prince Hal, Falstaff, and the wonderful Mistress Quickly. The last one on the right is my closest friend, The Bard, or TB for short."

As Nicole watched, Richard activated a switch near the head of his bed and TB climbed down a ladder from the shelf to the bed. The twenty-centimeter-high robot carefully navigated the folds in the bed coverings and came over to greet Nicole.

"And what be your name, fair lady?" TB said.

"I am Nicole des Jardins," she replied.

"Sounds French," the robot said immediately. "But you don't look French. At least not Valois." The robot appeared to be staring at her. "You look more like a child of Othello and Desdemona."

Nicole was astonished. "How did you do that?" she asked.

"I'll explain later," Richard said with a wave of his hand. "Do you have a favorite Shakespearean sonnet?" he now inquired. "If you do, recite a line, or give TB a number."

"Full many a glorious morning . . ." recalled Nicole.

". . . have I seen," the robot added,

"Flatter the mountain tops with sovereign eye,
Kissing with golden face the meadows green,
Gilding pale streams with heavenly alchemy . . ."

The little robot recited the sonnet with fluid head and
arm movements as well as a wide range of facial expressions. Again Nicole was impressed by Richard Wakefield's
creativity. She remembered the key four lines of the sonnet from her university days and mumbled them along
with TB:

"Even so my sun one early morn did shine,
With all-triumphant splendor on my brow;
But, out alack, he was but one hour mine,
The region cloud hath masked him from
      me now . . ."

After the robot finished the final couplet, Nicole, who
was moved by the almost forgotten words, found herself
applauding. "And he can do all the sonnets?" she asked.

Richard nodded. "Plus many, many of the more poetic
dramatic speeches. But that's not his most outstanding
capability. Remembering passages from Shakespeare only
requires plenty of storage. TB is also a very intelligent
robot. He can carry on a conversation better than—"

Richard stopped himself in midsentence. "I'm sorry,
Nicole. I'm monopolizing the time. You said you had some
business to discuss."

"But you've already used my two minutes," she said
with a twinkle in her eye. "Are you certain that you won't
die of starvation if I take five more minutes of your time?"

Nicole quickly summarized her investigation into the
RoSur software malfunction, including her conclusion that
the fault protection algorithms must have been disabled
by manual commands. She indicated that she could go no
further with her own analysis and that she would like
some help from Richard. She did not discuss her suspicions.

"Should be a snap," he said with a smile. "All I have to
do is find the place in memory where the commands are
buffered and stored. That could take a little time, given
the size of the storage, but these memories are generally

designed with logical architectures. However, I don't understand why you're doing all this detective work. Why don't you simply ask Janos and the others if they input any commands?"

"That's the problem," Nicole replied. "Nobody recalls commanding RoSur at any time after the final load and verify. When Janos hit his head during the maneuver, I thought his fingers were on the control box. He doesn't remember and I can't be certain."

Richard's brow furrowed. "It would be very unlikely that Janos just happened to toggle the fault protection enable switch with a random command. That would mean the overall design was stupid." He thought for a moment. "Oh well," he continued, "there's no need to speculate. Now you've aroused my curiosity. I'll look at the problem as soon as I have—"

"Break break. Break break." Otto Heilmann's voice on the communicator interrupted their conversation. "Will everyone come immediately to the science control center for a meeting. We have a new development. The lights inside Rama just came on again."

Richard opened the door and followed Nicole into the corridor. "Thanks for your help," Nicole said. "I appreciate it very much."

"Thank me after I do something," Richard said with a grin. "I'm notorious for promises. . . . Now, what do you think is the meaning of all these games with the lights?"

26

SECOND SORTIE

David Brown had placed a single large sheet of paper on the table in the middle of the control center. Francesca had divided it into partitions, representing hours, and was now busy writing down whatever he told her. "The damn mission planning software is too inflexible to be useful in a situation like this," Dr. Brown was saying to Janos Tabori and Richard Wakefield. "It's only good when the sequence of activities being planned is consistent with one of the preflight strategies."

Janos walked over to one of the monitors. "Maybe you can use it better than I can," Dr. Brown continued, "but I have found it much easier this morning to rely on pencil and paper." Janos called up a software program for mission sequencing and began to key in some data.

"Wait a minute," Richard Wakefield interjected. Janos stopped typing on the keyboard and turned to listen to his colleague. "We're getting all worked up over nothing. We don't need to plan the entire next sortie at this moment. In any case, we know the first major activity segment must be the completion of the infrastructure. That will take another ten or twelve hours. The rest of the sortie design can be done in parallel."

"Richard's right," Francesca added. "We're trying to do everything too fast. Let's send the space cadets into Rama to finish setting up. While they're gone we can work out the details of the sortie."

"That's impractical," Dr. Brown replied. "The academy graduates are the only ones who know how long each of the various engineering activities should take. We can't make meaningful timelines without them."

"Then one of us will stay here with you," Janos Tabori

said. He grinned. "And we can use Heilmann or O'Toole inside, as an extra worker. That shouldn't slow us down too much."

A consensus decision was reached in half an hour. Nicole would stay onboard the Newton again, at least until the infrastructure was completed, and represent the cadets in the mission planning process. Admiral Heilmann would go into Rama with the four other professional cosmonauts. They would finish the remaining three infrastructure tasks: the assembly of the rest of the vehicles, the deployment of another dozen portable monitoring stations in the Northern Hemicylinder, and the construction of the Beta campsite/communications complex on the north side of the Cylindrical Sea.

Richard Wakefield was in the process of reviewing all the detailed subtasks with his small team when Reggie Wilson, who had been virtually silent during the entire morning, suddenly jumped up from his chair. "This is all bullshit," he shouted. "I can't believe all the nonsense I'm hearing."

Richard stopped his review. Brown and Takagishi, who had already started discussing the sortie design, were suddenly silent. All eyes were focused on Reggie Wilson.

"A man died here four days ago," he said. "Killed, most likely, by whoever or whatever is operating that gigantic spacecraft. But we went inside exploring anyway. Next the lights go on and off unexpectedly." Wilson looked around the room at the rest of the crew. His eyes were wild. His forehead was sweating. "And what do we all do? Huh? How do we respond to this warning from alien creatures far superior to us? We sit down calmly and plan the rest of our exploration of their vehicle. Don't any of you get it? They don't want us in there. They want us to *leave*, to go home to Earth."

Wilson's outburst was greeted by an uncomfortable silence. At length General O'Toole walked over beside Reggie Wilson. "Reggie," he said quietly, "we were all upset by General Borzov's death. But none of the rest of us see any connection—"

"Then you're blind, man, you're blind. I was up in that goddamn helicopter when the lights went out. One minute it was bright as a summer day and the next, poof, it was pitch black. It was fucking weird, man. Somebody turned out *all* the lights. In this discussion never once have I heard anybody ask *why* the lights went out. What's the matter with you people? Are you too smart to be afraid?"

Wilson ranted for several minutes. His recurring theme was always the same. The Ramans had planned Borzov's death, they were sending a warning with the lights going on and off, there would be more disasters if the crew insisted on continuing with the exploration.

General O'Toole stood beside Reggie during the entire episode. Dr. Brown, Francesca, and Nicole had a hurried discussion on the side and then Nicole approached Wilson. "Reggie," she said informally, interrupting his diatribe, "why don't you and General O'Toole come with me? We can continue this conversation without delaying the rest of the crew."

He looked at her suspiciously. "You, Doctor? Why should I come with you? You weren't even in there. You haven't seen enough to know anything." Wilson moved over in front of Wakefield. "You were there, Richard," he said. "You saw that place. You know what kind of intelligence and power it would take to make a space vehicle that large and then launch it on a trip between the stars. Hey, man, we're *nothing* to them. We're less than ants. We haven't got a chance."

"I agree with you, Reggie," Richard Wakefield said calmly after a moment's hesitation. "At least where our comparative capabilities are concerned. But we have no evidence they're hostile. Or even care about whether or not we explore their craft. On the contrary, the very fact that we are alive—"

"*Look*," shouted Irina Turgenyev suddenly. "Look at the monitor."

A solitary image was frozen on the giant screen in the control center. A crablike creature filled the entire frame. It had a low, flat body, about twice as long as it was wide. Its weight was supported on six triple-jointed legs. Two scissorlike claws extended in front of the body and a whole row of manipulators, which looked uncannily like tiny human hands at first glance, nestled close to some kind of opening in the carapace. On closer inspection the manipulators were a veritable hardware store of capabilities—there were pincers, probes, rasps, and even something that resembled a drill.

Its eyes, if that's indeed what they were, were deeply recessed in protective hoods and raised like periscopes above the top of the shell. The eyeballs themselves were crystal or jelly, vivid blue in color, and utterly expressionless.

From the legend on the side of the image it was clear that the photograph had been taken just moments before, by one of the long-range drones, at a spot roughly five kilometers south of the Cylindrical Sea. The frame, filmed with a telescopic lens, covered an area roughly six meters square.

"So we have company in Rama," said Janos Tabori. The rest of the cosmonauts stared at the monitor in amazement.

All of the crew later agreed that the image of the crab biot on the giant screen would not have been so frightening if it had not occurred at that precise moment. Although Reggie's behavior was definitely aberrant, there was enough sense in what he was saying to remind each of them of the dangers in their expedition. None of the crew was completely free from fear. All of them had, in some private moment, confronted the disquieting fact that the super-advanced Ramans might not be friendly.

But most of the time they pushed aside their fears. It was part of their job. Like the early space shuttle astronauts in America, who knew that every so often the vehicle would crash or explode, the Newton cosmonauts accepted that there were uncontrollable risks associated with their mission. Healthy denial caused the group to avoid discussion of the unsettling issues most of the time and to focus on the more bounded (and therefore more controllable) items, such as the sequence of events for the following day.

Reggie's outburst and the simultaneous appearance of the crab biot on the monitor triggered one of the few philosophical group discussions that ever occurred on the project. O'Toole staked out his position early. Although he was fascinated by the Ramans, he did not fear them. God had seen fit to place him on this mission and, if He so chose, could decide that this extraordinary adventure would be O'Toole's last. In any case, whatever happened would be God's will.

Richard Wakefield articulated a point of view that was apparently shared by several of the other crew members. To him, the entire project was both a challenging voyage of discovery and a test of personal mettle. The uncertainties were there, to be sure, but they produced excitement as well as danger. The intense thrill of new learning, together with the possible monumental significance of this extraterrestrial encounter, more than compensated for the risks. Richard had no qualms about the mission. He was certain that this was the apotheosis of his life; if he didn't live beyond the end of the project, it would still have been worth it. He would have done something important during his brief existence on Earth.

Nicole listened attentively to the discussion. She didn't say much herself, but she found her own opinions crystallizing as she followed the flow of the conversation. She enjoyed watching the responses, both verbal and nonverbal, from the other cosmonauts. Shigeru Takagishi was clearly in the Wakefield camp. He was vigorously nodding his head the entire time Richard was talking about the excitement of participating in such a significant effort. Reggie Wilson, now subdued and probably embarrassed by his earlier tirade, did not say much. He commented only when asked a direct question. Admiral Heilmann looked uncomfortable from the beginning to the end. His entire contribution was to remind everyone of the passage of time.

Surprisingly, Dr. David Brown did not add much to the philosophical discussion. He made several short comments and once or twice seemed on the verge of launching into a long, amplifying explanation. But he never did. His true beliefs about the nature of Rama were not revealed.

Francesca Sabatini initially acted as a kind of moderator or interlocuter, asking questions of clarification and keeping the conversation on an even keel. Toward the end of the discussion, however, she offered several personal, can-

did comments of her own. Her philosophical view of the
Newton mission was altogether different from that expressed by O'Toole and Wakefield.

"I think you're making this entire thing much too complex and intellectual," she said after Richard had delivered
a long panegyric on the joys of knowledge. "There was no
need for me to do any deep soul-searching before I applied to be a Newton cosmonaut. I approached the issue
the same way I do all my major decisions. I did a risk/
reward trade-off. I judged that the rewards—considering
all the factors, including fame, prestige, money, even
adventure—more than warranted the risks. And I absolutely disagree with Richard in one respect. If I die on this
mission I will not be at all happy. For me, most of the
rewards from this project are delayed; I cannot benefit
from them if I do not return to Earth."

Francesca's comments aroused Nicole's curiosity. She
wanted to ask the Italian journalist some more questions,
but Nicole didn't think it was the proper time or place.
After the meeting was over, she was still intrigued by
what Francesca had said. *Can life really be that simple to
her?* Nicole thought to herself. *Can everything be evaluated in terms of risks and rewards?* She remembered
Francesca's lack of emotion when she drank the abortion
liquid. *But what about principles or values? Or even
feelings?* As the meeting broke up Nicole admitted to
herself that Francesca was still very much a puzzle.

Nicole watched Dr. Takagishi carefully. He was handling himself much better today. "I have brought a printout of the official sortie strategy, Dr. Brown," he was
saying, waving a four-inch-thick set of papers in his hand,
"to remind us of the fundamental tenets of sortie design
that resulted from over a year of unhurried mission planning. May I read from the summary?"

"I don't think you need to do that," David Brown responded. "We're all familiar with—"

"I'm not," interrupted General O'Toole. "I would like
to hear it. Admiral Heilmann asked me to pay close attention and brief him on the issues."

Dr. Brown waved for Takagishi to continue. The diminutive Japanese scientist was borrowing a page from Brown's own portfolio. Even though he knew that David Brown personally favored going after the crab biots on the second sortie, Takagishi still was attempting to convince the other cosmonauts that the top-priority activity should be a scientific foray into the city of New York.

Reggie Wilson had excused himself an hour earlier and had gone to his room for a nap. The remaining five crew members onboard the Newton had spent most of the afternoon struggling, without success, to reach an agreement on the activities for the second sortie. Since the two scientists Brown and Takagishi had radically different opinions on what should be done, no consensus was possible. Meanwhile, behind them on the large monitor, there had been intermittent views of the space cadets and Admiral Heilmann working inside Rama. The current picture showed Tabori and Turgenyev at the campsite adjoining the Cylindrical Sea. They had just finished assembling the second motorboat and were checking its electrical subsystems.

". . . The sequence of sorties has been carefully designed," Takagishi was reading, "to be consistent with the mission policies and priorities document, ISA–NT–0014. The primary goals of the first sortie are to establish the engineering infrastructure and to examine the interior on at least a superficial level. Of particular importance will be the identification of any characteristics of this second Rama spacecraft that are in any way different from the first.

"Sortie number two is designed to complete the mapping of the inside of Rama, focusing particularly on regions unexplored seventy years ago, as well as the collections of buildings called cities and any interior differences identified on the first sortie. Encounters with biots will be *avoided* on the second sortie, although the presence and location of the various kinds of biots will be part of the mapping process.

"Interaction with the biots will be delayed until the third sortie. Only after careful and *prolonged* observation will any attempt be made—"

"That's enough, Dr. Takagishi," David Brown interrupted. "We all have the gist of it. Unfortunately that sterile document was prepared months before launch. The situation we face now was never contemplated. We have the lights going on and off. And we have located and are tracking a herd of six crab biots just beyond the southern edge of the Cylindrical Sea."

"I disagree," said the Japanese scientist respectfully. "You said yourself that the unpredicted lighting profile did not represent a fundamental difference between the two spacecraft. We are not facing an unknown Rama. I submit that we should implement the sorties in accordance with the original mission plan."

"So you favor dedicating this entire second sortie to mapping, including or perhaps even featuring a detailed exploration of New York?" asked O'Toole.

"Exactly, General O'Toole. Even if one takes the position that the strange sound heard by cosmonauts Wakefield, Sabatini, and myself does not constitute an official difference, the careful mapping of New York is clearly one of the highest priority activities. And it is vital that we accomplish it on this sortie. The temperature in the Central Plain has already risen to minus five degrees. Rama is carrying us closer and closer to the Sun. The spacecraft is heating from the outside in. I predict the Cylindrical Sea will begin to melt from the bottom in three or four more days—"

"I have never said that New York was not a legitimate target for exploration," David Brown interrupted again, "but I have maintained from the very beginning that the biots are the true scientific treasure of this voyage. Look at these amazing creatures," he said, filling the center screen with a film of the six crab biots moving slowly across a bland region in the Southern Hemicylinder. "We may never have another opportunity to capture one. The drones have almost finished reconnoitering the entire interior and no other biots have been spotted."

The rest of the crew members, including Takagishi, looked at the monitor with rapt attention. The bizarre assemblage of aliens, arranged in a triangular formation with a slightly larger specimen in the lead, approached a jumbled mound of loose metal. The lead crab moved directly into the obstacle, paused a few seconds, and then used its claws to chop the elements of the mound into still

smaller pieces. The two crabs in the second row transferred the metal fragments onto the backs of the remaining
three members of the troop. This new material increased
the size of the small piles already on the tops of the shells
of the three crab biots in the back row.

"They must be the Raman garbage crew," Francesca
said. Everyone laughed.

"But you can see why I want to move quickly," David
Brown continued. "Right now the short film we just saw is
on its way to all the television networks on Earth. Over a
billion of our fellow men and women will watch it today
with the same mixture of fear and fascination that all of
you just felt. Imagine what kind of laboratories we will be
able to build to study such a creature. Imagine what we
will learn—"

"What makes you think you can capture one?" General
O'Toole asked. "They look as if they could be quite
formidable."

"We are certain that these creatures, although they
appear to be biological, are actually robots. Hence the
name 'biots,' which became popular during and after the
first Rama expedition. Based on all the reports from Norton and the other Rama I cosmonauts, each of these biots
is designed to perform a singular function. They have no
intelligence as we know it. We should be able to outsmart
them . . . and capture them."

A camera close-up of the scissorlike claws appeared on
the giant screen. They were obviously very sharp. "I don't
know," said General O'Toole. "I'd be inclined to follow
Dr. Takagishi's suggestion and observe them for quite a
while before trying to catch one."

"I disagree," said Francesca. "Speaking as a journalist,
no story could be bigger than the attempted capture of
one of those things. Everyone on Earth will watch. We
may never have another chance like this." She paused for
a moment. "The ISA has been pushing us for some upbeat
news. The Borzov incident didn't exactly convince the
taxpayers of the world that their space money is being
wisely spent."

"Why can't we do both tasks on the same sortie?" General O'Toole asked. "One subteam could explore New York and the other would go after a crab."

"No way," replied Nicole. "If the goal of this sortie is to seize a biot, then all of our resources should be applied in that direction. Remember, we are limited in both manpower and time."

"Unfortunately," David Brown now said with a wan smile, "we can't make this decision by committee. Since we don't have complete agreement, I must make the choice. . . . Therefore, the purpose of the next sortie will be to capture a crab biot. I presume that Admiral Heilmann will agree with me. If he doesn't, we will submit the issue to a vote of the crew."

The meeting broke up slowly. Dr. Takagishi wanted to offer one more argument, to point out that the majority of the biot species seen by the first Rama explorers did not materialize until *after* the thawing of the Cylindrical Sea. But nobody wanted to listen anymore. Everyone was tired.

Nicole approached Takagishi and clandestinely activated her biometry scanner. The warning file was empty. "Clean as a whistle," she said with a smile.

Takagishi looked at her very seriously. "Our decision is a mistake," he said somberly. "We should be going into New York."

27

TO CATCH A BIOT

"Be very careful," Admiral Heilmann said to Francesca. "It makes me nervous to see you leaning out like that."

Signora Sabatini had hooked her ankles underneath the seats of the helicopter and was now stretching out beyond the plane of the door. She was holding a small video camera in her right hand. Three or four meters below her, apparently oblivious to the whirring machine overhead, the six crab biots plodded methodically along. They were still in their phalanx formation, arranged like the first three rows of a set of bowling pins.

"Move out over the sea," Francesca shouted to Hiro Yamanaka. "They're coming to the edge and will be turning again."

The helicopter veered sharply to the left and flew over the side of the five-hundred-meter cliff that separated the southern half of Rama from the Cylindrical Sea. The bank here was ten times higher above the water than its northern counterpart. David Brown gasped as he looked down at the frozen sea half a kilometer below him.

"This is ridiculous, Francesca," he said. "What do you hope to accomplish? The automatic camera in the nose of the copter will take adequate pictures."

"This camera was specifically designed for zoom action," she said. "Besides, a little jitter gives the images more verisimilitude." Yamanaka steered back toward the bank. The biots were now about thirty meters directly ahead. The lead biot came up to within half a body length of the edge, paused for a fraction of a second, and then turned abruptly to its right. Another quick ninety-degree right turn completed the maneuver and left the biot heading in the exact opposite direction. The other five crabs followed their leader, executing their turns row by row with military precision.

"I got it that time," Francesca said happily, pulling herself back into the helicopter. "Head on and full frame. And I think I caught a glimmer of movement in the leader's blue eye just before it turned."

The biots were now ambling away from the cliff at their normal speed of ten kilometers per hour. Their movement caused a slight indentation in the loamy soil. Their heading was along a path parallel to their last previous sweep toward the sea. From above, the whole region looked like a suburban yard in which part of the grass had been mowed—on one side the ground was neat and packed, while in the territory not yet covered by the biots there was no orderly pattern in the soil markings.

"This could get boring," Francesca said, playfully reaching up and putting her arms around David Brown's neck. "We may have to amuse ourselves with something else."

"We'll only watch them one more strip. Their pattern is fairly simple." He ignored Francesca's light tickling on his neck. It seemed as if he were going through some kind of checklist in his mind. At length Brown spoke into the communicator. "What do you think, Dr. Takagishi? Is there anything else we should do at this time?"

Back in the scientific control center on the Newton, Dr. Takagishi was following the progression of the biots on the monitor. "It would be extremely valuable," he said, "if we could find out more about their sensory capabilities before we try to capture one of them. So far they have not responded to noises or to distant visual stimuli. In fact, they have apparently not even noticed our presence. As I'm sure you would agree, we don't have enough data yet to come to any definitive conclusions. If we could expose them to an entire range of electromagnetic frequencies and calibrate their responses, then we might have a better idea—"

"But that would take *days*," Dr. Brown interrupted. "And in the final analysis we would still have to take our chances. I can't imagine what we might learn that would materially alter our plans."

"If we found out more about them first," Takagishi

argued, "then we could design a better, safer capture procedure. It might even occur that we would learn something that would dissuade us altogether—"

"Unlikely," was David Brown's abrupt response. As far as he was concerned, this particular discussion was over. "Hey there, Tabori," he now shouted. "How are you guys coming with the huts?"

"We're almost finished," the Hungarian answered. "Another thirty minutes at the most. Then I'll be ready for a nap."

"Lunch comes first," Francesca interjected. "You can't go to sleep on an empty stomach."

"What are you cooking, beautiful?" Tabori bantered.

"Osso buco a la Rama."

"That's enough," Dr. Brown said. He paused for a couple of seconds. "O'Toole," he then continued, "can you handle the Newton all by yourself? At least for the next twelve hours?"

"Affirmative," was the response.

"Then send down the rest of the crew. By the time we all meet at the new campsite, it should be ready for occupancy. We'll have some lunch and a brief nap. Then we'll plan our biot hunt."

Below the helicopter the six crablike creatures continued their relentless march across the barren soil. The four human beings watched them encounter a distinct boundary, where the floor changed from dirt and small rocks into a fine wire mesh. As soon as they touched the narrow lane dividing the two sections, the biots executed a U-turn. They then headed back toward the sea along a parallel line adjacent to their last track. Yamanaka banked the helicopter, increased his altitude, and headed for the Beta campsite ten kilometers across the Cylindrical Sea.

They were all correct, Nicole was thinking. *Seeing it on the monitor is nothing by comparison.* She was descending on the chairlift into Rama. Now that she was beyond the halfway point, she had a breathtaking view in every direction. She remembered a similar feeling once, when she had been standing on the Tonto Plateau in the Grand Canyon National Park. *But that was made by nature and took over a billion years,* she said to herself. *Rama was actually built by somebody. Or something.*

The chair momentarily slowed. Shigeru Takagishi climbed off a kilometer below her. Nicole couldn't see him, but she could hear him talking to Richard Wakefield on the communicator. "Hurry up," she heard Reggie Wilson shout. "I don't like sitting here in the middle of nowhere." Nicole enjoyed being suspended on the chairlift. The amazing scene around her was temporarily almost static and she could study at her leisure any feature that was particularly interesting.

After one more stop for Wilson to disembark, Nicole was at last approaching the bottom of the Alpha chairlift herself. She watched, fascinated, as the resolution of her eyes improved quickly during the last three hundred meters of her descent. What had been a jumble of indistinct images resolved itself into a rover, three people, some equipment, and a small surrounding camp. After a few more seconds she could identify each of the three men. She had a quick flashback to another chairlift ride, this one in Switzerland some two months before. An image of King Henry flitted momentarily through her mind. It was replaced by the smiling face of Richard Wakefield just below her. He was giving her instructions on how best to ease herself out of the chair.

"It will never come to a complete stop," he was saying, "but it will slow down a lot. Unfasten your belt and then hit the ground walking, as if you were coming off a moving sidewalk."

He grabbed her by the waist and lifted her off the platform. Takagishi and Wilson were already in the backseat of the rover. "Welcome to Rama," Wakefield said.

"All right, Tabori," he then spoke into the communicator. "We're all here and ready to go. We're switching now to the listen-only mode for our drive."

"Hurry," Janos urged him. "We're having a hard time not eating your lunch. . . . By the way, Richard, will you bring tool box C when you come? We've been talking about nets and cages and I may need a wider variety of gadgets."

"Roger," Wakefield replied. He jogged over to the campsite and entered the only large hut. He emerged with a long rectangular metal box that was obviously very heavy. "Shit, Tabori," he said into the radio, "what in the world is in here?"

They all heard a laugh. "Everything you could possibly need to catch a crab biot. And then some."

Wakefield switched off the transmitter and climbed in the rover. He started driving away from the stairway in the direction of the Cylindrical Sea. "This biot hunt is the stupidest goddamn idea I've ever heard," Reggie Wilson groused. "Somebody is going to get hurt."

There was quiet in the rover for almost a minute. To the right, at the limit of their vision, the cosmonauts could barely see the Raman city of London. "Well, how does it feel to be part of the second team?" Wilson said to nobody in particular.

After an awkward silence, Dr. Takagishi turned to address him. "Excuse me, Mr. Wilson," he said politely, "are you talking to me?"

"Sure I am," Wilson replied, nodding his head up and down. "Didn't anyone ever tell you that you were the number *two* scientist on this mission? I guess not," Wilson continued after a short pause. "But that's not surprising. Down on Earth I never knew that I was the number two journalist."

"Reggie, I don't think—" Nicole said before she was interrupted.

"As for you, Doctor"—Wilson leaned forward in the rover—"you may be the only member of the *third* team. I overheard our glorious leaders Heilmann and Brown talking about you. They'd like to leave you on the Newton permanently. But since we may need your skills—"

"That's enough," Richard Wakefield broke in. There was a threatening edge in his voice. "You can stop being so unpleasant." Several tense seconds passed before Wakefield spoke again. "By the way, Wilson," he said in a friendlier tone, "if I remember correctly, you're a racing fanatic. Would you like to drive this buggy?"

It was the perfect suggestion. A few minutes later Reggie Wilson was in the driver's seat beside Wakefield, laughing wildly as he accelerated the rover around a tight circle.

Cosmonauts des Jardins and Takagishi were bumping around in the backseat.

Nicole was observing Wilson very carefully. *He's erratic again,* she was thinking. *That's at least three times in the last two days.* Nicole tried to recall when she had last done a full scan on Wilson. *Not since the day after Borzov died. I've checked the cadets twice in the interim. . . . Dammit,* she said to herself, *I let my preoccupation with the Borzov incident make me careless.* She made a mental note to scan everyone as soon as possible after she arrived at the Beta campsite.

"Say, my good professor," Richard Wakefield said once Wilson had finally straightened out and was heading for camp, "I have a question for you." He turned around and faced the Japanese scientist. "Have you figured out our strange sound from the other day? Or has Dr. Brown convinced you that it was just a figment of our collective imagination?"

Dr. Takagishi shook his head. "I told you at the time that it was a new noise." He stared off in the distance, across the unexplained mechanical fields of the Central Plain. "This is a different Rama. I know it. The checkerboard squares in the south are laid out in an entirely new pattern and no longer extend to the shore of the Cylindrical Sea. The lights now go on before the sea melts. And they go off abruptly, without dimming for several hours as the first Rama explorers reported. The crab biots now appear in herds instead of individually." He paused, still looking out across the fields. "Dr. Brown says that all these differences are trivial, but I think they mean something. It's just possible," Takagishi said softly, "that Dr. Brown is wrong."

"It's also possible that he's a complete son of a bitch," said Wilson bitterly. He accelerated the rover to its maximum speed. "Beta campsite, here we come!"

28

EXTRAPOLATION

Nicole completed her lunch of pressed duck, reconstituted broccoli, and mashed potatoes. The rest of the cosmonauts were still eating and it was temporarily quiet at the long table. In the corner, by the entrance, a monitor tracked the location of the crab biots. Their pattern had not changed. The blip representing the crabs would move in one direction for slightly more than ten minutes and then reverse itself.

"What happens after they finish this parcel?" Richard Wakefield asked. He was looking at a computer map of the area that was posted on a temporary bulletin board.

"Last time they followed one of those lanes between the checkerboard partitions until they came to a hole," Francesca responded from the other end of the table. "Then they dumped their garbage in it. They haven't picked up anything in this new territory, so what they will do when they finish is anybody's guess."

"Everyone is convinced that our biots are in fact garbagemen?" Richard asked.

"The evidence is fairly strong," David Brown said. "A similar solitary crab biot encountered by Jimmy Pak inside the first Rama was also believed to be a garbage collector."

"Excuse me," Janos Tabori interjected, "but just what garbage are these crabs collecting?"

"We flatter ourselves," Shigeru Takagishi said softly after a long silence. He finished chewing his last bite and swallowed. "Dr. Brown himself was the one who first said that it was unlikely we human beings could comprehend what Rama was about. Our conversation reminds me of that old Hindu proverb about the blind men who felt the elephant. They all described it differently, for each of them touched only a small part of the animal. None of them was correct."

"So, you don't think our crabs work for the Rama Sanitation Department?" Janos inquired.

"I didn't say that," Takagishi replied. "I merely suggested that it's hubris on our part to conclude so quickly that those six creatures have no purpose except cleaning up the garbage. Our observational data is woefully inadequate."

"Sometimes it is necessary to extrapolate," Dr. Brown rejoined testily, ". . . and even speculate, based on minimal amounts of data. You know yourself that new science is based on maximum likelihood rather than certainty."

"Before we become involved in an esoteric discussion about science and its methodology," Janos now interrupted with a grin, "I have a sporting proposition for you all." He stood up at his place. "Actually it was Richard's idea originally, but I've figured out how to make it into a game. It has to do with the lights."

Janos took a quick drink of water from his cup. "Since we first arrived here in Ramaland," he intoned formally, "there have been three transitions in the illumination state."

"Boo. Hiss," shouted Wakefield. Janos laughed.

"Okay, you guys," the little Hungarian then continued in his normal offhand way, "what's the deal with the lights? They've come on, gone off, and now come on again. What's going to happen in the future? I propose that we have a pool and contribute, say, twenty marks apiece. Each of us will make a prediction about the behavior of the lights for the rest of the mission and whoever is closest will win the pot."

"Who will judge the winner?" Reggie Wilson inquired sleepily. He had yawned several times during the preceding hour. "Despite the impressive set of brains around this table, I don't think anyone has figured out Rama yet. My personal belief is that the lights will not follow any pattern. They will go on and off at random times to keep us guessing."

"Write it down and send it on the modem to General O'Toole. Richard and I agreed that he would make a perfect judge. When the mission is over, he'll compare the predictions with actuality and someone will win a lucky dinner for two."

Dr. David Brown pushed his chair back from the table. "Are you finished with your game, Tabori?" he asked. "If so," he added, without waiting for an answer, "perhaps we can clean up this lunch mess and get on with our schedule."

"Hey skipper," Janos replied, "I'm just trying to loosen things up. Everybody's getting tense—"

Brown walked out of the hut before Cosmonaut Tabori had finished his sentence.

"What's bothering him?" Richard asked Francesca.

"I guess he's anxious about the hunt," Francesca answered. "He has been in a bad mood since this morning. Maybe he's feeling all the responsibility."

"Maybe he's just a jerk," said Wilson. He too rose from his seat. "I'm going to take a nap."

As Wilson was leaving the large hut Nicole remembered that she wanted to check everyone's biometry before the hunt. It was a simple enough task. All she needed was to stand close to each cosmonaut for about forty-five seconds with her activated scanner and then read the critical data off the monitor. If there were no entries in the warning files, the entire procedure was quite straightforward. On this particular check everyone was clean, including Takagishi. "Nice going," Nicole said to her Japanese colleague very quietly.

She walked outside to look for David Brown and Reggie Wilson. Dr. Brown's hut was at the far end of the campsite. Like the rest of the individual dwellings, his hut resembled a tall skinny hat sitting on the ground. All the huts were off-white in color, about two and a half meters tall, with a circular base just under two meters in diameter. They were manufactured with super-lightweight, flexible materials that combined easy packing and storage with formidable strength. Nicole remarked to herself that the huts looked something like native American Indian teepees.

David Brown was in his hut, sitting cross-legged on the ground in front of a portable computer monitor. On the screen was text from the chapter on biots in Takagishi's

Atlas of Rama. "Excuse me, Dr. Brown," Nicole said as she stuck her head in his door.

"Yes," he said, "what is it?" He made no attempt to hide his annoyance at the interruption.

"I need to check your biometry data," Nicole said. "You haven't been dumped since right before the first sortie."

Brown gave her an irritated glance. Nicole held her ground. The American shrugged his shoulders, half grunted, and turned back to the monitor. Nicole knelt beside him and activated her scanner.

"There are some folding chairs over in the supply hut," Nicole offered as Dr. Brown shifted his weight uncomfortably on the ground. He ignored her comment. *Why is he so rude to me?* Nicole found herself wondering. *Is it because of that report on Wilson and him? No,* she thought, answering her own question, *it's because I have never been properly deferential.*

Data began to appear on Nicole's screen. She carefully keyed in several inputs that permitted a synopsis of the warning data to be shown. "Your blood pressure has been too high for intermittent intervals during the last seventy-two hours, including almost all of today," she said without emotion. "This particular kind of pattern is usually associated with stress."

Dr. Brown stopped reading about biots and turned to face his life science officer. He looked at the displayed data without understanding it. "This graph shows the amplitudes and durations of your out-of-tolerance excursions," Nicole said, pointing at the screen. "None of the individual occurrences would be serious by itself. But the overall pattern is cause for concern."

"I have been under some pressure," he mumbled. David Brown watched while Nicole called up other displays showing data that corroborated her original statements. Many of Brown's warning files were overflowing.

The lights continued to flash on the monitor. "What's the worst-case scenario?" he inquired.

Nicole eyed her patient. "A stroke with paralysis or death," she replied. "If the condition persists or worsens."

He whistled. "What should I do?"

"In the first place," Nicole answered, "you must start by

getting more sleep. Your metabolic profile shows that since the death of General Borzov you have only had a total of eleven hours of solid rest. Why didn't you tell me you were having trouble sleeping?"

"I thought it was just excitement. I even took a sleeping pill one night and it had no effect."

Nicole's brow furrowed. "I don't remember giving you any sleeping pills."

Dr. Brown smiled. "Shit," he said, "I forgot to tell you. I was talking to Francesca Sabatini about my insomnia one night and she offered me a pill. I took it without thinking."

"Which night was that?" Nicole asked. She changed displays again on her monitor and called for more data from the storage buffers.

"I'm not certain," Dr. Brown said after some hesitation. "I think it was—"

"Oh, here it is," Nicole said. "I can see it in the chemical analysis. That was March third, the second night after Borzov's death. The day you and Heilmann were selected as joint commanders. From the breakout in this spectrometry data, I would guess that you took a single medvil."

"You can tell *that* from my biometry data?"

"Not exactly," Nicole said with a smile. "The interpretation is not unique. What was it you said at lunch? Sometimes it's necessary to extrapolate . . . and speculate."

Their eyes met for a moment. *Could that be fear?* Nicole wondered as she tried to interpret what she was seeing in his gaze. Dr. Brown looked away. "Thank you, Dr. des Jardins," he said stiffly, "for your report on my blood pressure. I will try to relax and get plenty of sleep. And I apologize for not informing you about the sleeping pill." He dismissed her with a wave of his hand.

Nicole started to protest her dismissal but decided against it. *He wouldn't follow my advice anyway,* she said to herself as she walked toward Wilson's hut. *And his blood pressure was certainly not dangerously high.* She thought about the strained final two minutes of their conversation, after she had astonished Dr. Brown by correctly identifying the type of sleeping pill. *There's something not quite right here. What is it that I am missing?*

She could hear Reggie Wilson snoring before she arrived at the door of his tent. After a brief debate with herself, Nicole decided that she would scan him after his nap. She then returned to her own hut and quickly fell asleep.

"Nicole. Nicole des Jardins." The voice intruded in her dream and awakened her. "It's me. Francesca. I need to tell you something."

Nicole sat up slowly on her cot. Francesca had already entered the hut. The Italian was wearing her friendliest smile, the one that Nicole had thought was always saved for the camera.

"I was talking to David just a few minutes ago," Francesca said as she approached the cot, "and he told me about your conversation after lunch." Francesca kept talking as Nicole yawned and swung her legs around to the floor. "I was, of course, very concerned to learn about his blood pressure—don't worry, he and I have already agreed that I won't use it—but what really bothered me was he reminded me that we never told you about the sleeping pill. I'm so embarrassed. We should have told you immediately."

Francesca was talking too fast for Nicole. Just moments before she had been in a deep sleep, dreaming of Beauvois, and now all of a sudden she was expected to listen to a staccato confession from the Italian cosmonaut.

"Could you wait a minute until I wake up?" Nicole asked crossly. She leaned around Francesca to a makeshift table and took a cup of water. She drank slowly.

"Now am I to understand," Nicole said, "that you have awakened me to tell me that you gave Dr. Brown a sleeping pill? Something I already know?"

"Yes," Francesca said with a smile. "I mean, that's part of it. But I realized that I had forgotten to tell you about Reggie also."

Nicole shook her head. "I'm not following you, Francesca. Are you talking about Reggie Wilson now?"

Francesca hesitated for a second. "Yes," she said. "Didn't you check him with your scanner right after lunch?"

Nicole shook her head again. "No, he was already asleep." She looked at her watch. "I had planned to scan him before the meeting started. Maybe an hour from now."

Francesca was flustered. "Well," she said, "when David told me that the medvil showed up in his biometry data, I thought . . ." She stopped herself in midsentence. She seemed to be collecting her thoughts. Nicole waited patiently.

"Reggie started complaining of headaches over a week ago," Francesca eventually continued, "after the two Newton ships joined for the rendezvous with Rama. Since he and I have been close friends and he knew about my knowledge of drugs—you know, from all that work on my documentary series—he asked me if I would give him something for headaches. I refused at first, but finally, after he kept badgering me, I gave him some nubitrol."

Nicole frowned. "That's a very strong medicine for a simple headache. There are still doctors who believe it should never be prescribed unless everything else has failed—"

"I told him all that," Francesca said. "He was adamant. You don't know Reggie. Sometimes you can't reason with him."

"How much did you give him?"

"Eight pills altogether, a total of two hundred milligrams."

"No wonder he's been acting so strangely." Nicole leaned over and picked up her pocket computer sitting on the end table. She accessed her medical data base and read the short entry about nubitrol. "Not much here," she said. "I'll have to ask O'Toole to transmit the full entry from the medical encyclopedia. But if I remember correctly, wasn't there a controversy about nubitrol remaining in the system for weeks?"

"I don't recall," Francesca replied. She looked at the monitor in Nicole's hand and quickly read the text. Nicole was irritated. She started to lambast Francesca verbally but at the last moment changed her mind. *So you gave drugs to both David and Reggie,* she was thinking. Out of her memory came a vague recollection of Francesca handing Valeriy Borzov a glass of wine several hours before he died. A strange chill ran through Nicole's body. Could her intuition be correct?

Nicole turned around and fixed Francesca with a cold stare. "Now that you have confessed to playing doctor and pharmacist for both David and Reggie, is there anything else you want to tell me?"

"What do you mean?" Francesca asked.

"Have you given drugs to any other member of the crew?"

Nicole felt her heart race as Francesca blanched, ever so slightly, and hesitated before replying.

"No. No, of course not," was her answer.

29

THE HUNT

The helicopter very slowly dropped the rover to the ground. "How much farther?" Janos Tabori asked over the communicator.

"About ten meters," Richard Wakefield replied from below. He was standing in a spot about a hundred meters south of the edge of the Cylindrical Sea. Above him the rover dangled at the end of two long cables. "Be careful to let it down gently. There are some delicate electronics in the chassis."

Hiro Yamanaka commanded the helicopter into its tightest possible altitude control loop while Janos electronically extended the cables a few centimeters at a time. "Contact," shouted Wakefield. "On the rear wheels. The front needs to come down another meter."

Francesca Sabatini raced around to the side of the rover to record its historic touchdown in the Southern Hemicylinder of Rama. Fifty meters farther from the cliff, in the neighborhood of a hut that was serving as a temporary headquarters, the rest of the cosmonauts were preparing for the hunt to begin. Irina Turgenyev was checking the installation of the cable snare in the second helicopter. David Brown was by himself a few meters away from the hut, talking on the radio with Admiral Heilmann back at the Beta campsite. The two men were reviewing the details of the capture plan. Wilson, Takagishi, and des Jardins were watching the conclusion of the rover landing operation.

"Now we know who's really the boss of this outfit," Reggie Wilson was saying to his two companions. He pointed at Dr. Brown. "This damn hunt is more like a military operation than anything we've done, yet our senior scientist is in charge and our ranking officer is man-ning the phones." He spat on the ground. "Christ, do we have enough equipment here? Two helicopters, a rover, three different kinds of cages—not to mention several large boxes of electrical and mechanical shit. Those poor bastard crabs don't have a chance."

Dr. Takagishi put the laser binoculars to his eyes. He found the target quickly. Half a kilometer to the east the crab biots were nearing the edge of the cliff again. Nothing about their motion had changed. "We need all the equipment because of the uncertainty," Takagishi said quietly. "Nobody really knows what is going to happen."

"I hope the lights go out," Wilson said with a laugh.

"We're prepared for that," David Brown interjected tersely as he walked up to join the other three cosmonauts. "The shells of the crabs have been sprayed with a light fluorescent material and we have plenty of flares. While you were complaining about the length of our last meeting, we were finishing the contingency plans." He stared truculently at his countryman. "You know, Wilson, you could try—"

"Break break," the voice of Otto Heilmann interrupted him. "News. Hot news. I just received word from O'Toole that INN will be carrying our feed *live*, beginning twenty minutes from now."

"Good work," replied Brown. "We should be ready by then. I see Wakefield heading this way in the rover." He glanced at his watch. "And the crabs should be turning again in another few seconds. Incidentally, Otto, do you still disagree with my suggestion to snare the lead biot?"

"Yes, David, I do. I think it's an unnecessary risk. What little we do know suggests that the lead crab has the most capability. Why take a chance? Any biot would be an incredible treasure to carry back to Earth, particularly if it's still functional. We can worry about the leader after we already have one in the bag."

"Then I guess I'm outvoted on this one. Dr. Takagishi and Tabori both agree with you. So does General O'Toole. We'll proceed with Plan B. The target biot will be number four, the back right biot as we approach from the rear."

The rover carrying Wakefield and Sabatini arrived at the hut area at almost the same time as the helicopter.

"Good job, men," Dr. Brown said as Tabori and Yamanaka jumped down from the 'copter. "Take a short breather, Janos. Then go over and make sure Turgenyev and the cable snare are both ready to go. I want you airborne in five minutes.

"All right," Brown said, turning to the others, "this is it. Wilson, Takagishi, and des Jardins in the rover with Wakefield. Francesca, you come with me in the second helicopter with Hiro."

Nicole started walking toward the rover but Francesca intercepted her. "Have you ever used one of these?" The Italian journalist extended a video camera the size of a small book.

"Once," Nicole answered, studying the camera in Francesca's hand, "eleven or twelve years ago. I recorded one of Dr. Delon's brain operations. I guess—"

"Look," interrupted Francesca, "I could use some help. I'm sorry I didn't discuss it with you earlier, but I didn't know— Anyway, I need another camera, one on the ground, especially now that we're live on INN. I'm not asking for miracles. You're the only one who—"

"What about Reggie?" Nicole replied. "He's the other journalist."

"Reggie won't help," Francesca said quickly. Dr. Brown called for her to come to the helicopter. "Will you do it, Nicole? Please? Or should I ask someone else?"

Why not? ran through Nicole's mind. *I have nothing else to do unless an emergency comes up.* "Sure," she replied.

"Thanks a million," Francesca shouted as she handed Nicole the camera and dashed off to the waiting helicopter.

"Well, well," said Reggie Wilson as Nicole approached the rover with the camera cradled in her hands. "I see that our crew doctor has been recruited by the number one journalist. I hope you asked for the minimum wage."

"Lighten up, Reggie," Nicole replied. "It doesn't bother me to help others when I have nothing specific to do myself."

Wakefield switched on the rover and began to drive east toward the biots. The headquarters had been intentionally established in the area already "cleaned" by the crabs.

The packed soil made progress very easy for the rover. They were within a hundred meters of the biots in less than three minutes. Overhead the two helicopters circled around the crabs.

"What exactly do you want me to do?" Nicole called to Francesca on the rover transmitter.

"Try to move parallel to the biots," Francesca answered. "You can probably run alongside, at least for some of the time. The most important moment is when Janos tries to close the snare."

"We're all ready here," Tabori announced a few seconds later. "Just give the word."

"Are we on the air?" Brown asked Francesca. She nodded. "All right," he said to Janos. "Go ahead."

From out of one of the helicopters came a long, thick cable with what looked like an inverted basket on the end. "Janos will try to center the snare on the target biot," Wakefield explained to Nicole, "and let the sides drape naturally over the corner of the shell. Then he will increase the tension and pull the biot off the ground. We will cage the crab after we return it to the Beta campsite."

"Let's see what they look like from down there," Nicole heard Francesca say. The rover was now right next to the biots. Nicole climbed out and jogged beside them. She was frightened at first. For some reason she had not expected them to be so large or so strange looking. Their metallic sheen reminded her of the cold exterior of many of the new buildings in Paris. As she ran along on the soil, the biots were only about two meters away from her. With the automatic focusing and framing of the camera, it was not difficult for Nicole to take the proper pictures.

"Don't get in front of them," Dr. Takagishi warned her. He didn't need to worry. Nicole had not forgotten what they had done to that mound of metal.

"Your pictures are really very good," Francesca's voice boomed on the rover receiver. "Nicole, try to speed up to the lead biot and then fall back little by little, letting the camera pan across each of the ranks." She waited while Nicole moved to the front of the biots. "Wow. That's superb. Now I know why we brought an Olympic champion with us."

On his first two attempts Janos missed with the snare. However, on the third try it landed perfectly on the number four crab's back. The edges of the net or basket spread out to the limit of the shell. Nicole was starting to sweat. She had been running already for four minutes. "From now on," Francesca said to her from the helicopter, "focus on the single target crab. Move up as close as you dare."

Nicole reduced her distance from the closest biot to about a meter. She nearly slipped once and a cold chill swept over her. *If I were to fall across their path,* she thought, *they'd make mincemeat out of me.* Her camera was fixed on the right rear crab as Janos tightened the cables.

"Now!" he shouted. The snare, with the biot entrapped, began to rise off the ground. Everything happened very fast. The target biot used its scissorlike claws to snap through one of the metal threads of the snare. The other five biots came to a brief halt, for maybe one full second, and then immediately all attacked the snare with their claws. The metal net was completely shredded and the biot was freed in five seconds.

Nicole was amazed by what she was seeing. Despite her pounding heart she continued to film. The lead biot now sat down on the ground. The other five surrounded it in an extremely tight circle. Each of the biots attached one claw to the crab in the center and the other to its neighbor on the right. The formation was finished in less than five more seconds. The biots were locked and motionless.

Francesca was the first to speak. "Absolutely incredible," she screamed in elation. "We just made the hair stand up on every human being on Earth."

Nicole felt Richard Wakefield beside her. "Are you all right?" he asked.

"I think so," she said. She was still shaking. The two of them glanced over at the biots. There was no movement.

"They're in a huddle," Reggie Wilson said from the rover. "The score is now Biots seven, Humans zero."

"Since you are so convinced that there is no danger, I'll agree to go ahead. But I must confess that I myself am nervous about another attempt. Those things clearly communicate with each other. And I don't think they want to be captured."

"Otto, Otto," Dr. Brown replied. "This procedure is only a straightforward refinement of what we tried the first time. The line nexus will adhere to the shell of the crab and will wrap its thin cables tightly around the entire carapace. The other biots will not be able to use their claws. There will be no room between the line and the shell."

"Admiral Heilmann, this is Dr. Takagishi." There was definite concern in his voice as he spoke into the communicator. "I must register my strongest objection to proceeding with this hunt. We have seen already how little we understand about these creatures. As Wakefield said, our attempt to snare one of them has obviously triggered their main fault protection responses. We have no idea at all how they will react next."

"We all understand that, Dr. Takagishi," David Brown interjected before Heilmann could respond. "But there are extenuating factors that override the uncertainties. First, as Francesca pointed out, the entire Earth will again be watching if we go after the biots right away. You heard what Jean-Claude Revoir said twenty minutes ago—we have already done more for space exploration than anyone since the original Soviet and American cosmonauts back in the twentieth century. Second, we are prepared to complete the hunt now. If we abandon the attempt and return all our equipment to Beta, then we will have wasted a huge amount of time and effort. Finally, there is no obvious danger. Why do you insist on making such dire predictions? All we saw the biots do was engage in some kind of self-defense activity."

"Professor Brown," the eminent Japanese scholar tried one last rational appeal, "please look around you. Try to imagine the capabilities of the creatures who made this amazing vehicle. Try to appreciate the possibility that perhaps, just perhaps, what we are trying to do might be viewed as a hostile act and has somehow been communicated to whatever intelligence is managing this spacecraft. Suppose as a result that we, as representatives of the human species, are condemning not only ourselves, but also, in some larger sense, all of our fellow—"

"Poppycock," David Brown scoffed. "How can anyone ever accuse *me* of wild speculation? . . ." He laughed heartily. "This is absurd. The evidence overwhelmingly indicates that this Rama has the same purpose and function as its predecessor and is completely oblivious to our existence. Just because one single subfamily of robots bands together when threatened does not have overwhelming significance." He looked around at the others. "I say that's enough talk, Otto. Unless you object, we're going out to capture a biot."

There was a short hesitation from across the Cylindrical Sea. Then the cosmonauts heard Admiral Heilmann's affirmative reply. "Go ahead, David. But don't take any unnecessary chances."

"Do you think we're really in danger?" Hiro Yamanaka asked Dr. Takagishi while the new capture tactics were being reviewed by Brown, Tabori, and Wakefield. The Japanese pilot was staring off in the distance at the massive structures in the southern bowl, thinking, perhaps for the first time, of the vulnerability of their position.

"Probably not," his countryman replied, "but it's insane to take such—"

"Insane is a perfect word for it," Reggie Wilson interrupted. "You and I were the only two vocal opponents of continuing this stupidity. But our objections were made to sound foolish and even cowardly. Personally, I wish one of those goddamn things would challenge the esteemed Dr. Brown to a duel. Or better still, a bolt of lightning would come shooting out of those spires over there."

He pointed at the great horns that Yamanaka had been regarding earlier. Wilson's voice changed and there was a fearful edge to it. "We are over our heads here. I can feel it in the air. We are being warned of danger by powers that none of us can begin to understand. But we are ignoring the warnings."

Nicole turned away from her colleagues and glanced at the lively planning meeting taking place fifteen meters away from her. Engineers Wakefield and Tabori were definitely enjoying the challenge of outwitting the biots.

Nicole wondered if perhaps Rama really was sending them some kind of a warning. *Poppycock,* she said to herself, repeating David Brown's expression. She shuddered involuntarily as she recalled the several seconds when the crab biots had devastated the metal snare. *I'm overreacting. And so is Wilson. There's no reason to be afraid.*

Yet, as she turned again and looked through the binoculars to study the biot formation half a kilometer away, there was a palpable fear in her that would not be assuaged. The six crabs had not moved in almost two hours. They were still locked in their original arrangement. *What are you really all about, Rama?* Nicole asked herself for the umpteenth time. Her next question startled her. She had never verbalized it before. *And how many of us will make it back to Earth to tell your tale?*

On the second capture attempt Francesca wanted to be on the ground beside the biots. As before, Turgenyev and Tabori were up in the prime helicopter along with the most important equipment. Brown, Yamanaka, and Wakefield were in the other helicopter. Dr. Brown had invited Wakefield to provide him with real-time advice; Francesca had of course persuaded Richard to take some aerial pictures for her to complement the automatic images from the helicopter system.

Reggie Wilson drove the ground-based cosmonauts to the biot site in the rover. "Now here's a good job for me," he said as they approached the location of the alien crabs. "Chauffeur." He gazed up at the distant ceiling of Rama. "You hear that, you guys? I'm versatile. I can do many things." He looked over at Francesca beside him in the front seat. "By the way, Mrs. Sabatini, were you planning to thank Nicole for her spectacular work? It was her action shots on the ground that captured the audience in your last transmission."

Francesca was busy checking all her video equipment and at first ignored Reggie's comment. When he repeated his jibe, she responded, without looking up, "May I remind Mr. Wilson that I do not need his unsolicited advice on how to conduct my business?"

"There was a time," Reggie mused out loud, shaking his

head, "when things were very different." He glanced at Francesca. There was no indication that she was even listening. "Back when I still believed in love," he said in a louder voice. "Before I knew about betrayal. Or ambition and its selfishness."

He jerked the rover wheel vigorously to the left and brought it to a stop about forty meters west of the biots. Francesca jumped out without a word. Within three seconds she was chattering to David Brown and Richard Wakefield on the radio about the video coverage of the capture. The ever polite Dr. Takagishi thanked Reggie Wilson for driving the rover.

"We're coming in," Tabori shouted from above. He managed to position the dangling nexus properly on his second attempt. The nexus was a round, heavy sphere about twenty centimeters in diameter, with a dozen small holes or indentations on its surface. It was slowly dropped onto the center of the shell of one of the outside biots. Next Janos, transmitting a barrage of commands from the hovering helicopter to the processor in the nexus, ordered the extension of the massed threads of metal rolled up inside the sphere. The crabs did not stir as the threads wrapped themselves around the target biot.

"What do you think, inspector?" Janos hollered at Richard Wakefield in the other helicopter.

Richard surveyed the strange apparatus. The thick cable was attached to a ring stanchion at the rear of the helicopter. Fifteen meters below, the metal ball sat on the back of the target biot, thin filaments extending from inside the ball around the top and bottom of the carapace. "Looks fine," Richard replied. "Now there's only the single question remaining. Is the helicopter stronger than their collective grip?"

David Brown commanded Irina Turgenyev to lift the prey. She slowly increased the speed of the blades and tried to ascend. The tiny slack in the cable disappeared but the biots barely moved. "They're either very heavy or they're holding onto the ground somehow," Richard said. "Hit them with a sharp burst."

The sudden jolt in the cable lifted the entire biot formation momentarily skyward. The helicopter strained as the biot mass dangled two or three meters off the ground. The two crabs not attached to the target biot dropped first, falling into a motionless heap seconds after takeoff. The other three crabs lasted longer, ten seconds altogether before they finally disengaged their claws from their companion and fell to the ground below. There were universal cries of joy and congratulations as the helicopter climbed higher into the sky.

Francesca was filming the capture sequence from a distance of about ten meters. After the last three biots, including the leader, had released their grips on the target crab and fallen onto the Raman soil, she leaned back to record the helicopter as it headed for the banks of the Cylindrical Sea with its prey. It took her two or three seconds to realize that everyone was shouting at her.

The lead biot and its final two companion crabs had not crumbled into a heap when they had hit the ground. Although slightly damaged, they were active and on the move within moments after landing. While Francesca was filming the departure of the helicopter, the lead biot sensed her presence and headed toward her. The other two followed a step behind.

They were only four meters away when Francesca, still filming, finally understood that she was now the prey. She turned around and started to run. "Run to the side," Richard Wakefield screamed into the communicator, "they can only go in straight lines."

Francesca zigged and zagged but the biots continued to follow her. Her original burst of adrenaline enabled her to extend the distance separating her from the crabs to ten meters. Later, however, as she began to tire, the relentless biots were closing in on her. She slipped and almost fell. By the time Francesca regained her stride the lead biot was no more than three meters away.

Reggie Wilson had raced toward the rover as soon as it was clear that the biots were chasing Francesca. Once he was at the controls of the vehicle, he headed for her rescue at top speed. He had originally intended to pick her up and move her out of the way of the biot onslaught. They were too close to her, however, so Reggie decided to smash into the three crabs from the side. There was a crash of metal on metal as the lightweight vehicle rammed the biots. Reggie's plan worked. The momentum of the crash carried Reggie and the crabs several meters to the side. The threat to Francesca was over.

But the biots were not incapacitated. Far from it. Despite the fact that one of the follower crabs had lost a leg and the lead biot had a slightly damaged claw, within seconds all three of them were at work in the wreckage. They started slicing the rover into chunks with their claws, and then they used their fearful collection of probes and rasps to tear the chunks into still smaller pieces.

Reggie was momentarily stunned by the impact of the rover against the biots. The alien crabs had been heavier than he had anticipated and the damage to his vehicle was severe. As soon as he realized that the biots were still active, he started to jump out of the rover. But he couldn't. His legs were wedged underneath the collapsed dashboard.

His unmitigated terror lasted no longer than ten seconds. There was nothing anyone could do. Reggie Wilson's horrified shrieks echoed through the vastness of Rama as the biots chopped him apart exactly as if he were part of the rover. It was accomplished swiftly and systematically. Both Francesca and the automatic camera in the helicopter filmed the final seconds of his life. The pictures were transmitted live back to the Earth.

30

POSTMORTEM II

Nicole sat quietly in her hut at the Beta campsite. She could not erase from her mind the horrible image of Reggie Wilson's face, contorted in terror as he was being hacked to pieces. She tried to force herself to think of something else. *So what now,* she wondered. *What will happen to the mission now?*

Outside it was dark again in Rama. The lights had vanished abruptly three hours before, after a period of illumination thirty-four seconds less than during the previous Raman day. The disappearance of the lights should have prompted much discussion and speculation. But it didn't. None of the cosmonauts wanted to talk about anything. The awful memory of Wilson's death weighed too heavily on everyone.

The normal crew meeting after dinner had been postponed until morning because David Brown and Admiral Heilmann were in an extended conference with ISA officials back on Earth. Nicole had not participated in any of the conversations, but it was not difficult for her to imagine their content. She realized that there was a very real possibility the mission would now be aborted. The hue and cry from the public might demand it. After all, they had witnessed one of the most gruesome scenes. . . .

Nicole thought of Genevieve sitting in front of the television at Beauvois, watching while Cosmonaut Wilson was being methodically subdivided by the biots. She shuddered. Then she chastised herself for being self-centered. *The real horror,* she said to herself, *must have been in Los Angeles.*

She had met the Wilson family twice during the early parties right after the crew selections were announced.

Nicole remembered the boy particularly. Randy was his name. He was seven or eight, wide-eyed and beautiful. He loved sports. He had brought Nicole one of his prized possessions, a program from the 2184 Olympics in nearly perfect condition, and had asked her to sign the page featuring the women's triple jump. She had tousled his hair as he had thanked her with a huge smile.

The image of Randy Wilson watching his father die on television was too much for her. Several tears wedged themselves into the corners of her eyes. *What a nightmare this year has been for you, little boy,* she thought. *The roller coaster of life. First the joy of having your father selected as a cosmonaut. Then all the Francesca nonsense and the divorce. Now this terrible tragedy.*

Nicole was becoming depressed and her mind was still too active for sleep. She decided that she wanted some company. She walked over to the next hut and knocked softly on the door.

"Is someone out there?" she heard from inside.

"*Hai,* Takagishi-san," she replied. "It's Nicole. May I come in?"

He walked over to the door and opened it. "This is an unexpected surprise," he said. "Is the visit professional?"

"No," she answered as she entered. "Strictly informal. I was not ready to sleep. I thought—"

"You are welcome to visit me anytime," he said with a friendly smile. "You do not need a reason." He looked at her for several seconds. "I am deeply disturbed by what happened this afternoon. I feel responsible. I don't think I did enough to stop—"

"Come on, Shigeru," Nicole replied. "Don't be ridiculous. You're not to blame. At least you spoke up. I'm the doctor and I didn't even say anything."

Her eyes wandered aimlessly around Takagishi's hut. Beside his cot, sitting on a small piece of cloth on the floor, Nicole saw a curious white figurine with black markings. She walked over to it and bent down on her knees. "What's this?" she asked.

Dr. Takagishi was slightly embarrassed. He came over beside Nicole and picked up the tiny fat oriental man. He held it between his index finger and his thumb. "It's a netsuke heirloom from my wife's family," he said. "It's made from ivory."

He handed the little man to Nicole. "He is the king of the gods. His companion, a similarly plump queen, rests on the table beside my wife's bed in Kyoto. Back before elephants became endangered, many people collected figures like this. My wife's family has a superb collection."

Nicole studied the little man in her hand. He had a benign, serene smile on his face. She imagined the beautiful Machiko Takagishi back in Japan and for a few seconds she envied their marital bond. *It would make events like Wilson's death much easier to deal with,* she thought.

"Would you like to sit down?" Dr. Takagishi was saying. Nicole positioned herself on a box next to the cot and they talked for twenty minutes. Mostly they shared memories of their families. They referred obliquely to the afternoon disaster several times, but they avoided detailed discussion of Rama and the Newton mission altogether. What they both needed were the comforting images of their daily lives on Earth.

"And now," Takagishi said, finishing his cup of tea and putting it on the end table beside Nicole's, "I have a strange request for Dr. des Jardins. Would you please go over to your hut and bring back your biometry equipment? I would like to be scanned."

Nicole started to laugh but noticed the seriousness in her colleague's face. When she returned with her scanner several minutes later, Dr. Takagishi told her the reason for his request. "This afternoon," he said, "I felt two very sharp pains in my chest. It was during the excitement, after Wilson crashed into the biots, and I realized . . ." He did not complete his sentence. Nicole nodded and activated the scanning instrument.

Neither of them said anything for the next three minutes. Nicole checked all the warning data, displayed graphs and charts of his cardiac performance, and shook her head regularly. When she was finished she faced her friend with a grim smile. "You've had a slight heart attack," she said to Dr. Takagishi. "Maybe two very close together. And your heart has been irregular ever since." She could tell that he had expected the news. "I'm sorry," she said.

"I have some medicine with me that I can give you, but it's only a stopgap measure. We must go back to the Newton immediately so we can treat this problem properly."

"Well." He smiled wanly. "If our predictions are correct, then it will be light again in Rama in about twelve hours. I assume we'll go then."

"Probably," she answered. "I'll talk to Brown and Heilmann about it right away. My guess is that you and I will leave first thing in the morning."

He reached out and took her hand. "Thank you, Nicole," he said.

She turned away. For the second time in an hour there were tears in the corners of her eyes. Nicole left Takagishi's hut and headed for the edge of camp to talk to David Brown.

"Ah, it *is* you." She heard Richard Wakefield's voice in the dark. "I thought for certain you were asleep. I have some news for you."

"Hello, Richard," Nicole said as the figure holding the flashlight emerged from the darkness.

"I couldn't sleep," he said. "Too many grisly pictures in my head. So I decided to work on your problem." He smiled. "It was even easier than I thought. Would you like to come to my hut for an explanation?"

Nicole was confused. She had been preoccupied with what she was going to say to Brown and Heilmann about Takagishi. "You do remember, don't you?" Richard inquired. "The problem with the RoSur software and the manual commands."

"You've been working on *that*?" she asked. "Down here?"

"Certainly. All I had to do was have O'Toole transmit the data that I needed. Come on, let me show you."

Nicole decided seeing Dr. Brown could wait for a few more minutes. She walked beside Richard. He knocked on another hut as they went by. "Hey Tabori, guess what?" he shouted. "I found our lovely lady doctor wandering around in the dark. Do you want to join us?"

"I explained some of it to him first," Richard said to Nicole. "Your hut was dark and I figured you were asleep."

Janos stumbled out of his door less than a minute later

and acknowledged Nicole with a smile. "All right, Wakefield," he said, "but let's not prolong it. I was finally drifting off."

Back in Wakefield's hut, the British engineer thoroughly enjoyed recounting what had happened to the robot surgeon when the Newton had experienced the unexpected torque. "You were right, Nicole," he said, "that there were manual commands input to RoSur. And these commands did indeed shut down the normal fault protection algorithms. But none of them was input until *during* the Raman maneuver."

Wakefield smiled and continued, watching Nicole carefully to ensure that she was following his explanation. "Apparently, when Janos fell and his fingers hit the control box, he generated three commands. At least that's what RoSur thought; it was told that there were three manual commands in its queue. Of course they were all garbage. But RoSur had no way of knowing this.

"Maybe now you can appreciate some of the nightmares that plague system software designers. There's just no way anybody could ever anticipate all possible contingencies. The designers had protected against *one* inadvertent garbage command—someone brushing the control box during an operation, for example—but not *several* bad commands. Manual commands were essentially considered to be emergencies by the overall system design. Hence they had the highest priority in the interrupt structure of the RoSur software and were always processed immediately. The design acknowledged, however, that there could be a single 'bad' manual command and had the capability of rejecting it and moving on to the next priority interrupts, which included fault protection."

"Sorry," said Nicole. "You've lost me. How could a design be structured to disregard a single bad command, but not several? I thought this simple processor operated in series."

Richard turned to his portable computer and, working from notes, called up on the monitor a mass of numbers arrayed in rows and columns. "Here are the operations, instruction by instruction, that the RoSur software implemented after there were manual commands in its queue."

"They repeat," Janos observed, "every seven operations."

"Exactly," Richard replied. "RoSur tried three times to process the first manual command, was unsuccessful in each attempt, and then went on to the next command. The software operated exactly as it was designed—"

"But why," Tabori asked, "did it go back to the first command afterward?"

"Because the software designers never considered the possibility of *multiple* bad manual commands. Or at least never designed for the condition. The internal question the software asks after finishing with the processing of each command is whether or not there is another manual command in the buffer. If there is *not*, then the software rejects the first command and is free to handle another interrupt. If there *is*, however, the software is told to store the rejected command and process the next command. Now, if two commands in a row are rejected, the software *assumes* that the command processor *hardware* is broken, swaps to the redundant hardware set, and tries again to process the same manual commands. You can understand the reasoning. Suppose one . . ."

Nicole listened for several seconds as Richard and Janos talked about redundant subsystems, buffered commands, and queue structures. She had very little training in either fault protection or redundancy management and could not follow the exchange. "Just a moment," she interjected at length, "you've lost me again. Remember, I'm not an engineer. Can't somebody give me a summary in normal English?"

Wakefield was apologetic. "Sorry, Nicole," he said. "You know what an interrupt-driven software system is?" She nodded. "And you are familiar with the way priorities operate in such a system? Good. Then the explanation is simple. The fault protection interrupts based on the accelerometer and imaging data were lower priority than the manual commands inadvertently entered by Janos when he was falling. The system became locked in a software loop trying to process the bad commands and never had a chance to heed the fault signals from the sensor subsystems. That's why the scalpel kept cutting."

For some reason Nicole was disappointed. The explanation was clear enough, and she had certainly not wanted the analysis to implicate Janos or any other member of the crew. But it was too simple. It had not been worth all her time and energy.

Nicole sat down on the cot in Richard Wakefield's hut. "So much for my mystery," she said.

Janos sat beside her. "Cheer up, Nicole," he said. "This is good news. At least now we know for certain that we didn't foul up the initialization process. There's a logical explanation for what happened."

"Great," she replied sarcastically. "But General Borzov is still dead. And now Reggie Wilson is too." Nicole thought about the American journalist's erratic behavior over the last several days and remembered her earlier conversation with Francesca. "Say," she said spontaneously, "did either of you ever hear General Borzov complain of headaches or any other discomfort? Especially on the day of the banquet?"

Wakefield shook his head. "No," said Janos. "Why do you ask?"

"Well, I asked the portable diagnostician, based on Borzov's biometry data, to give me the possible causes of his symptoms, given that the general was *not* having an appendicitis. The most likely cause was listed as drug reaction. Sixty-two percent probable. I thought that maybe he might have had an adverse reaction to some medication."

"Really?" Janos said, his curiosity piqued. "Why have you never said anything about this to me before?"

"I was going to . . . several times," Nicole answered. "But I didn't think you were interested. Remember when I stopped by your room on the Newton the day after General Borzov died? It was right after the crew meeting. From the way you responded I concluded that you didn't want to rehash—"

"Goodness." Janos shook his head. "How we humans fail to communicate. It was just a headache. Nothing more or less. I certainly didn't mean to give you the impression that I was unwilling to talk about Valeriy's death."

"Speaking of communicating," Nicole said as she rose wearily from the cot, "I must go to see Dr. Brown and Admiral Heilmann before I go to bed." She looked at

Wakefield. "Thanks a lot for your help, Richard. I wish I could say that I felt better now."

Nicole walked over beside Janos. "I'm sorry, friend," she said. "I should have shared my whole investigation with you. It probably would have been over much faster—"

"It's fine," Janos replied. "Don't worry about it." He smiled. "Come on, I'll walk with you as far as my suite."

Nicole could hear the loud conversation inside before she knocked on the door to the hut. David Brown, Otto Heilmann, and Francesca Sabatini were arguing about how to reply to the latest directions from Earth.

"They're overreacting," Francesca was saying. "And they'll realize it as soon as they have some time to reflect. This is not the first mission to suffer a loss of human life. They didn't cancel the American space shuttle when that school-teacher and her crew were killed."

"But they have *ordered* us to return to the Newton as soon as possible," Admiral Heilmann protested.

"So tomorrow we'll talk to them again and explain why we want to survey New York first. Takagishi says the sea will start to melt in another day or two and we'll have to leave anyway. Besides, Wakefield and Takagishi and I did hear something that night, even if David doesn't believe us."

"I don't know, Francesca," Dr. Brown was starting to respond when he finally heard Nicole's knock. "Who's there?" he asked crossly.

"Cosmonaut des Jardins. I have some important medical information—"

"Look, des Jardins," Brown interrupted quickly, "we're very busy. Can't it wait until morning?"

All right, Nicole said to herself. *I can wait until morning.* She wasn't anxious to answer Dr. Brown's questions about Takagishi's heart condition anyway. "Roger," she said out loud, laughing at herself for using the expression.

Within seconds Nicole could hear the discussion start again behind her. She walked slowly back to her hut. *Tomorrow has to be a better day*, she said as she crawled onto her cot.

31

ORVIETO PRODIGY

"Good night, Otto," David Brown said as the German admiral left his hut. "See you in the morning." Dr. Brown yawned and stretched. He looked at his watch. It was a little more than eight hours until the lights should come on again.

He pulled off his flight suit and had a drink of water. He had just laid down on his cot when Francesca entered his hut. "David," she said, "we have more problems." She walked over and gave him a short kiss. "I've been talking to Janos. Nicole suspects that Valeriy was drugged."

"Whaaat?" he replied. He sat up on his cot. "How could she? There was no way—"

"Apparently there was some evidence in his biometry data and she cleverly found it. She mentioned it to Janos tonight."

"You didn't react when he told you, did you? I mean, we must be absolutely—"

"Of course not," Francesca answered. "Anyway, Janos would never suspect anything in a thousand years. He is a total innocent. At least where things like this are concerned."

"Damn that woman," David Brown said. "And damn her biometry." He rubbed his face with his hands. "What a day. First that stupid Wilson tries to be a hero. Now this. . . . I told you we should have destroyed all the data from the operation. It would have been an easy matter to wipe out the central files. Then things would never—"

"She would still have his biometry records," Francesca countered. "That's where the prime evidence is. You would have to be an absolute genius to take the data from the operation itself and deduce anything." She sat down and cradled Dr. Brown's head against her chest. "Our big mistake was not when we failed to destroy the files. That would have aroused suspicion at the ISA. Our error was in underestimating Nicole des Jardins."

Dr. Brown shook free from the embrace and stood up. "Dammit, Francesca, it's your fault. I never should have let you talk me into it. I knew at the time—"

"You knew at the time," Francesca sharply interrupted, "that you, Dr. David Brown, were not going on the first sortie into Rama. You knew at the time that your future millions as the hero and perceived leader of this expedition would be seriously compromised if you stayed onboard the Newton." Brown stopped pacing and faced Francesca. "You knew at the time," she continued more softly, "that I too had a vested interest in your going on the sortie. And that I could be counted on to provide you with support."

She took his hands and pulled him back toward the cot. "Sit down, David," Francesca said. "We've been over and over this. We did not kill General Borzov. We simply gave him a drug that created the symptoms of an appendicitis. We made the decision together. If Rama had not maneuvered and the robot surgeon had not malfunctioned, then our plan would have worked perfectly. Borzov would be on the Newton today, recovering from his appendectomy, and you and I would be here leading the exploration of Rama."

David Brown removed his hands from hers and started to wring them. "I feel so . . . so unclean," he said. "I've never done anything like this before. I mean, whether we like it or not, we are partially responsible for Borzov's death. Maybe even for Wilson's as well. We could be indicted." He was shaking his head again. There was a forlorn expression on his face. "I'm supposed to be a scientist," he said. "What has happened to me? How did I get mixed up in these things?"

"Spare me your righteousness," Francesca said harshly. "And don't try to kid yourself. Aren't you the man who stole the decade's most important astronomical discovery from a woman graduate student? And then married her to keep her quiet forever? Your integrity was compromised a long, long time ago."

"That's unfair," Dr. Brown said petulantly. "I have mostly been honest. Except—"

"Except when it was important and worth a lot to you. What a pile of shit!" Francesca now stood up and paced around the hut herself. "You men are so damn hypocritical. You preserve your lofty self-images with amazing rationalizations. You never admit to yourselves who you really are and what you really want. Most women are more honest. We acknowledge our ambitions, our desires, even our basest wants. We admit our weaknesses. We face ourselves as we are, not as we would like to be."

She returned to the cot and took David's hands in hers again. "Don't you see, darling?" she said earnestly. "You and I are soulmates. Our alliance is based on the strongest bond of all—mutual self-interest. We are both motivated by the same goals of power and fame."

"That sounds awful," he said.

"But it's true. Even if you don't want to admit it to yourself. David, darling, can't you see that your indecisiveness comes from your failure to acknowledge your true nature? Look at me. I know exactly what I want and am never confused about what to do. My behavior is automatic."

The American physicist sat quietly beside Francesca for a long time. At length he turned and put his head on her shoulder. "First Borzov, now Wilson," he said with a sigh. "I feel whipped. I wish none of this had happened."

"You can't give up, David," she said, stroking his head. "We've come too far. And the big prize is now within our reach."

Francesca reached across him and started to remove his shirt. "It's been a long and trying day," she said soothingly. "Let's try to forget it." David Brown closed his eyes as she caressed his face and chest.

Francesca bent over and kissed him slowly on the lips. A few moments later she abruptly stopped. "You see," she said, slowly removing her own clothes, "as long as we are in this together, we can derive strength from each other." She stood up in front of David, forcing him to open his eyes.

"Hurry," he said impatiently, "I was already—"

"Don't worry so much about it," Francesca replied,

lazily pulling down her pants, "you've never had a problem with me." Francesca smiled again as she pushed his knees apart and pressed his face against her breasts. "Remember," she said, tugging easily at his shorts with her free hand, "I'm not Elaine."

She studied David Brown as he slept beside her. The strain and anxiety that had dominated his face just minutes before had been replaced by the carefree smile of a boy. *Men are so simple,* Francesca was thinking. *Orgasm is the perfect pain reliever. I wish it were that easy for us.*

She slipped off the small cot and put her clothes on again. Francesca was very careful not to disturb her sleeping friend. *But you and I still have a real problem,* she said to herself as she finished dressing, *which we need to address quickly. And it will be more difficult because we are dealing with a woman.*

Francesca walked outside her hut, into the black of Rama. There were a few lights near the supplies at the other end of the camp, but otherwise the Beta campsite was dark. Everyone else was asleep. She switched on her small flashlight and walked away in a southerly direction, toward the Cylindrical Sea.

What is it that you want, Madame Nicole des Jardins? she thought as she walked along. *And where's your weakness, your Achilles' heel?* For several minutes Francesca flipped through her entire memory bank on Nicole, attempting to find any personality or character flaw that could be exploited. *Money's not the answer. Sex isn't either, at least not with me.* She laughed involuntarily. *And certainly not with David. Your dislike for him is obvious.*

What about blackmail? Francesca asked herself as she drew near to the banks of the Cylindrical Sea. She remembered Nicole's strong reaction to her question about Genevieve's father. *Maybe,* she thought, *if I knew the answer to that question . . . But I don't.*

Francesca was temporarily stumped. She could not figure out any way to compromise Nicole des Jardins. By this time the lights from the campsite behind her were barely visible. Francesca extinguished her flashlight and very cautiously sat down to dangle her feet over the edge of the cliff.

Having her legs suspended above the frozen ice of the Cylindrical Sea brought back a suite of poignant memories from her childhood in Orvieto. At the age of eleven, despite the barrage of health warnings that assaulted her from every direction, the precocious Francesca had decided to start smoking cigarettes. Every day after school she would wind her way down the hill to the plain below the town and sit on the bank of her favorite creek. There she would smoke in silence, an act of solitary rebellion. On those lazy afternoons she would inhabit a fantasy world of castles and princes, millions of kilometers away from her mother and stepfather.

The memory of those adolescent moments produced an irresistible desire to smoke in Francesca. She had been taking her nicotine pills throughout the mission, but they satisfied only the physical addiction. She laughed at herself and reached into one of the special pockets of her flight suit. Francesca had hidden away three cigarettes in a special container that would preserve them in fresh condition. She had told herself before leaving the Earth that the cigarettes were there "in case of an emergency" . . .

Smoking a cigarette inside an extraterrestrial space vehicle was even more outrageous than smoking at the age of eleven. Francesca wanted to hoot with delight when she threw back her head and expelled the smoke into the Raman air. The act made her feel free, liberated. Somehow the threat represented by Nicole des Jardins did not seem so serious.

While she was smoking, Francesca recalled the acute loneliness of that young girl stealing down the slopes of old Orvieto. She also remembered the terrible secret that she had kept locked forever in her heart. Francesca had never told anyone about her stepfather, certainly not her mother, and she rarely thought about it anymore. But as she sat on the banks of the Cylindrical Sea, the anguish of her childhood appeared to her in sharp relief.

It began right after my eleventh birthday, she thought, plunging back into the details of her life eighteen years before. *I had no idea what the bastard wanted at first.*

She took another deep drag from her cigarette. *Even after he started bringing me gifts for no reason.*

He had been the principal of her new school. When she had taken her first full set of aptitude tests, Francesca had made the highest scores in the history of Orvieto. She was off the scale, a prodigy. Until then he had never noticed her. He had married her mother eighteen months before and fathered the twins almost immediately. Francesca had been a nuisance, another mouth to feed, nothing more than a part of her mother's furniture.

For several months he was especially nice to me. Then Mother went to visit Aunt Carla for a few days. The painful memories came fast, rushing like a torrent through her mind. She remembered the smell of wine on her stepfather's breath, his sweat against her body, her tears after he had left her room.

The nightmare had lasted for over a year. He had forced himself upon her whenever her mother was not in the house. Then one evening, while he was putting on his clothes and looking in the other direction, Francesca had smacked him in the back of the head with an aluminum baseball bat. Her stepfather had fallen to the floor, bloody and unconscious. She had dragged him into the living room and left him there.

He never touched me again, Francesca remembered, putting out her cigarette in the Raman dirt. *We were strangers in the same house. From then on I spent most of my time with Roberto and his friends. I was just waiting for my chance. I was ready when Carlo came.*

Francesca was fourteen during the summer of 2184. She spent most of her time that summer loitering around the main square of Orvieto. Her older cousin Roberto had just completed his certificate to be a tour guide for the cathedral in the square. The old Duomo, the chief tourist attraction of the town, had been built in phases, starting in the fourteenth century. The church was an artistic and architectural masterpiece. The frescoes by Luca Signorelli inside its San Brizio chapel were widely hailed as the finest examples of imaginative fifteenth century painting outside of the Vatican museum.

To have become an official Duomo guide was considered quite an accomplishment, especially at the age of nineteen. Francesca was very proud of Roberto. She sometimes accompanied him on his tours, but only if she agreed beforehand not to embarrass him with her wisecracks.

One August afternoon, right after lunch, a sleek limousine pulled into the piazza around Il Duomo and the chauffeur requested a guide from the tourist bureau. The gentleman in the limousine had not made a reservation and Roberto was the only guide available. Francesca watched with great curiosity as a short, handsome man in his late thirties or early forties climbed out of the back of the car and introduced himself to Roberto. Automobiles had been banned from upper Orvieto, except by special permit, for almost a hundred years, so Francesca knew the man must be an unusual individual.

As he always did, Roberto began his tour with the reliefs sculptured by Lorenzo Maitani on the outside portals of the church. Still curious, Francesca stood just off to the side, smoking quietly, while her cousin explained the significance of the weird demonic figures at the bottom of one of the columns. "This is one of the earliest representations of Hell," Roberto said, pointing at a group of Dantesque figures. "The fourteenth century concept of Hell involved an extremely literal interpretation of the Bible."

"Hah!" Francesca had suddenly interjected, dropping her cigarette on the cobblestones and walking toward Roberto and the handsome stranger. "It was also a very masculine concept of Hell. Notice that many of the demons have breasts and most of the sins depicted are sexual. Men have always believed that they were created perfect; it is women who have taught them to sin."

The stranger was astonished by the appearance of this gangly teenager expelling smoke from her mouth. His trained eye immediately recognized her natural beauty and it was clear that she was very bright. Who was she?

"This is my cousin, Francesca," Roberto said, obviously flustered by her interruption.

"Carlo Bianchi," the man said, extending his hand. His hand was moist. Francesca looked up at his face and could see that he was interested. She could feel her heart pounding in her chest. "If you listen to Roberto," she said coyly, "then all you'll get is the official tour. He leaves out the juicy bits."

"And you, young lady—"

"Francesca," she said.

"Yes, Francesca. Do you have a tour of your own?"

Francesca gave him her prettiest smile. "I read a lot," she said. "I know all about the artists who worked on the cathedral, particularly the painter Luca Signorelli." She paused for a moment. "Did you know," she continued, "that Michelangelo came here to study Signorelli's nudes before he painted the ceiling at the Sistine Chapel?"

"No, I didn't," Carlo said, laughing heartily. He was already fascinated. "But I do now. Come. Join us. You can add to what your cousin Roberto says."

She loved the way he kept staring at her. It was as if he were appraising her, as if she were a fine painting or a jeweled necklace, his eyes missing nothing as they roamed unabashedly over her figure. And his easy laughter spurred her on. Francesca's comments became increasingly outrageous and bawdy.

"You see that poor girl on the demon's back?" she said while they were gazing at the bewildering range of genius exhibited by Signorelli's frescoes inside the San Brizio chapel. "She looks like she's humping the demon in the butt, right? You know who she is? Her face and naked body are portraits of Signorelli's girlfriend. While he was slaving in here day after day, she became bored and decided to diddle a duke or two on the side. Luca was really pissed. So he fixed her. He condemned her to ride a demon in perpetuity."

When he stopped laughing, Carlo asked Francesca if she thought the woman's punishment was fair. "Of course not," the fourteen-year-old replied, "it's just another example of the male chauvinism of the fifteenth century. The men could screw anybody they wanted and were called virile; but let a woman try to satisfy herself—"

"*Francesca!*" Roberto interrupted. "Really. This is too much. Your mother would kill you if she heard what you are saying—"

"My mother is irrelevant at this moment. I'm talking about a double standard that still exists today. Look at . . ."

Carlo Bianchi could hardly believe his good fortune. A rich clothes designer from Milano, one who had established an international reputation by the time he was thirty, he had just happened to decide, on a whim, to hire a car to take him to Rome instead of going on the usual high-speed train. His sister, Monica, had always told him about the beauty of Il Duomo in Orvieto. It had been another last-minute decision to stop. And now. My, my. The girl was such a splendid morsel.

He invited Francesca to dinner when the tour was over. But when they reached the entrance to the fanciest restaurant in Orvieto, the young woman balked. Carlo understood. He took her to a store and bought her an expensive new dress with matching shoes and accessories. He was astonished by how beautiful she was. And only fourteen!

Francesca had never before drunk really fine wine. She drank it as if it were water. Each dish was so delicious that she positively squealed. Carlo was enchanted with his woman-child. He loved the way she let her cigarette dangle from the corner of her lips. It was so unspoiled, so perfectly gauche.

When the meal was over it was dark. Francesca walked with him back to the limousine parked in front of Il Duomo. As they went down a narrow alley, she leaned over and playfully bit his ear. He spontaneously pulled her to him and was rewarded with an explosive kiss. The surge in his loins overwhelmed him.

Francesca had felt it too. She did not hesitate a second when Carlo suggested they go for a ride in the car. By the time the limousine had reached the outskirts of Orvieto, she was sitting astride him in the backseat. Thirty minutes later, when they finished making love the second time, Carlo could not bear the thought of parting with this incredible girl. He asked Francesca if she would like to accompany him to Rome.

"*Andiamo*," she replied with a smile.

So we went to Rome and then Capri, Francesca remembered. *Paris for a week. In Milano you had me live with*

*Monica and Luigi. For appearances. Men are always so
worried about appearances.*

Francesca's long reverie was broken when she thought
she heard footsteps in the distance. She cautiously stood
up in the dark and listened. It was hard for her to hear
anything over her own breathing. Then she heard the
sound again, off to the left. Her ears told her the sound
was out on the ice. A burst of fear flooded her with an
image of bizarre creatures attacking their camp from across
the ice. She listened again very carefully, but heard nothing.

Francesca turned back toward the camp. *I loved you,
Carlo,* she said to herself, *if I ever loved any man. Even
after you began to share me with your friends.* More
long-buried pain came to the surface and Francesca fought
it with hard anger. *Until you started hitting me. That
ruined everything. You proved that you were a real bastard.*

Francesca very deliberately pushed aside the memories.
Now, where were we? she thought as she approached her
hut. *Ah yes. The issue was Nicole des Jardins. How much
does she really know? And what are we going to do about
it?*

32

NEW YORK EXPLORER

The tiny bell on his wristwatch awakened Dr. Takagishi from a deep sleep. For a few moments he was disoriented, unable to remember where he was. He sat up on his cot and rubbed his eyes. At length he recalled that he was inside Rama and that the alarm had been set to wake him up after five hours of sleep.

He dressed in the dark. When he was finished he picked up a large bag and fumbled around inside for several seconds. Satisfied with its contents, he threw the strap over his shoulder and walked to the door of his hut. Dr. Takagishi peered out cautiously. He could not see lights in any of the other huts. He took a deep breath and tiptoed out the door.

The world's leading authority on Rama walked out of the camp in the direction of the Cylindrical Sea. When he reached the shore, he climbed slowly down to the icy surface on the stairs cut into the fifty-meter cliff. Takagishi sat on the bottom rung, hidden against the base of the cliff. He removed some special cleats from his bag and attached them to the bottom of his shoes. Before walking out on the ice, the scientist calibrated his personal navigator so that he would be able to keep a constant heading once he left the shoreline.

When he was about two hundred meters away from the shore, Dr. Takagishi reached in his pocket to pull out his portable weather monitor. It dropped on the ice, making a short clacking sound in the quiet night. Takagishi picked it up a few seconds later. The monitor told him that the temperature was minus two degrees Centigrade and that a soft wind was blowing across the ice at eight kilometers per hour.

Takagishi inhaled deeply and was astonished by a peculiar but familiar odor. Puzzled, he inhaled again, this time concentrating on the smell. There was no doubt about it—it was cigarette smoke! He hurriedly extinguished his flashlight and stood motionless on the ice. His mind raced into overdrive, searching for an explanation. Francesca Sabatini was the only cosmonaut who smoked. Had she somehow followed him when he left the camp? Had she seen his light when he checked his weather monitor?

He listened for noises but heard nothing in the Raman night. Still he waited. When the cigarette smell had been gone for several minutes, Dr. Takagishi continued his trek across the ice, stopping every four or five steps to ensure that he was not being followed. Eventually he convinced himself that Francesca was not behind him. However, the cautious Takagishi did not turn on his flashlight again until he had walked more than a kilometer and had become worried that he might have drifted off course.

Altogether it took him forty-five minutes to reach the opposite edge of the sea and the island city of New York. When he was a hundred meters from the shore, the Japanese scientist took a larger flashlight from his bag and switched on its powerful beam. The ghostly silhouettes of the skyscrapers sent an exhilarating chill down his spine. At last he was here! At last he could seek the answers to his lifetime of questions unencumbered by someone else's arbitrary schedule.

Dr. Takagishi knew exactly where he wanted to go in New York. Each of the three circular sections of the Raman city was further subdivided into three angular portions, like a pie divided into slices. At the center of each of the three main sections was a central core, or plaza, around which the rest of the buildings and streets were arranged. As a boy in Kyoto, after reading everything he could find about the first Raman expedition, Takagishi had wondered what it would be like to stand in the center of one of those alien plazas and stare upward at buildings created by beings from another star. Takagishi felt certain not only that the secrets of Rama could be understood by studying New York, but also that its three plazas were the most likely locations for clues to the mysterious purpose of the interstellar vehicle.

The map of New York drawn by the earlier Raman explorers was as firmly etched in Takagishi's mind as the map of Kyoto, where he was born and raised. But that first Raman expedition had had only a limited time to survey New York. Of the nine functional units, only one had been mapped in detail; the prior cosmonauts had simply assumed, on the basis of limited observations, that all the other units were identical.

As Takagishi's brisk pace carried him deeper and deeper into the foreboding quiet of one part of the central section, some subtle differences between this particular segment of Rama and the one studied by Norton's crew (they had surveyed an adjacent slice) began to emerge. The layout of the major streets in the two units was the same; however, as Dr. Takagishi drew closer to the plaza, the smaller streets broke into a slightly different pattern from the one that had been reported by the first explorers. The scientist in Takagishi forced him to stop often and note all the variations on his pocket computer.

He entered the region immediately surrounding the plaza, where the streets ran in concentric circles. He crossed three avenues and found himself standing opposite a huge octahedron, about a hundred meters tall, with a mirrored exterior. His powerful flashlight beam reflected off its surface and then bounced from building to building around him. Dr. Takagishi walked slowly around the octahedron, searching for an entrance, but he did not find one.

On the other side of the eight-sided structure, in the center of the plaza, was a broad circular space without tall buildings. Shigeru Takagishi moved deliberately around the entire perimeter of the circle, studying the surrounding buildings as he walked. He gained no new insights about the purpose of the structures. When he turned inward at regular intervals to survey the plaza area itself, he saw nothing unusual or particularly noteworthy. Nevertheless, he did enter into his computer the location of the many short, nondescript metallic boxes that divided the plaza into partitions.

When he was again in front of the octahedron, Dr. Takagishi reached into his bag and pulled out a thin hexagonal plate densely covered with electronics. He deployed the scientific apparatus in the plaza, three or four meters away from the octahedron, and then spent ten minutes verifying with his transceiver that all the scientific instruments were properly working. When the Japanese scientist had completed checking the payload, he quickly left the plaza area and headed for the Cylindrical Sea.

Takagishi was in the middle of the second concentric avenue when he heard a short but loud popping noise behind him in the plaza. He turned around but didn't move. A few seconds later he heard a different sound. This one Takagishi recognized from his first sortie, both the dragging of the metal brushes and the embedded high-frequency singing. He shone his flashlight in the direction of the plaza. The sound stopped. He switched off his flashlight and stood quietly in the middle of the avenue.

Several minutes later the brush dragging began again. Takagishi moved stealthily across the two avenues and started around the octahedron in the direction of the noise. When he was almost to the plaza, a *beep, beep* from his bag broke his concentration. By the time he turned off the alarm, which was indicating that the scientific package he had just deployed in the plaza had already malfunctioned, there was total quiet in New York. Again Dr. Takagishi waited, but this time the sound did not recur.

He took a deep breath to calm himself and summoned all his courage. Somehow his curiosity won out over his fear and Dr. Takagishi returned to the plaza opposite the octahedron to find out what had happened to the scientific payload. His first surprise was that the hexagonal package had vanished from the spot where he had left it. Where could it have gone? Who or what could have taken it?

Takagishi knew that he was on the verge of a scientific discovery of overwhelming importance. He was also terrified. Fighting a powerful desire to flee, he shone his large flashlight around the plaza, hoping to find an explanation for the disappearance of the science station. The beam reflected off a small piece of metal some thirty to forty meters closer to the center of the plaza. Takagishi realized immediately that the reflection was coming from the instrument package. He hurried over to it.

He bent down on his knees and examined the electronics. There was no damage that was obvious. He had just pulled out his transceiver to begin a methodical check of all the science instruments when he noticed a ropelike object about fifteen centimeters in diameter at the edge of the flashlight beam illuminating the science package. Dr. Takagishi picked up his light and walked over to the object. It was striped, black and gold, and stretched off into the distance for twelve meters or so, disappearing behind an odd metal shed about three meters tall. He felt the thick rope. It was soft and fuzzy on the top. When he tried to turn it over to feel the bottom, the object began to move. Takagishi dropped it immediately and watched it slither slowly away from him toward the shed. The motion was accompanied by the sound of brushes dragging against metal.

Dr. Takagishi could hear the sound of his own heartbeat. Again he fought the urge to run away. He remembered his dawn meditations as a college student in the garden of his Zen master. He would not be afraid. He ordered his feet to march in the direction of the shed.

The black and gold rope disappeared. There was silence in the plaza. Takagishi approached the shed with his light beam on the ground at the spot where the thick rope had last been visible. He came around the corner and thrust the beam into the shed. He could not believe what he saw. A mass of black and gold tentacles writhed underneath the light.

A high-frequency whine suddenly exploded in his ears. Dr. Takagishi looked over his left shoulder and was thunderstruck. His eyes bugged out of his head. His scream was lost as the noise intensified and three of the tentacles reached out to touch him. The walls of his heart gave way and he slumped, already dead, into the grasp of the amazing creature.

33

MISSING PERSON

"Admiral Heilmann."

"Yes, General O'Toole."

"Are you by yourself?"

"Certainly. I just woke up a few minutes ago. My meeting with Dr. Brown is not for another hour. Why are you calling so early?"

"While you were sleeping I received a coded top secret message from COG military headquarters. It's about Trinity. They wanted to know the status."

"What do you mean, General?"

"Is this line secure, Admiral? Have you turned off the automatic recorder?"

"Now I have."

"They asked two questions. Did Borzov die without telling anyone his RQ? Does anyone else on the crew know about Trinity?"

"You know the answers to both questions."

"I wanted to be certain that you hadn't talked to Dr. Brown. They insisted that I check with you before encoding my answer. What do you think this is all about?"

"I don't know, Michael. Maybe somebody down on Earth is getting nervous. Wilson's death probably scared them."

"It certainly scared me. But not to the point that I would think about Trinity. I wonder if they know something that we don't."

"Well, I guess we'll find out soon enough. All the ISA officials have been insisting that we should evacuate Rama at the first available opportunity. They didn't even like our decision to rest the crew for several hours first. This time I don't think they will change their minds."

"Admiral, do you remember that hypothetical discussion we had with General Borzov during the cruise, about the conditions under which we would activate Trinity?"

"Vaguely. Why?"

"Do you still disagree with his insistence that we must know *why* the Trinity contingency is being called for? You said at the time that if the Earth thought great danger was imminent, you didn't personally need to understand the rationale."

"I'm afraid I'm not following you, General. Why are you asking me these questions?"

"I would like your permission, Otto, when I encode the response to COG military headquarters, to find out why they are asking about the status of Trinity at this particular time. If we are in danger, we have a right to know."

"You may request additional information, Michael, but I would bet that their inquiry is strictly routine."

Janos Tabori awakened while it was still dark inside Rama. As he pulled on his flight suit, he made a mental list of the activities that would be required to transport the crab biot to the Newton. If the order to leave Rama was confirmed, they would be departing soon after dawn. Janos consulted the formal evacuation procedure stored on his pocket computer and updated it by adding the new tasks associated with the biot.

He checked his watch. Dawn was only fifteen minutes away, assuming of course that the Rama diurnal cycle was regular. Janos laughed to himself. Rama had produced so many surprises already that there was no certainty the lights would return on schedule. If they did, however, Janos wanted to watch the Raman "sunrise." He could eat his breakfast after dawn.

A hundred meters from his hut the caged crab biot was immobile, as it had been since it was hoisted away from its companions the previous day. Janos shone his flashlight through the tough, transparent cage wall and checked to see if there were any signs that the biot might have moved during the night. Having established that the biot had not changed position, Janos walked away from the Beta campsite in the direction of the sea.

As he waited for the burst of light, he found himself thinking about the very end of his conversation with Nicole the night before. There was something not quite right about her offhand revelation of the possible cause of General Borzov's pain on the night he died. Janos remembered vividly the healthy appendix; there was no doubt that the primary diagnosis had been incorrect. But why had Nicole not talked to him about the backup drug diagnosis? Especially if she was conducting an investigation into the issue. . . .

Janos reached the inescapable conclusion that Dr. des Jardins had either lost faith in his ability or somehow suspected that he might have himself administered the drugs to General Borzov without consulting her. Either way he should find out what she was thinking. A strange idea, born from his own feelings of guilt, next crossed his mind. *Could it be,* he mused, *that Nicole somehow knows about the Schmidt and Hagenest project and suspects all four of us?*

For the first time, Janos himself wondered if perhaps Valeriy Borzov's pain had not been natural. He recalled the chaotic meeting the four of them had had two hours after David Brown had learned that he would be left onboard the Newton during the first sortie. "You must talk to him, Otto," a frustrated Dr. Brown had said to Admiral Heilmann. "You must convince him to change his mind."

Otto Heilmann had then admitted it was unlikely General Borzov would change the personnel assignments based on his request. "In that case," Dr. Brown had replied angrily, "we can say good-bye to all the incentive awards in our contract."

Throughout the meeting Francesca Sabatini had remained quiet and seemingly unworried. As he was leaving, Janos had overheard Dr. Brown berating her. "And why are you so calm?" he had said. "You stand to lose as much as anyone else. Or do you have a plan I don't know about?"

Janos had glimpsed Francesca's smile for only a fraction of a second. But he had remarked to himself at the time that she had seemed oddly confident. Now, as Cosmonaut Tabori awaited dawn on Rama, that smile returned to haunt him. With Francesca's knowledge of drugs it would have been well within her capability to give General Borzov something that would induce appendicitis symptoms. But would she have done something so . . . so blatantly dishonest, just to enhance the value of their postmission media project?

Again Rama was instantaneously flooded with light. As always, it was a feast for the eyes. Janos turned around slowly, looking in all directions and studying both bowls of the immense structure. With the light now brightly shining, he resolved to talk to Francesca at the first opportunity.

It was Irina Turgenyev, strangely enough, who asked the question. The cosmonauts were almost finished with their breakfast. Dr. Brown and Admiral Heilmann, in fact, had already left the table to conduct another of their interminable conference calls with ISA management. "Where's Dr. Takagishi?" she said innocently. "He's the last member of the crew that I would expect to be late for anything."

"He must have slept through his alarm," Janos Tabori answered, pushing his folding chair away from the table. "I'll go check on him."

When Janos returned a minute later he was perplexed. "He wasn't there," he said with a shrug of his shoulders. "I guess he went out for a walk."

Nicole des Jardins had an immediate sinking feeling in her stomach. She rose abruptly without finishing her breakfast. "We should go look for him," she said, her concern undisguised, "or he won't be ready when we leave."

The other cosmonauts all noticed Nicole's agitation. "What's going on here?" Richard Wakefield said good-naturedly. "One of our scientists takes a little morning walk on his own and the company doctor goes into panic?" He switched on his radio. "Hello, Dr. Takagishi, wherever you are. This is Wakefield. Will you please let us know that you're all right so that we can finish our breakfast."

There was a long silence. Every member of the crew knew that it was an absolutely mandatory requirement to carry a communicator at all times. You could choose to turn off the transmission capability, but you had to listen under any and all circumstances.

"Takagishi-san," Nicole said next with an urgent edge in her voice. "Are you all right? Please respond." During the extended silence, Nicole's sinking feeling in her stomach turned into a large knot. Something terrible had happened to her friend.

"I've explained that to you twice, Dr. Maxwell," David Brown said in exasperation. "It makes no sense to evacuate part of the crew. The most efficient way to search for Dr. Takagishi is to use the entire staff. Once we find him we will clear out of Rama with great haste. And to answer your last question, no, this is not a ploy on the part of the crew to avoid compliance with the evacuation order."

He turned to Admiral Heilmann and handed him the microphone. "Dammit, Otto," he muttered, "you talk to that bureaucratic nincompoop. He thinks he can command this mission better than we can, even though he's a hundred million kilometers away."

"Dr. Maxwell, this is Admiral Heilmann. I am in complete agreement with Dr. Brown. Anyway, we really can't afford to argue with such long delay times. We are going to proceed with our plan. Cosmonaut Tabori will stay here with me at Beta and pack all the heavy equipment, including the biot. I will coordinate the search. Brown, Sabatini, and des Jardins will cross the ice to New York, the most likely destination if the professor went under his own power. Wakefield, Turgenyev, and Yamanaka will look for him in the helicopters."

He paused for a moment. "There's no need for you to respond to this transmission in a hurry. The search will already have begun before your next message will arrive."

Back in her hut, Nicole very carefully packed her medical supplies. She criticized herself for not foreseeing that Takagishi might try one last time to visit New York. *You made another mistake*, Nicole said to herself. *The least you can do is make certain you're prepared when you find him.*

She knew the personal packing procedure by heart.

Nevertheless, she skimped on her own supplies of food and water to ensure that she had whatever an injured or sick Takagishi might need. Nicole had mixed emotions about her two companions on the quest to find the Japanese scientist, but it never occurred to her that the grouping might have been purposely planned. Everyone knew Takagishi's fascination with New York. Given the circumstances, it was not surprising that Brown and Sabatini were accompanying her to the primary search area.

Just before Nicole left the hut, she saw Richard Wakefield at her door. "May I come in?" he asked.

"Certainly," she replied.

He walked in with an uncharacteristic uncertainty, as if he were confused or embarrassed. "What is it?" Nicole asked after an awkward silence.

He smiled. "Well," he said sheepishly, "it seemed like a good idea a few minutes ago. Now it strikes me as a little stupid—maybe even childish." Nicole noticed he was holding something in his right hand. "I brought you something," he continued. "A good luck charm, I guess. I thought you might take it with you to New York."

Cosmonaut Wakefield opened his hand. Nicole recognized the figurine of Prince Hal. "You can say what you will about valor and discretion and all that, but sometimes a little luck is more important."

Nicole was surprisingly touched. She took the little figurine from Wakefield and studied its intricate detail with admiration. "Does the prince have any special qualities I need to know about?" she asked with a smile.

"Oh yes." Richard brightened. "He loves to spend witty evenings in pubs with fat knights and other unsavory characters. Or battle renegade dukes and earls. Or court beautiful French princesses."

Nicole blushed slightly. "If I'm lonely and want the prince to amuse me, what do I do?" she asked.

Richard came over beside Nicole and showed her a tiny keyboard just above Prince Hal's buttocks. "He'll respond to many commands," Richard said, handing her a very small baton the size of a pin. "This will fit perfectly into any of the key slots. Try T for talk or A for action if you want him to show you his stuff."

Nicole put the little prince and the baton in the pocket of her flight suit. "Thank you, Richard," she said. "This is very sweet."

Wakefield was flustered. "Well, you know, it's no big deal. It's just that we've had a spate of bad luck and I thought, I mean, maybe—"

"Thanks again, Richard," Nicole interrupted, "I appreciate your concern." They walked out of her hut together.

34

STRANGE COMPANIONS

Dr. David Brown was the kind of abstract scientist who neither liked nor trusted machines. Most of his published papers were written about theoretical subjects because he abhorred the formality and detail of empirical science. Empiricists had to contend with instrumentation and, even worse, engineers. Dr. Brown considered all engineers to be nothing more than glorified carpenters and plumbers. He tolerated their existence only because some of them were necessary if his theories were ever to be proved by actual data.

When Nicole innocently asked Dr. Brown some simple questions about the workings of the icemobile, Francesca could not restrain a cackle. "He has absolutely no idea," the Italian journalist responded, "and he couldn't care less. Would you believe that the man doesn't even know how to drive an electric cart? I've seen him stare at a simple food processing robot for over thirty minutes, trying without success to figure out how to use it. He would starve to death if nobody helped him."

"Come on, Francesca," Nicole replied as the two women climbed into the front seat of the icemobile, "he can't be that bad. After all, he has to use all the crew computers and communication devices, as well as the image processing system onboard the Newton. So you must be exaggerating."

The tenor of the conversation was light and harmless. Dr. David Brown slumped in the backseat and heaved a sigh. "Surely you two exceptional women have something more important to discuss. If not, perhaps you could explain to me why a lunatic Japanese scientist takes off from our camp in the middle of the night."

"According to Maxwell's assistant, that obsequious cipher named Mills, many people on Earth think our good Japanese doctor was kidnapped by the Ramans."

"Come on, Francesca. Be serious. Why would Dr. Takagishi decide to strike out on his own?"

"I have an idea," Nicole said slowly, "that he was impatient with the scheduled exploration process. You know how fervently he believes in the importance of New York. After the Wilson incident . . . well, he was fairly certain that an evacuation would be ordered. By the time we come back inside, *if* we come back, the Cylindrical Sea may have melted and it will be more difficult to reach New York."

Nicole's natural honesty was urging her to tell Brown and Sabatini about Takagishi's heart problems. But her intuitive sense told her not to trust her two companions. "He just doesn't seem like the type to go off half-cocked," Dr. Brown was saying. "I wonder if he heard or saw something."

"Maybe he had a headache or couldn't sleep for some other reason," Francesca offered. "Reggie Wilson used to prowl around at night when his head was bothering him."

David Brown leaned forward. "By the way," he said to Nicole, "Francesca tells me that you think Wilson's instability might have been exacerbated by the headache pills he was using. You certainly seem to know your drugs. I was extremely impressed by how quickly you identified the particular sleeping pill I had taken."

"Speaking of drugs," Francesca added after a short pause. "Janos Tabori mentioned something about a discussion he had with you concerning Borzov's death. I may not have understood him correctly, but I thought he said that you believe a drug reaction may have been involved."

They were driving steadily across the ice. The conversation had been even in tone, apparently casual. There was no obvious reason to be suspicious. *Nevertheless,* Nicole said to herself as she framed a response to Francesca's remarks, *those last two comments seemed too smooth. Almost practiced.* She turned to look at David Brown. She suspected that Francesca could dissemble without effort, but Nicole was certain she would be able to tell from Dr.

Brown's facial expression whether or not their questions were rehearsed. He squirmed slightly under her unblinking gaze.

"Cosmonaut Tabori and I were having a conversation about General Borzov and we started speculating about what might have caused his pain," Nicole said blandly. "After all, his appendix was perfectly healthy, so something else must have been responsible for his acute discomfort. In the course of our conversation, I mentioned to Janos that an adverse drug reaction should be considered as one possible cause. It was not a very strong statement."

Dr. Brown seemed relieved and immediately changed the subject. However, Nicole's statement had not satisfied Francesca. *Unless I am mistaken, our lady journalist has more questions,* Nicole mused. *But she isn't going to ask them right now.* She watched Francesca and could tell that the Italian woman was not paying attention to Dr. Brown's monologue in the backseat. While he was discussing the reaction on Earth to Wilson's death, Francesca was deep in thought.

There was a momentary quiet after Brown finished his commentary. Nicole glanced around her at the miles of ice, the imposing cliffs on the sides of the Cylindrical Sea, and the skyscrapers of New York in front of her. Rama was a glorious world. She had a momentary pang of guilt about her distrust of Francesca and Dr. Brown. *It's a shame that we humans are never able to pull in the same direction,* Nicole said to herself. *Not even when confronted by infinity.*

"I can't imagine how you have managed it," Francesca said, suddenly breaking the silence. She had turned to address Nicole. "Even after all this time, not even the tabloid videos have a legitimate lead. And it doesn't take a genius to figure out when it must have occurred."

Dr. Brown was completely lost. "What in the world are you talking about?" he asked.

"Our famous life science officer," Francesca replied. "Don't you find it fascinating that after all this time, the identity of her daughter's father is still unknown to the public?"

"Signora Sabatini," Nicole said immediately, switching to Italian, "as I told you once before, this subject is none of your business. I will not tolerate this kind of intrusion into my private affairs—"

"I just wanted to remind you, Nicole," Francesca interrupted quickly, also in Italian, "that you have secrets you might not want exposed."

David Brown stared blankly at the two women. He had not understood a word in the last exchange and was confused by the obvious tension. "So, David," Francesca said in a patronizing tone, "you were telling us about the mood on Earth. Do you think we're going to be ordered home? Or are we merely going to abort this particular sortie?"

"The COG Executive Council has been called into special session for later this week," he answered after a puzzled hesitation. "Dr. Maxwell's current guess is that we will be told to abandon the project."

"That would be a typical overreaction from a group of government officials whose primary objective has always been to minimize the downside risk. For the first time in history, adequately prepared human beings are exploring the interior of a vehicle built by another intelligence. Yet on Earth, the politicians continue to act as if nothing unusual has happened. They are incapable of vision. It's amazing."

Nicole des Jardins did not listen to the rest of Francesca's conversation with Dr. Brown. Her mind was still focused on their earlier exchange. *She must think I have proof about the drugs in Borzov,* Nicole said to herself. *There's no other possible explanation for the threat.*

When they reached the edge of the ice, Francesca spent ten minutes setting up the robot camera and sound equipment for a sequence showing the three of them preparing to search the alien city for their missing colleague. Nicole's complaints to Dr. Brown about the waste of time went unheeded. She did, however, make the fact that she was annoyed obvious by refusing to participate in the video sequence. While Francesca was completing her preparations, Nicole climbed the nearby stairway and studied the amazing city of skyscrapers. Behind and below her, Nicole could hear Francesca invoking the drama of the moment for the millions of viewers back on Earth.

"Here I stand on the outskirts of the mysterious island

city of New York. It was near this very spot that Dr.
Takagishi, Cosmonaut Wakefield, and I heard some strange
sounds earlier this week. We have reason to suspect that
New York may have been the professor's destination when
he took off from Beta campsite last night to do some
solitary and unauthorized exploration. . . .

"What has happened to the professor? Why does he not
respond when called on the commpak? Yesterday we witnessed a terrible tragedy when journalist Reggie Wilson,
risking his own life to save this reporter, was trapped
inside the rover and was unable to escape the powerful
claws of the crab biots. Has a similar fate befallen our
Rama expert? Did the extraterrestrials who built this amazing vehicle eons ago perhaps create a sophisticated trap
designed to subdue and ultimately destroy any unsuspect-
ing visitors? We don't know for certain. But we . . ."

From her vantage point on top of the wall, Nicole tried
to ignore Francesca and imagine in what direction Dr.
Takagishi might have gone. She consulted the maps stored
in her pocket computer. *He would have gone toward the
exact geometrical center of the city,* she concluded. *He
was certain there was meaning in the geometry.*

35

INTO THE PIT

They had walked the bewildering maze of streets for only twenty minutes, but they would have already been hopelessly lost without their personal navigators. They had no thorough plan for the search. They simply wandered up and down streets in a quasi-random pattern. Every three or four minutes there would be another transmission from Admiral Heilmann to Dr. Brown and the search party would have to look for a location where the signal strength was satisfactory.

"At this rate," Nicole remarked as once again they faintly heard Otto Heilmann's voice on the communicator, "our search is going to take forever. Dr. Brown, why don't you just stay in one spot? Then Francesca and I—"

"Break break," they heard Otto more clearly as David Brown moved into a space between two tall buildings. "Did you copy that last transmission?"

"Afraid not, Otto," Dr. Brown replied. "Would you please repeat it."

"Yamanaka, Wakefield, and Turgenyev have covered the bottom third of the Northern Hemicylinder. No sign of Takagishi. It's unlikely that he could have gone farther north, unless he went to one of the cities. In that case we should have seen his footprints somewhere. So you're probably on the right track.

"Meanwhile we have big news here. Our captured crab biot started to move about two minutes ago. It is trying to escape, but so far its tools have barely dented the cage. Tabori is working feverishly to build a larger, stronger cage that will go around the entire apparatus. I'm bringing Yamanaka's 'copter back to Beta so he can give Tabori a hand. He should be here in a minute— Wait. . . . There's an urgent coming through from Wakefield. . . . I'll put him on."

Richard Wakefield's British accent was unmistakable, though he could barely be heard by the trio in New York. "Spiders," he shouted in response to a question from Admiral Heilmann. "You remember the spider biot dissected by Laura Ernst? Well, we can see six of them just beyond the southern cliff. They're all over that temporary hut we built. And something has apparently repaired those two dead crab biots, for our prisoner's brothers are trundling toward the South Pole—"

"Pictures!" Francesca Sabatini screamed into the radio. "Are you taking pictures?"

"What's that? Sorry, I did not copy."

"Francesca wants to know if you're taking pictures," Admiral Heilmann clarified.

"Of course, love," Richard Wakefield said. "Both the automatic imaging system in the helicopter and the hand camera you gave me this morning have been running without interruption. The spider biots are amazing. I've never seen anything move so fast. . . . By the way, any sign of our Japanese professor?"

"Not yet," David Brown hollered from New York. "It's slow going in this maze. I feel as if I'm looking for a needle in a haystack."

Admiral Heilmann repeated the status of the missing person search for Wakefield and Turgenyev in the helicopter. Richard then said that they were coming back to Beta to refuel. "What about you, David?" Heilmann asked. "In view of everything, including the need to keep those bastards on Earth informed, don't you think you should return to Beta yourself? Cosmonauts Sabatini and des Jardins can continue the search for Dr. Takagishi. If necessary we can send someone to replace you when the helicopter picks you up."

"I don't know, Otto, I haven't—" Francesca turned off the transmit switch on David Brown's radio in the middle of his reply. He shot her an angry glance that quickly softened.

"We need to talk about this," she said firmly. "Tell him you'll call him back in a couple of minutes."

Nicole was flabbergasted by the conversation that ensued between Francesca Sabatini and David Brown. Neither one of them seemed to be even slightly concerned
about the fate of Dr. Takagishi. Francesca insisted that she
had to return to Beta immediately to cover *all* the breaking stories. Dr. Brown was anxious because he was away
from the "primary" action of the expedition.

Each argued that his reasons for returning were more
important. What if they both left New York? No, that
would leave cosmonaut des Jardins alone. Maybe she should
come with them and they could reinitiate the search for
Takagishi when things calmed down in several hours. . . .

Nicole finally exploded. "*Never*," she shouted suddenly
at them, "never in my life have I seen such egotistical
. . ." She could not think of a good noun. "One of our
colleagues is missing and almost certainly needs our help.
He may be injured or dying, yet all you two can do is
argue about your own petty prerogatives. It's really
disgusting."

She paused a second to catch her breath. "Let me tell
you one thing," Nicole continued, still fuming. "I am not
going back to Beta right now. I don't give a damn if you
order me. I am staying here and finishing the search. At
least I have my priorities straight. I know a man's life is
more important than image or status or even a stupid
media project."

David Brown blinked twice, as if he had been slapped
in the face. Francesca smiled. "Well, well," she said, "so
our reclusive life science officer knows more than we have
given her credit for." She looked over at David and then
back at Nicole. "Will you excuse us for a moment, dear?
We have a few matters to discuss in private."

Francesca and Dr. Brown moved over beside the base
of a skyscraper about twenty meters away and began an
animated conversation. Nicole turned the other way. She
was angry with herself for losing her temper. She was
especially irritated that she had revealed her knowledge of
their contract with Schmidt and Hagenest. *They will assume Janos told me,* she thought. *After all, we have been
close friends.*

Francesca walked back to join Nicole while Dr. Brown

radioed Admiral Heilmann. "David is calling for the helicopter to meet him next to the icemobile. He assures me that he can find his way out. I will stay here with you and search for Takagishi. At least that way I can photograph New York."

There was no emotion in Francesca's pronouncement. Nicole was unable to read her mood. "One other thing," Francesca added. "I promised David we would conclude our search and be ready to return to camp in four hours or less."

The two women hardly talked during the first hour of their search. Francesca was content to let Nicole choose the path. Every fifteen minutes they stopped to radio the Beta camp and obtain an updated fix on their position. "You're now about two kilometers south and four kilometers east of the icemobile," Richard Wakefield told them when they stopped for lunch. He had been delegated the job of keeping track of their progress. "You're just east of the central plaza."

They had gone to the central section first, for Nicole had thought that Takagishi would have headed there. They had found the open circular plaza with many low structures, but no sign of their colleague. Since then, Francesca and Nicole had visited the two other plazas and carefully combed the length of two of the central pie portions. They had found nothing. Nicole admitted she was running out of ideas.

"This is quite an astonishing place," Francesca responded as she began to eat her lunch. They were sitting on a square metal box about a meter high. "My photographs can barely begin to capture it. Everything is so quiet, so tall, so . . . alien."

"Some of these buildings could not be described without your pictures. The polyhedrons, for example. There's at least one in each slice, with the biggest one always right around the plaza. I wonder what they signify, if anything? And why are they located where they are?"

The emotional tension just below the surface in the two women remained suppressed. They chatted a little about what they had seen in their trek across New York. Francesca had been especially fascinated by a large trellis arrangement that they had found connecting two tall skyscrapers in the central unit. "What do you suppose that lattice or net thing was all about?" she asked idly. "It must have had twenty thousand loops and must have been fifty meters tall."

"I guess it's ridiculous for us to try to understand any of this," Nicole said with a wave of her hand. She finished her lunch and glanced at her companion. "Ready to continue?"

"Not quite," Francesca said purposefully. She cleaned up the remains of her lunch and put them in the garbage pouch of her flight suit. "You and I still have some unfinished business."

Nicole looked at her quizzically. "I think it's time we took off the masks and faced each other honestly," Francesca said in what was a deceptively friendly manner. "If you suspect that I gave Valeriy Borzov some medication on the day that he died, why don't you ask me directly?"

Nicole stared at her adversary for several seconds. "Did you?" she asked at length.

"Do you think I did?" Francesca replied coyly. "And if so, why did I do it?"

"You're just playing the same game at another level," Nicole said after a pause. "You're not willing to admit anything. You just want to find out how much I know. But I don't need a confession from you. Science and technology are supporting me. Eventually the truth will be obvious."

"I doubt it," Francesca said casually. She jumped down from the box. "The truth always eludes those who search for it." She smiled. "Now let's go find the professor."

On the western side of the central plaza the two women encountered another unique structure. From a distance it resembled a huge barn. The peak of its black roof was easily forty meters above the ground and it was more than a hundred meters long. There were two especially fascinating features about the barn. First, the two ends of the building were open. Second, although one could not see into it from the outside, all the walls and the roof were transparent from the *inside*. Francesca and Nicole took turns proving that it was not an optical illusion. Someone inside the barn could indeed see in all directions except down. In fact, the adjacent reflective skyscrapers had been precisely aligned so that all the nearby streets were visible from inside the barn.

"Fantastic," said Francesca as she photographed Nicole standing on the other side of the wall.

"Dr. Takagishi told me," Nicole said as she came around the corner, "that it was impossible to believe that New York was purposeless. The rest of Rama? Maybe. But nobody could have spent this much time and effort without some reason."

"You almost sound religious," Francesca said.

Nicole stared quietly at her Italian colleague. *She's needling me now,* Nicole said to herself. *She doesn't really care what I think. Maybe what anybody thinks.*

"Hey. Look at this," Francesca said after a short silence. She had walked a short way into the interior of the barn and was pointing at the ground. Nicole came up beside her. In front of Francesca a narrow rectangular pit was cut in the floor. The pit was about five meters long, a meter and a half wide, and quite deep, maybe as much as eight meters. Most of the bottom was in shadow. The walls of the pit were straight up and down, without any sign of indentation.

"There's another one over here. And another there. . . ." Altogether there were nine pits, each constructed in exactly the same manner, that were scattered over the south half of the barn. In the north half, nine small spheres rested on the surface in a carefully measured array. Nicole found herself wishing for a legend of some kind, an instructional guide that would explain the meaning or purpose of all these objects. She was starting to feel bewildered.

They had crossed almost the entire length of the barn when they heard a faint emergency signal on their communicators. "They must have found Dr. Takagishi," Nicole said out loud as she rushed out one of the open ends of the barn. As soon as she was no longer underneath the roof, the volume of the emergency signal nearly shattered her eardrums. "Okay. Okay," she radioed. "We can hear you. What's up?"

"We've been trying to call you for over two minutes," she heard Richard Wakefield say. "Where in the hell have you been? I only used the emergency signal because of its higher gain."

"We were inside this amazing barn," Francesca replied from behind Nicole. "It's like a surrealistic world, with one-way mirrors and weird reflections—"

"That's great," Richard interrupted, "but we don't have time to chat. You ladies are to march forthwith to the closest spot on the Cylindrical Sea. A helicopter will pick you up in ten minutes. We'd come into New York itself if there was a place for us to land."

"Why?" Nicole asked. "What's the hurry all of a sudden?"

"Can you see the South Pole from where you are?"

"No. We have too many tall buildings in the way."

"Something weird is happening around the little horns. Huge arcs of lightning are bouncing from spire to spire. It's an impressive display. We all feel something unusual is about to happen." Richard hesitated a second. "You should leave New York immediately."

"Okay," Nicole answered. "We're on our way."

She switched off the transmitter and turned to Francesca. "Did you hear how loud the emergency signal was the moment we came out of the barn?" Nicole thought for several seconds. "The material in the walls and roof of that building must block radio signals." Her face now brightened. "That explains what happened to Takagishi—he must be inside a barn, or something similar."

Francesca was not following Nicole's line of thought. "So what?" she said, taking one last panoramic image of the barn with her video camera. "It's really not important now. We must hurry out to meet the helicopter."

"Maybe he's even in one of those very pits," Nicole continued excitedly. "Sure. It could have happened. He was exploring in the dark. He could have fallen . . . Wait here," she said to Francesca. "I'll only be a minute."

Nicole dashed back inside the barn and bent down beside one of the holes. Holding the side of the pit with her hand, she shone the beam from her flashlight down into the bottom. Something was there! She waited a few seconds for her eyes to focus. It was a pile of material of some kind. She moved quickly to the next pit. "Doctor Takagishi," she yelled. "Are you here, Shig?" she shouted in Japanese.

"Come on!" Francesca hollered at Nicole from the end of the barn. "Let's go. Richard sounded very serious."

At the fourth pit the shadows made it very difficult for Nicole to see the bottom even with the beam from her flashlight. She could make out some objects, but what were they? She laid down on her stomach and eased slightly into the pit at an angle to try to confirm that the shapeless mass below her was not the body of her friend.

The lights in Rama began flashing on and off. Inside the barn, the optical effect was startling. And disorienting. Nicole glanced up to see what was happening and lost her balance. Most of her body slid into the pit. "Francesca," she yelled, pressing her hands against the opposite wall of the pit for support. "Francesca, I need some help," Nicole shouted again.

Nicole waited almost a minute before she concluded that Cosmonaut Sabatini must have already left the barn area. Her arms were tiring rapidly. Only her feet and the very bottoms of her legs were safely resting on the barn floor. Her head was next to one of the pit walls about eighty centimeters below floor level. The remainder of her body was suspended in midair, prevented from falling only by her intense arm pressure against the wall.

The lights continued to flash off and on at short intervals. Nicole lifted her head to see if she could possibly reach the top of the pit with one of her arms, while holding her position secure with the other. It was hopeless. Her head was too deep in the hole. She waited several more seconds, her desperation growing as the fatigue in her arms increased. Finally Nicole made an attempt both to throw her body upward and to grab onto the lip of the pit in one connected motion. She was almost successful. Her arms could not stop her downward momentum when she fell. Her feet followed her body into the hole and she smacked her head against the wall. She tumbled unconscious to the bottom of the pit.

36

IMPACT COURSE

Francesca had also been startled when the lights of Rama had suddenly begun to flash. Her initial impulse had been to run inside, just under the roof of the barn. Once there, she felt slightly more protected. *What's going on now?* she thought as the reflected lights from the adjacent buildings forced her to close her eyes to keep from becoming dizzy.

When she heard Nicole's cry for help, Francesca started to rush over to help her fellow cosmonaut. However, she tripped on one of the spheres and banged her knee as she fell. When she rose, Francesca could see in the strobing light that Nicole's position was very precarious. Only the backs of Nicole's shoes were visible. Francesca stood quite still and waited. Her mind had already raced ahead. She had a nearly perfect image of the pits in her memory, including a fairly accurate assessment of the depth. *If she falls she'll be injured,* she thought, *maybe even killed.* Francesca remembered the smooth walls. *She won't be able to climb out.*

The flashing lights gave an eerie overtone to the scene. As Francesca watched, she saw Nicole's body rise barely out of the pit and her hands scramble for a hold on the lip. In the next flashes of light the shoes changed angle with respect to the pit and then abruptly disappeared. Francesca heard no scream.

If she had not controlled herself, Francesca would have hurried over to the pit and looked into it. *No,* she said to herself, still standing amid the small spheres, *I must not look. If by chance she is still conscious, she might see me. Then I will have no options.*

Already Francesca was thinking about the possibilities offered by Nicole's fall. She was certain, based on their earlier exchange, that Nicole intended to do her utmost to prove that Borzov had ingested a pain-inducing drug on the last day of his life. It might be possible for Nicole even to identify the particular compound and then eventually, since it was not common, to trace its purchase back to Francesca. The scenario was unlikely, even implausible. But it could happen.

Francesca remembered using her special permits to buy the dimethyldexil, along with a batch of other items, at a hospital pharmacy in Copenhagen two years earlier. At the time there had been a suggestion that the drug, in very small doses, could produce mild feelings of euphoria in highly stressed individuals. A single journal article in an obscure Swedish mental health publication the following year had contained the information that sizable doses of dimethyldexil would produce acute pain that simulated an appendicitis.

As Francesca walked rapidly away from the barn in a northerly direction, her agile mind worked through all the possibilities. She was performing her usual risk/reward trade-off. The primary issue she was facing, now that she had left Nicole in the pit, was whether or not to tell the truth about Nicole's fall. *But why did you leave her there?* somebody would ask. *Why didn't you radio us that she had fallen and stand by until help could arrive?*

Because I was confused and frightened and the lights were flashing. And Richard had sounded so very concerned about our leaving. I thought it would be easier for us to all talk together at the helicopter. Was that believable? Barely. But it was easy to keep straight. *So I still have the partial truth option,* Francesca thought as she passed the octahedron near the central plaza. She realized she had walked too far to the east, checked her personal navigator, and then changed her direction. The lights of Rama continued to flash.

And what are my other choices? Wakefield talked with us just outside the barn. He knows where we were. A search party would definitely find her. Unless . . . Francesca thought again about the possibility that Nicole might eventually implicate her in the drugging of General Borzov. The resulting scandal would certainly result in a messy investigation and probably a criminal indictment. In any case, Francesca's reputation would be sullied and her future career as a journalist would be seriously compromised.

With Nicole out of the picture, on the other hand, there was virtually zero probability that anyone would ever learn that Francesca had drugged Borzov. The only person who knew the facts was David Brown, and he had been a co-conspirator. Besides, he had even more to lose than she did.

So the issue, Francesca thought, *is whether or not I can make up a believable story that both reduces the chance Nicole will be found and does not implicate me if she is. That's a very difficult task.*

She was nearing the Cylindrical Sea. Her personal navigator told her that she was only six hundred meters away. *Dammit,* Francesca answered herself after thinking very carefully about her situation, *I don't really have a completely safe option. I will have to choose one or the other. Either way there's a significant risk.*

Francesca stopped moving north and paced back and forth between two skyscrapers. As she was walking, the ground underneath her feet began to tremble. Everything was shaking. She dropped to her knees to steady herself. She heard Janos Tabori's voice very faintly on the radio. "It's all right, everybody, don't be alarmed. It looks as if our vehicle is undergoing a maneuver. That must have been what the warnings were all about. . . . By the way, Nicole, where are you and Francesca? Hiro and Richard are about to take off in the helicopter."

"I'm close to the sea, maybe two minutes away," Francesca answered. "Nicole went back to check on something."

"Roger," Janos replied. "Are you there, Nicole? Do you copy, cosmonaut des Jardins?"

There was silence on the radio.

"As you know, Janos," Francesca interjected, "communications are very spotty from here. Nicole knows where to meet the helicopter. She'll be along quickly, I'm certain." She paused a moment. "Say, where are the others? Is everyone all right?"

"Brown and Heilmann are on the radio with Earth. ISA management will be completely freaked out now. They were already demanding that we leave Rama before this maneuver began."

"We're just boarding the helicopter," Richard Wakefield said. "We'll be there in a few minutes."

It's done. I've made my choice, Francesca said to herself when Richard was finished. She was surprisingly elated. Immediately she began to rehearse her story. "We were near the large octahedron in the central plaza when Nicole spotted an alley off to our right that we had not noticed before. The street leading to the alley was extremely narrow and she remarked that it was probably a region where communications could not penetrate. I was already tired—we had been walking so fast. She told me to go ahead to the helicopter. . . ."

"And you never saw her again?" Richard Wakefield interrupted. Francesca shook her head. Richard was standing on the ice next to her. Beneath them the ice was vibrating as the long maneuver continued. The lights were now on. They had stopped their flashing when the maneuver began.

Pilot Yamanaka was sitting in the cockpit of his helicopter. Richard checked his watch. "It's almost five minutes since we landed here. Something must have happened to her." He glanced around. "Maybe she's coming out somewhere else."

Richard and Francesca climbed into the helicopter and Yamanaka took off. They cruised up and down the island coast, twice circling over the solitary icemobile. "Edge into New York," Wakefield commanded. "Maybe we'll be able to spot her."

From the helicopter it was virtually impossible to see the ground in the city. The 'copter had to fly above the tallest buildings. The streets were very narrow and the shadows played games with the eyes. Once Richard thought he saw something moving between the buildings, but it turned out to be an optical illusion.

"All right, Nicole, all right. Where in the hell are you?"

"Wakefield," Dr. David Brown's sonorous voice sounded in the helicopter, "I want you three to come back to Beta immediately. We need to have a meeting." Richard was surprised to hear that it was Dr. Brown. Janos had been the one monitoring their communication link since they had left Beta.

"What's the hurry, boss?" Wakefield replied. "We still haven't made our scheduled rendezvous with Nicole des Jardins. She should be coming out of New York any minute."

"I'll give you the details when you get here. We have some difficult decisions to make. I'm certain that des Jardins will radio when she reaches the shore."

It did not take them long to cross the frozen sea. Near the Beta campsite, Yamanaka landed the helicopter on the shaking ground and the three cosmonauts descended. The remaining four members of the crew were waiting for them.

"This is one incredibly long maneuver," Richard said with a smile as he approached the others. "I hope the Ramans know what they're doing."

"They probably do," Dr. Brown said somberly. "At least the Earth thinks that they do." He looked carefully at his watch. "According to the navigation section in mission control, we should expect this maneuver to last another nineteen minutes, give or take a few seconds."

"How do they know?" inquired Wakefield. "Have the Ramans landed on Earth and handed out a flight plan while we've been up here exploring?"

Nobody laughed. "If the vehicle stays at this attitude and acceleration rate," Janos said with uncharacteristic seriousness, "then in nineteen more minutes it will be on an impact course."

"Impact with what?" Francesca asked.

Richard Wakefield did some quick mental computations. "With the Earth?" he guessed. Janos nodded.

"Jesus!" Francesca exclaimed.

"Exactly," David Brown said. "This mission has become an Earth security concern. The COG Executive Council is meeting at this very moment to consider all contingencies. We have been told in the strongest possible language that we must leave Rama as soon as the maneuver is completed. We are to take nothing except the crab biot and our personal belongings. We are—"

"What about Takagishi? And des Jardins?" Wakefield asked.

"We will leave the icemobile where it is, along with a rover here at Beta. They are both easy to operate. We will still be in radio contact from the Newton." Dr. Brown stared directly at Richard. "If this spacecraft is really on an Earth impact course," he said dramatically, "our individual lives are no longer very important. The entire course of history is about to be changed."

"But what if the navigation engineers are wrong? What if Rama has just happened to make a maneuver that momentarily intersects an Earth impact trajectory? It could be—"

"Extremely unlikely. You remember that group of short-burst maneuvers at the time of Borzov's death? They changed the orientation of Rama's orbit so that an Earth impact could be achieved with one long maneuver at exactly the right time. The engineers on Earth figured it out thirty-six hours ago. They radioed O'Toole before dawn this morning to expect the maneuver. I didn't want to say anything while everyone was out looking for Takagishi."

"That explains why everyone is so anxious for us to clear out of here," Janos noted.

"Only partially," Dr. Brown continued. "There is clearly a different feeling about Rama and the Ramans down on Earth. ISA management and the world leaders on the COG Executive Council are apparently convinced that Rama is implacably hostile."

He stopped for several seconds, as if he were reassessing his own attitude. "I think they are reacting emotionally myself, but I cannot persuade them differently. I personally see no evidence of hostility, only a disinterest in and disregard for a wildly inferior being. But the televised account of Wilson's death has done its damage. The world's populace cannot be here beside us, cannot grasp the majesty of this place. They can only react viscerally to the horror—"

"If you don't think the Ramans have hostile intentions," Francesca interrupted, "then how do you explain this maneuver? It can't be coincidence. They or it has decided for some reason to head for the Earth. No wonder the people down there are traumatized. Remember, the first Rama never acknowledged its visitors in any way. This is a dramatically different response. The Ramans are telling us they know—"

"Hold it. Hold it," Richard said. "I think we're jumping to conclusions a little too fast. We have twelve more minutes before we should start pushing the panic buttons."

"All right, Cosmonaut Wakefield," Francesca said, now remembering that she was a reporter and activating her video camera, "for the record, what do you think it will mean if this maneuver does culminate in a trajectory that impacts the Earth?"

When Richard finally spoke he was very serious. "People of the Earth," he said dramatically, "if Rama has indeed changed its course to visit our planet, it is not necessarily a hostile act. There is nothing, I repeat nothing, that any of us have seen or heard that indicates the species that created this space vehicle wishes us any harm. Certainly Cosmonaut Wilson's death was disturbing, but it was probably an isolated response from a specific set of robots rather than a part of a sinister plan.

"I see this magnificent spacecraft as a single machine, almost organic in its complexity. It is extraordinarily intelligent and programmed for long-term survival. It is neither hostile nor friendly. It could easily have been designed to track any incoming satellites and compute where the visiting spacecraft must have originated. Rama's orbit change to fly in the vicinity of the Earth might therefore be nothing more than its standard response to an encounter initiated by another spacefaring species. It may simply be coming to find out more about us."

"Very good," Janos Tabori said with a grin. "That was borderline philosophical."

Wakefield laughed nervously.

"Cosmonaut Turgenyev," Francesca said as she changed the direction of the camera, "do you agree with your colleague? Right after General Borzov died, you openly expressed some concern that perhaps some 'higher force,' meaning the Ramans, might have had a hand in his death. What are your feelings now?"

The normally taciturn Soviet pilot stared directly into

the camera with her sad eyes. *"Da,"* she said, "I think Cosmonaut Wakefield is a very brilliant engineer. But he has not answered the difficult questions. Why did Rama maneuver during General Borzov's operation? Why did the biots cut Wilson to pieces? Where is Professor Takagishi?"

Irina Turgenyev paused a moment to control her emotions. "We will not find Nicole des Jardins. Rama may be only a machine, but we cosmonauts have already seen how dangerous it can be. If it is heading for the Earth, I fear for my family, my friends, for all humanity. There is no way to predict what it might do. And we would be powerless to stop it."

Several minutes later Francesca Sabatini carried her automatic video equipment out beside the frozen sea for one final sequence. She carefully checked the time before switching on the camera at precisely fifteen seconds before the maneuver was expected to end. "The picture you are seeing is jumping up and down," she said in her best journalistic voice, "because the ground underneath us here on Rama has been shaking continuously since this maneuver started forty-seven minutes ago. According to the navigation engineers, the maneuver will stop in the next few seconds if Rama has changed course to impact the Earth. Their calculations are, of course, based on assumptions about Rama's intentions—"

Francesca stopped in midsentence and took a deep breath. "The ground is no longer shaking. The maneuver is over. Rama is now on an Earth impact trajectory."

37

MAROONED

When Nicole awakened the first time she was groggy and had great difficulty holding any idea fixed in her mind. Her head hurt and she could feel sharp pains in her back and legs. She did not know what had happened to her. She was barely able to find her water flask and take a drink. *I must have a concussion*, she thought as she fell back asleep.

It was dark when Nicole woke up again. But her mind was no longer in a fog. She knew where she was. She remembered looking for Takagishi and sliding into the pit. Nicole also remembered calling for Francesca and the painful, terrible fall. She immediately took her communicator from the belt of her flight suit.

"Hello there, Newton team," she said as she stood up slowly. "This is cosmonaut des Jardins checking in. I've been, well, indisposed might be a good word. I fell down into a hole and knocked myself out. Sabatini knows where I am. . . ."

Nicole broke off her monologue and waited. There was no response from her receiver. She turned up the gain but only succeeded in picking up some strange static. *It's dark already,* she thought, *and it had only been light for two hours at most.* . . . Nicole knew that the periods of light inside Rama had been lasting about thirty hours. Had she been unconscious that long? Or had Rama thrown them another curveball? She looked at her wristwatch, which showed time elapsed since the start of the second sortie, and did a quick calculation. *I have been down here for thirty-two hours. Why has nobody come?*

Nicole thought back to the last minutes before she fell. They had talked to Wakefield, and then she had dashed in to check the pits. Richard always did a navigation fix when they were in two-way lock and Francesca knew exactly . . .

Could something have happened to the entire crew? But if not, why had nobody discovered her? Nicole smiled to herself as she fought the onset of panic. *Of course,* she reasoned, *they found me, but I was unconscious, so they decided* . . . Another voice in her head told her that her thought pattern didn't make sense. Under any circumstances, she would have been retrieved from the pit if they had found her.

She shuddered involuntarily as she feared, for a brief moment, that perhaps she would *never* be found. Nicole forced her mind to change subjects and began an assessment of the physical damage she had suffered during the fall. She ran her fingers carefully across all portions of her skull. There were several bumps, including a large one on the very back of her head. *That must have been responsible for the concussion,* she surmised. But there were no skull fractures and what little bleeding there had been had stopped hours ago.

She checked her arms and legs, then her back. There were bruises everywhere, but miraculously no bones were broken. The occasional sharp pain just below her neck suggested that she had either crushed part of a vertebra or pinched some nerves. Other than that, she would heal. The discovery that her body had survived more or less intact temporarily buoyed her spirits.

Nicole next surveyed her new domain. She had fallen in the middle of a deep but narrow rectangular pit. It was six paces from end to end and one and a half paces across. Using her flashlight and outstretched arm, she estimated the depth of the hole at eight and a half meters.

The pit was empty except for a jumbled collection of small metallic pieces, ranging in length from five to fifteen centimeters, that were stacked over at one end of the hole. Nicole examined them carefully under the beam from her flashlight. There were over a hundred altogether and maybe a dozen different individual types. Some were long and straight, others curved, a few jointed—they reminded Nicole of industrial trash from a modern steel mill.

The walls of the pit were absolutely straight. The wall material felt like a metal/rock hybrid to Nicole. It was cold, very cold. There were no anomalies, no wrinkles that might have been used as footholds, nothing that would encourage her to believe she could climb out. She tried to chip or scrape the wall surface using her portable medical tools. She was unable to make any mark.

Discouraged by the perfect construction of the pit walls, Nicole walked back to the metal pile to see if there was any way she could put together a ladder or scaffold, some kind of support that would elevate her to the point where she could climb out using her own strength. It was not encouraging. The metal pieces were small and thin. A quick mental calculation told her there was not enough mass to support her weight.

Nicole became even more discouraged when she ate a small snack. She remembered that she had brought very little food and water with her because she had wanted to carry extra medical supplies for Takagishi. Even if she rationed it carefully, her water would only last a day and her food no more than thirty-six hours.

She shone her flashlight directly upward. The beam bounced off the roof of the barn. Thinking about the barn reminded her again of the events preceding her fall. Nicole remembered the increased amplitude of the emergency signal once she exited the building. *Great*, she thought despondently. *The interior of this fantastic barn is probably a radio blackout zone. No wonder nobody heard me.*

She slept because there was nothing else to do. Eight hours later Nicole woke up with a start from a frightening dream. She had been sitting with her father and daughter in a lovely provincial restaurant in France. It was a magnificent spring day; Nicole could see flowers in the garden adjoining the restaurant. When the waiter had come, he had placed a plate of escargots smothered in herbs and butter in front of Genevieve. Pierre received a mountainous serving of chicken cooked in a mushroom and wine sauce. The waiter had smiled and left. Slowly it had dawned on Nicole that there was nothing for *her*. . . .

She had never dealt with real hunger before. Even during the Poro, after the lion cubs took her food, Nicole had not been seriously hungry. She had told herself before she slept that she would carefully ration her remaining food, but that was before the hunger pangs had become overpowering. Now Nicole tore into her food packets with trembling hands and just barely stopped herself from eating all the food that was left. She wrapped the paltry remainder, put it back into one of her pockets, and buried her face in her hands. Nicole allowed herself to cry for the first time since she had fallen.

She also allowed herself to acknowledge that starving to death would be a terrible way to die. Nicole tried to imagine what it would feel like to weaken from hunger and then ultimately to perish. Would it be a gradual process, each successive stage more horrible than the one before? "Then let it come soon," Nicole said out loud, momentarily abandoning all hope. Her digital watch was glowing in the dark, counting off the last precious seconds of her life. *How much longer will it be before I die?* she wondered.

Several hours passed. Nicole grew weaker and more despondent. She sat with her head bowed in the cold corner of the pit. Just as she was about to give up completely and accept her death, however, from inside her there came a different voice, an assertive, optimistic voice that refused to let her quit. It told her that *any* time of being alive was precious and wonderful, that simply being conscious at all, *ever*, was an overwhelming miracle of nature. Nicole took a slow, deep breath and opened her eyes. *If I'm to die here*, she said to herself, *then at least let me do it with élan.* She resolved that she would spend whatever time remained concentrating on the outstanding moments of her thirty-six years.

Nicole still retained a tiny hope of being rescued. But she had always been a practical woman, and logic told her that what was left of her life was probably measured in hours. During her unhurried trip into her treasured memories, Nicole wept several times, without inhibition, tears of joy at the past recaptured, bittersweet tears because she knew, as she relived each episode, that it was probably her last visit to that particular portion of her memory.

There was no pattern to her wanderings through the life that she had lived. She did not categorize, measure, or compare her experiences. Nicole simply lived them again as they came to her, each old event transformed and enriched by her heightened awareness.

Her mother occupied a special place in her memory. Because she had died when Nicole was only ten, her mother had retained all the attributes of a queen or goddess. Anawi Tiasso had indeed been beautiful and regal, a jet-black African woman of uncommon stature. All Nicole's images of her were bathed in soft, glowing light.

She remembered her mother in the living room of their home in Chilly-Mazarin, gesturing to Nicole to come sit upon her lap. Anawi read a book to her daughter every night before bedtime. Most of the stories were fairy tales about princes and castles and beautiful, happy people who overcame every obstacle. Her mother's voice was soft and mellow. She would sing lullabies to Nicole as the little girl's eyes grew heavier and heavier.

The Sundays of her childhood were special days. In the spring they would go to the park and play on the wide fields of grass. Her mother would teach Nicole how to run. The little girl had never seen anything as beautiful as her mother, who had been an international class sprinter as a young woman, racing gracefully across the meadow.

Of course Nicole remembered vividly all the details of her trip with Anawi to the Ivory Coast for the Poro. It was her mother who had held her during the nights in Nidougou before the ceremony. During those long, frightening nights, the little girl Nicole had struggled with all her fears. And each day, calmly and patiently, her mother had answered all her questions and had reminded her that many, many other girls had passed through the transitional rite without undue difficulty.

Nicole's fondest memory from that trip was set in the hotel room in Abidjan, the night before she and Anawi returned to Paris. She and her mother had discussed the Poro only slightly during the thirty hours since Nicole and the other girls had finished the ceremonies. Anawi had not yet offered any praise. Omeh and the village elders had told Nicole that she had been exceptional, but to a seven-year-old girl no appraisal is as important as the one from her mother. Nicole had summoned her courage just before dinner.

"Did I do all right, Mama?" the little girl had said tentatively. "At the Poro, I mean?"

Anawi had burst into tears. "Did you do all right? Did you do all right?" She had wrapped her long sinuous arms around her daughter and picked her up off the floor. "Oh, darling," her mother had said as she had held Nicole high above her head. "I'm so proud of you that I could split." Nicole had jumped into her mother's arms and they had hugged and laughed and cried for fifteen minutes.

Nicole lay on her back in the bottom of the pit, the tears from her memories rolling sideways across her face and down into her ears. For almost an hour she had been thinking about her daughter, starting with her birth and then going through each of the major events of Genevieve's life. Nicole was recalling the vacation trip to America that they had taken together, three years earlier when Genevieve had been eleven. How very close they had been on that trip, especially on the day they had hiked down the South Kaibab trail into the Grand Canyon.

Nicole and Genevieve had stopped at each of the markers along the trail, studying the imprint of two billion years of time on the surface of the planet Earth. They had lunched on a promontory overlooking the desert desiccation of the Tonto plateau. That night, mother and daughter had spread their sleeping mats, side by side, right next to the mighty Colorado River. They had talked and shared dreams and held hands throughout the night.

I would not have taken that trip, Nicole mused, beginning to think about her father, *if it hadn't been for you. You were the one who knew it was the right time to go.* Nicole's father was the cornerstone of her life. Pierre des Jardins was her friend, confessor, intellectual companion, and most ardent supporter. He had been there when she was born and at every significant moment of her life. It was he whom she missed the most as she lay in the bottom of the pit inside Rama. It was he with whom she would have chosen to have had her final conversation.

There was no single memory of her father that jumped out at her, that demanded renewal above all the rest. Nicole's mental montage of Pierre framed all the events of her own life. Not all of them were happy. She remembered clearly, for example, the two of them in the savanna not far from Nidougou, silently holding hands as they both wept quietly while the funeral pyre for Anawi burned into the African night. She could also still feel his arms around her as she sobbed without cease following her failure, at the age of fifteen, to win the nationwide Joan of Arc competition.

They had lived together at Beauvois, an unlikely pair, from a year after the death of her mother until Nicole had finished her third year of studies at the University of Tours. It had been an idyllic existence. Nicole roamed through the woods around their villa after she bicycled home from school. Pierre wrote his novels in the study. In the evening Marguerite rang the bell and called them both to dinner before the lady climbed on her own bicycle, her day's work complete, and returned to her husband and children in Luynes.

During the summers Nicole traveled with her father throughout Europe, visiting the medieval towns and castles that were the primary venues of his historical novels. Nicole knew more about Eleanor of Aquitaine and her husband Henry Plantagenet than she knew about the active political leaders of France and Western Europe. When Pierre won the Mary Renault Prize for historical fiction in 2181, she went with him to Paris to receive the award. Nicole sat on the first row in the large auditorium, dressed in the tailored white skirt and blouse that Pierre had helped her choose, and listened to the speaker extol her father's virtues.

Nicole could still recite parts of her father's acceptance speech from memory. "I have often been asked," her father had said near the end of his delivery, "if I have accumulated any wisdom that I would like to share with future generations." He had then looked directly at her in the audience. "To my precious daughter Nicole, and all the young people of the world, I offer one simple insight. In my life I have found two things of priceless worth—learning and loving. Nothing else—not fame, not power, not achievement for its own sake—can possibly have the same lasting value. For when your life is over, if you can say 'I have learned' and 'I have loved,' you will also be able to say 'I have been happy.' "

I have been happy, Nicole said as another group of tears ran down the side of her face, *and mostly because of you. You never disappointed me. Not even in my most difficult moment.* Her memory turned, as she knew it would, to the summer of 2184, when her life had accelerated at such a fantastic pace that she had lost control of its direction. In one six-week period Nicole won an Olympic gold medal, conducted a short but torrid affair with the Prince of Wales, and returned to France to tell her father that she was pregnant.

Nicole could remember the key events from that period as if they had happened only yesterday. No emotion in her life had ever quite matched the joy and exhilaration that she had felt when she was standing on the victory stand in Los Angeles, the gold medal around her neck and the cheers of a hundred thousand people echoing in her ears. It was her moment. For almost a week she was the darling of the world media. She was on the front page of every newspaper, highlighted in every major broadcast on sports.

After her final interview in the television studio adjoining the Olympic stadium, a young Englishman with an engaging smile had introduced himself as Darren Higgins and handed her a card. Inside was a handwritten invitation to dinner from none other than the Prince of Wales, the man who would become Henry XI of Great Britain.

The dinner was magical, Nicole recalled, her desperate situation in Rama temporarily forgotten. *He was charming. The next two days were absolutely wonderful.* But thirty-nine hours later, when she awakened in Henry's bedroom suite in Westwood, her fairy tale was suddenly over. Her prince who had been so attentive and affectionate was now frowning and fretful. As the inexperienced Nicole tried unsuccessfully to understand what had gone wrong, it slowly dawned on her that her flight of fantasy was over. *I was just a conquest,* she remembered, *the celebrity of the moment. I was unsuitable for any permanent relationship.*

Nicole would never forget the last words the prince had said to her in Los Angeles. He had been circling her while she was hurriedly packing. He could not understand why she was so distraught. Nicole had not replied to any of his questions and had resisted his attempts to embrace her. "What did you expect?" he had asked finally, his frustration obvious. "That we would ride off into the sunset and live happily ever after? Come on, Nicole, this is the real world. You must know that the English people would never accept a half-black woman as their queen."

Nicole had escaped before Henry saw her tears. *And so, my darling Genevieve,* Nicole said to herself in the bottom of the pit in Rama, *I left Los Angeles with two new treasures. I had a gold medal and a wonderful baby girl within my body.* Her thoughts quickly skipped across the following weeks of anxiety to the desperate, lonely moment when she finally summoned her courage to talk to her father.

"I . . . I don't know what to do," Nicole had said tentatively to Pierre on that September morning in the living room of their villa at Beauvois. "I know that I have disappointed you terribly—I have disappointed myself—but I want to ask you if it's all right. I mean, if I want to, Papa, can I stay here and try—"

"Of course, Nicole," her father had interrupted her. He was softly crying. It was the only time Nicole had seen him cry since the death of her mother. "We'll do whatever's right," he had said as he pulled her into his embrace.

I was so lucky, Nicole thought. *He was so accepting. He never faulted me. He never asked anything. When I told him that Henry was the father and that I never wanted anyone else to know, least of all Henry or the child, he promised he would keep my secret. And he has.*

The lights came on suddenly and Nicole stood up to survey her prison under the new conditions. Only the center of the pit was fully lighted; both the ends were in shadow. Considering her situation, she was feeling amazingly cheerful and upbeat.

She looked up to the roof of the barn and through it to the nondescript sky of Rama. Nicole thought about her last few hours and had a sudden impulse. She had not said a prayer in over twenty years but she dropped down on her knees in the full light in the middle of the pit. *Dear God*, she said, *I know it's a little late, but thank you for my father, my mother, and my daughter. And all the wonders of life.* Nicole glanced up at the ceiling. She was smiling and had a twinkle in her eye. *And right now, dear God, I could use a little help.*

38

VISITORS

The tiny robot strode out into the light and unsheathed his sword. The English army had arrived at Harfleur.

"Once more into the breach, dear friends, once more,
Or close the wall up with our English dead.
In peace there's nothing so becomes a man
As modest stillness and humility:
But when the blast of war blows in our ears,
Then imitate the action of the tiger . . ."

Henry V, new king of England, continued to exhort his imaginary soldiers. Nicole smiled as she listened. She had spent the better part of an hour following Wakefield's Prince Hal from the debauchery of his youth, onto the battlefields fighting against Hotspur and the other rebels, and thence to the throne of England. Nicole had only once read the three Henry plays, and that had been years before, but she was well aware of the historical period because of her lifelong fascination with Joan of Arc.

"Shakespeare made you into something you never were," she said out loud to the little robot as she bent beside it to insert Richard's baton in the OFF slot. "You were a warrior, to be sure, nobody would argue with that. But you were also a cold and heartless conqueror. You made Normandy bleed under your powerful yoke. You almost crushed the life out of France."

Nicole laughed nervously at herself. *Here I am,* she thought, *talking to a senseless ceramic prince twenty centimeters high.* She remembered her feelings of hopelessness an hour earlier after she had tried one more time to figure out a way to escape. The fact that her time was running out had been reinforced when she had drunk the next to last swig of water. *Oh well,* she mused, turning back to Prince Hal, *at least this is better than feeling sorry for myself.*

"And what else can you do, my little prince?" Nicole said. "What happens if I insert this pin in the slot marked c?"

The robot activated, walked a few steps, and finally approached her left foot. After a long silence Prince Hal spoke, not in the rich actor's voice he had used during his earlier recitals, but instead in Wakefield's British twang. "C stands for converse, my friend, and I have a considerable repertoire. But I don't speak until you say something first."

Nicole laughed. "All right, Prince Hal," she said after a moment's thought, "tell me about Joan of Arc."

The robot hesitated and then frowned. "She was a witch, dear lady, burned at the stake in Rouen a decade after my death. During my reign the north of France had been subjugated by my armies. The French witch, claiming she was sent by God—"

Nicole stopped listening and jerked her head up as a shadow crossed over them. She thought she saw something flying above the roof of the barn. Her heart pounded furiously. "Here. I'm here," she shouted at the top of her voice. Prince Hal droned on in the background about how Joan of Arc's success had sadly resulted in the return of his conquests to the realm of France. "So English. So typically English," Nicole said as she once again inserted the baton in Prince Hal's OFF button.

Moments later the shadow was large and completely darkened the bottom of the pit. Nicole looked up and her heart caught in her throat. Hovering over the pit, its wings spread and flapping, was a gigantic birdlike creature. Nicole shrunk back and screamed involuntarily. The creature stuck its neck into the pit and uttered a set of noises. The sounds were harsh yet slightly musical. Nicole was paralyzed. The thing repeated almost the same set of noises and then tried, without success because its wings were too large, to lower itself slowly into the narrow pit.

During this brief period Nicole, her traumatic terror

giving way to normal fear, studied the great flying alien. Its face, except for two soft eyes that were a deep blue surrounded by a brown ring, reminded her of the pterodactyls that she had seen in the French museum of natural history. The beak was quite long and hooked. The mouth was toothless and the two talons, bilaterally symmetrical about the main body, each had four sharp digits.

Nicole would have guessed the avian's mass at about a hundred kilograms. Its body, except for the face and beak, the ends of the wings, and the talons, was covered by a thick black material that resembled velvet. When it was clear to the avian that it would not be able to fly down to the bottom of the pit, it sounded two sharp notes, pulled itself up, and disappeared.

Nicole did not move at all during the first minute after the creature departed. Then she sat down and tried to collect her thoughts. The adrenaline from her fright was still coursing through her body. She tried to think rationally about what she had seen. Her first idea was that the thing was a biot, like all the rest of the mobile creatures that had been seen previously in Rama. *If that's a biot,* she said to herself, *then it's extremely advanced.* She pictured the other biots she had seen, both the crabs from the Southern Hemicylinder and the wide variety of weird creations filmed by the first Raman expedition. Nicole could not convince herself that the avian was a biot. There was something about the eyes . . .

She heard wings flapping in the distance and her body tensed. Nicole cowered in the shadowy corner just as the light in the pit was again obscured by a huge hovering body. Actually it was two bodies. The first avian had returned with a companion, the second one considerably the larger. The new bird stuck its neck down and stared at Nicole with its blue eyes while it hovered over the pit. It made a sound, louder and less musical than the other, and then craned its neck around to look at its companion. While the two avians jabbered back and forth, Nicole noticed that this one was covered with a polished surface, like linoleum, but in all other respects except size was identical to her first visitor. At length the new bird ascended and the strange pair landed on the side of the pit, still jabbering. They observed Nicole quietly for a minute or two. Then, after a brief conversation, they were gone.

Nicole was exhausted after her bout with fear. Within minutes after her flying visitors departed, she was curled up and asleep in the corner of the pit. She slept soundly for several hours. She was awakened by a loud noise, a crack that resounded through the barn like the report of a gun. She woke up quickly, but heard no more unexplained sounds. Her body reminded her that she was hungry and thirsty. She pulled out what was left of her food. *Should I make two tiny meals out of this?* she asked herself wearily, *or should I eat it all now and accept whatever comes?*

With a deep sigh, Nicole decided to finish off her food and water with one last meal. She was thinking that the two combined might give her enough sustenance that she could temporarily forget about food. She was wrong. While Nicole was drinking the last sip of water from her water flask, her mind was bombarded with images of the bottled spring water that she and her family always had on the table at Beauvois.

There was another loud crack in the distance after Nicole had finished her meal. She stopped to listen, but again there was silence. Her thoughts were dominated by escape ideas, all of them using the avians in some way to help her out of the pit. She was angry with herself for not having tried to communicate with them while she had the chance. Nicole laughed to herself. *Of course, they might have decided to eat me. But who's to say starving to death is to be preferred over being eaten?*

Nicole was certain that the avians would come back. Perhaps her certainty was reinforced by the hopelessness of her situation, but nevertheless she started making plans for what she would do when they did return. *Hello,* she imagined herself saying. She would stand up with an outstretched palm and walk forcefully to the center of the pit, right under the hovering creature. Nicole would then use a special set of gestures to communicate her plight: Pointing repeatedly first at herself and then the pit would indicate that she couldn't escape; waving at both the avians and the barn roof would ask them for their help.

Two loud sharp noises brought Nicole back to reality. After a brief pause she heard still another crack. Nicole searched through the "Environments" chapter in her computerized *Atlas of Rama* and then laughed at herself for not having recognized immediately what was occurring. The loud reports were the sound of the ice breaking up as the Cylindrical Sea melted from the bottom. Rama was still inside the orbit of Venus (although the last midcourse maneuver had placed it onto a trajectory whose distance from the sun was now increasing again), and the solar input had finally brought the temperature inside Rama to above the freezing point of water.

The *Atlas* warned of fierce windstorms, hurricanes that would be created by the atmospheric thermal instabilities following the melting of the sea. Nicole walked to the center of the pit. "Come on, you birds, or whatever you are," she yelled. "Come get me now and let me have a chance to escape."

But the avians did not come back. Nicole sat awake in the corner for ten hours, slowly growing weaker as the frequency of the loud reports reached a peak and then gradually diminished. The wind began to blow. At first it was just a breeze, but it became a gale by the time the cracks from the ice breaking up had stopped. Nicole was completely discouraged. When she fell asleep again she told herself that she would probably not be awake more than one or two more times.

The winds pummeled New York as the hurricane raged for hours. Nicole huddled lifelessly in a corner. She listened to the howling wind and remembered sitting in a ski chalet during a blizzard in Colorado. She tried to remember the pleasures of skiing but she could not. Her hunger and fatigue had weakened her imagination as well. Nicole sat very still, her mind devoid of thoughts except for wondering occasionally what it would feel like to die.

*   *   *

She couldn't remember falling asleep, but then she couldn't remember waking up either. She was very weak. Her mind was telling her that something had blown into her hole. It was dark again. Nicole crawled from her end of the pit toward the end with the jumbled metal. She did not switch on her flashlight. She bumped into something and started, then she felt it with her hands. The object was big, as large as a basketball. It had a smooth exterior and was oval in shape.

Nicole became more alert. She found her flashlight in her flight suit and illuminated the object. It was off-white and shaped like an egg. She examined it thoroughly. When she pressed on it hard, it gave some under the pressure. *Can I eat it?* her mind asked, her hunger so severe that she had no worries about what it might do to her.

Nicole pulled out her knife and was able to cut it with difficulty. She feverishly chopped off a chunk and forced it into her mouth. It was tasteless. Nicole spat it out and started to cry. She kicked the object angrily and it rolled over. She thought she heard something. Nicole reached out and pushed it hard, rolling it over again. *Yes*, she said to herself, *yes. That was a sloshing sound.*

It was slow cutting through the outside with her knife. After several minutes Nicole retrieved her medical equipment and started working on the object with her power scalpel. Whatever it was, the object was made of three separate and distinct layers. The covering was tough, like the skin of a football, and relatively difficult to manipulate. The second layer was a soft, moist, royal blue compound the consistency of a melon. Inside, in the center, were several quarts of a greenish liquid. Trembling with anticipation, Nicole stuck a cupped hand into the incision and pulled the liquid to her lips. It had an odd, medicinal taste, but it was refreshing. She drank two hurried swallows and then her years of medical training interceded.

Fighting against her desire to drink more, Nicole inserted the probe from her mass spectrometer into the liquid to analyze its chemical constituents. She was in

such a hurry that she made a mistake with the first specimen and had to repeat the process. When the results of
the analysis were displayed on the tiny modular monitor
that could be affixed to any of her instruments, Nicole
began to weep with joy. The liquid would not poison her.
On the contrary, it was rich in proteins and minerals in
the kinds of chemical combinations that the body could
process.

"All right, all right!" Nicole shouted out loud. She stood
up quickly and nearly fainted. More cautious now, she sat
back down on her knees and began the feast of her life.
She drank the liquid and ate the moist meat until she was
absolutely stuffed. Then she fell into a deep, satisfied
sleep.

Nicole's primary concern when she awakened was to
determine the quantity of "manna melon," as she called it,
that was available to her. She had been a glutton, and
knew it, but that was in the past. What she needed to do
now was to husband the manna melon until she could
somehow enlist the aid of the avians.

Nicole measured the melon carefully. Its gross weight
had originally been almost ten kilograms, but only a little
over eight remained. Her approximate assessment indicated that the inedible outer portion comprised roughly
two kilograms, leaving her six kilograms of nourishment
split roughly evenly between the liquid and the royal blue
meat. *Let's see*, she was thinking, *three liquid kilograms
makes* . . .

Nicole's thought processes were interrupted as the
lights came on again. *Yessirree*, she said to herself,
checking her wristwatch, *right on time, with the same
secular drift*. She looked up from her watch and saw the
egg-shaped object for the first time in the full light.
Her recognition was immediate. *Oh my God,* Nicole
thought as she walked over and traced with her fingers
the brown lines wriggling on the creamy-white surface.
I had almost forgotten. She reached into her flight suit
and pulled out the polished stone that Omeh had given
her on New Year's Eve in Rome. She stared at it and

then glanced over at the oval object in the pit. *Oh my God,* Nicole repeated.

She replaced the stone in her pocket and removed the small green vial. "Ronata will know the time to drink," she heard her great-grandfather say again. Nicole sat down in the corner and emptied the vial in one gulp.

39

WATERS OF WISDOM

Immediately Nicole's vision began to blur. She closed her eyes for a second. When she opened them again she was blinded by a riot of bright colors, streaming by her in geometrical patterns as if she were moving very fast. In the center of her sight, way off in the distance, a black dot emerged from the background amid a brilliant set of alternating red and yellow forms. Nicole concentrated on the dot as it continued to grow. It rushed toward her and expanded to fill her vision. She saw a man, an old black man, running across the African savanna on a perfect starry night. Nicole clearly saw his face as he turned to climb a mountain of rocks. The man looked like Omeh but also, somewhat strangely, like her mother.

He raced up the rock mountain with amazing agility. At the top he stood in silhouette, his arms outspread, and stared into the sky at the crescent moon on the horizon. Nicole heard the sound of a firing rocket engine and turned to her left. She watched a small spacecraft descend to the surface of the moon. Two men in space suits started down a ladder. She heard Neil Armstrong say, "That's one small step for man, one giant leap for mankind."

Buzz Aldrin joined Armstrong on the lunar surface and they both pointed off to their right. They were staring at an old black man standing on a nearby lunar scarp. He smiled. His teeth were very white.

His face loomed ever larger in Nicole's vision as the lunar landscape behind him began to fade. He started to chant slowly, in Senoufo, but at first Nicole could not comprehend what he was saying. All of a sudden she realized that he was talking to *her* and that she could understand every word. "I am one of your ancestors from long ago," he said. "As a boy I went out to meditate the night that people landed on the moon. Because I was thirsty, I drank deeply the waters from the Lake of Wisdom. I flew first to the moon, where I talked with the astronauts, and then to other worlds. I met The Great Ones. They told me you would come to bring the story of Minowe to the stars."

As Nicole watched, the old man's head began to grow. His teeth became vicious, long, his eyes yellow. He transformed into a tiger and leapt for her throat. Nicole screamed as she felt the teeth upon her neck. She prepared to die. But the tiger became limp, an arrow was buried deep in its side. Nicole heard a noise and looked up. Her mother, wearing a magnificent flowing red robe and carrying a golden bow, was running gracefully toward a gilded chariot parked in the middle of the air. "Mother . . . wait," Nicole shouted.

The figure turned. "You were seduced," her mother said. "You must be more careful. Only three times can I save you. Beware of what you cannot see but know is there." Anawi climbed into the chariot and took the reins. "You must not die. I love you, Nicole." The winged red horses arched higher and higher until Nicole could no longer see them.

The color pattern returned to her vision. Nicole heard music now, first far off in the distance, then much closer. It was synthetic, like the sound of crystal bells. Beautiful, haunting, ethereal. There was loud applause. Nicole was sitting in the front row at a concert with her father. On the stage an Oriental man with hair down to the floor, his eyes fixed in a gaze of rapture, stood next to three odd-shaped instruments. The sound was all around her. It made her want to cry.

"Come on," her father said. "We must go." As Nicole was watching her father turned into a sparrow. He smiled at her. She flapped her own sparrow wings and they were airborne together, leaving the concert behind. The music faded. The air rushed by them. Nicole could see the lovely Loire Valley and a glimpse of their villa at Beauvois. She was content to be going home. But her sparrow father descended instead at Chinon, farther down the Loire. The two sparrows landed in a tree on the castle grounds.

Beneath them, standing in the crisp December air, Henry Plantagenet and Eleanor of Aquitaine were arguing about the succession to the throne of England. Eleanor walked over under the tree and noticed the sparrows. "Why hello, Nicole," she said, "I didn't know you were there." Queen Eleanor reached up and stroked the sparrow's underbelly. Nicole thrilled to the softness of her touch. "Remember, Nicole," she said, "destiny is more important than love of any kind. You can endure anything if you are certain of your destiny."

Nicole smelled fire and sensed they were needed somewhere else. She and her father ascended, turning north toward Normandy. The fire smell grew stronger. They heard a cry for help and urgently flapped their wings.

In Rouen a plain girl with lights in her eyes looked up at them as they approached. The fire below had reached her feet, the first smell of burning flesh was in the air. The girl lowered her eyes in prayer as a makeshift cross was held above her head by a priest. "Blessed Jesus," she said, tears running down her cheeks.

"We'll save you, Joan," Nicole shouted as she and her father dropped into the crowded square. Joan embraced them as they untied her from the stake. The fire exploded around them and everything went black. In the next instant Nicole was flying again, but this time as a great white heron. She was alone, inside Rama, flying high over the city of New York. She banked to avoid one of the avians, who regarded her with shock.

Nicole could see everything in New York in incredible detail. It was as if she had multispectral eyes with a wide range of lenses. She could spot movement in four different places. Close to the barn, a centipede biot was trudging slowly toward the south end of the building. From the vicinity of each of the three central plazas, heat was emanating from underground sources, causing colored patterns in her infrared vision. Nicole circled down toward the barn and landed safely in her pit.

40

ALIEN INVITATION

I must be prepared for rescue, Nicole said to herself. She had finished filling her flask with the greenish liquid from the center of the manna melon. After carefully sectioning the moist melon flesh and putting the pieces in her old food container packets, Nicole sat back down in her usual corner.

Whew! she thought, returning to the wild mental excursion she had taken after drinking the contents of the vial. *What in the world was that all about?* Nicole recalled her vision during the Poro, when she was still a child, and the brief conversation about it that she had had with Omeh three years later when Nicole had returned to Nidougou for the funeral of her mother.

"Where did Ronata go?" Omeh had asked one evening when the old man and the girl had been alone together.

She had known immediately what he was asking. "I became a big white bird," she had answered. "I flew beyond the Moon and Sun to the great void."

"Ah," he had said, "Omeh thought so."

And why didn't you ask him then what had happened to you? the scientist in the adult Nicole asked her former ten-year-old self. *Then maybe some of this would make sense.* But somehow Nicole knew that the vision was beyond analysis, that it existed in a realm as yet unfathomed by the deductive processes that made science so powerful. She thought instead about her mother, about how beautiful she had been in her long flowing red robes. Anawi had saved her from the tiger. *Thank you, Mother*, Nicole thought. She wished that she had talked longer with her.

It was a weird sound, like dozens of unshod baby feet on a linoleum floor, and it was definitely coming in her direction. Nicole didn't have much time to wonder. Seconds later the head and antennae of a centipede biot appeared at the edge of her pit and, without slowing down in any way, proceeded directly down the wall at the opposite end.

Altogether the biot was four meters long. It clambered down the wall without difficulty, placing each of its sixty legs directly against the smooth surface and holding on by some kind of suction. Nicole put on her backpack and watched for her opportunity. She was not *that* surprised by the appearance of the biot. After what she had seen in her vision, she was certain that she was going to be rescued by some means.

The centipede biot consisted of fifteen attached, jointed segments, each with four legs, and an insectlike head with a bizarre array of sensors, two of which were long and thin and resembled antennae. The jumbled pile of metal at the other end of the pit was apparently its spare parts. While Nicole was watching, the biot replaced three of its legs, the carapace for one of its segments, and two knobby protuberances on the side of its head. The entire process took no more than five minutes. When it was finished, the biot started again up the wall.

Nicole jumped on the centipede biot's back when three-fourths of its body was heading upward. The sudden extra weight was too much. The biot lost its grasp and fell, along with Nicole, back into the pit. Moments later it tried again to scale the wall. This time Nicole waited until the entire length of the centipede was heading up the wall, hoping that the strength of the extra segments would make the difference. It was to no avail. The biot and Nicole collapsed into a heap.

One of its front legs had been severely injured during the second fall, so the biot made the necessary repairs before trying to ascend the wall a third time. Nicole, meanwhile, pulled all her strongest suture material out of her medical pack and tied one end of a long octuple thickness around the three back sections of the biot. In the other end of the suture thread she made a loop. After she first put on gloves to protect her hands and then fashioned a waistband to keep the thread from cutting, Nicole tied the loop around her waist.

This could be a disaster, Nicole realized as she imagined all the possible outcomes of her scheme. *If the thread does not hold, I could fall. The second time I might not be so lucky.*

The centipede inched its way up the wall as before. Several small steps after it was completely elongated, the biot felt Nicole's weight from below. This time, however, it did not fall. The struggling biot managed to continue slowly on its upward path. Nicole kept her body perpendicular to the surface, as if she were rock climbing, and held onto the suture thread with both her hands.

Nicole was about forty centimeters behind the last segment of the biot as they scaled the wall. When the head of the centipede reached the top of the pit, Nicole was almost halfway out. Her slow and steady climb continued as, segment after segment, a portion of the biot left the pit above her. A few minutes later, however, her progress slowed markedly, stopping altogether when the number of centipede segments remaining on the wall dropped to four. Nicole could almost touch the rear segment of the centipede if she stretched her arms above her. Only about one meter's length of the biot was still on the wall, but nevertheless it was apparently stuck. Nicole was putting too much strain on the joints attaching the rear segments.

Grim scenarios ran through Nicole's mind as she dangled more than six meters above the floor of the pit. *This is great,* she thought sarcastically, as she pulled tightly on the suture line and placed her feet firmly against the wall. *There are three possible outcomes, none of them good. The thread could break. The biot could collapse. Or I might remain suspended here forever.*

Nicole considered her alternatives. The only plan she could conceive with even a reasonable probability of success, and it was still very risky, was for her to climb up the suture thread to the last segment and then, somehow using the body or legs of the centipede as handholds, to muscle her way to the top of the pit.

Nicole glanced down and remembered her first fall. *I think I'll wait awhile first and see if this machine gets moving again.* A minute passed. Then another. Nicole took a deep breath. She reached up high on the suture line and pulled herself up the wall. She repeated the process with the other hand. She was now right behind the last segment. Nicole reached out and grabbed one of the legs, but as soon as she tried to put any weight on it, it pulled free from the wall.

So much for that plan, she thought after a moment's fright. She had restabilized herself just behind the biot. Nicole studied the centipede again very carefully. The carapace of each segment was made of overlapping pieces. *It might be possible to grab one of those flaps.* . . . Nicole reconstructed her first two attempts to ride on the back of the biot. *It was the suction force of the feet that gave out,* she thought. *Now most of the biot is on the level ground above. It should be able to hold me.*

Nicole realized that once she was on the back of the biot, she no longer had any protection against falling. To test the concept, she pulled herself to the top of the suture line and grabbed the carapace flap. She was able to get a firm grip. The only question was whether the flap could support her weight. Nicole tried to assess its strength while holding on to the suture with her other hand for safety. So far, so good.

Nicole grasped the flap on the rear biot segment and cautiously pulled herself up. She released her grip on the suture thread. Then she wrapped her legs around the side of the centipede's body and scooted along until she could reach the next flap. The legs of the rear segment popped off the wall, but the centipede did not move otherwise.

She repeated the process twice more, moving from segment to segment. Nicole was almost to the top. While she was on her final climb, she had a brief scare when the biot slipped a few centimeters back into the pit. Holding on breathlessly, she waited until the biot was stable and then crawled forward to the first segment that was on level ground. As she was crawling, the biot began walking again, but Nicole just rolled off sideways and landed on her back on the ground. "Hallelujah," she shouted.

As she stood on the wall around New York and stared

out at the moiling waters of the Cylindrical Sea, Nicole wondered why there had been no answer to her call for help. The self-test status flag on her radio indicated that it was working properly, yet she had tried three separate times without success to establish contact with the rest of the crew. Nicole was well aware of the commlinks available to the cosmonauts. Failure to receive a reply meant both that no crew members were within six to eight kilometers of her at present *and* that the Beta relay station was not operational. *If Beta were working,* Nicole thought, *then they would be able to talk to me from anywhere, even the Newton.*

Nicole told herself that the crew was doubtless onboard their own spacecraft, preparing for another sortie, and that the Beta communications station had probably been disabled by the hurricane. What bothered her, though, was that it had already been forty-five hours since the onset of the melting and more than ninety hours since she had fallen into the pit. Why was nobody looking for her?

Nicole's eyes scanned the sky for some sign of a helicopter. The atmosphere now contained clouds, as predicted. The melting of the Cylindrical Sea had substantially altered the weather patterns on Rama. The temperature had warmed up considerably. Nicole glanced at her thermometer and confirmed her estimate, that it was now four degrees above freezing.

The most likely situation, Nicole reasoned, returning to the question of the whereabouts of her colleagues, *is that they will return soon. I need to stay close to this wall so that I can be easily seen.* Nicole did not waste much time thinking about other, less likely scenarios. She considered only briefly the possibility that the crew had had a major disaster and nobody had yet been available to look for her. *But even in that case,* she said to herself, *I should follow the same approach. They would come sooner or later.*

To pass the time, Nicole took a sample of the sea and tested it. It had very few of the organic poisons found by the first Raman expedition. *Maybe they flourished and died while I was still in the pit,* she thought. *Anyway they're virtually all gone now.* Nicole noted to herself that in an emergency a strong swimmer might be able to make it across without a boat. However, she recalled the pictures of the shark biots and other denizens of the sea reported by Norton and his crew and slightly modified her assessment.

Nicole walked along the ramparts for several hours. While she was sitting down quietly eating her manna melon lunch (and thinking about methods she could employ to retrieve the rest of the melon, in the event that she still wasn't rescued in another seventy-two hours), she heard what she thought was a cry coming from New York. She thought immediately of Dr. Takagishi.

She tried her radio one more time. Nothing. Again Nicole checked the sky for some sign of a helicopter. She was still debating whether or not to forsake her lookout on the wall when she heard another cry. This time she had a better fix on its location. She located the nearest stairway and walked south into the center of New York.

Nicole had not yet updated the map of New York stored in her computer. After she crossed the annular streets near the central plaza, she stopped near the octahedron and entered all her new discoveries, including the barn with the pits and anything else she could remember. A moment later, while Nicole was admiring the beauty of the bizarre, eight-sided building, she heard a third cry. Only this time it was more like a shriek. If it was Takagishi, he was certainly making a peculiar noise.

She jogged across the open plaza, trying to close in on the sound while it was still fresh in her mind. As Nicole approached the buildings on the opposite side, the shriek sounded again. This time she also heard an answer. She recognized the voices. They sounded like the avian pair that had visited her while she was in the pit. Nicole became more cautious. She walked in the direction of the sound. It seemed to be coming from the area around the lattice nets that Francesca Sabatini had found so fascinating.

In less than two minutes, Nicole was standing between two tall skyscrapers that were connected at the ground by a thick mesh lattice that rose fifty meters into the air. About twenty meters above the ground, the velvet-bodied avian struggled against its trap. The avian's talons and wings were ensnared in the cords of the stringy lattice. It screamed again when it saw Nicole. Its larger companion, presently circling near the top of the buildings, dove down in her direction.

Nicole cowered against the facade of one of the buildings as the avian drew near. It jabbered at Nicole, as if it were scolding her, but it did not touch her. The velvet avian then said something and, after a short exchange, the huge linoleum bird withdrew to a nearby ledge about twenty meters away.

After she had calmed herself (and keeping one eye on the linoleum avian on its perch), Nicole walked over to the lattice and inspected it. She and Francesca had not had any time to spare when they had been searching for Takagishi, so this was Nicole's first chance for a detailed examination. The lattice was made of a ropelike material, about four centimeters thick, that had some elasticity. There were thousands of intersections in the lattice, and at each one of them there was a small knot, or node. The nodes were a little sticky, but not enough to make Nicole think that the whole lattice was some kind of spider web for catching flying creatures.

While she was studying the bottom of the lattice, the free avian flew over Nicole's head and landed close to its trapped friend. Being very careful to avoid becoming snared itself, it played with the individual strands with its talons. It also stretched and twisted the cords, with some difficulty. Next the linoleum bird gingerly stepped over to where its companion was trapped and made an awkward attempt either to break or untie the lattice links holding the other avian. When it was finished, the huge bird stepped back and stared at Nicole.

What is it doing? Nicole said to herself. *I'm certain that it's trying to tell me something. . . .* When Nicole did not move, the avian laboriously repeated the entire demonstration. This time Nicole thought she understood that the alien creature was trying to tell her that it couldn't free its friend. Nicole smiled and waved. Then, still staying at the bottom of the lattice, she tied a few of the adjacent cords together. When she subsequently untied them, the two avians shrieked their approval. She repeated the process twice and then pointed, first at herself and then at the velvet creature trapped above her.

There was a flurry of talk in their loud, sometimes musical tongue and the larger of the pair returned to his ledge. Nicole stared up at the velvet creature. It was caught in three different places; in each case its struggle had resulted in its being wedged more tightly in the elastic cord. Nicole surmised that the avian must have been caught in the violent hurricane winds and had been blown into the lattice during the preceding night. The cords had probably deformed under the momentum of the contact, and when they had snapped back to their normal size, the great bird was trapped in the mesh.

It was not a difficult climb. The lattice was carefully anchored to the two buildings and the rope itself was heavy enough that Nicole did not sway very much. But twenty meters off the ground is a considerable height, taller than a normal six-story building, so Nicole was having some second thoughts when she finally reached the altitude where the avian was trapped.

Nicole was panting from the effort of her climb. She eased gingerly over to the avian to ensure that she had not misunderstood anything in their strange communication. The alien bird followed her fixedly with its huge blue eyes.

One of the wings was snared very close to the avian's head. Nicole began trying to free the wing, first wrapping strands of the lattice around her own ankles to make certain that she would not fall. It was slow work. At one point Nicole caught a whiff of the creature's powerful breath. *I know that smell*, Nicole said to herself. It only took an instant for Nicole to connect the smell with the manna melon that she had been eating earlier. *So you eat the same thing?* Nicole thought. *But where does it come from?* Nicole wished that she could talk to these strange and wonderful creatures.

She struggled with the first knot. It was very tight. She was afraid she might injure the creature's wing if she pulled with more force. Nicole reached into her pack and retrieved her power scalpel.

Instantly the other avian was upon her, jabbering and

shrieking and scaring Nicole half to death. It would not go away and permit her to proceed until Nicole moved away from the trapped bird and showed its companion how the scalpel could cut through the lattice cord.

Using the scalpel the freeing operation was completed quickly. The velvet avian soared into the air, its musical cries of happiness resounding throughout the area. Its companion joined in the celebration with shrieks of its own as the two played, almost like lovebirds, in the air above the lattice. They disappeared a moment later and Nicole climbed slowly down to the ground.

Nicole was pleased with herself. She was ready now to return to the wall and wait for the rescue that she was certain was imminent. She walked toward the north, singing a folk song of the Loire that she remembered from her adolescence.

After several minutes Nicole had company again. More accurately, she had a guide. Whenever she would make a wrong turn, the velvet avian, flying overhead, would make an incredible racket. The noise would only cease when Nicole would go in the proper direction. *I wonder where we're going?* Nicole asked herself.

In the plaza area, not more than forty meters from the octahedron, the avian swooped down on an utterly unobtrusive portion of the metallic ground. It tapped its talons several times and then hovered over the spot. A covering of some kind slid away and the creature disappeared under the plaza. Twice it flew out, said something in Nicole's direction, and then descended.

Nicole understood the message. *I think I'm being invited home to meet the family,* she said to herself. *Let's just hope that I'm not the dinner.*

41

A FRIEND INDEED

Nicole had no idea what to expect. She was not fearful as she walked over and gazed at the hole in the ground. Curiosity was her dominant feeling. She worried momentarily that her rescue team might arrive while she was under the ground, but Nicole convinced herself that they would return later.

The rectangular cover was large, about ten meters long and six meters wide. When the avian saw that Nicole was following, it flew into the hole and waited on the third ledge. Nicole squatted beside the opening and stared into the depths. She could see some lights close by and more were flickering in the distance below her. She could not estimate accurately to what depth the corridor descended, but it was obviously more than twenty or thirty meters.

The downward climb was not easy for a nonflying species. The vertical corridor was essentially a large hole with a series of broad ledges along its sides. Each of the ledges was exactly the same size, about five meters long and one meter wide, and they were separated one from another by about two meters in depth. Nicole had to be very careful.

What light there was in the vertical corridor came from the opening to the plaza and some lanterns hanging on the walls every four ledges along the descent. The lanterns were enclosed in transparent wrappings that were very flimsy and paperlike. Each lantern contained a small, burning fire, together with some liquid substance that Nicole assumed was the fuel.

Nicole's velvet-bodied friend watched her patiently throughout the descent, always staying three ledges below her. Nicole had the feeling that if she were to slip, the avian would catch her in midair, but she didn't want to test her hypothesis. Her mind was running at a rapid pace. Nicole had already decided that the creatures were definitely not biots. That meant they were an alien species of some kind. *But they couldn't possibly be the Ramans,* Nicole reasoned. *Their level of technological development is totally inconsistent with this incredible spacecraft.*

Nicole remembered from her history courses the poor and backward Mayans found in Mexico by the conquistadors. The Spanish had deemed it impossible that the ancestors of those ignorant and impoverished people could possibly have built such impressive ceremonial centers. *Could that have happened here?* Nicole wondered. *Might these strange avians be all that is left of the master species that constructed this vehicle?*

About twenty meters below the surface Nicole heard what sounded like running water. The noise increased as she dropped onto a ledge that was actually an extension of a horizontal tunnel heading off behind her. Across the vertical corridor Nicole could see a similar dark hallway going in the opposite direction, also parallel to the surface.

Her avian guide was, as usual, three ledges below. Nicole pointed down the tunnel at her rear. The creature flew up close to her and systematically hovered over each of the two ledges immediately below Nicole, making it perfectly clear that Nicole was expected to descend.

Nicole was not willing to give up so easily. She took out her flask and made a drinking motion. Then Nicole pointed behind her at the dark tunnel. The avian fluttered about, apparently weighing the decision, and then flew over Nicole's head into the blackness. Forty seconds later Nicole saw a light in the distance that continued to grow as it approached her. The avian returned carrying a large torch in one of its talons.

Nicole followed the avian for about fifteen meters. They came to a room, off to the left of the tunnel, that contained a large cistern full of water. Fresh water fell into the cistern from a pipe embedded in the wall. Nicole pulled out her mass spectrometer and tested the liquid. It was virtually pure H_2O; no other chemicals were present above one part in a million. Careful to remember her manners, Nicole cupped her hands and drank from the waterfall. It was unbelievably delicious.

After she had finished drinking, Nicole continued to walk down the tunnel in the same direction. The avian went into a frenzy, flying up and down and jabbering incessantly, until Nicole reversed her direction and returned to the main vertical corridor. When she renewed her descent, she noticed that the ambient light level had dropped considerably. Nicole glanced above her. The opening to the plaza in New York was now closed. *I hope that doesn't mean I'm here for good,* she thought.

Twenty meters more below the surface, another pair of dark horizontal tunnels ran perpendicular to the main corridor. At this second level the velvet avian, still carrying the torch, led Nicole down one of the horizontal tunnels for about two hundred meters. She followed the bird into a large, circular room with a high ceiling. The avian used its torch to light several wall lanterns around the room. Then it disappeared. It was gone for almost an hour. Nicole sat as patiently as she could, at first staring around the black room that reminded her of a cave or grotto. There were no decorations. At length Nicole began to concentrate on how she would inform the avians that she was ready to leave.

When her velvet friend eventually returned, it brought four associates. Nicole heard them flapping their wings in the hallway and jabbering intermittently. Her avian's companion (who Nicole assumed was a mate of some kind) and two additional linoleum-surfaced creatures flew in first. They landed and then awkwardly walked up very close to Nicole to conduct a visual examination. After they had sat down on the opposite side of the room, another velvet-bodied creature, this one brown instead of black, flew in last. It was carrying a small manna melon in its talons.

The melon was placed in front of Nicole. All of the avians watched expectantly. Nicole neatly cut a one-eighth section out of the melon with her scalpel, picked it up to drink a small draft from the greenish liquid in the middle, and then carried the remaining melon over to her

hosts. They shrieked appreciatively, admiring the precision of the cut as they passed the melon among themselves.

Nicole watched the avians eat. They shared the melon,
one with another, and at no time were any portions meted
out. The two velvet avians were surprisingly deft and
dainty with their talons, making as little mess as possible
and leaving no waste whatsoever. The larger avians were
much clumsier; their eating reminded Nicole of animals
on Earth. Like Nicole, none of the avians ate the tough
outer covering of the manna melon.

When the meal was over the avians, who had not talked
at all while they were eating, huddled in a circle for
several seconds. The huddle broke up after the brown
velvet one jabbered something that sounded to Nicole like
a song. One at a time, they then flew over for another
close-up look at her and disappeared out the door.

Nicole sat quietly and wondered what would happen
next. The avians had left the lights on in the dining room
(or banquet hall, or whatever it was), but it was pitch
black in the corridor outside. They clearly intended for
her to stay where she was, at least for the time being. It
had been a long time since Nicole had had any sleep and
she was pleasantly full from the meal. *Oh well*, she thought
to herself, curling up on the floor after a short internal
debate, *maybe a short nap will refresh me.*

In her dream she heard someone calling her name, but
it was very far away. She had to strain to hear the voice.
Nicole woke with a start and tried to remember where she
was. She listened carefully but didn't hear anything. When
she checked her watch, she learned that she had been
asleep for four hours. *I'd better get out of here*, Nicole
thought. *It will be dark soon and I don't want to miss my
chance to be rescued.*

She moved out into the hallway and switched on her
small flashlight. Nicole reached the vertical corridor in
less than a minute. Immediately she began scrambling up
the ledges. Just below where she had stopped during her
descent for a drink of water, Nicole heard a strange noise
above her. She stopped to catch her breath. She leaned
slightly into the gaping hole and shone her light above, in

the direction of the sound. Something large was moving back and forth on the portion of the first level that jutted out into the vertical corridor.

Nicole cautiously climbed up to the ledge directly underneath the new phenomenon and crouched beneath it. Whatever it was, it was covering each square centimeter of the ledge in front of the tunnel entrance once every five seconds. There was no way Nicole could avoid it. She couldn't possibly pull herself up and then climb to the next ledge above in less than five seconds.

She moved down to one end of her ledge and listened intently to the sound above her. When the thing turned and went in the opposite direction, Nicole pulled her head over the edge of the next level. The object was moving rapidly on treads and looked altogether like an armored tank from the rear. She had only a brief glimpse, for the top half of the tank spun around quickly at the other end as it prepared to reverse its field.

One thing is certain, Nicole said to herself as she stood on the ledge below. *That tank is some kind of sentinel.* Nicole wondered whether or not it had any sensors— certainly it had given no indication that it had heard her—but decided that she couldn't afford to find out. *It wouldn't be much of a guard if it couldn't at least stop an intruder.*

Nicole climbed slowly down the ledges to the dining room level. She was sorely disappointed and now angry with herself for having come into the avian lair in the first place. It still did not make sense to her that the avians might be holding her as a captive. After all, hadn't the creature invited her to visit after Nicole had saved its life?

Nicole was also puzzled by the tank sentinel. Its existence was baffling, and completely inconsistent with the level of technological development of everything else in the lair. What was its purpose? Where did it come from? *Things just get curiouser and curiouser,* Nicole thought, recalling a phrase from one of her favorite books.

When she was back on the second underground level, Nicole looked around to see if there was any other way she could get out of the lair. There was an identical set of ledges on the opposite side of the vertical corridor. If she could jump across, then maybe . . .

Before considering seriously such a plan, Nicole had to determine whether or not a tank, or equivalent sentinel, was guarding the opposite horizontal tunnel on the first level. She couldn't tell from where she was standing, so Nicole, muttering to herself about her stupidity, climbed back up the ledges on her side to obtain a good view across the corridor. She was in luck. The ledge in front of the opposite tunnel was empty.

By the time she returned to the second underground level again, Nicole was fatigued from all the climbing. She stared across the corridor and at the lights in the abyss below her. She would almost certainly die if she fell. Nicole was a very good judge of distance and correctly reckoned that it was about four meters from the edge of the ledge extension in front of her tunnel to the edge on the opposite side. *Four meters*, she mused, *four and a half at the most. Allowing for some room at both ends, I need a five-meter jump to clear it. In flight suit with backpack.*

Nicole remembered a Sunday afternoon at Beauvois four years earlier, when Genevieve was ten and both mother and daughter were watching the 2196 Olympics on television. "Can you still jump a long way, Mama?" the little girl had asked, having a hard time picturing her mother as an Olympic champion.

Pierre had cajoled her into taking Genevieve to the athletics field adjacent to the secondary school at Luynes. Her timing had been way off in the triple jump, but after thirty minutes of warmup and practice Nicole had managed to long jump six and a half meters. Genevieve had not been that impressed. "Shoot, Mama," her daughter had said while they were bicycling home through the green countryside, "Danielle's big sister can jump almost that far, and she's only a university student."

The memory of Genevieve stirred a profound sadness in Nicole. She longed to hear her daughter's voice, help her with her hair, or go boating with her on their small private pond beside the Bresme. *We never value enough the time we have*, she thought, *until they're no longer around.*

Nicole started back down the tunnel to where the avians had left her. She wouldn't try the jump. It was too dangerous. If she slipped . . .

"Nicole des Jardins, where the hell are you?" Nicole froze the moment she heard the call, very faint, off in the distance. Had she imagined it? "Nicole," she heard again. It was definitely Richard Wakefield's voice. She ran back to the vertical corridor and started to shout. *No,* she thought rapidly, *that will wake them. It will not take me more than five minutes. I can jump . . .*

Nicole's adrenaline was pumping at an incredible rate. She marked off her steps and soared across the chasm with plenty of room to spare. She climbed up the ledges at breakneck speed. Toward the top she heard Wakefield calling her again.

"I'm here, Richard. Below you," she shouted. "Underneath the plaza."

Nicole reached the top ledge and started pushing on the covering. It wouldn't budge. "Shit," she shouted as the puzzled Richard paced around in the vicinity. "Richard, come over here. Where you hear my voice. Beat on the ground."

Richard began to knock hard on the covering. They were shouting at each other. The noise was deafening. From far below Nicole heard the flapping of wings. As the avians rose in the corridor, they began to shriek and jabber.

"Help me," Nicole hollered at them as they drew close. She pointed up at the cover. "My friend is out there."

Richard continued to pound. Only the two avians who had originally found Nicole in the pit came up to where she was. They hovered around her, flapping their wings and jabbering back at the five others who were one level below. The creatures were apparently having an argument, for the black velvet avian twice extended its neck down toward its associates and uttered a fearsome screech.

The covering suddenly opened. Richard had to scramble to keep from falling in. When he looked down into the hole he saw Nicole and two gigantic bird creatures, one of which flew right by him as Nicole crawled out of the opening. *"Holy shit!"* he exclaimed, his eyes following the flight of the avian.

Nicole was overcome with joy. She ran into Wakefield's arms. "Richard, oh Richard," she said, "I'm so glad to see you."

He grinned at her and returned the hug. "If I had known you felt like this," he said, "I would have come earlier."

42

TWO EXPLORERS

"Let me get this straight. You're telling me that you're *alone*? And we have no way to cross the Cylindrical Sea?"

Richard nodded. It was too much for Nicole. Five minutes earlier she had been exultant. Her ordeal had finally been over. She had imagined returning to the Earth and seeing her father and daughter again. Now he was telling her . . .

She walked away quickly and leaned her head against one of the buildings surrounding the plaza. Tears rolled down her cheeks as she gave vent to her disappointment. Richard followed her at a distance.

"I'm sorry," he said.

"It's not your fault," Nicole replied after she had regained her composure. "It just never occurred to me that I might see one of the crew again and *still* not be rescued—" She stopped herself. It was not fair for her to make Richard suffer. She walked over to him and forced a smile.

"I'm not usually this emotional," Nicole said. "And I interrupted your story right in the middle." She paused a second to wipe her eyes. "You were telling me about the shark biots chasing the motorboat. You saw them first when you were about halfway across the sea?"

"More or less," Richard replied. Her disappointment had subdued him. He tried a nervous laugh. "Do you remember, after one of the simulations, when the review board criticized us for not having sent a pilotless version of our motorboat into the water first, just to make sure that there wasn't something peculiar to the new design that would disturb the 'ecological equilibrium' in some way? Well, I thought their suggestion at the time was ridiculous. Now I'm not so certain. Those shark biots hardly bothered the Newton vessels, but they were definitely angry about my high-speed motorboat."

Richard and Nicole had sat down together on one of the gray metal boxes that dotted the plaza area. "I managed to dodge them once," Richard continued, "but I was extremely lucky. When I had no other choice I simply jumped out and swam. Fortunately for me, they were mostly after the boat. I didn't see one again while I was swimming until I was only a hundred meters from shore."

"How long have you been inside Rama altogether now?" Nicole asked.

"About seventeen hours. I left the Newton two hours after dawn. I spent too much damn time trying to repair the communications station at Beta. But it was impossible."

Nicole felt his flight suit. "Except for your hair, I can't even tell you've been wet."

Richard laughed. "Oh, the miracles of fabric engineering. Would you believe that this suit was almost dry by the time I changed my thermals? By then I was having a hard time convincing even myself that I had spent that twenty minutes swimming in the cold water." He looked at his companion. She was loosening up very slowly. "But I'm surprised at you, Cosmonaut des Jardins. You haven't even asked me the most important question. How did I know where you were?"

Nicole had pulled out her scanner and was reading Richard's biometry. Everything was within tolerances, despite his recent harrowing swim. She was a little slow to understand his question. "You *knew* where I was?" she said finally, knitting her brow. "I figured you were just wandering around—"

"Come on, lady. New York is small, but not *that* small. There's twenty-five square kilometers of territory inside these walls. And radio around here is completely unreliable." He grinned. "Let's see, if I stood and called your name in each square meter, I would have to call you twenty-five million times. At one call every ten seconds—allowing myself time to listen for a response and move to the next square meter—that would be six calls a minute. So it would take four million minutes, which is slightly

more than sixty thousand hours, or twenty-five hundred
Earth days—"

"Okay. Okay," Nicole interrupted. She was finally laughing. "Tell me how you knew where I was."

Richard stood up. "May I?" he said dramatically, extending his fingers toward the breast pocket of Nicole's
flight suit.

"I suppose so," she answered. "Although I can't imagine
what—"

Richard reached into her pocket and pulled out Prince
Hal. "He led me to you," Wakefield said. "You're a good
man, my prince, but for a while I thought you'd failed
me."

Nicole had no idea what Richard was talking about.
"Prince Hal and Falstaff have matching navigation beacons," he explained. "They put out fifteen strong pulses a
second. With Falstaff fixed in my hut at Beta and with an
equivalent transceiver over at Alpha campsite, I could
follow you by triangulation. So I knew exactly where you
were—at least in terms of x–y coordinates. My simple
tracking algorithm wasn't designed for excursions in z."

"That's what an engineer would call my visit to the
avian lair?" Nicole said with another smile. "An excursion
in z?"

"That's one way of describing it."

Nicole shook her head. "I don't know about you, Wakefield. If you really knew where I was all this time, why the
hell did you wait so long—"

"Because we lost you, or thought we had, before we
found you . . . after I came back to retrieve Falstaff."

"Have I become a dullard in the last week, or is this
roundabout explanation incredibly confusing?"

It was Richard's turn to laugh. "Maybe I should try to
make my presentation more orderly." He paused to arrange his mental notes. "I was really irritated," he began,
"back in June when the Engineering Steering Group decided not to use navigation beacons as backup personnel
locators. I had argued, unsuccessfully, that there might be
emergency situations, or unforeseen circumstances, in which
the signal-to-noise ratio on the regular voice link would be

below threshold. So I equipped three of my own robots just in case . . ."

Nicole studied Richard Wakefield while he talked. She had forgotten that he was both amazing and amusing. She was certain that if she asked the right questions, he could talk on this subject alone for a full hour.

". . . Then Falstaff lost the signal," he was saying. "I wasn't present myself at the time, for I was preparing to come with Hiro Yamanaka to pick you and Francesca up in the helicopter. But Falstaff has a small recorder and timetags all the data. After you didn't show up, I replayed the data from the recorder and found that the signal had abruptly disappeared.

"It came back on only briefly, while we were talking on the radio a few minutes later, but several seconds after our last conversation the signal was gone for good. The signature suggested a hardware failure to me. I thought Prince Hal had malfunctioned. When Francesca said that you had been with her up until the plaza, then I was virtually certain that Prince Hal—"

Nicole had only been listening with one ear but she bolted to attention when Richard mentioned Francesca. "Stop," Nicole interrupted, holding up her hand. "What did you say she told you?"

"That you and she had left the barn together and that you had walked away from her several minutes later to look for Takagishi—"

"That's complete bullshit," Nicole said.

"What do you mean?" Richard asked.

"It's a lie. An absolute and total untruth. I fell into that pit I told you about while Francesca was there, or at least no more than a minute after she left. She never saw me again."

Richard thought for a moment. "That explains why Falstaff lost you. You were in the barn all that time and the signal was blocked." Now it was his turn to be puzzled. "But why would Francesca make up such a story?"

That's what I would like to know, Nicole thought to herself. *She must have poisoned Borzov on purpose. Otherwise why would she deliberately . . .*

"Was there something between the two of you?" Richard was saying. "I always thought I detected—"

"Probably some jealousy," Nicole interrupted, "going both ways. Francesca and I are light-years apart."

"You can say that again," Richard said with a chuckle. "I've spent the better part of a year giving off signals that I find you intelligent and interesting and attractive. Yet I've never received anything but a restrained and courteous professional response. Francesca, on the other hand, notices if you happen to even glance at her."

"There are other, more substantive differences," Nicole replied, not altogether displeased that Richard had finally verbalized his interest in her as a woman.

There was a momentary pause in the conversation. Nicole glanced at her watch. "But I don't want to spend any more time talking about Francesca Sabatini," she said, "it's going to be dark again in an hour and we have an escape from this island to plan. We also have certain, uh, logistical issues to address, such as food, water, and other unmentionable items that made confinement in a small pit reasonably disgusting."

"I brought a portable hut—if we need one."

"That's great," Nicole replied. "I'll remember that when it rains." She reached automatically into her backpack for some manna melon but did not pull it out. "By the way," she said to Richard, "did you bring any *human* food?"

The hut came in handy when they were ready for sleep. They decided to pitch it just to the side of the central plaza. Nicole felt safer being close to the avians. In some sense they were her friends and they might help if an emergency arose. They were also the only known source of food. Between them, Richard and Nicole had barely enough food and water to last for another two Raman days.

Nicole had not objected to Richard's suggestion that they share the hut. He had gallantly offered to sleep outside, "if that would make you more comfortable," but the huts were plenty large enough for two sleeping mats as long as there were no other furnishings. Lying about half a meter apart made their conversation very easy. Nicole gave a detailed rendition of her hours alone, omitting only the part about the vial and the vision. That was too personal for her to share. Richard was fascinated by her entire story and absolutely intrigued by the avians.

"I mean, look," he said, propping his head up on his elbow, "try to figure out how the hell they got here. From what you've said, except for that tank sentinel—and I completely agree with you that it's an anomaly—they're no more advanced than prehistoric man. What a boggle it would be to learn their secret.

"You can't rule out completely that they're biots," he continued, barely able to contain his enthusiasm. "They might not be impressive as biology, but Jesus, as artificial intelligence they would be state of the art." He sat up on his mat. "Just think about what it would mean either way. We must find out all these answers. You're a linguist—maybe you could learn to talk to them."

Nicole was amused. "Has it occurred to you, Richard," she asked, "that all of this discussion will be academic if nobody ever rescues us?"

"A couple of times," Richard said with a laugh. He was lying down again. "That damn Heilmann took me aside, right before I came back inside Rama, and told me that I was acting 'in violation of all procedures' by returning here. He promised me that they would not come after me under *any* circumstances."

"So why did you come back?"

"I'm not completely certain," he said slowly. "I know I wanted to pick up Falstaff and see if, by some wild happenstance, he had ever received any more signals from your beacon. But I think there were other reasons. The mission was becoming more politics than science. It was obvious to me that the bureaucrats on Earth were going to abort the mission, 'for security reasons,' and the crew was not going to return to Rama. I knew the political discussions would continue for another day or two." He paused a second. "And I wanted one last look at the most incredible sight of my life."

Nicole was quiet for a moment. "You obviously weren't afraid," she said softly, "because you show no sign of fear even now. Doesn't the thought of being left to die on-board Rama bother you at all?"

"A little," Richard answered. "But dying in an exciting situation is much better than living in a boring one." Again he propped himself up on his elbow. "I have been looking forward to this mission for three years. I thought from the beginning that I had a good chance of being selected. Except for my robots and Shakespeare, there is nothing in my life but my work. I have no family or friends to think of . . ."

His voice trailed off. "And I'm as much afraid of going back as I am of dying. At least Richard Wakefield, Newton cosmonaut, has a clearly defined purpose." He started to say something else but stopped himself. Richard lay back down and closed his eyes.

43

EXOBIOLOGICAL
PSYCHOLOGY

"There's another reason not to give up hope," Richard said cheerfully as soon as he saw Nicole open her eyes, "and I forgot to mention it last night."

Nicole had always awakened very slowly. Even as a child. She liked to savor the last part of her dream state before confronting harsh reality. At home Genevieve and Pierre both knew not to talk to her about anything important until after she had had her morning coffee. She blinked at Richard, who was shining his small flashlight in the gap between them.

"This space vehicle is now headed for the Earth," he said. "Even if the Newton leaves, there might be another human spacecraft here sooner or later."

"What's that?" Nicole said, sitting up and rubbing her eyes.

"In all the excitement last night," Richard replied, "I left out one of the most important points. The maneuver—I guess you missed it because you were unconscious at the bottom of that pit—put Rama on an Earth impact course. That made our evacuation imperative."

Richard noticed that Nicole was staring at him as if he had lost his mind. "The spaceship is still on a hyperbola with respect to the Sun," he clarified, "but it's blasting full speed toward the Earth. We will impact in twenty-three days."

"Richard," Nicole said, longing intensely for that fresh cup of coffee, "I do not like jokes early in the morning. If you have spent your energy making up—"

"No, no," he interrupted. "I'm serious. It's true. Believe me."

Nicole pulled out her pocket thermometer and checked it. "Then tell me, my engineering genius, why is the temperature in here still increasing? If we are now going away from the Sun, shouldn't it be dropping?"

"You're smarter than that, Nicole." Richard shook his head. "The thermal input from the Sun on the exterior of Rama diffuses very slowly through the outer shell and then into the interior. The thermal conductivity is obviously very low. I wouldn't expect the temperatures to reach a peak for another two weeks at least."

Nicole remembered enough of her basic thermodynamics to realize he was making sense. It was too early in the morning for thermal diffusion. Nicole struggled with the idea that Rama was now bound for the Earth. She asked Richard for a drink of water. *What is going on here?* she thought. *Why is Rama now headed for our planet?*

Richard must have been reading her mind. "You should have heard the silly discussions about why Rama had changed its trajectory and what it was likely to do. There was a seven-hour conference call on the subject."

He laughed out loud. "The ISA has an employee—a Canadian, I think—whose specialty is exobiological psychology. Can you believe it? This jerk actually participated in the conference call and offered insights into the motives behind the Raman maneuver." Richard shook his head vigorously. "All bureaucracies are the same. They drain the life out of the truly creative people and develop mindless paper-pushers as their critical mass."

"What was the final result of the call?" Nicole asked after a short silence.

"Most of the sane people guessed that Rama would go into orbit around the Earth and conduct passive remote observations. But they were in the minority. Sanity and logic took a holiday, in my opinion. Even David Brown—who acted very strangely, it seemed to me, after we returned to the Newton—acknowledged that there was a high probability that Rama would do something hostile. He clarified his position by stating that it would *not*, in reality, be a hostile act; however, its attempt to learn more about the Earth might result in actions that would be *perceived* by us as hostile."

The agitated Richard was now standing up. "Have you ever heard such gobbledygook in your life? And Dr. Brown was one of the more coherent speakers. The entire ISA Advisory Board was polled as to which of the projected scenarios each of them favored. Do you think that bunch of plenipotentiaries could respond simply with 'I believe in Option A, direct impact with resultant destruction and climate alteration,' or 'I favor Option C, Earth orbit with bellicose intentions'? Hell no! Each one of them had to deliver a lecture of some kind. That weird Dr. Alexander, the one who asked you all the questions after your open biometry meeting in November, even spent fifteen minutes explaining how Rama's existence had exposed a flaw in the ISA charter. As if anybody gave a shit!" Richard sat down again and put his hands on his cheeks. "The whole thing was unbelievable."

Nicole was now fully awake. "I assume," she said, sitting up on her mat, "judging from your obvious irritation, that you disagreed with the consensus."

Richard nodded. "Almost three fourths of the large group participating in the call—which included all the Newton cosmonauts as well as most of the senior scientists and executives in the ISA—were convinced that the Raman maneuver was likely to be harmful to the Earth in some significant way. Almost all of them focused on the same issue. Since the first Rama apparently ignored our existence altogether, they argued, the fact that Rama II altered its trajectory to achieve a rendezvous with the Earth shows that this spacecraft is operating under different principles. I certainly agree with that conclusion. But what I cannot understand is why everyone necessarily assumes that the Raman action is hostile. It seems just as likely to me that the aliens could be motivated by curiosity, or even a desire to be our benefactors in some way."

The British engineer paused for a moment to reflect. "Francesca says that the polls on Earth are indicating that a huge majority of the average people as well, almost ten to one according to her, is terrified by Rama's approach. They are clamoring for the politicians to do something."

Richard opened the hut and walked out into the dark plaza. He idly shone his flashlight on the octahedron. "At a second meeting eighteen hours later it was decreed that the Newton team would not go inside Rama again. Technically, I am not in violation of that order, because I left the Newton before the official proclamation. But it was obvious that the order was coming."

"While the leaders of the planet Earth are discussing what to do with a spacecraft the size of an asteroid that is aimed directly at them," Nicole said as she walked out into the plaza behind him, "you and I have a more tractable problem. We must cross the Cylindrical Sea." She managed a wan smile. "Shall we do a little exploring while we talk?"

Richard directed his flashlight beam into the bottom of the pit. The manna melon was clearly identifiable but the individual pieces in the pile of jumbled metal were very hard to resolve. "So those are spare parts from a centipede biot?"

Nicole nodded. They were kneeling side by side on the lip. "Even in the daylight the ends of the pit are in shadows. I needed to be certain that I wasn't looking at Takagishi's body."

"I would love to see a centipede biot repair itself." Richard stood up and walked over to the wall of the barn. He knocked. "And the material scientists would love this stuff. Normal radio waves are blocked both ways and you can't see in from the outside. Yet the wall is somehow transparent if you're inside the barn looking out." He turned to Nicole. "Bring your scalpel over here. Let's see if we can cut off a piece."

Nicole was trying to decide if one of them should drop down into the pit and retrieve the melon. It wouldn't be too difficult, assuming the suture line would hold. At length she pulled out her scalpel and walked over beside Richard.

"I'm not certain we should do this," she said. She hesitated before applying the scalpel to the barn wall. "In the first place, the scalpel could be damaged. We might need it later. Second, uh, it might be considered vandalism."

"Vandalism?" he said rhetorically. Richard regarded Nicole with a peculiar look. "What a curiously homocentric concept." He shrugged his shoulders and headed toward one end of the barn. "Never mind," he said, "you're probably right about the scalpel."

Richard had entered some data into his pocket computer and was studying the small monitor when Nicole came over beside him. "You and Francesca were standing right about here, correct?" Nicole gave him an affirmative reply. "Then you went back into the barn to look into one of the pits?"

"We've been over this before," Nicole replied. "Why are you asking again?"

"I think Francesca saw you fall into one of the pits and purposely misled us with that story about your wandering off to search for our Japanese professor. She didn't want anybody to find you."

Nicole stared at Richard in the dark. "I agree," she responded slowly. "But why do *you* think so?"

"It's the only explanation that makes any sense. I had a bizarre encounter with her right before I came back inside. She came into my room under the pretense of wanting an interview, supposedly to find out why I was returning to Rama. When I mentioned Falstaff and your navigation beacon, she switched off her camera. Then she became quite animated and asked me many detailed technical questions. Before she left, she told me she was convinced that none of us should ever have entered Rama in the first place. I thought she was going to beg me not to go back.

"I can understand her not wanting me to find out that she had tried to maroon you in the pit," Richard continued after a brief pause. "What I can't fathom is why she left you there in the first place."

"You remember the night you explained to me why RoSur's fault protection had failed?" Nicole said after a moment's reflection. "That same night I also asked you and Janos if either of you had seen General Borzov . . ."

As they walked back in the direction of the central plaza and their hut, Nicole spent fifteen minutes explaining to Richard her entire hypothesis about the conspiracy. She told him about the media contract, the drugs Francesca

had given to both David Brown and Reggie Wilson, and
Nicole's personal interactions with all the principals. She
did not tell him about the data cube. Richard agreed that
the evidence was very compelling.

"So you think she left you there in the pit to avoid being
unmasked as a conspirator?"

Nicole nodded.

Richard whistled. "Then everything fits. It was apparent
to me that Francesca was running the show when we
returned to the Newton. Both Brown and Heilmann were
taking orders from her." He put his arm around Nicole. "I
wouldn't want that woman as my enemy. She clearly has
no scruples whatsoever."

44
ANOTHER LAIR

Richard and Nicole had bigger concerns than Francesca. When they returned to the central plaza, they found their hut had disappeared. Repeated knocks on the avian cover produced no response. The precariousness of their situation became clearer to both of them.

Richard grew moody and uncommunicative. He apologized to Nicole, saying that it was a characteristic of his personality for him to withdraw from people when he felt insecure. He played with his computer for several hours, only stopping occasionally to ask Nicole questions about the geography of New York.

Nicole lay down on her sleeping mat and thought about swimming across the Cylindrical Sea. She was not an exceptionally good swimmer. During training it had taken her about fifteen minutes to swim one kilometer. That had been in a placid swimming pool. To cross the sea she would be forced to swim five kilometers through cold, choppy water. And she might be accompanied by lovely creatures like the shark biots.

A jolly fat man twenty centimeters high interrupted her contemplation. "Would you like a drink, fair lass?" Falstaff asked her. Nicole rolled over and studied the robot from up close. He hoisted a large mug of fluid and drank it, spilling some on his beard. He wiped it off with his sleeve and then he burped. "And if you want nothing to drink," he said in a heavy British accent, thrusting his hand down into his codpiece, "then perhaps Sir John could teach you a thing or two between the sheets." The tiny face was definitely leering. It was crude, but very funny.

Nicole laughed. So did Falstaff. "I am not only witty in

myself," the robot said, "but the cause that wit is in other men."

"You know," Nicole said to Richard, who was watching from several meters away, "if you ever became tired of being a cosmonaut, you could make millions in children's toys."

Richard came over and picked up Falstaff. He thanked Nicole for her compliment. "As I see it, we have three options," he then said very seriously. "We can swim the sea, we can explore New York to see if we can forage enough material to construct some kind of boat, or we can wait here until someone comes. I'm not optimistic about our chances in any of the cases."

"So what do you suggest?"

"I propose a compromise. When it's light, let's carefully search the key areas of the city, particularly around the three plazas, and see if we can find anything that could be used to build a boat. We'll allot one Raman day, maybe two, to the exploration. If nothing turns up, we'll swim for it. I have no faith we'll ever see a rescue team."

"Sounds all right to me. But I would like to do one other thing first. We don't have a lot of food, to make a rather obvious understatement. I'd feel better if we pulled up the manna melon first, before we did any more exploring. That way we could be protected against any surprises."

Richard agreed that establishing the food supply would probably be a prudent initial action. But he didn't like the idea of using the suture thread again. "You were lucky in many ways," he told Nicole. "Not only did the line not break, it didn't even slip off that waistband you made. However, it did cut completely through your gloves in two places and almost through the waistband."

"You have another idea?" Nicole asked.

"The lattice material is the obvious choice," Richard replied. "It should be perfect, provided that we don't have any trouble obtaining it. Then I can go down in the pit and spare you the trouble—"

"Wrong," Nicole interrupted. She smiled. "With all due respect, Richard, now is not the time for any macho derring-do. Using the lattice is a great idea. But you're too heavy. If something happened, I would never be able to pull you out." She patted him on the shoulder. "And I hope it doesn't hurt your feelings, but I'm probably the more athletic of the two of us."

Richard feigned hurt pride. "But whatever happened to tradition? The man always performs the feats of physical strength and agility. Don't you remember your childhood cartoons?"

Nicole laughed heartily. "Yes, my dear," she said lightly. "But you aren't Popeye. And I'm not Olive Oyl."

"I'm not certain I can deal with this," he said, shaking his head vigorously. "To discover at the age of thirty-four that I'm not Popeye. . . . What a blow to my self-image." He cuddled Nicole gently. "What do you say?" he continued. "Should we try to sleep some more before it's light?"

Neither of them was able to sleep. They lay side by side on their mats in the open plaza, each occupied with his own thoughts. Nicole heard Richard's body move. "You're awake too?" she said in a whisper.

"Yeah," he answered. "I've even counted Shakespearean characters with no success. I was up to more than a hundred."

Nicole propped herself up on an elbow and faced her companion. "Tell me, Richard," she said, "where did this preoccupation of yours with Shakespeare come from? I know you grew up in Stratford, but it's hard for me to imagine how an engineer like you, in love with computers and calculations and gadgets, could become so fascinated with a playwright."

"My therapist told me it was an 'escapist compulsion,' " Richard replied a few seconds later. "Since I didn't like the real world or the people in it, he said, I made up another one. Except that I didn't create it from scratch. I just extended a wonderful universe already fabricated by a genius.

"Shakespeare was my God," Richard continued after a moment. "When I was nine or ten, I would stop in that park along the Avon—the one beside all the theaters, with the statues of Hamlet, Falstaff, Lady Macbeth, and Prince Hal—and spend the afternoon hours making up additional stories about my favorite characters. That way I put off going home until the last possible moment. I dreaded being around my father. . . . I never knew what he would do—

"But you don't want to hear this," Richard interrupted himself suddenly, "everyone has memories of childhood pain. We should talk about something else."

"We should talk about whatever we're feeling," Nicole responded, surprising even herself. "Which is something I hardly ever do," she added softly.

Richard turned and looked in her direction. He extended his hand slowly. She gently wrapped her fingers around his. "My father worked for British Rail," he said. "He was a very smart man, but socially clumsy, and he had difficulty finding a job that fit him after he finished the university at Sussex. Times were still tough. The economy had just started to recover from The Great Chaos. . . .

"When my mother told him that she was pregnant, he was overwhelmed by the responsibility of it all. He looked for a safe, secure position. He had always scored well on tests and the government had forced all the national transportation monopolies, including the rail system, to staff positions based on objective test results. So my father became the manager of operations at Stratford.

"He hated the job. It was boring and repetitive, no challenge at all for a man who had an honors degree. Mother told me that when I was very small he applied for other positions, but he always seemed to botch the interviews. Later on, when I was older, he never even tried. He sat at home and complained. And drank. And then made everyone around him miserable."

There was a long silence. Richard was having a difficult time struggling with the demons of his childhood. Nicole squeezed his hand. "I'm sorry," she said.

"So was I," Richard replied with a slight break in his voice. "I was just a small child with an incredible sense of wonder and love of life. I would come home enthusiastic about something new I had learned or something that had happened at school, and my Dad would just growl.

"Once, when I was only eight, I came home from school in the early afternoon and I got into an argument with him. It was his day off and he had been drinking, as usual.

Mother was out at the store. I don't remember what it was about now, but I do recall telling him that he was wrong about some trivial fact. When I continued to argue with him, he suddenly hit me in the nose with all his might. I fell against the wall with my broken nose gushing blood. From that time on, until I was fourteen and felt I could protect myself, I never walked in that house when he was there unless I was certain that my mother was home."

Nicole tried to imagine an adult man slugging an eight-year-old child. *What kind of human being could break his own son's nose?* she wondered.

"I had always been very shy," Richard was saying, "and had convinced myself that I had inherited my father's social clumsiness, so I didn't have many friends my own age. But I still yearned for human interaction." He looked over at Nicole and paused, remembering. "I made Shakespeare's characters my friends. I read his plays every afternoon in the park and immersed myself in his imaginative world. I even memorized entire scenes. Then I talked to Romeo or Ariel or Jaques while I was walking home."

It was not difficult for Nicole to visualize the rest of Richard's story. *I can picture you as an adolescent,* she thought. *Solitary, awkward, emotionally repressed. Your obsession with Shakespeare gave you an escape from your pain. All the theaters were near your home. You saw your friends become alive on the stage.*

On impulse Nicole leaned over and kissed Richard lightly on the cheek. "Thanks for telling me," she said.

As soon as it was daylight they walked over to the lattice. Nicole was surprised to find that the incisions she had made when she had freed the avian had all been repaired. The lattice was like new. "Obviously a repair biot has already been here," Richard commented, no longer extremely impressed after all the wonders he had already witnessed.

They cut off several long strands of the lattice and headed for the barn. On the way Richard tested the elasticity of the material. He found that it stretched about fifteen percent and always restored itself, albeit very slowly at times, to its original length. The restoration time varied

significantly, depending on how long the piece had been
fully stretched. Richard had already begun his examination of the inside structure of the cord when they arrived
at the barn.

Nicole did not waste any time. She tied one end of the
lattice material around a stumpy object just outside the
barn and lowered herself down the wall. Richard's function was to make certain that nothing untoward occurred
and to be available if there was some kind of an emergency. Down in the bottom of the pit Nicole shuddered
once as she remembered how helpless she had felt there
just a few days earlier. But she quickly turned her attention to her task, inserting a makeshift handle made from
her medical probes deep into the manna melon and then
securing the other end of the handle to her backpack. Her
ascent was vigorous and uneventful.

"Well." She smiled at Richard as she handed him the
melon to carry. "Should we now continue with Plan A?"

"Roger," he replied. "Now we know where our next ten
meals are coming from."

"Nine," Nicole corrected with a laugh. "I've made a
slight adjustment in the estimate now that I've watched
you eat a couple of times."

Richard and Nicole marched quickly from the barn to
the western plaza. They crisscrossed the open area and
combed the narrow alleys nearby, but they did not find
anything that would help them build a boat. Richard did
have an encounter with a centipede biot, however; in the
middle of their search one had entered the plaza and then
moved diagonally across it. Richard had done everything
possible, including lying in front of it and beating it over
the head with his backpack, to try to induce the biot to
stop. He had not been successful. Nicole was laughing at
him when Richard returned, a little frustrated, to her
side.

"That centipede is absolutely useless," he complained.
"What the hell is it for? It's not carrying anything. It has
no sensors that I can see. It just travels merrily along."

"The technology of an advanced extraterrestrial species," she reminded Richard of one of his favorite quotes, "will be indistinguishable from magic."

"But that damn centipede's not magic," he replied, a little annoyed at Nicole's laughter, "it's goddamn stupid!"

"And what would you have done if it had stopped?" Nicole inquired.

"Why, I would have examined it, of course. What did you think?"

"I think we'd be better off concentrating our energy in other areas," she replied. "I don't imagine a centipede biot is going to help us get off this island."

"Well," Richard said a little brusquely, "it's obvious to me already we're going about this process all wrong. We're not going to find anything on the surface. The biots probably clean it up regularly. We should be looking for another hole in the ground, like the avian's lair. We can use the multispectral radar to identify any places where the ground is not solid."

It took them a long time to find the second hole, even though it was not more than two hundred meters from the center of the western plaza. At first Richard and Nicole were much too restrictive in their search. After an hour, though, they finally convinced themselves that the ground underneath the plaza area was solid everywhere. They expanded their search to include the small streets and lanes nearby, off the concentric avenues. On a dead-end alley with tall buildings on three sides, they found another covering in the center of the road. It was not camouflaged in any way. This second cover was the same size as the one at the avian lair, a rectangle ten meters long and six meters wide.

45

NIKKI

"Do you think the avian cover opens in the same way?"
Nicole asked, after Richard had very carefully searched
the environs and found a flat plate on one of the buildings
that looked decidedly out of place. Pressing hard against
the plate had caused the cover to open.

"Probably," he answered. "We'll have to go back and
check."

"Then these places are not very secure," Nicole said.
The two of them walked back onto the street and knelt
down to look in the hole. A broad, steep ramp descended
from beside them and disappeared into the darkness below. They could only see about ten meters into the hole.

"It looks like one of those ancient parking lots," Richard
remarked. "Back when everybody had automobiles." He
stepped on the ramp. "It even feels like concrete."

Nicole watched as her companion moved slowly down
the ramp. When Richard's head was below the ground
level, he turned and spoke to her. "Aren't you coming?"
he asked. He had switched on his flashlight beam and had
illuminated a small landing another few meters below.

"Richard," Nicole said from above, "I think we should
discuss this. I don't want to be stuck—"

"Ah-ha!" Richard exclaimed. As soon as his foot hit the
first landing, some lights around him automatically lit the
next phase of the descent. "The ramp doubles back," he
shouted, "and continues down. Looks just the same." He
turned and disappeared from Nicole's field of view.

"Richard," Nicole now yelled, a little exasperated, "will
you please stop for a minute? We must talk about what
we're doing."

A few seconds later Richard's smiling face reappeared.

The two cosmonauts discussed their options. Nicole insisted that she was going to stay outside, in New York, even if Richard was going to continue with his exploration. At least that way, she argued, she could guarantee that they would not be stranded in the hole.

While she was talking, Richard was standing on the first landing and surveying the area around him. The walls were made of the same material Nicole had found in the avian lair. Small strip lights, looking not unlike normal fluorescent lights on Earth, ran along the wall to illuminate the path.

"Move away just a second, will you?" Richard shouted in the middle of their conversation.

At first puzzled, Nicole backed away from the entrance to the rectangular hole. "Farther," she heard Richard yell. Nicole walked over and stood against one of the surrounding buildings.

"Is this far enough?" she had just finished shouting when the covering on the hole began to close. Nicole ran forward and tried to stop the motion of the cover, but it was much too heavy. "Richard," she cried as the hole disappeared beneath her.

Nicole pounded on the cover and remembered her own feelings of frustration when she had been locked in the avian lair. She quickly ran back over to the building and pressed the embedded flat panel. Nothing happened. Almost a minute passed. Nicole became anxious. She ran back into the street and called for her colleague.

"I'm right here, under the cover," he answered, bringing Nicole considerable relief. "I found another plate near the first landing and pressed it. I think it toggles the cover closed or open, but it may have a timing delay constraint. Give me a few minutes. Don't you try to open the cover. And don't stand too near it."

Nicole backed away and waited. Richard had been correct. Several minutes later the cover opened and he emerged from the hole with a big grin on his face. "See," he said, "I told you not to worry. . . . Now what's for lunch?"

As they descended the ramp, Nicole heard the familiar

sound of running water. In a little room about twenty
meters behind the landing, they found the identical piping
and cistern that had been in the avian lair. Richard and
Nicole both filled their flasks with the fresh, delicious
water.

Outside the room there were no horizontal tunnels leading off in both directions, only another descending ramp
dropping five more meters beneath the floor. Richard's
flashlight beam crawled slowly across the dark walls near
the water room. "Look here, Nicole," he said, pointing at
what was a very subtle variation in building material.
"See, it arches around to the other side."

She followed his beam as it inscribed a long circular arc
on the wall. "It looks as if there were at least two phases of
construction."

"Exactly," he replied. "Maybe there were horizontal
tunnels here as well, at least in the beginning, and they
were sealed off later." Neither of them said anything else
as they continued their descent. Back and forth went the
identical ramps. Whenever Richard and Nicole touched a
new landing, the next descending ramp was illuminated.

They were fifty meters underneath the surface when the
ceilings above them opened up and the ramps terminated
in a large cavern. The circular floor of the cave was about
twenty-five meters in diameter. There were four dark
tunnels, five meters in height and equally spaced at ninety
degrees around the circle, that exited from the cavern.

"Eenie, Meenie, Mynie, Moe," Richard said.

"I'll take Moe," Nicole said. She headed toward one of
the tunnels. When she was within a few meters of the
entrance, the lights in the near portion of the tunnel
switched on.

This time it was Richard's turn to be hesitant. He stared
cautiously into the tunnel and made some quick entries
into his computer. "Does it look to you as if this tunnel
curves slightly to the right? See, there at the end of the
lights?"

Nicole nodded. She looked over Richard's shoulder to
see what he was doing. "I'm making a map," he said in
response to her curiosity. "Theseus had string and Hansel

and Gretel had bread. We have them both beat. Aren't computers wonderful?"

She smiled. "So what's your guess?" Nicole said while they were walking along in the near part of the tunnel. "Will it be a Minotaur or a gingerbread house with a wicked witch?"

We should be so lucky, Nicole thought. Her fear was increasing as they penetrated deeper and deeper into the tunnel. She recalled that awful moment of terror in the pit when she had first seen the avian hovering over her with its beak and talons extending in her direction. An icy chill ran down her spine. *There it is again,* she said to herself, *that feeling that something terrible is going to happen.*

She stopped. "Richard," she said, "I don't like this. We should turn back—"

They both heard the noise at the same time. It was definitely *behind* them, back in the vicinity of the circular cavern they had just left. It sounded like hard brushes dragging against metal.

Richard and Nicole huddled together. "That's the same sound," he whispered, "that I heard the first night in Rama, when we were at the walls of New York."

The tunnel behind them curved slightly to the left. When they looked back in that direction, the lights were off at the limit of their vision. The second time they heard the sound, however, some lights came on in the far distance almost simultaneously, indicating something was near the entrance to their tunnel.

Nicole bolted. She must have covered the next two hundred meters in thirty seconds, despite her flight suit and backpack. She stopped and waited for Richard. Neither of them heard the sound again and no new lights were illuminated in the distant reaches of the tunnel.

"I'm sorry," Nicole said when Richard finally arrived. "I panicked. I think I've been in this alien wonderland too long."

"Jesus," Richard responded with a disapproving frown. "I've never seen anybody run that fast." His frown changed into a smile. "Don't feel bad, Nikki," he said. "I was scared shitless too. But I was frozen in place."

Nicole continued taking deep breaths and stared at Rich-

ard. "What did you call me?" she asked, somewhat
belligerently.

"Nikki," he replied. "I thought it was time for me to
have my own special name for you. Don't you like it?"

Nicole was speechless for ten full seconds. Her mind
was millions of kilometers and fifteen years away, in a
hotel suite in Los Angeles, her body experiencing wave
after wave of pleasure. "That was remarkable, Nikki, truly
wonderful," the prince had said several minutes later. She
had told Henry on that night fifteen years before not to
call her Nikki, that it sounded like a name for a buxom
showgirl or a tart.

Richard was snapping his fingers in front of her face.
"Hello, hello. Anybody home?"

Nicole smiled. "Sure, Richard," she replied. "Nikki's
just fine—as long as you don't use it all the time."

They continued to walk slowly along the tunnel. "So
where did you go back there?" Richard asked.

Somewhere I can never tell you about, Nicole mused.
*Because each of us is the sum of all we have ever experi-
enced. Only the very young have a clean slate. The rest of
us must live forever with everything we have ever been.*
She slid her arm through Richard's. *And must have the
good sense to know when to keep it private.*

The tunnel seemed endless. Richard and Nicole had
almost decided to turn around when they came to a dark
entryway off to their right. With no hesitation they both
walked inside. The lights came on immediately. Inside the
room, on the big wall to the left of them, were twenty-five
flat rectangular objects, arranged in five orderly rows with
five columns each. The opposite wall was empty. Within
seconds after their entrance, the two cosmonauts heard a
high-frequency squeaky sound coming from the ceiling.
They tensed briefly, but relaxed as the squeaking continued and there were no new surprises.

They held hands and walked to one end of the long
narrow room. The objects on the wall were photographs,
most of them recognizable as having been taken somewhere inside Rama. The great octahedron near the central
plaza was featured in several of the photos. The remaining

pictures were a balance between scenes of the buildings of New York and wide-angle shots of panoramas around the interior of Rama.

Three of the photographs were particularly fascinating to Richard. They depicted sleek, aerodynamically curved boats plying the Cylindrical Sea; in one of the photographs a great wave was about to crash over the top of a large boat. "Now there's what we need," Richard said to Nicole excitedly. "If we could find one of them, our troubles would be over."

The squeaking above them continued with very little modulation. A spotlight moved from picture to picture at moments when there was a pause in the squeak. Nicole and Richard easily concluded that they were in a museum on some kind of tour, but there was nothing else they could know for certain. Nicole sat down against a side wall. "I'm having a lot of trouble with all this," she said. "I feel totally out of control."

Richard sat down beside her. "Me too," he said, nodding. "And I just arrived in New York. So I can imagine what all this is doing to you."

They were silent for a moment. "You know what bothers me the most?" Nicole said, trying to give some expression to the helplessness she was feeling. "It's how very little I understood and appreciated my own ignorance. Before I came on this voyage, I thought I knew the general dimensions of the relationship between my own knowledge and the knowledge of mankind. But what is staggering about this mission is how very small the *entire range* of human knowledge might be compared to what *could* be known. Just think, the sum of everything all human beings know or have ever known might be nothing more than an infinitesimal fraction of the *Encyclopedia Galactica*—"

"It *is* really frightening," Richard interrupted enthusiastically. "And thrilling at the same time. . . . Sometimes when I'm in a bookstore or a library, I am overwhelmed by all the things that I do not know. Then I am seized by a powerful desire to read all the books, one by one. Imagine what it would be like to be in the *true* library, one that combined the knowledge of all the species in the universe. . . . The very thought makes me woozy."

Nicole turned to him and slapped his leg. "All right, Richard," she said jokingly, changing the mood, "now that we have reaffirmed how incredibly stupid we are, what's our plan? I figure we have already covered about a kilometer in this tunnel. Where do we go from here?"

"I propose we walk another fifteen minutes in the same direction. In my experience tunnels always lead someplace. If we don't find anything, we'll turn around."

He helped Nicole up and gave her a small hug. "All right, Nikki," he said with a wink. "Half a league onward."

Nicole frowned and shook her head. "Twice is enough for one day," she said, extending her hand toward Richard.

46

THE BETTER PART OF VALOR

The huge circular hole below them extended into the darkness. Only the top five meters of the shaft were lit. Metal spikes, about a meter long, protruded from the wall, each separated from its neighbors by the same distance.

"This is definitely the destination of the tunnels," Richard muttered to himself. He was having some difficulty integrating this huge, cylindrical hole with its walls of spikes into his overall conception of Rama. He and Nicole had walked around the perimeter twice. They had even backtracked several hundred meters down the other, adjacent tunnel, concluding from its slight curvature to the right that it had probably originated at the same cavern as the tunnel they had followed earlier.

"Well," Richard said at length, shrugging his shoulders, "here we go." He put his right foot on one of the spikes to test its ability to hold his weight. It was firm. He moved his left leg down to another of the spikes and descended one more level with his right leg. "The spacing is nearly perfect," he said, glancing back at Nicole. "It shouldn't be a difficult climb."

"Richard Wakefield," Nicole said from the rim of the hole, "are you trying to tell me that you intend to climb down into that chasm? And that you expect me to follow?"

"I don't expect anything of you," he replied. "But I can't see turning back now. What's our alternative? Should we go back down the tunnel to the ramps and exit? For what? To see if anyone has found us yet? You saw the photographs of the boats. Maybe they're right here at the bottom. Maybe there's even a secret river that runs underground into the Cylindrical Sea."

"Maybe," Nicole said, starting to descend slowly now

that Richard's progress had triggered another bank of lights below them, "one of those things that made the bizarre noise is waiting for us down at the bottom."

"I'll find out," Richard said. "Hallooo, down there. We two human-type beings are coming down." He waved and momentarily lost his balance.

"Don't be a show-off," Nicole said, coming down beside him. She paused to catch her breath and look around. Her two feet were resting on spikes and she was holding tightly to two others with her hands. *I must be insane*, she said to herself. *Just look at this place. It's easy to imagine a hundred gruesome deaths.* Richard had dropped down to another pair of spikes. *And look at him. Is he totally immune to fear? Or just reckless? He actually seems to be enjoying all this.*

The third bank of lights illuminated a lattice on the opposite wall below them. It was hanging among all the spikes and, from a distance in the dim light, looked startlingly like a smaller version of the object that had been attached to the two skyscrapers in New York. Richard hurried around the cylinder to examine the lattice. "Come over here," he shouted at Nicole. "I think it's the same damn material."

The lattice was anchored to the wall by small bolts. At Richard's insistence, Nicole cut off a piece and handed it to him. He stretched it and watched it regain its shape. He studied its internal structure. "It *is* the same stuff," he said. His brow knitted into furrows. "But what the hell does it mean?"

Nicole stood beside him and idly shone her flashlight into the depths below them. She was about to suggest that they climb out and head for more familiar terrain when she thought she saw a reflection from a floor about twenty meters below. "I'm going to make you a proposition," Nicole said to Richard. "While you're studying that lattice cord, I'll drop down another several meters. We may be near the bottom of this bizarre well of spikes, or whatever it is. If not, then we'll abandon this place."

"All right," Richard said absentmindedly. He was already involved in his examination of the lattice cord using the microscope he had taken from his backpack.

Nicole nimbly descended to the floor. "I guess you'd better come down," she called to Richard. "There are two more tunnels, one large and one small. Plus another hole in the center—" He was beside her immediately. He had climbed down as soon as he had seen the lower platform illuminated by lights.

Richard and Nicole were now standing on a ledge three meters wide at the bottom of the spiked cylinder. The ledge formed a ring around another smaller descending hole that also had spikes growing out of its walls. To their left and right, dark arched tunnels were cut into the rock or metal that was the base construction material for the extensive underground world. The tunnel on their left was five to six meters high; the tiny tunnel on the opposite side, one hundred and eighty degrees around the ring, was only half a meter tall.

Running out of each of the two tunnels, and penetrating half a ledge-width into the ring, were two small parallel strips of unknown material that were fastened to the floor. The strips were very close together in the smaller tunnel and more widely spaced in the other. Richard was sitting on his knees examining the strips in front of the large tunnel when he heard a distant rumble. "Listen," he said to Nicole, as the two of them instinctively backed away from the entrance.

The rumbling increased and changed into a whining sound, as if something were moving swiftly through the air. Far off in the tunnel, which ran straight as an arrow, Richard and Nicole could see some lights switch on. They tensed. They didn't need to wait long for an explanation. A vehicle that resembled a hovering subway burst into view and sped toward them, stopping suddenly with its front edge just over the farthest extension of the strips on the floor.

Richard and Nicole had recoiled as the vehicle had hurtled toward them. Both were dangerously close to the edge of the ring. For several seconds they stood in silence, each staring at the aerodynamic shape hovering in front of them. Then they looked at each other and laughed simultaneously. "Okay," Nicole said nervously, "I get it. We've crossed into some new dimension. In this one it's just a little difficult to find the subway station. . . . This is so totally absurd. We climb down a spiked barrel and end up in a Metro station. . . . I don't know about you, Richard, but I've had enough. I'll take a few *normal* avians and manna melon any day of the week. . . ."

Richard had walked over beside the vehicle. A door in the side had opened and they could both see the lit interior. There were no seats, only thin cylindrical poles, spaced in no obvious pattern, that ran the three meters from the ceiling to the floor. "It can't go far," Richard said, sticking his head inside the door but leaving his feet on the ledge outside. "There's no place to sit down."

Nicole came over to inspect for herself. "Maybe they have no old or crippled people—and the grocery stores are all close to home." She laughed again as Richard leaned farther into the car so he could see the ceiling and walls more clearly. "Don't get any crazy ideas," she said. "It would be certifiably insane for us to climb aboard that car. Unless we were out of food and it was our last hope."

"I guess you're right," Richard replied. He was definitely disappointed as he withdrew from the subway car. "But what an amazing—" He stopped himself in midsentence. He was staring across the platform at the opposite side of the ledge. There, in the middle of the now illuminated entrance to the tiny tunnel, an identical vehicle, one tenth the size of the one next to them, was hovering off the floor. Nicole followed Richard's gaze.

"That must be the road to Lilliput over there," Nicole said. "Giants descend another floor and normal-size creatures take this subway. It's all very simple."

Richard walked swiftly around the ring. "That's perfect," he said out loud, taking off his backpack and setting it on the ledge beside him. He began to rummage in one of the large pockets.

"What are you doing?" Nicole asked.

Richard pulled two tiny figures out of the pack and showed them to her. "It's perfect," he repeated, his excitement unmistakable. "We can send Prince Hal and Falstaff. I'll only need a few minutes to adjust their software."

Already Richard had spread his pocket computer out on

the ledge beside the robots and was busily working away. Nicole sat down with her back against the wall between two spikes. She glanced over at Richard. *He is truly a rare species,* she said with admiration, thinking back over their hours together. *A genius, that's obvious. Almost without guile or meanness. And somehow he has retained the curiosity of a child.*

Nicole suddenly felt very tired. She smiled to herself as she was watching Richard. He was absorbed in his work. Nicole closed her eyes for a moment.

"I'm sorry that I took so long," Richard was saying. "I kept thinking of new things to add and I needed to re-arrange the linkage . . ."

Nicole woke up from her nap very slowly. "How long have we been here?" she said as she yawned.

"A little over an hour," Richard answered sheepishly. "But everything is all set. I'm ready to put the boys in the subway."

Nicole glanced around her. "Both the cars are still here," she commented.

"I think they work like all the lights. I bet they will stay in the station as long as we're on the platform."

Nicole stood up and stretched. "So here's the plan," Richard said. "I have the controlling transceiver in my hand. Hal and Sir John each have audio, video, and infra-red sensors that will acquire data continuously. We can choose which channel to monitor on our computers and send new commands as necessary."

"But will the signals penetrate the walls?" Nicole asked, remembering her experience inside the barn.

"As long as they don't have to travel through too much material. The system is way overdesigned in terms of signal to noise to accommodate some attenuation. . . . Besides, the large subway came at us along a straight line. I'm hoping this one will be similar."

Richard gingerly set the two robots down on the ledge and commanded them to walk toward the subway. Doors opened on both sides as they drew near. "Remember me to Mistress Quickly," Falstaff said as he climbed aboard. "She was a stupid lass, but with a good heart."

Nicole gave Richard a puzzled glance. "I didn't over-write all their earlier programming," he said with a laugh. "From time to time they will probably make some absurd random comments."

The two robots stood on the subway for a minute or two. Richard hastily checked their sensors and made one more set of calibrations on the monitor. At length the doors of the subway closed, the vehicle waited for another ten seconds, and then it rushed away into the tunnel.

Richard commanded Falstaff to face the front, but there was not much to be seen out the window. It was a surprisingly long ride at a very high speed. Richard estimated that the little subway had traveled more than a kilometer before it finally slowed to a stop.

Richard waited before commanding the two robots to leave the subway. He wanted to make certain that they did not get off at an intermediate stop. However, there was no need to worry: the first full set of imaging data from Prince Hal and Falstaff showed that the subway had indeed reached the end of the line.

The two robots walked around the flat platform beside the vehicle and photographed more of their surroundings. The subway station had arches and columns, but it was basically one long, connected room. Richard estimated from the images that the ceiling height was about two meters. He commanded Hal and Falstaff to follow a long hallway that moved off to the left, perpendicular to the subway track.

The hallway terminated in front of another tunnel, this one barely five centimeters high. As the robots examined the floor, finding two tiny strips extending almost to their feet, a subway of minuscule proportions arrived in the station. With its doors open and its interior lit, Richard and Nicole could see that the new subway car was identical, except for its size, to the two they had seen before.

The cosmonauts were sitting together with their knees on the ledge, both avidly watching the small computer monitor. Richard commanded Falstaff to take a picture of Prince Hal standing next to the tiny subway. "The car itself," Richard said to Nicole after studying the image, "is less than two centimeters tall. What's going to ride in it? Ants?"

Nicole shook her head and said nothing. She was feeling bewildered again. At that moment she was also thinking about her initial reactions to Rama. *Never in my wildest imagination,* she thought, recalling her awe at that first panoramic sight, *did I foresee that there would be so many new mysteries. The first explorers hardly scratched the surface—*

"Richard," Nicole said, interrupting her own thoughts.

He commanded the robots to walk back down the hallway and then glanced up from the monitor. "Yes?" he said.

"How thick is the outer shell of Rama?"

"I think the ferry covers about four hundred meters altogether," he said with a slightly puzzled expression. "But that's at one of the ends. We have no definite way of knowing how thick the shell is anywhere else. Norton and crew reported that the depth of the Cylindrical Sea was highly variable—as little as forty meters in some places and as much as a hundred and fifty elsewhere. That would suggest to me a shell thickness of several hundred meters at least."

Richard checked the monitor quickly. Prince Hal and Falstaff were almost back at the station where they had climbed off the subway. He transmitted a stop command and turned to Nicole. "Why are you asking? It's not like you to ask idle questions."

"There's obviously an entire unexplored world down here," Nicole replied. "It would take a lifetime—"

"We don't have that long," Richard broke in with a laugh. "At least not a normal lifetime. . . . But back to your thickness question, remember the entire Southern Hemicylinder has a floor level four hundred and fifty meters above the north. So unless there are some major structural irregularities—and we certainly haven't seen any from the outside—the thickness should be substantially greater in the south."

Richard waited for Nicole to say something additional. When she remained silent for several seconds, he turned back to the monitor and continued his surrogate exploration with the robots.

There had been a good reason for Nicole's question about the thickness of the shell. She had a picture in her mind that she could not shake. Nicole was imagining coming to the end of one of these long underground tunnels, opening a door, and then being blinded by the light of the Sun. *Wouldn't it be incredible,* she was thinking, *to be an intelligent creature living in this maze of dim light and tunnels and then, by chance, to stumble onto something that would irrevocably change your entire concept of the Universe? How could you return—*

"Now what in the world is that?" Richard was asking. Nicole stopped her mental drifting and focused on the monitor. Prince Hal and Falstaff had entered a large room at the opposite end of the subway station and were standing in front of a conglomeration of loose, spongelike webbing. The infrared image of the scene showed a nested sphere, inside the web, that was radiating heat. At Nicole's suggestion, Richard commanded the robots to walk around the object and survey the rest of this new domain.

The room was immense. It extended into the distance farther than the resolution of the video devices carried by the robots. The ceiling was about twenty meters high and the two side walls were separated by more than fifty meters. Several other similar spherical objects encased in spongy masses could be seen scattered about the room in the distance. A lattice, stretching almost all the way across the room but stopping five meters above the floor, dangled from the high ceiling in the foreground. Another lattice could barely be discerned a hundred meters or so behind the first one.

Richard and Nicole discussed what the robots should do next. There were no other exits from either the subway station or the large room. A panoramic image around the room revealed nothing nearby of interest except the sphere embedded in its spongy exterior. Nicole wanted to bring the robots back and leave the lair altogether. Richard's curiosity demanded at least a cursory investigation of one of the spherical objects.

The two robots were able, with some difficulty, to climb

around and through the webbed material to reach the sphere in the center. The ambient temperature increased as they neared the sphere. One of the purposes of the external material was clearly to absorb heat. When the robots reached the nested sphere, their internal monitors flashed a warning that the outside temperatures exceeded their safe operating limits.

Richard moved quickly. Directing the robots on a nearly continuous basis, he determined that the sphere was virtually impenetrable and was probably made of a thick metal alloy with a very hard surface. Falstaff banged on the sphere several times with his arm; the resulting sound damped quickly, indicating the sphere was full, possibly with a liquid. The two robots were weaving their way out of the sponge webbing when their audio systems picked up the sound of brushes dragging against metal.

Richard tried to speed up their escape. Hal was able to increase his pace but Falstaff, whose subsystem temperatures had risen too high during his proximity to the sphere, was prevented by his own internal processor logic from accelerating his actions. The brush sound continued to grow louder.

The computer monitor on the ledge between the two cosmonauts was changed to split screen. Prince Hal reached the edge of the sponge, hit the floor, and headed for the subway without waiting for his companion. Falstaff continued to climb slowly through the webbing. " 'Tis too much work for a drinking man," he mumbled, as he crawled over another barrier.

The dragging metal sound abruptly stopped and Falstaff's camera recorded an image of a long, skinny object with black and gold stripes. Moments later the camera frame went to all black and the little robot's "Terminal Fault Imminent" alarm began to sound. Richard and Nicole had one more fleeting glimpse of a picture from Falstaff; it showed what might have been a giant eye, from up close, a black gelatinous mixture tinged with blue. Then all transmissions from the robot, including emergency telemetry, abruptly ceased.

Meanwhile Hal had entered the waiting subway. During the several seconds before the subway left the station,

the ominous dragging sound was heard again. But the
subway departed anyway, with the robot inside, and started
speeding through the tunnel toward the two cosmonauts.
Richard and Nicole breathed a sigh of relief.

Not more than a second later a loud sound like breaking
glass was picked up by Prince Hal's audio system. Richard
commanded the robot to turn in the direction of the sound
and Hal's camera photographed a solitary black and gold
tentacle in midair. The tentacle had broken the window
and was moving inexorably toward the robot. Both Richard and Nicole realized what was happening at the same
moment. The thing was on top of the subway! And it was
coming toward them!

Nicole was climbing the spikes in a flash. Richard wasted
several valuable seconds picking up his computer monitor
and putting all his equipment in the backpack. He heard
Prince Hal's Terminal Fault Imminent alarm when he was
halfway up the spikes. Richard turned around to look just
as the subway pulled into the tunnel below him.

What he saw made his blood run cold. On top of the
subway was a large dark creature whose central body, if
that's indeed what it was, was flattened against the roof.
Striped tentacles extended in all directions. Four of them
had pierced the windows of the train and grabbed the
robot. The thing quickly climbed off the subway and
wrapped one of its eight tentacles around the lowest spikes.
Richard didn't watch anymore. He clambered up the rest
of the cylinder and started racing through the tunnel at
the top, following the steps of Nicole far ahead of him in
the distance.

As he ran, Richard noticed that the tunnel was curving
slightly to the right. He reminded himself that even though
this was not the same tunnel they had used before, it
should still lead them to the ramps. After several hundred
meters Richard stopped to listen for the sound of his
pursuer. He heard nothing. Richard had just taken two
deep breaths and started to run again when his ears were
assaulted by a terrible wail in front of him. It was Nicole.
Oh shit, he thought, as he rushed forward to find her.

47

PROGRESSIVE MATRICES

"Never, never in my entire life," Nicole said to Richard, "have I ever seen anything that terrified me like that." The two cosmonauts were sitting with their backs against the bottom of one of the skyscrapers surrounding the western plaza. They were both still breathing heavily, exhausted from their frantic escape. Nicole took a long drink of water.

"I had just started to relax," she continued. "I could hear you behind me—and nothing else. I decided I would stop in the museum and wait for you to catch up. It hadn't yet occurred to me that we were in the 'other' tunnel.

"It should have been obvious, of course, because the opening was on the wrong side. But I wasn't thinking logically at the moment. . . . Anyway, I stepped inside the room, the lights came on, and there he was, not more than three meters in front of me. I thought my heart had stopped altogether. . . ."

Richard remembered Nicole running into his arms in the tunnel and sobbing for several seconds. "It's Takagishi . . . stuffed like a deer or a tiger . . . in the opening to the right," she had said in fits and starts. After Nicole had regained her composure, the two of them had walked back down the tunnel together. Inside the opening, standing upright just opposite the entrance, Richard had been shocked to see Newton cosmonaut Shigeru Takagishi. He was dressed in his flight suit and looked exactly as he had the last time they had seen him at the Beta campsite. His face was fixed in a pleasant smile and his arms were at his sides.

"What the hell?" Richard had said, blinking twice, his curiosity only slightly stronger than his terror. Nicole had averted her eyes. Even though she had seen the sight before, the stuffed Takagishi was much too lifelike for her.

They had only stayed in the large room for a minute. Alien taxidermy had also performed wonders on an avian with a broken wing that was hanging from the ceiling next to Takagishi. Against the wall behind the Japanese scientist was Richard and Nicole's hut that had disappeared the day before. The hexagonal electronics board from the Newton portable science station was on the floor next to Takagishi's feet, not far from a full-scale model of a bulldozer biot. Other biot replicas were scattered around the room.

Richard had started to study the varied collection of biots in the room when they had faintly heard the familiar dragging noise coming from behind them in the tunnel. They had not wasted any more time. Their flight down the tunnel and up the ramps had been broken only by a brief stop at the cistern to replenish their supply of fresh water.

"Dr. Takagishi was a gentle, sensitive man," Nicole was saying to Richard, "with passionate feelings about his work. Just before launch I visited him in Japan and he told me that his lifelong ambition had been to explore a second Rama spacecraft."

"It's a shame he had to die such an unpleasant death," Richard grimly replied. "I guess that octospider, or one of its friends, must have dragged him down here for a visit to the taxidermist almost immediately. They certainly wasted no time putting him on display."

"You know, I don't think they killed him," Nicole said. "Maybe I'm hopelessly naive, but I didn't see any evidence of foul play in his . . . his statue."

"You think they just scared him to death?" Richard retorted sarcastically.

"Yes," said Nicole firmly. "At least it's possible." She spent the next five minutes explaining Takagishi's heart situation to Richard.

"I'm surprised at you, Nicole," Richard replied after listening carefully to her disclosure. "I had you figured all wrong. I thought you were Miss Prim and Proper, play it by the rules all the way. I never gave you credit for having a mind of your own. Not to mention a strong streak of compassion."

"In this instance it's not clear that either was an asset. If I had faithfully enforced the rules, Takagishi would be alive and living with his family in Kyoto."

"And he would have missed the singular experience of his life . . . which brings me to an interesting question, my dear doctor. Surely you are aware, as we sit here, that the odds do not favor our escape. We are both likely to die without ever seeing another human face. How do you feel about that? Where does your death—or any death, for that matter—fit into your overall scheme of things?"

Nicole looked at Richard. She was surprised by the tenor of his question. She tried without success to read the expression on his face. "I'm not afraid, if that's what you mean," she answered carefully. "As a doctor I've thought often about death. And of course since my mother died when I was very young, even as a child I was forced to have some perspective on the subject."

She paused for a moment. "For myself, I know that I would like to stay alive until Genevieve is grown—so that I can be a grandmother to her children. But just being alive is not the most important thing. Life must have quality to be worthwhile. And to have quality we must be willing to take a few risks. . . . I'm not being very focused, am I?"

Richard smiled. "No," he said, "but I like your general drift. You have mentioned the key word. Quality. . . . Have you ever considered suicide?" he asked suddenly.

"No," Nicole replied, shaking her head. "Never. There's always been too much to live for." *There must be some reason for his question,* she was thinking. "What about you?" she said after a short silence. "Did you think about suicide during any of that pain with your father?"

"No, strangely enough," he answered. "My father's beatings never made me lose my zest for life. There was too much to learn. And I knew that I would outgrow him and be on my own eventually." There was a long pause before he continued. "But there was one period in my life when I did seriously consider suicide," Richard said. "My pain and anger were so great that I did not think I could endure them."

He became silent, locked in his thoughts. Nicole waited patiently. Eventually she slipped her arm through his. "Well, my friend," she said lightly, "you can tell me about it someday. Neither of us is accustomed to sharing our deepest secrets. Maybe in time we can learn. I'm going to start by telling you why I believe we are not going to die and why I think we should go over to search the area around the eastern plaza next."

Nicole had never told anyone, not even her father, about her "trip" during the Poro. Before she finished telling her story to Richard, not only had Nicole covered what had happened to her as a seven-year-old at the Poro, but also she had recounted the story of Omeh's visit to Rome, the Senoufo prophecies about the "woman without companion" who scatters her progeny "among the stars," and the details of her vision after drinking the vial at the bottom of the pit.

Richard was speechless. The entire set of stories was so foreign to his mathematical mind that he did not even know how to react. He stared at Nicole with awe and amazement. At length, embarrassed by his silence, he started to speak. "I don't know what to say . . ."

Nicole put her fingers to his lips. "You don't need to say anything," she said. "I can read your reaction in your face. We can talk about it tomorrow, after you've had some time to think about what I told you."

Nicole yawned and looked at her watch. She pulled her sleeping mat out of her backpack and unrolled it on the ground. "I'm exhausted," she said to Richard. "Nothing like a little terror to produce instant fatigue. I'll see you in four hours."

"We've been searching now for an hour and a half," Richard said impatiently. "Look at this map. There's no place within five hundred meters of the plaza center that we haven't covered at least twice."

"Then we're doing something wrong," Nicole replied. "There were *three* heat sources in my vision." Richard frowned. "Or be logical, if you prefer. Why would there be three plazas and only two underground lairs? You said yourself that the Ramans always followed a reasonable plan."

They were standing in front of a dodecahedron that faced the eastern plaza. "And another thing," Richard growled to himself, "what's the purpose of all these damn polyhedrons? There's one in every sector and the three biggest are in the plazas. . . . Wait a minute," he said, as his eyes went from one of the twelve faces of the dodecahedron to an opposite skyscraper. His head then turned quickly around the plaza. "Could it be?" he said. "No," he answered, "that would be impossible."

Richard saw that Nicole was staring at him. "I have an idea," he said excitedly. "It may be completely far-fetched. . . . Do you remember Dr. Bardolini and his progressive matrices? With the dolphins? . . . What if the Ramans also left a pattern here in New York of subtle differences that change from plaza to plaza and section to section? . . . Look, it's no crazier than your visions."

Already Richard was on his knees on the ground, working with his maps of New York. "Can I use your computer too?" he said to Nicole a few minutes later. "That will speed up the process."

For hours Richard Wakefield sat beside the two computers, mumbling to himself and trying to solve the puzzle of New York. He explained to Nicole, when he took a break for dinner at her insistence, that the location of the third underground hole could only be determined if he thoroughly understood the geometric relationships between the polyhedrons, the three plazas, and all the skyscrapers immediately opposite the principal faces of the polyhedrons in each of the nine sectors. Two hours before dark Richard dashed off hurriedly to an adjacent section to obtain extra data that had not been recorded on their computer maps.

Even after dark he did not rest. Nicole slept the first part of the fifteen-hour night. When she awoke after five hours, Richard was still working feverishly on his project. He didn't even hear Nicole clear her throat. She arose quietly and put her hands on his shoulders. "You must get some sleep, Richard," she said quietly.

"I'm almost there," he said. She saw the bags under his eyes when he turned around. "No more than another hour."

Nicole returned to her mat. When Richard awakened her later, he was full of enthusiasm. "Wouldn't you know it?" he said with a grin. "There are three possible solutions, each of which is consistent with all the patterns." He paced for almost a minute. "Could we go look now?" he then said pleadingly. "I don't think I can sleep until I find out."

None of Richard's three solutions for the location of the third lair was close to the plaza. The nearest one was over a kilometer away, at the edge of New York opposite the Northern Hemicylinder. He and Nicole found nothing there. They then marched another fifteen minutes in the dark to the second possible location, a spot very near the southeast corner of the city. Richard and Nicole walked down the indicated street and found the covering in the exact spot that Richard had predicted. "Hallelujah," he shouted, spreading out his sleeping mat beside the cover. "Hooray for mathematics."

Hooray for Omeh, Nicole thought. She was no longer sleepy but she wasn't anxious to explore any new territory in the dark. *What comes first,* she asked herself after they had returned to camp and she was lying awake on her mat, *intuition or mathematics? Do we use models to help us find the truth? Or do we know the truth first, and then develop the mathematics to explain it?*

They were both up at daylight. "The days are still growing slightly shorter," Richard mentioned to Nicole. "But the sum of daytime and nighttime is remaining constant at forty-six hours, four minutes, and fourteen seconds."

"How long before we reach the Earth?" Nicole inquired as she was stuffing her sleeping mat into its protective package.

"Twenty Earth days and three hours," he replied after consulting his computer. "Are you ready for another adventure?"

She nodded. "I presume you also know where to find the panel that opens this cover?"

"No, but I bet it's not hard to find," he said confidently. "And after we find this one, the avian lair opening will be duck soup because we'll have the whole pattern."

Ten minutes later Richard pushed on a metal plate and the third covering swung open. The descent into this third hole was down a wide staircase broken by occasional landings. Richard took Nicole's hand as they walked down the stairs. They used their flashlights to find their way, as no lights illuminated their descent.

The water room was in the same place as in the other underground lairs. There were no sounds in the horizontal tunnels that led off from the central stairway at either of the two main levels. "I don't think anyone lives here," Richard said.

"At least not yet," Nicole answered.

48

WELCOME EARTHLINGS

Richard was puzzled. In the first room off one of the top horizontal tunnels he had found an array of strange gadgets that he had decoded in less than an hour. He now knew how to regulate the lights and temperature throughout each particular portion of the underground lair. But if it was that easy, and all the lairs were similarly constructed, why did the avians not use the lights that had been provided? While they were eating breakfast Richard quizzed Nicole about the details of the avian lair.

"You're overlooking more fundamental issues," Nicole said, as she took a bite of manna melon. "The avians aren't that important by themselves. The real question is, where are the Ramans? And why did they put these holes under New York in the first place?"

"Maybe they're all Ramans," Richard replied. "The biots, the avians, the octospiders—maybe they all came originally from the same planet. At the beginning they were all one happy family. But as the years and generations passed, different species evolved in separate ways. Individual lairs were constructed and the—"

"There are too many problems with that scenario," Nicole interrupted. "First, the biots are definitely machines. The avians may or may not be. The octospiders almost certainly aren't, although a technological level that could create this spaceship in the first place might have progressed further in artificial intelligence than we can possibly imagine. My intuitive sense, however, says that those things are organic."

"We humans would never be able to distinguish between a living creature and a versatile machine created by a truly advanced species."

"I agree with that. But we can't possibly resolve this argument by ourselves. Besides, there is another question that I want to discuss with you."

"What's that?" Richard asked.

"Did the avians and the octospiders and these underground regions exist also on Rama I? If so, how did the Norton crew miss them altogether? If not, why are they on this spacecraft and not the first one?"

Richard was quiet for several seconds. "I see where you're heading," he said finally. "The fundamental premise has always been that the Rama spacecraft were created millions of years ago, by unknown beings from another region of the galaxy, and that they were totally uninvolved with and disinterested in whatever they encountered during their trek. If they were created that long ago, why would two vehicles that were presumably built at virtually the same time have such striking differences?"

"I'm starting to believe that our colleague from Kyoto was right," Nicole answered. "Maybe there *is* a meaningful pattern to all this. I'm fairly confident that the Norton crew was thorough and accurate in its survey and that all the distinctions between Rama I and Rama II are indeed real. As soon as we acknowledge that the two spacecraft are different, we face a more difficult issue. *Why* are they different?"

Richard had finished eating and was now pacing in the dimly lit tunnel. "There was a discussion just like this before it was decided to abort the mission. At the teleconference the main question was, why did the Ramans change course to encounter the Earth? Since the first spacecraft had not done so, it was considered hard evidence that Rama II was different. And the people participating in that meeting knew nothing of the avians or octospiders."

"General Borzov would have loved the avians," Nicole commented after a short silence. "He thought that flying was the greatest pleasure in the world." She laughed. "He once told me that his secret hope in life was that reincarnation was on the level and that he would come back as a bird."

"He was a fine man," Richard said, stopping his pacing

momentarily. "I don't think we ever properly appreciated all his talents."

As Nicole replaced part of the manna melon in her backpack and prepared to continue the exploration, she smiled at her peripatetic friend. "One more question, Richard?"

He nodded.

"Do you think we've met any Ramans yet? By that I mean the creatures who made this vehicle. Or any of their descendants."

Richard shook his head vigorously. "Absolutely not," he said. "Maybe we've met some of their creations. Or even other species from the same planet. But we haven't seen the main characters yet."

They found the White Room off to the left of a horizontal tunnel at the second level below the surface. Until then the exploration had been almost boring. Richard and Nicole had walked down many tunnels and had peered into one empty room after another. Four times they had found a set of gadgets for regulating the lights and temperature. Until they reached the White Room, they had seen nothing else of interest.

Both Richard and Nicole were astonished when they entered a room whose walls were painted a crisp white. In addition to the paint, the room was fascinating because one corner was cluttered with objects that turned out, on closer inspection, to be quite familiar. There was a comb and a brush, an empty lipstick container, several coins, a collection of keys, and even something that looked like an old walkie-talkie. In another pile there was a ring and a wristwatch, a tube of toothpaste, a nail file, and a small keyboard with Latin letters. Richard and Nicole were stunned. "Okay, genius," she said with a wave of her hand. "Explain all this, if you can."

He picked up the tube of toothpaste, opened the cap, and squeezed. A white material came out. Richard put his finger in it and then placed the finger in his mouth. "Yuck," he said, spitting out the paste. "Bring your mass spectrometer over here."

While Nicole was examining the toothpaste with her

sophisticated medical instruments, Richard picked up each of the other objects. The watch in particular fascinated him. It was indeed keeping proper time, second by second, although its reference point was completely unknown. "Did you ever go to the space museum in Florida?" he asked Nicole.

"No," she answered distractedly.

"They had a display of the common objects taken by the crew on the first Rama mission. This watch looks exactly like the one in the display—I remember it well because I bought a similar one in the museum shop."

Nicole walked over with a puzzled look on her face. "This stuff isn't toothpaste, Richard. I don't know what it is. The spectra are astonishing, with an abundance of super-heavy molecules."

For several minutes the two cosmonauts rummaged in the odd collection of items, trying to make some sense out of their latest discovery. "One thing is certain," Richard said as he was trying unsuccessfully to open up the walkie-talkie, "these objects are definitely associated with human beings. There's simply too many of them for some kind of strange interspecies coincidence."

"But how did they get here?" Nicole asked. She was trying to use the brush but its bristles were far too soft for her hair. She examined it in more detail. "This is not really a brush," she announced. "It *looks* like a brush, and *feels* like a brush, but it's useless in the hair."

She bent down and picked up the nail file. "And this can't be used to file any human's fingernails." Richard came over to see what she was talking about. He was still struggling with the walkie-talkie. He dropped it in disgust and took the nail file that Nicole had extended toward him.

"So these things look human, but aren't?" he said, pulling the file against the end of his longest fingernail. The nail was unchanged. Richard gave the file back to Nicole. "What's going on here?" he shouted in a frustrated tone.

"I remember reading a science fiction novel while I was at the university," Nicole said a few seconds later, "in which an extraterrestrial species learned about human beings solely from our earliest television programs. When they finally met us, they offered cereal boxes and soaps and other objects the aliens had seen on our television commercials. The packages were all properly designed, but the contents were either nonexistent or absolutely wrong."

Richard had not been listening carefully to Nicole. He had been fiddling with the keys and surveying the collection of objects in the room. "Now what do all these things have in common?" he said, mostly to himself.

They both arrived at the same answer several seconds later. "They were all carried by the Norton crew," Richard and Nicole said in unison.

"So the two Rama space vehicles must have some kind of communication linkup," Richard said.

"And these objects have been planted here on purpose, to show us that the visit to Rama I was observed and recorded."

"The spider biots that inspected the Norton campsites and the equipment must have contained imaging sensors."

"And all of these things were fabricated from pictures transmitted from Rama I to Rama II."

After Nicole's last comment both of them were silent, each following his own thought pattern. "But why do they want us to know all this? What is it we're supposed to do now?" Richard stood up and began to pace around the room. Suddenly he started laughing. "Wouldn't it be amazing," he said, "if David Brown was right after all, if the Ramans really were completely uninterested in anything they found, but programmed their space vehicles to *act* interested in any visitors? They could flatter whatever species they encountered by making midcourse corrections and by fashioning simple objects. What an incredible irony. Since all immature species are probably hopelessly self-centered, the visitors to the Raman craft would be totally occupied trying to understand an assumed message—"

"I think you're getting carried away," Nicole interrupted. "All we know at this point is that this spacecraft apparently received pictures from Rama I, and that reproductions of small, everyday objects that were carried by the Norton crew have been placed here in this room for us to find."

"I wonder if the keyboard is as useless as everything else," Richard said as he picked it up. He spelled the word "Rama" with the keys. Nothing happened. He tried "Nicole." Still nothing.

"Don't you remember how the old models worked?" Nicole said with a grin. She took the keyboard. "They all had a separate power key." She pressed the unmarked button in the upper right-hand corner of the keyboard. A portion of the opposite wall slid away, revealing a large black square area about one meter on a side.

The small keyboard was based on the ones that had been attached to the portable computers on the first Rama mission. It had four rows of twelve characters, with an extra power button in the upper right-hand corner. The twenty-six Latin letters, ten Arabic numerals, and four mathematical operands were marked on forty of the individual keys. The other eight keys contained either dots or geometrical figures on their surfaces and, in addition, could be set in either an "up" or "down" position. Richard and Nicole quickly learned that these special keys were the true controls of the Raman system. By trial and error they also discovered that the result from striking any individual action key was a function of the positioning of the *other* seven keys. Thus, pressing any specific command key could produce as many as 128 different results. Altogether, then, the system provided for 1,024 separate actions that could be initiated from the keyboard.

Making a command dictionary was a laborious process. Richard volunteered for the duty. Using their own computers to keep notes, he began the process of developing the rudiments of a language to translate the special keyboard commands. The initial goal was simple—to be able to use the Raman computer like one of their own. Once the translation was developed, any given input into the Newton portable computers would contain, as part of its output, what set of key impressions on the Raman board would produce a similar response on the square black screen.

Even with Richard's intelligence and computer expertise, the task was a formidable one. It was also not something that could easily be shared. At Richard's suggestion, Nicole climbed out of the lair twice during the first Raman

day they were in the White Room. Both times she took
long walks around New York, casting her eyes to the sky
from time to time to look for a helicopter. On the second
excursion Nicole went back to the barn where she had
fallen in the pit. Already so much had happened that her
frightening experience at the bottom seemed like ancient
history.

She thought often about Borzov, Wilson, and Takagishi.
All the cosmonauts had known when they left the Earth
that there were uncertainties in the mission. They had
trained often to handle vehicle emergencies, problems
with their own spacecraft that might prove to be life
threatening . . . but none of them had actually believed
that there would be any fatalities on the mission. *If Richard and I perish here in New York,* Nicole remarked to
herself, *then almost half the crew will have died. That will
be the worst disaster since we started flying piloted missions again.*

She was standing outside the barn, in almost the exact
spot where she and Francesca had talked to Richard on
the communicator the last time. *So why did you lie,
Francesca?* Nicole wondered. *Did you think somehow my
disappearance would silence all suspicion?*

On the final morning at the Beta campsite, before she
and the others had set out to look for Takagishi, Nicole
had transmitted all the notes in her own portable computer in Rama through the networking system to the
desktop in her room on the Newton. At the time Nicole
had made the data transfer to give herself extra memory, if
she should need it, in her traveling computer. *But it's all
there,* she recalled, *if some diligent detective ever looks
for it. The drugs, Jason's blood pressure, even a cryptic
reference to the abortion. And of course Richard's solution to the RoSur malfunction.*

On her two walks Nicole saw several centipede biots,
and even a bulldozer once, at the far limit of her vision.
She didn't see any avians and neither heard nor saw an
octospider. *Maybe they only come out at night,* she mused
as she returned to have dinner with Richard.

49

INTERACTION

"We're almost out of food," Nicole said. They packed up what remained of the manna melon and stuffed it in Richard's backpack.

"I know," he replied. "I have a plan for you to obtain some more."

"*Me?*" asked Nicole. "Why is it my job?"

"Well, first of all, it only requires one person. Working with graphics on the Raman computer gave me the idea. Second, I can't spare the time. I think I'm on the verge of breaking into the operating system. There are about two hundred commands that I can't explain unless they allow entry into another level, some kind of higher order space in the hierarchy."

Richard had explained to Nicole during dinner that he had now figured out how to use the Raman computer like one on the Earth. He could store and retrieve data, perform mathematical computations, design graphics, even create new languages. "But I haven't begun to tap its potential," he had said. "Tonight and tomorrow I must discover more of its secrets. We're running out of time."

His plan for obtaining food was, indeed, deceptively simple. After the long Raman night (during which Richard could not have slept more than three hours), Nicole walked over to the central plaza to implement the plan. Based on his progressive matrix analysis, Richard gave her three possible locations for the panel to open the covering above the avian lair. He was so confident of his analysis that he wouldn't even discuss what she should do if she didn't find the plate. Richard was correct. Nicole found the panel easily. Then she opened the cover and shouted down the vertical corridor. There was no response.

She shone her flashlight into the darkness below her. The tank sentinel was on duty, going to and fro in front of the horizontal tunnel that led past the water room. Nicole shouted again. If she could avoid it, she did not want to descend even to the first ledge. Even though Richard had assured her he would come to her rescue if she was overdue, Nicole did not relish the prospect of being hemmed in with the avians again.

Was that a distant jabbering she heard? Nicole thought so. She took one of the coins that she had found in the White Room and dropped it into the vertical corridor. It sailed far down, hitting a ledge somewhere near the second main level. This time there was loud jabbering. One of the avians flew up into her flashlight beam and over the tank sentinel's head. Moments later the cover began to close and Nicole had to move away.

She had discussed this contingency with Richard. Nicole waited several minutes and then pushed the panel again. When she yelled into the depths of the avian lair the second time, there was an immediate response. This time her friend, the black velvet avian, flew up to within five meters of the surface and jabbered at her. It was clear to Nicole that she was being told to go away. Before the avian turned around, however, Nicole pulled out her computer monitor and activated a stored program. Two manna melons appeared on the screen in graphic depiction. As the avian watched, the melons became colored and then a neat incision displayed the texture and color inside one of them.

The black velvet avian had flown up closer to the opening for a better look. Now it turned and screeched back into the dark below. Within seconds a second familiar bird, the likely mate for the black velvet one, flew up and landed on the first ledge below the ground. Nicole repeated the display. The two birds talked and then flew deeper into the lair.

Minutes went by. Nicole could hear occasional jabbering from the depths of the corridor. At length her two friends returned, each carrying a small manna melon in its talons. They landed in the plaza near the opening. Nicole walked over toward the melons, but the avians continued to clutch them. What followed was (Nicole assumed) a long lecture. The two birds jabbered both individually and together, always looking at her and often tapping on the melons. Fifteen minutes later, apparently satisfied that they had communicated their message, the avians took flight, swooped around the plaza, and vanished into their lair.

I think they were telling me that melons are in short supply, Nicole thought as she walked back toward the eastern plaza. The melons were heavy. She had one in each of the two backpacks that she had emptied that morning before she left the White Room. *Or maybe that I should not disturb them in the future. Whatever it was, we will not be welcome anymore.*

She thought that Richard would be ecstatic when she returned to the White Room. He was, but not because of Nicole and the manna melons. He had a grin on his face from one ear to the other and was holding one hand behind his back. "Wait until I show you what I have," he said as Nicole unloaded the backpacks. Richard brought his hand around in front of him and opened it. The hand contained a solitary black ball about ten centimeters in diameter.

"I'm nowhere near figuring out all the logic, or how much information can go in the request," Richard said. "But I have established a fundamental principle. We can ask for and receive 'things' using the computer."

"What do you mean?" Nicole asked, still not certain why Richard was so excited about a small black ball.

"They made this for me," he said, handing her the ball again. "Don't you understand? Somewhere here they have a factory and can make things for us."

"Then maybe 'they,' whoever they are, can start making us some food," said Nicole. She was a little annoyed that Richard had neither congratulated her nor thanked her for the melons. "The avians are not likely to give us any more."

"It will be no problem," Richard said. "Eventually, once we learn the full range of the request process, we may be able to order fish and chips, steak and potatoes, anything, as long as we can state what we want in unambiguous scientific terms."

Nicole stared at her friend. With his unkempt hair, his unshaven face, the bags under his eyes, and his wild grin, he looked at the moment like a fugitive from an insane asylum. "Richard," she asked, "will you slow down a little? If you've found the Holy Grail, can you at least spend a second explaining it to me?"

"Look at the screen," he said. Using the keyboard he drew a circle, then scratched it out and made a square. In less than a minute Richard had carefully drawn a cube in three dimensions. When he was finished with the graphics, he put the eight action keys into a predetermined configuration and then pressed the key with the small rectangle designator. A set of strange symbols appeared on the black monitor. "Don't worry," Richard said, "we don't need to understand the details. They are just asking for the dimensional specifications on the cube."

Richard next made a string of entries from the normal alphanumeric keys. "Now," he said, turning back to face Nicole, "if I have done it correctly, we will have a cube, made from the same material as that ball, in about ten minutes."

They ate some of the new melon while they waited. It tasted the same as the others. *Steak and potatoes would be unbelievably good,* Nicole was thinking, when suddenly the end wall lifted up half a meter above the floor and a black cube appeared in the gap.

"Wait a minute, don't touch it yet," Richard said as Nicole went over to investigate. "Look here!" He shone his flashlight into the darkness behind the cube. "There are vast tunnels beyond these walls," he said, "and they must lead to factories so advanced we couldn't even recognize them. Imagine! They can even make objects on request."

Nicole was beginning to understand why Richard was so ecstatic. "We now have the capability to control our own destiny in some small way," he continued. "If I can break the code fast enough, we should be able to request food, maybe even what we need to build a boat."

"Without loud motors, I hope," quipped Nicole.

"No motors," agreed Richard. He finished his melon and turned back to the keyboard.

Nicole was becoming worried. Richard had succeeded in making only one new breakthrough in a full Raman day. All he had to show for thirty-eight hours of work (he had only slept eight hours during the entire period) was one new material. He could make "light" black objects like the first ball, whose specific gravity was close to balsa wood, or he could make "heavy" black objects of density similar to oak or pine. He was wearing himself out with his work. And he could not, or would not, share any of the load with Nicole.

What if his first discovery was just blind luck? Nicole said to herself as she climbed the stairs for her dawn walk. *Or what if the system cannot make anything but two kinds of black objects?* She could not help worrying about wasted time. It was only sixteen more days until Rama would encounter the Earth. There was no sign of a rescue team. At the back of her mind was the thought that perhaps she and Richard had been abandoned altogether.

She had tried to talk to Richard about their plans the previous evening, but he had been exhausted. Richard hadn't responded in any way when Nicole had mentioned to him that she was very concerned. Later, after she had carefully outlined all their options and asked his opinion about what they should do, she noticed that he had fallen asleep. When Nicole awakened after a brief nap herself, Richard was already working again at the keyboard and refused to be distracted by either breakfast or conversation. Nicole had stumbled over the growing array of black objects on the floor as she had exited the White Room for her early morning exercise.

Nicole was feeling very lonely. The last fifty hours, which she had spent mostly by herself, had passed very slowly. Her only escape had been the pleasure of reading. She had the text of five books stored in her computer. One was her medical encyclopedia, but the other four were all for recreation. *I bet all of Richard's discretionary memory is filled with Shakespeare,* she thought as she sat on the wall surrounding New York. She stared out at the

Cylindrical Sea. In the far distance, barely visible in her binoculars through the mist and clouds, she could see the northern bowl where they had entered Rama the first time.

She had two of her father's novels stored in the computer. Nicole's personal favorite was *Queen for All Ages*, the story of Eleanor of Aquitaine's younger years, beginning with her adolescence at the ducal court in Poitiers. The story line followed Eleanor through her marriage to Louis Capet of France, their crusade to the Holy Land, and her extraordinary personal appeal for an annulment from Pope Eugenius. The novel culminated with Eleanor's divorce from Louis and betrothal to the young and exciting Henry Plantagenet.

The other Pierre des Jardins novel in her computer's memory was his universally acclaimed chef d'oeuvre, *I Richard Coeur de Lion*, a mixture of first-person diary and interior monologue, set during two winter weeks at the end of the twelfth century. In the novel Richard and his soldiers, embarked on another crusade, are quartered near Messina under the protection of the Norman king of Sicily. While there the famous warrior-king and homosexual son of Eleanor of Aquitaine and Henry Plantagenet, in a burst of self-examination, relives the major personal and historical events of his life.

Nicole remembered a long discussion with Genevieve after her daughter had read *I Richard* the previous summer. The young teenager had been fascinated by the story, and had surprised her mother by asking extremely intelligent questions. Thoughts of Genevieve made Nicole wonder what her daughter might be doing at Beauvois at the very moment. *They have told you that I have disappeared*, Nicole surmised. *What does the military call it? Missing in action?*

In her mind's eye Nicole could see her daughter riding home from school each day on her bicycle. "Any news?" Genevieve would probably say to her grandfather as she crossed the portal of the villa. Pierre would just shake his head sorrowfully.

It has been two weeks now since anyone has officially seen me. Do you still have hope, my darling daughter?

The bereft Nicole was struck by an overwhelming desire to talk to Genevieve. For a moment, suspending reality, Nicole could not accept the fact that she was separated from her daughter by millions of kilometers and had no way to communicate with her. She rose to return to the White Room, thinking in her temporary confusion that she could phone Genevieve from there.

When her sanity returned several seconds later, Nicole was astonished at how easily her mind had tricked itself. She shook her head and sat down on the wall overlooking the Cylindrical Sea. She remained on the wall for almost two hours, her thoughts roaming freely over a variety of subjects. Toward the end of the time, when she was preparing to return to the White Room, her mind focused on Richard Wakefield. *I have tried, my British friend,* Nicole said to herself. *I have been more open with you than with anyone since Henry. But it would be just my luck to be here with someone even less trusting than myself.*

Nicole was feeling an undefined sadness as she trekked down the stairs to the second level and turned right at the horizontal tunnel. Her sadness changed to surprise when she entered the White Room. Richard jumped up from his small black chair and greeted her with a hug. He had shaved and brushed his hair. He had even cleaned his fingernails. Laid out on the black table in the middle of the room was a neatly sectioned manna melon. One piece sat on each of the two black plates in front of the chairs.

Richard pulled out her chair and indicated for Nicole to sit down. He went around the table and sat in his own seat. He reached across the table and took both of Nicole's hands. "I want to apologize," he said with great intensity, "for being such a boor. I have behaved very badly these last few days.

"I have thought of thousands of things to tell you during these hours I've been waiting," he continued hesitantly, a strained smile playing across his lips, "but I can't remember most of them. . . . I know I wanted to explain to you how very important Prince Hal and Falstaff were to me. They were my closest friends. . . . It has not been easy for

me to deal with their deaths. My grief is still very
intense. . . ."

Richard took a drink of water and swallowed. "But most
of all," he said, "I'm sorry that I have not told you what a
spectacular person you are. You are intelligent, attractive,
witty, sensitive—everything I ever dreamed of finding in a
woman. Despite our situation, I've been afraid to tell you
how I felt. I guess my fear of rejection runs very deep."

Tears welled out of the corner of Richard's eyes and ran
down his cheeks. He was trembling slightly. Nicole could
tell what an incredible effort it had been for him. She
brought his hands up against her cheeks. "I think you're
very special too," she said.

50

HOPE SPRINGS ETERNAL

Richard continued to work with the Rama computer, but he limited himself to short sessions and involved Nicole whenever he could. They took walks together and chatted like old friends. Richard entertained Nicole by acting out entire scenes from Shakespeare. The man had a prodigious memory. He tried to play both sides in the love scenes from *Romeo and Juliet*, but every time he broke into his falsetto, Nicole would erupt with laughter.

One night they talked for over an hour about Omeh, the Senoufo tribe, and Nicole's visions. "You understand that it's difficult for me to accept the physical reality of some of these stories," Richard said, attempting to qualify his curiosity. "Nevertheless, I admit that I find them absolutely fascinating." Later he showed keen interest in analyzing all the symbolism in her visions. It was obvious that he acknowledged Nicole's mystical attributes as just another component in her rich personality.

They slept nuzzling together before they made love. When they did finally have intercourse, it was gentle and unhurried, surprising both of them with its ease and satisfaction. A few nights later, Nicole was lying with her head on Richard's chest, quietly drifting in and out of sleep. He was in deep thought. "Several days ago," he said, nudging her awake, "back before we became so intimate, I told you that I considered committing suicide once. At the time I was afraid to tell you the story. Would you like to hear it now?"

Nicole opened her eyes. She rolled over and put her chin on his stomach. "Uh-huh," she said. She reached up and kissed him on the eyes before he began his tale.

"I guess you know I was married to Sarah Tydings when

both of us were very young," he began. "It was also before she was famous. She was in her first year with the Royal Shakespeare Company and they were performing *Romeo and Juliet, As You Like It,* and *Cymbeline* in repertory at Stratford. Sarah was Rosalind and Juliet and fantastic at both.

"She was eighteen at the time, just out of school. I fell in love with her the first night I saw her as Juliet. I sent her roses in the dressing room every evening and used most of my savings to see all the performances. We had two long dinners together and then I proposed. She accepted more from astonishment than love.

"I went to graduate school at Cambridge after the summer was over. We lived in a modest flat and she commuted to the theater in London. I would go with her whenever I could, but after several months my studies demanded more of my time."

Richard stopped his narrative and glanced down at Nicole. She had not moved. She was lying partially across him, a smile of love on her face. "Go on," she said softly.

"Sarah was an adrenaline junkie. She craved excitement and variety. The mundane and tedious angered her. Grocery shopping, for example, was a colossal bore. It was just too much trouble for her to turn on the set and decide what to order. She also found any kind of schedule incredibly constraining.

"Lovemaking had to be performed in a different position or be accompanied by some different music every time; otherwise it was old hat. For a while I was creative enough to satisfy her. I also took care of all the routine tasks to free her from the drudgery of housework. But there were only so many hours in the day. Ultimately, despite my considerable abilities, my graduate studies began to suffer because I was spending all my energy making life interesting for her.

"After we had been married for a year, Sarah wanted to rent a flat in London, so that she didn't need to make the long commute every night after a performance. Actually she had already been spending a couple of nights a week in London, ostensibly with one of her actress friends. But her career was soaring and we had plenty of money, so why should I say no?

"It was not long before rumors about her behavior became quite widespread. I chose to ignore them, fearing, I guess, that she wouldn't deny them if I asked her. Then one night, late, while I was studying for an examination, I received a phone call from a woman. She was very polite, although obviously distraught. She told me that she was the wife of the actor Hugh Sinclair, and that Mr. Sinclair—who at that time was starring with Sarah in the American drama *In Any Weather*—was having an affair with my wife. 'In fact,' she told me, 'he is over at your wife's flat at this very moment.' Mrs. Sinclair started crying and then hung up."

Nicole reached up and softly caressed Richard's cheek with her hand. "I felt as if my chest had exploded," he said, remembering the pain. "I was angry, terrified, frantic. I went to the station and took the late train to London. When the taxi dropped me at Sarah's place, I ran to the door.

"I did not knock. I bolted up the stairs and found the two of them sleeping naked in the bed. I picked Sarah up and flung her against the wall—I can still remember the sound of her head smashing into the mirror. Then I fell on him in a rage, punching his face over and over, until it was nothing but a mass of blood. It was awful. . . ."

Richard stopped himself and began to cry noiselessly. Nicole put her arms around his heaving chest and wept with him. "Darling, darling," she said.

"I was an animal," he cried. "I was worse than my father ever was. I would have killed them both if the people in the next flat hadn't restrained me."

Neither of them said anything for several minutes. When Richard spoke again his voice was subdued, almost remote. "The next day, after the police station and the tabloid reporters and all the recriminations with Sarah, I wanted to kill myself. I would have done it, too, if I had owned a gun. I was considering the gruesome alternatives—pills, slitting my wrists with a razor blade, jumping off a bridge—when another student called to ask me a detailed question on relativity. There was no way, after fifteen minutes of thinking about Mr. Einstein, that suicide was still a viable option. Divorce, certainly. Celibacy, highly likely. But death was out of the question. I could never have prematurely terminated my love affair with physics." His voice trailed off.

Nicole wiped her eyes and placed her hands in his. She leaned her naked body across Richard's and kissed him. "I love you," she said.

Nicole's sounding alarm indicated that it was daylight again in Rama. *Ten more days*, she noted after a quick mental calculation. *We'd better have a serious talk now.*

The alarm had awakened Richard as well. He turned and smiled at his sleeping partner. "Darling," Nicole said, "the time has come—"

"The walrus said, to speak of many things."

"Come on now, be serious. We have to decide what we're going to do. It's fairly obvious that we're not going to be rescued."

"I agree," said Richard. He sat up and reached across Nicole's mat for his shirt. "I have been dreading this moment for days. But I guess we have finally reached the point where we should consider swimming across."

"You don't think there's any chance of making a boat out of our black stuff?"

"No," he answered. "One material is too light and the other too heavy. We could probably build a hybrid that would be seaworthy, *if* we had some nails, but without any sails we would still have to row across. . . . Our best bet is to swim."

Richard stood up and walked over to the black square on the wall. "My fancy plans didn't pan out, did they?" He thumped lightly on the square. "And I was going to produce steak and potatoes as well as a boat."

"The best laid plans of mice and men gang aft agley."

"What a weird poet old Scottish Robbie was. I never could understand what people saw in him."

Nicole finished dressing and started doing some stretching exercises. "Whew," she said, "I'm out of shape. I haven't had any heavy physical activity in days." She smiled at Richard, who was looking at her coyly. "*That* doesn't count," she added, shaking her head.

"It's almost the only exercise I've ever liked," Richard replied with a grin. "I used to hate it at the academy when we had those special physical training weekends."

Richard had laid out small portions of manna melon on the black table. "Three more meals after this one," he said without emotion. "I guess we swim before it's dark again."

"You don't want to go this morning?" Nicole asked.

"No," he replied. "Why don't you go survey the coast and pick a spot. I found something last night on the computer that has me baffled. It won't give us food or sailboats, but it looks as if I may have finally broken through into another kind of structure."

After breakfast, Nicole kissed Richard good-bye and wandered up to the surface. It did not take her long to reconnoiter the coast. There really were no reasons to pick one embarkation point over another. The grim reality of the coming swim oppressed Nicole. *The odds are good,* she told herself, *that neither Richard nor I will be alive when it is dark again in Rama.*

She tried to imagine what it would be like to be eaten by a shark biot. Would it be a quick death? Or would you drown aware that your legs had just been amputated? Nicole shuddered at the idea. *Maybe we should try to obtain another melon. . . .* She knew that was useless. Sooner or later, they had to swim.

Nicole turned her back on the sea. *At least these last few days have been good,* she said to herself, not wanting to think anymore about their predicament. *He has been an excellent companion. In every way.* She allowed herself the momentary luxury of recalling their shared pleasure. Then Nicole smiled and started walking back toward the lair.

"But what am I looking at?" Nicole asked as another image flashed up on the black square.

"I'm not completely certain," Richard replied. "All I know is that I have tapped into a long list of some kind. You remember that one particular command configuration that produces the lines of symbols that look like Sanskrit?

Well, I was scrolling through the gibberish and eventually I noticed a pattern. I stopped at the beginning of the pattern, changed the position of the last three keys, and then hit the double dot again. Suddenly an image was on the screen. And every time I hit an alphanumeric, the picture changed."

"But how do you know you're looking at sensor output?"

Richard entered a command and there was a change in the image. "Occasionally I see something I recognize," he said. "Look at that one, for example. Couldn't that be the Beta stairway viewed from a camera in the middle of the Central Plain?"

Nicole studied the picture. "Possibly," she said, "but I don't see how you could ever tell for certain."

Richard commanded the screen to change again. The next three pictures were unintelligible. The fourth one showed a feature tapering to a point at the top of the frame. "And that one," he said. "Couldn't it be one of the little horns, as seen from a sensor near the top of the Big Horn?"

No matter how hard she tried, Nicole could not visualize what the view would be like from the top of the giant spire in the center of the southern bowl. Richard continued to flip through the pictures. Only about one in five was even partially clear. "Somewhere in this system there must be some enhancement algorithms," he said to himself. "Then I can sharpen up all the images."

Nicole could tell that Richard was about to begin another long work session. She walked over to him and put her arms around his neck. "Could I talk you into a little distraction first?" she said, reaching up and kissing him on the mouth.

"I guess so," he replied, dropping the keyboard on the floor. "It will probably be good for me to clear my mind."

Nicole was in the middle of a beautiful dream. She was home again at her villa in Beauvois. Richard was sitting beside her on the couch in the living room and was holding her hand. Her father and daughter were opposite them in the soft chairs.

Her dream was broken by Richard's insistent voice.

When Nicole opened her eyes her lover was standing over her, his voice crackling with excitement. "Wait until you see this, darling," he said, extending a hand to pull her up. "It's fantastic! Somebody is still here."

Nicole shook the dream from her mind and looked over at the black square where Richard was pointing. "Can you believe it?" he said, jumping up and down. "There's no doubt about it. The military ship is still docked."

Only then did Nicole realize that she was looking at a picture of the outside of Rama. She blinked her eyes and listened to Richard's rambling explanation. "Once I figured out the code for the enhancement parameters, almost every frame became clear. That set of pictures I showed you earlier must be the real-time output from hundreds of Rama's imaging sensors. And I think I have figured out how to access the other sensor data bases as well."

Richard was exultant. He threw his arms around Nicole and lifted her off the ground. He hugged and kissed her and bounced around the room like a lunatic.

When he finally calmed down a little, Nicole spent almost a full minute studying the image that was projected on the black square. It was definitely the Newton military ship; she could read the markings. "So the science spacecraft has gone home," she commented to Richard.

"Yes," he answered, "as I expected. I was afraid they would *both* be gone and that after we swam across the sea, we would find ourselves still trapped, this time in a larger prison."

The same concern had bothered Nicole. She smiled at Richard. "It's relatively straightforward, then, isn't it? We swim across the Cylindrical Sea and walk over to the chairlift. Someone will be waiting for us at the top."

Nicole started packing her belongings. Richard, meanwhile, continued to flash new images on the screen. "What are you doing now, darling?" Nicole asked gently. "I thought we were going to make our swim."

"I haven't made a full pass through the sensor list since I located the enhancement parameters," Richard replied. "I just want to make certain we're not missing anything critical. It will only take another hour or so."

Nicole stopped packing and sat down in front of the screen beside Richard. The pictures were indeed interesting. Some were exterior shots, but most were images of different regions inside Rama, including the underground lairs. One magnificent photo was taken from the top of the large room where the hot spheres in their sponge webbing rested on the floor beneath the hanging lattices. Richard and Nicole watched the picture for a moment, hoping to see a black and gold octospider, but they detected no movement.

They were near the end of the list when an image of the bottom third of the Alpha stairway stunned them both. There, climbing down the stairs, were four human figures in space suits. Richard and Nicole watched the figures descend for five seconds and then exploded with joy. "They're coming!" Richard said, throwing his arms into the air. "We're going to be rescued!"

51

ESCAPE HARNESS

Richard was becoming impatient. He and Nicole had been standing on the walls of New York for over an hour, scanning the skies for some sign of a helicopter. "Where the hell are they?" he grumbled. "It only takes fifteen minutes by rover from the bottom of Alpha stairway to the Beta campsite."

"Maybe they're looking somewhere else," Nicole said encouragingly.

"That's ridiculous," Richard said. "Surely they would go to Beta first—and even if they couldn't repair the comm system, at least they'd find my last message. I said I was taking one of the motorboats to New York."

"They probably know that there's no place for a helicopter to land in the city. They may be coming across in a boat themselves."

"Without first seeing if they could spot us from the helicopter? That's unlikely." Richard turned his eyes to the sea and searched for a sail. "A boat. A boat. My kingdom for a boat."

Nicole laughed but Richard barely managed a little smile. "Two men could assemble the sailboat in the supply hut at Beta in less than thirty minutes," he fretted. "Dammit, what's holding them up?"

In his frustration Richard switched on the transmitter in his communicator. "Now hear this, you guys. If you're anywhere near the Cylindrical Sea, identify yourselves. And then hurry your asses over here. We're standing on the wall and we're tired of waiting."

There was no response. Nicole sat down on the wall. "What are you doing?" Richard asked.

"I think you're worrying enough for both of us," she

responded. "And I'm tired of standing up and waving my arms." She stared across the Cylindrical Sea. "It would be so much easier," Nicole said wistfully, "if we could just fly across ourselves."

Richard cocked his head to one side and looked at her. "What a great idea," he said several seconds later. "Why didn't we think of it before?" He immediately sat down and started doing some calculations on his computer. "Cowards die many times before their deaths," he mumbled to himself, "the valiant never taste of death but once."

Nicole watched her friend furiously pounding his keyboard. "What are you doing, dear?" she inquired, glancing over his shoulder at the computer monitor.

"Three!" he shouted, after finishing a computation. "Three should be enough." Richard looked up at the puzzled Nicole. "Do you want to hear the most outrageous plan in interplanetary history?" he asked her.

"Why not?" she said with a doubtful smile.

"We are going to build ourselves harnesses out of the lattice material and the avians are going to fly us across the Cylindrical Sea."

Nicole stared at Richard for several seconds. "Assuming we can make the harnesses," she said skeptically, "how do we talk the avians into doing their part?"

"We convince them it's in their own best interest," Richard replied. "Or alternatively we threaten them in some way. . . . I don't know, you can work on that issue."

Nicole was incredulous. "Anyway," Richard continued, grabbing her hand and walking down the wall, "it beats standing around here waiting for the helicopter or the boat."

Five hours later there was still no sign of the rescue team. When they had finished making the harnesses, Richard had left Nicole at the wall and gone back to the White Room to check through the sensor set again. He returned with the news that he thought he had seen the human figures in the vicinity of the Beta campsite, but that the resolution on that particular frame had been very poor. As they had agreed, Nicole had been calling every half hour on the communicator. There had been no response.

"Richard," she said, while he was programming some graphics on his computer, "why do you think the rescue team was using the stairway?"

"Who knows?" he replied. "Maybe the chairlift malfunctioned and there were no engineers left."

"It seems strange to me," Nicole mused. *Something about this is bothering me*, she thought, *but I don't dare share it with Richard until I can explain it. He doesn't believe in intuition.* Nicole glanced at her watch. *It's a good thing we rationed the melon. If the rescue team doesn't show up and this wild scheme doesn't work, we won't be swimming until next daylight.*

"Preliminary design complete," Richard stated emphatically. He waved to Nicole to join him. "If you approve the line drawing," he said, pointing at the monitor in his hand, "then I will proceed with the detailed graphics."

In the picture three large avians, each with one line wrapped around its body, were flying in formation across a sea. Dangling underneath them, and attached by three lines, was a stick figure human being sitting in a flimsy harness. "Looks good to me," said Nicole, never thinking for a minute that such an event would actually happen.

"I can't believe we're doing this," Nicole remarked, pushing the plate to open the avian lair for the second time.

Their first attempt to renew contact had resulted in the expected cold shoulder. This second time it was Richard who shouted into the avian lair. "Listen to me, you avians," he growled in his fiercest voice, "I need to talk to you. Right *now*. Get up here on the double." Nicole had to restrain a laugh.

Richard began dropping black objects into the lair. "See," he said with a grin, "I knew these damn things would be good for something." Eventually they could hear some activity at the bottom of the vertical corridor. The same pair of avians they had seen before flew up to the top of the lair and started screeching at Richard and Nicole. They did not even look at the monitor when Richard held it out for them. When they were finished screeching, the

pair flew over the top of the tank sentinel and the cover
closed again.

"It's no use, Richard," Nicole said when he asked her to
open the cover a third time. "Even our friends are against
us." She paused before pressing the plate. "What are we
going to do if they attack us?"

"They won't attack," Richard said, indicating for Nicole
to open the cover. "But just in case, I want you to stay
over there. I will deal with our feathered friends."

There was jabbering from the lair as soon as the cover
opened the third time. Richard immediately started shouting back and pitching black objects down the corridor.
One of them hit the tank sentinel and prompted a small
explosion, like a gunshot.

The two familiar avians flew up to the opening and
screamed at Richard. Three or four of their comrades were
just behind. The noise was unbelievable. Richard did not
back down. He kept yelling and pointing at the computer
monitor. Finally he was able to get their attention.

The group of avians watched the graphic depiction of
the flight across the sea. Richard then held up one of the
harnesses in his left hand and started running the demonstration on his monitor again. Frantic conversation among
the avians ensued. At the end, however, Richard sensed
that he had lost. As a pair of the other avians flew over the
top of the tank sentinel, Richard climbed down into the
lair, onto the first ledge. "Hold it," he shouted at the top
of his lungs.

The mate of the black velvet avian lunged forward, its
threatening beak no more than a meter from Richard's
face. The noise from all the screeching and jabbering was
deafening. Richard was undaunted. Despite the avian pro-
tests, he descended to the second ledge. Now he would
not be able to escape if the cover started to close.

Again he held up the harness and pointed at the monitor. A chorus of screeches told him the response. Then,
above the avian howl, he heard another sound, like a
Klaxon alarm announcing a fire drill at a school or hospital.
All the avians immediately calmed down. They settled
quietly on the ledges and stared down at the tank sentinel.

The lair was strangely silent. After a few seconds Richard heard the beating of wings and moments later a new avian flew into the vertical corridor. It rose slowly up to his level and hovered just opposite him. It had a gray velvet body and sharp gray eyes. Two thick rings of bright cherry red were wrapped around its neck.

The creature studied Richard and landed on the ledge opposite him, across the corridor. The avian that had been in that spot scurried out of the way. When the gray velvet bird spoke, it was soft and very clear. After the speech was finished, the black velvet avian flew up beside the new arrival and apparently explained the furor. Several times the two avians stared across at Richard. The last time, thinking that perhaps their nodding heads were a cue, Richard displayed the graphic flight one more time and held up the harnesses. The bird with the cherry rings flew over beside him for a closer look.

The creature made a sudden movement, frightening Richard, and he nearly fell off the ledge. What may have been avian laughter was silenced by a few words from the gray velvet leader, who then sat quite still, as if it were thinking, for over a minute. At length the avian leader gestured toward Richard with one talon, opened its huge wings, and soared out through the opening into daylight.

For several seconds Richard did not move. The great creature rose up, up into the sky above the lair and was soon followed by the two more familiar avians. Moments later Nicole's head appeared in the opening. "Are you coming?" she asked. "I don't know how you did it, but it looks as if our friends are ready."

52

FLIGHT 302

Richard pulled the harness tight around Nicole's waist and buttocks. "Your feet will dangle," he said, "and at first, when the lattice cord is stretching, you will have the feeling that you're falling."

"What if I hit the water?" Nicole asked.

"You have to trust the avians to fly high enough that you won't," Richard replied. "I think they're quite intelligent, especially the one with the red rings."

"Do you think it's the king?" Nicole asked, adjusting the harness for comfort.

"Probably their equivalent," Richard answered. "He has made it clear from the beginning that he intends to fly in the middle of the formation."

Richard walked up the steep incline to the wall, carrying all three harness lines in his hands. The avians were sitting quietly together, staring out at the sea. They acquiesced as he tied the harness around their midsections, just behind the backs of the wings. Then they watched his computer monitor as he again showed them the graphics of the takeoff. The avians were to lift off together, slowly, pull the harness lines taut directly over Nicole's head, and then lift her straight up before flying north across the sea.

He checked that the knots were secure and then returned to Nicole's side at the bottom of the incline. She was only about five meters from the water. "If, by some chance, the avians do not return for me," Richard told her, "don't wait forever. Once you find the rescue team, assemble the sailboat and come across. I will be down in the White Room." He took a deep breath. "Be safe, my darling," he added. "Remember that I love you."

Nicole could tell from the pounding of her heart that

the moment of takeoff had finally arrived. She kissed Richard slowly on the lips. "And I love you," she murmured.

When they broke their embrace, Richard waved at the avians on the wall. The gray velvet avian cautiously rose in the air, followed immediately by its two companions. They hovered in formation directly over Nicole. She felt the three lines pull tight and was momentarily lifted into the air.

Seconds later, as the elastic cord began to stretch, Nicole was falling toward the ground again. The avians flew higher, heading out over the water, and Nicole felt as if she were a yo-yo, bouncing up and down as the cord would stretch and then contract with a jerk when the avians rose swiftly to a higher altitude.

It was an exciting flight. She touched the water once, just barely, while she was still close to shore. She was temporarily frightened, but the avians lifted her quickly before anything more than her feet were wet. Once the lattice cord was at its full extension, the ride was fairly smooth. Nicole sat in her harness, her hands holding on to two of the three lines, her feet dangling below her about eight meters from the tops of the waves.

The middle of the sea was quite calm. About halfway across Nicole saw two great, dark figures swimming along beneath her, parallel to her course. She was certain they were shark biots. She also detected two or three other species in the water, including one, long and skinny like an eel, that reared itself out of the sea and watched her fly by. *Whew,* Nicole thought as she surveyed the water, *I'm certainly glad that I didn't swim.*

The landing was easy. Nicole had been concerned that the avians might not realize there was a fifty-meter cliff on the opposite side of the sea. She needn't have worried. As they approached landfall in the Northern Hemicylinder, the avians gently increased their altitude. Nicole was set down gingerly about ten meters from the edge.

The huge birds landed close by. Nicole climbed out of her harness and walked over to the avians. She thanked them profusely and tried to pat them on the backs of their heads, but they jerked away from her touch. The creatures rested for several minutes and then, at a signal from their leader, they flew off across the sea toward New York.

Nicole was surprised at the intensity of her emotions. She knelt down and kissed the ground. It was only then that she realized she had never really expected to escape safely from New York. For a moment, before she started searching for the rescue team with her binoculars, she reviewed everything that had happened to her since that fateful crossing in the icemobile. *Before New York is a lifetime ago*, she said to herself. *Now everything has changed*.

Richard untied the harness from the avian leader and dropped it on the ground. All the birds were now free. The creature with the gray velvet body craned its neck around to see if Richard was finished. The rich cherry red of its rings was even clearer in the full daylight. Richard wondered about the rings and what they signified, knowing there was a high likelihood he would never see these magnificent aliens again.

Nicole came over beside Richard. When he had landed she had embraced him passionately. The avians had boldly stared, signaling their curiosity. *They too*, Nicole thought, *must be wondering about us*. The linguist in her imagined what it would be like actually to talk to an extraterrestrial species, to begin to understand how an altogether different intelligence might operate. . . .

"I wonder how we say good-bye and thank you," Richard was saying.

"I don't know," Nicole replied, "but it would be nice—"

She stopped to watch the avian leader. It had called the other two creatures to come beside it and the three birds were standing facing Richard and Nicole. On a signal they all spread their wings, to their full extent, and formed into a circle. They turned around one full revolution and then fell back into a straight line facing the humans.

"Come on," Nicole said. "We can do that."

Nicole and Richard stood side by side, their arms outstretched, and faced their avian friends. Nicole then put her arms on Richard's shoulders and led him through a

circular turn. Richard, who was sometimes not very graceful, stumbled once but managed to complete the movement. Nicole imagined that the avian leader was smiling
when she and Richard straightened out after their revolution.

The three avians took off seconds later. Higher and
higher in the sky they rose, until they were at the limit of
Nicole's vision. Then they flew south, across the sea toward home.

"Good luck," Nicole whispered as they departed.

The rescue team was not in the vicinity of the Beta
campsite. In fact, Richard and Nicole had not seen any
sign of them during a thirty-minute drive in the rover
along the coast of the Cylindrical Sea. "These guys must
really be stupid," Richard groused. "My message was in
plain view there at Beta. Could it be that they haven't
even come down this far yet?"

"It's less than three hours until dark," Nicole replied.
"They may have returned to the Newton already."

"All right, then, to hell with them," Richard said. "Let's
have a bite to eat and then head for the chairlift."

"Do you think we should save any of the melon?" Nicole asked a few minutes later, while they were eating.
Richard gave her a puzzled glance. "Just in case," she
added.

"Just in case what?" Richard rejoined. "Even if we don't
find that idiotic rescue bunch and must climb all the stairs
ourselves, we'll still be out of here right after dark. Remember, we become weightless again at the top of the
stairway."

Nicole smiled. "I guess I'm naturally more cautious,"
she said. She put several bites of melon back into her
pack.

They had driven three fourths of the way toward the
chairlift and the Alpha stairway when they spotted the
four human figures in space suits. It looked as if they were
leaving the conglomeration of buildings that had been
designated as the Raman Paris. The figures were walking
in the opposite direction from the rover.

"I told you the guys were idiots," Richard exclaimed.
"They don't even have the sense to take off their space

suits. It must be a special team, sent up in the spare Newton vehicle just to find us and bring us back."

He steered the rover across the Central Plain in the direction of the humans. Richard and Nicole both started shouting when they were within a hundred meters, but the men in the space suits continued their slow procession toward the west. "They probably can't hear us," Nicole offered. "They still have on their helmets and communication gear."

A frustrated Richard drove up to within five meters of the single-file line, stopped the rover, and jumped out in a hurry. He ran quickly around to the leader, shouting all the way. "Hey, guys," he yelled. "We're here, behind you. All you have to do is turn around—"

Richard stopped cold as he stared at the blank expression of the man in the lead. He recognized the face. Jesus, it was Norton! He shuddered involuntarily as a tingle ran down his spine. Richard barely jumped out of the way as the four-man procession walked slowly past him. Numb from the shock, he quietly studied the other three faces, none of which changed expression as they marched past. They were three other cosmonauts from the Rama I crew.

Nicole was at his side only seconds after the final figure passed him. "What's the matter?" she said. "Why didn't they stop?" The blood had all drained out of Richard's face. "Darling, are you all right?"

"They're biots," Richard mumbled. "Goddamn human biots."

"Whaaat?" Nicole replied, a streak of terror in her voice. She ran quickly to the head of the line and stared at the face behind the helmet glass. It was definitely Norton. Every feature of the face, even the color of the eyes and the slight mustache, was absolutely perfect. But the eyes didn't say anything.

The motion of the body, too, now that she noticed it, seemed artificial. Each pair of steps was a repeated pattern. There were only slight variations from figure to figure. *Richard is right,* Nicole thought. *These are human biots. They must have been made from the images, just like the toothpaste and the brush.* A momentary panic swelled in her chest. *But we don't need a rescue team,* she told herself, calming her anxiety. *The military ship is still docked at the top of the bowl.*

Richard was stunned by the discovery of the human biots. He sat in the rover for several minutes, unwilling to drive, asking questions of Nicole and himself that he could not possibly have answered. "So what's going on here?" he said over and over again. "Are all these biots based on real species, found somewhere in the universe? And why are they being fabricated in the first place?"

Before they drove over to the chairlift, Richard insisted that they both shoot many minutes of video footage of the human biots. "The avians and octospiders are fascinating," he said as he took a special close-up of "Norton's" leg motion, "but this tape will blow everyone away."

Nicole reminded him that it was less than two hours until dark and that it still might be necessary for them to climb the Stairway of the Gods. Satisfied that he had recorded the bizarre procession for posterity, Richard slid into the driver's seat of the rover and headed toward the Alpha stairway.

There was no need to perform any tests to see if the chairlift was working properly; it was running when they drove up beside it. Richard jumped out of the rover and ran into the control room.

"Someone's coming down," he said, pointing up the lift.

"Or something," Nicole said grimly.

The five-minute wait seemed like an eternity. At first neither Richard nor Nicole said anything. Later, however, Richard suggested that maybe they should sit in the rover in case they needed to make a quick escape.

Each of them trained binoculars on the long cable stretching upward to the heavens. "It's a man!" cried Nicole.

"It's General O'Toole!" said Richard a few moments later.

Indeed it was. General Michael Ryan O'Toole, American air force officer, was descending in the chairlift. He was still several hundred meters above Richard and Nicole, but had not yet seen them. He was busy studying with his binoculars the beauty of the alien landscape around him.

General O'Toole had been preparing to leave Rama for
the final time when, as he rode up in the chairlift, he had
spotted what looked like three birds flying far to the south
in the Rama sky. The general had decided to return to see
if he could find those birds again. He was unprepared for
the joyous greeting that awaited him when he reached the
bottom of his ride.

53

TRINITY

When Richard Wakefield had left the Newton to go back inside Rama, General O'Toole had been the last crew member to say good-bye. The general had waited patiently while the other cosmonauts had finished their conversations with Richard. "You're really certain you want to do this?" Janos Tabori had said to his British friend. "You know the full committee is going to declare Rama off limits within hours."

"By then"—Richard had grinned at Janos—"I will be on my way to Beta. Technically I will not have violated their order."

"That's bullshit," Admiral Heilmann had interjected tersely. "Dr. Brown and I are in charge of this mission. We have both told you to stay onboard the Newton."

"And I've told you several times," Richard said firmly, "that I left some personal items inside Rama that are very important to me. Besides, you know as well as I do that there's nothing for any of us here to do over the next couple of days. Once the abort decision is definitely made, all the major scheduling activities will be on the ground. We will be told when to undock and head for Earth."

"I will remind you, one more time," Otto Heilmann had replied, "that I consider what you are doing an act of insubordination. When we return to Earth I intend to prosecute to the fullest—"

"Save it, will you, Otto?" Richard interrupted. There was no rancor in his tone. He adjusted his space suit and started to put on his helmet. As always Francesca was recording the scene on her video camera. She had been strangely silent since her private conversation with Richard an hour earlier. She seemed detached, as if her mind were somewhere else.

General O'Toole walked up to Richard and extended his hand. "We haven't spent much time together, Wakefield," he said, "but I've admired your work. Good luck in there. Don't take any unnecessary chances."

Richard had been surprised by the general's warm smile. He had expected the American military officer to try to talk him out of leaving. "It's magnificent in Rama, General," Richard had said. "Like a combination of the Grand Canyon, the Alps, and the Pyramids all at once."

"We've lost four crew members already," O'Toole replied. "I want to see you back here safe and sound. God bless you."

Richard finished shaking the general's hand, put on his helmet, and stepped across into the airlock. Moments later, when Wakefield was gone, Admiral Heilmann was critical of General O'Toole's behavior. "I'm disappointed in you, Michael," he said. "From that warm send-off the young man might have concluded that you actually approved of his action."

O'Toole faced the German admiral. "Wakefield has courage, Otto," he said. "And conviction as well. He is not afraid of either the Ramans or the ISA disciplinary process. I admire that kind of self-confidence."

"Nonsense," Heilmann rejoined. "Wakefield is a brash, arrogant schoolboy. You know what he left inside? A couple of those stupid Shakespearean robots. He just doesn't like taking orders. He wants to do what's uppermost on his own personal agenda."

"That makes him a lot like the rest of us," Francesca remarked. The room was quiet for a moment. "Richard is very smart," she said in a subdued tone. "He probably has reasons for going back into Rama that none of us understand."

"I just hope he comes back before dark, as he promised," Janos said. "I'm not certain I could stand to lose another friend."

The cosmonauts filed out of the atrium into the hallway. "Where's Dr. Brown?" Janos asked Francesca as he walked along beside her.

"He's with Yamanaka and Turgenyev. They're reviewing possible crew assignments for the trip home. As short-handed as we are, a lot of cross training will be necessary before we leave." Francesca laughed. "He even asked me if I could be a backup navigation engineer. Can you imagine that?"

"Easily," Janos replied. "You probably could learn any of the engineering assignments at this point."

Behind them Heilmann and O'Toole shuffled down the corridor. When they reached the hall leading to the private crew quarters, General O'Toole started to leave. "Just a minute," Otto Heilmann said. "I need to talk to you about something else. This damn Wakefield thing almost made it slip my mind. Can you come to my office for an hour or so?"

"Essentially," Otto Heilmann said, pointing at the unscrambled cryptogram on the monitor, "this is a major change to the Trinity procedure. It's not surprising. Now that we know much more about Rama, you would expect the deployment to be somewhat different."

"But we never anticipated using all five weapons," O'Toole responded. "The extra pair were only loaded onboard in case of failures. That much megatonnage could vaporize Rama."

"That's the intent," Heilmann said. He sat back in his chair and smiled. "Just between us chickens," he said, "I think there's a lot of pressure on the general staff down there. The feeling is that Rama's capabilities were vastly underrated initially."

"But why do they want to put the two largest weapons in the ferry passageway? Surely one of the bombs would accomplish the desired result."

"What if it didn't explode for some reason? There has to be a backup." Heilmann leaned forward eagerly on his desk. "I think this change to the procedure clearly defines the strategy. The two at the end will ensure that the structural integrity of the vehicle will be absolutely destroyed—that's essential to guarantee that it is impossible for Rama to maneuver again after the blast. The other three bombs are scattered around the interior to make

certain that no part of Rama is safe. It's equally important
that the explosions should result in enough velocity change
that all the remaining pieces miss the Earth."

General O'Toole constructed a mental image of the
giant spacecraft being annihilated by five nuclear bombs.
It was not a pleasant picture. Once, fifteen years before,
he and twenty other members of the COG general staff
had flown into the South Pacific to watch a hundred-
kiloton weapon explode. The COG system engineering
personnel had convinced the political leaders, and the
world press, that one nuclear test was necessary "every
twenty years or so" to ensure that all the old weapons
would indeed fire in an emergency. O'Toole and his team
had observed the demonstration, ostensibly to learn as
much as possible about the effects of nuclear weapons.

General O'Toole was deep in his memory, recalling the
spine-tingling horror of that fireball rising in the peaceful
South Pacific sky. He was not aware that Admiral Heilmann
had asked him a question. "I'm sorry, Otto," he said. "I
was thinking about something else."

"I had asked you how long you thought it might take to
get approval for Trinity."

"You mean in our case?" O'Toole said with disbelief.

"Of course," Heilmann responded.

"I can't imagine it," O'Toole said quickly. "The weapons
were included in the mission manifest solely to guard
against openly hostile actions by the Ramans. I even remember the baseline scenario—an unprovoked attack against
the Earth by the alien spacecraft, using high-technology
weapons beyond the capabilities of our defenses. The current situation is altogether different."

The German admiral studied his American colleague.
"No one ever envisioned the Rama spacecraft on a collision course with the Earth," Heilmann said. "If it does not
alter its trajectory, it will gouge an enormous hole in the
surface and kick up such dust that the temperatures will
drop all over the world for several years. . . . At least,
that's what the scientists say."

"But that's preposterous," O'Toole argued. "You heard
all the discussion during the conference call. No rational
person really believes that Rama will actually hit the Earth."

"Impact is only one of several disaster scenarios. What would you do if you were chief of staff? Destroying Rama now is a safe solution. Nobody loses."

Visibly shaken by the conversation, Michael O'Toole excused himself from the meeting with Admiral Heilmann and headed for his room. For the first time in his entire association with the Newton mission, O'Toole thought that he might actually be ordered to use his RQ code to activate the weapons. Never before, never for a moment, had he considered that the bombs in the metal containers at the back of the military ship were anything more than a palliative for the fears of the civilian politicians.

Sitting at the computer terminal in his room, the concerned O'Toole recalled the words of Armando Urbina, the Mexican peace activist who had advocated a total dismantling of the COG nuclear arsenal. "As we have seen both at Rome and Damascus," Señor Urbina had said, "if the weapons exist, they can be used. Only if there are no weapons at all can we guarantee that human beings will never again suffer the horror of nuclear devastation."

Richard Wakefield did not return before the Raman nightfall. Since the communication station at Beta had been knocked out of commission by the hurricane (the Newton had monitored the breakup of the Cylindrical Sea and the onset of the windstorm through telemetry relayed by Beta before it was silenced), Richard had moved out of communications range when he was halfway across the Central Plain. His last transmission to Janos Tabori, who had volunteered to man the commlink, had been typically Wakefield. As the signal from inside Rama was fading, Janos, in a lighthearted tone, had asked Richard how he wanted to be remembered "to your fans" in case he was "swallowed by the Great Galactic Ghoul."

"Tell them that I loved Rama not wisely, but too well," Richard had shouted into his communicator.

"What's that?" Otto Heilmann had puzzled. The admiral had come looking for Janos to discuss a Newton engineering problem.

"He killed her," Janos had said, trying without success to lock up the signal again.

"Who killed— What are you talking about?"

"It's not important," Janos had answered, spinning around in his chair and floating into the air. "Now, what can I do for you, Herr Admiral?"

Richard's failure to return was not considered serious until several hours after the following Raman dawn. The cosmonauts remaining on the Newton had convinced themselves the night before that Wakefield had become absorbed in some task ("Probably fixing the Beta comm station," Janos had offered), had lost track of the time, and had decided not to take a solitary ride out in the dark. But when he didn't return in the morning, a feeling of gloom began to pervade the conversation of the crew.

"I don't know why we won't admit it," Irina Turgenyev said suddenly during a period of quiet at dinnertime. "Wakefield is not coming back either. Whatever got Takagishi and des Jardins got him as well."

"That's ridiculous, Irina," Janos replied heatedly.

"*Da,*" she remarked. "That's what you've always said. Ever since the beginning when General Borzov was cut to pieces. Then it was an accident that the crab biot attacked Wilson. Cosmonaut des Jardins disappears down an alley—"

"Coincidence," Janos shouted, "all coincidence!"

"You're stupid, Janos," Irina shouted back. "You trust everybody and everything. We should blow the damn thing to pieces before it does any more—"

"Stop, stop, you two," David Brown said loudly as the two Soviet colleagues continued to argue.

"All right, now," added General O'Toole. "We're all a little tense. There's no need for us to quarrel."

"Will anyone be going in to look for Richard?" the emotional Janos asked no one in particular.

"Who would be crazy enough—" Irina began to respond.

"No," interrupted Admiral Heilmann firmly. "I told him that his visit was unauthorized and that we would not come after him under any circumstances. Besides, Dr. Brown and the two pilots tell me that we can barely fly the two Newton ships home with the manpower remaining— and their analysis assumed Wakefield was with us. We cannot take any more risks."

There was a long and somber silence at the dinner

table. "I had planned to tell everyone when the meal was over," David Brown then said, standing up beside his chair, "but it looks to me as if this group could use some good news now. An hour ago we received our orders. We're to depart for Earth at I–14 days, a little over a week from now. Between now and then we will cross train the personnel, rest for the voyage home, and make certain that all the Newton engineering systems are working properly."

Cosmonauts Turgenyev, Yamanaka, and Sabatini all shouted their approval. "If we're going to leave without returning to Rama," Janos inquired, "why are we waiting so long? Surely we can be well enough prepared in three or four days."

"As I understand it," Dr. Brown replied, "our two military colleagues have a special task that will occupy most of their time—and some of ours—for much of the next three days." He glanced over at Otto Heilmann. "Do you want to tell them?"

Admiral Heilmann stood up at his place. "I need to discuss the details first with General O'Toole," he said in a ringing voice. "We'll explain it to everyone else in the morning."

O'Toole didn't need Otto Heilmann to show him the message that had been received only twenty minutes before. He knew what it said. In compliance with the procedure, there were only three words: PROCEED WITH TRINITY.

54

ONCE A HERO

Michael O'Toole could not sleep. He tossed and turned, switched on his favorite music, and repeated both the "Hail Mary" and "Our Father" litanies over and over. Nothing worked. He longed for a distraction, something that would make him forget his responsibilities and allow his soul some repose.

Proceed with Trinity, he thought to himself at last, focusing on the true cause of his disquiet. What exactly did that mean? Use the teleoperator forklifts, open up the containers, pick up the weapons (they were about the size of refrigerators), check out the subsystems, put the bombs in a pod, carry them over to the Rama seal, ferry them to the heavy load elevator . . .

And what else? he thought. One more thing. It wouldn't take much more than a minute at each weapon, but it was by far the most important. Each bomb had a redundant pair of tiny numerical keyboards on its side. He and Admiral Heilmann each had to use the keyboards to input a special sequence of digits, an RQ code it was called, before the weapons could be activated. Without those codes the bombs would remain absolutely dormant, forever.

The original debates over whether or not to include nuclear weapons in the limited Newton supply manifest had echoed through the corridors of COG military headquarters in Amsterdam for several weeks. The ensuing vote had been close. It was decided that the Newton would carry the nuclear weapons, but to allay widespread concerns it was also decided to implement rigorous safety measures that would guard against their unwarranted use.

During these same meetings, the COG military leadership avoided public outcry by placing a top secret classification on the fact that the Newton was transporting nuclear bombs to its rendezvous with Rama. Not even the civilian members of the Newton crew had been told about the existence of the weapons.

The secret working group on Trinity safety procedures had met seven times at four different locations around the world prior to the Newton launch. To make the deployment process immune to untoward electronic inputs, manual action had been chosen as the method of activation for the nuclear weapons. Thus neither a lunatic on the Earth nor a frightened cosmonaut on the Newton could trigger the process with a simple electronic command. The current COG chief of staff, a brilliant but passionless disciplinarian named Kazuo Norimoto, had expressed concern that without electronic command capability the military was unduly dependent upon the humans selected for the mission. He had been persuaded, however, that it was far better to depend on the Newton military officers than to worry about a terrorist or fanatic somehow gaining possession of the activation code.

But what if one of the Newton military officers were seized by panic? How could the system be protected against a unilateral act of nuclear warfare by a crew member? When all the discussions were completed, the resultant safety system was relatively simple. There would be three military officers in the crew. Each of them would have an RQ code known only to himself. Manual input of any two of the long numerical sequences would arm the nuclear devices. The system was thus protected against either a recalcitrant officer or a frightened one. It sounded like a foolproof system.

But our current situation was never considered in the contingency analyses, O'Toole thought as he lay in his bed. *In the event of any dangerous action, either military or civilian, each of us was supposed to designate an alternate to learn our code. But who would have thought that an appendectomy was dangerous? Valeriy's RQ died with him. Which means the system now requires two for two.*

O'Toole rolled over on his stomach and pressed his face against the pillow. He now clearly understood why he was still awake. *If I don't input my code those bombs cannot be used.* He remembered a luncheon on the military ship with Valeriy Borzov and Otto Heilmann during the leisurely cruise toward Rama. "It's a perfect set of checks and balances," the Soviet general had joked, "and probably played a role in our individual selections. Otto would pull the trigger at the slightest provocation and you, Michael, would agonize over its morality even if your life were threatened. I'm the tie breaker."

But you are dead, General O'Toole said to himself, *and we have been ordered to activate the bombs.* He rose from the bed and walked over to his desk. As he had done all his life when facing a tough decision, O'Toole pulled a small electronic notebook from his pocket and made two short lists, one summarizing the reasons for following his orders to destroy Rama and the other presenting arguments against it. He had no strictly logical reasons to oppose the destruction command—the giant vehicle was probably a lifeless machine, his three colleagues were almost certainly dead, and there was a nontrivial implied threat to the Earth. But still O'Toole hesitated. There was something about committing such a flagrantly hostile act that offended his sensibilities.

He returned to his bed and rolled over on his back. *Dear God,* he prayed, staring at the ceiling, *how can I possibly know what is right in this situation? Please show me the way.*

Only thirty seconds after his morning alarm, Otto Heilmann heard a soft knock on his door. General O'Toole walked in moments later. The American was already dressed for the day. "You're up early, Michael," Admiral Heilmann said, fumbling for his morning coffee that had been automatically heating for five minutes already.

"I wanted to talk to you," O'Toole said pleasantly. He courteously waited for Heilmann to pick up his coffee packet.

"What is it?" the admiral asked.

"I want you to call off the meeting this morning."

"Why?" Heilmann replied. "We need some assistance from the rest of the crew, as you and I discussed last night. The longer we wait to get started, the more chance we will delay our departure."

"I'm not ready just yet," O'Toole said.

Admiral Heilmann's brow furrowed. He took a long sip from his coffee and studied his companion. "I see," he said quietly. "And what else is needed before you will be ready?"

"I want to talk to someone, General Norimoto perhaps, to understand why we are destroying Rama. I know you and I talked about it yesterday, but I want to hear the reasons from the person giving the order."

"It is a military officer's duty to follow orders. Asking questions could be viewed as a disciplinary breach—"

"I understand all that, Otto," O'Toole interrupted, "but this is not a battlefield situation. I am not refusing to comply with the order. I just want to be certain . . ." His voice trailed off and O'Toole stared off in the distance.

"Certain of what?" Heilmann asked.

O'Toole took a deep breath. "Certain that I'm doing the right thing."

A video conference with Norimoto was arranged and the Newton crew meeting was delayed. Since it was the middle of the night in Amsterdam, it was some time before the encoded transmission could be translated and presented to the COG chief of staff. In his typical manner, General Norimoto then requested several more hours to prepare his response, so that he could obtain "staff consensus" on what he was going to say to O'Toole.

The general and Admiral Heilmann were sitting together in the Newton military control center when the transmission from Norimoto began. General Norimoto was dressed in his full military uniform. He did not smile when he greeted the Newton officers. He put on his glasses and read from a prepared text.

"General O'Toole, we have carefully reviewed the questions contained in your last transmission. All your concerns were included on the issues list that was discussed here on Earth before we reached the decision to proceed with Trinity. Under the unique provisions contained in the ISA-COG operating protocols, you and the other Newton military personnel are temporarily part of my special staff; therefore, I am your commanding officer. The message that was transmitted to you should be treated as an order."

General Norimoto managed just a glimmer of a smile. "Nevertheless," he continued reading, "because of the significance of the action contained in your order and your obvious concern about its repercussions, we have prepared three summary statements that should help you to understand our decision:

"One: We do not know if Rama is hostile or friendly. We have no way of obtaining additional data to resolve the issue.

"Two: Rama is hurtling toward Earth. It might impact our home planet, take hostile action once it's in our neighborhood, or perform benign activities that we can't define.

"Three: By implementing Trinity when Rama is still ten or more days away, we can guarantee the safety of the planet, regardless of Rama's intentions or future actions."

The general paused for the briefest of moments. "That is all," he then concluded. "Proceed with Trinity."

The screen went blank. "Are you satisfied?" Admiral Heilmann asked.

"I guess so," O'Toole said with a sigh. "I didn't hear anything new, but I shouldn't have expected anything else."

Admiral Heilmann looked at his watch. "We've wasted almost an entire day," he said. "Should we have the crew meeting after dinner?"

"I'd rather not," O'Toole replied. "This episode has exhausted me and I hardly slept at all last night. I'd prefer to wait until the morning."

"All right," Heilmann said after a pause. He stood up and put his arm on O'Toole's shoulder. "We'll get started first thing after breakfast."

In the morning General O'Toole did not attend the scheduled crew meeting. He phoned Heilmann and asked the admiral to proceed with the discussion without him. O'Toole's excuse was that he had a "vicious stomach upset." He doubted if Admiral Heilmann really believed his explanation, but it didn't really matter.

O'Toole watched and listened to the meeting on the video monitor in his room, never interrupting or adding to the proceedings. None of the other cosmonauts seemed particularly surprised that the Newton was carrying a nuclear arsenal. Heilmann did a thorough job of explaining what was to be done. He enlisted the help of Yamanaka and Tabori, as he and O'Toole had discussed, and outlined a sequence of events that would be complete with the weapons deployed inside Rama in seventy-two hours. That would leave the crew another three days to prepare for departure.

"When will the bombs detonate?" Janos Tabori asked nervously after Admiral Heilmann was finished.

"They will be set to explode sixty hours after our scheduled departure. According to the analytical models, we should be out of the debris field in twelve hours, but for safety we have specified, in our procedure, that the weapons will not be exploded unless we are at least twenty-four hours away. . . . If our departure is delayed because of some crisis, we can always overwrite the detonation time by electronic command."

"That's reassuring," Janos remarked.

"Any more questions?" Heilmann asked.

"Just one," Janos said. "As long as we're inside Rama putting these things in their proper locations, I assume that it's all right if we look around for our lost friends. In case they may be wandering—"

"The timeline is very tight, Cosmonaut Tabori," the admiral replied, "and the deployment itself, inside the structure, only takes a few hours. Unfortunately, due to our delays in starting the procedure, we will place the weapons in their designated positions during the time that Rama is dark."

Great, O'Toole thought in his room, *that's something else that can be blamed on me.* All in all, though, he felt that Admiral Heilmann had handled the meeting very well. *It was nice of Otto not to say anything about the code,* O'Toole told himself. *He probably figures I'll come around. And he's probably right.*

*   *   *

When O'Toole woke up from a short nap it was past lunchtime and he had a ravenous appetite. There was nobody in the dining room except Francesca Sabatini; she was finishing her coffee and studying some kind of engineering data on a nearby computer monitor.

"Feeling better, Michael?" she said when she saw him.

He nodded. "What are you reading?" O'Toole asked.

"I'm looking at the executive software manual," Francesca replied. "David is very concerned that without Wakefield we won't even know if the Newton software is working properly or not. I'm learning how to read the self-test diagnostic output."

"Whew." O'Toole whistled. "That's pretty heavy for a journalist."

"It's really not that complicated," Francesca said with a laugh. "And it's extremely logical. Maybe in my next career I'll be an engineer."

O'Toole made himself a sandwich, picked up a package of milk, and joined Francesca at the table. She put a hand on his forearm. "Speaking of next careers, Michael, have you given any thought to yours?"

He looked at her quizzically. "What are you talking about?"

"I'm trapped in the usual professional dilemma, my dear friend. My duties as a journalist are in direct conflict with my feelings."

O'Toole stopped chewing. "Heilmann told you?"

She nodded. "I'm not stupid, Michael. I would have found out sooner or later. And this is a big, big story. Maybe one of the biggest of the mission. Can't you see the trailer on the nightly news? 'American general refuses to follow order to destroy Rama. Tune in at five.' "

The general became defensive. "I haven't refused. The Trinity procedure does not call for me to input my code until after the weapons are out of the containers—"

"—and ready for placement in the pods," Francesca finished. "Which is about eighteen hours from now. Tomorrow morning, as near as I can figure. . . . I plan to be on hand to record the historic event." She rose from the table. "And Michael, in case you're wondering, I haven't mentioned your call to Norimoto in any of my reports. I may refer to your conversation with him in my memoirs, but I won't publish them for at least five years."

Francesca turned and looked directly in O'Toole's eyes. "You're about to crap in your mess kit, my friend. You will go from being an international hero to a bum overnight. I hope you've considered your decision very, very carefully."

55

THE VOICE OF MICHAEL

General O'Toole spent the afternoon in his room, watching on the video monitor as Tabori and Yamanaka checked out the nuclear weapons. He was excused, on the basis of his presumed stomach upset, from his assigned task of checking out the weapon subsystems. The procedure was surprisingly straightforward; no one would have suspected that the cosmonauts were initiating an activity designed to destroy the most impressive work of engineering ever seen by humans.

Before dinner O'Toole placed a call to his wife. The Newton was rapidly approaching the Earth now and the delay time between transmission and reception was under three minutes. Old-fashioned two-way conversations were even possible. His talk with Kathleen was cordial and mundane. General O'Toole thought briefly about sharing his moral dilemma with his wife, but he realized that the videophone was not secure and decided against it. They both expressed excitement about being reunited again in the very near future.

The general ate dinner with the crew. Janos was in one of his boisterous moods, entertaining the others with stories about his afternoon with "the bullets," as he insisted on calling the nuclear bombs. "At one point," Janos said to Francesca, who had been laughing nonstop since his narrative began, "we had all the bullets lightly anchored to the floor and lined up in a row, like dominoes. I scared the shit out of Yamanaka. I pushed the front one over and they all fell, clang, bang, in every direction. Hiro was certain they were going to explode."

"Weren't you worried that you might injure some critical components?" David Brown asked.

"Nope," Janos replied. "The manuals that Otto gave me said that you couldn't hurt those things if you dropped them from the top of the Trump Tower. Besides," he added, "they aren't even armed yet. Right, Herr Admiral?"

Heilmann nodded and Janos launched into another story. General O'Toole drifted away, into his own mind, struggling impossibly with the relationship between those metal objects in the military ship and the mushroom-shaped cloud in the Pacific. . . .

Francesca interrupted his reverie. "You have an urgent call on your private line, Michael," she said. "President Bothwell will be on in five minutes."

The conversation at the table stopped. "Well," said Janos with a grin, "you must be some special person. It's not just everybody that receives a call from Slugger Bothwell."

General O'Toole excused himself politely from the table and went to his room. *He must know,* he was thinking as he waited impatiently for the call to connect. *But of course. He's the president of the United States.*

O'Toole had always been a baseball fan and his favorite team, naturally enough, was the Boston Red Sox. Baseball had gone into receivership at the height of The Great Chaos, in 2141, but a new group of owners had put the leagues back in business four years later. When Michael was six, in 2148, his father had taken him to Fenway Dome to watch a game between the Red Sox and the Havana Hurricanes. It was the beginning of a lifelong love affair for O'Toole.

Sherman Bothwell had been a left-handed, power-hitting first baseman for the Red Sox between 2172 and 2187. He had been immensely popular. A Missouri boy by birth, his genuine modesty and old-fashioned dedication to hard work were as exceptional as the 527 home runs he had hit during his sixteen years in the major leagues. During the last year of his baseball career, Bothwell's wife had died in a terrible boating accident. Sherman's uncomplaining courage in facing the responsibility of raising his children as a single parent was applauded in every American home.

Three years later, when he married Linda Black, the darling daughter of the governor of Texas, it was obvious to many people that old Sherman had a political career in mind. He advanced through the ranks with great speed. First lieutenant governor, then governor and presidential hopeful. He was elected to the White House by a landslide in 2196; it was anticipated that he would soundly defeat the Christian Conservative candidate in the forthcoming general election of 2200.

"Hello, General O'Toole," the man in the blue suit with the friendly smile said when the screen was no longer blank. "This is Sherman Bothwell, your president."

The president was using no notes. He was leaning forward in a simple chair, his elbows resting on his thighs and his hands folded in front of him. He was talking as if he were sitting beside General O'Toole in someone's cozy living room.

"I have been following your Newton mission with great interest—as has everybody in my family, including Linda and the four kids—ever since you launched. But I have been *especially* attentive these last several weeks, as the tragedies have rained down upon you and your courageous colleagues. My, my. Who would have ever thought that such a thing as that Rama ship could exist? It is truly staggering . . .

"Anyway, I understand from our COG representatives that the order has been given to destroy Rama. Now, I know that decisions like that are not made lightly, and that it places quite a large responsibility on folks like yourself. Nevertheless, I'm certain it's the right action.

"Yessirree, I know it's correct. Why, you know, my daughter Courtney—that's the eight-year-old—she wakes up with nightmares almost every night. We were watching when you all were trying to capture that *bi-ot*, the one that looked like a crab, and my, it was positively awful. Now, Courtney knows—it's been all over the television— that Rama is heading *di-rectly* for the Earth and she is really scared. Terrified. She thinks the whole country will be overrun by those crab things and that she and all her friends will be chopped up just like journalist Wilson.

"I'm telling you all this, General, because I know you're facing a big decision. And I've heard on the grapevine that you may be hesitant to destroy that humongous spacecraft and all its wonders. But General, I've told Courtney about you. I've told her that you and your crew are going to blow Rama to smithereens long before it reaches the Earth.

"That's why I called. To tell you that I'm counting on you. And so is Courtney."

General O'Toole had thought, before listening to the president, that he might take advantage of the call and lay his dilemma in front of the leader of the American people. He had imagined that he might even question Slugger Bothwell about the nature of a species that destroys to protect against an unlikely downside risk. But after the practically perfect short speech from the ex–first baseman, O'Toole had nothing to say. After all, how could he refuse to respond to such a plea? All the Courtney Bothwells on the entire planet were counting on him.

After sleeping for five hours O'Toole awakened at three o'clock. He was aware that the most important action of his life was facing him. It seemed to him that everything he had done—his career, his religious studies, even his family activities—had been preparing him for this moment. God had trusted him with a monumental decision. But what did God want him to do? His forehead broke out in a sweat as O'Toole knelt before the image of Jesus on the cross that was behind his desk.

Dear Lord, he said, clasping his hands earnestly, *my hour approaches and I still do not see Thy will clearly. It would be so easy for me just to follow my orders and do what everyone wants. Is that Thy desire? How can I know for certain?*

Michael O'Toole closed his eyes and prayed for guidance with a fervor surpassing any he had ever felt previously. As he prayed, he recalled another time, years before, when he had been a young pilot working as part of a temporary peacekeeping force in Guatemala. O'Toole and his men had awakened one morning to find their small air base in the jungle completely surrounded by the right-wing terrorists that were trying to bring the fledgling democratic government to its knees. The subversives wanted the planes. In exchange they would guarantee safe passage to O'Toole and his men.

Major O'Toole had taken fifteen minutes to deliberate and pray before deciding to fight it out. In the ensuing battle the planes were destroyed and almost half his men were killed, but his symbolic stand against terrorism emboldened the young government and many others throughout Central America at a time when the poor countries were struggling desperately to overcome the ravages of two decades of depression. O'Toole had been awarded the Order of Merit, the highest COG military accolade, for his exploits in Guatemala.

Onboard the Newton years later, General O'Toole's decision process was much less straightforward. In Guatemala the young major had not had any questions about the morality of his actions. His order to destroy Rama, however, was altogether different. In O'Toole's opinion, the alien ship had not taken any overtly bellicose actions. In addition, he knew that the order was based primarily on two factors: fear of what Rama *might* do and the uproar of xenophobic public opinion. Historically, both fear and public opinion were notoriously unconcerned about morality. If somehow he could learn what Rama's true purpose was, then he could . . .

Below the painting of Jesus on the desk in his room was a small statue of a young man with curly hair and wide eyes. This figure of St. Michael of Siena had accompanied O'Toole on every journey he had made since his marriage to Kathleen. Seeing the statue gave him an idea. General O'Toole reached into one of the desk drawers and pulled out an electronic template. He switched on the power, checked the template menu, and accessed a concordance indexing the sermons of St. Michael.

Under the word "Rama," the general found a host of different references in the concordance. The one that he was looking for was the only one marked in a bold font. That specific reference was the saint's famous "Rama sermon," delivered in camp to a group of five thousand of Michael's neophytes three weeks before the holocaust in Rome. O'Toole began to read.

"As the topic for my talk to you today, I am going to address an issue raised by Sister Judy in our council, namely what is the basis for my statement that the extraterrestrial spacecraft called Rama might well have been the first announcement of the second coming of Christ. Understand that at this point I have had no clear revelation one way or the other; God has, however, suggested to me that the heralds of Christ's next coming will have to be extraordinary or the people on Earth will not notice. A simple angel or two blowing trumpets in the heavens won't suffice. The heralds must do things that are truly spectacular to engage attention.

"There is a precedent, established in the old testament prophecies foretelling the coming of Jesus, of prophetic announcements originating in the heavens. Elijah's chariot was the Rama of its time. It was, technologically speaking, as much beyond the understanding of its observers as Rama is today. In that sense there is a certain conforming pattern, a symmetry that is not inconsistent with God's order.

"But what I think is most hopeful about the arrival of the first Rama spacecraft eight years ago—and I say first because I am certain there will be others—is that it forces humanity to think of itself in an extraterrestrial perspective. Too often we limit our concept of God and, by implication, our own spirituality. We belong to the universe. We are its children. It's just pure chance that our atoms have risen to consciousness here on this particular planet.

"Rama forces us to think of ourselves, and God, as beings of the universe. It is a tribute to His intelligence that He has sent such a herald at this moment. For as I have told you many times, we are overdue for our final evolution, our recognition that the entire human race is but a single organism. The appearance of Rama is another signal that it is time for us to change our ways and begin that final evolution."

General O'Toole put down the template and rubbed his eyes. He had read the sermon before—right before his meeting with the pope in Rome, in fact—but somehow it had not seemed as significant then as it did now. *So which are you, Rama?* he thought. *A threat to Courtney Bothwell or a herald of Christ's second coming?*

*   *   *

During the hour before breakfast General O'Toole was still vacillating. He genuinely did not know what his decision would be. Weighing heavily upon him was the fact that he had been given an explicit order by his commanding officer. O'Toole was well aware that he had sworn, when he had received his commission, not only to follow orders, but also to protect the Courtney Bothwells of the planet. Did he have any evidence that this particular order was so immoral that he should abrogate his oath?

As long as he thought of Rama as only a machine, it was not too difficult for General O'Toole to countenance its destruction. His action would not, after all, kill any Ramans. But what was it that Wakefield had said? That the Raman spaceship was probably more intelligent than any living creatures on Earth, including human beings? And shouldn't superior machine intelligence have a special place among God's creations, perhaps even above lower life forms?

Eventually General O'Toole succumbed to fatigue. He simply had no energy left to deal with the unending stream of questions without answers. He reluctantly decided to cease his internal debate and prepared to implement his orders.

His first action was to rememorize his RQ code, the specific string of fifty integers between zero and nine that was known only by him and the processors inside the nuclear weapons. O'Toole had personally entered his code and checked that it had been properly stored in each of the weapons before the Newton mission had been launched from Earth. The string of digits was long to minimize the probability of its being duplicated by a repetitive, electronic search routine. Each of the Newton military officers had been counseled to derive a sequence that met two criteria: The code should be almost impossible to forget and should not be something straightforward, like all the phone numbers in the family, that an outside party might figure out easily from the personnel files.

For sentimental reasons, O'Toole had wanted nine of the numbers in his code to be his birthdate, 3–29–42, and the birthdate of his wife, 2–7–46. He knew that any decryption specialist would immediately look for such obvious selections, so the general resolved to hide the birthdates in the fifty digits. But what about the other forty-one digits? That particular number, forty-one, had intrigued O'Toole ever since a beer and pizza party during his sophomore year at MIT. One of his associates then, a brilliant young number theorist whose name he had long forgotten, had told O'Toole in the middle of a drunken discussion that forty-one was a "very special number, the initial integer in the longest continuous string of quadratic primes."

O'Toole never fully comprehended what exactly was meant by the expression "quadratic prime." However, he did understand, and was fascinated by, the fact that the string 41, 43, 47, 53, 61, 71, 83, 97, where each successive number was computed by increasing the difference from the previous number by two, resulted in exactly forty consecutive prime numbers. The sequence of primes ended only when the forty-first number in the string turned out to be a nonprime, namely $41 \times 41 = 1681$. This little known piece of information O'Toole had shared only one time in his life, with his wife Kathleen on her forty-first birthday, and he had received such a lackluster reponse that he had never told anybody about it again.

But it was perfect for his secret code, particularly if he disguised it properly. To build his fifty-digit number, General O'Toole first constructed a sequence of forty-one digits, each coming from the sum of the first two digits in the corresponding term in the special quadratic prime sequence beginning with 41. Thus "5" was the initial digit, representing 41, followed by "7" for 43, "1" for 47 (4 + 7 = 11 and then truncate), "8" for 53, etc. O'Toole next scattered the numbers of the two birthdates using an inverse Fibonacci sequence (34, 21, 13, 8, 5, 3, 2, 1, 1) to define the locations of the nine new integers in the original forty-one-digit string.

It was not easy to commit the sequence to memory, but the general did not want to write it down and carry it with him to the activation process. If his code were written down, then anyone could use it, with or without his permission, and his option to change his mind again would be precluded. Once he had rememorized the sequence, O'Toole destroyed all his computations and went to the dining room to have breakfast with the rest of the cosmonauts.

"Here's a copy of my code for you, Francesca, and one for you, Irina, and the final one goes to Hiro Yamanaka. Sorry, Janos," Admiral Heilmann said with a big smile, "but I'm all out of bullets. Maybe General O'Toole will let you enter his code into one of the bombs."

"It's all right, Herr Admiral," Janos said wryly. "Some privileges in life I can do without."

Heilmann was making a big production out of activating the nuclear weapons. He had had his fifty-digit number printed out multiple times and had enjoyed explaining to the other cosmonauts how clever he had been in the conception of his code. Now, with uncharacteristic flair, he was allowing the rest of the crew to participate in the process.

Francesca loved it. It was definitely good television. It occurred to O'Toole that Francesca had probably suggested such a staging to Heilmann, but the general didn't spend much time thinking about it. O'Toole was too busy being astonished by how calm he himself had become. After his long and agonizing soul-searching, he was apparently going to perform his duty without qualms.

Admiral Heilmann became confused during the entering of his code (he admitted that he was nervous) and temporarily lost track of where he was in his sequence. The system designers had foreseen this possibility and had installed two lights, one green and one red, right above the numerical keyboards on the side of the bomb. After every tenth digit one of the two lights would illuminate, indicating whether or not the previous decade of code was a successful match. The safety committee had expressed concern that this "extra" feature compromised the system (it would be easier to decrypt five ten-digit strings than one fifty-digit string), but repeated human engineering tests prior to launch had shown that the lights were necessary.

At the end of his second decade of digits, Heilmann was greeted by the flashing red light. "I've done something wrong," he said, his embarrassment obvious.

"Louder," shouted Francesca from where she was filming. She had neatly framed the ceremony so that both the weapons and the pods appeared in the picture.

"I've made a mistake," Admiral Heilmann proclaimed. "All this noise has distracted me. I must wait thirty seconds before I can start again."

After Heilmann had successfully completed his code, Dr. Brown entered the activation code on the second weapon. He seemed almost bored; certainly he didn't push the keyboard with anything approaching enthusiasm. Irina Turgenyev activated the third bomb. She made a short but passionate comment underscoring her belief that the destruction of Rama was absolutely essential.

Neither Hiro Yamanaka nor Francesca said anything at all. Francesca, however, did impress the rest of the crew by doing her first thirty digits from memory. Considering that she had supposedly never seen Heilmann's code until an hour earlier, and had not been alone for more than two minutes since then, her feat was quite remarkable.

Next it was General O'Toole's turn. Smiling comfortably, he walked easily up to the first weapon. The other cosmonauts applauded, both showing their respect for the general and acknowledging his struggle. He asked everyone please to be quiet, explaining that he had committed his whole sequence to memory. Then O'Toole entered the first decade of digits.

He stopped for a second as the green light flashed. In that instant an image flashed into his mind of one of the frescoes on the second floor of the shrine of St. Michael in Rome. A young man in a blue robe, his eyes uplifted to the heavens, was standing on the steps of the Victor Emmanuel Monument, preaching to an appreciative multitude. General O'Toole heard a voice, loudly and distinctly. The voice said "No."

The general spun around quickly. "Did anybody say anything?" he said, staring at the other cosmonauts. They shook their heads. Befuddled, O'Toole turned back to the bomb. He tried to remember the second decade of digits. But it was no good. His heart was racing at breakneck speed. His mind kept saying, over and over again, *What was that voice?* His resolve to perform his duty had vanished.

Michael O'Toole took a deep breath, turned around again, and walked across the huge bay. When he passed his stunned colleagues he heard Admiral Heilmann yell, "What are you doing?"

"I'm going to my room," O'Toole said without breaking stride.

"Aren't you going to activate the bombs?" Dr. Brown said behind him.

"No," replied General O'Toole. "At least not yet."

56

AN ANSWERED PRAYER

General O'Toole stayed in his room the rest of the day. Admiral Heilmann dropped by about an hour after O'Toole's failure to enter his code. After some meaningless small talk (Heilmann was terrible at that sort of thing), the admiral asked the all-important question.

"Are you ready to proceed with the activation?"

O'Toole shook his head. "I thought I was this morning, Otto, but . . ." There was no need for him to say anything more.

Heilmann rose from his chair. "I've given orders for Yamanaka to take the first two bullets to the passageway inside Rama. They'll be there by dinner if you change your mind. The other three will be left in the bay for the time being." He stared at his colleague for several seconds. "I hope you come to your senses before too much longer, Michael. We're already in deep trouble at headquarters."

When Francesca came in with her camera two hours later, it was clear from her choice of words that the attitude toward the general, at least among the remaining cosmonauts, was that O'Toole was suffering from acute nervous tension. He wasn't being defiant. He wasn't making a statement. None of the rest of the crew could have tolerated those alternatives, because they would all look bad by association. No, it was obvious that there was something wrong with his nerves.

"I've told everyone not to bother you with calls," Francesca said compassionately as she glanced around the room, her television mind already framing the images of the coming interview. "The phones have been ringing like coming interview. "The phones have been ringing like crazy, especially since I sent down the tape from this morning." She walked over to his desk, checking the objects on its top. "Is this Michael of Siena?" Francesca asked, picking up the small statue.

O'Toole managed a wan smile. "Yes," he said. "And I think you know the man on the cross in the picture."

"Very well," Francesca replied. "Very well indeed. . . . Look, Michael, you know what's coming. I would like for this interview to paint you in the best possible light. Not that I'm going to treat you with kid gloves, you understand, but I want to make certain that those wolves down there hear your side of the story—"

"They're already screaming for my hide?" O'Toole interrupted.

"Oh, yes," she answered. "And it will get much worse. The longer you delay activating the bombs, the more wrath will be aimed at you."

"But why?" O'Toole protested. "I haven't committed a crime. I've simply delayed activating a weapon whose destructive power exceeds—"

"That's irrelevant," Francesca retorted. "In *their* eyes you haven't done your job, namely to protect the people on the planet Earth. They're frightened. They don't understand all this extraterrestrial crap. They've been told that Rama will be destroyed and now you've refused to remove their nightmares."

"Nightmares," mumbled O'Toole, "that's what Bothwell—"

"What about President Bothwell?" inquired Francesca.

"Oh, nothing," he said. He looked away from her probing eyes. "What else?" O'Toole asked impatiently.

"As I was saying, I want you to look as good as possible. Comb your hair again and put on a fresh uniform, not a flight suit. I'll daub a little makeup on your face so you don't look washed out." She returned to the desk. "We'll place your family photos in full view next to Jesus and Michael. Think carefully about what you're going to say. Of course I'll ask why you failed to activate the weapons this morning."

Francesca walked over and put her hand on O'Toole's

shoulder. "In my introduction I will have suggested that you've been under a strain. I don't want to put words in your mouth, but admitting a little weakness will probably play well. Particularly in your country."

General O'Toole squirmed while Francesca finished the preparations for the interview. "Do I have to do this?" he asked, becoming more and more uncomfortable as the journalist essentially rearranged his room.

"Only if you want anybody to think you're not Benedict Arnold," was her curt reply.

Janos came in to visit just before dinner. "Your interview with Francesca was very good," he lied. "At least you raised some moral issues that all of us should consider."

"It was dumb of me to bring up all that philosophical crap," O'Toole fretted. "I should have followed Francesca's advice and blamed everything on my fatigue."

"Well, Michael," said Janos, "what's done is done. I didn't come in here to review the events of the day. I'm certain you've done that plenty of times already. I came in here to see if I could be any help."

"I don't think so, Janos," he replied. "But I do appreciate the thought."

There was a long hiatus in the conversation. At length Janos stood up and shuffled toward the door. "What do you do now?" he asked quietly.

"I wish I knew," O'Toole answered. "I don't seem to be able to come up with a plan."

The combined Rama–Newton spacecraft continued to hurtle toward the Earth. With each passing day the Rama threat loomed greater, a huge cylinder moving at hyperbolic speed toward what would be a calamitous impact if no new midcourse corrections were made. The estimated crash point was in the state of Tamil Nadu, in south India, not far from the city of Madurai. Physicists were on the network news every night, explaining what could be expected. "Shock waves" and "ejecta" became terms bandied about at dinner parties.

Michael O'Toole was vilified by the global press. Francesca had been right. The American general became the focus of a world's fury. There were even suggestions that he should be court-martialed and executed, onboard the Newton, for his failure to follow orders. A lifetime of important accomplishments and selfless contributions was forgotten. Kathleen O'Toole was forced to leave the family apartment in Boston and take refuge with a friend in Maine.

The general was tortured by his indecision. He knew that he was doing irreparable damage to his family and his career by his failure to activate the weapons. But each time he convinced himself he was ready to execute the order, that loud and resounding "No" echoed again in his ears.

O'Toole was only marginally coherent in his final interview with Francesca, the day before the scientific ship left to return to the Earth. She asked some very tough questions. When Francesca asked him why, if Rama were going to orbit the Earth, it had not yet made a deflection maneuver, the general perked up momentarily and reminded her that aerobraking—dissipating energy in the atmosphere as heat—was the most efficient method of achieving orbit around a planetary body with an atmosphere. But when she gave him a chance to amplify his statement, to discuss how Rama might reconfigure itself to have aerodynamic surfaces, O'Toole did not answer. He just stared at her distractedly.

O'Toole came out of his room for the final dinner the night before Brown, Sabatini, Tabori, and Turgenyev departed for home. His presence spoiled the last supper. Irina was extremely nasty to him, upbraiding the general venomously, and refusing to sit at the same table. David Brown ignored him altogether, choosing instead to discuss in excruciating detail the laboratory being designed in Texas to accommodate the captured crab biot. Only Francesca and Janos were friendly, so General O'Toole returned to his room right after dinner without formally saying good-bye to anyone.

The next morning, less than an hour after the scientific

ship had left, O'Toole buzzed Admiral Heilmann and asked for a meeting. "So you have finally changed your mind?" the German said excitedly when the general entered his office. "Good. It's not too late yet. It's only I–12 days. If we hurry we can still detonate the bombs at I–9."

"I'm getting closer, Otto," O'Toole replied, "but I'm not there yet. I've been thinking about all this very carefully. There are two things I would still like to do. I'd like to talk to Pope John-Paul and I want to go inside to see Rama for myself."

O'Toole's response left Heilmann deflated. "Shit," he said. "Here we go again. We'll probably—"

"You don't understand, Otto," the American said. He stared fixedly at his colleague. "This is good news. Unless something totally unexpected occurs, either during my call to the pope or while I'm exploring Rama, I'll be ready to enter my code the minute I come out."

"Are you certain?" Heilmann asked.

"I give you my word," O'Toole replied.

General O'Toole held nothing back in his long, emotional transmission to the pope. He was aware that his call was being monitored, but it no longer mattered. A single thing was uppermost in his mind: making the decision to activate the nuclear weapons with a clear conscience.

He waited impatiently for the reply. When Pope John-Paul V finally appeared on the screen, he was sitting in the same room in the Vatican where O'Toole had had his audience just after Christmas. The pope was holding a small electronic pad in his right hand and occasionally glanced down as he spoke.

"I have prayed with you, my son," the pontiff began in his precise English, "particularly during this last week of your personal turmoil. I cannot tell you what to do. I do not have the answers any more than you do. We can only hope together that God, in His wisdom, will provide unambiguous answers to your prayers.

"In response to some of your religious inquiries, however, I can make a few comments. I offer them to you in the hope that they will be helpful. . . . I cannot say whether or not the voice you heard was that of St. Michael, or if you had what is known as a religious experience. I can affirm that there is a category of human experience, usually called religious for lack of a better term, that exists and cannot be explained in purely rational or scientific terms. Saul of Tarsus was definitely blinded by a light from the heavens as part of his conversion to Christianity, before he became the apostle Paul. Your voice may have been St. Michael. Only you can decide.

"As we discussed three months ago, God certainly created the Ramans, whoever they were. But he also created the viruses and bacteria that cause human death and suffering. We cannot glorify God, either individually or as a species, if we do not survive. It seems unlikely to me that God would expect us to take no action if our very survival were threatened.

"The possible role of Rama as a herald for the second coming of Christ is a difficult issue. There are some priests inside the church who agree with St. Michael, although they are a distinct minority. Most of us feel that the Rama craft are too spiritually sterile to be heralds. They are incredible engineering marvels, to be sure, but there is nothing about them that suggests any warmth or compassion or any other redeeming characteristic that is associated with Christ. It therefore seems very unlikely that Rama has any strictly religious significance.

"In the end it is a decision you must make yourself. You must continue your prayers, as I'm certain you realize, but maybe expect a little less fanfare in God's response. He does not speak to everyone in the same way; nor will each of His messages to you come in the same form. Please remember one more thing. As you explore Rama in search of God's will, the prayers of many on Earth will go with you. You can be certain that God will give you an answer; your challenge is to identify and interpret it."

John-Paul ended his transmission with a blessing and a recitation of the Lord's prayer. General O'Toole knelt automatically and spoke the words along with his spiritual leader. When the screen was blank, he reviewed what the pontiff had said and felt reassured. *I must be on the right track,* O'Toole said to himself. *But I should not expect a heavenly proclamation with accompanying trumpets.*

O'Toole was not prepared for his powerful emotional response to Rama. Perhaps it was the sheer scale of the spacecraft, so much larger than anything ever built by human beings. Perhaps also his long confinement on the Newton and heightened emotional state contributed to the intensity of his feelings. Whatever the reasons, Michael O'Toole was totally overwhelmed by the spectacle as he made his solitary way into the giant spacecraft.

There was no specific feature that dominated the rest in O'Toole's mind. His throat caught and his eyes brimmed with tears of wonder on several different occasions: riding down the chairlift on his initial descent and looking out across the Central Plain with its long illuminated strips that were Rama's light; standing beside the rover on the shores of the Cylindrical Sea and staring through his binoculars at the mysterious skyscrapers of New York; and gawking many times, like all the cosmonauts before him, at the gigantic horns and buttresses that adorned the southern bowl. O'Toole's dominant feelings were awe and reverence, much as he had felt the first time he had entered one of the old European cathedrals.

He spent the Raman night at Beta, using one of the extra huts left by the cosmonauts on the second sortie. He found Wakefield's message dated two weeks earlier, and had a momentary desire to assemble the sailboat and cross over to New York. But O'Toole restrained himself and focused on the true purpose of his visit.

He admitted to himself that although Rama was a spectacular achievement, its magnificence should not be a relevant factor in his evaluation process. Was there anything he had seen that would cause him to alter his tentative conclusion? No, he grudgingly answered. When the lights came on again inside the giant cylinder, O'Toole was confident that before the next Raman nightfall he would activate the weapons.

Still he procrastinated. He drove the entire length of the coastline, examining New York and the other vistas from different vantage points and observing the five-hundred-meter cliff on the opposite side of the sea. On one last pass through the Beta campsite, O'Toole decided to pick up some odds and ends, including a few personal mementos left behind by the other crew members in their hasty retreat from Rama. Not many items had escaped the hurricane, but he found some souvenirs that had been trapped in corners against the supply crates.

General O'Toole took a long nap before he guided the rover back to the bottom of the chairlift. Realizing what he was going to do when he reached the Newton, O'Toole knelt down and prayed one last time before ascending. Shortly into his ride, when he was still less than half a kilometer above the Central Plain, he turned in his chair and looked back across the Raman panorama. *Soon this will all be gone,* O'Toole thought, *enveloped in a solar furnace unleashed by man.* His eyes lifted from the plain and focused on New York. He thought he saw a moving black speck in the Raman sky.

With trembling hands he lifted his binoculars to his eyes. In a few seconds O'Toole located the enlarged speck. He quickly changed the binocular resolution and the speck split into three parts, each a bird soaring in formation far off in the distance. O'Toole blinked but the image did not change. There were indeed three birds flying in the Raman sky!

Joy filled General O'Toole. He yelled with delight as he followed the birds with his binoculars until he could no longer see them. The remaining thirty minutes of the ride to the top of the Alpha stairway seemed like a lifetime.

The American officer immediately climbed into another chair and descended again into Rama. He wanted desperately to see those birds one more time. *If I could somehow photograph them,* he thought, planning to drive back to the Cylindrical Sea if necessary, *then I could prove to everyone that there are also living creatures in this amazing world.*

Starting two kilometers above the floor O'Toole searched in vain for the birds as he descended. Only slightly disheartened by his failure to find them, he was subsequently dumbfounded by what he saw when he dropped his binoculars from his eyes and prepared to disembark from the chair. Richard Wakefield and Nicole des Jardins were standing side by side at the bottom of the lift.

General O'Toole embraced them each with a vigorous hug and then, with tears of happiness running down his cheeks, he knelt on the soil of Rama. "Dear God," he said as he offered his silent prayer of thanks. "Dear God," he repeated.

57

THREE'S COMPANY

The three cosmonauts talked avidly for over an hour. There was so much to tell. When Nicole told of her fright upon encountering the dead Takagishi in the octospider lair, O'Toole was momentarily silent and then shook his head. "There are so many unanswered questions here," he said, staring up at the high ceiling. "Are you really malevolent after all?" he asked rhetorically.

Richard and Nicole both praised the general's courage in not entering his code to activate the weapons. They were also both horrified that the COG had ordered the destruction of Rama. "It is absolutely unforgivable for us to use nuclear weapons against this spaceship," Nicole said. "I am convinced that it is not fundamentally hostile. And I believe that Rama maneuvered to intercept the Earth because it has a specific message for us."

Richard lightly chided Nicole for developing her opinion more on the basis of emotions than facts. "Perhaps," she rejoined, "but there is a serious logical flaw as well in this decision to destroy. We now have hard evidence that this vehicle communicated with its predecessor. There is good reason to suspect that a Rama III is out there somewhere, probably coming in this direction. If the Rama fleet *is* potentially hostile, there is no way the Earth will be able to escape. We may succeed in destroying this second craft—but in so doing we will almost certainly alert their next ship. Since their technology is so much more advanced than ours, we would have no possibility of surviving their concerted attack."

General O'Toole looked at Nicole with admiration. "That's an excellent point," he said. "It's a shame you weren't available for the ISA discussions. We never considered—"

"Why don't we postpone the rest of this conversation until we're back on the Newton?" Richard said suddenly. "According to my watch, it will be dark again in another thirty minutes, before any of us have reached the top of the lift. I don't want to ride in the dark any longer than is necessary."

The three cosmonauts believed that they were leaving Rama for the last time. As the remaining minutes of light dwindled, each cosmonaut gazed intently at the magnificent alien landscape that stretched out into the distance. For Nicole, the dominant feeling was one of elation. Cautious by nature with her expectations, until this moment in the chairlift she had not allowed herself the intense pleasure of believing that she would ever again hold her beloved Genevieve in her arms. Her mind was now flooded by the bucolic beauty of Beauvois and she imagined in detail the joy of her reunion scene with her father and daughter. *It could be as little as a week or ten days,* Nicole said to herself expectantly. By the time she reached the top she was having difficulty containing her jubilation.

During his ride Michael O'Toole reviewed, one more time, his activation decision. When dark came to Rama, suddenly and at the predicted moment, he had finished developing his plan for communicating his decision to the Earth. They would phone ISA management immediately. Nicole and Richard would summarize their stories and Nicole would present her reasons for thinking that the destruction of Rama would be "unforgivable." O'Toole was convinced that his order to activate the weapons would then be rescinded.

The general switched on his flashlight just before his chair reached the top of the stairway. He stepped off in the weightless environment and stood beside Nicole. They waited for Richard Wakefield before proceeding together around the ramp to the ferry passageway, only a hundred meters away. After the trio had boarded the ferry and were ready to move through the Rama shell toward the Newton, Richard's flashlight beam fell on a large metal object on the side of the passage. "Is that one of the bombs?" he asked.

The nuclear weapon system did indeed resemble an oversized bullet. *How curious*, Nicole thought, recoiling as an instant shudder ran through her system. *It could be any shape, of course. I wonder what subconscious aberration made the designers choose that particular form. . . .*

"But what's that weird contraption at the top?" Richard was asking O'Toole.

The general's brow furrowed as he stared at a bizarre object illuminated by the center of the beam of light. "I don't know," he confessed. "I've never seen it before." He disembarked from the ferry. Richard and Nicole followed him.

General O'Toole shuffled over to the weapon and studied the strange attachment fixed above the numerical keyboard. It was a flat plate, slightly larger than the keyboard itself, that was anchored by angular joints to the sides of the weapon. On the underside of the plate, momentarily retracted, were ten tiny punches—at least that's what they looked like to O'Toole. His observation was confirmed seconds later when one of the punches extended and hit the number "5" on the keyboard several centimeters below. The "5" was followed in rapid succession by a "7," and then by eight more numbers before a green light flashed the successful completion of the first decade.

Within seconds the apparatus entered ten more digits and another green light flashed. O'Toole froze in terror. *My God*, he thought, *that's my code! Somehow they've broken—* His panic subsided an instant later when, after the third decade of digits, the red light announced that an error had been made.

"Apparently," General O'Toole said a short time later in response to an inquiry from Richard, "they have jerryrigged this scheme to try to enter the code in my absence. They only have the first two decades correct. For a moment I was afraid . . ." O'Toole paused, aware of strong emotions stirring within him.

"They must have assumed you weren't coming back," Nicole said in a matter-of-fact tone.

"If Heilmann and Yamanaka did it,." O'Toole replied. "Of course we can't rule out completely the possibility that the contraption might have been placed there by the aliens . . . or even the biots."

"Extremely unlikely," Richard commented. "The engineering is much too crude."

"At any rate," O'Toole said, opening his backpack for some tools to disconnect the apparatus, "I'm not taking any chances."

At the Newton end of the passageway, O'Toole, Wakefield, and des Jardins found the second bomb fitted with the same apparatus. The trio watched it punch out one code attempt—with the same result, a failure somewhere in the third decade—and then they disabled it as well. Afterward they opened up the seal and exited from Rama.

Nobody greeted them when they stepped inside the Newton military ship. General O'Toole assumed that both Admiral Heilmann and Yamanaka were asleep and went immediately to the bedrooms. He wanted to talk to Heilmann in private anyway. But the two men were not in their rooms. It did not take long to confirm, in fact, that the other two cosmonauts were nowhere in the comparatively small living and working area of the military ship.

A search of the supply area in the back of the ship was also futile. However, the threesome did discover that one of the extravehicular activity (EVA) pods was missing. This discovery raised another perplexing set of questions. Where could Heilmann and Yamanaka have gone in the pod? And why had they violated the top-priority project policy that at least one crew member should always stay onboard the Newton?

The three cosmonauts were puzzled as they returned to the control center to discuss their possible courses of action. O'Toole was the first to raise the specter of foul play. "Do you think those octospiders, or even some of the biots, might have come onboard? After all, it's not difficult to enter the Newton unless it's in Self-Protection Mode."

Nobody wanted to say what all three of them were thinking. If someone or something had captured or killed their two colleagues on the ship, then it might still be around and *they* might be in danger themselves. . . .

"Why don't we call the Earth and announce that we're alive?" Richard said, breaking the silence.

"Great idea." General O'Toole smiled. He moved over to the control center console and activated the panel. A standard system status display appeared on the large screen. "That's strange," the general commented. "According to this, we have no video link with the Earth presently. Only low-rate telemetry. Now, why would the data system configuration have been changed?"

He keyed in a simple set of commands to establish the normal multichannel high-rate link with the Earth. A swarm of error messages appeared on the monitor. "What the hell?" Richard exclaimed. "It looks as if the video system has died." He turned to O'Toole. "This is your specialty, General, what do you make of all this?"

General O'Toole was very serious. "I don't like it, Richard. I've only seen this many error messages one time before—during one of our early simulations when some nincompoop forgot to load the communications software. We must have a major software problem. The probability of that many hardware failures in such a short time span is essentially zero."

Richard suggested that O'Toole subject the video communications software to its standard self-test. During the test, the diagnostic printout reported that the error buffers in the self-test algorithm had overflowed when the procedure was less than one percent complete. "So the vidcomm software is definitely the culprit," Richard said, analyzing the data in the diagnostic. He entered some commands. "It's going to take a while to straighten it out—"

"Just a minute," Nicole interrupted. "Shouldn't we spend our time trying to make some sense out of all this new information before we start on any specific tasks?" The two men stopped their activity and waited for her to continue. "Heilmann, Yamanaka, and one pod are missing from this ship," Nicole said, walking slowly around the control center, "and someone was trying to automatically activate the two nuclear bombs in the passageway. Meanwhile the vidcomm software, after functioning properly for hundreds of days—counting all the preflight simulations—has suddenly gone haywire. Does either of you have a coherent explanation for all this?"

There was a long silence. "General O'Toole's suggestion of a hostile invasion of the Newton might work," Richard offered. "Heilmann and Yamanaka might have fled to save themselves and the aliens could have purposely screwed up the software."

Nicole was not convinced. "Nothing I have seen suggests that any aliens—or even any biots, for that matter—have been inside the Newton. Unless we see some evidence—"

"Maybe Heilmann and Yamanaka were trying to break the general's code," Wakefield invented, "and they were afraid—"

"Stop. Stop," Nicole shouted suddenly. "Something's happening to the screen." The two men turned around just in time to see Admiral Otto Heilmann's face materialize on the monitor.

"Hello, General O'Toole," Heilmann said with a smile from the huge screen. "This videotape was triggered by your entering the Newton airlock. Cosmonaut Yamanaka and I prepared it just before we departed in one of the pods three hours before I–9 days. We were ordered to evacuate less than an hour after you went inside to explore Rama. We delayed as long as we could but eventually had to follow our instructions.

"Your personal orders are simple and straightforward. You are to enter your activation code into the two weapons in the ferry passageway and the three remaining in the bay. You should depart in the final pod no more than eight hours thereafter. Don't be concerned about the electronic devices in operation on the two bombs in the Raman shell. COG military headquarters ordered them put in place to test some new top secret decryption techniques. You will discover they can easily be disabled with pliers and/or wirecutters.

"An extra, emergency propulsion system has been added to the pod and its software has been programmed to guide you to a safe location, where you will rendezvous with an ISA tug. All you need to do is code in the exact time of

your departure. However, I must stress that the new pod
navigation algorithms are valid *only* if you leave the Newton *before* I–6 days. After that time, I am told the guidance parameters become increasingly invalid and it will be
almost impossible to rescue you."

There was a short pause in Heilmann's delivery and his
voice took on an increased sense of urgency. "Don't waste
any more time, Michael. Activate the weapons and go
directly to the pod. We have already supplied it with the
food and other essentials that you will need. . . . Good
luck on your voyage home. We'll see you back on Earth."

58

HOBSON'S CHOICE

"I'm certain that Heilmann and Yamanaka were being extremely cautious," Richard Wakefield explained. "They probably left early so they could take extra supplies. And with these lightweight pods, each extra kilogram can be critical."

"*How* critical?" asked Nicole.

"Well—it could make all the difference between getting into a safe orbit around Earth—or shooting past it so quickly that we couldn't be rescued."

"Does that mean," O'Toole inquired somberly, "that only one of us might be able to use the pod?"

Richard paused before answering. "I'm afraid that's possible; it's a function of the time of departure. We'll have to do some quick calculations to determine exactly. But personally I see no reason why we shouldn't consider flying this entire spacecraft. I was trained as a backup pilot, after all. . . . We have only limited control authority, since the ship is so large, but if we jettison everything we don't absolutely need, we may be able to do it. . . . Again, we'll need to do the computations."

Nicole's assignments from General O'Toole and Richard were to check the supplies that had been placed in the pod, determine their adequacy, and then approximate both the mass and packaging volume required to support either two or three travelers. In addition Richard, still favoring flying back to Earth in the military ship, asked Nicole to go through the Newton supply manifest and estimate how much mass could be thrown overboard.

While O'Toole and Wakefield used the computers in the control center, Nicole worked alone in the huge bay. First she examined the remaining pod very carefully. Although the pods were normally used by a single person for local extravehicular activity (EVA), they had also been designed as emergency escape vehicles. Two people could sit behind the tough, transparent front window with a week's supplies on the shelves at the rear of the small cabin. *But three people?* Nicole wondered. *Impossible. Someone would have to squeeze into the shelf space. And then there would not be adequate room for the supplies.* Nicole thought momentarily about being confined to the tiny shelves for seven or eight days. *It would be even worse than the pit in New York.*

She looked through the supplies that had been hastily thrown into the pod by Heilmann and Yamanaka. The food allocation was more or less correct, both in quantity and variety, for a one-week voyage; the medical kit, however, was woefully inadequate. Nicole made a few notes, constructed what she considered to be a proper supply list for either a two- or three-person crew, and estimated the mass and packaging requirements. She then started to cross the bay.

Her eyes were drawn to the bullet-shaped nuclear weapons lying placidly on their sides right beside the pod airlock. Nicole walked over and touched the bombs, her hands idly running across the polished metal surface. *So these are the first great weapons of destruction,* she thought, *the outcome of the brilliant physics of the twentieth century.*

What a sad commentary on our species, Nicole mused, as she was walking among the nuclear bombs. *A visitor comes to see us. It cannot speak our language, but it does discover where we live. When it turns the corner onto our street, while its purpose is still utterly unknown, we blast it into oblivion.*

She shuffled across the bay toward the living quarters, aware of a profound feeling of sadness deep within her. *Your problem,* Nicole said to herself, *is that you always expect too much. From yourself. From those you love. Even from the human race. We are yet too immature a species.*

A momentary wave of nausea forced Nicole to stop for a moment. *What's this?* she thought. *Are these bombs making me ill?* In the back of her mind Nicole recalled a similar feeling of nausea fifteen years before, two hours into her flight from Los Angeles to Paris. *It can't be,* she told herself. *But I'll check just to be certain. . . .*

"That's the second reason why the three of us cannot all fit in a single pod. Don't feel bad, Nicole. Even if the physical space could accommodate our bodies and the needed supplies, the velocity change capability of the pod with all that mass is barely enough to close the orbit around the Sun. Our chances of being rescued would be virtually nil."

"Well," Nicole replied to Richard, trying to be cheerful, "at least we still have the other option. We can go home in this big vehicle. According to my estimates, we can dump in excess of ten thousand kilograms—"

"I'm afraid it doesn't matter," General O'Toole interrupted. Nicole looked at Richard. "What's he talking about?"

Richard Wakefield stood up and walked over to Nicole. He took her hands in his. "They screwed up the navigation system too," Richard said. "Their automatic search algorithms, the big number crunchers being used to try to decrypt O'Toole's code, were overlaid into the general purpose computers on top of the vidcomm and navigation subroutines. This ship is useless as a transportation module."

General O'Toole's voice was distant and lacked its usual upbeat timbre. "They must have started only minutes after I left. Richard read the command buffers and found out that the decryption software was uplinked less than two hours after my departure."

"But why would they incapacitate the Newton?" Nicole asked.

"Don't you understand?" O'Toole said with passion. "The priorities had changed. Nothing was as important as detonating the nuclear weapons. They didn't want to waste the time for the radio signals to go back and forth to Earth. So they moved the computations up here, where each successive candidate code could be commanded from the computer without delay."

"In fairness to mission control," Richard interjected, now pacing around the room, "we should acknowledge that the fully loaded Newton military ship actually has less orbit change capability than a two-person pod with an auxiliary propulsion system. In the eyes of the ISA safety manager, there was no increased risk associated with making this craft inoperable."

"But none of this should have happened in the first place," the general argued. "Dammit! Why couldn't they just have waited for my return?"

Nicole sat down abruptly in one of the available chairs. Her head was spinning and she felt momentarily dizzy. "What's the matter?" Richard said, approaching her with alarm.

"I have been having occasional periods of nausea today," Nicole replied. "I think I'm pregnant. I'll know for certain in about twenty minutes." She smiled at the dumbfounded Richard. "It's extremely rare for a woman to become pregnant within ninety days of an injection of neutrabriolate. But it has happened before. I don't suppose—"

"Congratulations," an enthusiastic General O'Toole suddenly interrupted. "I had no idea that the two of you were planning to have a family."

"Nor did I," Richard replied, still looking shocked. He gave Nicole a vigorous hug and held her close. "Nor did I," he repeated.

"There will be no more discussion of this subject," General O'Toole said emphatically to Richard. "Even if Nicole weren't pregnant with your child, I would insist that the two of you go in the pod and leave me here. It's the only sensible decision. In the first place, we both know that mass is the most critical parameter and I am the heaviest of the three of us by far. In addition, I am old and you two are both quite young. You know how to fly the pod; I've never even trained inside it a single time. Besides," he added dryly, "I will be court-martialed on Earth for refusing to follow orders."

"As for you, my good doctor," O'Toole continued moments later, "I don't need to tell you that you are carrying a very special baby. He or she will be the only human child that was ever conceived inside an extraterrestrial space vehicle." He stood up and glanced around. "Now," he said, "I propose we open a bottle of wine and celebrate our last evening together."

Nicole watched General O'Toole glide over to the larder. He opened it and started rummaging around. "I'm perfectly happy with fruit juice, Michael," she said. "I shouldn't drink more than a single glass of wine now anyway."

"Of course," he replied quickly. "I temporarily forgot. I was hoping that we could do something special on this last night. I wanted to share one last time—" General O'Toole stopped himself and brought the wine and juice back to the table. He handed cups to both Richard and Nicole. "I want you both to know," he said quietly, his mood now subdued, "that I cannot imagine a finer pair of people than the two of you. I wish you every success, especially with the baby."

The three cosmonauts drank in silence for several seconds. "We all know it, don't we?" General O'Toole said in a barely audible tone. "The missiles must be on their way. How long do you figure I have, Richard?"

"Judging from what Admiral Heilmann said on the tape, I would say that the first missile will reach Rama at 1–5 days. That would be consistent both with the pod being outside the debris field and the deflection velocities that must be imparted to the surviving pieces of the spacecraft."

"I'm afraid I'm lost," Nicole said. "What missiles are we talking about?"

Richard leaned over toward her. "Both Michael and I are certain," he said gravely, "that the COG has ordered a missile strike against Rama. They had no assurance that the general would ever return to the Newton and enter his code. And the search algorithm with the automatic punch was a long shot at best. Only a missile strike could guarantee that Rama would not have the capability of harming our planet."

"So I have a little more than forty-eight hours to make my final peace with God," General O'Toole said after reflecting for several seconds. "I have lived a fabulous life. I have much to be thankful for. I will go into His arms without regret."

59

DREAM OF DESTINY

As Nicole stretched her arms over her head and to her sides, she brushed against Richard on her left and one of the water containers hanging slightly out of the shelf behind her. "It's going to be crowded," she observed, squirming in her seat.

"Yes, it is," Richard replied distractedly. His attention was focused on the display in front of the pilot's seat in the pod. He entered some commands and waited for the response. When it finally came, Richard frowned.

"I guess I'll make one more attempt to repackage the supplies," Nicole said with a sigh. She turned around in her seat and stared at the shelves. "I could save us some room and fourteen kilograms if our rescue was guaranteed in seven days," she said.

Richard did not respond. "Dammit," he muttered when a set of numbers appeared on the display.

"What's the matter?" Nicole asked.

"There's something not quite right here," Richard said. "The navigation code was developed for considerably less payload mass—it may not converge if we lose one of the accelerometers." Nicole waited patiently for Richard to explain. "So if we have any hiccoughs along the way, we will probably have to stop for several hours and reinitialize."

"But I thought you said there was plenty of fuel for the two of us."

"Plenty of fuel, yes. However, there are some subtleties in the reprogrammed navigation algorithms that assume the pod contains less than a hundred kilograms, basically only O'Toole and his supplies."

Nicole could read the concern in Richard's brow. "We're all right, I think, if there are no malfunctions," he continued. "But no pod has ever been operated under conditions like this."

Through the front window they could see General O'Toole walking across the bay toward them. He was carrying a small object in his hand. It was TB, one of Richard's tiny Shakespearean robots.

"I almost forgot I had him," O'Toole said a minute later after he had been thanked profusely by Richard. Cosmonaut Wakefield was soaring around the supply depot like a joyous child, a wide smile on his delighted face.

"I thought I'd never see any of them again," Richard yelled from one of the side walls where his exuberant momentum had carried him.

"I was passing your room," General O'Toole shouted back, "right before the scientific ship departed. Cosmonaut Tabori was arranging your things. He asked me to keep that particular robot, just in case—"

"Thank you, thank you, Janos," Richard said. He walked carefully down the wall and anchored himself to the floor. "This is a very special one, Michael," he said with a gleam in his eye. He switched on TB's power. "Do you know any Shakespearean sonnets?"

"There's one that Kathleen especially likes, if I can recall it. I think the first line is, 'That time of year thou mayst'— "

"That time of year thou mayst in me behold
When yellow leaves, or none, or few, do hang
Upon those boughs which shake against the cold,
Bare ruined choirs where late the sweet birds sang.
In me thou seest the twilight of such day
As after sunset fadeth in the west . . ."

The feminine voice coming from TB startled both Nicole and General O'Toole. The words struck a resonant chord in O'Toole; he was deeply moved and a few tears welled up in the corners of his eyes. Nicole took the general's hand and squeezed it compassionately after TB had finished the sonnet.

"You didn't say anything to Michael about the problems

you found with the pod navigation," Nicole said. She and Richard were lying side by side in one of the small bedrooms on the military ship.

"No," replied Richard quietly. "I didn't want to worry him. He believes that we are going to be safe and I don't want him to think differently."

Nicole extended her arm and touched Richard. "We could stay here, darling—then at least Michael would survive."

He rolled over toward her. She could tell he was looking at her, even though she couldn't see him very clearly in the dark. "I thought about that," Richard said. "But he would never accept it. . . . I even thought about sending you by yourself. Would you want to do that?"

"No," Nicole answered after thinking for a moment. "I don't think so. I'd rather go with you, unless . . ."

"Unless what?"

"Unless there really is a big difference in the odds. If one of us can survive but two of us are almost certainly doomed, it doesn't make much sense—"

"I can't give you an accurate probabilistic assessment," Richard interrupted. "But I don't think there's a major difference if we go together. My knowledge of the pod and its system might almost be worth the extra mass. But either way, we're better off in the pod than if we stay here."

"You're absolutely convinced that missiles are on the way, aren't you?"

"Yes, indeed. Nothing else makes sense. I would bet that such a contingency plan was under development as soon as Rama changed course and headed for the Earth."

They were silent again. Nicole tried to sleep but was unsuccessful. They had both decided to rest for six hours before departing so that they could store some energy for what would doubtless be an exhausting voyage. Nicole's mind, however, would not turn off. She kept imagining General O'Toole perishing in a nuclear fireball.

"He really is a wonderful man," Nicole said very quietly. She wasn't certain if Richard was still awake.

"Yes, he is," Richard answered in the same tone. "I envy his inner strength. I can't imagine giving up my own life for someone else so willingly." He paused for a moment. "I guess that comes from his deep religious beliefs. He doesn't see death as an end, only as a transition."

I could do it, Nicole thought. *I could give up my life for Genevieve. Maybe even for Richard and this unborn baby. Perhaps in O'Toole's religion everyone is part of his family.*

Richard, meanwhile, was struggling with his own emotions. Was he being selfish in not insisting that Nicole go alone? Could he really justify the extra risk of his presence in terms of his extra skills? He dismissed the questions and tried to think of something else.

"You haven't said much about the baby," Nicole said softly after another short silence.

"I haven't really had time to integrate him, or her, into what's going on," Richard replied. "I guess I've been insensitive. . . . You know I'm happy about it. I just want to wait until we're rescued before I seriously start thinking about what it will be like to be a father." He leaned over and gave Nicole a kiss. "Now, darling, I hope you won't think I'm being rude, but I'm going to try to sleep. It could be a long time before we have another opportunity—"

"Of course," she said. "I'm sorry." Nicole's mind drifted to another picture, this one of a small baby. *I wonder if he'll be intelligent,* she thought. *And will he have Richard's blue eyes and long fingers?*

Nicole was curled up in a ball in the corner of the dimly lit room. The taste of manna melon was still in her mouth. She was awakened by a strange tapping on her shoulder. Nicole glanced up and saw the gray velvet avian bending over her. The cherry rings around its neck glowed in the dark. "Come," it said pleadingly. "You must come with us."

She followed the avian into the hallway and turned to the right, away from the vertical corridor. The other avians were standing quietly against the wall. They were all watching her carefully. The whole procession followed the gray avian down the tunnel.

In a few moments the tunnel expanded into a large room. There was a solitary small light on the far wall, but otherwise the room was dark. Others were present, but

Nicole could not see them clearly. Occasionally she glimpsed their silhouettes as they moved across the beam from the single light source. Nicole started to say something but the avian leader interrupted her. "*Shh,*" it said, "they will be here soon."

Nicole heard a noise coming toward them from the opposite side of the room. It sounded like a cart with wooden wheels moving on a dirt path. As it approached, the avians around Nicole backed up and pressed against her. Moments later there was a fire in front of them.

A bier was resting on top of a burning cart. Nicole gasped. Her mother's body, dressed in regal green robes, lay on top of the bier. In the light from the fire Nicole could see some of the others in the room. Richard was smiling at her, holding the hand of a dark little girl about two years old. General O'Toole was very close to the fire, kneeling in prayer beside it. Behind him were a variety of biots and two or three odd forms that must have been octospiders.

The flames consumed the bier and began to burn her mother's body. Her mother rose slowly from her supine position. When Anawi turned in Nicole's direction, her face changed. It was Omeh's head on top of her mother's body.

"Ronata," he said distinctly, "the prophecies must be heeded. The Senoufo blood will be spread, even unto the stars. Minowe will be left behind. Ronata must travel with those who come from far away. Go now, and save the strange ones and Ronata's children."

60

RETURN TO RAMA

I *can't believe I'm doing this*, Nicole said to herself as she carried her final ferryload of supplies to the heavy elevator at the top of the Beta stairway. It was dark inside Rama. The beam from her flashlight shone into the black void.

The dream had been so incredibly vivid that Nicole had been completely discombobulated for more than five minutes after she woke up. Even now, almost two hours later, when she closed her eyes Nicole could see Omeh's face perfectly and hear his magical voice intoning the words. *I hope Richard doesn't wake up before I'm gone*, Nicole thought. *There's no way he would ever understand.*

She returned to the ferry and made one last trip through the shell toward the Newton. For thirty minutes she had been drafting her good-bye remarks in her mind, but now that the moment had come, Nicole was apprehensive. "Dear Michael and dearest Richard," she would begin, "last night I had the most compelling dream of my life. The old Senoufo chieftain Omeh appeared to me and told me that my destiny was with Rama."

Nicole passed through the airlock and entered the control center. She sat down in front of the camera and cleared her voice. *This is ridiculous*, she thought, just before she turned on the lights. *I must be insane.* But the power of Omeh's image in her mind calmed all of her last-minute doubts. Moments later she continued with her final remarks to her friends.

"There is no way I can summarize in this short farewell the importance of Omeh and my African background in my life. Michael, Richard can tell you some of the Senoufo stories as the two of you fly home to Earth. Suffice it to say that I have never been misled by the old shaman. I know well that voices in a dream have no substance and are most likely creations of my own subconscious, but nevertheless I have decided to follow the directions Omeh gave me.

"I intend to do whatever I can to communicate to Rama that nuclear missiles may be on the way. I don't know exactly how I will accomplish this, but I will have some hours to plan while I am assembling the sailboat to cross the Cylindrical Sea. I do remember, Richard, our discussion about the keyboard commands that might lead into the higher hierarchy. . . .

"It is extremely difficult for me to say good-bye like this, and I am keenly aware that it is a poor substitute for a final embrace. But if you two were awake, you would never let me go back inside Rama. . . . I love you, Richard, never doubt it for a moment. I know it's unlikely, but maybe somehow, someday we will be united in another place. I promise you that if I survive to give birth to our child, I will never cease telling her about the intelligence, wit, and sensitivity of her father.

"I have one last request. If it turns out that either of you reaches home safely and I never return to the Earth, please explain to Genevieve what happened to me. Tell her the whole story, about the dream, the vial and the vision, and the Poro when I was a child. And tell her that I loved her with all my heart."

Tears were flowing down Nicole's cheeks when she finished her message. She stood up and rewound the tape. She played it for a minute, to make certain that it had recorded properly, and then walked over to the airlock. *Goodness*, she thought as she put on her helmet, *I'm really going to do it*.

During Nicole's eerie descent on the chairlift in the dark she had strong misgivings about her decision to return. It was only her supreme self-discipline that allowed her to chase away the lingering fears. As she climbed into the rover and started to drive toward the Cylindrical Sea, Nicole thought about how she would communicate with the intelligence governing Rama. *I'll definitely use pictures,* she said to herself, *and wherever possible the precise language of science. That much I have learned from Richard.*

The thought of Richard rekindled her anxieties. *He'll think that I have abandoned him,* she worried. *And how can I really expect him to think otherwise?* Nicole recalled the depressing first days of her pregnancy with Genevieve and how very lonely she had been having nobody with whom she could share her feelings. Again she felt a strong call to turn around and leave Rama. Her introspection was broken by the spectacular arrival of light. Dawn had come again to Rama. As before, Nicole was mesmerized by the sights around her. *There's nothing like this anywhere in the universe.*

When she reached what had been the Beta campsite, she first found and started to unpack the large sailboat. It was in good shape. It had been packed at the bottom of a large storage container. Working to assemble the sailboat kept Nicole from brooding too much about her decision to leave the Newton. Mechanical assembly was not her forte. She almost despaired once when she had to disassemble a major fitting that had taken her ten minutes to put together in the first place. The entire exercise reminded her of several frustrating Christmas Eves at Beauvois when she and Pierre had worked almost all night to put Genevieve's new toys together. "There ought to be a law that stores can only sell assembled toys," Nicole laughingly muttered as she struggled with the directions for the sailboat.

Nicole carried the hull of the boat down the steps and placed it right next to the water. Each of the major substructures she assembled on the cliff above, where the light was brighter. She was so engrossed in her work that she did not hear the footsteps until they were only two or three meters away. When Nicole, who was working on her knees, turned to her right and saw something approaching her from very close, she was frightened almost out of her wits.

Moments later she and Richard were kissing and hugging joyously. "O'Toole's coming too," he said, sitting down next to Nicole and immediately beginning to work on the sailboat. "At first, when I explained that I wasn't leaving without you, that whatever life I could have on Earth wouldn't mean anything if you weren't with me, he told me that you and I were both crazy. But after we talked, and I explained to him that I thought we had a decent probability of warning the Ramans, he decided that he'd rather spend his last hours with us than take a chance on a lonely and painful death in the pod."

"But I thought you said that it would be a safe trip for a solitary passenger."

"It's not completely clear. The software loaded in the pod is a nightmare. You can tell from the programming that it was done hastily. And how could it have been properly checked? O'Toole by himself might have had a better chance than the two of us together. . . . But remember, he would face serious problems upon his arrival on Earth. That court-martial comment was not idle chatter."

"I don't think that Michael was afraid of a court-martial. He might have wanted to spare his family, but—"

A shout from the distance interrupted their conversation. General O'Toole was waving at them from an approaching rover. "But I don't understand," Nicole said. "How did he get here so quickly? You didn't walk, did you?"

Richard laughed. "Of course not. I left a beacon at the bottom of the chairlift. After I arrived at Beta and saw that you had removed the sailboat and its parts, I sent the rover back on automatic."

"That was brave of you," Nicole said. "What if I had set sail during the extra time that it took you to find me on foot?"

Richard peered over the cliff at the boat's hull down next to the water. "Actually you've done better than I expected," he said with a tease in his voice. "You might have finished in another hour or two."

He grabbed Nicole's hands as she tried to hit him.

General O'Toole was the only practiced sailor among

the three of them. Soon after they reached the midpoint of their sail, he relegated Richard to holding an oar as a possible weapon in case the pair of shark biots that were shadowing them decided to attack. "It's not Marblehead or the Cape," O'Toole said as he stared across at New York, "but it's definitely an interesting sail."

During the voyage Richard tried, without success, to convince a nervous Nicole that the shark biots were unlikely to bother them. "After all," he told her, "they didn't bother the boats at all during the first Rama expedition. They must have capsized me because of something special in the design of our new motorboats."

"How can you be so certain?" Nicole asked, staring uncomfortably at the gray shadows in the water beside them. "And if they are not going to attack us, why have they been following us for so long?"

"We're a curiosity, that's all," Richard replied. Nevertheless, he braced himself when one of the shadows suddenly veered toward the boat. It disappeared underneath them and joined its companion on the other side. "See," he said, releasing his grip on the oar, "I told you there was nothing to worry about."

They moored the sailboat on the New York side before climbing up the nearby stairway. Since General O'Toole had never been to New York before and was naturally very curious about what he was seeing, Richard went ahead to start working on the computer while Nicole gave the briefest of tours to O'Toole along the way.

By the time Nicole and the general reached the White Room, Richard already had some progress to report. "My hypothesis was correct," he said only seconds after the other two had joined him. "I'm fairly certain that I now have accessed the entire sensor list. They must have radar or its equivalent onboard. While I'm trying to locate it, why don't you two develop a flow diagram for how we will communicate our warning. Remember, keep it simple. We probably don't have more than twenty-four hours until the first missile arrives."

Twenty-four hours, Nicole said to herself. *One more day.* She glanced over at Richard, hard at work at the keyboard, and General O'Toole, who was looking at some of the black objects still scattered in one of the corners. Nicole's momentary feelings of fondness for the two men were quickly truncated by a sharp burst of fear. The reality of their predicament overpowered her. *Will we all die tomorrow?* she wondered.

61

ENDANGERED SPACECRAFT

"We really shouldn't be surprised," Richard said without emotion. The three of them were sitting in front of the large black screen. "All of us expected it."

"But we hoped otherwise," O'Toole interjected. "Sometimes it's depressing to be proven correct."

"Are you positive, Richard," Nicole asked, "that each of those blips represents an object in space?"

"I don't think there's any doubt," Richard replied. "We know for certain that we're looking at sensor output. And look, I'll show you how to change the fields." Richard called to the screen a display that showed a cylinder, definitely Rama, at the center of a set of concentric circles. Next he keyed in another pair of commands, resulting in motion on the screen. The cylinder became smaller and smaller, ultimately collapsing to a point. The size of the concentric circles around the cylinder also diminished during the motion and new circles appeared at the edge of the screen. Eventually a group of dots, sixteen in all, appeared on the right side of the display.

"But how do you know they are missiles?" Nicole queried, indicating the small points of light.

"I don't," Richard said. "But I do know they are flying objects nearly on a straight line between Rama and the Earth. I suppose they might be peace envoys, but I doubt it seriously."

"How long?" O'Toole asked.

"It's hard to tell exactly," Richard answered after a moment's pause. "I'd estimate eighteen to twenty hours until the first one. They're spread out more than I would have expected. If we track them for an hour or so, we'll have a more precise estimate of the impact time."

General O'Toole whistled and then reflected for several seconds before speaking. "Before we try to tell this spacecraft that it's about to undergo a nuclear attack, will you answer one simple question for me?"

"If I can," Richard replied.

"What makes you think that Rama can protect itself from these incoming missiles, even if we are able to communicate the warning?"

There was a protracted silence. "Do you remember one time, Michael, almost a year ago," Richard said, "when we were flying together from London to Tokyo and we started talking about religion?"

"You mean when I was reading Eusebius?"

"I think so. You were telling me about the early history of Christianity. . . . Anyway, right in the middle of the discussion I suddenly asked you why you believed in God. Do you remember your answer?"

"Of course," O'Toole replied. "It's the same response I gave my oldest son when he declared himself an atheist at the age of eighteen."

"Your answer on the plane perfectly captures my attitude in this current situation. We know that Rama is extremely advanced technologically. Certainly when it was designed there must have been some consideration of a possible hostile attack. . . . Who knows, maybe it even has a powerful propulsion system that we haven't yet discovered and will be able to maneuver out of the way. I bet—"

"Can I interrupt for a second?" Nicole said. "I wasn't with you two on the flight to Tokyo. I'd like to know how Michael answered your question."

The two men stared at each other for several seconds. Finally General O'Toole responded. "Faith informed by thought and observation," he said.

"The first part of your plan is not too difficult, and I agree with the approach, but I have no mental picture of how we will communicate the yield, or how to tie the nuclear chain reaction to the incoming missiles unambiguously."

"Michael and I will work on those items while you

develop the graphics for the first segment. He says he remembers his nuclear physics reasonably well."

"Remember not to make too many assumptions," Richard reminded Nicole. "We must make certain that each part of the message is self-contained."

General O'Toole was not with Richard and Nicole at the moment. After two hours of intense work he had walked away, out into the tunnel, about five minutes earlier. His two colleagues suddenly worried about his absence. "He's probably going to the bathroom," Richard said.

"He might be lost," Nicole replied.

Richard moved over to the entrance to the White Room and hollered into the corridor. "Hullo, Michael O'Toole," he said. "Are you all right?"

"Yes," came the answer from the direction of the central stairway. "Can you and Nicole come around here for a minute?"

"What's up?" Richard inquired a few moments later when he and Nicole joined the general at the foot of the stairway.

"Who built this lair?" O'Toole asked, his eyes focused on the ceiling high above him. "And why do you think it was created in the first place?"

"We don't know," Richard answered impatiently, "and I don't think we'll resolve the issue in the next few minutes, or even hours. Meanwhile, we have work—"

"Indulge me for a little while," O'Toole interrupted firmly. "I need to have this discussion before I can proceed." Richard and Nicole waited for him to continue. "We are rushing pell-mell toward sending a warning to whatever intelligence is in control of this vehicle. Presumably, we are doing this so that Rama will be able to take measures to protect itself. How do we know that's the right action for us? How do we know that we're not being traitors to our species?"

General O'Toole waved his arms at the large cavern around him. "There must be some reason, some grand plan for all this. Why were all those fake human objects left in the White Room? Why did the Ramans invite us to communicate with them? Who and what are the avians and the octospiders?" He shook his head, frustrated by all the unanswered questions. "I was uncertain about destroying Rama; but I'm equally uncertain about sending the warning. What if Rama escapes the nuclear attack because of us and then destroys the Earth anyway?"

"That's extremely unlikely, Michael. The first Rama sailed through the solar system—"

"Just a minute, Nicole, if you don't mind," Richard interrupted softly. "Let me try to answer the general."

He walked over and put his arm on General O'Toole's shoulder. "Michael," Richard said, "what has impressed me the most about you since the first time we met has been your ability to understand the difference between the answers we can know, as a result of deduction or the scientific method, and those questions for which there is not even a valid logical approach. There is no way whatsoever that we can understand what Rama is all about at this juncture. We don't yet have enough data. It's like trying to solve a system of simultaneous linear equations when there are many more variables than constraints. Multiple hypersurfaces of correct solutions exist."

O'Toole smiled and nodded his head. "What we do know," Richard continued, "is that a fleet of missiles is now approaching Rama. They are probably armed with nuclear warheads. We have a choice, to warn or not to warn, and we must make it based on the information available to us at this moment."

Richard pulled out his small computer and walked over beside O'Toole. "You can represent this entire problem as a three-by-two matrix," he said. "Assume there are three possible descriptions of the Raman threat: never hostile, always hostile, and hostile only if attacked. Let these three situations represent the rows of the matrix. Now consider the decision facing us. We can either warn them, or choose not to. Note that it is only a *successful* warning that matters. So there are two columns to the matrix, Rama warned and Rama not warned."

O'Toole and Nicole both looked over Richard's shoulder as he constructed the matrix and displayed it on his small monitor. "If we now look at the outcomes of the six events represented by the individual elements in this matrix, and try to assign some probabilities wherever we can, we will have all the information we need to make our decision. Do you agree?"

General O'Toole nodded, impressed by how quickly and concisely Richard had structured their dilemma. "The outcome of the second row is always the same," Nicole now offered, "independent of whether or not we warn them. If Rama is truly hostile, with their more advanced technology it makes no difference whether we warn them or not. Sooner or later, with this vehicle or one that comes in the future, they will either subjugate or destroy the human race."

Richard paused a moment to ensure that O'Toole was following the conversation. "Similarly," he then said slowly, "if Rama is *never* hostile, it cannot be wrong to warn them. In neither case, warned or unwarned, is the Earth in danger. And if we are successful in telling them about the nuclear missiles, then something extraordinary will have been saved."

The general smiled. "So the only possible problem, O'Toole's Anxiety, if you want to call it that, comes if Rama was not originally intending to be hostile, but will change its mind and attack the Earth once it learns that nuclear missiles have been launched against it."

"Precisely," said Richard. "And I would argue that our warning itself would probably be a mitigating factor in that potentially hostile case. After all—"

"All right. All right," O'Toole replied. "I see where you're headed. Unless a very high probability is assigned to the case I'm worried about, the overall analysis suggests a better result from warning the Ramans." He suddenly laughed. "It's a good thing you don't work for COG military headquarters, Richard. You might have convinced me with logic to activate the code—"

"I doubt it," Nicole said. "Nobody could have made a solid case for that kind of paranoia."

"Thank you." The general smiled. "I'm satisfied. You were very persuasive. Let's go back to work."

Driven by the relentless approach of the missiles, the threesome worked tirelessly for hours. Nicole and Michael

O'Toole designed the warning message in two discrete segments. The first segment, much of which was background to establish the basic communication technique, presented all the trajectory mechanics, including the Rama orbit as the vehicle entered the solar system, the two Newton craft leaving the Earth and joining just before rendezvous with the alien ship, the two Raman maneuvers changing its trajectory, and finally the sixteen missiles blasting off from the Earth toward a Rama intercept. Richard, his long hours of work at the keyboard and black screen now paying off, transformed all these orbital events into graphic line drawings while the other two cosmonauts struggled with the complexity of the remainder of the message.

The second segment was exceedingly difficult to design. In it the humans wanted to explain that the incoming missiles carried nuclear warheads, that the explosive power of the bombs was generated by a chain reaction, and that the heat, shock, and radiation resulting from the explosion were all enormously powerful. Presenting the fundamental picture was not the challenge; quantifying the destructive power in any terms that could be understood by an extraterrestrial intelligence was a formidable obstacle.

"It's impossible," an exasperated Richard exclaimed when both O'Toole and Nicole insisted that the warning was not complete without some indication of the explosion temperature and the magnitude of the shock and radiation fields. "Why don't we just indicate the quantity of fissionable material in the process? They must be great at physics. They can compute the yield and other parameters."

Time was running out and all three of them were becoming exhausted. In the final hours, General O'Toole succumbed to fatigue and, at Nicole's insistence, took a substantial nap. His biometry output had indicated that his heart was in stress. Richard even slept for ninety minutes. But Nicole never allowed herself the luxury of rest. She was determined to figure out some way to depict in pictures the destructive power of the weapons.

When the men awakened, Nicole convinced them to append to the second segment an additional short section demonstrating what would happen to a city or forest on

Earth if a one-megaton nuclear bomb exploded in the vicinity. For these pictures to make any sense, of course, Richard had to expand his earlier glossary, in which he had defined the chemical elements and their symbols with mathematical precision, to include some more measures of size. "If they understand this," he grumbled as he laboriously included scale tick marks beside his line drawings of buildings and trees, "then they're smarter than even I gave them credit for."

Finally the message was completed and stored. They reviewed the entire warning one last time and made a few corrections. "Of the commands that I have never been able to understand," Richard said, "there are five that I have reason to suspect may be links to a different level processor. Of course, I am only guessing, but I believe it's an educated guess. I will transmit our message five times, using each of these particular commands a single time, and hope that our warning somehow reaches the central computer."

While Richard entered all the proper commands into the keyboard, Nicole and General O'Toole went for a walk. They climbed up the stairway and wandered around the skyscrapers of New York. "You believe that we were meant to board Rama and find the White Room, don't you?"

"Yes," Nicole answered.

"But for what purpose?" asked the general. "If the Ramans just wanted to make contact with us, why did they go to such elaborate lengths? And why are they risking our misinterpretation of their intent?"

"I don't know," Nicole said. "Maybe they're testing us in some way. To find out what we're like."

"Goodness," O'Toole replied, "what a terrible thought. We may be catalogued as the creatures who launch nuclear attacks against visitors."

"Exactly," said Nicole.

Nicole showed O'Toole the barn with the pits, the lattice where she had rescued the avian, the stunning polyhedrons, and the entrances to the other two lairs. She was becoming very tired, but she knew that she would not sleep until everything was resolved.

"Should we head back?" O'Toole said after he and Nicole had walked down to the Cylindrical Sea and verified that the sailboat was still intact where they had left it.

"All right," Nicole answered wearily. She checked her watch. It was exactly three hours and eighteen minutes until the first nuclear missile would arrive at Rama.

62

THE FINAL HOUR

Nobody had spoken for five minutes. Each of the three cosmonauts sat enmeshed in his own private world, aware that the first missile was now less than an hour away. Richard raced through all the sensor outputs hurriedly, searching vainly for any indication that Rama was taking some protective action. "Shit," he muttered, looking again at the close-up radar picture that showed the lead missile drawing closer and closer.

Richard walked over to where Nicole was sitting in the corner. "We must have failed," he said quietly. "Nothing has changed."

Nicole rubbed her eyes. "I wish I weren't so tired," she said. "Then maybe we could do something interesting for our last fifty minutes." She smiled grimly. "Now I know what it must be like to be on Death Row."

General O'Toole approached from the other side of the room. He was holding two of the small black balls in his left hand. "You know," he said, "often I have wondered what I would do if I ever had a specified, finite time before I died. Now here I am, and my mind keeps focusing on a single thing."

"What's that?" Nicole asked.

"Have either of you ever been baptized?" he replied tentatively.

"Whaaat?" exclaimed Richard with a laugh of surprise.

"I thought not," said General O'Toole. "What about you, Nicole?"

"No, Michael," she answered. "My father's Catholicism was more tradition than ceremony."

"Well," persisted the general. "I'm offering to baptize you both."

"Here? Now?" inquired the astounded Wakefield. "Are my ears deceiving me, Nikki, or did I just hear this gentleman suggest that we spend the last hour of our life being baptized?"

"It won't take—" O'Toole started to say.

"Why not, Richard?" Nicole interrupted. She stood up with a bright smile on her face. "What else do we have to do? And it's a hell of a lot better than morbidly sitting around here waiting for the great fireball."

Richard almost cackled. "This is wonderful!" he exclaimed. "I, Richard Wakefield, lifelong atheist, am considering being baptized on an extraterrestrial spaceship as the final action of my life. I love it!"

"Remember what Pascal wrote," Nicole teased.

"Ah, yes," Richard replied. "A simple matrix from one of the world's great thinkers. 'There may or may not be a God; I may or may not believe in Him. The only way I can lose is if there is a God and I do not believe in Him. Therefore I shall believe in Him to minimize my downside risk.'" Richard chuckled. "But I did not agree to believe in God, only to being baptized."

"So you'll do it," Nicole said.

"Why not?" he replied, parroting her earlier comment. "Maybe that way I don't have to stay in Limbo with the virtuous pagans and unbaptized children." He grinned at O'Toole. "All right, General, we're all yours. Do your thing."

"Now you listen closely to this, TB," Richard said. "You're probably the only robot ever to be in a human's pocket during a baptism."

Nicole nudged Richard in the ribs. The patient General O'Toole waited a few moments and then began the ceremony.

At Richard's insistence, they had left the lair and walked out into the open plaza. Richard had wanted the sky of Rama overhead and neither of the other two had objected. Nicole had gone over to the Cylindrical Sea to fill the baptismal flask with water while General O'Toole completed his preparations. The American general was taking the baptism seriously but was apparently not offended by Richard's lighthearted banter.

Nicole and Richard knelt down in front of O'Toole. He sprinkled water on Richard's head. "Richard Colin Wakefield, I baptize thee in the name of the Father, and the Son, and the Holy Spirit."

When O'Toole had finished baptizing Nicole in the same simple way, Richard stood up and grinned. "I don't feel any different," he said. "I'm just like I was before—scared shitless about dying in the next thirty minutes."

General O'Toole had not moved. "Richard," he said softly, "could I ask you to kneel again? I would like to say a short prayer."

"What's this?" Richard asked. "First a baptism, now a prayer?" Nicole looked up at him. Her eyes asked him to accede. "All right," he said, "I guess I might as well go all the way."

"Almighty God, please hear our prayer," the general said in a strong voice. He also was kneeling now. His eyes were closed and his hands were clasped in front of him. "We three have gathered here in what may be our final hour to pay homage to Thee. We beseech Thee to consider how we may serve Thee if we continue to live and, if it be Thy will, we ask Thee to spare us a painful and horrible death. If we are to die, we pray that we may be accepted into Thy heavenly kingdom. Amen."

General O'Toole stopped for just a moment and then began to recite the Lord's prayer. After he had said, "Our Father, Who art in heaven, hallowed be Thy name—" the lights in the great spaceship were abruptly extinguished. Another Raman day was over. Richard and Nicole waited respectfully until their friend had finished the prayer before pulling out their flashlights.

Nicole thanked the general and gave him a small hug. "Well, here we are," Richard jabbered nervously. "Twenty-seven minutes and counting. We've had a baptism and a prayer. What should we do now? Who has an idea for the last, and I mean the very last, amusement? Should we sing? Dance? Play some kind of game?"

"I would prefer to remain up here by myself," General

O'Toole said solemnly, "and face my death in atonement and prayer. And I imagine the two of you would like to be alone together."

"All right, Nikki," Richard said. "Where shall we share our final kiss? On the shore of the Cylindrical Sea or back in the White Room?"

Nicole had been awake for thirty-two consecutive hours and was absolutely exhausted. She fell into Richard's arms and closed her eyes. At that moment scattered flashes of light intruded upon the new blackness of the Raman night.

"What's that?" General O'Toole asked anxiously.

"It must be the horns," Richard answered excitedly. "Come on, let's go."

They ran to the south edge of the island and stared at the massive, enigmatic structures in the southern bowl. Filaments of light were darting between different pairs of the six spires surrounding the great monolith in the center. The yellow arcs seemed to sizzle in the air, undulating gently back and forth in the middle while remaining connected to one of the little horns at each end. A distant cracking sound accompanied the spectacular sight.

"Amazing," said O'Toole, overcome with awe. "Absolutely amazing."

"So Rama is going to maneuver," Richard said. He could hardly contain himself. He hugged Nicole, then O'Toole, and finally kissed Nicole on the lips. "Whoopee!" he yelled as he danced along the wall.

"But Richard," Nicole shouted after him, "isn't it too late? How can Rama move out of the way in such a short time?"

Richard ran back to his colleagues. "You're right," he said breathlessly. "And those damn missiles probably have terminal guidance anyway." He started running again, this time heading back toward the plaza. "I'm going to watch on the radar."

Nicole glanced over at General O'Toole. "I'm coming," he said. "But I've already run enough for one day. I want to watch this show for another few seconds. You can go on without me if you want."

Nicole waited. As the two of them walked briskly toward the plaza, General O'Toole thanked Nicole for allowing him to baptize her. "Don't be silly," she replied. "I'm the one who should thank you." She put her hand on his shoulder. *The baptism itself wasn't that important,* she continued in her private thoughts. *It was obvious that you were concerned about our souls. We agreed primarily to show our affection for you.* Nicole smiled to herself. *At least I think that was the reason. . . .*

The ground underneath them began to shake vigorously and General O'Toole stopped, momentarily frightened. "That's apparently what happened during the last maneuver," Nicole said, steadying both of them by taking the general's hand, "although I was personally lying unconscious at the bottom of a pit and missed the entire event."

"Then the light show was just an announcement of the maneuver?"

"Probably. That's why Richard was so elated."

They had barely opened the lair covering when Richard bolted up the stairs. "They've done it!" he exclaimed. "They've done it!"

O'Toole and Nicole stared at him as he caught his breath. "They've deployed some kind of mesh or net—I don't know exactly what it is—about six, maybe eight hundred meters thick—all around the spacecraft." He turned around. "Come on," he said, dashing down the steps three at a time.

Despite her fatigue, Nicole responded to his excitement with a final burst of adrenaline. She bounded down the stairs after Richard and ran to the White Room. He was standing in front of the black screen, flipping back and forth from the exterior image that showed the new material around the vehicle to the radar view that depicted the incoming missiles.

"They must have understood our warning," he said to Nicole. Richard jubilantly picked her up off the ground, gave her a kiss, and held her in the air. "It worked, darling," he shouted. "Thank you, oh thank you."

Nicole too was excited. But she was not yet convinced that Rama's action would prevent the destruction of the vehicle. After General O'Toole came in and Richard explained to him what they were seeing on the screen, there were only nine minutes left. Nicole had butterflies the size of basketballs in her stomach. The ground continued to shake as Rama extended its maneuver.

The nuclear missiles obviously had terminal guidance, for despite the fact that Rama was definitely changing its trajectory, the missiles continued to approach along a straight line. The close-up radar picture showed that the sixteen attackers were quite spread out. Their estimated impact times ranged over a period slightly less than an hour.

Richard's frenetic activity increased. He paced wildly around the room. At one point he pulled TB out of his pocket, put him down on the floor, and began talking rapidly to the little robot as if TB were his closest friend. What Richard said was barely coherent. One moment Richard was telling TB to prepare for the coming explosion; a second later he was explaining to him how Rama was going to miraculously evade the oncoming missiles.

General O'Toole was trying to remain calm, but it was impossible with Richard flying around the room like a Tasmanian devil. He started to say something to Richard, but decided instead to step outside into the tunnel for some quiet.

During one of the rare moments that Richard was not moving, Nicole walked over to him and grabbed his hands. "Darling," she said, "relax. There's nothing we can do."

Richard looked down for a second at his friend and lover and then threw his arms around her. He kissed her wildly and then sat down on the shaking floor, pulling her down beside him. "I'm scared, Nicole," he said, his body trembling. "I'm really scared. I hate not being able to do anything."

"I'm frightened too," she replied gently, taking his hands again. "And so is Michael."

"But neither of you *act* scared," Richard said. "I feel like an idiot, bouncing around here like Tigger in *Winnie the Pooh*."

"Every person confronts death in a different way," Nicole said. "All of us feel fear. We just deal with it in our own individual fashion."

Richard was calming down. He glanced over at the big monitor and then at his watch. "Three more minutes until the first impact," he said.

Nicole put her hands on his cheeks and kissed him softly on the lips. "I love you, Richard Wakefield," she said.

"And I love you," he answered.

Richard and Nicole were sitting quietly on the floor, holding hands and watching the black screen, when the first missile reached the edge of the dense mesh that surrounded Rama. General O'Toole was standing behind them in the doorway—he had returned to the room about thirty seconds earlier. At the moment the missile made contact, the impacted part of the mesh yielded, cushioning the blow but allowing the missile to penetrate deeper into the netting. Simultaneously, other pieces of the mesh wrapped themselves rapidly about the missile, spinning a thick cocoon with amazing speed. It was all over in a fraction of a second. The missile was about two hundred meters from the outer shell of Rama, already enclosed in a thick wrapping, when its nuclear warhead detonated. The mesh on the screen flew around a little, but there was only a barely perceptible nudge inside the White Room.

"Wow!" said Richard first. "Did you see that?"

He jumped up and approached the screen. "It happened so fast," Nicole commented, coming up beside him.

General O'Toole mumbled a very short prayer of thanks and joined his colleagues in front of the screen. "How do you think it did that?" he asked Richard.

"I have no idea," Richard replied. "But somehow that cocoon contained the explosion. It must be a fantastic material." He flipped back to the radar image. "Let's watch this next one more closely. It should be here in a few—"

There was a brilliant flash of light and the screen went blank. Less than a second later a sharp lateral force hit them hard, knocking them to the floor. The lights went out in the White Room and the ground stopped shaking. "Is everyone all right?" Richard asked, groping for Nicole's hand in the dark.

"I think so," O'Toole replied. "I hit the wall, but only with my back and elbow."

"I'm fine, darling," Nicole answered. "What happened?"

"Obviously that one exploded early, before it reached the net. We were hit by the shock wave."

"I don't understand," O'Toole said. "The bomb exploded in a vacuum. How could there be a shock wave?"

"It wasn't technically just a shock wave," Richard replied, standing up as the lights came back on and the ground began to shake again. "Hey, how about that!" he interrupted himself. "The famous Raman redundancy scores again. You okay?" he said to Nicole, who looked unsteady as she was standing up.

"I bruised my knee," she answered, "but it's not serious."

"The bomb destroyed the rest of its own missile," Richard said, now answering O'Toole's question as he searched through the sensor list for the redundant imaging and radar outputs, "vaporizing most of the casing and reducing the rest to fragments. The gas and debris moved outward at enormous speeds, creating the wave that hit us. The mesh attenuated the size of the shock."

Nicole moved over against the wall and sat down. "I want to be ready for the next one," she said.

"I wonder how many bumps like that Rama can survive," Richard said.

General O'Toole came over and sat down beside Nicole. "Two down and fourteen to go," he said. They all smiled. At least they weren't dead yet.

Richard located the redundant sensors a few minutes later. "Uh-oh," he said as he surveyed the remaining blips on the screen. "Unless I'm mistaken, the last bomb that exploded was many kilometers away. We were lucky. We'd better hope one doesn't detonate just outside the mesh."

The trio watched while two more missiles were trapped and wrapped in the material surrounding Rama. Richard stood up. "We have a brief respite now," he said. "It will be three minutes or so before our next impact—then we'll have four more missiles in a hurry."

Nicole rose to her feet also. She saw that General O'Toole was holding his back. "Are you sure you're all right, Michael?" she asked. He nodded, still watching the screen. Richard came over beside Nicole and took her hand. A minute later they sat down together against the wall to wait for the next impacts.

They didn't wait long. A second lateral force, much stronger than the first one, hit them within twenty seconds. Again the lights went out and the floor stopped shaking. Nicole could hear O'Toole's labored breathing in the dark. "Michael," she said, "are you hurt?"

When there was no immediate reply, Nicole started crawling in his direction. That was a mistake. She was not braced against anything when the powerful third blast hit. Nicole was thrown savagely into the wall, hitting it with the side of her head.

General O'Toole stayed beside Nicole while Richard went up into New York to survey the city. The men spoke quietly when Richard returned. He reported only minor damage. Thirty minutes after the final missile had been trapped, the lights came back on and the ground started shaking again. "You see," Richard said with a grin, "I told you we'd be all right. They always do everything important in threes."

Nicole remained unconscious for almost another hour. During the last few minutes she was vaguely aware of both the vibration of the floor and the conversation on the opposite side of the room. Nicole opened her eyes very slowly.

"The net effect," she heard Richard say, "is to increase our velocity along the hyperbola. So we will cross the Earth's orbit much earlier than previously, long before the planet itself has arrived."

"How close will we come to the Earth?"

"Not too close. It depends on when this maneuver ends. If it stopped now we would miss by a million kilometers or so, more than twice the distance to the Moon."

Nicole sat up and smiled. "Good morning," she said cheerfully.

The two men came over beside her. "Are you all right, darling?" Richard asked.

"I think so," Nicole said, feeling the bump on the side of her head. "I may have occasional headaches for a while." She looked at the two men. "What about you, Michael? I seem to remember being worried about you right before the big blast."

"The second one knocked the wind out of me," O'Toole replied. "Luckily I was better prepared for the third bomb. And my back seems fine now."

Richard started to explain what he had learned from the output of Rama's celestial sensors. "I heard the last part of it," Nicole said. "I gather we're now going to miss the Earth altogether." Richard helped her to stand up. "But where are we headed?"

Richard shrugged his shoulders. "No planetary or asteroidal targets are anywhere close to our present trajectory. Our hyperbolic energy is increasing. If nothing changes we will escape from the solar system altogether."

"And become interstellar travelers," Nicole said quietly.

"If we live that long," added the general.

"For my part," Richard said with a playful smile, "I am not going to worry about what happens next. At least not yet. I plan to celebrate our escape from the nuclear phalanx. I vote we go upstairs and introduce Michael to some new friends. Should it be the avians or the octospiders?"

Nicole shook her head and smiled. "You're hopeless, Wakefield. Let me not in any way inhibit—"

"Let me not to the marriage of true minds
Admit impediments . . ."

TB suddenly interrupted. All three of the cosmonauts were startled. They stared down at the tiny robot and then erupted with laughter.

". . . love is not love
Which alters when it alteration finds
Or bends with the remover to remove.
Oh no, it is an ever-fixed mark . . ."

Richard picked up TB and switched him off. Nicole and Michael were still laughing. Richard embraced each of them individually. "I can't think of three better traveling companions," he said, holding the little robot over his head, "wherever it is we're going."

ACKNOWLEDGMENTS

Many different people contributed to this novel during numerous conversations over a two-year period. Those whose comments or insights were especially valuable include Bebe Barden, Paul Chodas, Clayton Frohman, Michael Glassman, Bruce Jakosky, Roland Joffe, Gerry Snyder, and Ian Stewart.

Lou Aronica, Malcolm Edwards, and Russ Galen each made significant contributions to the book. Their editing insights were essential in shaping the final structure of the novel.

Special thanks are extended to Father Martin Slaught, whose religious acumen was indispensable in creating General O'Toole, and Peter Guber, who enabled the authors to meet for the first time over three years ago.

Finally, no acknowledgment would be complete without bouquets for Mr. Lee's family. His wife, Stacey, and five young sons, Cooper, Austin, Robert, Patrick, and Michael, generously allowed him to make the necessary trips halfway around the world to Sri Lanka and granted him the private time that was required for the integration of this novel.

About the Authors

ARTHUR C. CLARKE is one of the most famous science fiction writers of all time. In addition to *Rendezvous with Rama*, he has written such million-copy bestsellers as *Childhood's End*, *2001: A Space Odyssey*, *2010: Odyssey Two*, and *2061: Odyssey Three*. He cobroadcast the *Apollo 11, 12*, and *15* missions with Walter Cronkite and Captain Wally Schirra, and shared an Oscar nomination with Stanley Kubrick for the film version of *2001: A Space Odyssey*.

GENTRY LEE has been chief engineer on Project Galileo, director of science analysis and mission planning for NASA's *Viking* mission to Mars, and partner with Carl Sagan in the design, development, and implementation of the television series *Cosmos*.

Mr. Clarke and Mr. Lee previously collaborated on the novel *Cradle*.

Arthur C. Clarke is legendary. He's a science fiction writer whose imaginings reverberate outside the realm of fiction. A true visionary, he conceived of communications satellites in geostationary orbits—a speculation soon realized. He also cobroadcast the Apollo 11, 12, and 15 missions with Walter Cronkite and Captain Wally Schirra.

No less remarkable are his literary works. His 1973 novel *Rendezvous with Rama* swept the Hugo, Nebula, and Campbell awards. Author of more than fifty books, Clarke has fifty million copies in print. *2001: A Space Odyssey* is the Oscar-nominated product of his collaboration with film director Stanley Kubrick.

At the heart of every Arthur C. Clarke novel lies a small puzzle with large ramifications. He is an author who takes an idea and drops it into a quiet pool of thought. There's a splash—that's the intriguing nature of Clarke's scientific genius. Then the ripples spread out, washing up on character, society, soaking the whole book in wonder. It laps around your toes as you read. . . .

The Fountains of Paradise

What follows is a quite dramatic moment excerpted from Clarke's 1978 novel The Fountains of Paradise. *Set in a country modeled on Sri Lanka, it was Clarke's research for this book that drew him to this exotic land, where he has now lived for many years. This scene is exemplary of Clarke's style: A captivating idea, grounded in pure science, lies at the heart of the story, promising to change the world forever.*

He released the PAUSE button on the projector, and the frozen statue came instantly to life.

"My name is Vannevar Morgan. I am Chief Engineer of Terran Construction's Land Division. My last project was the Gibraltar Bridge. Now I want to talk about something incomparably more ambitious."

Rajasinghe glanced around the room. Morgan had hooked them, just as he had expected.

He leaned back in his chair and waited for the now familiar, yet still almost unbelievable, prospectus to unfold. Odd, he thought, how quickly one accepted the conventions of the display, and ignored quite large errors of the TILT and LEVEL controls. Even the fact that Morgan "moved" while staying in the same place, and the totally false perspective of exterior scenes, failed to destroy the sense of reality.

"The Space Age is almost two hundred years old. For more than half that time, our civilization has been utterly dependent upon the host of satellites that now orbit the earth.

"Global communications, weather forecasting and control, land and ocean resources, banks, postal and information services—if anything happened to their spaceborne systems, we would sink back into a dark age. During the resultant chaos, disease and starvation would destroy much of the human race.

"And looking beyond the earth, now that we have self-sustaining colonies on Mars, Mercury, and the moon, and are mining the incalculable wealth of the asteroids, we see the beginnings of true interplanetary commerce. Though it took a little longer than the optimists predicted, it is now obvious that the conquest of the air was only a modest prelude to the conquest of space.

"But now we are faced with a fundamental problem, an obstacle that stands in the way of all future progress. Although the research work of generations has made the rocket the most reliable form of propulsion ever invented . . ."

"Has he considered bicycles?" muttered Sarath.

". . . space vehicles are still grossly inefficient. Even worse, their effect on the environment is appalling. Despite all attempts to control approach corridors, the noise of take-off and re-entry disturbs millions of people. Exhaust products dumped in the upper atmosphere have triggered climatic changes, which may have very serious results. Everyone remembers the skin-cancer crisis of the twenties, caused by ultraviolet breakthrough—and the astronomical cost of the chemicals needed to restore the ozonosphere.

"Yet if we project traffic growth to the end of the century, we find that earth-to-orbit tonnage must be increased almost fifty percent. This cannot be achieved without intolerable costs to our way of life—perhaps to our very existence. And there is nothing that the rocket engineers can do. They have almost reached the absolute limits of performance, set by the laws of physics.

"What is the alternative? For centuries, men have dreamed of antigravity and of 'spacedrives.' No one has ever found the slightest hint that such things are possible; today we believe that they are only fantasy.

"In the very decade that the first satellite was launched, however, one daring Russian engineer conceived a system that would make the rocket obsolete. It was years before anyone took Yuri Artsutanov seriously. It has taken two centuries for our technology to match his vision."

Each time he played the recording, it seemed to Rajasinghe that Morgan really came alive at this point. It was easy to see why; now he was on his own territory, no longer relaying information from an alien field of expertise. And despite all his reservations and fears, Rajasinghe could not help sharing some of that enthusiasm. It was a quality that, nowadays, seldom impinged upon his life.

"Go out of doors any clear night," continued Morgan, "and you will see that commonplace wonder of our age— the stars that never rise or set, but are fixed motionless in the sky. We, and our parents, and *their* parents have long taken for granted the synchronous satellites and space stations, which move above the equator at the same speed as the turning earth, and so hang forever above the same spot.

"The question Artsutanov asked himself had the child-like brilliance of true genuis. A merely clever man could never have thought of it—or would have dismissed it instantly as absurd.

"*If* the laws of celestial mechanics make it possible for an object to stay fixed in the sky, might it not be possible to lower a cable down to the surface, and *so to establish an elevator system linking earth to space?* . . .

Morgan faded out, like a ghost that had been suddenly exorcised. He was replaced by a football-sized earth, slowly revolving. Moving an arm's breadth above it, and keeping always poised above the same spot on the equator, a flashing star marked the location of a synchronous satellite.

From the star, two thin lines of light started to extend— one directly down toward the earth, the other in exactly the opposite direction, out into space.

"When you build a bridge," continued Morgan's disembodied voice, "you start from the two ends and meet in the middle. With the Orbital Tower, it would be the exact opposite. You have to build upward *and* downward simultaneously from the synchronous satellite, according to a careful program. The trick is to keep the structure's center of gravity always balanced at the stationary point. If you don't, it will move into the wrong orbit, and start drifting slowly around the earth."

The descending line of light reached the equator; at the same moment, the outward extension also ceased.

"The total height must be at least forty thousand kilometers, and the lowest hundred, going down through the atmosphere, may be the most critical part, because there the Tower may be subject to hurricanes. It won't be stable until it's securely anchored to the ground.

"And then, for the first time in history, we will have a

stairway to heaven—a bridge to the stars. A simple elevator system, driven by cheap electricity, will replace the noisy and expensive rocket, which will then be used only for its proper job of deep-space transport.

This excerpt gives ample proof as to why The Fountains of Paradise, *a Hugo and Nebula award winner, is the kind of book that inspires reviewers to use superlatives:*

"Arthur C. Clarke once again sounds his grand theme . . . man is most himself when he strives greatly, when he challenges the very laws of the universe."
—The New York Times Book Review

The City and the Stars

In The City and the Stars *all it takes is one restless young man to topple the conventions that his civilization is built upon. Here, young Alvin is on the verge of the discovery. . . . Two isolated nations remain on a world otherwise devastated by apocalypse, and the leaders have decided that cutting off all further communication is the only way to avoid absolute destruction.*

Ten million inhabitants of Alvin's city have since been living in ignorance of the other city's existence. Alvin is about to bring an end to this carefully insulated way of life.

Alystra had found it very easy to follow Alvin and Khedron without their knowledge. They seemed in a great hurry—something which in itself was most unusual—and never looked back. It had been an amusing game to pursue them along the moving ways, hiding in the crowds yet always keeping them in sight. Toward the end their goal had been obvious; when they left the pattern of streets and went into the park, they could only be heading for the Tomb of Yarlan Zey. The park contained no other buildings, and people in such eager haste as Alvin and Khedron would not be interested merely in enjoying the scenery.

Because there was no way of concealing herself on the last few hundred yards to the Tomb, Alystra waited until Khedron and Alvin had disappeared into the marbled gloom. Then, as soon as they were out of sight, she hurried up the grass-covered slope. She felt fairly sure that she could hide behind one of the great pillars long enough to discover what Alvin and Khedron were doing; it did not matter if they detected her after that.

The Tomb consisted of two concentric rings of columns, enclosing a circular courtyard. Except in one sector, the columns screened off the interior completely, and Alystra avoided approaching through this opening, but entered the Tomb from the side. She cautiously negotiated the first ring of columns, saw that there was no one in sight, and tiptoed across to the second. Through the gaps, she could see Yarlan Zey looking out through the entrance, across the park he had built, and beyond that to the city over which he had watched for so many ages.

And there was no one else in all this marble solitude. The Tomb was empty.

At that moment, Alvin and Khedron were a hundred feet underground, in a small, boxlike room whose walls seemed to be flowing steadily upward. That was the only indication of movement; there was no trace of vibration to show that they were sinking swiftly into the earth, descending toward a goal that even now neither of them fully understood.

It had been absurdly easy, for the way had been prepared for them. (By whom? wondered Alvin. By the Central Computer? Or by Yarlan Zey himself, when he transformed the city?) The monitor screen had shown them the long, vertical shaft plunging into the depths, but they had followed its course only a little way when the image had blanked out. That meant, Alvin knew, that they were asking for information that the monitor did not possess, and perhaps never had possessed.

He had scarcely framed this thought when the screen came to life once more. On it appeared a brief message, printed in the simplified script that machines had used to communicate with men ever since they had achieved intellectual equality:

> STAND WHERE THE STATUE GAZES—AND
> REMEMBER:
> DIASPAR WAS NOT ALWAYS THUS

The last five words were in larger type, and the meaning of the entire message was obvious to Alvin at once. Mentally framed code messages had been used for ages to unlock doors or set machines in action. As for "Stand where the statue gazes"—that was really *too* simple.

"I wonder how many people have read this message?" said Alvin thoughtfully.

"Fourteen, to my knowledge," replied Khedron. "And there may have been others." He did not amplify this rather cryptic remark, and Alvin was in too great a hurry to reach the park to question him further.

They could not be certain that the mechanisms would still respond to the triggering impulse. When they reached the Tomb, it had taken them only a moment to locate the single slab, among all those paving the floor, upon which the gaze of Yarlan Zey was fixed. It was only at first sight that the statue seemed to be looking out across the city; if one stood directly in front of it, one could see that the eyes were downcast and that the elusive smile was directed toward a spot just inside the entrance to the Tomb. Once the secret was realized, there could be no doubt about it. Alvin moved to the next slab, and found that Yarlan Zey was no longer looking toward him.

He rejoined Khedron, and mentally echoed the words that the Jester spoke aloud: "Diaspar was not always thus." Instantly, as if the millions of years that had lapsed since their last operation had never existed, the waiting machines responded. The great slab of stone on which they were standing began to carry them smoothly into the depths.

Overhead, the patch of blue suddenly flickered out of existence. The shaft was no longer open; there was no danger that anyone should accidentally stumble into it.

Alvin wondered fleetingly if another slab of stone had somehow been materialized to replace the one now supporting him and Khedron, then decided against it. The original slab probably still paved the Tomb; the one upon which they were standing might only exist for infinitesimal fractions of a second, being continuously re-created at greater and greater depths in the earth to give the illusion of steady downward movement.

Neither Alvin nor Khedron spoke as the walls flowed silently past them. Khedron was once again wrestling with his conscience, wondering if this time he had gone too far. He could not imagine where this route might lead, if indeed it led anywhere. For the first time in his life, he began to understand the real meaning of fear.

Alvin was not afraid; he was too excited. This was the sensation he had known in the Tower of Loranne, when he had looked out across the untrodden desert and seen the stars conquering the night sky. He had merely gazed at the unknown then; he was being carried toward it now.

The walls ceased to flow past them. A patch of light appeared at one side of their mysteriously moving room, grew brighter and brighter, and was suddenly a door. They stepped through it, took a few paces along the short corridor beyond—and then were standing in a great, circular cavern whose walls came together in a sweeping curve three hundred feet above their heads.

The column down whose interior they had descended seemed far too slim to support the millions of tons of rock above it; indeed, it did not seem to be an integral part of the chamber at all, but gave the impression of being an afterthought. Khedron, following Alvin's gaze, arrived at the same conclusion.

"This column," he said, speaking rather jerkily, as if anxious to find something to say, "was built simply to house the shaft down which we came. It could never have carried the traffic that must have passed through here when Diaspar was still open to the world. *That* came through those tunnels over there; I suppose you recognize what they are?"

Alvin looked toward the walls of the chamber, more than a hundred yards away. Piercing them at regular intervals were large tunnels, twelve of them, radiating in all directions exactly as the moving ways still did today. He could see that they sloped gently upward, and now he recognized the familiar gray surface of the moving ways. These were only the severed stumps of the great roads; the strange material that gave them life was now frozen into immobility. When the park had been built, the hub of the moving way system had been buried. But it had never been destroyed.

Alvin began to walk toward the nearest of the tunnels. He had gone only a few paces when he realized that something was happening to the ground beneath his feet. *It was becoming transparent.* A few more yards, and he seemed to be standing in midair without visible support. He stopped and stared down into the void beneath him.

"Khedron!" he called. "Come and look at this!"

In The City and the Stars *Clarke has created an eerily sterile world of the far, far future in a novel that leaves a lingering impression.*

Imperial Earth

What kind of book could inspire reviewers at the Washington Post *to choose words like "scintillating" and "consummate"? Clarke's 1976 novel* Imperial Earth *garnered terrific review attention. Harper's Bookletter described the writer's prowess with a succinct accuracy:*

"A what-if voyage of the imagination, re-creating our conception of the present by an intricate fabrication of the future."

As the book begins, a ten-year-old boy picks up a human sound on the surface of the planet Titan, where he has lived underground his entire life. The call is a portent of things to come, for Duncan Makenzie, destined to be ruler of Titan, must heed the voice of his forefathers and return to Earth. . . .

Duncan Makenzie was ten years old when he found the magic number. It was pure chance; he had intended to call Grandma Ellen, but he had been careless and his fingers must have touched the wrong keys. He knew at once that he had made a mistake, because Grandma's viddy had a two-second delay, even on Auto/Record. This circuit was live immediately.

Yet there was no ringing tone, and no picture. The screen was completely blank, with not even a speckling of interference. Duncan guessed that he had been switched into an audio-only channel, or had reached a station where the camera was disconnected. In any case, this certainly wasn't Grandma's number, and he reached out to break the circuit.

Then he noticed the sound. At first, he thought that someone was breathing quietly into the microphone at the far end, but he quickly realized his mistake. There was a random, inhuman quality about this gentle susurration; it lacked any regular rhythm, and there were long intervals of complete silence.

As he listened, Duncan felt a growing sense of awe. Here was something completely outside his normal, everyday experience, yet he recognized it almost at once. In his ten years of life, the impressions of many worlds had been inprinted on his mind, and no one who had heard this most evocative of sounds could ever forget it. He was listening to the voice of the wind, as it sighed and whispered across the lifeless landscape a hundred meters above his head.

Duncan forgot all about Grandma, and turned the volume up to its highest level. He lay back on the couch, closed his eyes, and tried to project himself into the unknown, hostile world from which he was protected by all the safety devices that three hundred years of space technology could contrive. Someday, when he had passed his survival tests, he would go up into that world and see with his own eyes the lakes and chasms and low-lying orange clouds, lit by the thin, cold rays of the distant sun. He had looked forward to that day with calm anticipation rather than excitement—the Makenzies were noted for their lack of excitement—but now he suddenly realized what he was missing. So might a child of Earth, on some dusty desert far from the ocean, have pressed a shell against his ear and listened with sick longing to the music of the unattainable sea.

There was no mystery about the sound, but how was it reaching him? It could be coming from any of the hundred million square kilometers lying above his head. Somewhere— perhaps in an abandoned construction project or experimental station—a live microphone had been left in circuit, exposed to the freezing, poisonous winds of the world above. It was not likely to remain undetected for long; sooner or later it would be discovered and disconnected. He had better capture this message from the outside while it was still there; even if he knew the number he had accidentally called, he doubted if he could ever establish the circuit again.

The amount of audio-visual material that Duncan had stored under MISC was remarkable, even for an inquisitive ten-year-old. It was not that he lacked organizing ability— that was the most celebrated of all the Makenzie talents— but he was interested in more things than he knew how to index. He had now begun to discover, the hard way, that information not properly classified can be irretrievably lost.

He thought intently for a minute, while the lonely wind sobbed and moaned and brought the chill of space into his warm little cubicle. Then he tapped out APHA INDEX* WIND SOUNDS* PERM STORE #.

From the moment he touched the # or EXECUTE key, he had begun to capture that voice from the world above. If all went well, he could call it forth again at any time by using the index heading WIND SOUNDS. Even if he had made a mistake, and the console's search program failed to locate the recording, it would be *somewhere* in the machine's permanent, nonerasable memory. There was always the hope that he might one day find it again by chance, as was happening all the time with information he had filed under MISC.

He decided to let the recording run for another few

minutes before completing the interrupted call to Grandma. As luck would have it, the wind must have slackened at about the time he keyed EXECUTE, because there was a long, frustrating silence. Then, out of that silence, came something new.

It was faint and distant, yet conveyed the impression that mounted second by second in intensity, but somehow never came any closer. The scream rose swiftly to a demonic shriek, with undertones of thunder—then dwindled away as quickly as it had appeared. From beginning to end it lasted less than half a minute. Then there was only the sighing of the wind, even lonelier than before.

Imperial Earth not only attests to Clarke's facility with the icons of science fiction—spaceships, clones, and so on— but it bears witness to Clarke's other obsession: the ocean. In 2276, Duncan Makenzie is entertained aboard the raised ship Titanic, *in a chapter entitled "The Ghost from Grand Banks."*

*Clarke couldn't get enough of the idea, and in 1990 he wrote a new novel—*The Ghost from the Grand Banks, *a magnificent near-future story of a project that undertakes to raise the* Titanic *for the one hundredth anniversary of its sinking.*

The Deep Range

There are vast, unexplored expanses of our universe, dark and silent places where humanity has yet to go. Space, of course, is what first leaps to mind, but our mysterious oceans are vast and dark too; and equally intriguing to Clarke's questioning mind. The fields of the ocean bed are the playgrounds for strange creatures and heroic men in The Deep Range. . . .

"We're just passing my record, Walt. Ten thousand's the deepest I've ever been."

"And we're only halfway there. Still, what difference does it make if you've got the right ship? It just takes a bit longer to go down, and a bit longer to come up. These subs would still have a safety factor of five at the bottom of the Philippine Trench."

"That's true enough, but you can't convince me there's no psychological difference. Don't *you* feel two miles of water on your shoulders?"

It was most unlike Don to be so imaginative; usually it was Franklin who made such remarks and was promptly laughed at. If Don was getting moody, it would be best to give him some of his own medicine.

"Tell me when you've got to start bailing," said Franklin. "If the water gets up to your chin, we'll turn back."

He had to admit the feeble joke helped his own morale. The knowledge that the pressure around him was rising steadily to five tons per square inch did have a definite effect on his mind—an effect he had never experienced in shallow-water operations where disaster could be just as instantaneous, just as total. He had complete confidence in his equipment and knew that the sub would do all that he asked it to; but he still felt that curious feeling of depression which seemed to have taken most of the zest out of the project into which he had put so much effort.

Five thousand feet lower down, that zest returned with all its old vigor. They both saw the echo simultaneously, and for a moment were shouting at cross purposes until they remembered their signals discipline. When silence had been restored, Franklin gave his orders.

"Cut your motor to quarter speed," he said. "We know the beast's very sensitive and we don't want to scare it until the last minute."

"Can't we flood the bow tanks and glide down?"

"Take too long—he's still three thousand feet below. And cut your sonar to minimum power; I don't want him picking up our pulses."

The animal was moving in a curiously erratic path at a constant depth, sometimes making little darts to right or left as if in search of food. It was following the slopes of an unusually steep submarine mountain, which rose abruptly some four thousand feet from the sea bed. Not for the first time, Franklin thought what a pity it was that the world's most stupendous scenery was all sunk beyond sight in the ocean depths. Nothing on the land could compare with the hundred-mile-wide canyons of the North Atlantic, or the monstrous potholes that gave the Pacific the deepest soundings on earth.

They sank slowly below the summit of the submerged mountain—a mountain whose topmost peak was three miles below sea level. Only a little way beneath them now that mysteriously elongated echo seemed to be undulating through the water with a sinuous motion which reminded Franklin irresistibly of a snake. It would, he thought, be ironic if the Great Sea Serpent turned out to be exactly that. But that was impossible, for there were no water-breathing snakes.

Neither man spoke during the slow and cautious approach to their goal. They both realized that this was one of the great moments of their lives, and wished to savor it to the full. Until now, Don had been mildly skeptical, believing that whatever they found would be no more than some already-known species of animal. But as the echo on the screen expanded, so its strangeness grew. This was something wholly new.

The mountain was now looming above them; they were skirting the foot of a cliff more than two thousand feet high, and their quarry was less than half a mile ahead. Franklin felt his hand itching to throw on the ultraviolet searchlights which in an instant might solve the oldest mystery of the sea, and bring him enduring fame. How important to him was that? he asked himself, as the seconds ticked slowly by. That it was important, he did not attempt to hide from himself. In all his career, he might never have another opportunity like this. . . .

Suddenly, without the slightest warning, the sub trembled as if struck by a hammer. At the same moment Don cried out: "My God— what was that?"

"Some damn fool is letting off explosives," Franklin replied, rage and frustration completely banishing fear. "Wasn't everyone notified of our dive?"

"That's no explosion. I've felt it before—it's an earthquake."

No other word could so swiftly have conjured up once

more all that terror of the ultimate depths which Franklin had felt brushing briefly against his mind during their descent. At once the immeasurable weight of the waters crushed down upon him like a physical burden; his sturdy craft seemed the frailest of cockleshells, already doomed by forces which all man's science could no longer hold at bay.

He knew that earthquakes were common in the deep Pacific, where the weights of rock and water were forever poised in precarious equilibrium. Once or twice on patrols he had felt distant shocks—but this time, he felt certain, he was near the epicenter.

"Make full speed for the surface," he ordered. "That may be just the beginning."

"But we only need another five minutes," Don protested. "Let's chance it, Walt."

Franklin was sorely tempted. That single shock might be the only one; the strain on the tortured strata miles below might have been relieved. He glanced at the echo they had been chasing; it was moving much faster now, as if it, too, had been frightened by this display of Nature's slumbering power.

"We'll risk it," Franklin decided. "But if there's another one we'll go straight up."

"Fair enough," answered Don. "I'll bet you ten to one—"

He never completed the sentence. This time the hammer blow was no more violent, but it was sustained. The entire ocean seemed to be in travail as the shock waves, traveling at almost a mile a second, were reflected back and forth between surface and sea bed. Franklin shouted the one word "Up!" and tilted the sub as steeply as he dared toward the distant sky.

But the sky was gone. The sharply defined plane which marked the water-air interface on the sonar screen had vanished, replaced by a meaningless jumble of hazy echoes. For a moment Franklin assumed that the set had been put out of action by the shocks; then his mind interpreted the incredible, the terrifying picture that was taking shape upon the screen.

"Don," he yelled, "run for the open sea—the mountain's falling!"

The billions of tons of rock that had been towering above them were sliding down into the deep. The whole face of the mountain had split away and was descending in a waterfall of stone, moving with a deceptive slowness and an utterly irresistible power. It was an avalanche in slow motion, but Franklin knew that within seconds the waters through which his sub was driving would be torn with falling debris.

He was moving at full speed, yet he seemed motionless. Even without the amplifiers, he could hear through the hull the rumble and roar of grinding rock. More than half the sonar image was now obliterated, either by solid fragments or by the immense clouds of mud and silt that were now beginning to fill the sea. He was becoming blind; there was nothing he could do but hold his course and pray.

The Fountains of Paradise, The City and the Stars, Imperial Earth, and *The Deep Range: four of Arthur C. Clarke's mostly richly imaginative novels. Even a small sampling from this incredibly prolific author is ample evidence of Clarke's invaluable contribution to imaginative fiction—for any science fiction author today would be hard pressed to deny his/or her debt to Clarke. From the golden age of science fiction in the 1950s into the 1990s, the grand master has been changing the way people think about the future. Arthur C. Clarke truly is, as christened by* The New York Times, *"the colossus of science fiction."*

In Rama II, *the stunning sequel to Arthur C. Clarke's 1973 masterpiece* Rendezvous with Rama, *a military and scientific mission is mounted to board the second mysterious Raman spaceship that has entered our solar system. And just like the first Raman ship, the second leaves our neighborhood of space just as silently and enigmatically as the first—with one minor difference. On board are three humans, who have cast their fates with that of the massive spaceship.* Rama II *is leaving our solar system—carrying them to an unknown destination, light-years away.*

In Garden of Rama, *the third Rama book, Richard Wake-field, Nicole des Jardins, and Michael O'Toole are on-board* Rama II *for years before even a hint of their destination is revealed. Nicole has borne children, and they all have aged considerably on their strange voyage that is taking them farther and farther from home. What follows is an excerpt from Nicole's journal, in which she recounts the final moments of their long journey and the wonders that are their destination.*

8 July 2213—

The maneuver began four days ago, right on schedule, as soon as the third and final light show was finished. We didn't see or hear any avians or octospiders, as we haven't for four years now. Katie was very disappointed. She wanted to see the octospiders all return to New York.

Yesterday a pair of the mantis biots came into our lair and went straight to the deceleration tank. They were carrying a large container, in which were the five new webbed beds (Simone, of course, needs a different size now) and all the helmets. We watched them from the distance while they installed the beds and checked out the tank system. The children were fascinated. The short visit from the mantises confirmed that we will soon be under-going a major change in velocity.

Richard was apparently correct with his hypothesis about the connection between the main propulsion system and the overall thermal control of *Rama*. The temperature has already started to drop topside. In anticipation of a long maneuver, we have been busy using the keyboard to order cold-weather clothing for all the children.

The constant shaking is again disrupting our lives. At first it was amusing for the kids, but they are already complaining about it. Poor Benjy is in a state of continual distress. He moans often and not even Simone can com-fort him. Katie wants to go up and wander around New York. She is irritated that we won't let her.

I am praying that our destination is near. Michael prays

that "God's will be done"—sometimes I'm afraid my prayers are more selfish than that.

1 September 2213—

Something new is definitely happening. Again I am so excited that I can hardly sit still.

For the last ten days, ever since we finished in the tank and the maneuver ended, we have been approaching a solitary light source situated about thirty astronomical units away from the star Sirius. Richard has ingeniously manipulated the sensor list and the black screen so that this source is dead center on our monitor at all times, regardless of which particular Raman telescope is observing it.

Two nights ago we began to see some definition in the object—we could tell that there were actually many separate sources of light. We speculated that perhaps it was an inhabited planet and Richard rushed around computing the heat input from Sirius on a planet whose distance was roughly equal to Neptune's distance from our sun. Even though Sirius is much larger, brighter, and hotter than the Sun, Richard concluded that our paradise, if this was indeed our destination, was still going to be very cold.

Last night our target began to resolve itself more clearly. It is an elongated construction (Richard says it therefore cannot be a planet—anything "that size" that is decidedly nonspherical "must be artificial"), shaped like a cigar, with two rows of lights along the top and bottom and a few more at each end. Because we don't know exactly how far away it is, we don't know for certain its size. However, Richard has been making some "guesstimates" based on our closing velocity, and he thinks the cigar is roughly a hundred and fifty kilometers long and fifty kilometers tall.

The entire family sits in our main room and stares at the monitor. This morning we had another surprise. Katie identified the other two vehicles before anyone else. Richard had shown her earlier how to change the Raman sensors feeding into the black screen and, while the rest of us were talking, she accessed the distant radar sensor that we had first used thirteen years ago to identify the nuclear missiles coming from Earth. The cigar-shaped object was at the edge of the radar field of view. Standing right in front of the cigar, almost indistinguishable from it in the wide field, were two other blips. If the giant cigar is indeed our target, then perhaps we are about to have company.

8 September 2213—

There is no way I can adequately describe the astounding events of the last five days. The language does not have adjectives superlative enough to capture what we have seen and experienced. Michael has even commented that heaven may pale by comparison beside the wonders that we have witnessed.

At this moment our family is onboard a driverless small shuttle craft, no larger than a city bus on Earth, that is whizzing us from the waystation to an unknown destination. The cigar-shaped waystation is still visible, but just barely, out the domed window at the rear of the craft. To our left, our home for thirteen years, the cylindrical spaceship we call Rama, appears to be headed in a slightly different direction than we are. It departed from the waystation a few hours after we did, lit like a Christmas tree on the outside, and we are presently separated from it by about two hundred kilometers.

We came to a stop, relative to the waystation at least, four days and eleven hours ago. We were the third spacecraft in the queue, behind a spinning starfish only one tenth the size of *Rama* and a giant wheel, with a hub and spokes, that entered the waystation within hours after our final vernier correction maneuver.

The waystation itself was hollow inside. The ends, top, and bottom of the cigar, the portions that we could see from a distance because of the lights, were structures of some kind. When the giant wheel moved into the hollow center (and it just barely fit, so its diameter, according to Richard, must be at least forty kilometers), deployable elements of the waystation rolled out to meet the wheel and fix it in place.

While the wheel was entering the waystation, we moved up to the second spot in the queue, about three hundred kilometers from the waystation. Because of the lights and the superb quality of the Raman telescopes, we were able to watch what was going on in the waystation with a resolution of several hundred meters.

A suite of special vehicles in three unusual shapes (one looked like a balloon, another like a blimp, and the third resembled a bathysphere on Earth) entered the wheel during the next twelve hours. We couldn't see what was going on inside the wheel, but the vehicles were there for quite a while. They came out singly at odd intervals over the next two days. When each vehicle emerged, it was met by a shuttle, like ours except much larger in all cases. The shuttles were all parked in the dark in the right-hand side of the cigar. Each of them moved into place thirty minutes or so before the appointed time for its rendezvous with one of the special vehicles that had been inside the wheel.

As soon as they were loaded, the shuttles always took off in a direction directly opposite the queue. About an hour after the final vehicle had emerged from the wheel and the last shuttle had departed, the many pieces of mechanical equipment attached to the wheel were retracted and the great circular spacecraft itself eased out of the waystation.

Although we nominally took turns sleeping during all the activity, I hardly slept at all. My mind was bombarded by dreams and my high level of excitement made it impossible for me to stay asleep longer than two hours at a time. Each time I woke up I would ask someone if anything significant had changed before trying to force myself to doze off again.

The starfish had already entered the waystation and was being handled by another set of gantries and attachments when a loud whistle summoned us topside in Rama. The whistle was followed, as before, by a light show in the southern bowl, but this one was completely different from the ones that had preceded the maneuvers. The Big Horn was the star this time. Circular rings of color would form slowly near its tip and then glide north, centered along the spin axis of Rama. The rings were huge. Richard estimated they were at least a kilometer in diameter, with a ring thickness of forty meters.

The dark Raman night was illuminated by as many as eight of these rings at a time. The order remained the same—red, orange, yellow, green, blue, brown, pink, and purple—for three repetitions. As a ring would break up and disappear near the Alpha relay station at the northern bowl of Rama, a new ring of the same color would form back near the tip of the Big Horn.

We stood transfixed, our mouths agape, as this spectacle took place. As soon as the last ring disappeared from the third set, another astonishing event occurred. All the lights came on inside Rama! The Raman night had only begun three hours earlier—for thirteen years the sequence of night and day had been completely regular. Now, all of a sudden, it was changed. And it wasn't just the lights. There was music as well; at least I guess you could call it music. It sounded like millions of tiny bells and it seemed to be coming from everywhere.

None of us could move for several minutes. Benjy began to cry. High in the sky, toward the north, Richard (who had the best pair of binoculars) then spied something flying slowly toward us. "It's the avians," he shouted, jumping up and down. "I just remembered something. I visited them in their new home in the north while I was on my odyssey."

One at a time we each looked through his binoculars. At first it wasn't certain that Richard was correct in his identification, but as they came closer the fifty or sixty specks resolved themselves into the great birdlike creatures we know as the avians. They headed straight for New York. Half the avians hovered in the sky, maybe three hundred meters above their lair, as the other half dove down to the surface.

"Come on, Daddy," Katie yelled. "Let's go see." Before I could raise any objection, father and daughter were off at a sprint. I watched Katie run. She is already very fast. In my mind's eye I could see my mother's graceful stride across the grass in the park at Chilly-Mazarin—Katie has definitely inherited some characteristics from her mother's side of the family even though she is first and foremost her father's daughter.

Simone and Benjy had already started toward our lair. Patrick was concerned about the avians. "Will they hurt Daddy and Katie?" he asked.

I smiled at my handsome five-year-old son. "No, darling," I answered, "not if they're careful." Michael, Patrick, Ellie, and I returned to the lair to watch the starfish being processed in the waystation.

We couldn't see much because all the ports of entry to the starfish were on the opposite side, away from the Raman cameras. But we assumed a similar unloading activity was occurring, because eventually the three shuttles left for some new destination. The smaller starfish was finished with its processing very quickly. It had already left the waystation before Richard and Katie returned.

"Start packing," Richard said breathlessly as soon as they came back to the lair. "We're leaving. We're all leaving."

"You should have seen them," Katie said to Simone almost simultaneously. "They were huge. And ugly. They went down in their lair . . ."

"The avians returned to get some special things from their lair," Richard interrupted her. "Maybe they were mementos of some kind. Anyway, everything fits. We're getting out of here."

As I raced around trying to put our essentials into a few of the sturdy boxes, I criticized myself for not having figured everything out sooner. We had watched both the wheel and the starfish "unload" at the waystation. But it had not occurred to us that *we* might be the cargo to be unloaded by Rama.

It was impossible to decide what to pack. We had been living in those six rooms (including the two we had fixed up for storage) for thirteen years. We had probably requested an average of five items a day using the keyboard. Granted, most of the objects had long since been thrown away, but still. . . . We didn't know where we were going. How could we know what to take?

"Do you have any idea what's going to happen to us?" I asked Richard.

My husband was beside himself trying to figure out how to take his large computer. "Our history, our science—all that remains of our knowledge is there," he said, pointing at the computer in agitation. "What if it's irretrievably lost?"

It weighed only eighty kilograms altogether. I told him

we could all help him carry the computer after we had packed clothing, personal items, and some food and water.

"Do you have any idea where we're going?" I repeated.

Richard shrugged his shoulders. "Not the slightest," he replied. "But wherever it is, I bet it will be amazing."

Katie came into our room. She was holding a small pouch and her eyes were alive with energy. "I'm packed and ready," she said. "Can I go topside and wait?"

Her father's affirmative nod was barely in motion when Katie bolted out the door. I shook my head, giving Richard a disapproving look, and went down the hall to help Simone with the other children. The process of packing for the boys was an ordeal. Benjy was cranky and weepy. Even Patrick was irritable. Simone and I had just finished (the job was impossible until we forced the boys to take a nap) when Richard and Katie returned from topside.

"Our vehicle is here," Richard said calmly, suppressing his excitement.

"It's parked on the ice," Katie added, taking off her heavy jacket and gloves.

"How do you know it's ours?" Michael asked. He had entered the room only moments after Richard and Katie.

"It has seven seats and room for our bags," my ten-year-old daughter replied. "Who else could it be for?"

"*Whom*," I said mechanically, trying to integrate this latest new information. I felt as if I had been drinking from a fire hose for four consecutive days.

"Did you see any octospiders?" Patrick asked.

"Oc-to-spi-der," Benjy repeated carefully.

"No," answered Katie, "but we did see four mammoth planes, real flat, with wide wings. They flew over our heads, coming from the south. We think the flat planes were carrying the octos, don't we, Dad?"

Richard nodded.

I took a deep breath. "All right then," I said. "Bundle up, everybody. Let's go. Carry the bags first. Richard, Michael, and I will make a second trip for the computer."

An hour later we were all in the vehicle. We had climbed the stairs of our lair for the last time. Richard pressed a flashing red button and our Raman helicopter (I call it that because it went straight up, not because it had any rotary blades) lifted off the ground.

Our flight path was slow and vertical for the first five minutes. Once we were close to the spin axis of Rama, where there was no gravity and very little atmosphere, the vehicle hovered in place for two or three minutes while it changed its external configuration.

It was an awesome final view of Rama. Many kilometers below us, our island home was but a small patch of grayish brown in the middle of the frozen sea that circled the giant cylinder. I could see the horns in the south clearer than ever before. Those amazing long structures, supported by massive flying buttresses larger than small towns on the Earth, all pointed directly north.

I felt strangely emotional as our craft began to move again. After all, Rama had been my home for thirteen years. I had given birth to five children there. I also have matured, I remember telling myself, and may finally be growing into the person I have always wanted to be.

There was very little time to dwell on what had been. Once the configuration change was complete, our vehicle zipped along the spin axis to the northern hub in a matter of a few minutes. Less than an hour later we were all safely in this shuttle. We had left Rama. I knew we would never return. I wiped the tears from my eyes as the shuttle pulled out of the waystation.

The Ghost from the Grand Banks, *Arthur C. Clarke's first solo novel in years, forays not into space but other equally unexplored territories. It is Earth,* A.D. *2012—the one hundredth anniversary of the sinking of the* Titanic—*and a massive recovery operation is under way. In this dramatic story of the near future, Clarke plumbs the uncharted depths of the North Atlantic, as well as another strangely beautiful landscape found in the realm of higher mathematics.*

For it is a mathematical function called the Mandelbrot Set that is inextricably linked to the raising of the great ship. When charted on a graph, the Mandelbrot Set takes the shape of an infinitely complicated landscape. The Craigs, whose role in bringing the Titanic *to the surface is integral, have a brilliant daughter named Ada, who is obsessed with any and all manifestations of the M-set (as it is called).*

In the following scene, Ada is explaining to Jason Bradley, another member of the recovery team, about the poetry of the M-set. The ramifications are overwhelming; and ironically, Ada's obsession with the M-set will soon threaten her very life.

Into the M-set

It was hard to believe, Jason Bradley told himself, that people actually *lived* like this, only a few generations ago. Though Conroy Castle was a very modest example of its species, its scale was still impressive to anyone who had spent most of his life in cluttered offices, motel rooms, ship's cabins—not to mention deep-diving minisubs, so cramped that the personal hygiene of your companions was a matter of crucial importance.

The dining room, with its ornately carved ceiling and enormous wall mirrors, could comfortably seat at least fifty people. Donald Craig felt it necessary to explain the little four-place table that looked lost and lonely at its center.

"We've not had time to buy proper furniture—the castle's own stuff was in terrible shape—most of it had to be burned. And we've been too busy to do much entertaining. But one day, when we've finally established ourselves as the local nobility . . ."

Edith did not seem to approve of her husband's flippancy, and once again Bradley had the impression that she was the leader in this enterprise, with Donald a reluctant—or at best passive—accomplice. He could guess the scenario: People with enough money to squander on expensive toys often discovered that they would have been happier without them. And Conroy Castle—with all its surrounding acres and maintenance staff—must be a very expensive toy indeed.

When the servants (Servants! That was another novelty) had cleared the remnants of an excellent Chinese dinner flown in specially from Dublin, Bradley and his hosts retreated to a set of comfortable armchairs in the adjoining room.

"We won't let you get away," said Donald Craig, "without giving you our Child's Guide to the M-set. Edith can spot a Mandelvirgin at a hundred meters."

Bradley was not sure if he qualified for this description. He had finally recognized the odd shape of the lake, though he had forgotten its technical name until reminded of it. In the last decade of the century, it had been impossible to escape from manifestations of the Mandelbrot Set—they were appearing all the time on video displays, wallpaper, fabrics, and virtually every type of design. Bradley recalled that someone had coined the word *Mandelmania* to describe the more acute symptoms; he had begun to suspect that it might be applicable to this odd household. But he was quite prepared to sit with polite interest through whatever lecture or demonstration his hosts had in store for him.

He realized that they, too, were being polite, in their own way. They were anxious to have his decision, and he was equally anxious to give it.

He only hoped that the call he was expecting would come through before he left the castle. . . .

Bradley had never met the traditional stage mother, but he had seen her in movies like—what was that old one called?—ah, *Fame*. Here was the same passionate determination on the part of a parent for a child to become a star, even if there was no discernable talent. In this case, he did not doubt that the faith was fully justified.

"Before Ada begins," said Edith, "I'd like to make a few points. The M-set is the most complex entity in the whole of mathematics—yet it doesn't involve anything more advanced than addition and multiplication—not even subtraction or division! That's why many people with a good knowledge of math have difficulty in grasping it. They simply can't believe that something with too much detail to be explored before the end of the universe can be generated without using logs or trig functions or higher transcendentals. It doesn't seem reasonable that it's all done merely by adding numbers together."

"Doesn't seem reasonable to me, either. If it's so simple, why didn't anyone discover it until 1980?"

"Very good question! Because so much adding and multiplying is involved, with such huge numbers, that we had to wait for high-speed computers. If you'd given abacuses to Adam and Eve and *all* their descendants right up to now, they couldn't have found some of the pictures Ada can show you by pressing a few keys. Go ahead, dear. . . ."

The holoprojector was cunningly concealed; Bradley could not even guess where it was hiding. Very easy to make this old castle a haunted one, he thought, and scare away any intruders. It would beat a burglar alarm.

The two crossed lines of an ordinary x-y diagram appeared in the air, with the sequence of integers 0, 1, 2, 3, 4 . . . marching off in all four directions.

Ada gave Bradley that disconcertingly direct look, as if she was once again trying to estimate his IQ so that her presentation could be appropriately calibrated.

"Any point on this plane," she said, "can be identified by two numbers—its x and y coordinates. OK?"

"OK," Bradley answered solemnly.

"Well, the M-set lies in a very small region near the origin—it doesn't extend beyond plus or minus 2 in either direction. So we can ignore all the larger numbers."

The integers skittered off along the four axes, leaving only the numbers 1 and 2 marking distances away from the central zero.

"Now suppose we take any point inside this grid, and join it to the center. Measure the length of this radius—let's call it r."

This, thought Bradley, is putting no great strain on my mental resources. When do we get to the tricky part?

"Obviously, in this case r can have any value from 0 to just under 3—about 2.8, to be exact. OK?"

"OK."

"Right. Now Exercise One. Take any point's r value, and square it. *Keep on squaring it.* What happens?"

"Don't let me spoil your fun, Ada."

"Well, if r is exactly one, it stays at that value—no matter how many times you square it. One times 1 times 1 times 1 is always 1."

"OK," said Bradley, just beating Ada to the draw.

"If it's even a *smidgen* more than 1, however, and you go on squaring it, sooner or later it will shoot off to infinity. Even if it's 1.0000 . . . 0001, and there are a million 0s to the right of the decimal point. It will just take a bit longer.

"But if the number is *less* than 1—say .99999999 . . . with a million 9s—you get just the opposite. It may stay close to 1 for ages, but as you keep on squaring it, suddenly it will collapse and dwindle away down to 0—OK?"

This time Ada got there first, and Bradley merely nodded. As yet, he could not see the point in this elementary arithmetic, but it was obviously leading somewhere.

"Lady, stop bothering Mr. Bradley! So you see, simply squaring numbers—and going on squaring them, over and over—divides them into two distinct sets. . . ."

A circle had appeared on the two crossed axes, centered on the origin and with radius unity.

"Inside that circle are all the numbers that disappear when you keep on squaring them. Outside are all those that shoot off to infinity. You could say that the circle radius 1 is a fence—a boundary—a *frontier*—dividing the two sets of numbers. I like to call it the S-set."

"S for squaring?"

"Of cour—yes. Now, here's the important point. The numbers on either side are totally separated; yet though nothing can pass through it, the boundary hasn't any thickness. It's simply a line—you could go on magnifying it forever and it would stay a line, though it would soon appear to be a straight one because you wouldn't be able to see its curvature."

"This may not seem very exciting," interjected Donald, "but it's absolutely fundamental—you'll soon see why. Sorry, Ada."

"Now, to get the M-set we make one teeny, *weeny* change. We don't just square the numbers. We square and *add* . . . square and *add*. You wouldn't think it would make all that difference—but it opens up a whole new universe. . . .

"Suppose we start with 1 again. We square it and get 1. Then we add them to get 2.

"Two squared is 4. Add the original 1 again—answer, 5.

"Five squared is 25—add 1—26.

"Twenty-six squared is 676—you see what's happening! The numbers are shooting up at a fantastic rate. A few more times around the loop, and they're too big for any computer to handle. Yet we started with—1! So that's the first big difference between the M-set and the S-set, which has its boundary at 1.

"But if we started with a much smaller number than 1—say 0.1—you'll probably guess what happens."

"It collapses to nothing after a few cycles of squaring and adding."

Ada gave her rare but dazzling smile.

"*Usually*. Sometimes it dithers around a small, fixed value—anyway, it's trapped inside the Set. So once again we have a map that divides all the numbers on the plane into two classes. Only this time, the boundary isn't something as elementary as a circle."

"You can say that again," murmured Donald. He collected a frown from Edith, but pressed on. "I've asked quite a few people what shape they thought would be produced; most suggested some kind of oval. No one came near the truth: no one ever could. All *right*, Lady! I won't interrupt Ada again!"

"Here's the first approximation," continued Ada, scooping up her boisterous puppy with one hand while tapping the keyboard with the other. "You've already seen it today."

The now-familiar outline of Lake Mandelbrot had appeared superimposed on the grid of unit squares, but in far more detail than Bradley had seen it in the garden. On the right was the largest, roughly heart-shaped, figure, then a smaller circle touching it, a much smaller one touching *that*—and the narrow spike running off to the extreme left and ending at -2 on the x axis.

Now, however, Bradley could see that the main figures were barnacled—that was the metaphor that came instantly to mind—with a myriad of smaller subsidiary circles, many of which had short jagged lines extending from them. It was a much more complex shape than the pattern of lakes in the garden—strange and intriguing, but certainly not at all beautiful. Edith and Ada, however, were looking at it with a kind of reverential awe, which Donald did not seem entirely to share.

"This is the complete Set with no magnification," said Ada, in a voice that was now a little less self-assured—in fact, almost hushed.

"Even on this scale, though, you can see how different it is from the plain, zero-thickness circle bounding the S-set. You could zoom *that* up forever and ever, and it would remain a line—nothing more. But the boundary of the M-set is *fuzzy*—it contains infinite detail: you can go in anywhere you like, and magnify as much as you please—and you'll always discover something new and unexpected. Look!"

The image expanded; they were diving into the cleft between the main cardioid and its tangent circle. It was, Bradley told himself, very much like watching a zip-fastener being pulled open—except that the teeth of the zipper had the most extraordinary shapes.

First they looked like baby elephants, waving tiny trunks. Then the trunks became tentacles. Then the tentacles sprouted eyes. Then, as the image continued to expand, the eyes opened up into black whirlpools of infinite depth. . . .

"The magnification's up in the millions now," Edith whispered. "The picture we started with is already bigger than Europe."

They swept past the whirlpools, skirting mysterious islands guarded by reefs of coral. Flotillas of sea horses sailed by in stately procession. At the screen's exact center, a tiny black dot appeared, expanded, began to show a haunting familiarity—and seconds later revealed itself as an exact replica of the original Set.

This, Bradley thought, is where we came in. Or is it? He could not be quite sure; there seemed to be minor differences, but the family resemblance was unmistakable.

"Now," continued Ada, "our original picture is as wide as the orbit of Mars—so this miniset's really far smaller than an atom. But there's just as much detail all around it. And so on forever."

The zooming stopped; for a moment it seemed that a sample of lacework, full of intricate loops and whorls that teased the eye, hung frozen in space. Then, as if a paintbox had been spilled over it, the monochrome image burst into colors so unexpected, and so dazzlingly beautiful, that Bradley gave a gasp of astonishment.

The zooming restarted, but in the reverse direction, and in a microuniverse now transformed by color. No one said a word until they were back at the original complete M-set, now an ominous black fringed with a narrow border of golden fire, and shooting off jagged lightnings of blues and purples.

"And where," asked Bradley when he had recovered his breath, "did all those colors come from? We didn't see them on the way in."

Ada laughed.

"No—they're not really part of the Set—but aren't they gorgeous? I can tell the computer to make them anything I like."

"Even though the actual colors are quite arbitrary," Edith explained, "they're full of meaning. You know the way map makers put shades of blue and green between contour lines, to emphasize differences in level?"

"Of course: we do just the same thing in oceanography. The deeper the blue, the deeper the water."

"Right. In this case, the colors tell us how many times the computer's had to go around the loop before it decides whether a number definitely belongs to the M-set—or not. In borderline cases, it may have to do the squaring and adding routine thousands of times."

"And often for hundred-digit numbers," said Donald. "*Now* you understand why the Set wasn't discovered earlier."

"Mighty good reason."

"Now watch this," said Ada.

The image came to life as waves of color flowed outward. It seemed that the borders of the Set itself were continually expanding—yet staying in the same place. Then Bradley realized that nothing was really moving; only the colors were cycling around the spectrum, to produce this completely convincing illusion of movement.

I begin to understand, Bradley thought, how someone could get lost in this thing—even make it a way of life.

"I'm almost certain," he said, "that I've seen this program listed in my computer's software library—with a couple of thousand others. How lucky I've never run it. I can see how addictive it could get."

He noticed that Donald Craig glanced sharply at Edith, and realized that he had made a somewhat tactless remark. However, she still seemed engrossed by the flow of colors, even though she must have seen this particular display countless times.

"Ada," she said dreamily, "give Mr. Jason our favorite quotation from Einstein."

That's asking a lot from a ten-year-old, thought Bradley—even one like this; but the girl never hesitated, and there was no trace of mechanical repetition in her voice. She understood the words, and spoke from the heart:

"The most beautiful thing we can experience is the mysterious. It is the source of all true art and science. He to whom this emotion is a stranger, who can no longer pause to wonder and stand wrapped in awe, is as good as dead."

I'll go along with that, thought Bradley. He remembered calm nights in the Pacific, with a skyful of stars and a glimmering trail of bioluminescence behind the ship; he recalled his first glimpse of the teeming life-forms—as alien as any from another planet—gathered around the scalding cornucopia of a Galapagos midocean vent, where the continents were slowly tearing apart; and he hoped that before long he would feel awe and wonder again, when the tremendous knife-edge of *Titanic*'s prow came looming up out of the abyss.

The dance of colors ceased: the M-set faded out. Although nothing had ever been *really* there, he could somehow sense that the virtual screen of the holograph projector had switched off.

"So now," said Donald, "you know more about the Mandelbrot Set than you want to." He glanced momentarily at Edith, and once again Bradley felt that twinge of sympathy toward him.

It was not at all the feeling he had expected, when he came to Conroy Castle: envy would have been a better word. Here was a man with great wealth, a beautiful home, and a talented and attractive family—all the ingredients that were supposed to guarantee happiness. Yet something had obviously gone wrong. I wonder, Bradley thought, how long it is since they went to bed together. It could be as simple as that—though *that*, of course, was seldom simple. . . .

The Ghost From the Grand Banks *will be available in November 1990, wherever Bantam Books are sold.*